Essentials
of

Engineering
Fluid
Mechanics

Essentials of

Engineering Fluid Mechanics

second edition

Reuben M. Olson

Associate Professor
Department of Civil Engineering
Ohio University

International Textbook Company
Scranton, Pennsylvania

Consulting Editor

Edward F. Obert

Professor of Mechanical Engineering
University of Wisconsin

Preface to the Second Edition

This second edition contains some rearrangement of material which appeared in the first edition, some new material, and many new problems.

A review of thermodynamics and mathematics is combined. Development of various forms of the continuity equation are placed together in the chapter on fluid dynamics. Flow in ducts deals first with uniform (fully-developed) flow, then with nonuniform flow, including flow in the entrance region of ducts and compressible gas flow.

Material introducing the student to non-Newtonian fluids, the use of vectors in deriving the continuity and momentum equations, the Navier-Stokes equations, conformal mapping, and oblique shocks has been added. Additional material on laminar flow in noncircular ducts is included.

Some problems from the first edition have been changed, and many new problems have been added. An attempt has been made to keep a balance between theory and engineering applications both in the text and in the problems.

I would like to express my appreciation to the many people who have used the first edition and who have made constructive suggestions concerning revisions and additions. Comments of Professor E. Silberman, Director, and J. M. Wetzel of the St. Anthony Falls Hydraulic Laboratory, University of Minnesota, have been especially useful.

REUBEN M. OLSON

Athens, Ohio
July, 1966

Preface to the First Edition

This text is an outgrowth of experience in the fields of hydraulics, thermodynamics, and heat transfer and in teaching courses in fluid mechanics for aeronautical, civil, electrical, mining, and mechanical engineers and applied mathematicians. It is based on the premise that fluid mechanics is fluid mechanics, and that the same fundamentals should be taught to all engineering students.

The student should develop a good understanding of the properties of fluids and the principles of fluid behavior and should be able to solve practical problems. He should not emphasize one aspect at the expense of the other. The understanding of principles involves physical ideas, as well as mathematical ones, and includes derivations and analysis of resulting equations which describe fluid behavior. Problem solving involves numerical calculations from working formulas, often with the inclusion of experimentally determined coefficients. Both approaches are included in the text.

Application of the continuity principle, the steady-flow energy equation (from the first law of thermodynamics), the equations of motion, and the momentum theorem (from Newton's second law) are stressed throughout. Particular emphasis is placed on the similarities and differences between the steady-flow energy equation and the integrated forms of the differential equation of motion for nonviscous fluids, known as the Bernoulli equations.

No sharp distinction is made between incompressible flow and compressible flow, although some chapters are devoted exclusively to one or the other. One chapter is devoted to a discussion of the similarities between open-channel flow and gas flow.

An introduction to potential flow and to boundary layer flow is given. The boundary layer treatment is extended to include a chapter on a brief introduction to thermal boundary layers in order to show the interrelationships between them and the hydrodynamic boundary layer.

A system of units adaptable to fluid mechanics (the slug-foot-second system) is used. Factors of proportionality such as g_c and conversion factors such as J are omitted from equations and need not be used if appropriate property values are introduced. Equations appear in a form common in hydraulics, hydrodynamics, and gas dynamics.

Dimensionless groups and numbers are used freely after their introduction, in which case the system of units used becomes immaterial.

It is difficult to acknowledge all original sources in a book of this type, but where appropriate they are given. A list of supplementary reading for students is included at the end of the text. Many of these books are beautifully written, and the student should find them interesting. An additional list of references is also included.

I wish to thank my colleagues in both the Mechanical Engineering and the Civil Engineering departments here at the University of Minnesota, especially those at the St. Anthony Falls Hydraulic Laboratory, for many discussions on the teaching of fluid mechanics and on the specific contents of various portions of this text. I am indebted to Alvin G. Anderson, Warren E. Ibele, Albert G. Mercer, and John F. Ripken for their comments on particular chapters; to Joseph M. Wetzel for his reading of and his critical comments on the entire manuscript; to James R. Steven of the City College of New York and Edward F. Obert of the University of Wisconsin for their thorough reviews and comments; and to Mrs. Donald W. Wray for her capable editing and typing of the manuscript. I take personal responsibility for any errors and would appreciate their being called to my attention.

REUBEN M. OLSON

Minneapolis, Minnesota
June, 1961

Contents

Contents

1

Introduction

Fluid mechanics is a study of the behavior of fluids at rest and in motion. The study takes into account the various properties of fluids and their effects on the resulting flow patterns, in addition to the forces within the fluid and forces interacting between the fluid and its boundaries. The study also includes the mathematical application of some fundamental laws—conservation of matter, Newton's laws of motion, and the first and second laws of thermodynamics—to explain observed facts and to predict as-yet unobserved fluid behavior. An engineer should approach the study of fluid mechanics with the idea of extending his previous contact with physics, mathematics, and mechanics and with two purposes in mind: 1) to obtain an understanding of and a feeling for the behavior of fluids, and 2) to solve numerical problems of a type encountered in engineering practice.

1–1. DEFINITION OF A FLUID

A fluid may be defined as a substance which continuously deforms when subjected to shear stresses. This definition implies that shear stresses may exist only when a fluid is in motion. In order that shear stresses may exist, however, the fluid must be *viscous*, a characteristic exhibited by all *real* fluids. An *ideal* fluid may be defined as one which has no viscosity (it may be called *nonviscous* or *inviscid*), and hence no shear stresses may exist within the fluid whether this ideal fluid is in motion or not. These statements apply to liquids as well as gases (including vapors).

Shear stresses are set up in all real fluids as a result of relative motion between the fluid and its boundaries or between adjacent layers of the fluid. The greater this relative motion, the greater are the shear stresses for a given fluid. Also, for a given relative motion, the shear stresses are greater when the fluid viscosity is greater. It is this viscous shear which causes resistance to flow, either directly or indirectly—directly in the case of pressure drop in a pipe, for example, and indirectly in the case of drag on a golf ball or any similar situation where the flow separates from the boundary and creates a wake which contributes to a significant if not major portion of the drag. At high speeds in gases, however, drag may be largely due to compressible effects rather than viscous effects.

The flow of ideal, irrotational fluids is called potential flow, and may be analyzed by the same mathematical methods (using vectors or complex variables, for example) as are used for other potential fields—

electric and magnetic fields, the flow of electricity in a conductor, and the flow of heat by conduction are examples. The study of ideal fluids is of engineering interest because real fluids act like ideal fluids in many instances. Ideal fluids in fluid mechanics are analogous to reversible processes in thermodynamics; neither exist but are approached by real viscous fluids and by real irreversible processes, respectively.

The treatment of fluids at rest in Chapter 4 applies to both nonviscous as well as viscous fluids, since the effects of viscosity do not appear when a fluid is at rest, but only when a fluid is in motion. The basic laws of fluid dynamics introduced in Chapter 5 apply to both types of fluid. An introduction to the flow of ideal incompressible fluids is given in Chapter 6, and high-speed flow of ideal compressible gases is introduced in Chapter 9. Essentially all the rest of the book deals with real fluids.

1–2. EVERYDAY EXPERIENCES WITH FLUIDS

Prehistoric man's contact with fluids was probably confined largely to the air he breathed and the water he drank and swam in. Later he made use of hydrostatic principles not only in swimming but in making rafts, and he used dynamic principles of fluid motion (or motion in a fluid) when he developed crude boats or canoes and spears and arrows. Throughout history man has increased his everyday contact with fluids.

In the home we are all familiar with water piping and the·water hammering which results when a faucet is closed rapidly. Hydraulic engineers must make mathematically elaborate designs for surge tanks in water turbine systems in order to prevent water-hammer damage. The vortex we see when a bathtub is drained is fundamentally the same as a tornado and the swirls in the wake downstream of a bridge pier or behind a canoe. Hot water or steam radiators to heat homes and the radiators for cooling in an automobile depend on the growth of a thermal and a fluid boundary layer for their effectiveness as heat convectors.

When we say that something or someone is "slower than molasses in January," we are using a qualitative measure of fluid viscosity because we are aware that molasses flows slowly when cold. Lubricating oils for our automobiles are purchased according to a viscosity rating, the SAE number (10 or 20, for example), though we may request a thick or thin oil or a light or heavy oil instead. Few of us are aware that cold water is twice as viscous as warm water (this variation exists in tap water in northern states between winter and summer).

The windmill on a farm has its counterpart in ship, boat, and airplane propellers, in pumps, blowers, fans, turbines, kitchen blenders, and malted milk mixers. In each, a torque and thrust is applied either to a fluid or by a fluid, and all are examples of a lifting vane.

The shifting of snow or sand in a high wind, both along the ground and in the air above it, has a counterpart in rivers, where sediment is carried to them by smaller streams and then in them to be deposited as sand bars or carried to the sea to form deltas.

Deposits of snow behind snow fences and the hollow regions around a tree trunk or pole following a blizzard are due to the same type of flow pattern which exists behind a golf ball in flight. Incidentally, ship hulls and aircraft wings and fuselages are made *smooth* in order to reduce drag, but golf balls are made *rough* in order to reduce their drag.

Even a physiologist is concerned with fluid mechanics. The heart is a pump which pumps a fluid (blood) through a piping system (vessels and arteries).

Rockets sent skywards by small boys on the Fourth of July are essentially the same in principle as the rockets used to send man-made satellites into interstellar space. Rocket nozzles have the same general shape as nozzles in gas and steam turbines and the aspirators used in a garden hose to draw liquid fertilizer into the water stream for sprinkling.

We are all aware of aerodynamic drag if we have ever walked or cycled against or with a high wind. In rowing a boat or paddling a canoe we find that we must row or paddle faster and harder in order to go faster, not only to accelerate but also to maintain a higher speed.

The crack of a whip in air induces a shock wave because the tip of the whip travels at supersonic speed. A hunter shooting a rifle sends a supersonic missile to hit a target. Many of us have seen shooting stars disappear because they were traveling so fast they burned up because of "friction."

Thus we all are continually dealing with fluids at rest and in motion although we are seldom aware of them quantitatively, if even qualitatively.

1–3. HISTORICAL BACKGROUND[1]

The application of fluid mechanics began in connection with the motion of stones, spears, and arrows. Ships with oars and sails were used as early as 3000 B.C. Irrigation systems have been found in prehistoric ruins in both Egypt and Mesopotamia. The early Greeks recognized air and water as two of the four forms of matter (the others were fire and earth). Aristotle (4th century B.C.) studied the motions of bodies in thin media and in voids. Archimedes (3rd century B.C.) formulated the well-known laws of floating bodies.

The Roman aqueducts were built in the 4th century B.C., although written evidence indicates the builders did not understand pipe resistance. Da Vinci (1452–1519) hinted he advocated an experimental approach to

---

[1]Hunter Rouse and Simon Ince, *History of Hydraulics* (Iowa City Iowa Institute of Hydraulic Research, State University of Iowa, 1957).

science, saying, "Remember when discoursing on the flow of water to adduce first experience and then reason." He correctly described many flow phenomena. Galileo (1564–1642) contributed much to the science of mechanics.

The Italian school of hydraulics included Castelli (1577–1644), Torricelli (1608–1647), and Guglielmini (1655–1710), and ideas concerning the steady flow continuity equation in rivers, flow from a container, the barometer, and some qualitative concepts of flow resistance in rivers came from them. A Frenchman, Mariotte (1620–1684), made experiments in which he measured forces of jets and of the wind. In addition to his well-known laws of motion, Newton (1642–1727) proposed that fluid resistance is proportional to what we now call velocity gradient, and he also made experiments on the drag of spheres.

The mathematical science of fluid mechanics—hydrodynamics—was due to four 18th century mathematicians: Daniel Bernoulli and Leonhard Euler (Swiss) and Clairaut and d'Alembert (French). These were followed by Lagrange (1736–1813), Laplace (1749–1827), and an engineer, Gerstner (1756–1832) who contributed ideas on surface waves.

Experimentalists of the 18th century added much. These men included Poleni, who derived an equation for weir flow; de Pitot, who developed a tube for measuring velocities; Chezy, who developed a resistance formula for open channels; Borda, who performed experiments on resistance with rotating arms and analyzed flow through orifices; Bossut, who built a towing tank; Du Buot, who pioneered the French school of hydraulics; and Venturi, who experimented with flow in changing cross sections.

In the 19th century, the Frenchmen Coulomb (1736–1806) and Prony (1755–1839) conducted tests and drew conclusions regarding flow resistance; the German brothers Ernst (1795–1878) and Wilhelm Weber (1804–1891) conducted tests on wave motion; the French engineers Burdin (1790–1873), Fourneyman (1802–1867), Coriolis (1792–1843), and the American engineer Francis (1815–1892) contributed towards the development and analysis of hydraulic turbines; the Scotsman Russell (1808–1882) and the Alsatian Reech (1805–1880) conducted tests on waves and towed ship models; the Englishman Smith (1808–1874) and the Swede Ericsson (1803–1889) developed the screw propeller; the German Hagen (1797–1889), the Frenchman Poiseuille (1799–1869), and the Saxon Wiesbach (1806–1871) did extensive work on pipe flow; the Frenchman Saint-Venant (1797–1886) analyzed the sonic orifice and contributed to open channel hydraulics; the Frenchmen Dupuit (1804–1866), Bresse (1822–1883), and Bazin (1829–1917) and the Irishman Manning (1816–1897) did extensive work in open channel hydraulics; the Frenchman Darcy (1803–1858) did work on pipe flow and percolating flow; the German Lilienthal (1848–1896) and the Englishmen Phillips (1845–1912) and Lanchester (1868–1946) did extensive pioneering work on the lift of vanes, Lanchester introducing a theory of lift; and the Englishmen William Froude (1810–1879) and his son Robert Froude (1846–1924) did extensive ship model testing.

Classical and applied hydrodynamics were advanced during the 19th century by Navier (1785–1836), Cauchy (1789–1857), Poisson (1781–1840), Saint-Venant, and Boussinesq (1842–1929) in France; Stokes (1819–1903), Airy (1801–1892), Reynolds (1842–1912), Lord Kelvin (1824–1907), Lord Rayleigh (1842–1919), and Lamb (1849–1934) in England; Helmholtz (1821–1894) and Kirchhoff (1824–1887) in Germany; and Joukowsky (1847–1921) in Russia.

At the end of the 19th century, theoretical hydrodynamics, based on Euler's equations of motion for an ideal (nonviscous) fluid, had reached a comparatively high level of development. It did not explain, however, many observed effects, such as the pressure drop in pipes, and thus practicing engineers developed their own empirical science of hydraulics. These two fields—hydrodynamics and hydraulics—had much too little in common at that time. In 1904 Prandtl (1875–1953) in Germany introduced the concept of a boundary layer, a thin region adjacent to a boundary, in which the viscous effects were concentrated. This proved to be the concept which unified all aspects of modern fluid mechanics—aerodynamics, hydraulics, gas dynamics, and convective heat transfer. Prandtl is properly considered to be the father of modern fluid mechanics.

1–4. CURRENT RESEARCH ACTIVITIES IN FLUID MECHANICS

It might be more informative to discuss current research in fluid mechanics at the end of the text. However, mention of current research at this point should prepare the reader to accept the treatment for what it is. In spite of the level of knowledge of fluid behavior at the present time, there are surprisingly many gaps in that knowledge.

Exact solutions of the mathematical equations describing fluid flow (the Navier-Stokes equations, given in Chapter 5) have been carried out for only a relatively few instances. It may be said that our knowledge is quite complete only for situations in which laminar flow occurs and in which the fluid is nonviscous (potential flow).

Thus nearly all current investigations involve turbulent flow, especially on the mechanism of the origin or initiation of turbulent flow in boundary layers, and flow in regions where this boundary layer separates from a boundary. Included in these investigations are studies on the effects of surface roughness. Engineering practice makes use of an equivalent size of sand-grain roughness, though it is believed that roughness element spacing and shape are also important. This is of interest in pipe flow, aeronautics, naval architecture, and convective heat transfer.

The mechanism and prediction of sediment transportation in rivers and streams and the prediction and prevention of beach erosion due to waves in coastal waters is of current interest in hydraulics. The effects of cavitation—formation of gas or vapor cavities in liquids— are known to a degree, but the actual mechanism is not yet completely known, and the prediction of its inception and effects especially in model tests as well as in prototype (full scale) performance of pumps, turbines, propellers, and hydrofoils is difficult.

Investigations of two-phase flow—flow of liquids and gases or vapors, solids and gases, and solids and liquids together—are being carried out. Supersonic gas flow involving the combined effects of boundary layers (viscous effects) with shocks (compressible effect) in relation to drag, stability, and heat transfer is being studied in connection with rocketry and space flight. Recently the study of magnetohydrodynamics and plasmas— effects of ionized gases in magnetic fields at high temperatures—became of interest.

Both fluid dynamic and heat transfer phenomena in film and transpiration cooling and in separated flows are being studied. The viscous behavior of non-Newtonian fluids such as slurries, molten plastics, and suspended paper pulp is of current interest.

Laminar flows may be generally analyzed mathematically, but the analytical description of turbulent flows is not yet complete. The most useful studies of turbulent flows have been experimental investigations coupled with analysis based on physical models of the flow. Mathematical analyses of laminar flow are generally easier to make than experimental studies; conversely, experimental studies of turbulent flow are easier to make than analytical studies. A number of experimental studies have been recently undertaken in order to verify boundary-condition assumptions made in laminar flow analyses. These experimental studies are generally difficult to make owing to the small magnitude of the velocities and pressure differences encountered. Stable and symmetrical laminar flow without secondary flows is often difficult to obtain.

Pure or theoretical research at the one extreme and applied research at the other are merged and overlap in many instances. Model testing in all fields of fluid mechanics becomes more and more complicated when attempts are made to separate one of a number of effects occurring together. In many instances all prototype conditions cannot be modeled precisely, and in these instances the practice of modeling becomes an art as well as a science.

It is the duty of engineers, even though they are not engaged in research, to keep abreast of current developments in order that they may be applied expeditiously in engineering designs.

1–5. NOTES ON SYMBOLS AND UNITS

Fluid mechanics encompasses the traditional fields of classical hydro-dynamics, hydraulics, thermodynamics, heat transfer, gas dynamics, chemical engineering, and theoretical mechanics. No single system of symbols or units is common to all these fields.

A list of symbols, which is a composite of those recommended by the American Standards Association (ASA) in various fields, is given in Appendix 1. The only exception involves dimensionless numbers named in honor of individuals who have distinguished themselves in their respective fields. For example, the ASA recommends that N_R be used for the Reynolds number. But when subscripts (and in some instances, subscripts *on* subscripts) are needed this becomes cumbersome. More commonly used are (usually) the first two letters of the individual's name, such as Re for the Reynolds number and Pr for the Prandtl number. The sole exception is M for the Mach number in gas dynamics.

Physical quantities may be designated in terms of a few primary dimensions such as force, length, time, and temperature (F, L, T, and θ), or as mass, length, time, and temperature (M, L, T, and θ). Many physical quantities require more than one primary dimension in order that they may be described. Each one of these primary dimensions, in turn, may be specified by any one of a variety of units. The dimension of length, for example, may be expressed in units of microns, inches, feet, meters, fathoms, rods, or miles, to cite just a few possibilities.

That there is no universal system of units in the United States may be verified by a brief perusal of a few engineering texts chosen at random. The problem of consistent units increases when other countries' texts and publications enter the picture.[2]

The major difference in units between the various fields encompassed in fluid mechanics is for the unit for mass. Both pound-mass and slug-mass units are used, 32.174 $\mathrm{lb_m}$ being equal to 1 slug. The force unit is usually the pound force, the length unit the foot (or inch), and the time unit the second.

Newton's second law states that force is proportional to time rate of change of momentum. Thus

$$F \propto ma$$

and we may write

$$F = \frac{ma}{g_c} \tag{1–1a}$$

where g_c is the factor of proportionality. In the pound-mass system, a

---

[2]Carl F. Kayan, Ed., *Systems of Units* (Washington, D. C.: American Association for the Advancement of Science, 1959).

1 lb$_f$ will accelerate a 1 lb$_m$ 32.174 ft/sec^2. Thus Eq. 1–1a becomes

$$1 \text{ lb}_f = \frac{(1 \text{ lb}_m) \ (32.174 \text{ ft/sec}^2)}{32.174 \text{ lb}_m \text{ ft/lb}_f \text{ sec}^2} \tag{1–1b}$$

which is correct from the point of view of both units and numbers, and

$$g_c = 32.174 \text{ lb}_m \text{ ft/lb}_f \text{ sec}^2$$

In the slug-mass system, a 1 lb$_f$ will accelerate a 1 slug mass 1 ft/sec^2. Thus Eq. 1–1a becomes

$$1 \text{ lb}_f = \frac{(1 \text{ slug}) \ (1 \text{ ft/sec}^2)}{1 \text{ slug ft/lb}_f \text{ sec}^2} \tag{1–1c}$$

which is also correct from the point of view of both units and numbers and $g_c = 1$ slug ft/lb$_f$ sec^2. The first method is common in engineering thermodynamics, and the second method is common in fluid mechanics, aerodynamics, and engineering mechanics. The g_c in the slug-mass system, however, is usually omitted in equations, since its numerical value is unity. This is equivalent to defining

$$1 \text{ lb}_f = 1 \text{ slug ft/sec}^2 \tag{1–2a}$$

or
$$1 \text{ slug} = 1 \text{ lb}_f \text{ sec}^2/\text{ft} \tag{1–2b}$$

In any system a consistent set of units must be employed within any given equation, since only quantities all with the same units may be added numerically. For example, the expression

$$L = 3 \text{ yd} + 2 \text{ ft} + 7 \text{ in.}$$

must be converted to

$$L = (3 \text{ yd}) \left(\frac{36 \text{ in.}}{\text{yd}}\right) + (2 \text{ ft}) \left(\frac{12 \text{ in.}}{\text{ft}}\right) + 7 \text{ in.}$$

before adding to get

$$L = 108 \text{ in.} + 24 \text{ in.} + 7 \text{ in.}$$
$$= 139 \text{ in.}$$

Fluid properties are usually given in reference sources in units commonly used in thermodynamics, chemistry, or physics. They may, however, be expressed in other equivalent units. For example, the specific heat capacity at constant pressure for air is commonly given as

$$c_p = 0.240 \text{ Btu/lb}_m \text{ F}$$

which is equivalent to

$$\left(0.24 \frac{\text{Btu}}{\text{lb}_m \text{ F}}\right) \left(778 \frac{\text{ft lb}_f}{\text{Btu}}\right) = 186.5 \text{ ft lb}_f/\text{lb}_m \text{ F}$$

or
$$\left(0.24 \frac{\text{Btu}}{\text{lb}_m \text{ F}}\right) \left(32.174 \frac{\text{lb}_m}{\text{slug}}\right) = 7.72 \text{ Btu/slug F}$$

or
$$\left(0.24 \frac{\text{Btu}}{\text{lb}_m \text{ F}}\right) \left(778 \frac{\text{ft lb}_f}{\text{Btu}}\right) \left(32.174 \frac{\text{lb}_m}{\text{slug}}\right) = 6000 \text{ ft lb}_f/\text{slug F}$$

Thus, in a similar manner, terms in an equation may be converted to a consistent set of units before adding (or multiplying). A few examples will illustrate this.

EXAMPLE 1–1. The Bernoulli equation may be written as

$$p + \frac{\rho V^2}{2} = p_0$$

where p is the static pressure (force per unit area), ρ is the mass density (mass per unit volume), V is the speed (distance per unit time), and p_0 is the stagnation pressure (force per unit area). For a fluid density of 62.4 lb_m/ft^3 (1.94 slugs/ft^3), if the static pressure is 20 $lb_f/in.^2$ and the velocity 50 ft/sec, what is the stagnation pressure?

Solution: The stagnation pressure is

$$p_0 = 20 \frac{lb_f}{in.^2} + \left(62.4 \frac{lb_m}{ft^3}\right)\left(50 \frac{ft}{sec}\right)^2 \left(\frac{1}{2}\right)$$

which must be converted to

$$p_0 = \left(20 \frac{lb_f}{in.^2}\right)\left(144 \frac{in.^2}{ft^2}\right) + \left(62.4 \frac{lb_m}{ft^3}\right)\left(\frac{1}{32.2\ lb_m/slug}\right)\left(\frac{2500\ ft^2}{sec^2}\right)\left(\frac{1}{2}\right)$$

$$= 2880 \frac{lb_f}{ft^2} + 2425 \frac{slugs}{ft\ sec^2}$$

$$= 2880 \frac{lb_f}{ft^2} + 2425 \left(\frac{lb_f\ sec^2}{ft}\right)\left(\frac{1}{ft\ sec^2}\right)$$

$$= 2880 \frac{lb_f}{ft^2} + 2425 \frac{lb_f}{ft^2}$$

$$= 5305 \frac{lb_f}{ft^2}$$

Now if p has units of lb_f/ft^2, ρ has units of slugs/ft^3, and velocity has units of ft/sec, the value of p_0 may be calculated directly by inserting appropriate values. If ρ has units of lb_m/ft^3, it must be converted to units of slugs/ft^3 before making these direct calculations. In this case,

$$p_0 = 2880 \frac{lb_f}{ft^2} + \left(\frac{1}{2}\right)\left(1.94 \frac{slugs}{ft^3}\right)\left(50 \frac{ft}{sec}\right)^2$$

$$= 2880 \frac{lb_f}{ft^2} + 2425 \frac{lb_f}{ft^2}$$

$$= 5305 \frac{lb_f}{ft^2}$$

EXAMPLE 1–2. The adiabatic steady-flow energy equation for a perfect gas with zero work may be written as

$$c_p T_1 + \frac{V_1^2}{2} = c_p T_0$$

where c_p is the specific heat capacity at constant pressure, T_1 and T_0 are the static and stagnation temperatures, respectively, and V is the speed. For a static temperature $T_1 = 60$ F and a speed $V_1 = 1500$ ft/sec, what is the stagnation temperature?

Solution: The stagnation temperature is

$$T_0 = T_1 + \frac{V_1^2}{2c_p}$$

$$= 60 \text{ F} + \frac{(1500 \text{ ft/sec})^2}{2 (0.240 \text{ Btu/lb}_m \text{ F})}$$

$$= 60 \text{ F} + \frac{(2,250,000 \text{ ft}^2/\text{sec}^2)}{2 (0.240 \text{ Btu/lb}_m \text{ F}) (778 \text{ ft lb}_f/\text{Btu}) (32.2 \text{ lb}_m/\text{slug})}$$

$$= 60 \text{ F} + 187 \frac{\text{slug ft}}{\text{lb}_f \text{ sec}^2} \text{ F}$$

$$= 60 \text{ F} + 187 \text{ F}$$

$$= 247 \text{ F}$$

since a slug $= 1$ lb$_f$ sec^2/ft. If $c_p = 6000$ ft lb$_f$/slug F (equivalent to 6000 ft^2/sec^2 F) were used initially, the calculation is more direct, or

$$T_0 = 60 \text{ F} + \frac{2,250,000 \text{ ft}^2/\text{sec}^2}{2 (6000 \text{ ft}^2/\text{sec}^2 \text{ F})}$$

$$= 60 \text{ F} + 187 \text{ F} = 247 \text{ F}$$

EXAMPLE 1–3. The speed of sound in a perfect gas is given by

$$c = \sqrt{kRT}$$

where k is the ratio of specific heat capacities, R is the gas constant, and T is the absolute temperature. For air at 60 F, find the speed of sound.

Solution:

$$c = \sqrt{(1.4) \left(53.3 \frac{\text{ft lb}_f}{\text{lb}_m \text{ R}} \right) \left(\frac{32.2 \text{ lb}_m}{\text{slug}} \right) (520 \text{ R})}$$

$$= \sqrt{1,248,000 \frac{\text{ft lb}_f}{\text{slug}}}$$

$$= 1118 \sqrt{\frac{\text{ft lb}_f}{\text{lb}_f \text{ sec}^2/\text{ft}}}$$

$$= 1118 \sqrt{\frac{\text{ft}^2}{\text{sec}^2}}$$

$$= 1118 \frac{\text{ft}}{\text{sec}}$$

If $R = 1715$ ft lb$_f$/slug R (equivalent to 1715 ft^2/sec^2 R) were used directly,

$$c = \sqrt{(1.4) \left(1715 \frac{\text{ft}^2}{\text{sec}^2 \text{ R}} \right) (520 \text{ R})}$$

$$= 1118 \frac{\text{ft}}{\text{sec}}$$

In this text, conversion factors such as g_c and the mechanical equivalent of heat J (778 ft lb_f/Btu) generally will be omitted. If density in slugs per cubic foot and specific heat capacities and the gas constant in units of ft lb_f/slug R, or the equivalent ft^2/sec^2 R are used, numerical calculations may be made *directly* from the equations, with *no conversion factors necessary*. Exceptional cases will be mentioned individually.

PROBLEMS

1-1. A container with a volume of 1 ft^3 contains 62.4 lb_m of water. How many slugs of water does it contain?

1-2. The mass of standard air in a volume of 1 ft^3 is 0.0765 lb_m. What is the mass of 6 ft^3 of standard air in slugs?

1-3. One cubic centimeter of water represents a mass of 1 gm. What is the mass of 1 ft^3 of this water in slugs?

Ans. 1.94 slugs

1-4. A man "weighs" 190 lb_m on a beam balance. *a*) What is his mass in slugs? *b*) What force does this man exert on the beam balance in a gravitational field of 32.1 ft/sec^2?

Ans. 189.6 lb_f

1-5. The dynamic viscosity of water at 80 F is 1.80×10^{-5} lb_f sec/ft^2. What is the dynamic viscosity of this water in units of slug/ft sec?

Ans. 1.80×10^{-5} slug/ft sec

1-6. The dynamic viscosity of water at 100 F is 0.442×10^{-3} lb_m/ft sec. What is the dynamic viscosity in units of lb_f sec/ft^2?

1-7. The dynamic viscosity of an hydraulic oil at 100 F is 9.66×10^{-3} lb_m/ft sec. What is its dynamic viscosity in units of slug/ft sec?

1-8. The kinematic viscosity ν is defined as the ratio of the dynamic viscosity μ to the density ρ. What is the kinematic viscosity of water in units of ft^2/sec for a dynamic viscosity of 2.04×10^{-5} lb_f sec/ft^2 and a density of 1.94 slugs/ft^3?

1-9. Kinematic viscosity ν is defined as the ratio of dynamic viscosity μ to density ρ ($\nu = \mu/\rho$). Show that kinematic viscosity has units of ft^2/sec when dynamic viscosity has units of lb_f sec/ft^2 and density has units of slugs/ft^3.

1-10. Express a standard atmosphere of 14.696 lb_f/in.^{2} in units of lb_f/ft^2.

1-11. Show that the expression $\rho V^2/2$ (called the dynamic pressure) has units of pressure in lb_f/ft^2 when ρ is in slugs/ft^3 and V is the velocity in ft/sec.

1-12. The sum of dynamic pressure $\rho V^2/2$ and the static pressure p is called the stagnation or total pressure p_0. That is

$$\frac{\rho V^2}{2} + p = p_0$$

Let $\rho = 1.94$ slugs/ft^3, $V = 40$ mph, and $p = 14.5$ lb$_f$/in.^{2} What is the stagnation or total pressure in lb$_f$/in.^{2}?

Ans. 37.7 lb$_f$/in.^{2}

1–13. In Prob. 1–12, let $\rho = 0.002378$ slug/ft^3, $V = 200$ mph, and $p = 14.7$ lb$_f$/in.^{2} What is the stagnation or total pressure in lb$_f$/ft^2?

1–14. Let V represent velocity in ft/sec and g the acceleration of gravity in ft/sec^2. Show that $V^2/2g$ (called the velocity, kinetic, or dynamic head) has units of ft or ft lb$_f$/lb$_f$, which represents energy per unit weight.

1–15. For a velocity $V = 30$ ft/sec, what is the velocity head $V^2/2g$ for *a*) water of density $\rho = 1.94$ slugs/ft^3, *b*) air of density 0.002378 slug/ft^3, and *c*) mercury of density 26.3 slugs/ft^3?

1–16. Let V represent velocity in ft/sec. Show that the expression $V^2/2$ represents energy per unit mass in units of ft lb$_f$/slug.

1–17. What is the kinetic energy per unit mass $(V^2/2)$ for a velocity of $V = 40$ ft/sec for *a*) water of density $\rho = 1.94$ slugs/ft^3, *b*) air of density 0.002378 slug/ft^3, and *c*) mercury of density 26.3 slugs/ft^3?

1–18. From Example 1–1, $V = \sqrt{2(p_0 - p)/\rho}$ ft/sec, where p_0 and p are in units of lb$_f$/ft^2 and ρ is in units of slugs/ft^3. Write this expression with the appropriate numerical factor to give *a*) V in units of ft/sec for pressures in lb$_f$/in.^{2} and density ρ in units of lb$_m$/ft^3, *b*) V in units of miles per hour when pressures are in units of lb$_f$/in.^{2} and density ρ is in units of slugs/ft^3, and *c*) V in knots when pressures are in units of lb$_f$/in.^{2} and density ρ is in units of slugs/ft^3 [1 knot = 1 nautical mile (6080 ft)/hr].

Ans. *c*) $V = 7.11 \sqrt{2(p_0 - p)/\rho}$

1–19. From Example 1–2, $V = \sqrt{2c_p(T_0 - T)}$ ft/sec when temperatures are in units of degrees Rankine and c_p is in units of ft lb$_f$/slug R. *a*) Show that 1 ft lb$_f$/slug R = 1 ft^2/sec^2 R. *b*) Write an expression for velocity V in units of ft/sec with an appropriate numerical factor when c_p is given in units of Btu/lb$_m$ R and temperatures are given in degrees Rankine.

1–20. For perfect gases the difference between specific heat capacities at constant pressure and at constant volume is equal to the gas constant; that is, $c_p - c_v = R$. For air, $c_p = 0.240$ Btu/lb$_m$ R and the gas constant $R = 53.3$ ft lb$_f$/lb$_m$ R. What is c_v in units of ft lb$_f$/slug R?

1–21. Show that $\rho V^2/2$ represents pressure, as well as energy per unit volume. When ρ is in slugs per cubic foot and V is in ft/sec, show that the pressure is in lb$_f$/ft^2 and that the energy per unit volume is in ft lb$_f$/ft^3.

1–22. In Example 1–2, what is the stagnation temperature T_0 when the static temperature T_1 is 70 F, $c_p = 6000$ ft lb$_f$/slug R and $V_1 = 600$ miles/hr?

1–23. In Example 1–3, at what temperature in degrees F is the speed of sound in air 730 miles/hr? $k = 1.4$ and $c_p = 6000$ ft lb$_f$/slug R. Deg Rankine = 460 + Deg Fahrenheit.

Ans. 17 F

2

Fluid Properties

All real fluids have or exhibit certain measurable characteristics or properties which are of engineering importance. Fluid density, compressibility, capillarity, and vapor pressure may be of interest for fluids at rest; and in addition to these, viscosity is significant for real fluids in motion. The thermal properties, such as gas constant, internal energy, enthalpy and entropy for gases, and specific heat capacities and conductivity for both gases and liquids, are important in heat transfer and gas dynamics. Pressure and temperature are considered to be thermodynamic properties, though they might be considered as independent properties upon which the (other) tabular properties depend. Some fluid properties are actually combinations of the properties already mentioned. Thermal diffusivity, for example, involves thermal conductivity, density, and specific heat capacity at constant pressure, the Prandtl number involves viscosity, specific heat capacity at constant pressure, and thermal conductivity (or fluid viscosity and thermal diffusivity); and kinematic viscosity involves dynamic viscosity and density.

2–1. DENSITY, SPECIFIC VOLUME, SPECIFIC WEIGHT, AND SPECIFIC GRAVITY

The *density* ρ of a substance is a measure of the concentration of matter and is expressed in terms of mass per unit volume. It is determined by taking the ratio of the mass of a substance contained within a particular region divided by the volume of this region. The region should be both small enough and yet large enough so that there are no significant variations in density in subregions within it. Near the nose of a high-speed missile, for example, the concentration of matter may vary tenfold within a region much less than 1 in. in linear dimension. Thus the measured region should not be too large. If the measured region is too small, however, some subregions might not contain any molecules, or a measured region equal and adjacent to the particular one considered might contain a significantly different amount of matter.

Mass per unit volume may be expressed in terms of grams per cubic centimeter (cgs system), kilograms per cubic meter (mks system), pounds per cubic foot, or slugs per cubic foot (engineering practice). Both of the latter units are used in American practice. Since 1 slug $= 32.17$ lb$_m$, a density of 1 slug/ft^3 $= 32.17$ lb$_m$/ft^3.

Temperature and pressure have a slight effect on the density of liquids, and a pronounced effect on the density of gases.

The *specific volume* v is the volume occupied by a unit mass of a substance, and thus is the reciprocal of density.

$$v = \frac{1}{\rho} \tag{2-1}$$

Specific weight γ is the force of gravity on the mass contained in a unit volume of a substance. Thus

$$\gamma = \rho g \tag{2-2}$$

If the density of water is 1.94 slugs/ft^3 and the acceleration of gravity $g = 32.17$ ft/sec^2, the specific weight of water is

$$\gamma = \left(1.94 \ \frac{\text{slugs}}{\text{ft}^3}\right)\left(32.17 \ \frac{\text{ft}}{\text{sec}^2}\right) = 62.4 \ \text{lb}_f/\text{ft}^3$$

The numerical value of specific weight in lb$_f$/ft^3 is the same as the numerical value of the density in lb$_m$/ft^3 at locations where the acceleration of gravity is 32.17 ft/sec^2.

Strictly speaking, specific weight is not a true fluid property, since it depends on the value of the local gravitational acceleration. Hydrostatic forces exerted by fluids do depend on gravity, however, and it is customary to use the specific weight in calculations which involve them.

Specific gravity s is a term used to compare the density of a substance with that of water. Since the density of all liquids depends on temperature as well as pressure, the temperature of the liquid in question, as well as the reference temperature of water, should be stated in giving precise values of specific gravity.

$$s = \frac{\rho}{\rho_w} = \frac{\gamma}{\gamma_w} \tag{2-3}$$

EXAMPLE 2–1. The density of mercury at 50 F is 849.2 lb$_m$/ft^3 and at 100 F it is 845.0 lb$_m$/ft^3. The density of water at these temperatures is 62.4 lb$_m$/ft^3 and 62.0 lb$_m$/ft^3, respectively. a) What is the specific gravity of mercury at 50 F referred to water at 50 F? b) What is the specific gravity of mercury at 100 F referred to water at 100 F?

Solution: a)

$$s = \frac{849.2}{62.4} = 13.61$$

b)

$$s = \frac{845.0}{62.0} = 13.63$$

Values of density or specific gravity of liquids may be found in numerous references.[1] Some typical values for various liquids are given in Tables 2–1 and 2–2. More detailed data for water are given in Table 2–7.

TABLE 2–1

DENSITY OF SOME LIQUIDS

[lb_m/ft^3 and (slugs/ft^3)]

TEMPER-ATURE (deg F)	LIQUID				
	Water	Benzene	Glycerine	Mercury	Light Oil
32	62.4(1.94)		79.7(2.47)	851(26.4)	
40	62.4(1.94)		79.5(2.47)	850(26.4)	
50	62.4(1.94)		79.3(2.46)	849(26.4)	
60	62.4(1.94)	55.1(1.71)	79.1(2.46)	848(26.3)	57.0(1.77)
80	62.2(1.93)	54.6(1.70)	78.7(2.45)	847(26.3)	56.8(1.765)
100	62.0(1.93)	54.0(1.68)	78.2(2.43)	845(26.3)	56.0(1.74)
120	61.7(1.92)		77.8(2.42)	843(26.2)	
150	61.2(1.90)	53.5(1.66)		841(26.1)	54.3(1.69)
212	59.8(1.86)			836(26.0)	

TABLE 2–2

SPECIFIC GRAVITY OF SOME LIQUIDS AT 68 F

Liquid	Specific Gravity
Gasoline	0.66–0.69
Kerosene	0.82
Castor oil	0.97
Sea water	1.025 (typical)
Carbon tetrachloride	1.595
Acetylene tetrabromide	2.962
Methyl alcohol	0.796

The densities of gases may be calculated from any one of various gas equations as a function of pressure and temperature. We will assume a perfect gas, for which

$$p = \rho RT \qquad (2\text{–}4a)$$

or
$$pv = RT \qquad (2\text{–}4b)$$

in which p is the absolute pressure, ρ is the density, R is the gas constant (having dimensions of energy per unit mass and unit temperature), and T is the absolute temperature. Typical values of R for various gases are listed in Table 2–3.

[1]See, for example, *Handbook of Chemistry and Physics* (38th ed.; Cleveland: Chemical Rubber Publishing Company, 1956–1957). Also, *International Critical Tables* (New York: McGraw-Hill Book Company, Inc., 1926–1930).

TABLE 2-3

VALUES OF GAS CONSTANT

GAS OR MIXTURE	GAS CONSTANT	
	$\dfrac{\text{ft lb}_f}{\text{lb}_m\ R}$	$\dfrac{\text{ft lb}_f}{\text{slug R}}$
Air....................	53.3	1,715
Carbon dioxide..........	35.1	1,130
Carbon monoxide........	55.2	1,776
Hydrogen..............	766	24,660
Nitrogen..............	55.2	1,776
Oxygen................	48.3	1,555
Xenon.................	11.76	378

EXAMPLE 2-2. Compute the density of air at 20 lb$_f$/in.^{2} absolute and 100 F

Solution:

$$\rho = \frac{p}{RT} = \frac{2880 \text{ lb}_f/\text{ft}^2}{(1715 \text{ ft lb}_f/\text{slug R})\ (560 \text{ R})} = 0.00300 \text{ slug/ft}^3$$

$$\rho' = \left(0.00300 \frac{\text{slug}}{\text{ft}^3}\right)\left(32.17 \frac{\text{lb}_m}{\text{slug}}\right) = 0.0965 \text{ lb}_m/\text{ft}^3$$

2-2. VISCOSITY

Viscosity is that property of all real fluids which distinguishes them from ideal (nonviscous) fluids. The viscosity of a fluid is a measure of its resistance to flow. This resistance to flow is measured as a total shear force, a unit shear stress being the shear per unit area subjected to shear.

The viscosity of a gas increases with temperature because of the greater molecular activity as the temperature increases. The kinetic theory of gases (no intermolecular forces are considered) shows that as gas molecules move in random directions superimposed on the mean fluid motion, they collide with other molecules in adjacent fluid layers. The molecules with which they collide move (on the average) at a different fluid velocity, and the collisions will increase or decrease their mean fluid motion depending on whether they collide with faster or slower molecules. This interchange of molecular momentum is manifested as fluid viscosity. A perfect gas, then, may have viscosity and would be called a perfect real gas, as contrasted with a perfect ideal, or nonviscous, gas. It may be shown that the viscosity of a perfect gas is linearly related to the mean free path of the gas molecules. A measurement of gas viscosity, then, may be used to determine the molecular mean free path.

For liquids, molecular spacings are much less than for gases, and molecular cohesion is very strong. Increased temperatures decrease this molecular cohesion between molecules, and this is manifested as a reduction

in liquid viscosity as the temperature of the liquid
is increased.

Newton postulated that the shear stress within a fluid is proportional to the rate of change of
velocity normal to the flow. This rate of change of
velocity is also called the *velocity gradient*. In
Fig. 2–1, the velocity u at any distance y from the
boundary measured at a section A is as shown,
and the curve connecting the tips of the vectors
representing the velocities is called the *velocity
profile*. The velocity gradient at any value of y
is defined as

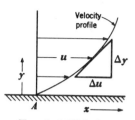

Fig. 2–1. Velocity
profile and veloc-
ity gradient.

$$\frac{du}{dy} = \lim_{\Delta y \to 0} \left(\frac{\Delta u}{\Delta y}\right) \tag{2-5}$$

and represents the inverse slope of the velocity profile as shown in Fig. 2–1.
Thus, Newton's law of viscosity may be written as

$$\tau \propto \frac{du}{dy} \tag{2-6}$$

where τ is the shear stress. If the fluid flows in parallel layers, the flow is
called *laminar* flow, and for this type of flow the proportionality factor
relating shear stress with velocity gradient is called the *dynamic viscosity* μ.
Then

$$\tau = \mu \left(\frac{du}{dy}\right) \tag{2-7}$$

and this is the definition of the fluid property known as dynamic or absolute
viscosity.[2] The dimensions of dynamic viscosity are those of shear stress
divided by velocity gradient, or

$$\left(\frac{\text{Force}}{\text{Area}}\right) \frac{1}{\text{velocity/length}} = \frac{(\text{force})(\text{time})}{\text{area}} = \frac{FT}{L^2} = \frac{M}{LT}$$

since Newton's second law may be expressed dimensionally as $F = ML/T^2$.

Kinematic viscosity ν is defined as the ratio of dynamic viscosity to
density. Thus

$$\nu = \frac{\mu}{\rho} \tag{2-8}$$

and has dimensions of area per unit time.

If shear stress is in units of lb_f/ft^2 and velocity gradient is in units of
(ft/sec)/ft, the units of dynamic viscosity are

[2]For non-parallel laminar flow, $\tau = \mu\left(\dfrac{du}{dy} + \dfrac{dv}{dx}\right)$ when there is a velocity
component v in the y direction which changes with respect to x. In turbulent flow,
$\tau = (\mu + \rho\epsilon)\,(du/dy)$, where ϵ is an eddy viscosity which is not a fluid property
since it depends largely on the flow. Values of $\rho\epsilon$ over 200 times larger than μ
have been measured.

$$\mu = \frac{lb_f\ sec}{ft^2} = \frac{slugs}{ft\ sec}$$

and those of kinematic viscosity are

$$\nu = \frac{ft^2}{sec}$$

Since 1 slug = 32.17 lb_m, 1 slug/ft sec = 32.17 lb_m/ft sec.

EXAMPLE 2–3. The dynamic viscosity of water at 60 F is 2.34×10^{-5} lb_f sec/ft². Express this in units of slug/ft sec and lb_m/ft sec, and calculate the kinematic viscosity in units of ft²/sec.

Solution: Equivalent values are

$$\mu = 2.34 \times 10^{-5}\ lb_f\ sec/ft^2 = 2.34 \times 10^{-5}\ slug/ft\ sec$$

$$= \left(2.34 \times 10^{-5}\ \frac{slug}{ft\ sec}\right)\left(32.17\ \frac{lb_m}{slug}\right) = 75.4 \times 10^{-5}\ lb_m/ft\ sec$$

The kinematic viscosity is

$$\nu = \frac{\mu}{\rho} = \left(2.34 \times 10^{-5}\ \frac{slug}{ft\ sec}\right)\frac{1}{1.94\ slug/ft^3} = 1.21 \times 10^{-5}\ ft^2/sec$$

or

$$\nu = \frac{\mu}{\rho'} = \left(75.4 \times 10^{-5}\ \frac{lb_m}{ft\ sec}\right)\frac{1}{62.4\ lb_m/ft^3} = 1.21 \times 10^{-5}\ ft^2/sec$$

The use of kinematic viscosity eliminates possible confusion regarding the system of mass units employed. Metric equivalents to American engineering units are shown in Table 2–4.

Special names are given some of the combinations of units, in honor of Reynolds, Poiseuille, and Stokes (see Sec. 1–3). Conversions from one set of units to another are easily made, and are tabulated in Table 2–5.

TABLE 2–4

UNITS OF VISCOSITY

	American Engineering		Metric (cgs)
Dynamic.......	$\dfrac{slug}{ft\ sec} = \dfrac{lb_f\ sec}{ft^2}$		$\dfrac{gm}{cm\ sec} = \dfrac{dyne\ sec}{cm^2}$ (Poise)
	$12\ \dfrac{slug}{in.\ sec} = \dfrac{lb_f\ sec}{in.^2}$ (Reyn)		
Kinematic.....	$\dfrac{ft^2}{sec}$		$\dfrac{cm^2}{sec}$ (Stoke)

TABLE 2–5

VISCOSITY CONVERSION FACTORS

1 poise = 100 centipoises = 1 dyne sec/cm²
    = 0.00209 slug/ft sec = 0.00209 lb_f sec/ft² = 0.0673 lb_m/ft sec
    = 0.0000145 reyns
1 stoke = 100 centistokes = 1 cm²/sec = 0.001076 ft²/sec

EXAMPLE 2–4. Express a viscosity of 1 slug/ft sec in poises.

Solution:

$$1 \frac{\text{slug}}{\text{ft sec}} = \left(1 \frac{\text{slug}}{\text{ft sec}}\right) \left(\frac{32.17 \text{ lb}_m}{\text{slug}}\right) \left(\frac{453.6 \text{ gm}}{\text{lb}_m}\right) \left(\frac{1}{30.48 \text{ cm/ft}}\right)$$

$$= 479 \frac{\text{gm}}{\text{cm sec}}$$

$$= 479 \text{ poises}$$

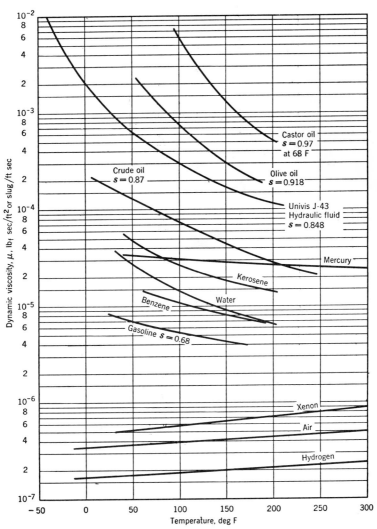

FIG. 2–2. Dynamic viscosity of some liquids and gases.
Values of specific gravity apply at about 70 F.

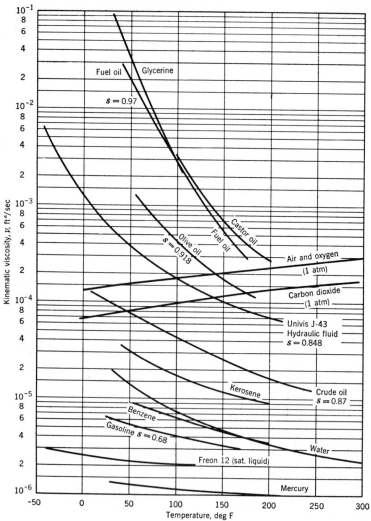

FIG. 2–3. Kinematic viscosity of some liquids and gases.
Values of specific gravity apply at about 70 F.

Various types of viscometers are used in the laboratory to measure kinematic viscosity. The time, in seconds, for a specified quantity of liquid to drain from a given cup or reservoir is measured and the viscosity expressed in seconds (Saybolt, if the viscometer is a Saybolt instrument). An equation to convert t seconds for various viscometers is

$$\nu = At - \frac{B}{t} \qquad \text{ft}^2/\text{sec} \tag{2–9}$$

where A and B are constants given in Table 2–6.

TABLE 2–6
Constants for Viscometers

Viscometer	A	B
Saybolt universal.......	0.236×10^{-5}	194×10^{-5}
Redwood..............	0.280×10^{-5}	185×10^{-5}
Engler.................	0.158×10^{-5}	405×10^{-5}

The viscosity of various liquids and gases as a function of temperature is shown in Figs. 2–2 and 2–3. The viscosity of standard air is $\mu = 3.72 \times 10^{-7}$ slug/ft sec and $\nu = 1.56 \times 10^{-4}$ ft^2/sec. More detailed data for water are given in Table 2–7.

TABLE 2–7
Properties of Water*

Temperature °F	Specific Gravity, s	Density, ρ		Viscosity	
		lb$_m$/ft^3	slugs/ft^3	Dynamic, μ slug/ft sec	Kinematic, ν ft^2/sec
32	0.9999	62.42	1.940	3.746×10^{-5}	1.931×10^{-5}
35	0.9999	62.42	1.940	3.536	1.823
39.2	1.0000	62.43	1.941	3.274	1.687
40	0.9999	62.43	1.940	3.229	1.664
50	0.9997	62.41	1.940	2.735	1.410
60	0.9990	62.37	1.938	2.359	1.217
70	0.9980	62.30	1.936	2.050	1.059
80	0.9966	62.22	1.934	1.799	0.930
90	0.9950	62.11	1.931	1.595	0.826
100	0.9931	62.00	1.927	1.424	0.739
110	0.9909	61.86	1.923	1.284	0.667
120	0.9885	61.71	1.918	1.168	0.609
130	0.9860	61.55	1.913	1.069	0.558
140	0.9832	61.38	1.908	0.981	0.514
150	0.9802	61.20	1.902	0.905	0.476
160	0.9770	61.00	1.896	0.838	0.442
170	0.9738	60.80	1.890	0.780	0.413
180	0.9704	60.58	1.883	0.726	0.385
190	0.9667	60.36	1.876	0.678	0.362
200	0.9630	60.12	1.868	0.637	0.341

*From *Hydraulic Models*, Am. Soc. Civil Engrs., 1942.

Newtonian and non-Newtonian fluids. A fluid for which the dynamic viscosity μ depends on temperature (and slightly on pressure) and is independent of the shear rate is called a Newtonian fluid. A graph relating shear stress and shear rate (velocity gradient) is a straight line through the origin whose slope is the dynamic viscosity, $\mu = \tau/(du/dy)$. This graph is often called the flow curve, and is shown in Fig. 2–4.

Fluids whose viscous behavior is not described by Eq. 2–7 are called *non-Newtonian* fluids. Although these non-Newtonian fluids are not uncommon, their viscous behavior is not yet completely understood.

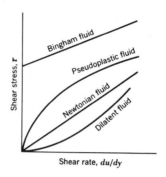

FIG. 2–4. Viscous behavior of fluids; flow curves.

Fluids have been classified according to their viscous behavior in different ways. Wilkinson [1][3] classifies them in two groups as Newtonian and non-Newtonian. The non-Newtonian group has three sub-groups:

1) Fluids for which the shear stress depends only on the shear rate, and although the relation between them is not linear it is independent of the time of application of the shear stress,

2) Fluids for which the shear stress depends not only on the shear rate, but also on the time the fluid has been sheared or on its previous history, and

3) Viscoelastic fluids which exhibit characteristics of both elastic solids and viscous fluids.

Metzner [2,3] classifies fluids into four general categories:

I. *Purely viscous fluids.* These include Newtonian fluids and non-Newtonian fluids for which the shear stress depends only on shear rate and is time-independent. Air and water are Newtonian. Gases and low-molecular-weight liquids are almost always Newtonian, and for them $\tau = \mu(du/dy)$ for parallel laminar flow (only one non-zero velocity component). A number of nonlinear constitutive equations have been used to describe the viscous behavior of non-Newtonian viscous fluids. For parallel flow they include:

a) The power-law equation

$$\tau = K(du/dy)^n \tag{2-10}$$

where K is a consistency index and n is a flow behavior index, which become μ and 1, respectively, for a Newtonian fluid.

b) The Ellis equation

$$du/dy = \frac{\tau_1}{\mu_0} + \left(\frac{\tau}{K}\right)^{1/n}$$

[3]Numbers in brackets refer to references at the end of the chapter.

which corrects for the inaccuracy of the power-law equation at low shear rates.

c) The Bingham equation

$$\tau = \tau_1 + \mu_B(du/dy)$$

which describes the behavior of a fluid which acts as a solid for shear stresses less than τ_1 and as a Newtonian fluid for shear stresses greater than τ_1 (Fig. 2–4).

d) The three-parameter Eyring-Powell equation

$$\tau = \mu(du/dy) + C_1 \sinh^{-1}\left(\frac{1}{C_2}\frac{du}{dy}\right)$$

which is not explicit in du/dy, but is more accurate over a larger range of shear rates than the preceding equations.

For power-law fluids most non-Newtonian slurries, polymer solutions, and molten polymers (including cellulose derivatives) have a flow behavior index n less than unity. These fluids are called *pseudoplastic* because the apparent viscosity decreases with increasing shear rate—the flow curve becomes flatter as the shear rate increases (Fig. 2–4). Suspensions of solids with high solid concentrations and highly-saturated polymer solutions have a flow behavior index n greater than unity. These fluids are called *dilatent* because the apparent viscosity increases with increasing shear rate—the flow curve steepens with increasing shear rate (Fig. 2–4). Different values of flow index n result in different shapes of velocity profiles for laminar flow in circular ducts (Appendix I) and exhibit different effects of flow rate on pressure drop for these flows.

Typical Bingham fluids include some slurries, drilling muds, oil paints, toothpaste, and sewage sludges.

II. *Time-dependent fluids.* Fluids for which the apparent viscosity decreases with time under a constant shear rate are called *thixotropic;* those for which the apparent viscosity increases with time are called *rheopectic.* This behavior is characteristic of gypsum pastes, slurries, and suspensions of solids in liquids. The time dependency is often significant for only short time periods of shear stress application. Thus the time-dependent fluids are often treated as purely viscous fluids. Thixotropic fluids often exhibit hysteresis effects.

III. *Viscoelastic fluids.* Materials such as pitch, flour dough, and some solid and molted polymers exhibit characteristics of both elastic solids and viscous fluids.

IV. *More complex rheological systems.* Some fluids exhibit characteristics of all three categories I, II, and III. In a superimposed magnetic field, a fluid may have a shear-rate-shear-stress relation which includes magnetohydrodynamic effects. For low density gases the fluid may have to be considered as made up of discrete particles, and not be treated as a continuum. These are typical of fluids in this fourth category.

Most of the work on non-Newtonian fluids during the past decade has been done by chemical engineers, but interest is being shown by people in other engineering areas. An informative discussion of the civil engineering aspects of non-Newtonian fluids is given by Bugliarello et al [4]. Engineers in many areas are becoming increasingly confronted with the flow of non-Newtonian fluids in pipes as well as in the design and selection of pumps for these fluids [5]. Experiments have shown that frictional effects for some non-Newtonian fluids are less than for a Newtonian fluid under equivalent turbulent flow conditions, resulting in a lower pressure drop in pipes and reduced drag on bodies submerged in liquids. This latter situation is of interest in naval hydrodynamics.

The study of non-Newtonian fluids is a part of the general science of rheology [6].

2–3. SURFACE TENSION AND CAPILLARITY

If a spoon is held under a dripping faucet, the water may rise nearly $\frac{1}{8}$ in. above the upper edges of the spoon before spilling. Similarly, water may be poured into a glass to a level nearly $\frac{1}{8}$ in. above the lip of the glass. If a small-bore tube is placed vertically in a free water surface, the water will rise in the tube; if the liquid is mercury, the mercury will be depressed within the tube. These are examples of the effects of surface tension and capillarity of liquids.

Surface tension is a characteristic of a liquid surface or skin, and its effects occur at liquid-gas or liquid-liquid interfaces. It is expressed in terms of energy per unit area, or its equivalent, force per unit length. The surface tension of water, for example, varies slightly with temperature, but it is about 0.005 lb_f/ft at ordinary temperatures. It may be reduced to about one-half that value by the addition of wetting agents.

Typical values of surface tension for some liquids are given in Table 2–8. It is seen that the surface tension is essentially the same for a liquid in contact with air or its own vapor. The higher the surface tension, the better is the interface in a manometer (see Sec. 4–3).

Attempts are usually made to avoid the effects of surface tension. Manometers (see Sec. 4–3) contain fluids which are chosen so as to have a readable meniscus (interface), that of mercury under water being exceptionally good, and that of carbon tetrachloride under water being poor. Manometer tubing, especially when an air-liquid interface is used in plastic tubing, should be selected carefully in order to avoid erroneous results.

TABLE 2–8

SURFACE TENSION OF LIQUIDS AT 77 F
IN CONTACT WITH AIR, WATER, OR THEIR OWN VAPOR*

Substance	Surface Tension (lb/ft)
Carbon tetrachloride-air.............	0.0018
Water-air........................	0.0050
Mercury-air.......................	0.032
Carbon tetrachloride-water..........	0.0031
Mercury-water.....................	0.026
Carbon tetrachloride-vapor..........	0.0018
Water-vapor......................	0.0050

*Handbook of Chemistry and Physics (38th ed.; Cleveland: Chemical Rubber Publishing Company, 1956–1957).

Some plastic tubes also exhibit hysteresis effects when used in this way—a falling liquid column comes to rest at a different position than a rising liquid column for the same external pressure condition. Hydraulic models are made large enough so that shallow depths, which otherwise might be affected by surface tension, are avoided. Wetting agents may be used to reduce these effects if the size of the model is made as large as possible, yet smaller than would be desirable. Surface tension plays a role in deterring the growth of small gas nuclei in liquids when they pass through low-pressure regions, yet the precise role is not understood. This rapid growth and collapse of bubbles in liquids is one form of cavitation.

Forces due to surface tension are, with the preceding exceptions, generally small compared with the forces due to gravity, viscosity, and pressure in engineering practice.

2–4. COMPRESSIBILITY OR ELASTICITY

Fluids may be deformed by viscous shear or compressed by an external pressure applied to a volume of fluid. All fluids are compressible by this method, liquids to a much smaller degree, however, than gases.

The compressibility is defined in terms of an average bulk modulus of elasticity

$$\overline{K} = - \frac{p_2 - p_1}{(V_2 - V_1)/V_1} \qquad (2\text{–}11)$$

where V_2 and V_1 are the volumes of the substance at pressure p_2 and p_1, respectively. The bulk modulus varies with the pressure for gases, and with both pressure and temperature (though but slightly) for liquids. Thus, the true bulk modulus of elasticity is the limiting value of Eq. 2–11 when the pressure and volume changes become infinitesimal.

$$K = -\frac{dp}{dV/V} \qquad (2\text{–}12\text{a})$$

If a unit mass of substance is considered,

$$K = -\frac{dp}{dv/v} \qquad (2\text{–}12\text{b})$$

and

$$K = +\frac{dp}{d\rho/\rho} \qquad (2\text{–}12\text{c})$$

The denominators of Eqs. 2–11 and 2–12 are dimensionless, so that K has the dimensions of a pressure, or force per unit area.

The value of K for water at 68 F is about 320,000 $lb_f/in.^2$ at atmospheric pressure, increasing essentially linearly to about 410,000 $lb_f/in.^2$ at a pressure of 15,000 $lb_f/in.^2$ Thus, in this range,

$$K = 320,000 + 6\,p \quad lb_f/in.^2$$

where p is the gage pressure in $lb_f/in.^2$

The change in volume of a gas for a change in pressure depends on the compression process. If *isothermal* (constant temperature), the gas equation may be expressed in logarithmic form as $\ln p = \ln \rho + \ln (RT)$ and differentiated to obtain $dp/p = d\rho/\rho$. Thus

$$K_{\text{isothermal}} = \frac{dp}{d\rho/\rho} = \frac{dp}{dp/p} = p \qquad (2\text{–}13)$$

and the elastic modulus equals the absolute pressure during an isothermal compression.

If the compression is adiabatic and is carried out slowly so that equilibrium conditions exist, the compression may be considered reversible and adiabatic, or *isentropic* (see Chapter 3). For this process, $p/\rho^k = $ constant (k is the ratio of specific heat capacities). The logarithmic form, $\ln p - k \ln \rho = \ln C$, may be differentiated to obtain $dp/p = k\,d\rho/\rho$. Thus

$$K_{\text{isentropic}} = \frac{dp}{d\rho/\rho} = \frac{dp}{dp/kp} = kp \qquad (2\text{–}14)$$

and the elastic modulus equals the absolute pressure times the ratio of specific heat capacities ($k = c_p/c_v = 1.4$ for air) during an isentropic compression.

The bulk modulus of elasticity K is of interest in acoustics as well as in fluid mechanics. The velocity of sound in any medium is

$$c = \sqrt{\frac{K}{\rho}} \qquad (2\text{–}15)$$

and for a gas, sound waves are transmitted essentially isentropically (see Sec. 9–1), so that the velocity of sound in a perfect gas is

$$c = \sqrt{\frac{kp}{\rho}} = \sqrt{kRT} \qquad (2\text{–}16)$$

EXAMPLE 2–5. What is the speed of sound in water at 68 F and atmospheric pressure?

Solution:

$$c = \sqrt{\frac{K}{\rho}} = \sqrt{\frac{(320{,}000 \text{ lb}_f/\text{in.}^2)\ (144 \text{ in.}^2/\text{ft}^2)}{1.94 \text{ slugs/ft}^3}} = 4870 \text{ ft/sec}$$

EXAMPLE 2–6. What is the speed of sound in air at 68 F at sea level and at an altitude where the pressure is 10 lb$_f$/in.^{2} absolute?

Solution: At either pressure,

$$c = \sqrt{kRT} = \sqrt{(1.4)\left(1715 \frac{\text{ft lb}_f}{\text{slug R}}\right)(528 \text{ R})} = 1126 \text{ ft/sec}$$

2–5. VAPOR PRESSURE

If a liquid and its vapor coexist in equilibrium, the vapor is called a saturated vapor, and the pressure exerted by this saturated vapor is called the *vapor pressure*. The vapor pressure is a function of temperature for a given substance.

The vapor pressure of liquids is of practical importance in barometers (see Sec. 4–3), pump-piping systems, and from an elementary point of view, in the formation of cavities in low-pressure regions within a liquid.

Values of vapor pressure for some liquids at various temperatures are shown in Table 2–9.

TABLE 2–9

VAPOR PRESSURE OF SOME LIQUIDS

TEMPERATURE (deg F)	LIQUID VAPOR PRESSURE (psia)				
	Water	Mercury	Kerosene	Propane	Methyl Alcohol
40	0.122		0.32	78	0.71
60	0.26	0.000025	0.44	107	1.42
100	0.95		0.86	187	4.42
160	4.74		1.23		

REFERENCES

1. W. L. Wilkinson, *Non-Newtonian Fluids* (New York: Pergamon Press, 1960).

2. A. B. Metzner, "Flow of Non-Newtonian Fluids," Section 7 of *Handbook*

of Fluid Dynamics, edited by V. L. Streeter (New York: McGraw-Hill Book Company, Inc., 1961).

3. A. B. Metzner, "Heat Transfer in Non-Newtonian Fluids," *Advances in Heat Transfer,* Vol. 2 (New York: Academic Press, 1965), pp. 357–397.

4. G. Bugliarello, V. C. Behn, C. E. Carver, E. M. Krokosky, J. F. Ripken, and R. L. Schiffman, "Non-Newtonian Flows," *Civil Eng.,* Vol. 35 (1965), pp. 68–70.

5. G. Bugliarello, "Some Considerations on the Analysis and Design of Hydraulic Machinery for Non-Newtonian Fluids," *Proc. Tenth Congress Intl. Assoc. for Hyd. Research,* Vol. 4 (1963), Paper No. 4.1.

6. A. G. Fredrickson, *Principles and Applications of Rheology* (Englewood Cliffs, New Jersey: Prentice-Hall Inc., 1964).

PROBLEMS

2–1. A gallon of sea water weighs 8.55 lb$_f$ where $g = 32.1$ ft/sec^2. What are the density and specific gravity of this sea water referred to water at 60 F? (7.48 gallons = 1 ft^3.)

Ans. $\rho = 1.99$ slugs/ft^3, $s = 1.026$

2–2. What is the specific gravity of mercury at 40 F, 60 F, and 120 F referred to water at the same temperature?

2–3. What volume of kerosene would be occupied by a mass of 0.6 slug?

2–4. What force does a standard gravitational field of 32.17 ft/sec^2 exert on a 1 ft^3 of water at 60 F?

2–5. Compute the density in slugs/ft^3 and the specific weight in lb$_f$/ft^3 for a standard gravitational field for each of the liquids listed in Table 2–2.

2–6. Distinguish between the density and the specific gravity of a liquid.

2–7. Compute the density of standard air ($p = 14.696$ psia and $T = 59$ F) in units of slug/ft^3.

Ans. 0.002378 slug/ft^3

2–8. Calculate the density of each gas listed in Table 2–3 at atmospheric pressure ($p = 14.696$ psia) and a temperature of 59 F.

Ans. $\rho_{hydrogen} = 0.0001653$ slug/ft^3, $\rho_{xenon} = 0.01079$ slug/ft^3

2–9. The temperature and pressure of the NACA standard atmosphere at 14,000 ft are 9.1 F and 1243 psfa, respectively. What is the air density at that altitude?

Ans. 0.001546 slug/ft^3

2–10. The temperature and pressure of the NACA standard atmosphere at 130,000 ft are 33 F and 6.071 psfa, respectively, and at sea level 59 F and 14.696 psia, respectively. What is the ratio of the number of molecules of air per unit volume at sea level to that at 130,000 ft, considering the air to have the same composition at each altitude?

2-11. Does the equation $p = \rho RT$ apply to

a) only a nonviscous perfect gas

b) only a viscous perfect gas

c) to both viscous and nonviscous (real and ideal) perfect gases?

2-12. What is the density of nitrogen at 2200 psfa and 100 F in units of slug/ft³?

2-13. Nitrogen in a high-pressure container is at 200 psig and 80 F. What is its density in slug/ft³?

Ans. 0.0323 slug/ft³

2-14. A gas at 20 psia and 40 F has a density of 0.00510 slug/ft³, and at 200 psia and 140 F the density is 0.0417 slug/ft³. Is the gas a perfect gas?

2-15. What property does a real fluid have that an ideal fluid does not have?

2-16. Define fluid viscosity, as though you were writing for Scientific American magazine.

2-17. From kinetic theory, the dynamic viscosity of a perfect gas increases with temperature and is independent of pressure. Under what conditions does the kinematic viscosity of a perfect gas also increase with temperature? Under what conditions does it decrease?

2-18. Show that the term *velocity gradient* is synonymous with *rate of angular deformation* and *time rate of shear strain*.

2-19. Verify the equivalences in Table 2–4.

2-20. Verify the conversion factors listed in Table 2–5.

2-21. From Fig. 2–3, determine the dynamic viscosity of fuel oil at 70 F.

Ans. $\mu = 1.64 \times 10^{-4}$ slug/ft sec

2-22. A fluid has a kinematic viscosity of 3 centistokes and a dynamic viscosity of 5×10^{-5} slug/ft sec. What is the density of the fluid in slug/ft³?

2-23. Show that the dynamic viscosity of mercury given in Fig. 2–2 is related to the kinematic viscosity given in Fig. 2–3 by the density values given in Table 2–1.

2-24. What is the dynamic viscosity of Univis J-43 hydraulic fluid at 100 F in Reyns?

Ans. 2.08×10^{-2} Reyns

2-25. What is the viscosity of Univis J-43 hydraulic fluid at 150 F in Saybolt seconds?

Ans. 56.8 sec

2-26. Repeat Prob. 2–25 for a) a Redwood viscometer, and b) an Engler viscometer.

2–27. In Fig. 2–1, is the shear stress greater at the boundary at A or out in the flow? Explain.

2–28. An oil ($\mu = 0.0016$ slug/ft sec, $\rho = 1.60$ slugs/ft^3) flows along a flat plate with a velocity profile near the plate given by the equation

$$u = 96y - 1152y^2 \qquad \text{ft/sec}$$

where y is the distance from the plate in feet. What is the shear stress at the plate surface?

Ans. 0.1536 lb$_f$/ft^2

2–29. The velocity profile in a fluid near a boundary is (Fig. 2–1)

$$u = 72y - 144y^2 \qquad \text{ft/sec}$$

where y is in feet. What is the velocity gradient a) at the boundary? b) at $y = 1.5$ in.? c) at $y = 3$ in.?

2–30. Air at 40 F and 12 psia flows past a smooth surface with a velocity profile (Fig. 2–1) given by

$$u = 960y - 3 \times 10^6 y^3 \qquad \text{ft/sec}$$

where y is in feet. The kinematic viscosity of the air is 1.79×10^{-4}ft^2/sec. What is the shear stress at the boundary surface?

2–31. A fluid flows along a surface with a velocity profile (Fig. 2–1) given by

$$u = 36y - 48y^2 \qquad \text{ft/sec}$$

where y is in feet. The specific gravity of the fluid is 0.8 and its kinematic viscosity is 0.0004 ft^2/sec. What is the shear stress at the boundary surface?

2–32. Air at 40 F and 15 psia flows along a flat surface with a velocity profile (Fig. 2–1) given by

$$u = 40y - 80y^3 \qquad \text{ft/sec}$$

where y is in feet. The measured shear stress is 1.44×10^{-5} lb$_f$/ft^2. What is the kinematic viscosity of the air?

2–33. The velocity profile for laminar flow in a round pipe is given by the equation

$$u = u_{\max} [1 - (r/R)^2]$$

where $u_{\max}$ is the center-line velocity, R is the pipe radius, and r is the radial distance from the pipe center line. a) What is the velocity gradient at the pipe wall? Note that the normal distance from the pipe wall is $y = R - r$; thus, $dy = - dr$ and $du/dy = - du/dr$. b) What is the wall shear stress when fuel oil at 50 F flows with an average velocity of 10 ft/sec ($u_{\max} = 20$ ft/sec) in a 6-in. diameter pipe? c) What is the shear stress at the pipe center line? d) Show that the velocity gradient, and hence shear stress, varies linearly with radius.

Ans. b) 6.02 lb$_f$/ft^3

2–34. A fluid flows along a flat surface with a laminar velocity profile given by
$$u = 24y - 36y^2 \quad \text{ft/sec}$$
where y is the distance from the surface in feet. *a*) What are the velocity gradients at the surface, 2 in. from the surface, and 4 in. from the surface? *b*) What are the shear stresses at these points for air, for water, and for crude oil at 100 F?

Ans. *a*) 12 (ft/sec)/ft at 2 in., *b*) 3.41 × 10⁻⁴ lb_f/ft² for water at the surface.

2–35. The velocity profile for laminar flow in a round pipe is given in Prob. 2–33. Show that the shear stress varies linearly from zero at the pipe center line to a maximum at the pipe wall.

2–36. Oil with a density of 1.75 slugs/ft³ flows through a 2-in. diameter pipe. Measurements of the pressure drop over a portion of the pipe indicate that the shear stress at the pipe wall is 0.048 lb_f/ft², and flow measurements indicate the velocity profile to be given by
$$u = 2 - 288r^2 \quad \text{ft/sec}$$
where r is the radial distance from the pipe center line in feet. What is the kinematic viscosity of the oil?

Ans. 5.71 × 10⁻⁴ ft²/sec

2–37. Fuel oil at 60 F flows in a 12-in. diameter pipe with a velocity profile given by
$$u = 8 - 32r^2 \quad \text{ft/sec}$$
where r is the radial distance from the pipe center line in feet. The flow is laminar. *a*) What is the total shearing force in 100 ft of pipe length? *b*) The total shear force over a given length of pipe equals the pressure drop over that length times the cross-sectional area of the pipe (this is discussed in Chapters 5 and 10). What is the pressure drop over the 100-ft length of pipe?

2–38. For laminar flow in a circular tube, the direct measurement of the tube diameter, the pressure drop over a given length of tube, and the flow rate will enable the experimenter to calculate the wall shear stress and the velocity profile. From these the fluid viscosity may be determined. For a velocity profile given by (Fig. 2–1)
$$u = 96y - 1152y^2 \quad \text{ft/sec}$$
where y is in feet, the wall shear stress is 0.048 lb_f/ft². What is the dynamic viscosity of the fluid?

2–39. A liquid fills the space between two parallel plates 0.02 in. apart. The lower plate is at rest and the upper plate is maintained in steady motion at 1 ft/sec by a force of 0.04 lb_f/ft². What is the dynamic viscosity of the fluid?

Ans $\mu = 6.67 \times 10^{-5}$ slug/ft sec

2–40. The space between two parallel plates ½ in. apart is filled with an oil of viscosity $\mu = 0.001$ slug/ft sec. A thin 1 × 2-ft rectangular plate is pulled through the oil ⅛ in. from one plate and ⅜ in. from the other. What force is required to pull the plate at 1 ft/sec?

2–41. A flat plate moves at a constant velocity V with respect to another flat plate at rest and parallel to the first. The space between the plates has a thickness h and is occupied by a viscous fluid of viscosity μ. *a*) What is the shape of the velocity profile in the viscous fluid? Justify your answer. *b*) What is the velocity gradient at the surface of the plate which is at rest?

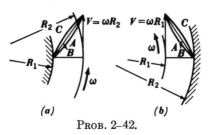

(a)　　　　　*(b)*

PROB. 2–42.

2–42. A viscous fluid of viscosity μ occupies the annular space between a fixed and a rotating cylinder. For laminar motion, is the shape of the velocity profile similar to curve A, B (linear), or C for the two situations shown? Prove your conclusions.

Ans. a) curve C

2–43. A thin-walled cylinder 10 in. long rotates at 60 rpm midway between two fixed concentric cylinders of 10.0-in. and 10.5-in. diameter, respectively. A torque of 2.8 lb$_f$ ft is required to maintain the motion. What is the viscosity of the oil which fills the space between the two fixed cylinders?

2–44. Two coaxial circular plates 1 ft in diameter are spaced 0.01 in. apart. The space between them is filled with an oil having a viscosity $\mu = 0.15$ lb$_m$/ft sec. The plates are horizontal, the bottom one is at rest, and the upper one rotates at 2 rps. What torque is required to maintain the given speed?

Ans. 6.9 lb$_f$ ft

2–45. A sleeve 12 in. long encases a vertical rod 1.000 in. in diameter with a uniform radial clearance of 0.002 in. When the sleeve and rod are immersed in olive oil at 60 F, the effective weight of the sleeve is 1 lb$_f$. How fast will the sleeve slide down the rod? Consider the drag on the outer portion of the sleeve to be negligible (it is about 0.002 lb$_f$).

Ans. 0.326 ft/sec

2–46. A 6.00-in. diameter shaft rotates at 1800 rpm in a stationary journal bearing 12 in. long with a 6.02-in. ID. The uniform space between shaft and bearing is filled with an oil of viscosity 3.6×10^{-4} slug/ft sec. What horsepower is required to overcome the viscous resistance in the bearing? NOTE: Power = force × velocity.

2–47. An 800-lb$_f$ hydraulic lift consists of a 7.990-in. diameter shaft in an 8.000-in. diameter sleeve 6 ft long. The shaft supporting the lift falls steadily at 2 in./sec. What is the viscosity of the oil between the shaft and sleeve?

2–48. A 6.000-in. diameter shaft rotates at 400 rpm in a bearing 6.010 in. in diameter. An oil film between the shaft and bearing is of uniform thickness. What is the velocity gradient in the oil film?

2-49. A 6.00-in. diameter shaft rotates in a 6.02-in. diameter bearing 12 in. long, the space between shaft and bearing being filled with an oil of viscosity $\mu = 0.001$ slug/ft sec. What torque is required to maintain a rotational speed of 400 rpm?

Ans. 4.93 lb_f ft

2-50. The dynamic viscosity of water at 68 F is 1 centipoise and the density is 0.9982 gm/cc. Calculate the dynamic viscosity in units of *a*) slug/ft sec, *b*) lb_m/ft sec, *c*) reyns, and *d*) lb_f sec/ft²; and the kinematic viscosity in *e*) stokes and *f*) ft²/sec.

Ans. *b*) 0.000673 lb_m/ft sec, *e*) 0.01002 stokes

2-51. An SAE 20 crankcase oil is one for which the range of Saybolt viscometer readings is from 120 to 185 sec at 130 F. *a*) What is the kinematic viscosity of this oil at the mid-point of this range (152.5 sec) in ft²/sec? *b*) What would be the viscosity of this oil in Redwood seconds? *c*) What would be the viscosity of this oil in Engler seconds?

2-52. The added pressure due to surface tension in a small bubble over the ambient pressure may be found by equating the pressure difference times the great circle area of the bubble to the surface tension times bubble circumference. Show that, for a small bubble of radius R, $\Delta p = 2\sigma/R$.

2-53. Calculate the excess pressure inside an 0.002-in. radius bubble over the ambient pressure for an air bubble in *a*) carbon tetrachloride, *b*) water, and *c*) mercury.

Ans. *b*) 60 psf

2-54. It is assumed that bubble nuclei may expand and produce a form of cavitation known as intermittent bubble cavitation when the ambient pressure is reduced or the nuclei pass through a low-pressure region in a liquid. Would a given reduction in pressure have a greater effect on the growth of a large or on a small bubble? Explain.

2-55. The elastic modulus is defined as $K = -dp/(dv/v)$. Show that this is equivalent to $K = +dp/(d\rho/\rho)$.

2-56. An external pressure of 6800 psi reduces the volume of a given quantity of water by 2 per cent. What is the bulk modulus of elasticity of the water?

Ans. $\overline{K} = 340{,}000$ lb_f/ft²

2-57. Estimate the elastic modulus for water at 68 F at a pressure of 1000 psi and at 10,000 psi.

2-58. The *Trieste* submerged to a depth of 36,198 ft in the Mariannas Trench early in 1960. The pressure at that depth is about 16,470 psi. *a*) What is the average elastic modulus K throughout this range of depth, assuming it to vary linearly and to be the same as for fresh water? *b*) What is the increase in density of sea water from the surface to a depth of 36,198 ft?

Ans. *b*) 4.6 per cent

2–59. What is the speed of sound in sea water at 68 F a) at the surface of the sea and b) at a depth of 35,800 ft? See Prob. 2–58 (a) for K_{avg}.

2–60. The speed of sound in any homogeneous medium is $c = \sqrt{K/\rho}$. Let subscripts m, w, and g refer to property values for the *mixture*, for *water*, and for the *gas*, respectively, in a gas-bubble-and-water mixture. Then for a nonresonant mixture, sound is considered to be propagated at constant temperature at low gas concentrations, and the sound speed is given by $c_m = \sqrt{K_m/\rho_m}$. Let x be the proportion of gas by volume. a) Show that the density of the mixture is $\rho_m = x\rho_g + (1 - x)\rho_w$. b) The elastic modulus K_m may be obtained by treating its reciprocal in a similar manner. Show that

$$\frac{1}{K_m} = \frac{x}{K_g} + \frac{1 - x}{K_w}$$

c) Show that

$$c_m = \sqrt{\frac{p_g K_w}{[xK_w + (1 - x)p_g][x\rho_g + (1 - x)\rho_w]}}$$

d) Calculate the speed of sound in water at 68 F at atmospheric pressure containing 0.1 per cent gas nuclei by volume, and compare with Example 2–5. The result applies at frequencies below bubble resonance. e) Repeat part d) for 1 per cent by volume of gas nuclei.

Ans. d) 1020 ft/sec, e) 331 ft/sec

2–61. The speed of sound in any medium is $c = \sqrt{K/\rho}$. Suppose water contains 100 parts per million by volume of minute gas nuclei evenly distributed. How does the speed of sound in this mixture compare with the speed of sound in pure water at the same temperature and pressure? Explain.

2–62. The speed of sound in any medium is $c = \sqrt{K/\rho}$. Suppose minute water droplets are sprayed into dry air at a low concentration. How would the speed of sound in this mixture compare with the speed of sound in dry air at the same pressure and temperature? Explain.

2–63. The elastic modulus K is evaluated at two different pressures for a given gas, p_2 being higher than p_1. Is K_2 equal to K_1, less than K_1, or greater than K_1? Explain.

2–64. Air expands from 40 to 20 psia. What is the elastic modulus K a) at the beginning of expansion for an isothermal expansion, b) at the end of expansion for a reversible adiabatic expansion, and c) at the end of a polytropic expansion for which the ratio of specific heat capacities k is replaced by $n = 1.2$?

2–65. Repeat Prob. 2–64 for a compression from 15 psia to 100 psia.

3

Thermodynamic and Mathematical Considerations

A treatment of fluid mechanics, especially one which includes gas flows, requires an inclusion of thermodynamic considerations. Only those concepts and equations which apply to fluid mechanics, or which will in many instances simplify the treatment in later discussions, will be included here. More detailed information is available in textbooks on thermodynamics.

Fundamental in this discussion is the concept of a system and of a control volume. A system contains a definite quantity of matter upon which we wish to focus our attention. The region outside the system boundaries is called its surroundings and could be a part of another system. The system may be either closed or open. In a closed system, no material or mass (fluid) crosses the boundaries, and thus the system contains a fixed amount of matter. In an open system, matter (fluid) crosses the boundaries, and the amount of matter within the system may or may not change with time. In fluid flow it is generally more convenient to deal with a fixed region in space rather than with a fixed quantity of matter. This fixed region is called a control volume; it is bounded by a control surface.

3–1. TEMPERATURE

If two systems or bodies, one which feels hot and one cold, are brought into contact, after some time they will feel less hot and less cold, respectively, and eventually they will be in a state of equilibrium where no further changes occur. They are then said to be at the same temperature. An arbitrary scale of temperature may be defined. An example is the well-known Fahrenheit scale, defined as 32 F at the temperature of an equilibrium mixture of pure ice and air-saturated water (ice point) and 212 F at the temperature of an equilibrium mixture of pure water and water vapor at a pressure of 1 atmosphere (steam point). The Rankine temperature scale is the so-called absolute Fahrenheit scale. Thus

Temperature in degrees Rankine =
temperature in degrees Fahrenheit + 459.67

The temperature of a substance is a property of that substance, that is, it is a characteristic of the equilibrium state.

3–2. WORK

Work flows from one system (to its surroundings or to another system) if the only effect outside the one system is equivalent to the raising of a weight (exerting a force through a distance). We will consider work to be positive if it is done *by* the one system we are considering. Examples of positive work are: an expansion of the boundaries of a system and work done by a substance (fluid) as it passes through a turbine. If work is received by a system, such as by a pump or compressor, then the work is considered to be negative. Work is *not* a property of a substance, since it is energy in transition. It will be designated by W, and if measured in terms of energy per unit mass of substance, w will be used.

Energy may be defined as the capacity to do work.

3–3. HEAT

If a system is not in thermal equilibrium with its surroundings, then energy will pass through the boundaries of the system. The energy which is being transferred is called heat. We will consider heat to be positive if it is added *to* the system we are considering and negative if it is removed from it. Heat, like work, is *not* a property of a substance since it is energy in transition. The quantity transferred will be designated by Q, and if measured in terms of energy per unit mass, q will be used.

3–4. THE FIRST LAW OF THERMODYNAMICS

The first law of thermodynamics is an expression of the conservation of energy. Whenever energy is transferred across the boundaries of a system, the energy of the system changes by an equal amount. The increase in energy of the system is equal to the decrease in energy of its surroundings, and vice versa.

One form of the first law states that if work is added to a substance in a closed system with no heat transfer to or from the system, the amount of work added depends only upon the end states of the process. Thus we may define a property E whose change represents this work. For a unit mass of substance

$$e_1 - e_2 = w'_{1\text{-}2}$$

The quantity e may be called the *energy content*. It consists of kinetic energy, potential energy, and internal energy.

If the process is accompanied by a transfer of heat, then the heat added to the substance within the system is the difference between the actual work added and the work added during a no-heat-transfer process between the same two end states. This may be expressed (per unit mass) as

$$q_{1\text{-}2} = w_{1\text{-}2} - w'_{1\text{-}2}$$

It follows that

$$q_{1\text{-}2} = e_2 - e_1 + w_{1\text{-}2} \tag{3-1}$$

For a closed system (the mass of the system is constant) the energy content consists of kinetic energy, potential energy, and internal energy u. For the closed system with negligible kinetic and potential energy

$$q_{1\text{-}2} = u_2 - u_1 + w_{1\text{-}2} \tag{3-2}$$

We will be concerned only with energy conversions between the various forms of mechanical energy and thermal energy and will not consider energy involved in chemical and nuclear reactions, or work done as a result of capillary, electric, or magnetic effects.

Equations 3-1 and 3-2 express the first law of thermodynamics, relating heat, work, and energy content. A more complete discussion of energy content is given in the development of the steady-flow energy equation for a control volume or an open system in Sec. 5-4.

3-5. THE SECOND LAW OF THERMODYNAMICS

The first law of thermodynamics contains no restrictions regarding the direction in which changes in the form of energy may take place. Thus mechanical energy may be transformed into thermal energy, and thermal energy may be transformed into mechanical energy according to the first law. The second law of thermodynamics, however, places restrictions on the direction of these energy transformations. For example, mechanical energy dissipated into thermal energy as a result of viscous shear in a real fluid cannot be recovered as mechanical energy; the process is irreversible according to the second law.

Of the many ways of expressing the second law of thermodynamics, the most useful in fluid mechanics is expressed as an axiom known as the inequality of Clausius. This states that if a system undergoes a complete cyclic process (the substance within the system is brought back to its original equilibrium state) the integral of dQ/T is equal to or less than zero.

$$\oint \frac{dQ}{T} \leqq 0$$

If the cycle is performed reversibly, the integral equals zero. A cyclic reversible process leaves no trace of its occurrence either within the system or in its surroundings—both are brought back to their respective initial states. No real or actual process is reversible because of friction, viscous shear, temperature difference, and so forth, although some real processes are very nearly reversible and may be considered to be so for purposes of analysis. For real processes, then, the integral is less than zero.

Another second law axiom states that the integral of dQ/T for a reversible process between a reference condition or state and some final condition or state defines the change in a new property, and this property is called *entropy*. If entropy per unit mass is designated as s,

$$ds = \frac{dq_{\text{rev}}}{T}$$

From the first law for a closed system (Eq. 3–2)

$$dq = du + dw$$

so that

$$ds = \frac{du + p\,dv}{T} \tag{3-3}$$

when only $p\,dv$ work is done. It follows that for a reversible process wherein no heat is transferred to or from the system (an *adiabatic* process), $ds = 0$ and for an irreversible adiabatic process, $ds > 0$.

Another property called the *enthalpy H* (or h per unit mass) is defined as the sum of the internal energy and the product of pressure and specific volume.

$$h = u + pv \tag{3-4}$$

In differential form, $dh = du + p\,dv + v\,dp$ so that Eq. 3–3 may be written as

$$T\,ds = dh - v\,dp \tag{3-5}$$

Equation 3–5 is perhaps the most useful form or expression of the first and second laws of thermodynamics for our purpose.

3–6. THE PERFECT GAS

For many engineering applications, assuming real gases to behave perfectly is a sufficiently accurate assumption. The equation of state is

$$pv = RT \qquad \text{or} \qquad p = \rho RT \tag{3-6}$$

where p is the absolute pressure, v the specific volume, T the absolute temperature, ρ the density, and R the gas constant. Values of the gas constant for a number of gases are listed in Table 3–1.

TABLE 3–1
SOME TYPICAL PROPERTIES OF GASES AT APPROXIMATELY 70 F

GAS	R		c_p		c_v		$k = \dfrac{c_p}{c_v}$
	$\dfrac{\text{ft lb}_f}{\text{lb}_m\ R}$	$\dfrac{\text{ft lb}_f}{\text{slug}\ R}$	$\dfrac{\text{Btu}}{\text{lb}_m\ F}$	$\dfrac{\text{ft lb}_f}{\text{slug}\ F}$	$\dfrac{\text{Btu}}{\text{lb}_m\ F}$	$\dfrac{\text{ft lb}_f}{\text{slug}\ F}$	
Air.............	53.3	1,715	0.240	6,000	0.171	4,285	1.40
Carbon dioxide...	35.1	1,130	0.196	4,900	0.151	3,770	1.30
Helium..........	386	12,420	1.237	30,960	0.741	18,540	1.67
Hydrogen.......	766	24,660	3.45	86,310	2.46	61,650	1.40
Methane........	96.2	3,095	0.522	13,080	0.399	9,985	1.31
Nitrogen........	55.2	1,776	0.248	6,216	0.177	4,440	1.40
Oxygen.........	48.3	1,555	0.217	5,440	0.155	3,885	1.40
Xenon..........	11.76	378	0.0376	942	0.0225	564	1.67

An indication of the accuracy of the perfect gas equation when applied to the mixture of gases known as air is shown in Fig. 3–1, where values of the compressibility factor Z ($Z = pv/RT$) are shown as a function of pressure and temperature. The shaded area indicates the range of pressures and temperatures in which the perfect gas equation is accurate within 1 per cent.

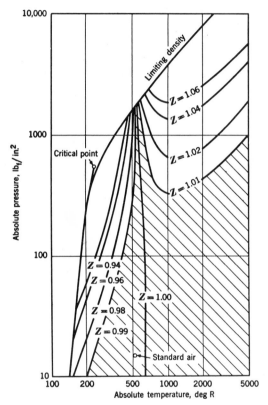

FIG. 3–1. Accuracy of the perfect gas equation for air. (Data from Newman A. Hall and Warren E. Ibele, "The Tabulation of Imperfect-Gas Properties of Air, Nitrogen, and Oxygen," *Trans. ASME*, Vol. 76, October, 1954, pp. 1039–1056. Used with permission of The American Society of Mechanical Engineers.)

The so-called specific heat capacities at constant pressure c_p and at constant volume c_v are defined as

$$c_p = \left(\frac{\partial h}{\partial T}\right)_p$$

or the change of enthalpy with respect to temperature at constant pressure and

$$c_v = \left(\frac{\partial u}{\partial T}\right)_v$$

or the change of internal energy with respect to temperature at constant volume. For a perfect gas, c_v is a function of temperature,

$$du = c_v \, dT$$

and if c_v is a constant,

$$u_2 - u_1 = c_v \, (T_2 - T_1) \tag{3-7}$$

Thus for *any* process or path between states 1 and 2 the internal energy change per unit mass equals c_v times the temperature change.

Also, $dh = c_p \, dT$ and if c_p is a constant,

$$h_2 - h_1 = c_p \, (T_2 - T_1) \tag{3-8}$$

Thus for *any* process or path between states 1 and 2 the enthalpy change per unit mass equals c_p times the temperature change.

From the definition of enthalpy it can be shown that, for a perfect gas,

$$c_p - c_v = R \tag{3-9}$$

We also may define a ratio for all substances as

$$k = \frac{c_p}{c_v} \tag{3-10}$$

so that for a perfect gas

$$c_v = \frac{R}{k-1} \tag{3-11}$$

and

$$c_p = \frac{Rk}{k-1} \tag{3-12}$$

Some typical values of the gas constant, specific heats, and the specific heat ratio are listed in Table 3–1.

3–7. FLOW PROCESSES

Substances (fluids) may undergo changes in state via a number of different paths or processes. Those already mentioned and some additional ones will be listed and defined for ready reference.

A system is *isothermal* if its temperature remains constant. The equation of state then indicates that $pv =$ constant for a perfect gas.

A system is *isobaric* if its pressure remains constant.

A system or process is *adiabatic* if no heat is transferred to or from the system to its surroundings. For this process $dq = 0$.

If the system or process is adiabatic and changes occur reversibly (often called a frictionless adiabatic process) then the process is called *isentropic*. The entropy during this process remains constant, and $ds = 0$. In special situations, the flow may be isentropic but neither adiabatic nor reversible. For example, if a real fluid flows through a pipe, there is an increase in internal entropy due to viscous shear or turbulence. If heat were removed in a manner such that the decrease in fluid entropy from the heat removed just balanced the increase in fluid entropy from internal causes, the flow could occur at constant entropy and be isentropic. However, it would be neither adiabatic (heat is transferred) nor reversible (internal friction exists). From Eqs. 3–5, 3–6, and 3–12

$$p_1 v_1^k = p_2 v_2^k = \text{constant} \qquad (3\text{–}13a)$$

$$\frac{p_1^{\frac{k-1}{k}}}{T_1} = \frac{p_2^{\frac{k-1}{k}}}{T_2} = \text{constant} \qquad (3\text{–}13b)$$

and
$$\frac{p_1^{1/k}}{\rho_1} = \frac{p_2^{1/k}}{\rho_2} = \text{constant} \qquad (3\text{–}13c)$$

A *polytropic* process is a general one for which

$$p_1 v_1^n = p_2 v_2^n = \text{constant} \qquad (3\text{–}14)$$

where $n = 1$ for an isothermal process,

$n = 0$ for a constant-pressure process,

$n = k$ for an isentropic (reversible or frictionless adiabatic) process.

Equations 3–13 apply to polytropic processes with k replaced by $n \neq 0$.

EXAMPLE 3–1. Ammonia enters a compressor-condenser system at a rate of 2 lb_m/min. The compressor adds energy at a rate of 3 hp to the ammonia, and the condenser removes 1100 Btu/min. What is the change in energy content of the ammonia? (1 hp = 33,000 ft lb_f/min.)

Solution: From Eq. 3–1,

$$e_2 - e_1 = q_{\text{added}} - w_{\text{done}}$$
$$= -550 - \frac{(-3)(33,000/2)}{778.2}$$
$$= -486.5 \text{ Btu/lb}_m$$
$$= -379,000 \text{ ft lb}_f/\text{lb}_m$$

EXAMPLE 3–2. If in Fig. 3–2, $p_1 = 15$ psia and $T_1 = 40$ F for air, what is the change in the internal energy, the change in enthalpy, the heat added to the air, and the work done by the air going from state *1* to states *2* and *3* ($p_2 = p_3 = 105$ psia)? The system does no shaft work, so only $p \, dv$ work is involved.

Solution:
$$v_1 = RT_1/p_1$$
$$= 12.33 \text{ ft}^3/\text{lb}_m$$

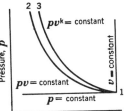

FIG. 3–2. Thermodynamic processes.

For process *1-2*, the temperature is constant, and the change in internal energy and in enthalpy are both zero and

$$v_2 = p_1 v_1/p_2 = (15)(12.33)/105 = 1.761 \text{ ft}^3/\text{lb}_m$$

$$w_{1\text{-}2} = \int_1^2 p\ dv = RT_1 \ln (v_2/v_1)$$

$$= (53.3)\ 500 \ln (1/7) = -51,800 \text{ ft lb}_f/\text{lb}_m$$

Then from Eq. 3–2,

$$q_{1\text{-}2} = u_2 - u_1 + w_{1\text{-}2}$$

$$= 0 - 51,800/778.2 = -66.6 \text{ Btu/lb}_m$$

For process *1-3*,

$$T_3 = T_1\ (p_3/p_1)^{\frac{k-1}{k}} = 500\ (7)^{0.286} = 870 \text{ R} = 410 \text{ F}$$

$$u_3 - u_1 = c_v(T_3 - T_1) = (0.171)(370) = 63.3 \text{ Btu/lb}_m$$

$$h_3 - h_1 = c_p(T_3 - T_1) = (0.240)(370) = 88.8 \text{ Btu/lb}_m$$

The heat added is zero, since the process is adiabatic, and from Eq. 3–2

$$q_{1\text{-}3} = u_3 - u_1 + w_{1\text{-}3}$$

$$0 = 63.3 + (w_{1\text{-}3}/778.2)$$

$$w_{1\text{-}3} = -49,300 \text{ ft lb}_f/\text{lb}_m$$

This represents work done *on* the gas (since the algebraic sign is negative). Comparable results per slug mass may be obtained by using R, c_p, and c_v per slug mass from Table 3–1.

3–8. PARTIAL AND TOTAL DERIVATIVES

Partial and total derivatives, vectors, and complex variables are used in the mathematical analysis of fluid flow. The treatment presented here will not include complex variables; only partial and total derivatives and vectors will be used.

If u (any continuous variable, such as pressure or velocity) is a function of several variables such that

$$u = u(x,y,z,t)$$

then for each fixed value of y, z, and t, u is a function of x. If this function is differentiable, the usual process of differentiation may be applied to it. The result is indicated by $\partial u/\partial x$ and is called the partial derivative of u with respect to x. Similarly, if x, z, and t; or x, y, and t; or x, y, and z are kept fixed, we may obtain the partial derivatives of u with respect to y, z, and t. These are indicated by $\partial u/\partial y$, $\partial u/\partial z$, and $\partial u/\partial t$, respectively.

The *total differential* of u for a given dx, dy, dz, and dt represents how much u changes if x, y, z, and t each change, and is defined as

$$du = \frac{\partial u}{\partial x} dx + \frac{\partial u}{\partial y} dy + \frac{\partial u}{\partial z} dz + \frac{\partial u}{\partial t} dt$$

EXAMPLE 3–3. If $u = xyz + y - 3z$, what is the total differential of u and du/dt?

Solution:
$$\frac{\partial u}{\partial x} = yz \qquad \frac{\partial u}{\partial y} = xz + 1 \qquad \frac{\partial u}{\partial z} = xy - 3$$

$$du = (yz)\,dx + (xz + 1)\,dy + (xy - 3)\,dz$$

and
$$\frac{du}{dt} = (yz)\frac{dx}{dt} + (xz + 1)\frac{dy}{dt} + (xy - 3)\frac{dz}{dt}$$

3–9. VECTORS

Velocities are vector functions, and thus velocity fields are represented by vector fields in fluid flow systems. A vector in a rectangular coordinate system may be expressed by means of three mutually perpendicular components. Hence, a flow field may be expressed in terms of one vector equation or three scalar equations. These are equivalent, but the vector form is more concise and is often preferred. Boldface type is sometimes used to indicate vectors, and will be used here.

A vector in space is a directed line segment and is a combination of a magnitude and a direction. It may have components in each of the x, y, and z rectangular coordinate directions. If we denote unit vectors (vectors whose length or magnitude equal one) in the x, y, and z directions by **i**, **j**, and **k**, respectively, *any* vector may be written in the form

$$\mathbf{A} = A_x\,\mathbf{i} + A_y\,\mathbf{j} + A_z\,\mathbf{k}$$

where A_x, A_y, and A_z are the magnitudes of the components of the vector **A** in the x, y, and z directions, respectively.

Vectors may be added or subtracted by adding or subtracting their components in the x, y, and z directions, respectively. Thus

$$\mathbf{A} + \mathbf{B} = (A_x + B_x)\,\mathbf{i} + (A_y + B_y)\,\mathbf{j} + (A_z + B_z)\,\mathbf{k}$$

and
$$\mathbf{A} - \mathbf{B} = (A_x - B_x)\,\mathbf{i} + (A_y - B_y)\,\mathbf{j} + (A_z - B_z)\,\mathbf{k}$$

Note that $(\mathbf{A} + \mathbf{B}) = (\mathbf{B} + \mathbf{A})$ and that $(\mathbf{A} - \mathbf{B}) = -(\mathbf{B} - \mathbf{A})$.

A vector may be multiplied by a scalar or by another vector. A scalar multiplier merely changes the length of the vector to which it is applied, or it reverses its direction. Thus, if $\mathbf{B} = -3\mathbf{A}$, the vector **B** points in the opposite direction as the vector **A**, and is three times the length of the vector **A**.

Vector multiplication is a bit more complicated. There are two kinds of vector multiplication which are useful: a *dot, or scalar, product* and a *cross, or vector, product*. The dot, or scalar, product of **A** and **B** is denoted by

$$\mathbf{A} \cdot \mathbf{B} = |\,\mathbf{A}\,|\,|\,\mathbf{B}\,|\cos\theta = A_x B_x + A_y B_y + A_z B_z$$

where $|\,\mathbf{A}\,|$ indicates the magnitude of the vector **A**, and θ is the angle between the vectors **A** and **B**. Work is an example of a product of a force

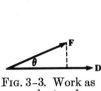

FIG. 3–3. Work as a product of a force and a displacement vector.

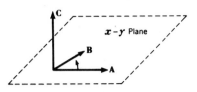

FIG. 3–4. Orientation of vector cross product $\mathbf{A} \times \mathbf{B} = \mathbf{C}$.

vector $\mathbf{F}$ and a displacement vector $\mathbf{D}$. If in Fig. 3–3 a force $\mathbf{F}$ acts on a body and the body moves in the direction of the vector $\mathbf{D}$, then the work done is the product of the component of the force $\mathbf{F}$ in the direction of the vector $\mathbf{D}$, times the displacement D.

$$W = |\mathbf{F}| \, |\mathbf{D}| \cos\theta$$

Note that if $\mathbf{A} \cdot \mathbf{B} = 0$, then $\mathbf{A}$ is normal to $\mathbf{B}$, since the cosine of the 90-deg angle between them is zero.

The cross, or vector, product of $\mathbf{A}$ and $\mathbf{B}$ is denoted by

$$\mathbf{A} \times \mathbf{B} = \begin{vmatrix} \mathbf{i} & \mathbf{j} & \mathbf{k} \\ A_x & A_y & A_z \\ B_x & B_y & B_z \end{vmatrix} = \mathbf{i}\begin{vmatrix} A_y & A_z \\ B_y & B_z \end{vmatrix} - \mathbf{j}\begin{vmatrix} A_x & A_z \\ B_x & B_z \end{vmatrix} + \mathbf{k}\begin{vmatrix} A_x & A_y \\ B_x & B_y \end{vmatrix} = \mathbf{C}$$

The magnitude of $\mathbf{A} \times \mathbf{B} = \mathbf{C}$ is the area of the parallelogram with sides $\mathbf{A}$ and $\mathbf{B}$. The direction of $\mathbf{A} \times \mathbf{B} = \mathbf{C}$ is normal to the plane of $\mathbf{A}$ and $\mathbf{B}$ and points in the direction of movement of a right-handed screw turning from $\mathbf{A}$ towards $\mathbf{B}$ (Fig. 3–4). Note that if $\mathbf{A} \times \mathbf{B} = 0$, then $\mathbf{A}$ and $\mathbf{B}$ are parallel. The form of the determinant indicates that $\mathbf{A} \times \mathbf{B} = -(\mathbf{B} \times \mathbf{A})$.

The velocity resulting from angular rotation is an example of a vector cross product. If a rigid body (or fluid in a forced vortex) rotates about an axis, the velocity at any point is $\mathbf{V} = \boldsymbol{\omega} \times \mathbf{P}$, where $\boldsymbol{\omega}$ is a vector of length ω parallel to the axis of rotation and pointing in the direction of advance of a right-handed screw rotating with the body, and $\mathbf{P}$ is any vector drawn from the axis of rotation to the point.

EXAMPLE 3–4. Let $\mathbf{A} = 2\mathbf{i} - \mathbf{j} + \mathbf{k}$ and $\mathbf{B} = \mathbf{i} + \mathbf{j} + 2\mathbf{k}$. What are the scalar and vector products of $\mathbf{A}$ and $\mathbf{B}$?

Solution: $\mathbf{A} \cdot \mathbf{B} = 2 - 1 + 2 = 3$

and

$$\mathbf{A} \times \mathbf{B} = \begin{vmatrix} \mathbf{i} & \mathbf{j} & \mathbf{k} \\ 2 & -1 & 1 \\ 1 & 1 & 2 \end{vmatrix} = \mathbf{i}(-2 -1) -\mathbf{j}(4 -1) +\mathbf{k}(2 +1) = -3\mathbf{i} -3\mathbf{j} +3\mathbf{k}$$

Further operations with vectors are needed, in addition to vector addition, subtraction, and multiplication. These involve a vector operator *del*.

The vector differential operator del is defined by

$$\nabla = \frac{\partial}{\partial x}\, \mathbf{i} + \frac{\partial}{\partial y}\, \mathbf{j} + \frac{\partial}{\partial z}\, \mathbf{k}$$

When this operates on a scalar function $f\,(x,y,z)$, the result is the *gradient* of that scalar function, which is a vector pointing in the direction of maximum increase of the function.

$$\operatorname{grad} f = \nabla f = \frac{\partial f}{\partial x}\, \mathbf{i} + \frac{\partial f}{\partial y}\, \mathbf{j} + \frac{\partial f}{\partial z}\, \mathbf{k}$$

It will be shown that a vector velocity field representing a fluid flow may be obtained from a scalar velocity potential in this manner.

The scalar product of the del operator and a vector is called the *divergence* of the vector.

$$\operatorname{div} \mathbf{A} = \nabla \cdot \mathbf{A} = \frac{\partial A_x}{\partial x} + \frac{\partial A_y}{\partial y} + \frac{\partial A_z}{\partial z}$$

It will be shown that the divergence of a vector velocity field for an incompressible fluid is zero, and that this is one form of the continuity equation.

The cross product of the del operator and a vector is called the *curl* of the vector.

$$\operatorname{curl} \mathbf{A} = \nabla \times \mathbf{A} = \begin{vmatrix} \mathbf{i} & \mathbf{j} & \mathbf{k} \\ \dfrac{\partial}{\partial x} & \dfrac{\partial}{\partial y} & \dfrac{\partial}{\partial z} \\ A_x & A_y & A_z \end{vmatrix}$$

It will be shown that the rotation of a vector velocity field is given by the curl of the velocity vector. The disappearance of the curl is a test of whether or not a velocity field is derivable from a potential function (see Chapter 6).

Successive operations, such as the divergence of the gradient, may be denoted by

$$\nabla \cdot \nabla f = \nabla^2 f = \frac{\partial^2 f}{\partial x^2} + \frac{\partial^2 f}{\partial y^2} + \frac{\partial^2 f}{\partial z^2}$$

When $\nabla^2 f = 0$, this is called the Laplace equation, and is a test of whether the function f is a possible potential function for incompressible flow.

The curl of a gradient is *always* zero.

$$\operatorname{curl} \operatorname{grad} f = \nabla \times \nabla f = 0$$

EXAMPLE 3–5. Let $f = x^2 + 2y + 3xz$. What is the gradient, and the divergence and the curl of the gradient?

Solution: $\nabla f = (2x + 3z)\,\mathbf{i} + 2\,\mathbf{j} + 3x\mathbf{k}$ (a vector)

$\nabla^2 f = 2 + 0 + 0 = 2$ (a scalar)

$$\nabla \times \nabla f = \begin{vmatrix} \mathbf{i} & \mathbf{j} & \mathbf{k} \\ \dfrac{\partial}{\partial x} & \dfrac{\partial}{\partial y} & \dfrac{\partial}{\partial z} \\ (2x + 3z) & 2 & 3x \end{vmatrix} = (0 - 0)\mathbf{i} - (3 - 3)\mathbf{j} + (0 + 0)\mathbf{k} = 0$$

PROBLEMS

3–1. For each of the following flow systems state whether a significant amount of work is done *by* or *on* the fluid, and whether a significant amount of heat is *added to* or *removed from* the fluid.

a) Water flowing through a centrifugal pump
b) Water flowing through a hydraulic turbine
c) Water flowing over the spillway of a large dam
d) Water flowing through the radiator of an automobile
e) Water flowing through the entire cooling system of an automobile
f) Air flowing through an automobile radiator
g) Air flowing through an automobile radiator and past the engine
h) Air flowing through the slipstream of an airplane propeller
i) Air passing through an air compressor
j) Steam passing through a steam turbine

> *Ans.* e) Heat removed from water in radiator and added to it in water jackets around cylinders. Work done on water by water pump.
> g) Heat added to air as it passes through radiator, and work done on air by the fan.

3–2. Temperatures may be expressed as absolute or relative (degrees Rankine or Fahrenheit, for example). Which *may* or *should* be used for making calculations involving a) temperature differences, b) temperature ratios, and c) calculations of gas densities from the perfect gas equation?

3–3. Determine the volume occupied by a mass of 1 slug of each of the gases listed in Table 3–1 at a temperature of 59 F and a pressure of 14.7 psia.

> *Ans.* For helium, $v = 3043$ ft^3

3–4. Because differences in internal energy and differences in enthalpy are of more general interest than absolute values, numerical values of u and of h for vapors and gases, as well as for liquids, are tabulated with respect to a reference state other than absolute zero temperature. May both u and h be assumed zero at this reference state? Explain.

3-5. An automobile tire has a constant volume of 4000 in.³ and contains 0.016 slug of air. At an atmospheric pressure of 14.6 psia, what will be the range of gage pressures in the tire for a temperature range from 60 F to 160 F?

3-6. Compute the change in internal energy and the change in enthalpy for the air in the tire for the temperature variation of Prob. 3–5.

Ans. $\Delta H = 12.3$ Btu

3-7. Show from Eq. 3–3 or Eq. 3–5 that the entropy change of the air in the tire of Prob. 3–5, as the temperature increases from $T_1 = 60$ F to $T_2 = 160$ F, is expressible as

$$s_2 - s_1 = c_v \ln \frac{T_2}{T_1} \qquad \text{per unit mass}$$

and then compute the change in entropy of the air in the tire. Does it increase or decrease as the temperature increases?

3-8. From Eqs. 3–5 and 3–13c show that, for an isentropic flow or process of a perfect gas, the change in enthalpy is given by

$$\Delta h = \frac{k}{k-1} \Delta \left(\frac{p}{\rho} \right)$$

From Eqs. 3–8 and 3–12 show that the isentropic requirement is needlessly restrictive, and that the change in enthalpy may be expressed by this equation for any type of flow or process.

3-9. What is the increase in internal energy of a unit mass of air, methane, and xenon if the temperature of each increases 100 F by means of *a*) a constant-pressure process, *b*) an adiabatic process, and *c*) a constant-volume process?

Ans.   *c*) $\Delta u = 17.1$ Btu/lb$_m$ for air and $\Delta u = 998,500$ ft lb$_f$/slug for methane.

3-10. Calculate the increase in enthalpy for the conditions of Prob. 3–9.

3-11. When 3.1 Btu are added to 1 ft³ of a gas initially at 50 psia and 62 F, the temperature increases to 132 F. Which of the gases listed in Table 3–1 might this be?

Ans.   Any gas for which $k = 1.4$

3-12. Rework Example 3–1 using the slug as the unit of mass throughout.

3-13. Rework Example 3–2 using the slug as the unit of mass throughout.

3-14. From Eqs. 3–5, 3–6, and 3–12 derive Eqs. 3–13a, b, and c for isentropic flow of a perfect gas.

3-15. Air at 100 psia and 140 F expands isentropically to a temperature of 40 F. *a*) What is the final pressure? *b*) What are the initial and final densities?

Ans.   *b*) $\rho_{\text{final}} = 0.00886$ slug/ft³

3-16. Air at 100 psia and 100 F expands isentropically to a pressure of 70 psia. *a*) What is the final temperature? *b*) What is the final air density?

Ans.   *a*) 46 F

3–17. Air at 100 psia and 100 F expands isentropically to a temperature of 6 F. What is the final air density?

3–18. Methane at 50 psia and 120 F expands isentropically to a pressure of 27.2 psia. *a*) What is the final temperature? *b*) What is the final gas density?

Ans.   *b*) 0.00252 slug/ft³

3–19. What is the density of air at 1000 psia and 540 F *a*) considering air to be a perfect gas and *b*) for actual air?

Ans.   *b*) 0.0815 slug/ft³

3–20. What is the density of air at 100 psia and -220 F *a*) considering air to be a perfect gas and *b*) for actual air?

3–21. Repeat Prob. 3–16 for a polytropic expansion with $n = 1.235$.

3–22. Repeat Prob. 3–17 for a polytropic expansion with $n = 0.824$.

3–23. For each $f(x,y,z)$, find grad f (∇f):
a) xy^2z^3
b) $x^2 - y^2 + 4z^2$
c) $\ln(x^2 - y^2 + z^2)$

Ans.   *b*) $2x\mathbf{i} - 2y\mathbf{j} + 8z\mathbf{k}$

3–24. For each $\mathbf{A}(x,y,z)$, find div $\mathbf{A}$ ($\nabla\cdot\mathbf{A}$) and curl $\mathbf{A}$ ($\nabla \times \mathbf{A}$):
a) $x\mathbf{i} + y\mathbf{j} + z\mathbf{k}$
b) $(y - z)\mathbf{i} + (x - 2z)\mathbf{j} + (y - x)\mathbf{k}$
c) $(x + y)\mathbf{i} - (y + z)\mathbf{j} + (x + z)\mathbf{k}$

Ans.   *a*) div $\mathbf{A} = 3$, curl $\mathbf{A} = 0$

3–25. For each $\mathbf{F}(x,y,z)$, show that curl $\mathbf{F} = 0$ and find an $f(x,y,z)$ such that $\mathbf{F} = \nabla f$.
a) $y^2z^3\mathbf{i} + 2xyz^3\mathbf{j} + 3xy^2z^2\mathbf{k}$
b) $e^x[(y + 2z)\mathbf{i} + \mathbf{j} + 2\mathbf{k}]$
c) $4(x^2 + y^2 + z^2)\,(x\mathbf{i} + y\mathbf{j} + z\mathbf{k})$
d) $2(x + y + 2z)\,(\mathbf{i} + \mathbf{j} + 2\mathbf{k})$

Ans.   *a*) $f = xy^2z^3$

3–26. Verify that each vector $\mathbf{V}$ has div $\mathbf{V} = 0$.
a) $2\mathbf{i} + 5\mathbf{j} - 7\mathbf{k}$
b) $y^2z\mathbf{i} + x^2z\mathbf{j} + x^2y\mathbf{k}$
c) $2y^2\mathbf{i} + (x^2 - z^2)\mathbf{j} + (x^2 - y^2)\mathbf{k}$

4

Fluid Statics

This chapter deals primarily with the variation in fluid pressure with elevation and the result of these pressure variations on surfaces submerged in fluids at rest. A study of these variations will enable us to determine, for example, pressure differences as measured with manometers, hydrostatic forces on dams and spillway gates, buoyancy on submerged objects, and the pressure-density-temperature variations with altitude in the atmosphere.

The subject of fluid statics is a special case of fluid dynamics. When terms involving fluid motion are omitted, the equations of motion of fluid dynamics (Chapter 5) become the equations of fluid statics.

It should be remembered that pressure (or pressure intensity) is a scalar quantity, and therefore, the pressure acts equally in any and all directions at a point in a fluid. *Areas and forces are vector quantities.* The area vector always points in a direction normal to the area, and its magnitude is equal to the magnitude of the area. Thus a force is a vector whose magnitude is the product of the pressure intensity and the magnitude of the area and which points in a direction normal to the area. Forces on surfaces resulting from pressure intensity always act normal to that surface.

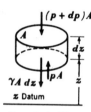

FIG. 4–1. Elemental cylinder of fluid at rest.

4–1. GENERAL DIFFERENTIAL EQUATION

A very simple differential equation will be derived which can then be integrated both for liquids (constant density) and for gases (variable density). Consider a right cylinder (circular or otherwise). Equilibrium of the external forces shown in Fig. 4–1 gives[1]

$$pA - (p + dp)\,A - \gamma A\,dz = 0$$

from which

$$dp = -\gamma\,dz = -\rho g\,dz \qquad (4\text{–}1)$$

(In vector form this equation is grad $p = \rho\mathbf{g}$ and since $\partial p/\partial x = \partial p/\partial y = 0$, the vector equation becomes $\partial p/\partial z = -\rho g$ because z is measured positively upwards and g is directed vertically downwards.) This equation expresses the familiar facts that 1) the pressure intensity decreases with elevation (dp is negative when dz is positive), and 2) the pressure intensity

[1]Recall that the specific weight $\gamma = \rho g$ and is thus not a true property of a fluid since it depends on the local gravitational acceleration.

49

remains the same if there is no change in elevation (dz is zero, and thus dp is zero). Thus, for example, a) the pressure intensity decreases as we go from a given depth towards the surface of a lake, or as we go upwards in the atmosphere; and b) the pressure intensity at a 20-ft depth in a lake at one point is the same as that at a 20-ft depth at some other point in the lake, but pressures at equal elevations in an open container accelerated linearly or rotationally are not the same because the fluids are not at rest.

4–2. HYDROSTATICS

Equation 4–1 can be integrated for a constant-specific-weight fluid.

$$\int_1^2 dp = -\gamma \int_1^2 dz$$

from which

$$p_2 - p_1 = -\gamma(z_2 - z_1)$$

where the pressure change is in pounds per square foot if the specific weight is in pounds per cubic foot and the elevation change is in feet. This equation is commonly expressed as

$$\Delta p = \gamma h \qquad (4\text{–}2)$$

where h is the height difference between points for which the pressure difference is to be calculated. Note that the equation gives only the magnitude of p; whether the pressure increases or decreases is determined from Eq. 4–1.

The term p/γ is defined as the *pressure head*, z is defined as the *potential head* with respect to an arbitrary datum, and $(p/\gamma) + z$ is defined as the *piezometric head*. Thus if we write $(p_2 - p_1)/\gamma = -(z_2 - z_1)$, we find that the increase in pressure head equals the decrease in potential head. If we write $(p_1/\gamma) + z_1 = (p_2/\gamma) + z_2$, we find that the piezometric head is constant in a liquid at rest.[2]

4–3. MANOMETRY

In order to determine pressures or pressure differences from manometer measurements, we apply Eqs. 4–1 and 4–2, starting at one end of the manometer system and writing pressure differences between successive fluid interfaces.

The simplest form of a manometer is a barometer (Fig. 4–2), which is used to determine the absolute atmospheric pressure intensity. Equations 4–1 and 4–2 for the barometer become

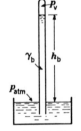

Fig. 4–2.
Barometer.

[2]Note that this is a special form of the Bernoulli equation (Section 5–4) when the velocity terms are zero.

$$p_v + \gamma_b h_b = p_a$$

The advantages of using mercury are apparent from a comparison (Table 4-1) of the vapor pressure p_v and the barometer height h_b for mercury, water, and benzene, for example. Not only is the specific weight of mercury such that a more reasonable height of barometer is possible, but the vapor pressure is low (it can be ignored). A standard atmosphere (2116.2 psfa)[3] is assumed at 59 F.

TABLE 4-1

COMPARISON OF BAROMETER LIQUIDS

Barometer Fluid	p_v (psfa)	γ (lb$_f$/ft^3)	γh_b (psf)	h_b (ft)
Mercury......	0.0036	848	2116.2	2.493
Water........	48.8	62.4	2067.4	33.1
Benzene......	208.8	55.2	1907.4	34.6

Water barometers are used, however, in connection with cavitation tests on propellers, water pumps, and water turbines. Note that liquid heights in barometers are *not* related by the specific weights of the liquids, nor are they the same for a given liquid, because of the variation in vapor pressure with different liquids or with temperature for a given liquid. The temperature correction applied to a common mercury barometer corrects for variations in specific weight of mercury, the expansion of the glass tube containing the mercury, and the expansion of the (usually) brass measuring scale.

Differential manometers are used to measure the difference in pressure intensity between a given point and the atmosphere, or between two points neither of which is at atmospheric pressure. Some manometers are so arranged that a relatively large pressure difference is measured in terms of a relatively small manometer deflection, while in others a relatively small pressure difference is measured in terms of a relatively large manometer deflection. (The term manometer deflection refers to the distance between pertinent liquid-liquid or liquid-gas interfaces.) Manometers of the latter type are often called micromanometers.

The manometer deflection generally depends on the relative specific weights of the two or more fluids used in the manometer. Not only should the specific weights be different but adjacent liquids must be compatible. Their surface tension properties should be such that a good

[3]The abbreviation psfa is for pressure in pounds per square foot absolute (lb$_f$/ft^2 absolute), psfg refers to pressure in pounds per square foot gage (lb$_f$/ft^2 gage), and psf refers to a pressure difference in pounds per square foot (lb$_f$/ft^2).

meniscus (interface) is obtained and so that they will not mix or dissolve together.

Some examples of manometer installations follow.

EXAMPLE 4–1. What is the suction pressure on a centrifugal pump as measured with a mercury manometer as shown in Fig. 4–3? Water is flowing.

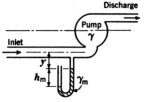

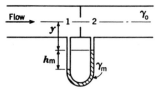

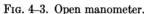

FIG. 4–3. Open manometer.   FIG. 4–4. Differential manometer.

Solution: In this instance the hydrostatic equations (Eqs. 4–1 and 4–2) are applied from the open end of the manometer to the inlet pipe center line, in terms of gage pressure.

$$0 - \gamma_m h_m - \gamma y = p_{\text{inlet}}$$

and if $h_m = 4.3$ in. and $y = 8$ in.,

$$p_{\text{inlet}} = -(848)(4.3/12) - (62.4)(8/12) = -345 \text{ psfg}$$

EXAMPLE 4–2. The pressure drop across an orifice in a pipeline can be measured with a manometer as shown in Fig. 4–4. What is the magnitude of $p_1 - p_2$?

Solution: The hydrostatic equations are applied from point *1* to point *2* to obtain

$$p_1 + \gamma_o (y + h_m) - \gamma_m h_m - \gamma_o y = p_2$$

so that

$$p_1 - p_2 = h_m (\gamma_m - \gamma_o)$$

and if $h_m = 14$ in., $\gamma_m = (2.95)(62.4)$ lb$_f$/ft^3, and $\gamma_o = (0.8)(62.4)$ lb$_f$/ft^3, then

$$p_1 - p_2 = \frac{14}{12} [(2.95)(62.4) - (0.8)(62.4)] = 156.5 \text{ psf}$$

The piezometric head difference between points *1* and *2* is

$$h_1 - h_2 = (p_1 - p_2)/\gamma_o = 3.14 \text{ ft of oil}$$

Note that the distance y does not appear in the solution, and thus a differential manometer of this type may be placed at any elevation with respect to the pipe, whereas in Example 4–1, the position of the manometer y was important.

It can be shown that a manometer connected as in Fig. 4–4 indicates the difference in piezometric pressure $(p_1 + \gamma_o z_1) - (p_2 + \gamma_o z_2)$, or the difference in piezometric head, $[(p_1/\gamma_o) + z_1] - [(p_2/\gamma_o) + z_2]$, between points *1* and *2*, and indicates the difference in pressure intensity or pressure head only for a horizontal system.

EXAMPLE 4–3. A sensitive manometer containing water and oil is shown in Fig. 4–5. What pressure difference is indicated if the liquid levels in the upper chambers were initially at the same level and the manometer deflection was zero when $p_A = p_B$? The level in A is $1/512$ in. higher, and that in B is $1/512$ in. lower than initially.

Solution: The hydrostatic equations give

$$p_A + \gamma_o[y + (1/512)(1/12)] + \gamma_w(1/12) - \gamma_o[y + (1/12) - (1/512)(1/12)] = p_B$$
$$p_B - p_A = [2\gamma_o/(12)(512)] - (\gamma_o/12) + \gamma_w/12 = [(\gamma_w - \gamma_o)/12] + 2\gamma_o/(12)(512)$$
$$= 1.04 + 0.016 = 1.056 \text{ psf} = 0.00733 \text{ psi}[4]$$

Note that the relative cross-sectional areas of chambers A and B and the manometer tubing determine the magnitude of the second term in the final expression for $p_B - p_A$, and this term often may be neglected.

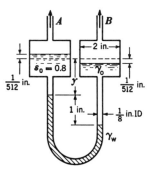

FIG. 4–5. Micromanometer.

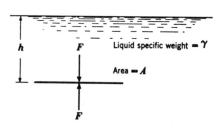

FIG. 4–6. Flat horizontal surface submerged in a liquid.

4–4. FLUID FORCES ON SUBMERGED SURFACES

A flat surface submerged horizontally at a depth h has the same pressure intensity imposed on every point of that surface (Fig. 4–6). Then the total force F acting downward on the top surface is

$$F = \bar{p}A = \gamma h A$$

This is also equal to the total force F acting upwards on the bottom surface, since the pressure intensity is the same on both the top and bottom surfaces.

If the flat surface is inclined from the horizontal at some arbitrary angle θ, the resultant force (acting normal to the flat surface) is equal in magnitude to the product of the pressure intensity at the centroid of the surface and the surface area. This is shown in Fig. 4–7.

The total force F acting on one side (equal in magnitude but oppositely directed to that on the opposite side) is the integral of the forces acting on each infinitesimal area dA.

[4]The abbreviation psi is for pressure in pounds per square inch (lb$_f$/in.²), psig refers to gage pressure in pounds per square inch (lb$_f$/in.² gage), and psia refers to absolute pressure in pounds per square inch (lb$_f$/in.² absolute).

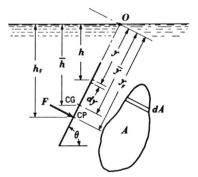

Fig. 4–7. Flat inclined surface
submerged in a liquid.

$$f = p\,dA = \gamma h\,dA = \gamma y \sin\theta\,dA$$
$$F = \int_A \gamma y \sin\theta\,dA = \gamma \sin\theta \int_A y\,dA$$

But $\int y\,dA$ is the first moment of the area about O, defined in terms of y, the distance from O to the centroid, as

so that
$$\int_A y\,dA = \bar{y}A$$
$$F = \gamma(\sin\theta)\,\bar{y}A = \gamma\bar{h}A = \bar{p}A \tag{4-3}$$

since the pressure $\bar{p}$ at the centroid is equal to $\gamma\bar{h}$.

The force F is *not* applied at the centroid of the area, but is always below it by an amount which diminishes with depth. If, in Fig. 4–7, h_F is the depth at which the resultant force F is applied at the center of pressure CP, we can determine a value of y_F, measured parallel to the flat surface, from which h_F may be determined. We define y_F in such a way that Fy_F, the first moment of the force F about the point O, is expressed in terms of the first moment of the forces on the infinitesimal area dA. Then

so that
$$Fy_F = \int_A \gamma y^2 \sin\theta\,dA$$
$$y_F = \frac{\gamma \sin\theta \int_A y^2\,dA}{\gamma \sin\theta \int_A y\,dA} = \frac{\int_A y^2\,dA}{\int_A y\,dA}$$

The numerator is the moment of inertia of the total area of the flat surface about O, which can be expressed in terms of the moment of inertia about the centroid of the flat area.

$$\int_A y^2\,dA = I_{CG} + \bar{y}^2 A$$

The denominator is simply $\bar{y}A$. Thus
$$y_F = \bar{y} + \frac{I_{CG}}{A\bar{y}} \tag{4-4}$$

It is convenient to express I_{CG} for any flat area in terms of that area, and this is done in Table 4–2.

TABLE 4–2
MOMENTS OF INERTIA FOR VARIOUS PLANE SURFACES
ABOUT THEIR CENTER OF GRAVITY

Surface	I_{CG}
Rectangle or square	$\dfrac{1}{12} Ah^2$
Triangle	$\dfrac{1}{18} Ah^2$
Quadrant of circle (or semicircle)	$\left(\dfrac{1}{4} - \dfrac{16}{9\pi^2}\right) Ar^2 = 0.0699\ Ar^2$
Quadrant of ellipse (or semiellipse)	$\left(\dfrac{1}{4} - \dfrac{16}{9\pi^2}\right) Aa^2 = 0.0699\ Aa^2$
Parabola	$\left(\dfrac{3}{7} - \dfrac{9}{25}\right) Ah^2 = 0.0686\ Ah^2$
Circle	$\dfrac{1}{16} Ad^2$
Ellipse	$\dfrac{1}{16} Ah^2$

EXAMPLE 4–4. What is the hydrostatic force, and its location, on a round vertical gate 4 ft in diameter if its top is submerged 6 ft in water as shown in Fig. 4–8?

Solution:

$$F_1 = \bar{p}A = \gamma \bar{y} A = (62.4)(8)\left(\frac{\pi 4^2}{4}\right) = 6280\ \text{lb}_f$$

$$y_F = \bar{y} + \frac{I_{CG}}{A\bar{y}} = 8 + \frac{\frac{1}{16} Ad^2}{A\,(8)} = 8 + \frac{1}{8} = 8.125\ \text{ft}$$

The force F_2 required to open the gate is obtained by equating moments about the gate hinge.

$$\left(2 + \frac{I_{CG}}{A\bar{y}}\right) F_1 = 4F_2 \quad \text{and} \quad F_2 = \frac{17}{32} F_1 = 3340 \text{ lb}_f$$

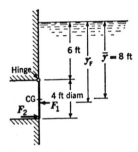

FIG. 4–8. Vertical gate.

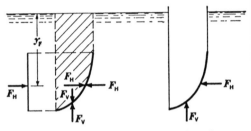

FIG. 4–9. Identical curved surfaces submerged in a liquid.

4–5. CURVED SURFACES

The static forces on a curved submerged surface are expressed in terms of the horizontal and vertical components (Fig. 4–9).

1. The horizontal component is equal (in magnitude and point of application) to the force exerted on a projection of the curved surface in a vertical plane.
2. The vertical component is equal to the weight of fluid directly above the surface, and is applied at the centroid of this fluid.

To be in equilibrium, the horizontal and vertical components on opposite sides of the surface are equal and opposite, respectively. The resultant force on either side is the vector sum of the two components, and again, are equal and opposite for the two sides of the curved surface. Note that the horizontal component F_H and the vertical component F_V are the same for each of the two similar curved surfaces shown in Fig. 4–9.

These generalizations regarding horizontal and vertical force components on curved surfaces are directly applicable to the horizontal and inclined flat surfaces discussed in Sec. 4–4. They can also be used to determine buoyant forces.

Buoyancy is the resultant of the surface forces due to pressure on a submerged body and is equal to the weight of fluid displaced.

In Fig. 4–10, the horizontal force on surface 1–2–3 is equal and opposite to that on surface 1–4–3, so that the net horizontal force is zero. The vertical force on the top surface 2–1–4 (F_{VT}) is equal to the weight of liquid above that surface (diagonally-hatched "volume"), and that on the bottom surface 2–3–4 (F_{VB}) is equal to the liquid above that surface (horizontally hatched "volume"), *even though liquid does not occupy all that volume*

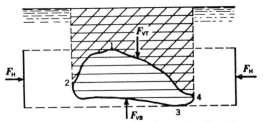

FIG. 4–10. Submerged volume in a liquid.

(see Fig. 4–9). The net vertical force is, then, represented by the weight of liquid in the "volume" *1–4–3–2*, the displaced volume. This is known as Archimedes' principle.

EXAMPLE 4–5. What is the resultant force per foot length on a horizontal circular cylinder of 4-ft diameter if water is 4 ft deep on one side and 2 ft deep on the other (Fig. 4–11)?

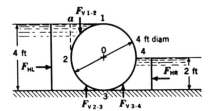

FIG. 4–11. Cylindrical dam.

Solution: The horizontal force on the left side is

$$F_{HL} = \bar{p}A = \gamma\bar{h}A = (62.4)(2)(4) = 499 \text{ lb}_f$$

and it acts $\frac{4}{3}$ ft above the bottom. The horizontal force on the right side is

$$F_{HR} = \bar{p}A = \gamma\bar{h}A = (62.4)(1)(2) = 125 \text{ lb}_f$$

and it acts $\frac{2}{3}$ ft above the bottom. The vertical force on surface *1–2* is equal to the weight of water in volume *1–a–2–1*.

$$F_{V1\text{-}2} = \gamma\left(r^2 - \frac{\pi r^2}{4}\right) = 62.4\left(2^2 - \frac{\pi 2^2}{4}\right) = 53.6 \text{ lb}_f$$

The vertical force on surface *2–3* is equal to the weight of water in volume *1–a–2–3–1*.

$$F_{V2\text{-}3} = \gamma\left(r^2 + \frac{\pi r^2}{4}\right) = 446 \text{ lb}_f$$

The vertical force on surface *3–4* is equal to the weight of water in volume *3–4–0–3*.

$$F_{V3\text{-}4} = \frac{\gamma\pi r^2}{4} = 196 \text{ lb}_f$$

The net vertical force is 588 lb$_f$ upwards, and the net horizontal force is 374 lb$_f$ towards the right. The resultant force is $\sqrt{588^2 + 374^2} = 697$ lb$_f$ at an angle 57.5 deg from the horizontal ($\tan^{-1} 1.57$).

4–6. AEROSTATICS

Aerostatics is a subject of interest in meteorology and aeronautics. We will integrate Eq. 4–1 for an isothermal atmosphere and a dry adiabatic atmosphere, and then show that the resulting equations for an isothermal atmosphere combined with certain departures from the equations for an adiabatic atmosphere will describe what is known as the NACA (National Advisory Committee for Aeronautics, now known as the NASA, the National Aeronautics and Space Administration) standard atmosphere. Equation 3–13 for a reversible adiabatic system will apply for an atmosphere with no heat transfer, since the air will be at rest and no entropy changes due to irreversibilities (such as turbulence) will occur. The atmosphere will be considered to be dry air as a perfect gas with no water vapor present.

4–7. ISOTHERMAL ATMOSPHERE

If we assume a specified temperature which does not vary with altitude, the variable specific weight can be expressed in terms of the varying pressure from the gas equation of state $\rho = p/RT$, and the hydrostatic equation $dp = -\gamma\, dz = -\rho g\, dz$ becomes[5]

$$\int_1^2 \frac{dp}{p} = -\frac{g}{RT} \int_1^2 dz$$

Integration gives

$$\frac{p_2}{p_1} = e^{-\frac{g(z_2 - z_1)}{RT}} \tag{4–5}$$

This equation indicates an exponential decrease in pressure with an increase in altitude, and that at an infinite altitude the pressure decreases to zero. Note that the pressures in Eq. 4–5 are absolute and may be expressed in any absolute units, such as pounds per square inch, pounds per square foot, atmospheres, inches of mercury, and so forth.

The density ratio is

$$\frac{\rho_2}{\rho_1} = e^{-\frac{g(z_2 - z_1)}{RT}}$$

4–8. POLYTROPIC ATMOSPHERE

Again, the hydrostatic equation $dp = -\gamma\, dz = -\rho g\, dz$ can be integrated by expressing the variable density in terms of the variable pressure.

---

[5]The acceleration of gravity g varies with both latitude and altitude (about 0.0031 ft/sec² per 1000 ft increase in altitude), but is considered constant at some average value for the range of elevations involved.

For a polytropic atmosphere, from Eq. 3–14,

$$\frac{p}{\rho^n} = \frac{p_1}{\rho_1^n}$$

where subscript 1 refers to any point where conditions are known. Then

$$\rho = \rho_1 \left(\frac{p}{p_1}\right)^{1/n}$$

and Eq. 4–1 becomes

$$\int_1^2 p^{-1/n}\, dp = -\rho_1\, p_1^{-1/n} \int_1^2 dz$$

Integrating and simplifying yields

$$z_2 - z_1 = \frac{n}{(n-1)} \frac{RT_1}{g} \left[1 - \left(\frac{p_2}{p_1}\right)^{\frac{n-1}{n}}\right] \tag{4-6a}$$

or

$$\frac{p_2}{p_1} = \left[1 - g\,\frac{(n-1)}{n}\,\frac{(z_2 - z_1)}{RT_1}\right]^{\frac{n}{n-1}} \tag{4-6b}$$

Equations 4–6 give the pressure or elevation in terms of the other for a given set of conditions at some known point 1. From Eqs. 3–13 and 4–6b

$$\frac{T_2}{T_1} = \left[1 - \frac{(n-1)}{n}\,\frac{g}{RT_1}\,(z_2 - z_1)\right] \tag{4-7a}$$

or

$$\frac{T_2 - T_1}{z_2 - z_1} = -\frac{g(n-1)}{nR} \tag{4-7b}$$

indicating a linear variation of temperature with altitude. Equations 4–7 imply a lapse rate (temperature change per foot of increase in altitude or elevation) of -0.00536 F/ft for a dry adiabatic atmosphere with $n = k$.[6] Any linear lapse rate may be expressed by Eqs. 4–7 if a suitable value of the polytropic exponent n is used.

4–9. NACA STANDARD ATMOSPHERE

The NACA standard atmosphere is defined as 14.696 psia and 59 F at sea level, a linear temperature drop to -67.0 F at 35,332 ft, a constant temperature to 104,987 ft, a linear temperature increase to 170.6 F at 164,042 ft, a constant temperature to 196,850 ft, and a linear temperature drop to -27.4 F at 255,905 ft. Appropriate values of the polytropic exponent n in Eqs. 4–6 and 4–7 are obtained by solving Eqs. 4–7 for n. This gives

[6]Combining the differential form of the first law of thermodynamics $(dq = c_p\, dT - dp/\rho)$ and the differential form of the hydrostatic equation $(dp = -\rho g\, dz)$ also shows that $dT/dz = -g/c_p = -0.00536$ F/ft for a dry adiabatic atmosphere.

Fluid Statics

$$n = \cfrac{1}{1 + \cfrac{R\,dT}{g\,dz}} \qquad (4\text{–}8)$$

and for temperature variations specified in the NACA standard atmosphere, values of n are listed in Table 4–3, and are shown in Fig. 4–12.

TABLE 4–3

LAPSE RATE AND POLYTROPIC EXPONENT FOR NACA STANDARD ATMOSPHERE

Range	Altitude (ft)	Type Atmosphere	Lapse Rate (deg F/ft)	n
1	0— 35,332	Polytropic	−0.00357	1.235
2	35,332—104,987	Isothermal	0	
3	104,987—164,042	Polytropic	0.00402	0.824
4	164,042—196,850	Isothermal	0	
5	196,850—255,905	Polytropic	−0.00335	1.217

If a certain air mass is displaced vertically and, as a result of buoyancy due to differences in temperature, the displaced air tends to return to its original position, the atmosphere is considered to be stable. If a displacement results in no tendency to return to the original position or to be

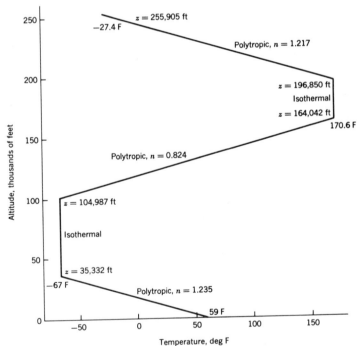

FIG. 4–12. NACA standard atmosphere (from NACA Technical Note No. 1428, 1947).

displaced further, the atmosphere is considered to be neutral. If a displacement results in a tendency for further displacement, the atmosphere is considered to be unstable.

An air mass moved vertically will be at the same pressure as the ambient air, and since there will be no heat transfer, the temperature will vary according to Eq. 3–13b.

$$\frac{T_2}{T_1} = \left(\frac{p_2}{p_1}\right)^{\frac{k-1}{k}}$$

If the atmosphere itself is truly adiabatic, the displaced air will always be at the same pressure and temperature as the ambient air, and there will be no buoyant forces tending to move the air mass. In order that $n < k$, the lapse rate would have to be greater algebraically than that for an adiabatic atmosphere (-0.00536 F/ft); thus when an air mass is moved vertically, its temperature would be less than ambient if moved upwards and greater than ambient if moved downwards, and buoyancy world tend to return it to its original level. Finally, if $n > k$, the lapse rate would have to be less algebraically than that for an adiabatic atmosphere; when an air mass is moved vertically, its temperature would be greater than ambient if moved upwards and less if moved downwards, and buoyancy would tend to displace the air mass further.

The NACA atmosphere is used for determining altitude from altimeters (pressure gages) and, since the altimeters do not correct for variations in the temperature of the air beneath them, they read too high in cold weather and too low in warm weather.

Thus, stability in the atmosphere may be defined in terms of the lapse rate or the polytropic exponent. If $n < k$, the atmosphere is stable; if $n = k$, the atmosphere is neutral; and if $n > k$, the atmosphere is unstable.

EXAMPLE 4–6. What are the air pressure, temperature, and density at 60,000 ft for the NACA standard atmosphere?

Solution: The pressure is obtained by stages for the first two ranges given in Table 4–3. From Eq. 4–6b, with $n = 1.235$,

$$\frac{p_2}{p_1} = \left[1 - \frac{(32.17)(0.235)(35,332)}{(1.235)(1715)(519)}\right]^{5.26} = 0.232$$

$$p_2 = (2116.2)(0.232) = 490 \text{ psfa}$$

From Eq. 4–5

$$\frac{p_3}{p_2} = e^{-\frac{(32.2)(24,668)}{(1715)(392.4)}} = \frac{1}{3.254}$$

$$p_3 = 150.5 \text{ psfa}$$

The temperature is -67.6 F. The density is

$$\rho_3 = \frac{p_3}{RT_3} = \frac{150.5}{(1715)(392.4)} = 0.000244 \text{ slug/ft}^3$$

PROBLEMS

4-1. Explain why the equations relating pressure changes with elevation (Eqs. 4-2, 4-5, and 4-6b) all involve the acceleration of gravity g, in addition to fluid properties.

4-2. The practical depth limit for a free diver is about 50 meters. What is the pressure intensity in fresh water at that depth?

4-3. The practical depth limit for a suit diver is about 185 meters. What is the pressure intensity in sea water at that depth?

Ans. 38,800 psfg

4-4. The Ewing camera has been used at a 5500-meter depth in the Atlantic Ocean. What is the pressure intensity at that depth? *a)* Assume constant density equal to that at the surface. *b)* Use answer to part *a)* and calculate the density at the 5500-meter depth, then calculate the pressure at that depth using the average density.

4-5. The Mohole platform will be anchored near the Hawaiian Islands in the Pacific to drill into the earth's crust, beginning at a depth of about 14,000 ft. Estimate the pressure intensity at that depth.

4-6. Seals are known to dive to depths of 200 ft or more, whalebone whales to depths as great as 1150 ft, and it is believed sperm whales dive to depths as great as 3000 ft. What is the range of pressures to which each of these mammals is exposed during these dives in the sea?

Ans. For sperm whales, 1333 psi

4-7. The specific weight of sea water is 64 lb_f/ft^3 at sea level. Estimate its specific weight at the bottom of the Mariannas Trench (depth = 36,198 ft), taking into account the compressibility of the water. Assume $\overline{K} = 368,000$ $lb_f/in.^2$ and that g is essentially constant.

4-8. In Prob. 4-7, estimate the pressure at the 35,800-ft depth by using an arithmetic mean specific weight.

Ans. 16,250 psi

4-9. What is the difference in pressure between the surface of a lake and a point 60 ft below the surface? What is the difference in piezometric head between these points?

4-10. Show diagrammatically that the piezometric head is constant in a liquid of constant density at rest. Assume any convenient datum plane for $z = 0$.

4-11. A spherical bubble migrates upwards in water. At a depth of 40 ft its diameter is 0.2 in. What is its diameter just as it reaches the water surface? Assume a standard atmospheric pressure above the water.

Ans. 0.259 in.

4-12. A mercury barometer reading is 29.0 in. Express this atmospheric pressure in terms of a) psia, b) psfa, c) psig, d) feet of water, and e) feet of carbon tetrachloride.

Ans.   e) 20.6 ft

4–13. A mercury barometer reads 29.90 in. A pressure gage on a steam turbine indicates a pressure of 55 psig. What is the absolute pressure of the steam?

4–14. Explain whether absolute or gage pressures *may* or *should* be used in making calculations involving a) pressure differences, b) pressure ratios, and c) the density of a gas from the perfect gas equation.

4–15. The atmospheric pressure is 2050 psfa. What is the height of a barometer containing any one of the following liquids at a temperature of 60 F? Assume specific gravity from Table 2–2 if not given for 60 F.

a) Mercury c) Kerosene

b) Water d) Methyl alcohol

Note that although methyl alcohol has a specific gravity less than that for kerosene, its barometer height is less.

4–16. How would the height of a water barometer on a warm summer day at 100 F compare with that on a cold fall day at 40 F, assuming the same atmospheric pressure exists on both days? Explain.

4–17. What is the specific gravity of fluid A?

4–18. What is the specific gravity of fluid B?

Ans. $s_B = 2.964$

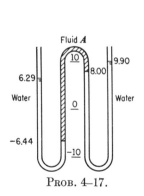

PROB. 4–17.

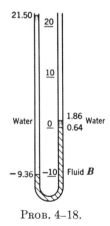

PROB. 4–18.

4–19. What difference in piezometric pressure head in feet of flowing fluid is indicated by a deflection of 12 in. of mercury (see Fig. 4–4) when the flowing fluid is a) water, b) fuel oil, and c) carbon tetrachloride? Assume $s = 13.59$ for mercury.

Ans.   a) 12.59 ft

4-20. In Fig. 4–3, acetylene tetrabromide is used in the manometer to measure the pump inlet pressure. The manometer deflection is 18.20 in. and $y = 7.50$ in. What is the pump inlet pressure *a*) in psig and *b*) in inches of mercury vacuum?

4-21. A mercury manometer is to be used to measure the pressure drop between two points along a horizontal pipe in which water flows. The maximum pressure drop to be measured is expected to be 20 psi. What is the corresponding manometer deflection? Assume $s = 13.59$ for mercury.

Ans.   3.67 ft

4-22. Repeat Prob. 4–21 with kerosene flowing in the pipe.

4-23. In a pipe in which oil flows, what is *a*) the pressure drop and *b*) the drop in piezometric head across an orifice if it is measured with a mercury manometer which indicates a deflection of 8.0 in.? Assume $s = 0.92$ for the oil. See Fig. 4–4.

4-24. Find $p_A - p_C$ and $p_A - p_B$.

4-25. An oil ($s = 0.9$) is to be used in a manometer to measure the pressure drop across a length of horizontal pipe. Draw a sketch showing the manometer arrangement, the relative position of the oil-water meniscus in each leg of the manometer, and the flow direction. The pressure drops in the direction of flow.

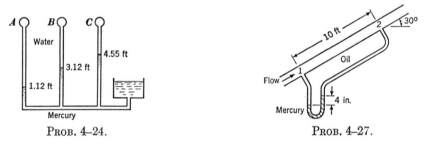

PROB. 4–24.   PROB. 4–27.

4-26. The deflection of a differential manometer is a direct indication of the difference in *piezometric* pressure or head between two piezometer holes to which the manometer is connected. It indicates the difference in pressure intensity or pressure head only for a horizontal flow system. Show that these statements are true by writing expressions for the difference in piezometric pressure or head, and the difference in pressure intensity or pressure head for the system shown in Fig. 4–4 when the pipe is inclined and when the pipe is horizontal.

4-27. A manometer is connected to piezometer taps 10 ft apart in a pipe inclined 30 deg from the horizontal. Oil of specific gravity $s = 0.9$ flows in the pipe. The pressure drop due to viscous shear is to be measured. The manometer contains mercury and shows a deflection of 4.0 in. *a*) What is $p_1 - p_2$? *b*) What is the pressure drop due to viscous shear? *c*) Explain the difference in answers for parts (*a*) and (*b*).

Ans.   *a*) 3.78 psi, *b*) 1.83 psi

4-28. Repeat Prob. 4–27*a* and *b* for water flowing in the pipe.

4–29. Show that the resultant force on any rectangular flat surface whose base is horizontal and whose top coincides with a free liquid surface at rest is located $2H/3$ from the liquid surface, H being the height of the rectangle.

4–30. A flat plate 2 x 10 ft is immersed in water with the 10-ft side vertical and the 2-ft side horizontal. The total resultant force acts 10 in. below the centroid of the plate. How deep is the upper edge submerged?

Ans. 5 ft

4–31. Repeat Prob. 4–30 for a resultant force 20 in. below the centroid.

4–32. A rectangular gate with a horizontal base of 6 ft and a height of 4 ft lies in a plane inclined 45 deg from the horizontal. Water is on one side of the gate and the top is submerged 10 ft. What is the minimum force which may be applied to the gate to hold it in position when it is hinged at the bottom?

PROB. 4–32.　　　　　　　　PROB. 4–36.

4–33. Repeat Example 4–4 (Fig. 4–8) for a) a 4-ft square gate, b) an elliptical gate 4 ft high and 8 ft wide, and c) a triangular gate 4 ft wide at the top and 4 ft high. Does the triangle have to be symmetrical about a vertical line or not?

4–34. An open channel 12 ft wide at the surface and 8 ft deep has a vertical dam at its end which projects above the water surface. Calculate the total hydrostatic force on the dam and locate its point of application for channels of the following cross sections: a) Rectangle. b) Isosceles triangle with axis of symmetry vertical. c) Parabola. d) Semiellipse.

Ans. c) $F = 12,800$ lb$_f$ applied 4.57 ft below water surface.

4–35. A vertical wall separates two bodies of water 10 ft and 15 ft deep, respectively. What is the resultant force, and its location, on the wall per lineal foot of wall?

4–36. A vertical plate has dimensions as shown. It is submerged in a liquid so that the upper edge coincides with the free surface of the liquid. Is the total force on the square portion greater, the same, or less than the total force on the semicircular portion?

4–37. Given a sea wall as shown, a) what is the resultant force per lineal foot of wall? b) Determine $\bar{x}$.

Ans. a) 15,350 lb$_f$ at 33.7 deg from horizontal

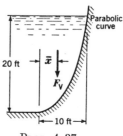

PROB. 4–37.

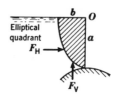

PROB. 4–38.

4–38. Show that the moment of F_H about O is a^2/b^2 times the moment of F_V about O, and thus is equal to it for a circular quadrant. For the general case of an elliptical quadrant, what are the conditions for which the resultant of F_H and F_V pass a) above O, b) through O, and c) below O?

4–39. The Mohole platform will displace about 21,500 tons of sea water. What is the weight of the platform?

4–40. A cork lifebuoy weighs 10 lb$_f$ and has a specific weight of 15 lb$_f$/ft^3. How much more weight can this lifebuoy support in sea water than in fresh water? Does this weight represent air weight or submerged weight? Explain.

Ans. 1.067 lb$_f$

4–41. A 2-ft cube weighing 464 lb$_f$ is lowered into a large tank containing 6 ft of water under 6 ft of oil ($s = 0.8$). If the sides of the cube remain vertical, a) how much of the cube protrudes above the oil-water interface and b) what is the total liquid force on one side of the cube?

4–42. A hollow sphere is filled with W lb$_f$ of liquid through a small hole in the top. What is the buoyant force on the top half of the sphere?

4–43. A hollow right circular cone is filled with W lb$_f$ of liquid through a small hole in its apex. What is the buoyant force on the conical surface of the cone? Its axis is vertical.

Ans. $2W$

4–44. Let W be the weight of a hydrometer whose stem has a cross-sectional area of A. Show that the distance between specific gravity markings for equal increments of s decreases as the specific gravity increases, and thus the marked scale is nonlinear. Let Δh be the stem distance between marks indicating specific gravities of s and $s + \Delta s$. Then show that

$$\Delta h = \frac{W}{A\gamma}\left[\frac{\Delta s}{s(s + \Delta s)}\right]$$

where γ is the specific weight of water.

4–45. A hydrometer weighs 0.08 lb$_f$ in air and has a ¼-in. diameter stem. What is the distance between specific gravity marks labeled 1.10 and 1.20?

4–46. One-eighth the total volume of an iceberg projects above the surface of the sea. *a)* What is the average density of the ice in the iceberg? *b)* What is its specific gravity?

Ans. *a)* $\rho = 1.74$ slugs/ft³

4–47. A long vertical pipe is 6 in. in diameter, weighs 500 lb_f, is closed at both ends, and floats in water. At what depth is the bottom end of the pipe?

4–48. Derive Eqs. 4–6a and 4–6b from the polytropic and hydrostatic equations (Eqs. 3–14 and 4–1).

4–49. Derive Eq. 4–8 from Eq. 4–7b.

4–50. A 10-ft constant-diameter balloon is filled with helium. The total weight of the balloon, gas, and payload is 20 lb_f. In an isothermal atmosphere, at what altitude will the balloon come to rest? Ground pressure and temperature are 14.5 psia and 70 F, respectively.

Ans. 18,600 ft

4–51. Repeat Prob. 4–50 for an NACA standard atmosphere.

4–52. Verify the lapse rates and polytropic exponents for the NACA standard atmosphere given in Table 4–3. Assume g constant at 32.174 ft/sec².

4–53. Calculate the pressure of the NACA standard atmosphere at altitudes of *a)* 35,332 ft, *b)* 104,987 ft, *c)* 164,042 ft, *d)* 196,850 ft, and *e)* 255,905 ft.

Ans. *a)* 490 psfa, *d)* 0.730 psfa

4–54. Calculate the pressure at each altitude in Prob. 4–53 for an isothermal atmosphere. Assume standard air at sea level.

4–55. What are the pressure, temperature, and air density at an altitude of 10,000 ft in the NACA standard atmosphere?

4–56. What are the pressure, temperature, and air density at an altitude of 20,000 ft in the NACA standard atmosphere?

4–57. Calculate the density of the air at the altitudes given in Prob. 4–53, assuming the air to have the same composition at all altitudes.

Ans. *c)* 0.00000179 slug/ft³

4–58. At what altitude is the pressure of the NACA standard atmosphere *a)* 50 per cent, *b)* 25 per cent, *c)* 10 per cent, and *d)* 1 per cent of that at sea level? Refer to Prob. 4–53 to determine range of altitudes in which these pressures exist.

Ans. *d)* 100,900 ft

4–59. Suppose the atmosphere were to be made up of air of constant density equal to that of standard air at sea level. *a)* What would be the height of the atmosphere? *b)* What per cent of the total atmosphere lies below this height in the NACA standard atmosphere? *c)* Repeat part *b)* for an isothermal atmosphere.

Ans. *c)* 63.2 per cent

4–60. A mercury barometer reads 29.50 in. at the foot of a mountain and 21.10 in. at its peak. Assume standard air at a barometer of 29.92 in. of mercury at sea level. What is the height of the mountain if the atmosphere is assumed to be a) isothermal, b) dry adiabatic, and c) the NACA standard atmosphere?

Ans.   a) 9270 ft above foot

4–61. What is the pressure gradient at the peak of the mountain for the three types of atmosphere assumed in Prob. 4–60?

Ans.   a) 0.0540 psf/ft

4–62. From Eqs. 4–6a and 4–8, show that the altitude z may be expressed in terms of known sea level conditions T_0 and p_0 and temperature gradient dT/dz, and a measured pressure p at the altitude z. That is, show that

$$z = \frac{T_0}{-\,dT/dz}\left[1 - \left(\frac{p}{p_0}\right)^{-\frac{R}{g}\left(\frac{dT}{dz}\right)}\right]$$

for a prescribed temperature gradient.

4–63. Given sea level conditions $p_0 = 29.92$ in. of mercury, $T_0 = 59$ F, $dT/dz = -0.00357$ F/ft, and a pressure $p = 20.0$ in. of mercury at some altitude. Estimate the error in measurement of altitude for a possible error of 2 per cent in measuring the pressure p. Use the equation derived in Prob. 4–62.

Ans.   512 ft error

4–64. Referring to Prob. 4–62, show that

$$p = p_0\left[1 + \left(\frac{dT}{dz}\right)\frac{z}{T_0}\right]^{-\frac{1}{\frac{R}{g}\left(\frac{dT}{dz}\right)}}$$

for a prescribed temperature gradient in a polytropic atmosphere.

4–65. The Empire State building in New York is 1248 ft high. Assume an NACA standard atmosphere and sea level conditions at the street level. Suppose you have a desk-type aneroid barometer which you carry to the top of the building. If the accuracy of the barometer is within 0.02 in. of mercury, with what accuracy can you measure the height of the building?

Ans.   38 ft maximum error

5 | Fluid Dynamics

In Chapter 4 we considered fluids at rest. In this chapter we will consider fluids in motion. The laws of conservation of mass, momentum, and energy apply to a *system*, made up of material of fixed identity; and it will be necessary to express these laws for a *control volume*, a volume fixed in space through which fluid flows [1]. Although the continuity and momentum equations and the equations of motion are developed for unsteady flow, application of these and the energy equation generally will be to steady flow situations. The conservation laws are valid for both ideal and real fluids, for gases as well as for liquids. Thus their principles and methods of application should be mastered thoroughly.

5–1. TYPES OF FLOW

There are many ways in which fluid flows may be classified. For example, flow may be steady or unsteady, one-, two-, or three-dimensional, uniform or nonuniform, laminar or turbulent, and incompressible or compressible. In addition, gas flows may be subsonic, transonic, supersonic, or hypersonic, and liquids flowing in open channels may be subcritical, critical, or supercritical.

Flow is *steady* when conditions do not vary with *time*, or when, in the case of turbulent flow, variations in velocity and pressure at a point are very small with respect to the mean values and the mean values do not vary with time. If the flow is not steady, it is *unsteady*. Constant flow of water in a pipe is steady, but during opening or closing of a valve the flow is unsteady. Air flow through a blow-down type of wind tunnel would be unsteady, but during a testing time of some 10-30 sec the flow would be steady. A given flow may be steady with respect to one observer, and unsteady with respect to another. For example, flow around the upstream portion of a bridge pier would appear steady to an observer on the pier, and it would appear unsteady to an observer floating by on the water.

Flow may be classified as one-, two-, or three-dimensional. Various definitions of flow on this basis are found in technical literature.

Mathematical or hydrodynamical treatments often consider the kinematics of the system, and the type of flow is determined by the number of velocity components which exist.

In this text we will use the following definitions, which are commensurate with current engineering practice. In general the definitions involve the *gradients* of velocity, for example, rather than the *components* of velocity.

One-dimensional flow is flow in which all fluid and flow parameters (velocity, pressure, and temperature—thus density and viscosity) are constant throughout any cross section normal to the flow [2]. Changes in both flow velocity and area may occur from section to section. Average fluid and flow parameters vary only along the mean streamline. The flow of real fluids cannot be completely one-dimensional, since the velocity at a boundary must be zero with respect to the boundary.[1] They may, however, be assumed to be one-dimensional in many instances. Whenever the flow is one-dimensional—actual *or* assumed—a one-dimensional *analysis* may be applied to the flow system, and average values of the fluid and flow parameters are used to describe the flow at a section. Examples of one-dimensional flow are shown in Fig. 5–1.

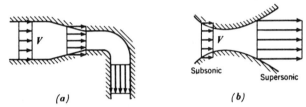

Fɪɢ. 5–1. One-dimensional flow.   *a*) Incompressible flow in a duct. *b*) Compressible gas flow in a nozzle. Velocity, pressure, and temperature are assumed constant throughout any section.

Two-dimensional flow is flow which is the same in parallel planes and which is not one-dimensional. It is also necessary that conditions be the same along any line normal to the planes. This prevents otherwise identical flow patterns from being staggered from plane to plane. Usually, two-dimensional flow may also be defined as flow in which either the fluid or flow parameters (or both) have spacial gradients in two directions, x and y, for example. Thus in Fig. 5–2(*a*) the velocity varies only in the y direction but the pressure varies in the x direction, so that gradients exist in two directions. Note that while the flow is one-*directional* since velocity vectors have only an x component, the flow is two-*dimensional*. In Fig. 5–2(*b*) the velocity varies in both the x and the y direction; and the pressure varies in the x direction, where streamlines are parallel, and in both the x and the y directions, where streamlines are curved (in the diverging section).

Three-dimensional flow is flow in which the fluid or flow parameters vary in the x, y, and z directions in a rectangular system of coordinates.

---

[1]There are instances of slip flow in rarefied gases, but treatment of these is beyond the scope of this text.

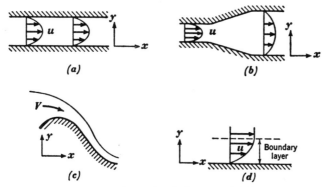

FIG. 5–2. Two-dimensional flow. *a*) Viscous flow
between parallel plates; $u = u(y)$ and $p = p(x)$.   *b*)
Viscous flow between diverging plates; $u = u(x,y)$ and
$p = p(x,y)$.   *c*) Flow over the central part of a wide
spillway; $V = V(x,y)$.   *d*) Boundary-layer flow past a
wide flat plate; $u = u(x,y)$. See also Fig. 7–2.   Flow
within boundary layer is two-dimensional. Flow outside
boundary layer may be essentially one-dimensional.

Thus, gradients of the fluid or flow parameters exist in all three directions.
Axisymmetric flow is sometimes considered to be two-dimensional, since
in cylindrical coordinates, gradients exist in only two directions—axial
and radial.

An exception to the statement that two-dimensional flow has gradients
in two directions is shown in Fig. 5–3. The flow is not one-dimensional
although one-directional, but since it is the same in parallel planes, we
may consider it to be two-dimensional.

Flow past airfoils of infinite span is two-
dimensional; flow near the ends of a finite-
span airfoil is three-dimensional. Flow past
the central portion of a completely submerged
hydrofoil is two-dimensional; for a hydrofoil
piercing a free-water surface, the flow is three-
dimensional near the water surface. Flow
over the central portion of a wide spillway in
a river is two-dimensional, and flow through
ducts is usually three-dimensional; they may
both be considered one-dimensional if average
values of fluid and flow parameters are
assumed to exist throughout any section

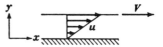

FIG. 5–3. Viscous flow
between parallel plates,
one at rest and the other
moving; $u = u(y)$; pres-
sure and temperature are
constant. Flow is not one-
dimensional, since velocity
is not constant across a
section. Since flow is the
same in parallel planes, the
flow is two-dimensional.

normal to the mean flow. Many real flow situations which are actually
two- or three-dimensional may be analyzed quite satisfactorily with the
assumption of one-dimensional flow.

Flow may be *uniform* or *nonuniform*, depending on the variation in flow area and the velocity in the direction of flow. If the mean velocity V and the cross-sectional area A are constant in the direction of flow, the flow is uniform. If not, the flow is nonuniform. Liquid flow in a pipe of constant area, and in an open channel of constant width and depth, are examples of uniform flow. Liquid flow in varying-area ducts, and all gas flows except low-velocity, constant-area gas flow, are examples of non-uniform flow because the velocity varies from section to section.

Laminar viscous flow exists when fluid layers flow alongside one another either at the same or at slightly different velocities. There is no macroscopic mixing of fluid particles. If a dye (nonsoluble and of the same density as the flowing fluid) is injected into a laminar flow, the dye will appear as a single thread or filament and will not disperse throughout the fluid. In *turbulent* flow there are small velocity fluctuations (both parallel and transverse to the mean velocity) superimposed on the mean motion. There is a mixing of the fluid, and a dye injected into a turbulent flow quickly disperses throughout the fluid. The straight filaments of smoke rising for a few inches from a cigarette held in still air is a well-known example of laminar flow, and the ensuing sinuous or haphazard motion of the smoke above the straight filaments is an example of turbulent motion. Whether the flow is laminar or turbulent depends on the relative magnitudes of the inertia and viscous forces in a fluid system, and there are quantitative values of the ratio of these forces for various flow systems from which the type of flow usually may be determined. There are instances of quasi-laminar-turbulent flow when turbulent flow is not fully established. This is called *transition* flow. This type of flow is usually intermittent at a point or section of the flow—laminar, then turbulent, then laminar, and so on—and is difficult to analyze, analytically as well as experimentally. Laminar flow may be analyzed analytically, but turbulent flow requires experimental results (combined with analytical) for complete analysis. Much is known about the behavior and decay of turbulence, but a satisfactory explanation of its origin is not yet available. Laminar flow is associated with low velocities, highly viscous fluids, or small flow passages. Turbulent flow is associated with high velocities, lower viscosity fluids, or larger flow passages. In engineering practice, turbulent flow is much more common than laminar flow.

Flow is considered *incompressible* if the density changes are negligible. All liquid flows and gas flows at low velocities may be considered to be incompressible flow. Gas flow above 200-300 ft/sec may be considered to be compressible flow. Actually all fluids are somewhat compressible, but generally an incompressible fluid is considered to be one for which the density is independent of pressure. It is customary to make a sharp distinction between compressible fluids and compressible flow.

Gas flows are considered *subsonic, transonic, supersonic,* or *hypersonic,* depending on whether the velocity is less, about the same, greater, or much greater than the speed of sound (see Fig. 9–2).

Water flowing in an open channel (a river or spillway) is considered *subcritical, critical,* or *supercritical,* depending on whether the velocity is less, the same, or greater than that of an elementary surface wave. A wave generated when a pebble is dropped into shallow water is considered to be an elementary wave (see Chapter 12).

5–2. CONSERVATION OF MASS AND THE CONTINUITY EQUATION

The equation of continuity may be written in different forms. It expresses the requirement that a fluid is continuous and that fluid mass is conserved—it is neither created nor destroyed. In rectangular coordinates it is expressed as

$$\frac{\partial \rho}{\partial t} + \frac{\partial (\rho u)}{\partial x} + \frac{\partial (\rho v)}{\partial y} + \frac{\partial (\rho w)}{\partial z} = 0 \qquad (5\text{–}1a)$$

and in vector form as

$$\frac{\partial \rho}{\partial t} + \nabla \cdot (\rho \mathbf{V}) = 0 \qquad (5\text{–}1b)$$

and is valid throughout all fluids, both viscous and nonviscous, except at isolated singularities such as sources and sinks (Chapter 6). In Eqs. 5–1 u, v, and w are the velocity components in the x, y, and z directions, respectively, and ρ is the fluid density. The velocity components as well as the density all may be functions of x, y, z, and t (time). $\mathbf{V}$ (x, y, z, t) is the resultant velocity vector $\mathbf{V} = u\mathbf{i} + v\mathbf{j} + w\mathbf{k}$.

For steady or unsteady flow of an *incompressible* fluid, the continuity equation may be written for a rectangular coordinate system as

$$\frac{\partial u}{\partial x} + \frac{\partial v}{\partial y} + \frac{\partial w}{\partial z} = 0 \qquad (5\text{–}2a)$$

and in vector form as

$$\nabla \cdot \mathbf{V} = 0 \qquad (5\text{–}2b)$$

For two-dimensional flow in the x-y plane ($\mathbf{w} = 0$) Eq. 5–1a becomes

$$\frac{\partial \rho}{\partial t} + \frac{\partial (\rho u)}{\partial x} + \frac{\partial (\rho v)}{\partial y} = 0 \qquad (5\text{–}3)$$

for the general situation of variable density, and

$$\frac{\partial u}{\partial x} + \frac{\partial v}{\partial y} = 0 \qquad (5\text{–}4)$$

for incompressible flow.

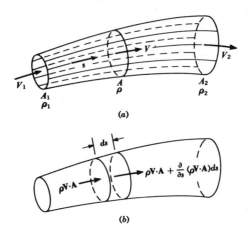

FIG. 5–4. A stream tube (bounded by
streamlines).

For *one-dimensional* flow in a streamline direction s, we may consider
the flow through a stream tube (Fig. 5–4). A stream tube is a flow passage
bounded by streamlines, and thus no fluid may pass through the walls of
the stream tube. Velocity vectors at all points are tangent to streamlines,
and hence no fluid can cross a streamline, nor can streamlines intersect
one another or become tangent to one another. Pipes and nozzles are
examples of stream tubes. The continuity equation for a stream tube is a
particular form of Eq. 5–1a. For unsteady flow it may be written as

$$\frac{\partial(\rho\mathbf{A})}{\partial t} + \frac{\partial(\rho\mathbf{A}\cdot\mathbf{V})}{\partial s} = 0 \tag{5–5}$$

and for steady flow as

$$\frac{\partial(\rho\mathbf{A}\cdot\mathbf{V})}{\partial s} = 0$$

or

$$\rho\mathbf{A}\cdot\mathbf{V} = \dot{m}, \text{ a constant mass flow rate} \tag{5–6a}$$

The area vector $\mathbf{A}$ is a vector whose magnitude is equal to the magnitude of the area, and whose direction is normal to the plane of the area.
Thus the dot product of area and velocity indicates that the velocity
component normal to the plane of the area and parallel to the vector $\mathbf{A}$
representing the area is multiplied by the magnitude of the area to get a
scalar product which represents a volumetric flow rate. Whenever the
product of a scalar velocity and a scalar area is given as VA, the dot product
$\mathbf{V}\cdot\mathbf{A}$ is implied.

Equation 5–6a may be written in scalar form as $\dot{m} = VA\rho$, where V

is the average velocity throughout the cross section A of the stream tube. If the fluid velocity u in the streamline direction varies throughout the area A, the average velocity may be found by integrating over the area or by averaging point velocities at the center of a number of equal sub-areas. Thus

$$\dot{m} = \rho V A = \int \rho u \, dA = \rho_1 V_1 A_1 = \rho_2 V_2 A_2 \qquad (5\text{-}6b)$$

Equation 5–6b may be simplified for special situations:

1. For incompressible flow ρ is a constant, and the constant volumetric flow rate Q is

$$Q = \mathbf{V} \cdot \mathbf{A} = VA = \int u \, dA = V_1 A_1 = V_2 A_2 \qquad (5\text{-}7)$$

2. For gas flow in a constant-area duct, the constant mass flow intensity $\mathbf{G}$ (a vector) is

$$\mathbf{G} = \rho \mathbf{V}, \text{ or in scalar form, } G = \rho_1 V_1 = \rho_2 V_2 \qquad (5\text{-}8)$$

3. For incompressible flow in a constant-area duct, the average velocity remains constant in magnitude.

$$V_1 = V_2 \qquad (5\text{-}9)$$

EXAMPLE 5–1. Air at 80 F and 50 psia flows through a 6-in. diameter pipe at an average velocity of 120 ft/sec. What is a) the mass-flow rate, b) the mass-flow intensity, and c) the velocity at a section where the pressure has dropped to 40 psia for constant temperature flow?

Solution:

$$\rho = p/RT = (50)(144)/(1715)(540) = 0.00777 \text{ slug/ft}^3$$
$$A = 0.1963 \text{ ft}^2$$

a) $VA\rho = (120)(0.1963)(0.00777) = 0.183$ slug/sec

b) $G = V\rho = (120)(0.00777) = 0.933$ slug/ft^2 sec

c) $V_1 \rho_1 = V_2 \rho_2$ so that

$$V_2 = \frac{V_1(p_1/RT_1)}{p_2/RT_2} = \frac{V_1 p_1}{p_2} = \frac{(120)(50)}{40} = 150 \text{ ft/sec}$$

The differential scalar form of Eq. 5–6 may be obtained by direct differentiation with respect to the stream tube direction s and division by $VA\rho$, or by differentiating the logarithmic form of the equation with respect to s. We obtain for flow through a conduit (stream tube)

$$\frac{1}{V}\frac{dV}{ds} + \frac{1}{A}\frac{dA}{ds} + \frac{1}{\rho}\frac{d\rho}{ds} = 0 \qquad (5\text{-}10a)$$

which is often written as

$$\frac{dV}{V} + \frac{dA}{A} + \frac{d\rho}{\rho} = 0 \qquad (5\text{-}10b)$$

From this it is apparent that the velocity, area, and density cannot all increase, nor can they all decrease, in the direction of flow (in the direction of positive s).

Derivation of the continuity equation. The various forms of the continuity equations for a control volume are derived by stating mathematically that the net rate of inflow of mass into a given region is equal to the rate of change of mass in that region, and this will be zero for an incompressible fluid. In Fig. 5-5, the mass-flow rate into the region consisting of a rectangular parallelopiped of sides Δx, Δy, and Δz in the $+x$ direction

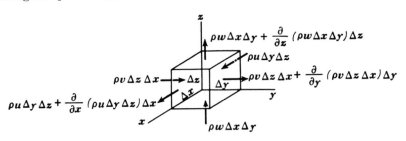

FIG. 5-5.   Mass flow rate in and out of an elemental control volume.

is $(\rho u\, \Delta y\, \Delta z)$, and out of it, in the $+x$ direction, it is the mass-flow rate in, plus the rate of change of the mass-flow rate in the $+x$ direction times Δx. This is

$$\rho u\, \Delta y\, \Delta z + \frac{\partial}{\partial x}(\rho u\, \Delta y\, \Delta z)\, \Delta x$$

The net inflow of mass in the $+x$ direction per unit time is the difference between these, which is

$$-\frac{\partial}{\partial x}(\rho u\, \Delta y\, \Delta z)\, \Delta x$$

Similarly, the net rate of mass flow into the region in the $+y$ and the $+z$ directions is

$$-\frac{\partial}{\partial y}(\rho v\, \Delta z\, \Delta x)\, \Delta y$$

and

$$-\frac{\partial}{\partial z}(\rho w\, \Delta x\, \Delta y)\, \Delta z$$

The rate of increase of mass in the region is (if not zero)

$$\frac{\partial}{\partial t}(\rho\, \Delta x\, \Delta y\, \Delta z)$$

and thus

$$-\frac{\partial}{\partial x}\left(\rho u\,\Delta y\,\Delta z\right)\Delta x - \frac{\partial}{\partial y}\left(\rho v\,\Delta z\,\Delta x\right)\Delta y - \frac{\partial}{\partial z}\left(\rho w\,\Delta x\,\Delta y\right)\Delta z$$

$$= \frac{\partial}{\partial t}\left(\rho\,\Delta x\,\Delta y\,\Delta z\right)$$

Since Δy and Δz do not vary with x; Δz and Δx do not vary with y; Δx and Δy do not vary with z; and Δx, Δy, and Δz do not vary with t, we can divide through by the quantity $\Delta x\,\Delta y\,\Delta z$, which is the volume of the region considered. We then obtain

$$\frac{\partial(\rho u)}{\partial x} + \frac{\partial(\rho v)}{\partial y} + \frac{\partial(\rho w)}{\partial z} = -\frac{\partial\rho}{\partial t}$$

for steady or unsteady flow of an incompressible or a compressible fluid.

In cylindrical coordinates this becomes

$$\frac{\partial v_r}{\partial r} + \frac{v_r}{r} + \frac{1}{r}\frac{\partial v_\theta}{\partial\theta} + \frac{\partial v_z}{\partial z} = 0 \qquad (5\text{--}11)$$

where r and θ are the polar radius and angle in the x-y plane and all planes parallel to it, v_r and v_θ are velocity components in the r and θ directions, and v_z is equivalent to w, the velocity in the z direction.

From the definition of the vector operator del, the divergence is readily shown to be zero, based on the preceding derivation, for an incompressible fluid.

$$\text{div }\mathbf{V} = \nabla\cdot\mathbf{V} = \frac{\partial V_x}{\partial x} + \frac{\partial V_y}{\partial y} + \frac{\partial V_z}{\partial z}$$

$$= \frac{\partial u}{\partial x} + \frac{\partial v}{\partial y} + \frac{\partial w}{\partial z} = 0$$

For one-dimensional flow in a stream tube (Fig. 5–4b), Eq. 5–5 may be derived by expressing mathematically that the net mass flow rate into a control volume of the stream tube of elemental length ds and area A equals the rate of change of mass within the control volume. Thus

$$\rho\mathbf{V}\cdot\mathbf{A} - \left[\rho\mathbf{V}\cdot\mathbf{A} + \frac{\partial}{\partial s}\left(\rho\mathbf{V}\cdot\mathbf{A}\right)ds\right] = \frac{\partial}{\partial t}\left(\rho A\,ds\right)$$

so that after division by ds (a fixed length)

$$\frac{\partial(\rho A)}{\partial t} + \frac{\partial}{\partial s}\left(\rho\mathbf{V}\cdot\mathbf{A}\right) = 0$$

Vector derivation of the continuity equation. A control volume $\mathcal{V}$ is

bounded by its control surface S (Fig. 5–6). As before, the net flow into
the control volume (the fluid enters through a part of the control surface
and leaves through other parts) equals the time rate of increase of mass
within the control volume V.

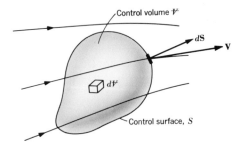

Fig. 5–6.   Control volume for vector derivation
of continuity equation.

Through an elemental area dS the mass flow rate outwards (positive)
is $\rho \mathbf{V} \cdot d\mathbf{S}$ and thus the net mass flow into the control volume through the
control surface is $-\iint_A \rho \mathbf{V} \cdot d\mathbf{S}$. The mass of an elemental volume within
the control volume is $\rho \, dV$, and the total mass within the control volume
is $\iiint_V \rho \, dV$, which increases at a rate of

$$\frac{\partial}{\partial t} \iiint_V \rho \, dV$$

Thus the principle of conservation of mass is written as

$$-\iint_S \rho \mathbf{V} \cdot d\mathbf{S} = \frac{\partial}{\partial t} \iiint_V \rho \, dV$$

Changing the surface integral to a volume integral gives

$$-\iint_S \rho \mathbf{V} \cdot d\mathbf{S} = -\iiint_V \nabla \cdot \rho \mathbf{V} \, dV = \frac{\partial}{\partial t} \iiint_V \rho \, dV$$

so that by changing the order of integration and differentiation, we have

$$\iiint_V \left[\nabla \cdot (\rho \mathbf{V}) + \frac{\partial \rho}{\partial t} \right] dV = 0$$

This equation holds for all control volumes, however small, and the integrand must therefore be zero. Thus

$$\nabla \cdot \rho \mathbf{V} + \frac{\partial \rho}{\partial t} = 0$$

as before.

5–3. ROTATION AND VORTICITY

An expression for fluid rotation and a condition for a fluid to be irrotational will be needed in the development of the equations of motion normal to a streamline in the next section.

The fluid rotation about any axis is defined as the average rotation of any two mutually perpendicular line segments (made up of fluid material) in a plane normal to this axis. The *vorticity* is defined as twice the fluid rotation and is measured by the curl of the velocity vector. If the fluid rotation or vorticity is zero, then the fluid is said to be *irrotational*. It will be shown that for zero rotation about any axis parallel to the z axis

$$\frac{\partial v}{\partial x} = \frac{\partial u}{\partial y} \tag{5–12a}$$

Similarly, for zero rotation about axes parallel to the x and y axes,

$$\frac{\partial w}{\partial y} = \frac{\partial v}{\partial z} \tag{5–12b}$$

and

$$\frac{\partial u}{\partial z} = \frac{\partial w}{\partial x} \tag{5–12c}$$

In vector notation, the curl of the velocity vector is equal to the fluid vorticity.

$$\text{Vorticity} = \text{curl } \mathbf{V} = \nabla \times \mathbf{V} = \begin{vmatrix} \mathbf{i} & \mathbf{j} & \mathbf{k} \\ \dfrac{\partial}{\partial x} & \dfrac{\partial}{\partial y} & \dfrac{\partial}{\partial z} \\ u & v & w \end{vmatrix}$$

$$= \left(\frac{\partial w}{\partial y} - \frac{\partial v}{\partial z}\right)\mathbf{i} + \left(\frac{\partial u}{\partial z} - \frac{\partial w}{\partial x}\right)\mathbf{j} + \left(\frac{\partial v}{\partial x} - \frac{\partial u}{\partial y}\right)\mathbf{k} \tag{5–12d}$$

For *irrotational* motion the curl of the velocity vector is zero, and the coefficients of $\mathbf{i}$, $\mathbf{j}$, and $\mathbf{k}$ are each zero. Thus for irrotational flow in the x-y plane, $\partial u/\partial y = \partial v/\partial x$. For *rotational* flow the curl of the velocity vector is non-zero, and one or more of the coefficients of $\mathbf{i}$, $\mathbf{j}$, and $\mathbf{k}$ are non-zero. For rotational flow in the x-y plane, the vorticity is twice the fluid rotation, or $\left(\dfrac{\partial v}{\partial x} - \dfrac{\partial u}{\partial y}\right)\mathbf{k}$.

An interesting discussion on vorticity and the role of eddies in fluid motion is given by Rouse [3].

Equations 5–12 are derived by considering in the x-y plane, for example, the average of the rotations of two mutually perpendicular line segments (those parallel to the x and the y axes may be used) of length Δx and Δy in Fig. 5–7. If the x component of velocity of the line segment Δy at (x, y) is u, then at $(x, y + \Delta y)$ it is $u + (\partial u/\partial y)\,\Delta y$; and if the y component of the velocity of the segment Δx at (x, y) is v, then at $(x + \Delta x, y)$ it is $v + (\partial v/\partial x)$ Δx. Note that if $\partial u/\partial x$ and $\partial v/\partial y$ are both zero, the line segments Δx and Δy can undergo only a translation, with no rotation possible. For a counterclockwise rotation considered positive, the rotation of the line segment Δx is the difference between the velocities at the ends of the line segment, divided by the length of the line segment. This may be written as

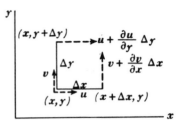

FIG. 5–7.   Rotation of two fluid-line segments.

$$\frac{v + (\partial v/\partial x) \Delta x - v}{\Delta x} = \frac{\partial v}{\partial x}$$

and for the line segment Δy the rotation is

$$-\frac{u + (\partial u/\partial y) \Delta y - u}{\Delta y} = -\frac{\partial u}{\partial y}$$

The average of these is the rotation about the z axis.

$$\omega_z = \frac{1}{2}\left(\frac{\partial v}{\partial x} - \frac{\partial u}{\partial y}\right)$$

$$= 0 \qquad \text{for no rotation}$$

Thus for an irrotational fluid,

$$\frac{\partial v}{\partial x} = \frac{\partial u}{\partial y}$$

and by a similar analysis for rotation about axes parallel to the x and y coordinate axes, Eqs. 5–12b and 5–12c are obtained. These are also obtainable by expansion of Eq. 5–12d.

EXAMPLE 5–2. Show that the following velocity components satisfy continuity and that they represent irrotational flow:

$$u = (2x + y + z)\, t$$
$$v = (x - 2y + z)\, t$$
$$w = (x + y)\, t$$

Solution: Solving, $\partial u/\partial x = 2t$, $\partial v/\partial y = -2t$, and $\partial w/\partial z = 0$. Thus continuity is satisfied, since $\partial u/\partial x + \partial v/\partial y + \partial w/\partial z = 0$. The flow is not steady because u, v, and w vary with time. If irrotational, Eqs. 6–2a, b, and c must be satisfied; they are, since $t = t$, $t = t$, and $t = t$, respectively. In vector form,

$$\mathbf{V} = (2x + y + z)t\ \mathbf{i} + (x - 2y + z)t\ \mathbf{j} + (x + y)t\ \mathbf{k}$$
$$\nabla \cdot \mathbf{V} = 2t - 2t + 0 = 0$$

and continuity is satisfied.

$$\nabla \times \mathbf{V} = \begin{vmatrix} \mathbf{i} & \mathbf{j} & \mathbf{k} \\ \partial/\partial x & \partial/\partial y & \partial/\partial z \\ (2x + y + z)t & (x - 2y + z)t & (x + y)t \end{vmatrix}$$

$$= (t - t)\,\mathbf{i} - (t - t)\,\mathbf{j} + (t - t)\,\mathbf{k} = 0$$

and the flow is shown to be irrotational.

5–4. CONSERVATION OF MOMENTUM

Newton's second law of motion states that force is proportional to the time rate of change of momentum. This law may be applied to fluid flow through a control volume to obtain the momentum theorem. It may also be applied to an element of fluid to obtain the equations of motion in differential form, and these equations may be integrated for certain conditions to obtain equations of practical use in solving flow problems.

Momentum theorem. The momentum theorem is concerned only with external forces and provides useful results without requiring a detailed knowledge of the internal processes within the fluid. It may be applied to flows which are steady or unsteady; one-, two-, or three-dimensional, compressible or incompressible.

As in the case of solids or discrete particles, fluids tend to continue in a state of uniform motion or rest unless acted upon by external forces. If the velocity of a group of fluid particles or of the entire fluid as it passes through the surface of a control volume changes either in magnitude, direction, or both, a net external force acting *on* the fluid is required to produce this change. We will consider
1) normal forces due to pressure,
2) tangential forces due to viscous shear,
3) body forces, such as gravity acting in the direction of the gravitational field.

The momentum theorem states that the net force acting externally *on* the fluid within a prescribed control volume equals the time rate of change of momentum of the fluid within the control volume plus the net rate of flow of momentum outward through the surface of the control volume.

Development of the momentum theorem. In Fig. 5–8 let $\mathbf{M}$ be the linear momentum of the particular fluid within the control volume bounded by the control surface S at time t. At time $t + \delta t$ this same fluid occupies the region bounded by S', and its momentum is

$$\left[\mathbf{M} + \frac{\partial \mathbf{M}}{\partial t}\, dt \right] + [\text{momentum of the fluid in II}]$$
$$- [\text{momentum of the fluid in I}]$$

The last two terms represent the momentum flow out of the control volume

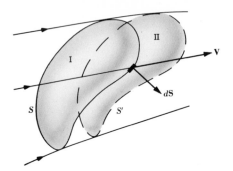

FIG. 5–8. Control volume for vector derivation
of momentum theorem.

through the control surface S during the time δt. Hence the time rate of
change of momentum of the fluid initially within S is

$$\frac{\partial \mathbf{M}}{\partial t} + \text{momentum flow rate outwards through the boundary } S \text{ of the}$$
$$\text{control volume}$$

The momentum of the fluid within the control volume for the fluid initially
within S is

$$\mathbf{M} = \iiint_{\mathcal{V}} \rho \mathbf{V} \cdot d\mathcal{V}$$

and the momentum flow rate (also called the momentum flux or the rate
of momentum transport) outward through the control surface S is

$$\iint_{S} \rho \, \mathbf{V} \, (\mathbf{V} \cdot d\mathbf{S})$$

Thus the time rate of change of momentum is equated to the net force
acting on the fluid within the control volume.

$$\Sigma \mathbf{F} = \frac{\partial \mathbf{M}}{\partial t} + \iint_{S} \rho \, \mathbf{V} \, (\mathbf{V} \cdot d\mathbf{S}) \qquad (5\text{–}13)$$

For steady flow $\partial \mathbf{M}/\partial t = 0$. The last term in Eq. 5–13 is the difference
between the flow of momentum of the fluid leaving through S and the
flow of momentum of the fluid entering through S. Thus for *steady* flow
we may write

$$\Sigma \mathbf{F} = (\dot{m}\mathbf{V})_{\text{leaving } S} - (\dot{m}\mathbf{V})_{\text{entering } S} \qquad (5\text{–}14a)$$

or in scalar form

$$\Sigma F_x = (\dot{m}V_x)_{\text{leaving } S} - (\dot{m}V_x)_{\text{entering } S} \qquad (5\text{–}14b)$$

with similar expressions for the y and z directions, respectively.
   Equations 5–14 may also be written as

$$\Sigma \mathbf{F} = \dot{m}(\mathbf{V}_{\text{leaving } S} - \mathbf{V}_{\text{entering } S}) \qquad (5\text{–}15a)$$

or in scalar form

$$\Sigma F_x = \dot{m}(V_x \text{ leaving } S - V_x \text{ entering } S) \qquad (5\text{-}15b)$$

with similar expressions for the y and z directions, respectively.

If gravity or other body forces are absent, ΣF represents only forces due to pressure and viscous shear. These are equal and opposite at all points within the control volume, and thus ΣF is the integral of these forces over the control surface S.

Application of the momentum theorem. In instances where the fluid velocity changes only in magnitude, the direction along which the momentum equation is written is well defined, and a scalar equation is sufficient. When the fluid changes direction, a vector equation may be used or scalar equations must be written in mutually perpendicular directions, and forces and velocities along these directions represent components of the resultant forces and velocities. The velocity change in Eq. 5–15 may be expressed in terms of absolute or relative velocity for *non-accelerating* control volumes; that is, the fluid velocities may be taken with respect to any non-accelerating moving reference or to a reference at rest, so long as a consistent reference is used. The earth is usually considered to be a reference at rest, though a fixed star should probably be used.

Forces due to pressure should be based on gage pressure (that is, with respect to the ambient atmospheric pressure) because forces resulting from atmospheric pressure completely envelop the control volume and thus they cancel and have no resultant effect.

The momentum theorem may be applied to a control volume in which two or more fluids enter and combine within the control volume, such as in the combustion chamber of a jet engine. For steady flow, the net force *on* the fluid is the difference between the flow of momentum of the fluid leaving the control volume and the total flow of momentum of the various fluids entering the control volume (Eq. 5–15).

The momentum theorem may be applied in the following manner: the region or control volume wherein a momentum change takes place is isolated, and a positive x direction (and a positive y and z direction if necessary) is arbitrarily assigned. The mass flow rate is expressed in terms of either the entrance or exit conditions, since Eqs. 5–14 and 5–15 are valid for steady flow only. Some examples, in which one-dimensional flow is assumed, will illustrate the application of the momentum principle. In all instances, the control volume wherein the momentum change takes place is indicated by dotted lines. Some unsteady flows may be transformed into steady flows by changing the frame of reference. The flow in Ex. 5–4 is a steady flow when viewed with respect to the rocket. The steady flow momentum theorem may be applied to a moving wave front (Secs. 9–1 and 12–2) when written with respect to the moving wave front, and to a tidal bore when written with respect to the moving hydraulic jump (Sec. 12–6).

EXAMPLE 5–3. Water flows through a reducing elbow at a rate of 8 ft³/sec. The area reduction is from 1 ft² to 0.5 ft². The pressure is 25 psig at inlet and 23.6 psig at exit. What is the resultant force of the water on the elbow? Assume the bend to be in a horizontal plane.

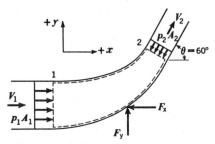

Solution: In Fig. 5–9, let F_x and F_y be the x and y components of the viscous shear and pressure forces of the elbow walls on the fluid be as shown. The

FIG. 5–9. Flow through a reducing elbow.

momentum equations written in the $+x$ and $+y$ directions are

$$p_1 A_1 - F_x - p_2 A_2 \cos \theta = V A \rho (V_2 \cos \theta - V_1)$$

and

$$F_y - p_2 A_2 \sin \theta = (V A \rho)(V_2 \sin \theta - 0)$$

Then

$$F_x = p_1 A_1 - p_2 A_2 \cos \theta - V_1 A_1 \rho (V_2 \cos \theta - V_1)$$

$$= (25)(144)(1) - (23.6)(144)(0.5)(0.5) - (8)(1)(1.94)\left[(16)\left(\frac{1}{2}\right) - 8\right]$$

$$= 2750 \text{ lb}_f \text{ on the water}$$

$$F_y = p_2 A_2 \sin \theta + V_1 A_1 \rho (V_2 \sin \theta - 0)$$

$$= (23.6)(144)(0.5)(0.866) + (8)(1)(1.94)[(16)(0.866) - 0]$$

$$= 1685 \text{ lb}_f \text{ on the water}$$

The resultant force of the water on the elbow is $\sqrt{2750^2 + 1685^2} = 3226$ lb$_f$ at an angle $\tan^{-1} 1685/2750$, or 31.5 deg from the x direction, downward and to the right.

EXAMPLE 5–4. A rocket travels at 1500 ft/sec and discharges its exhaust gases at 1800 ft/sec relative to the rocket at a rate of 0.33 slug/sec through an exit area of 0.5 ft². The absolute pressure at exit is 14 psia and the ambient air pressure is 12 psia. What is the thrust on the rocket?

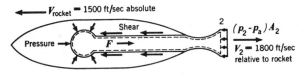

FIG. 5–10. Thrust on rocket.

Solution: The gases have a momentum change within the dotted-line region in Fig. 5–10. The external forces acting on the gases are due to pressure and viscous shear, as indicated. Let F be the resultant of these forces. Since the exit pressure is above the ambient pressure, two external forces act. The force F is applied by the rocket walls, and the force $(p_2 - p_a)A_2$ results from the positive gage pressure at exit.

$$F - (p_2 - p_a) A_2 = (V A \rho) (V_2 - 0)$$

Expressing the change in gas velocity as relative to the rocket,

$$F = (VA\rho)V_2 + (p_2 - p_a)A_2 = (0.33)(1800) + (2)(144)(0.5) = 738 \text{ lb}_f$$

The thrust of the gases *on* the rocket is equal and opposite to F. Note that the effect of a positive gage pressure at exit is to increase the thrust, so that a rocket designed to operate at one altitude will produce a higher thrust at a higher altitude, and conversely. This example is rather extreme, and in general, a rocket should be designed to expand the gases closer to the ambient pressure. If the gases expand fully, the exit pressure p_2 is fixed by the gas condition as it enters the nozzle and the nozzle design. Lowering the exit pressure will also increase the exit velocity.

EXAMPLE 5–5. A liquid jet strikes a curved blade and is deflected through an angle of 60 deg. The jet velocity is 80 ft/sec, the jet area is 0.1 ft², and the liquid density is 1.94 slugs/ft³. What force is exerted by the jet on the vane? Assume constant jet speed.

Solution: In Fig. 5–11,

$$- F_x = VA\rho \, (V \cos \theta - V)$$

$$F_x = (80)(0.1)(1.94) \left[80 - (80) \left(\frac{1}{2} \right) \right] = 621 \text{ lb}_f$$

$$F_y = VA\rho \, (V \sin \theta - 0) = (80)(0.1)(1.94) \, [(80)(0.866)] = 1076 \text{ lb}_f$$

The resultant force is $\sqrt{621^2 + 1076^2} = 1242 \text{ lb}_f$.

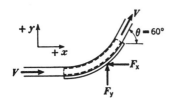

FIG. 5–11. Blade force on free jet of liquid.

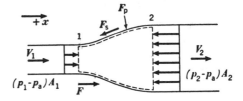

FIG. 5–12. Gas flowing through expansion.

EXAMPLE 5–6. A gas flows through an expanding section in a pipe. The area increases from A_1 to A_2, the velocity decreases from V_1 to V_2, the pressure increases from p_1 to p_2, and the gas density increases from ρ_1 to ρ_2. What is the net force of the walls of the expanding section on the fluid?

Solution: The walls of the expanding section exert both viscous shear (opposite to the flow direction) and a force due to pressure (axial component is in the flow direction). Let the resultant of these be F in the direction shown in Fig. 5–12. The atmospheric pressure is p_a.

$$(p_1 - p_a)A_1 + F - (p_2 - p_a)A_2 = V_1 A_1 \rho_1 (V_2 - V_1) = V_2 A_2 \rho_2 (V_2 - V_1)$$

$$F = p_2 A_2 - p_1 A_1 + V_1 A_1 \rho_1 (V_2 - V_1)$$

$$- p_a(A_2 - A_1)$$

The results of Example 5–6 may be used to define the *thrust function*, which is commonly used in gas dynamics. The resulting expression for the net force F may be rearranged to give

$$F = (p_2 A_2 + V_2{}^2 A_2 \rho_2) - (p_1 A_1 + V_1{}^2 A_1 \rho_1) - p_a(A_2 - A_1)$$

where the expression $(pA + V^2 A \rho)$ is called the thrust function. The net external force is thus equal to the change in the thrust function corrected for the effect of the atmosphere.

We have used the average velocity across a section in determining the momentum flux $V^2 A \rho$ through a section in a one-dimensional analysis. If the velocity varies across the section, the true momentum flux is greater than that based on the average velocity. The true momentum flux is found by integrating the product of the mass-flow rate and velocity over the area of flow. This is

$$\int_A (u\rho \, dA) \, u$$

while that based on the average velocity is

$$(V\rho A) \, V = V^2 A \rho$$

The ratio of the true momentum flux to that based on the average velocity is called the *momentum correction factor* β, where

$$\beta = \frac{\int_A u^2 \, dA}{V^2 A} \geq 1 \qquad\qquad (5\text{–}16)$$

For one-dimensional flow, $\beta = 1$, and this is an assumption often made. For laminar flow in a round pipe with a parabolic velocity profile, $\beta = \frac{4}{3}$, and for turbulent flow in a round pipe, $\beta \approx 1.05$.

EXAMPLE 5–7. An incompressible fluid of density ρ approaches a flat plate with a uniform free-stream velocity u_s and flows past one side of the plate. Because of viscous shear, the fluid motion is retarded within a thin layer of thickness δ.

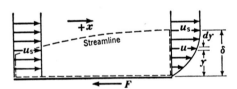

FIG. 5–13. Flow along a flat plate.

The velocity within this layer varies from zero at the wall to the free-stream velocity u_s at $y = \delta$. The fluid within the thin layer has had its momentum changed by an external force F applied along the surface or wall of the plate, as shown in Fig. 5–13. The momentum equation is

$$- F = \int_0^\delta (u\rho \, dy)(u - u_s)$$

which can be evaluated if u is expressed as a function of y, and this will be done in Chapter 7.

Equations of motion. We now consider the application of Newton's second law to an element of a nonviscous fluid moving along a streamline. (Flow of a real fluid with friction is treated in Chapter 10.) The result in differential form is called Euler's (or sometimes Bernoulli's) equation of motion along a streamline and is a special form of the more general Navier-Stokes equations which include viscous effects. Integration of the equation of motion for steady flow of an incompressible fluid yields what is known as Bernoulli's equation in hydraulics. It is common, however, to designate the integrated form of the equation of motion for compressible flow as Bernoulli's equation as well. Bernoulli's equation is often called an energy equation because of its similarity to the steady-flow energy equation obtained from the first law of thermodynamics for a frictionless (nonviscous) fluid with no heat transfer and no external shaft work. This similarity will be discussed in more detail in Sec. 5-6, after the steady-flow energy equation is developed.

If the velocity V of an elementary fluid particle is a function of position and time, we may write that $V = V(s,t)$. Thus (see Sec. 3-8),

$$dV = \frac{\partial V}{\partial s}\, ds + \frac{\partial V}{\partial t}\, dt \quad \text{or} \quad \frac{dV}{dt} = \frac{\partial V}{\partial s}\frac{ds}{dt} + \frac{\partial V}{\partial t}$$

and since the velocity along a streamline is $V = ds/dt$, the acceleration in that direction is

$$a_s = \frac{dV}{dt} = V\frac{\partial V}{\partial s} + \frac{\partial V}{\partial t} \tag{5-17}$$

The term $V\,\partial V/\partial s$ is the convective acceleration, or the variation in velocity along a streamline; $\partial V/\partial t$ is the local acceleration, or the variation of velocity at a point with respect to time.

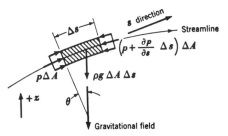

FIG. 5-14. Elementary ideal fluid particle moving along a streamline.

We will now apply Newton's second law to an element of a nonviscous fluid. From Fig. 5-14, writing $\Sigma F = ma_s$ along the streamline gives

$$p\,\Delta A - \left(p + \frac{\partial p}{\partial s}\,\Delta s\right)\Delta A - \rho g\,\Delta A\,\Delta s \sin\theta = \rho\,\Delta A\,\Delta s\left(V\frac{\partial V}{\partial s} + \frac{\partial V}{\partial t}\right)$$

and since $\sin \theta = \partial z / \partial s$, upon simplifying we get

$$V \frac{\partial V}{\partial s} + \frac{1}{\rho} \frac{\partial p}{\partial s} + g \frac{\partial z}{\partial s} = -\frac{\partial V}{\partial t} \qquad (5\text{--}18)$$

which is Euler's equation of motion along a streamline for a nonviscous fluid. For steady flow $\partial V / \partial t = 0$, and integration along a streamline for a constant-density fluid gives

$$\frac{V^2}{2} + \frac{p}{\rho} + gz = \text{constant} \qquad (5\text{--}19a)$$

which may also be written as

$$\frac{\rho V_1^2}{2} + p_1 + \rho g z_1 = \frac{\rho V_2^2}{2} + p_2 + \rho g z_2 = \text{constant total pressure} \quad (5\text{--}19b)$$

or $\qquad \dfrac{V_1^2}{2g} + \dfrac{p_1}{g\rho} + z_1 = \dfrac{V_2^2}{2g} + \dfrac{p_2}{g\rho} + z_2 = \text{constant total head} \quad (5\text{--}19c)$

In Eq. 5–19b the term $\rho V^2 / 2$ is known as the dynamic pressure, p is the static pressure, and $g\rho z$ is the potential pressure. In Eq. 5–19c, the term $V^2 / 2g$ is known as the velocity head, $p/g\rho$ (equivalent to p/γ) is the pressure head, and z is the potential head. The constant sum of these quantities is known as *Bernoulli's constant.*[2]

Equations 5–19a, 5–19b, and 5–19c are known as Bernoulli's equations for an incompressible fluid. They are valid for *a*) steady flow, *b*) an incompressible fluid, *c*) a fluid with no viscosity (shear or friction forces were neglected), and thus the flow may be considered thermodynamically reversible, and *d*) conditions where no external shaft work is involved.

Equations 5–19 may be applied to viscous fluids, in instances when the viscous effects are small, in order to obtain approximate results. Many times these results are very close to the actual results.

For a gas flowing without heat transfer and without viscous effects (frictionless adiabatic or isentropic flow), $p/\rho^k = \text{constant}$ and the equation of motion (Eq. 5–18) for steady flow is

$$V \frac{\partial V}{\partial s} + \frac{c^{1/k}}{p^{1/k}} \frac{\partial p}{\partial s} + g \frac{\partial z}{\partial s} = 0$$

which, upon integration along a streamline, becomes

$$\frac{V^2}{2} + \frac{k}{k-1} \left(\frac{p}{\rho}\right) + gz = \text{constant} \qquad (5\text{--}20a)$$

or $\qquad \dfrac{V_1^2}{2} + \dfrac{k}{k-1} \left(\dfrac{p_1}{\rho_1}\right) + gz_1 = \dfrac{V_2^2}{2} + \dfrac{k}{k-1} \left(\dfrac{p_2}{\rho_2}\right) + gz_2 \quad (5\text{--}20b)$

[2]It is constant throughout an irrotational fluid, but is generally different for different flow systems.

If $V_1 = 0$,

$$V_2 = \sqrt{\frac{2k}{k-1}\left[\frac{p_1}{\rho_1} - \frac{p_2}{\rho_2}\right]} \qquad (5\text{-}21a)$$

$$= \sqrt{\frac{2kR}{k-1}(T_1 - T_2)} \qquad (5\text{-}21b)$$

This equation was derived for a) steady flow, b) a compressible nonviscous perfect gas flowing isentropically (no heat transfer and constant entropy),[3] and c) conditions where no external work is involved.

If we consider the fluid element of Fig. 5–14 and apply Newton's second law in a direction *normal* to the streamline as in Fig. 5–15, variations in velocity head, pressure head, and potential head (or velocity or dynamic pressure, static pressure, and potential pressure) across streamlines, from one to another, may be determined.

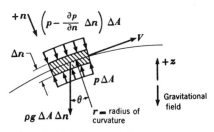

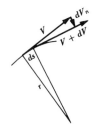

FIG. 5–15. Normal forces on elementary ideal fluid particle moving along a curved streamline.

FIG. 5–16. Flow along curved streamline.

Although the velocity V itself is always tangent to a streamline at any given point, if the streamline is curved, the velocity at an infinitesimal distance from the given point measured along the streamline will have changed direction. The component of this changed velocity in a direction normal to the streamline at the given point is designated as V_n. If V_n is a function of position and time, we may write that $V_n = V_n(s,t)$. Thus

$$dV_n = \frac{\partial V_n}{\partial s}\, ds + \frac{\partial V_n}{\partial t}\, dt$$

or

$$\frac{dV_n}{dt} = \frac{\partial V_n}{\partial s}\frac{ds}{dt} + \frac{\partial V_n}{\partial t}$$

[3] It can be shown (Sec. 5–6) that the steady-flow energy equation written for *any* adiabatic flow without external work, for both reversible *and* irreversible flow (with friction), has the same form as Eq. 5–20, which is derived for reversible flow only. This is pure coincidence.

From Fig. 5–16, $\partial V_n/\partial s = V/r$, and since $ds/dt = V$,

$$a_n = \frac{V^2}{r} + \frac{\partial V_n}{\partial t}$$

The term V^2/r is the convective, and $\partial V_n/\partial t$ the local acceleration, respectively.

As before, we will apply Newton's second law to an element of a nonviscous fluid. From Fig. 5–15, writing $\Sigma F = ma_n$ normal to the streamline gives

$$-p\,\Delta A + \left(p - \frac{\partial p}{\partial n}\,\Delta n\right)\Delta A + \rho g\,\Delta A\,\Delta n\cos\theta = \rho\,\Delta A\,\Delta n\left(\frac{V^2}{r} + \frac{\partial V_n}{\partial t}\right)$$

and since $\cos\theta = -\partial z/\partial n$, upon simplifying we get

$$\frac{V^2}{r} + \frac{1}{\rho}\frac{\partial p}{\partial n} + g\frac{\partial z}{\partial n} = -\frac{\partial V_n}{\partial t} \tag{5–22}$$

which is the equation of motion normal to a streamline.

If the streamlines are straight (the radius of curvature r is infinite and V^2/r and V_n are both zero), Eq. 5–22 may be integrated along the direction n to get, for a constant-density fluid,

$$p + \rho g z = \text{constant}$$

which indicates that in flow of constant-density fluids in which there is no curvature of the streamlines, the piezometric pressure is constant normal to the streamlines. In a horizontal plane under the same conditions, the pressure intensity is constant normal to the streamlines. For steady flow, $\partial V_n/\partial t = 0$ and the last term in Eq. 5–22 drops out.

We will integrate Eq. 5–22 for an irrotational fluid and for a rotational fluid. The definition of rotation (Sec. 5–3) in the s and n coordinates used here may be expressed as

$$\frac{\partial V_n}{\partial s} - \frac{\partial V}{\partial n} = 2\omega \tag{5–23}$$

where ω is the angular velocity of the fluid about an axis normal to s and n.

An irrotational fluid (Sec. 5–3) is one for which ω is zero. Since

$$\frac{\partial V_n}{\partial s} = \frac{V}{r}$$

we may write for an irrotational fluid

$$\frac{\partial V_n}{\partial s} = \frac{V}{r} = \frac{\partial V}{\partial n}$$

Therefore, $$\frac{V^2}{r} = V\frac{V}{r} = V\frac{\partial V}{\partial n}$$

For steady flow of an irrotational fluid, the equation of motion normal to a streamline (Eq. 5–22) becomes

$$V\frac{\partial V}{\partial n} + \frac{1}{\rho}\frac{\partial p}{\partial n} + g\frac{\partial z}{\partial n} = 0$$

Integration in a direction normal to the streamlines for a constant-density fluid gives

$$\frac{V^2}{2} + \frac{p}{\rho} + gz = \text{constant} \qquad (5\text{–}24\text{a})$$

or

$$\frac{V_1{}^2}{2} + \frac{p_1}{\rho} + gz_1 = \frac{V_2{}^2}{2} + \frac{p_2}{\rho} + gz_2 \qquad (5\text{–}24\text{b})$$

Thus in an incompressible, steady, irrotational fluid, the Bernoulli constant is the same along streamlines (Eq. 5–19a), as well as across streamlines (Eq. 5–24), and thus the same throughout the entire fluid.

In a *free* (irrotational) vortex

$$\frac{\partial V}{\partial n} = -\frac{\partial V}{\partial r} = \frac{V}{r}$$

since the n direction was taken opposite to the r direction (Fig. 5–15). Thus, from the last equality, $Vr = constant$ in a free vortex, and the tangential velocity varies inversely with distance from the axis of rotation. Recall that the derivation was based on a nonviscous fluid, and thus a true free vortex is limited to ideal fluids. Real fluids, however, exhibit characteristics of ideal fluids in some instances. The swirl produced by a canoe paddle, the vortex in a bathtub drain, vertical intakes for hydraulic turbines, volutes of centrifugal pumps, and a tornado (Sec. 6–3) approach a free vortex, except near the axis of rotation.

If the fluid rotates as a solid body, there is no relative motion between fluid particles and thus no shear, even though the fluid is viscous. The equation of motion normal to a streamline (Eq. 5–22) for steady flow may therefore be applied. For this *forced* vortex (called forced because an external torque has to be applied) the angular velocity is constant and is given by

$$\omega = \frac{V}{r}$$

Since $\partial V_n/\partial s = V/r$, Eq. 5–23 may be written as

$$\frac{V}{r} - \frac{\partial V}{\partial n} = 2\omega = 2\frac{V}{r}$$

so that

$$-\frac{\partial V}{\partial n} = \frac{V}{r} \quad \text{and} \quad \frac{V^2}{r} = -V\frac{\partial V}{\partial n}$$

Substitution of this expression for V^2/r in Eq. 5–22 for steady flow gives, upon integration in a direction normal to the streamlines for a constant-density fluid,

$$-\frac{V^2}{2} + \frac{p}{\rho} + gz = \text{constant} \qquad (5\text{--}25\text{a})$$

or $$-\frac{V_1^2}{2} + \frac{p_1}{\rho} + gz_1 = -\frac{V_2^2}{2} + \frac{p_2}{\rho} + gz_2 \qquad (5\text{--}25\text{b})$$

Note the difference between this equation for a forced vortex and Eq. 5–24 for a free vortex.

A forced vortex may be generated by rotating a cylindrical container about its axis, and the resulting free surface of the liquid in the container will assume the shape of a paraboloid (Fig. 5–17). Pressures at any point within the liquid are determined from the hydrostatic equation ($\Delta p = \rho g \, \Delta z$) or from Eq. 5–25. The liquid contained within the impeller of a centrifugal pump approximates that of a forced vortex. When there is flow through the pump, the pressure rise due to radial flow must be added to that produced by the rotation (tangential flow). If subscript 1 refers to the inlet and 2 to the outlet of an impeller, and V_T refers to the tangential velocity and V_R to the radial velocity, then the pressure head difference between outlet and inlet is, for radial impeller vanes,

$$\frac{p_2 - p_1}{\rho g} = \left(\frac{V_{2T}^2}{2g} - \frac{V_{1T}^2}{2g}\right) + \left(\frac{V_{1R}^2}{2g} - \frac{V_{2R}^2}{2g}\right) \qquad (5\text{--}26)$$

if friction is neglected.

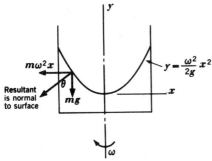

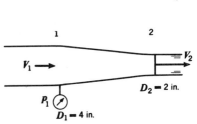

FIG. 5–17. Liquid rotated as a forced vortex; $dy/dx = \tan\theta = m\omega^2 x/mg = \omega^2 x/g$. Then $dy = (\omega^2 x/g)\,dx$ and $y = \omega^2 x^2/2g$, since the constant of integration is zero.

FIG. 5–18. Nozzle on end of pipe.

EXAMPLE 5–8. A 2-in. diameter nozzle is attached to the end of a 4-in. diameter pipe. The pressure in the pipe is 53 psig. What is the flow rate through the nozzle? Assume water flows without friction. See Fig. 5–18.

Solution: From Bernoulli's equation, $\rho(V_1^2/2) + p_1 = \rho(V_2^2/2)$, since p_2 is 0 psfg. From continuity, $V_1 A_1 = V_2 A_2$. Solving for V_2 gives

$$V_2 = \sqrt{\frac{2p_1}{\rho[1 - (A_2/A_1)^2]}} = \sqrt{\frac{(2)(53)(144)}{(1.94)\,[1 - (2/4)^4]}} = 91.6 \text{ ft/sec}$$

$$Q = V_2 A_2 = (91.6)(\pi/144) = 2.00 \text{ ft}^3/\text{sec}$$

Note that in order to state that the pressure at the nozzle exit is at atmospheric pressure, the streamlines must be parallel. If the nozzle consists of a straight taper, there would be a contraction of the flow beyond the end of the nozzle, the streamlines would be curved, and the pressure would vary across the exit section from atmospheric at the outer edge of the jet to a value above atmospheric at the jet axis.

EXAMPLE 5–9. Kerosene flows from a large open tank through a 2-in. diameter hole in its side. The free surface of the kerosene is 17 ft above the center line of the hole (see Fig. 5–19). What is the velocity of the jet issuing from the hole? Assume frictionless flow.

Solution: The Bernoulli equation may be applied from the free surface to a point in the jet where the pressure is known. As in Example 5–7, this is where the streamlines become parallel and the pressure is atmospheric.

The Bernoulli equation is

$$0 + 0 + 17 = \frac{V_2{}^2}{2g} + 0 + 0$$

so that $V_2 = \sqrt{(2g)(17)} = 33.1$ ft/sec. Note that the jet velocity is independent of the fluid density.

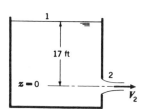

FIG. 5–19. Flow from an open tank.

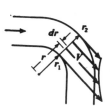

FIG. 5–20. Free-vortex flow around a square elbow.

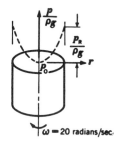

FIG. 5–21. Forced vortex in a rotating drum.

EXAMPLE 5–10. The pressure on the nose of a torpedo moving at a 60-ft depth in the sea ($\rho = 1.99$ slugs/ft^3) is 37 psig. What is the speed of the torpedo? Assume the torpedo at rest with sea water approaching it at a speed V_1.

Solution: The velocity of flow on the torpedo nose is zero. The flow may be assumed frictionless, and Bernoulli's equation is

$$\frac{\rho V_1{}^2}{2} + p_1 = p_2$$

where $p_1 = \rho g(60) = (1.99)(32.17)(60) = 3840$ psfg and $p_2 = 5328$ psfg. Thus $V_1 = \sqrt{2(p_2 - p_1)/\rho} = \sqrt{(2)(5328 - 3840)/1.99} = 38.6$ ft/sec.

EXAMPLE 5–11. The pressure on the nose of a subsonic aircraft is 20 psia at an altitude where the ambient pressure is 14 psia and the temperature is 30 F. What is the speed of the aircraft?

Solution: As in Example 5–10, the flow is the same as though the aircraft were at rest and an air stream approaches it at the speed of the aircraft in still air. The flow may be assumed adiabatic and reversible (frictionless) so that the Bernoulli equation given by Eq. 5–20b applies. In this equation, $V_2 = 0$ on the nose of the aircraft. From Eq. 5–20b and the isentropic relation $p_1/\rho_1^k = p_2/\rho_2^k$ we get

$$V_1 = \sqrt{\frac{2k}{k-1} RT_1 \left[\left(\frac{p_2}{p_1}\right)^{\frac{k-1}{k}} - 1 \right]}$$

$$= \sqrt{\frac{2.8}{0.4} (1715)(490) \left[\left(\frac{20}{14}\right)^{0.286} - 1 \right]}$$

$$= 795 \text{ ft/sec}$$

EXAMPLE 5–12. An elbow of 1 x 1-ft cross section is made up of two circular arcs with an inner radius $r_1 = 1$ ft and an outer radius $r_2 = 2$ ft (Fig. 5–20). Assume water flows through this elbow as a free vortex. The pressure difference between the inner and outer walls is 3 psi. What is the flow rate?

Solution: We use the fact that for a free vortex, $Vr = $ constant and Eq. 5–24b is used to find either the velocity at any radius or the value of the constant. Then we integrate across the section, since the velocity varies, to find the flow rate. $V_1 r_1 = V_2 r_2$ so that $V_1 = 2V_2$. From Eq. 5–24b,

$$p_2 - p_1 = \frac{\rho}{2} (V_1^2 - V_2^2) = \frac{c^2 \rho}{2} \left(\frac{1}{r_1^2} - \frac{1}{r_2^2}\right)$$

Thus
$$c^2 = \frac{2(p_2 - p_1)}{\rho[(1/r_1^2) - (1/r_2^2)]} = \frac{(2)(3)(144)}{(1.94)(1 - \frac{1}{4})} = 594$$

$$c = 24.4 \text{ ft}^2/\text{sec}$$

$$Q = \int_{r_1}^{r_2} V \, dr = \int_{r_1}^{r_2} \frac{c}{r} \, dr = 24.4 \ln\frac{r_2}{r_1} = (24.4)(0.693) = 16.9 \text{ ft}^3/\text{sec}$$

EXAMPLE 5–13. A closed cylindrical drum 3 ft in diameter and full of water is rotated about its axis (vertical) at 20 radians/sec (see Fig. 5–21). What is the increase in pressure at the outer edge of the drum due to rotation?

Solution: The pressure at the axis remains unchanged because of the rotation. Let p_R be the pressure at the outer radius and p_O be that at the axis. From Eq. 5–25b, $p_R - p_O = \rho V_R^2/2 = \rho \omega^2 R^2/2 = (1.94)(20^2)(1.5^2)/2 = 873$ psf.

5–5. CONSERVATION OF ENERGY

The steady-flow energy equation for fluid flow is obtained from the first law of thermodynamics, which considers both mechanical and thermal forms of energy. It states that the amount of heat added to the fluid as it passes through a system (region) is equal to the change in energy content of the fluid plus any work done by the fluid.

For the closed system (no fluid passes the system boundaries) the energy content is made up of kinetic energy, internal energy, and potential energy (see Chapter 3). For the open system (fluid flows through the system by passing across the system boundaries) the energy content is made up of kinetic energy, internal energy, potential energy, and displacement energy. This displacement energy is the energy, or work, required to push the fluid across the boundaries of the system. The steady-flow energy equation may be written as

$$q = \Delta(\text{kinetic energy}) + \Delta(\text{displacement energy}) + \Delta(\text{potential energy})$$
$$+ \Delta(\text{internal energy}) + (\text{work done by the fluid})$$

The heat added and the internal energy are considered to be forms of thermal energy and the remaining terms are considered to be forms of mechanical energy.

Kinetic energy. The kinetic energy of any mass m moving at a velocity V is $mV^2/2$, and in terms of kinetic energy per unit mass, it is $V^2/2$. For a fluid passing a section where the velocity is not uniform (two- or three-dimensional flow), the true kinetic energy per second is always greater than that based on the average velocity. The true kinetic energy is found by integrating the product of mass-flow rate through an infinitesimal area and the kinetic energy per unit mass over the entire flow area. The ratio of the true kinetic energy per unit time to that based on the average velocity is called the *kinetic energy correction factor* α, where

$$\alpha = \frac{\int_A (u^2/2)(u\rho \, dA)}{(V^2/2)(V\rho A)} = \frac{\int_A u^3 \, dA}{V^3 A} \geq 1 \tag{5-27}$$

For one-dimensional flow, $\alpha = 1$; for laminar flow in a round pipe with a parabolic velocity profile, $\alpha = 2$; for turbulent flow in a pipe, $\alpha \approx 1.1$.

Flow or displacement energy. Flow or displacement energy is the energy or work required to push a unit mass of fluid across the boundary of a system, at entrance or exit. Thus if the shaded area in Fig. 5-22 represents the volume occupied by a unit mass of fluid, its volume is the specific volume v; if the area through which it flows is A, the length of the shaded region is v/A. The work required to displace this volume from the shaded region to the dotted region across the boundary is the force times the distance moved. This is $(pA)(v/A) = pv$. The term pv is the flow or displacement work (or energy) per unit mass of fluid. Although pv has a value for both closed and open systems, only for the open system does it represent energy (flow or displacement work).

Potential energy. A unit mass of fluid has potential energy dependent upon its elevation above an arbitrary datum elevation where $z = 0$. The work required to bring it to any elevation other than the datum is gz ft lb$_f$ per unit mass, and this is its potential energy.

Internal energy. The internal energy (u per unit mass) is the form in which energy is stored within a substance, and in general, it is a function of pressure and temperature. For a perfect gas, it is a function only of the temperature (Eq. 3–7).

The steady-flow energy equation may now be written as (see Fig. 5–23)

$$\frac{V_1{}^2}{2} + p_1 v_1 + gz_1 + u_1 + q - w = \frac{V_2{}^2}{2} + p_2 v_2 + gz_2 + u_2 \qquad (5\text{–}28)$$

for one-dimensional flow with $\alpha_1 = \alpha_2 = 1$, and this is the steady-flow energy equation applicable to one-dimensional flow of all fluids (compressible or incompressible, with or without friction). In terms of enthalpy ($h = u + pv$), Eq. 5–28 may be written as

$$\frac{V_1{}^2}{2} + h_1 + gz_1 + q - w = \frac{V_2{}^2}{2} + h_2 + gz_2 \qquad (5\text{–}29a)$$

Recall from Eqs. 3–7 and 3–8 that for a perfect gas,

$$u_2 - u_1 = c_v(T_2 - T_1) \qquad \text{and} \qquad h_2 - h_1 = c_p(T_2 - T_1)$$

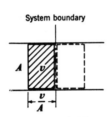

Fig. 5–22. Flow work or displacement energy.

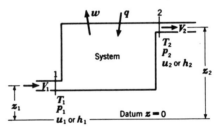

Fig. 5–23. Nomenclature for steady-flow energy equation.

In general, setting $\alpha_1 = \alpha_2 = 1$ for a one-dimensional analysis is acceptably accurate even though the flow is two- or three-dimensional. Equations 5–28 and 5–29 are the forms of the energy equation generally applicable to gas flows, although they are valid for liquid flows as well. According to the first law of thermodynamics, energy is neither created nor destroyed, so there are actually no energy losses—merely a conversion from one form of energy to another (from thermal to mechanical, or from mechanical to thermal).

Compressible gases. In thermodynamics, the steady-flow energy equation applied to gases or vapors is generally used in analyses involving heat and work transfer and enthalpy changes in systems such as boilers, compressors, gas or steam turbines, and condensers. In fluid mechanics, we are generally interested in systems involving heat transfer and enthalpy and velocity changes. Thus the work term and potential energy change are of secondary interest and may be considered zero. For open systems with heat transfer, Eq. 5–29a becomes

$$\frac{V_1{}^2}{2} + h_1 + q = \frac{V_2{}^2}{2} + h_2 \tag{5-29b}$$

For adiabatic flow (irreversible as well as reversible, that is, with or without friction),

$$\frac{V_1{}^2}{2} + h_1 = \frac{V_2{}^2}{2} + h_2 = h_0 \tag{5-29c}$$

where h_0 is the total or stagnation enthalpy, corresponding to a condition of zero velocity reached adiabatically. In general, the stagnation state corresponds to a condition of zero velocity reached isentropically. (See Chapter 9 for a more detailed treatment.)

For isothermal flow, $h_1 = h_2$ for a perfect gas and thus

$$\frac{V_1{}^2}{2} + q = \frac{V_2{}^2}{2} \tag{5-29d}$$

EXAMPLE 5–14. What is the temperature on the nose of a missile moving at 2000 ft/sec in standard air (59 F)?

Solution: This is supersonic flow, and the air must pass through a shock before it reaches the nose of the missile. The flow is *not* isentropic (not reversible), and Eq. 5–29c may be applied, or $V_1{}^2/2 + h_1 = h_0$, where we consider the missile to be at rest and the air is approaching it at the speed of the missile in still air. Thus $V_1{}^2/2 = c_p (T_0 - T_1)$ and $T_0 = T_1 + V_1{}^2/2c_p = 59 + (2000^2)/(2)(6000) = 59 + 333 = 392$ F. The subscript 0 refers to stagnation conditions, since the velocity on the missile nose (at rest) is zero.

Liquids and constant-density gases. We neglect the thermal terms, and to account for the conversion of some of the mechanical energy into thermal energy due to viscous dissipation or irreversibilities, this mechanical energy is included in a friction term h_L. Then the energy equation becomes

$$\frac{V_1{}^2}{2} + \frac{p_1}{\rho} + gz_1 - w = \frac{V_2{}^2}{2} + \frac{p_2}{\rho} + gz_2 + h_L' \tag{5-30a}$$

where $h_L' = (u_2 - u_1 - q)$ and represents the amount of mechanical energy converted into thermal energy.

It is easier to measure the available energy dissipation from pressure measurements than to account for it by temperature measurements. For example, if water flows through a 500-ft length of 6-in. pipe at a rate of 2 ft^3/sec, the available energy dissipation appears in the form of a pressure drop of about 13 psi, depending on the pipe roughness. If the pipe were perfectly insulated, there would be no heat loss ($q = 0$), and the increase in internal energy equivalent to the dissipation of mechanical energy would result in a temperature rise of a little less than 0.04 F ($\Delta T = \Delta p / \rho c_v$). The pressure drop can be measured with much more accuracy than the temperature rise, even for the limiting case when no heat is transferred through the pipe walls. If the pipe is not insulated, the temperature rise would be even less than 0.04 F.

Equations 5–28, 5–29, and 5–30a express the steady-flow energy equation in terms of energy per unit mass of fluid (ft lb$_f$/slug). The energy equation for liquids is usually written in a form obtained from Eq. 5–30a by dividing each term by the acceleration of gravity g. This gives (since the specific weight $\gamma = \rho g$)

$$\frac{V_1^2}{2g} + \frac{p_1}{\gamma} + z_1 - w = \frac{V_2^2}{2g} + \frac{p_2}{\gamma} + z_2 + h_L \qquad (5\text{–}30b)^4$$

where each term has the dimensions of energy per unit *weight* of fluid (ft lb$_f$/lb$_f$) or head (ft). Thus in hydraulics each term is often referred to as *head*—velocity head, pressure head, potential head, head removed by a turbine (w is positive) or added by a pump (w is negative), and head loss (h_L is always positive in the direction of flow), in the order appearing in Eq. 5–30b.

Equation 5–29a, in terms of energy per unit mass, will be used for compressible gas flow, and Eq. 5–30b, in terms of energy per unit weight, will be used for liquid flow and constant-density gas flow.

EXAMPLE 5–15. Oil ($s = 0.86$) flows in a pipe 2 ft in diameter with an average velocity of 5 ft/sec. The piezometric pressure drop in 1000 ft of pipe is 1.49 psi. What is the friction (head loss)?

Solution: Equation 5–30b applies since the flow is with friction. Thus, since the velocity remains constant ($V_1 = V_2$) and $\Delta(p + \gamma z) = (1.49)(144)$ psf,

$$\frac{p_1}{\gamma} + z_1 = \frac{p_2}{\gamma} + z_2 + h_L$$

$$h_L = \Delta\left(\frac{p}{\gamma} + z\right) = (1.49)(144)/(62.4)(0.86)$$

$$= 4.0 \text{ ft lb}_f/\text{lb}_f$$

EXAMPLE 5–16. Two open reservoirs of water (Fig. 5–24) are connected by 4000 ft of 10-in. pipe. The level of the higher reservoir is 120 ft above that of the lower reservoir. The steady-flow rate is 4.5 ft³/sec. *a*) What is the total head loss (available energy dissipation)? *b*) What is the pressure at the mid-point of the pipe, assuming one-half the head loss occurs upstream and one-half downstream of the mid-point? Assume the mid-point of the pipe to be at the same level or elevation as the lower reservoir.

----

[4] In the energy equation for gases (Eq. 5–28), pressures must be in absolute units. In the energy equation for liquids or incompressible fluids (Eqs. 5–30a and 5–30b), pressures may be either gage or absolute, since the terms involving pressure may be brought to the same side of the equal sign and become $\Delta p / \gamma$. Thus the difference in pressures Δp is the same whether gage or absolute pressures are used.

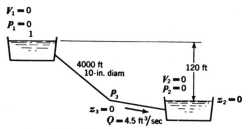

FIG. 5-24. Flow between open reservoirs.

Solution: a) Equation 5–30b may be written between the free surfaces of the reservoirs. The velocity at each point is zero, and the pressures are both atmospheric. Thus Eq. 5–30b becomes, with the z datum at the lower reservoir,

$$0 + 0 + 120 = 0 + 0 + 0 + h_L$$

$$h_L = 120 \text{ ft or ft lb}_f/\text{lb}_f$$

b) Equation 5–30b written between the upper reservoir surface and the pipe mid-point is

$$0 + 0 + 120 = \frac{V_3{}^2}{2g} + \frac{p_3}{\gamma} + 0 + 60$$

$$p_3 = (120 - 60 - 1.06)(62.4)/144$$

$$= 25.5 \text{ psig}$$

The pressure at the pipe mid-point obviously depends on its elevation.

5–6. COMPARISON OF EQUATIONS OF MOTION WITH STEADY-FLOW ENERGY EQUATION

Both the Euler and Bernoulli equations and the steady-flow energy equation are applicable along a stream tube, which comprises the closed portion of the boundaries of an open system. Thus they may be compared with one another. The Bernoulli equation for steady incompressible flow (Eq. 5–19) may be written as

$$\Delta\left(\frac{V^2}{2} + \frac{p}{\rho} + gz\right) = 0 \qquad\qquad (5\text{–}31)$$

and the steady-flow energy equation for incompressible flow (Eq. 5–30a) as

$$- w = \Delta\left(\frac{V^2}{2} + \frac{p}{\rho} + gz\right) + h_L \qquad\qquad (5\text{–}32)$$

Comparing Eq. 5–31 with Eq. 5–32, we may state that since Eq. 5–31 does not include friction (viscous shear) or external shaft work and Eq. 5–32 does, one difference between the flow of a real and an ideal incompressible fluid is that in order to keep the sum of kinetic, displacement, and potential energy constant, *external shaft work must be done on a real fluid to overcome the so-called head loss due to frictional effects.* If no external shaft work is done on the fluid, then the head loss due to frictional effects decreases the available energy of the fluid.

For gas flow, the Euler equation of motion for steady flow (Eq.5–18 with $\partial V/\partial t = 0$) is valid for a *nonviscous fluid only*. The steady-flow energy equation (Eq. 5–28 or Eqs. 5–29) is valid for *both* viscous and nonviscous fluids (both reversible and irreversible flow). If we compare them in differential form for conditions of *reversible* (frictionless) flow, the Euler equation of motion should remove the results of motion or flow from the steady-flow energy equation, and we should be left with the first law of thermodynamics for a nonflow (closed) system. That this is true is easily verified. Equation 5–28 in differential form with no external work is

$$dq = V\, dV + p\, dv + v\, dp + g\, dz + du$$

and Eq. 5–18 with $\partial V/\partial t = 0$ is

$$V\, dV + \frac{dp}{\rho} + g\, dz = 0$$

Subtraction gives

$$dq = du + p\, dv$$

which is an expression of the first law of thermodynamics for a closed system.

For an adiabatic gas flow (though not necessarily reversible, in which case $p/\rho^k \neq C$) with no external work, the steady-flow energy equation is

$$\frac{V_1^2}{2} + h_1 + gz_1 = \frac{V_2^2}{2} + h_2 + gz_2$$

and since for a perfect gas $h = c_p T = \dfrac{Rk}{k-1}\, T = \dfrac{k}{k-1}\left(\dfrac{p}{\rho}\right)$, we get

$$\frac{V_1^2}{2} + \frac{k}{k-1}\left(\frac{p_1}{\rho_1}\right) + gz_1 = \frac{V_2^2}{2} + \frac{k}{k-1}\left(\frac{p_2}{\rho_2}\right) + gz_2 \qquad (5\text{–}33)$$

for *either* reversible *or* irreversible adiabatic flow. This is identical in appearance to Eq. 5–20b obtained from the Euler equation for a *nonviscous* (frictionless) gas.

Equation 5–33 is a highly specialized form of the energy equation and at the same time a specialized integral of the equation of motion. The conditions required to specialize these two equations to produce the same form are not necessarily coincident, since we started from two entirely different initial points of consideration.

We may conclude that the steady-flow energy equation cannot be derived from the equations of motion, nor can the equations of motion be derived from the energy equation.

5–7. WORK AND POWER

Power expended in doing work is expressed as a product of the work done per unit mass of fluid times the mass rate of flow. In terms of the steady-flow energy equation, as written for liquids, it is the product of the work done per unit weight of fluid and the weight rate of flow.

$$P = w(VA\gamma) \qquad \text{ft lb}_f/\text{sec} \qquad (5\text{--}34)$$

The power available in a jet results from the kinetic energy of the jet, and the power represented is the product of this kinetic energy per unit mass and the mass rate of flow, or kinetic energy per unit weight of fluid times the weight rate of flow.

$$P = \frac{V^2}{2}(VA\rho) = \frac{V^2}{2g}(VA\gamma) \qquad \text{ft lb}_f/\text{sec} \qquad (5\text{--}35)$$

Power loss in a flow system from viscous dissipation is the product of energy loss per unit mass of fluid and the mass-flow rate, or the energy loss per unit weight of fluid times the weight rate of flow.

$$P = h_L (VA\gamma) \qquad \text{ft lb}_f/\text{sec} \qquad (5\text{--}36)$$

Power required to overcome a drag force is the product of the drag force and the velocity of the body moving through a fluid. Power is, in reality, a scalar product of two vectors—a force and a velocity. In scalar notation, the drag force is considered to be the component parallel to the velocity.

$$P = FV \qquad (5\text{--}37)$$

One horsepower is defined as 550 ft lb$_f$/sec, or 33,000 ft lb$_f$/min. Thus, for example, if w ft lb$_f$ of shaft work per unit mass were done on a hydraulic turbine, the horsepower given up for a flow rate of Q ft^3/sec is $Q\rho w/550$. If w ft lb$_f$ of shaft work per unit weight were done for a flow rate of Q ft^3/sec, the horsepower would be $Q\gamma w/550$.

EXAMPLE 5–17. Water flows from one reservoir at elevation 100 ft to another at elevation 48 ft through 2000 ft of 18-in. cast-iron pipe. The flow rate is 8 ft^3/sec and 40 hp are extracted from the water by a turbine. What is the head or energy loss experienced by the water in flowing from the higher to the lower reservoir?

Solution: Apply Eq. 5–30a between the reservoir surfaces after determining the work extracted from the water. Horsepower $= Q\gamma w/550$, so that $w = (550)(40)/(8)(62.4) = 44$ ft lb$_f$ per unit weight (lb$_f$). The velocity and pressure are both zero at each reservoir surface. Thus Eq. 5–30a becomes

$$0 + 0 + 100 - (+44) = 0 + 0 + 48 + h_L$$
$$h_L = 8 \text{ ft lb}_f/\text{lb}_f$$

5–8. THE NAVIER-STOKES EQUATIONS

Euler's equation of motion previously derived to apply along a streamline direction (Eq. 5–18) may also be written for the x, y, and z directions in a rectangular coordinate system. Equation 5–18 may be written as

$$\frac{\partial V}{\partial t} + V\frac{\partial V}{\partial s} = -g\frac{\partial z}{\partial s} - \frac{1}{\rho}\frac{\partial}{\partial s}(\gamma z + p) \qquad [5\text{--}18]$$

where $-(1/\rho)\,\partial(\gamma z)/\partial s$ is the body force per unit mass due to gravity.

The equivalent forms of the equations of motion for an inviscid fluid in the x, y, and z coordinates in terms of a body force $\mathbf{F} = X\mathbf{i} + Y\mathbf{j} + Z\mathbf{k}$ per unit mass are

$$\frac{\partial u}{\partial t} + u\frac{\partial u}{\partial x} + v\frac{\partial u}{\partial y} + w\frac{\partial u}{\partial z} = X - \frac{1}{\rho}\frac{\partial p}{\partial x} \tag{5-38a}$$

$$\frac{\partial v}{\partial t} + u\frac{\partial v}{\partial x} + v\frac{\partial v}{\partial y} + w\frac{\partial v}{\partial z} = Y - \frac{1}{\rho}\frac{\partial p}{\partial y} \tag{5-38b}$$

$$\frac{\partial w}{\partial t} + u\frac{\partial w}{\partial x} + v\frac{\partial w}{\partial y} + w\frac{\partial w}{\partial z} = Z - \frac{1}{\rho}\frac{\partial p}{\partial z} \tag{5-38c}$$

where for body forces due only to gravity, $X = -\dfrac{1}{\rho}\dfrac{\partial(\gamma h)}{\partial x}$, etc., h being measured vertically upwards. In vector form these equations become

$$\frac{D\mathbf{V}}{Dt} = \mathbf{F} - \frac{1}{\rho}\operatorname{grad} p \tag{5-38d}$$

For a viscous fluid, viscous forces must be included in the equations of motion, and the resulting equations are known as the Navier-Stokes equations. Terms to be added to the right side of the above Euler equations are of the form $\dfrac{\mu}{\rho}\left(\dfrac{\partial^2 u}{\partial x^2} + \dfrac{\partial^2 u}{\partial y^2} + \dfrac{\partial^2 u}{\partial z^2}\right) = \nu\,\nabla^2 u$, etc. Thus for an incompressible viscous fluid, the Navier-Stokes equations may be written as

$$\frac{\partial u}{\partial t} + u\frac{\partial u}{\partial x} + v\frac{\partial u}{\partial y} + w\frac{\partial u}{\partial z} = X - \frac{1}{\rho}\frac{\partial p}{\partial x} + \nu\left(\frac{\partial^2 u}{\partial x^2} + \frac{\partial^2 u}{\partial y^2} + \frac{\partial^2 u}{\partial z^2}\right) \tag{5-39a}$$

$$\frac{\partial v}{\partial t} + u\frac{\partial v}{\partial x} + v\frac{\partial v}{\partial y} + w\frac{\partial v}{\partial z} = Y - \frac{1}{\rho}\frac{\partial p}{\partial y} + \nu\left(\frac{\partial^2 v}{\partial x^2} + \frac{\partial^2 v}{\partial y^2} + \frac{\partial^2 v}{\partial z^2}\right) \tag{5-39b}$$

$$\frac{\partial w}{\partial t} + u\frac{\partial w}{\partial x} + v\frac{\partial w}{\partial y} + w\frac{\partial w}{\partial z} = Z - \frac{1}{\rho}\frac{\partial p}{\partial z} + \nu\left(\frac{\partial^2 w}{\partial x^2} + \frac{\partial^2 w}{\partial y^2} + \frac{\partial^2 w}{\partial z^2}\right) \tag{5-39c}$$

or in vector form as

$$\frac{D\mathbf{V}}{Dt} = \mathbf{F} - \frac{1}{\rho}\operatorname{grad} p + \nu\,\nabla^2\mathbf{V} \tag{5-39d}$$

These Navier-Stokes equations are nonlinear, and exact solutions have been obtained only for situations for which some of the terms are zero. Integration is then possible. Prandtl in 1904 simplified the equations for laminar boundary layer flow (see Appendix II) and these were later solved to obtain useful engineering results (Chapter 7).

Exact solutions of the Navier-Stokes equations have been carried out for laminar flow between parallel plates with and without pressure gradients, laminar flow in a pipe, flow between two concentric rotating cylinders, a suddenly accelerated plane wall, flow over an oscillating plate, flow near a stagnation point, flow over a rotating disc, and flow in convergent and divergent channels.

Solutions for very slow (creeping) motion have also been made. Results for parallel flow past a sphere were given by Stokes in 1851 and by Oseen in 1910, and for parallel flow past a circular cylinder by Lamb.

Reynolds in 1894 developed a modified form of the Navier-Stokes equations for turbulent flow by writing each velocity as an average value plus a fluctuating component. These modified equations indicated a shear stress in turbulent flow called the Reynolds stresses, and have been useful in the study of turbulent flow.

The derivation of the Navier-Stokes equations and the various solutions and developments are discussed in detail and summarized by Schlichting [4] and Rouse [5].

REFERENCES

1. A. H. Shapiro, "Basic Equations of Fluid Flow," Section 2 of *Handbook of Fluid Dynamics*, edited by V. L. Streeter (New York: McGraw-Hill Book Company, Inc., 1961). See also Reference 2.

2. A. H. Shapiro, *The Dynamics and Thermodynamics of Compressible Fluid Flow*, Vol. I (New York: The Ronald Press Company, 1953), pp. 73-74.

3. H. Rouse, "On the Role of Eddies in Fluid Motion," *American Scientist*, Vol. 51 (1963), pp. 285-314.

4. H. Schlichting, *Boundary Layer Theory* (Translated by J. Kestin), 4th ed. (New York: McGraw-Hill Book Company, Inc., 1960).

5. H. Rouse, *Fluid Mechanics for Hydraulic Engineers* (New York: McGraw-Hill Book Company, Inc., 1938 and reissued by Dover Publications).

PROBLEMS

5-1. Classify the following flows as steady or unsteady, uniform or non-uniform. Where there is reason for doubt, give conditions for which flow is as you state.
  a) Water in a garden hose
  b) Water flowing through the nozzles of a rotating sprinkler
  c) Flow through the nozzle attached to the end of a garden hose
  d) Flow of gases through a rocket nozzle
  e) Flow through a blow-down type of supersonic wind tunnel
  f) Flow of water over a wide spillway in a river

g) Liquid draining from a small tank

h) Gasoline in the fuel line of an automobile in city traffic; on a superhighway

5–2. Classify the following flows as one-, two-, or three-dimensional:

a) Flow of water over a wide spillway in a river.

b) Flow in a bend in a river.

c) Flow through the test section of a water tunnel or subsonic wind tunnel. Why is flow which is nearly one-dimensional desirable?

d) Flow of a nonviscous fluid through a rectangular elbow.

e) Flow of a viscous fluid through an elbow in a round pipe.

5–3. Classify the following as laminar or turbulent flow:

a) Summer-grade lubricating oil flowing from an oil can

b) Water issuing from a fire nozzle

c) Flow in a river

d) Flow through a hypodermic needle

e) Atmospheric winds

f) Flow of a viscous liquid at low velocity through a small pipe

g) Flow of a low-viscosity liquid at a relatively high velocity through a large pipe

5–4. Determine the v component of velocity to within an additive constant which will satisfy continuity for each of the following:

a) $u = x^2$

e) $u = \dfrac{-y}{x^2 + y^2}$

b) $u = 6x + xy$

f) $u = x$

c) $u = x^2 + x$

g) $u = 2xy^2$

d) $u = \dfrac{x}{x^2 + y^2}$

Ans.   *a)* $v = -2xy + f(x)$

b) $v = -6y - y^2/2 + f(x)$

5–5. In Prob. 5–4, which flows could be irrotational, and for what conditions regarding $f(x)$ would they be?

5–6. Which of the following flows satisfy continuity for an incompressible fluid flow, and of these, which are rotational (typical of a viscous fluid) and which are irrotational (typical of a nonviscous fluid)?

a) $u = x^2 \cos y$; and $v = -2x \sin y$

b) $u = x + 2$; and $v = 1 - y$

c) $u = xyt$; and $v = x^3 - y^2t/2$

d) $u = \ln x + y$; and $v = xy - y/x$

e) $u = x + y$; and $v = x - y$

Ans.   *a)* and *c)* satisfy continuity for a rotational fluid, *b)* and *e)* for an irrotational fluid; *d)* does not satisfy continuity.

5–7. Derive Eq. 5–11, the continuity equation for motion of a steady incompressible fluid in polar coordinates, for two-dimensional flow in the $x - y$ plane.

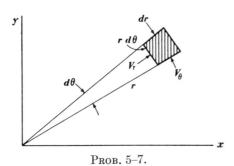

PROB. 5–7.

5–8. Extend the results of Prob. 5–7 to the general case when there is a z component of velocity v_z. This is the continuity equation for steady flow in cylindrical coordinates.

$$Ans. \quad \frac{\partial v_r}{\partial r} + \frac{v_r}{r} + \frac{1}{r}\frac{\partial v_\theta}{\partial \theta} + \frac{\partial v_z}{\partial z} = 0$$

5–9. In Prob. 5–8
a) Describe the flow when $v_\theta = v_z = 0$.
b) Describe the flow when $v_r = 0$.
c) Describe the flow when $v_r = v_z = 0$.
d) Describe the flow when $v_\theta = v_r = 0$.

5–10. A fluid flows radially from a point source with a velocity $v_r(r, t)$. Show that the continuity equation, except for the source itself, is

$$\frac{\partial \rho}{\partial t} + \frac{\rho}{r^2}\frac{\partial}{\partial r}(r^2 v_r) + v_r \frac{\partial \rho}{\partial r} = 0$$

5–11. Let the x and y components of velocity in steady, two-dimensional, incompressible flow be linear functions of x and y, such that

$$\mathbf{V} = (ax + by)\mathbf{i} + (cx + dy)\mathbf{j}$$

where a, b, c, and d are constants. a) For what conditions is continuity satisfied? b) What is the vorticity? c) For what conditions is the flow irrotational?

5–12. Given the velocity field in two-dimensional flow

$$\mathbf{V} = (x - 2y)t\mathbf{i} - (2x + y)t\mathbf{j}$$

a) Show that continuity is satisfied for incompressible flow. b) Is the flow steady or unsteady? Why? c) Is the flow that of an ideal or of a real fluid? Prove your answer.

5–13. Water flows in an 8-in. pipe at an average velocity of 12 ft/sec. What is the volumetric flow rate a) in ft³/sec and b) in gpm? What is the mass flow rate c) in lb$_m$/sec and d) in slugs/sec? e) What is the mass-flow intensity?

$Ans.$ d) 8.13 slugs/sec

5–14. An axial-flow pump circulates water through a water tunnel at an average speed of 50 ft/sec in the test section. The test section diameter is 6 in., the diameter just upstream of the pump is 13.2 in., and the upstream diameter of the contraction cone preceding the test section is 18.0 in. *a*) What are the average flow velocities at these two sections? *b*) What is the volumetric flow rate through the water tunnel?

5–15. A centrifugal pump has an 8-in. diameter inlet pipe and a 6-in. diameter discharge pipe. For a flow rate of 1000 gpm (1 ft³ = 7.48 gal) what is *a*) the average flow velocity at the pump inlet and *b*) what is the average flow velocity at the pump discharge?

5–16. Methane at 150 psia and 120 F flows in a 10-in. diameter pipe at an average velocity of 60 ft/sec. *a*) What is the mass-flow rate in slug/sec? *b*) What is the mass-flow rate in lb$_m$/sec? *c*) What is the mass-flow intensity in slug/ft² sec?

Ans.   *a*) 0.394 slug/sec

5–17. At one section in a 12-in. diameter pipe methane flows at a pressure of 120 psia, a temperature of 100 F, and an average velocity of 60 ft/sec. *a*) What is the mass flow rate in slug/sec? *b*) What is the average flow velocity at a downstream section where the pressure is 80 psia and the temperature 100 F? *c*) What is the pressure at a section yet farther downstream where the average flow velocity is 1000 ft/sec and the temperature is 62 F?

5–18. Atmospheric air heated at constant pressure to 150 F is drawn through a suitable entrance and nozzle to the 16 x 16-in. square test section of a supersonic wind tunnel. The average velocity in the test section is 1.5 times the speed of sound corresponding to the air temperature in the test section. Assume the air expands isentropically from the outside atmosphere after heating to 4.0 psia in the test section. *a*) What is the air temperature in the

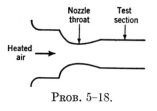

PROB. 5–18.

test section? *b*) What is the density of the air in the test section? *c*) What is the mass-flow rate of air through the wind tunnel? *d*) What is the flow rate of air in ft³/min of standard air?

Ans.   *c*) 2.14 slugs/sec

5–19. The pressure in the throat of the nozzle upstream of the test section of the wind tunnel in Prob. 5–18 is 7.76 psia. For isentropic flow, what is *a*) the air temperature in the nozzle throat and *b*) the width of the nozzle throat if the flow is two-dimensional? The velocity in the throat is sonic (Eq. 2–16).

5–20. A pair of 12-in. diameter cymbals are brought together coaxially at a relative speed of 15 ft/sec. At what radial velocity does the air pass the perimeter of the cymbals when they are ½ in. apart?

5–21. The velocity profile for laminar flow in a pipe is given by

$$u = u_m\left(1 - \frac{r^2}{R^2}\right)$$

where u_m is the center-line velocity, R is the pipe radius, and r is the radial distance from the pipe axis. a) Show that the average velocity of flow is $V = u_m/2$. b) Show that the ratio of the true rate of momentum transport to that based on the average velocity is $\beta = \frac{4}{3}$. c) Show that the ratio of the true rate of kinetic energy transport to that based on the average velocity is $\alpha = 2$.

5–22. The velocity profile for laminar flow between two parallel plates is given by

$$u = u_m\left(1 - \frac{b^2}{B^2}\right)$$

where u_m is the center-plane velocity, B is the half spacing between plates, and b is the normal distance from the center plane. a) What is the average velocity in terms of u_m? b) What is the momentum correction factor β? c) What is the kinetic energy correction factor α?

5–23. The velocity profile for turbulent flow in a circular tube is given by

$$u = u_m\left(\frac{y}{R}\right)^{\frac{1}{7}}$$

$$= u_m\left(1 - \frac{r}{R}\right)^{\frac{1}{7}}$$

where u_m is the centerline velocity, R is the tube radius, and y is the radial distance from the tube wall $(r = R - y)$. What is the average velocity in terms of u_m?

5–24. The velocity u within a turbulent boundary layer at a distance y feet from the boundary surface varies according to the equation

$$u = u_s\left(\frac{y}{\delta}\right)^{\frac{1}{7}}$$

where u_s is the free-stream velocity outside the boundary layer and δ is the boundary layer thickness (see Fig. 7–6). What is the mass flow rate within the boundary layer for standard air in a 4-ft width of flow for $u_s = 100$ ft/sec and $\delta = 0.093$ ft?

5–25. Show that for a finite number of point velocities measured at the centroids of n equal areas throughout a flow cross section,

a)
$$u_{avg} = V = \frac{\int_A u\, dA}{A} \approx \frac{1}{n}\sum_1^{i=n} u_i$$

b)
$$\beta = \frac{\int_A u^2\, dA}{V^2 A} \approx \frac{1}{V^2 n}\sum_1^{i=n} u_i^2$$

c)
$$\alpha = \frac{\int_A u^3\, dA}{V^3 A} \approx \frac{1}{V^3 n}\sum_1^{i=n} u_i^3$$

Velocities measured at the center of equal increments of $(r/R)^2$, representing equal increments of area, in circular ducts of various diameters are as listed; velocities are in ft/sec.

Problem	5–26	5–27	5–28	5–29	5–30
Duct diameter, in	6.0	12.0	18.0	1.399	1.397
$(r/R)^2$	Measured velocity u, in ft/sec				
0.05	46.6	18.2	5.29	135	168.5
0.15	46.6	16.8	5.28	130.5	162
0.25	46.6	14.9	5.26	126.5	155
0.35	46.55	12.75	5.21	122	148
0.45	46.5	10.9	5.19	117.5	141.5
0.55	46.6	9.4	5.11	113	134
0.65	46.5	7.9	5.06	108	126.5
0.75	46.0	6.5	4.93	102.5	118
0.85	44.5	5.6	4.66	96	107
0.95	43.0	4.5	4.19	82	87

5–26. Velocities were measured at the upstream end of a diffuser in a water tunnel. $a)$ What is the average velocity? $b)$ What is the momentum correction factor β? $c)$ What is the kinetic energy correction factor α? What is the volumetric flow rate in ft^3/sec?

Ans. c) $\alpha = 1.0014$

5–27. Velocities were measured at the downstream end of a diffuser in a water tunnel. $a)$ What is the average velocity? $b)$ What is the momentum correction factor β? $c)$ What is the kinetic energy correction factor α?

Ans. b) $\alpha = 1.18$

5–28. Velocities were measured at the upstream end of a contraction for a water tunnel. $a)$ What is the average velocity? $b)$ What is the momentum correction factor β? $c)$ What is the kinetic energy correction factor α? $d)$ What is the volumetric flow rate in ft^3/sec?

5–29. Velocities were measured in a circular tube at 76 F and 2077 psfa. $a)$ What is the average velocity? $b)$ What is the momentum correction factor β? $c)$ What is the kinetic energy correction factor α? $d)$ What is the mass flow rate in slug/sec?

Ans. d) 0.00273 slug/sec

5–30. Velocities were measured in a circular tube at 76 F and 2059 psfa. $a)$ What is the average velocity? $b)$ What is the momentum correction factor β? $c)$ What is the kinetic energy correction factor α? $d)$ What is the mass flow rate in slug/sec?

5–31. Express the fluid vorticity as a function of y for the following laminar boundary layer velocity profiles (see Fig. 7–6):

$$a)\ u = \frac{2u_s}{\delta} y - \frac{u_s}{\delta^2} y^2$$

$$b) \quad u = \frac{3u_s}{2\delta} y - \frac{u_s}{2\delta^3} y^3$$

$$c) \quad u = u_s \sin (\pi y / 2\delta)$$

5–32. What can be said about the vorticity of the flow from the surface to $y = \delta$, the outer edge of the boundary layer, in Prob. 5–31? What is the vorticity at $y > \delta$?

5–33. A 1-in. diameter nozzle on the end of a 3-in. diameter fire hose discharges water with a jet velocity of 90 ft/sec. The pressure in the hose is 55 psig. What is the magnitude and direction of the net force of the water on the nozzle?

Ans. 313 lb$_f$, downstream

5–34. Repeat Prob. 5–33 for a jet velocity of 60 ft/sec and a hose pressure of 21 psig.

5–35. A horizontal jet of water 0.01 ft² in area moving at 100 ft/sec is divided in half by a splitter on a stationary flat plate inclined 45 deg from the jet direction. What is the magnitude and direction of the resultant force on the plate?

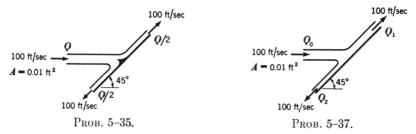

PROB. 5–35.   PROB. 5–37.

5–36. Repeat Prob. 5–35 for a jet velocity of 50 ft/sec. Obtain an answer based on that for Prob. 5–35 by physical reasoning.

5–37. A horizontal water jet 0.01 ft² in area moving at 100 ft/sec strikes a smooth flat plate inclined 45 deg from the jet direction. What is the magnitude and direction of the resulting force on the plate?

5–38. A vane is curved so that a jet of water is completely reversed in direction. The jet velocity is 100 ft/sec and the flow rate from the nozzle creating the jet is 2 ft³/sec. *a)* What is the force of the jet on the vane at rest, assuming no frictional effects? *b)* If the vane moves away from the jet at 40 ft/sec, what is the force of the jet on the vane, neglecting frictional effects?

Ans. *b)* 279 lb$_f$

5–39. Water enters a conical diffuser at an average velocity of $V_1 = 40$ ft/sec. The diffuser enlarges from a 6.00-in. diameter at inlet to 11.66 in. diameter at exit over a length of 4.57 ft. The measured pressure rise is $0.81\rho V_1^2/2$. The pressure at inlet is atmospheric. What is the resultant longitudinal force of the diffuser walls on the water?

Ans. 887 lb$_f$

5–40. Water flows through a well-designed contraction cone for a water tunnel at an average velocity at exit of $V_2 = 40.0$ ft/sec. The contraction inlet is 17.90 in. diameter and the exit is 6.00 in. diameter. The measured pressure drop is 1.00 $\rho V_2^2/2$. The exit is at atmospheric pressure. What is the resultant longitudinal force of the water on the contraction walls?

5–41. A water jet pump has a jet area $A_j = 0.05$ ft² and a jet velocity $V_j = 90$ ft/sec which entrains a secondary stream of water having a velocity $V_s = 10$ ft/sec in a constant-area pipe of total area $A = 0.6$ ft². At section *2* the water is thoroughly mixed. Assume one-dimensional flow and neglect wall shear. *a)* What is the average velocity of the mixed flow at section 2? *b)* What is the pressure rise $(p_2 - p_1)$, assuming the pressure of the jet and the secondary stream to be the same at section *1*?

Ans. b) 6.58 psi

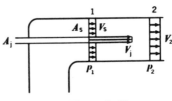

PROB. 5–41.

5–42. A rocket carries its own fuel and oxygen supply and discharges its exhaust gases at a velocity of 2000 ft/sec relative to the rocket and at ambient pressure. The flow rate is 1 slug/sec and the density of the exhaust gases is 0.001 slug/ft³. What is the thrust on the rocket?

5–43. A rocket-propelled craft flies at a speed of 1700 ft/sec in a westerly direction. The combustion gases exhaust through an exit area of 1 ft² at ambient pressure, at a density of 0.0005 slug/ft³, and at a speed of 300 ft/sec relative to the ground in an easterly direction. What is the thrust on the craft?

5–44. A rocket burns fuel at a rate of 8 lb$_m$/sec and ejects the exhaust gases at 4500 ft/sec relative to the rocket and at the same pressure as the surroundings. What is the thrust developed when the rocket travels at a forward speed of *a)* 500 ft/sec and *b)* 1500 ft/sec?

5–45. A jet aircraft takes in air at 150 lb$_m$/sec and burns fuel at a rate of 10 lb$_m$/sec. The combustion gases leave the aircraft at ambient pressure and at 4800 ft/sec relative to the aircraft. *a)* What thrust is produced if the aircraft is held at rest on a test stand? *b)* What thrust is produced if the aircraft flies at 800 ft/sec?

Ans. a) 23,840 lb$_f$, *b)* 20,120 lb$_f$

5–46. Can a rocket travel faster than the relative velocity of the exhaust gases which leave it? Explain.

5–47. A rocket exhausts 100 lb$_m$ of gas per second at an exit velocity of 4800 ft/sec relative to the rocket. What is the thrust produced *a)* when the rocket is held at rest on a test stand, *b)* when the rocket travels at 800 ft/sec, and *c)* if the rocket flies at an altitude where the ambient pressure is 4 psia? Exit pressure is 14.7 psia and exit diameter is 1 ft.

5–48. Water flows under a sluice gate as shown. Assume frictionless flow with one-dimensional flow at sections *1* and *2*. *a)* Show that the force of the water on the sluice gate is equal to the difference in thrust functions at sections *1* and *2* when the pressure terms are based on gage pressure. *b)* Sketch the variation of pressure on the gate as a function of depth.

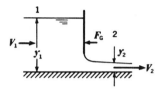

PROB. 5–48.

5–49. Show that the pressure gradient normal to streamlines for steady flow in a horizontal plane is

$$\frac{\partial p}{\partial n} = -\frac{\rho V^2}{r}$$

where the n direction is towards the center of curvature of the streamlines.

5–50. Two-dimensional flow of an ideal incompressible fluid occurs around a 90-deg bend as a free vortex (see Fig. 5–29). The center-line velocity is 8 ft/sec. *a)* What are the tangential and normal accelerations at the inner and outer walls of the bend? *b)* What are the pressure gradients normal to streamlines at the inner and outer walls of the bend? *c)* What is the pressure difference between the outer and the inner walls of the bend? $r_1 = 0.5$ ft; $r_2 = 1.5$ ft. Water flows.

Ans. *a)* $a_s = 0$, $a_n = 512$ ft/sec² at inner wall and 18.94 ft/sec² at outer wall, *c)* 221 psf

5–51. What force F is required to prevent the sprinkler from rotating about a vertical axis? The density of the flowing liquid is ρ.

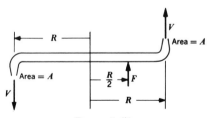

PROB. 5–51.

5–52. Fluid is accelerated as it passes through the slipstream of a propeller. Show that the average velocity of the fluid as it passes the plane of the propeller blades is the average of the upstream and downstream velocities V_1 and V_4. Assume $p_1 = p_4$, $V_2 = V_3$ and neglect viscous effects.

5–53. The drag on a circular cylinder of diameter D may be measured indirectly by determining the change in momentum flux through the control volume or surface indicated. The pressure is assumed to be constant over the entire control

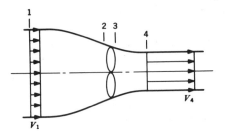

PROB. 5–52.

PROB. 5–53.

surface. *a*) What is the drag force on the cylinder per unit length of cylinder? *b*) The drag coefficient is defined here as $C_D = F/(\rho u_s{}^2/2)(D)$. What is the drag coefficient? Compare with that shown in Fig. 11–4 at Re_D between 10^4 and 10^5.

$$Ans. \quad F = \frac{2}{3} \rho u_s{}^2 D$$

5–54. The velocity of an ideal incompressible fluid as it steadily approaches the stagnation point at the leading edge of a cylinder of radius R held normal to the stream is

$$u = u_s\left(1 - \frac{R^2}{x^2}\right)$$

What is the fluid acceleration at *a*) $x = -3R$, *b*) $x = -2R$, and *c*) $x = -R$? *d*) If $u_s = 6$ ft/sec and $R = \frac{1}{12}$ ft, what is the magnitude of the acceleration at $x = -2R$?

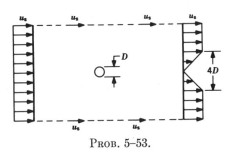

PROB. 5–54.   PROB. 5–56.

5–55. The tangential velocity V_t around the surface of a circular cylinder of radius R held normal to a steady ideal incompressible flow stream is

$$V_t = 2u_s \sin \theta$$

where u_s and θ are defined in Fig. 6–15. What are the tangential and the normal components of acceleration at a) $\theta = 0$, b) $\theta = \pi/4$, and c) $\theta = \pi/2$? Evaluate for $u_s = 10$ ft/sec and $R = 1$ in.

5-56. Water flowing into the vertical inlet of a diversion tunnel for a dam forms an irrotational vortex except near its axis. At a point 4 ft from the center of rotation, the tangential velocity is 3 ft/sec. a) How much lower is the water surface at a point 2 ft from the center of rotation than at a point 4 ft from the center of rotation? b) By how much is the water level at the 2-ft radius below the level of the water far from the axis of the vortex?

Ans. a) 0.42 ft

5-57. Barometer readings indicated a minimum pressure of 14.10 psia at 650 ft and 14.32 psia at 1460 ft from the center of a tornado. The flow approximated that of a free vortex. Estimate the wind speed at 650 ft for an air temperature of 60 F.

5-58. Water particles in a large reservoir move in horizontal circles about a fixed vertical axis. The motion out to a radius R is that of a forced vortex at an angular velocity ω; beyond R the motion is that of a free vortex. This is known as a cylindrical vortex. a) Sketch the shape of the water surface. (It is essentially like that produced by a canoe paddle.) b) What is the peripheral velocity V_θ of the particles for a radius $r > R$ in terms of r, R, and ω? c) What is the slope of the water surface at R in a radial direction?

Ans. c) $\omega^2 R/g$

5-59. Suppose particles in a swirling mass of air move in horizontal circles about a fixed vertical axis such that the motion out to a radius R is that of a forced vortex with angular velocity ω; beyond R the motion is that of a free vortex. This is known as a cylindrical vortex. a) What is the peripheral velocity V_θ for $r < R$ and for $r > R$? b) Indicate, by a sketch, the variation in pressure with radius in a horizontal plane. Compare with Prob. 5–39(a). c) What is the radial pressure gradient at $r = R$? Compare with Prob. 5–39(c). d) Why does the free vortex not extend to the axis of rotation in a real fluid? (This is essentially the motion of a tornado, or of dust and leaves or snow often observed on a windy day.)

5-60. Water flows through a 1×2-ft rectangular duct and through an elbow with a 1-ft inner radius and a 3-ft outer radius. The pressure difference between the outer and inner walls of the elbow is 1.50 psi. Assume a free-vortex flow through the elbow. What is the volumetric flow rate?

Ans. 17.4 ft³/sec

5-61. A centrifugal pump impeller rotates at 1450 rpm. The inlet radius is 2 in. and the outlet radius is 8 in. With no flow (pump discharge valve is shut off), the fluid within the impeller rotates as a forced vortex. What is the pressure difference in pounds per square inch and the pressure head difference in feet of fluid between impeller outlet and inlet a) if the impeller contains water and b) if the pump is not primed, so that the impeller rotates in standard air?

Ans. b) 0.0792 psi and 149 ft

5-62. Water flows through a horizontal conical contraction at a rate of 12 ft³/sec. The flow is steady and one-dimensional. The diameter of the contraction cone decreases from 2 ft to 1 ft in a length of 2 ft. What is a) the fluid acceleration and b) the pressure gradient at the midsection of the contraction?

5–63. In Prob. 5–62 the flow rate is increasing at a rate of 2 cfs/sec. What is the total fluid acceleration at the midsection of the contraction?

5–64. The tangential velocity around the surface of a cylinder normal to the flow of a nonviscous fluid at a free steam velocity u_s and density ρ is $v_\theta = -2u_s \sin \theta$ (see Fig. 6–15). a) Write an expression for the pressure at the surface of the cylinder in terms of the free stream pressure p_s, u_s, ρ and θ. b) At what values of θ is the velocity zero? These are the stagnation points. c) At what values of θ is the pressure on the surface of the cylinder equal to the free stream pressure p_s?

5–65. The tangential velocity around the surface of a sphere in a nonviscous fluid flowing past it at a free stream velocity of u_s is $v_\theta = -(3/2)\, u_s \sin \theta$. Answer parts a), b), and c) of Prob. 5–64.

5–66. In Prob. 5–65, a) what is the difference between the maximum and the minimum pressure on the surface of the sphere in terms of the fluid density ρ and the free stream velocity u_s. b) What is this pressure difference for $u_s = 10$ ft/sec, $\rho = 1.94$ slugs/ft^3 for a billiard ball of diameter 2.375 in. and c) for a basketball of diameter 9.5 in.? d) Does the size of the sphere affect the answer?

Ans.　c) 218 psf

5–67. The pressure on the nose of a sea lion as it swims in the sea is 9.0 psi above that of the surroundings. What is its speed?

5–68. A body is immersed in a river at a 20-ft depth. The pressure on its upstream face is 10.0 psi above the pressure of the atmosphere at the water surface. What is the velocity of the river at the 20-ft depth?

Ans.　14.1 ft/sec

5–69. A 12-in. diameter horizontal duct contracts gradually to 4 in. in diameter. Water at 100 F flows at a rate of 4 ft^3/sec through the system. For one-dimensional flow, what is the pressure drop, neglecting viscous effects?

Ans.　13.9 psi

5–70. A liquid flows from a large open tank through a round hole in the side of the tank located H ft below the free liquid surface within the tank. a) Where in the flow stream is the velocity equal to $\sqrt{2gH}$, neglecting friction? b) Explain why it is necessary to write the Bernoulli equation from a point within the tank to the section of the jet where the streamlines are parallel. c) Describe the pressure distribution throughout the flow section at the hole in the tank.

5–71. Write an expression for the volumetric flow rate for a liquid of density ρ flowing through a venturi meter [Fig. 13–11(a)] in terms of the diameters D_1 and D_2, and the pressure drop $p_1 - p_2$. Assume a nonviscous fluid. Viscous effects may be taken into account by multiplying the result of this problem by a discharge coefficient C_d.

5–72. Standard air enters a Venturi meter [Fig. 13–11(a)] which has a 4-in. diameter inlet and a 2-in. diameter throat. A water manometer connected between inlet and throat shows a deflection of 6 in. What is the flow rate through the tube in slug/sec? Neglect frictional effects and consider flow to be incompressible.

5-73. A duct with an area 3 ft² contracts gradually to an area of 1 ft². The pressure drop between the two sections is measured with a mercury manometer which indicates a deflection of 15 in. What is the flow of water through the system, neglecting losses?

Ans. 33.7 ft³/sec

5-74. The width of a rectangular open channel is reduced from 6 to 5 ft and the bottom is raised 1 ft at the contracted section. The depth upstream is 4 ft and the surface drops 3 in. at the contracted section. What is the flow rate? Neglect frictional effects.

Ans. 67.4 ft³/sec

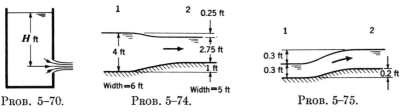

PROB. 5–70.   PROB. 5–74.   PROB. 5–75.

5-75. Water flows in a rectangular channel 10 ft wide at a depth of 0.3 ft. The channel bottom is gradually raised 0.2 ft. The water surface rises 0.3 ft as the water passes over the raised portion of the channel. What is the flow rate? Neglect frictional effects.

5-76. Suppose the gage pressure in the pipe of Example 5–8 is reduced to one-half its value, that is, to 26.5 psig. *a*) What is the flow rate? *b*) Make a quantitative statement on how the flow rate through a nozzle depends on the pressure at its inlet, assuming frictionless flow.

5-77. Suppose the head on the hole in the tank of Example 5–9 is reduced to one-half its value, that is, to 8.5 ft. *a*) What will be the jet velocity? *b*) What can you say regarding the effect of head on the velocity of a jet from a hole in the side of a tank?

5-78. In Prob. 5–75, what is the flow rate for a channel width of 9 ft at section 2? Neglect viscous effects.

5-79. Water is 12 ft deep upstream of a small dam, and flows over the downstream face of the dam at a rate of 12 cfs/ft width of dam. *a*) What is the water depth at the foot of the dam, assuming no losses? *b*) What is the resultant horizontal force of the water on the dam per foot width?

Ans. *b*) 3876 lb$_f$

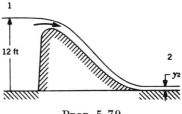

PROB. 5–79.

5-80. A liquid of density ρ flows steadily without friction in a horizontal duct whose shape is the frustum of a cone at a flow rate of Q. Show that the pressure gradient in the direction of flow $+ x$ in terms of the diameter D is

$$\frac{dp}{dx} = \frac{32\rho Q^2}{\pi^2 D^5}\frac{dD}{dx}$$

5-81. A Venturi meter [Fig. 13-11(a)] installed in a 12-in. pipeline has a throat diameter of 4 in. The pressure at inlet is 20 psig, and the barometric pressure is 14.7 psia. At what pipeline velocity will cavitation begin (vapor pressure occurs at the point of minimum pressure) when water at 90 F flows through the meter? Neglect frictional effects.

Ans. 7.96 ft/sec

5-82. For the NACA standard atmosphere, compare the dynamic pressure for a speed of 200 ft/sec at sea level with that at 10,000 ft ($\rho = 0.001756$ slug/ft^3) and at 20,000 ft ($\rho = 0.001267$ slug/ft^3).

Ans. 47.6, 35.1, and 25.3 psf, respectively.

5-83. Air flows through a horizontal insulated pipe. Frictional effects reduce pressure and density in the direction of flow so that the velocity is increased from 50 to 400 ft/sec. What is the reduction in temperature?

Ans. 13.1 deg F

5-84. The stagnation temperature on the nose of a rocket is 100 F. The rocket travels at an altitude where the ambient temperature is 10 F and the pressure is 9 psia. What is the speed of the rocket?

5-85. The second law of thermodynamics requires that if irreversibilities due to friction exist in a flow system, the entropy must increase for adiabatic flow. *a)* On the temperature-entropy diagram, show that for adiabatic gas flow in a duct from one pressure to another, the downstream temperature is higher for frictional flow than for frictionless flow. *b)* Compare the downstream enthalpy for frictional flow with that for frictionless adiabatic duct flow from one pressure to another. *c)* Compare the downstream velocity for frictional flow with that for frictionless adiabatic duct flow from one pressure to another. *d)* For

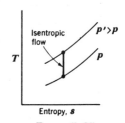

PROB. 5-85.

a given upstream condition, compare the downstream pressure for frictional flow with that for frictionless adiabatic flow to a given downstream temperature.

5-86. Air flows in a duct. At section A, the pressure is 30 psia and the temperature is 240 F. At section B, the pressure is 26 psia and the temperature is 215 F. The flow is adiabatic. In what direction is the flow? Refer to Prob. 5-85.

5-87. Air flows in a duct. At section A, the pressure is 30 psia and the temperature is 240 F. At section B, the pressure is 26 psia and the temperature is 200 F. The flow is adiabatic. In what direction is the flow? Refer to Prob. 5-85.

5-88. Air at 80 psia and 400 F flows from a reservoir through a converging nozzle and expands adiabatically to 44 psia and 272 F (see Fig. 9-3). *a)* What is the final velocity of the air? b) What would be the final velocity of the air if the expansion to 44 psia were frictionless?

Ans. a) 1240 ft/sec, b) 1273 ft/sec

5–89. The first law of thermodynamics states that for steady flow in the absence of heat transfer and work transfer the total energy of a fluid, for example, remains constant as the fluid passes through a control volume. Explain the loss term h_L in the energy equation for liquids in light of this statement.

5–90. In Prob. 5–40, what is the head loss based on one-dimensional flow?

Ans. 0.31 ft

5–91. In Prob. 5–39, what is the head loss based on one-dimensional flow? Compare this with the head loss based on a kinetic energy correction factor at entrance of $\alpha_1 = 1.004$ and at exit, $\alpha_2 = 1.56$.

5–92. Oil of specific gravity $s = 0.90$ flows in a 4-in. pipe. The pressure at section 1 is 50 psig, and the pressure at a downstream section 2, which is 55 ft lower in elevation than section 1, is 60 psig. What is the head loss?

5–93. At section A in a piping system the diameter is 6 in. and the pressure is 10 psig. At another section B, which is 20 ft higher in elevation than section A, the diameter is 12 in. and the pressure is 12 psig. For water flowing at a rate of 1 ft³/sec, determine the flow direction.

5–94. Kerosene flows in a pipe between points A and B. Point B is 80 ft higher than point A. The pressure at A is 60 psig and at B it is 40 psig. In which direction is the flow?

5–95. The average velocity of a jet of water issuing from a round hole in the side of an open tank is 39.5 ft/sec. The hole is 25 ft below the free surface of the water in the tank. What is the head loss due to viscous dissipation?

5–96. A 1.5-in. diameter jet of water issues from a nozzle connected to a 2.5-in. diameter pipe. The jet velocity is 60 ft/sec. a) Assuming no frictional losses, what is the pressure in the pipe? b) If this pressure in the pipe produces a jet velocity of only 59 ft/sec, what is the head loss due to frictional effects?

Ans. b) 1.7 ft

5–97. A turbine operates between a headwater pool 170 ft above the tailwater pool. The head loss in the system is 20 ft. The power output of the turbine is 8425 hp at an efficiency of 90 per cent. What is the flow rate through the turbine?

5–98. When water flows through a pipeline from one open reservoir to another whose free surface is 50 ft below the first, the flow rate is 2 ft³/sec. A pump is then installed in the pipeline and 2 ft³/sec are pumped from the lower to the higher reservoir. What is the horsepower added to the water by the pump?

Ans. 22.7 hp

5–99. Water flows at an average velocity of 45 ft/sec in a 6.00-in. diameter jet. What is the horsepower of the jet?

5–100. The design head for the Grand Coulee power plant was 330 ft. At a flow rate of 4660 ft³/sec, the power output is 154,000 horsepower. What is the plant efficiency?

Ans. 88.3 per cent

5–101. A turbine generates 3450 horsepower at 200 rpm under a head of 47 ft when the flow rate is 865 ft³/sec. What is the turbine efficiency?

5–102. Water is pumped through a centrifugal pump at a rate of 2.355 ft³/sec. The pump inlet is 6 in. ID and the discharge is 4 in. ID. The inlet pressure is 5 in. mercury vacuum, and the discharge pressure is 30 psig. What is the horsepower output of the pump?

5–103. A hydraulic turbine operates between a headwater and a tailwater 85 ft below the headwater elevation. The hydraulic losses in the intake and outlet total 14 ft. The flow rate is 600 ft³/sec. *a)* What is the horsepower input to the turbine? *b)* What is the output of the turbine if its efficiency is 92 per cent?

5–104. What is the over-all efficiency of a hydroelectric plant with an output of 8425 hp when the flow rate is 550 ft³/sec from a headwater pool 170 ft above the tailwater elevation? Compare with the turbine efficiency given in Prob. 5–96.

5–105. A jet of water issuing from a nozzle at Q ft³/sec with a velocity V_j strikes a series of vanes mounted on a wheel, called a Pelton wheel, which rotates with a peripheral velocity $V_b = \omega R$. The jet is split in half by the vanes, each half being deflected through an angle β. The entire system is at atmospheric pressure. *a)* What is the power in the jet? *b)* What power is given up by the jet to the blades? *c)* Show that the theoretical efficiency, defined as the ratio of power given up by the jet to the power in the jet, is independent of the flow rate and depends only on the speed ratio V_b/V_j and the blade angle β. *d)* Show that the theoretical efficiency is a maximum when the speed ratio is $V_b/V_j = 0.5$. *e)* The efficiency would be a maximum for a blade angle of 180 deg. Why are Pelton wheels made with blade angles of approximately 165 deg? *f)* What advantage results from splitting the jet in half?

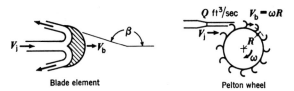

Blade element   Pelton wheel

Prob. 5–105

5–106. An air compressor takes in 12,000 ft³ of standard air per hour through an inlet of 1 ft² in area. It exhausts through a 3-in. pipe (0.0491 ft² in area) at 140 F and 120 psia. The heat lost by conduction, convection, and radiation is 950 Btu/slug of air. *a)* Show that the change in kinetic energy and in potential energy is negligible. *b)* What is the power output of the compressor?

Ans.   *b)* 17.66 hp

5-107. The cross-sectional area of a diffuser increases from 1 ft² at inlet to 4 ft² at exit. The inlet velocity is 40 ft/sec and is at a pressure of 10 psig. Assume one-dimensional flow of water without losses. What is the net force *on the walls of the diffuser* in the axial direction? See Fig. 5–12.   *Ans.* 7810 lb_f, upstream

5-108. A 4-ft diameter fan is mounted as shown. Standard air is drawn from the atmosphere and is discharged through a 2-ft diameter exit at 80 ft/sec. Assume one-dimensional, incompressible, frictionless flow. Note that the exit pressure is atmospheric. *a)* What is the pressure at section *1*? *b)* What is the pressure at section *2*? *c)* How much power is added to the air by the fan? Use Eq. 5–37. *d)* Using the steady-flow energy equation and Eq. 5–34, calculate the power added to the air by the fan. Compare with part *(c)*.

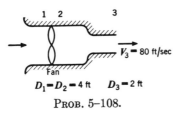

$D_1 = D_2 = 4$ ft $D_3 = 2$ ft

PROB. 5–108.

5-109. Methane at 175 psia and 100 F enters a rough, insulated, 6-in. diameter pipe at 60 ft/sec. At a downstream section, the velocity is 600 ft/sec. *a)* What is the temperature at the downstream section? *b)* What is the pressure at the downstream section? *c)* What is the total wall shear force?   *Ans.*   *c)* 4372 lb_f

5-110. Air flows at a constant temperature of 100 F in a pipe having a cross-sectional area of 0.1 ft². At inlet the pressure is 100 psia and the velocity is 100 ft/sec. At exit the pressure is 85 psia. *a)* What is the exit velocity? *b)* What is the total viscous shear force?

Ans.   *b)* 213 lb_f

5-111. A nozzle is attached to the end of a pipe by means of a bolted flange. The pipe area is 0.1 ft² and the nozzle tip area is 0.05 ft². The pressure in the pipe is 50.5 psig. Water flows without appreciable friction. What is the total tension on the flange bolts?

5-112. One arm of a rotating water sprinkler is 3 ft long. It consists of a ¾-in. pipe (0.82 in. ID) which terminates in a 90-deg reducing elbow with a ⅜-in. nipple (0.49 in. ID). The pressure in the ¾-in. pipe is 20 psig. Assume a loss of one pipe velocity head through the elbow. What is the torque on the sprinkler arm when it is held at rest?

5-113. In Prob. 5–112, *a)* What is the speed of rotation if the sprinkler rotates without friction? *b)* Explain why, when the sprinkler arm rotates, you cannot isolate only the fluid in the reducing elbow in making a momentum analysis, but must include the fluid in the arm of the sprinkler as well.

5–114. Air flows through a 6-in. diameter horizontal pipe. At inlet, the pressure is 120 psia, the temperature is 150 F, and the average velocity is 140 ft/sec. As a result of pipe friction and heat transfer, the exit pressure is 80 psia and the exit temperature is 180 F. *a*) What is the exit velocity? *b*) What is the total wall shear opposing the flow? *c*) How much heat must be added to the air or removed from it per unit time?

Ans. *b*) 1095 lb$_f$

5–115. A piston in a large tank of cross-sectional area A forces an incompressible ideal fluid of density ρ out of the tank and into the atmosphere through a small pipe of cross-sectional area a. The fluid jet has a cross-sectional area $C_c\, a$ in the smaller pipe. *a*) Write the continuity, momentum, and Bernoulli equations for this system to show that the contraction coefficient is

$$C_c = \frac{1}{2 - a/A}$$

b) As a becomes very small compared with A, the entrance to the small pipe is called a Borda mouthpiece. What is the contraction coefficient for a Borda mouthpiece?

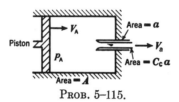

PROB. 5–115.

5–116. Water flows from a 2-in. diameter orifice at the end of a 4-in. diameter pipe at a rate of 0.5 ft³/sec. The jet contracts to an area 64.4 per cent of the orifice area before the streamlines become parallel. Assume no frictional losses. *a*) What is the pressure in the pipe upstream from the orifice? *b*) What is the force of the water on the orifice plate? *c*) What horsepower is required to maintain this flow?

6

Potential Flow

Potential flow refers to the flow of an ideal, irrotational fluid. A study of a system which in reality does not exist might seem fruitless, but real fluids in many instances exhibit the characteristics of ideal fluids. Many problems in fluid mechanics deal with the relative motion between bodies and fluids of low viscosity—airfoils in air, for example. The viscous fluid may be regarded as consisting of two regions: a thin layer adjacent to the body in which the viscous effects are large, and the rest of the fluid in which the viscous effects are negligible. In this outer region, the flow of the viscous fluid is essentially that of an ideal fluid. A knowledge of ideal fluid behavior is therefore useful in predicting or analyzing the behavior of real fluid flows.

We will consider the steady flow in two dimensions of an incompressible, irrotational fluid and show mathematically how to describe streamline patterns for various types of flow. Potential flow also exists in three dimensions and for compressible flow [1, 2, 3], but these will not be considered in detail. The differential equations of the velocity potential for incompressible flow are linear and solutions may be superposed. These equations for compressible flow are nonlinear and hence solutions may not be superposed.

From the streamline patterns, the velocity and pressure variations throughout a flow field may be obtained. From the pressure distribution around the surface of a body the drag and lift may be calculated. The drag is generally zero for steady motion in an infinite, continuous, irrotational fluid, but is non-zero for free-streamline flows and for some flows with the body near a boundary. The calculated lift for some airfoils is in remarkable agreement with the actual lift experienced by the airfoil in a real fluid. The streamline patterns, together with their associated potential lines, form a flow net which has an exact counterpart in other potential fields such as heat conduction, flow of electricity in a conductor or electrolyte, and electric and magnetic fields.

A method of obtaining flow patterns by a superposition of simpler flow patterns will be shown together with a number of examples. Other methods of obtaining potential flows by conformal transformations in the complex plane, including the Schwarz-Christoffel method, will be discussed. Finally, since an accelerating or converging real fluid flow behaves remarkably like a potential flow, some values of contraction coefficients calculated for potential flow by von Mises will be tabulated.

6–1. VELOCITY POTENTIAL AND STREAM FUNCTION
FOR TWO-DIMENSIONAL FLOW

If w is zero and both u and v are independent of z, then streamlines and the paths of particles lie in planes parallel to the x-y plane. If the motion in the x-y plane is known, the motion is everywhere known, and the flow is then two-dimensional.

It will be shown that a function (or variable) ϕ exists, called the velocity potential, such that the velocity components u and v, as well as their resultant $\mathbf{V}$, are obtainable from

$$u = -\frac{\partial \phi}{\partial x} \qquad (6\text{–}1a)$$

$$v = -\frac{\partial \phi}{\partial y} \qquad (6\text{–}1b)$$

and $\qquad \mathbf{V} = -\nabla \phi = -\text{grad } \phi = -\frac{\partial \phi}{\partial x}\,\mathbf{i} - \frac{\partial \phi}{\partial y}\,\mathbf{j} - \frac{\partial \phi}{\partial z}\,\mathbf{k} \qquad (6\text{–}1c)$

The velocity components u and v are also obtainable from a stream function ψ, defined such that

$$u = -\frac{\partial \psi}{\partial y} \qquad (6\text{–}2a)$$

and $\qquad\qquad v = \frac{\partial \psi}{\partial x} \qquad (6\text{–}2b)$

Combining Eqs. 6–1 and 6–2, we find that

$$\frac{\partial^2 \phi}{\partial x^2} + \frac{\partial^2 \phi}{\partial y^2} = 0 \qquad (6\text{–}3)$$

or in vector form $\qquad \nabla \cdot \nabla \phi = \nabla^2 \phi = 0$

Equation 6–3 is the Laplace equation. Similarly,

$$\frac{\partial^2 \psi}{\partial x^2} + \frac{\partial^2 \psi}{\partial y^2} = 0 \qquad (6\text{–}4)$$

or in vector form $\qquad \nabla \cdot \nabla \psi = \nabla^2 \psi = 0$

The similarity of Eqs. 6–3 and 6–4 suggests that the potential and stream functions for one flow could represent the potential and stream functions for another flow. That is, given stream and potential functions may be interchanged to produce another flow pattern. An example of this is the source, or sink, and the vortex described in Sec. 6–3.

Equipotential lines are lines of constant ϕ, and streamlines are lines of constant ψ. Equations 6–1 and 6–2 indicate that they always intersect at right angles, and the two families of intersecting lines form a system of curvilinear squares called a *flow net*. A graphical method of drawing flow nets will be described in Sec. 6–2. The derivation of the potential function and stream functions for a few simple flow patterns will be given in Sec. 6–3.

If ϕ_1 and ϕ_2 are two velocity potentials which satisfy the Laplace equation, then $(\phi_1 + \phi_2)$, which is the result of superposing the flows represented by ϕ_1 and ϕ_2 individually, will also satisfy the Laplace equation and thus will be the velocity potential for the combined flows. Similarly, the stream function for the resulting combined motion is the sum of the stream functions for each of the superposed flows.

The stream function is a consequence of the continuity equation and thus is applicable to *both* rotational and irrotational flows. The potential function, however, is a consequence of the condition for zero vorticity, and thus is applicable to *only* irrotational flows.

Derivation of velocity potential and stream function. A differential expression $u\,dx + v\,dy$ is called exact if there exists a function, say $-\phi(x, y)$, such that $d\phi = -(u\,dx + v\,dy)$, the test for exactness being that

$$\frac{\partial u}{\partial y} = \frac{\partial v}{\partial x}$$

This is the condition for two-dimensional irrotational flow. Since the total differential of ϕ is

$$d\phi = \frac{\partial \phi}{\partial x}\,dx + \frac{\partial \phi}{\partial y}\,dy$$

it follows that, by equating coefficients of dx and dy in the two expressions for $d\phi$,

$$u = -\frac{\partial \phi}{\partial x} \quad \text{and} \quad v = -\frac{\partial \phi}{\partial y}$$

The function $\phi(x,y)$ is the velocity potential, and irrotational flow is called potential flow. Use of the negative partial differentials of ϕ produces flow in a direction of decreasing potential.

Similarly, a differential expression $-u\,dy + v\,dx$ is called exact if there exists a function, say $\psi(x,y)$ such that $d\psi = -u\,dy + v\,dx$, the test for exactness being that

$$-\frac{\partial u}{\partial x} = \frac{\partial v}{\partial y}$$

This is the condition imposed by the continuity equation. Since the total differential of ψ is

$$d\psi = \frac{\partial \psi}{\partial x}\,dx + \frac{\partial \psi}{\partial y}\,dy$$

it also follows that, by equating coefficients of dx and dy in the two expressions for $d\psi$,

$$u = -\frac{\partial \psi}{\partial y} \quad \text{and} \quad v = \frac{\partial \psi}{\partial x}$$

and therefore equipotential lines and streamlines intersect everywhere at right angles. Along a potential line, $u\,dx + v\,dy = 0$, from which

$$\left(\frac{dy}{dx}\right)_\phi = -\frac{u}{v}$$

Along a streamline, $-u\,dy + v\,dx = 0$, or

$$\left(\frac{dy}{dx}\right)_\psi = \frac{v}{u}$$

Thus,

$$\left(\frac{dy}{dx}\right)_\phi = -\left(\frac{1}{dy/dx}\right)_\psi$$

and thus at any point of intersection the equipotential lines are normal to the streamlines.

In polar form, the radial component of velocity is

$$v_r = -\frac{1}{r}\frac{\partial \psi}{\partial \theta} = -\frac{\partial \phi}{\partial r} \tag{6–5a}$$

and the tangential component is

$$v_\theta = \frac{\partial \psi}{\partial r} = -\frac{1}{r}\frac{\partial \phi}{\partial \theta} \tag{6–5b}$$

The vector velocity $\mathbf{V}$ is expressed in terms of the potential function as follows:

$$\mathbf{V} = u\,\mathbf{i} + v\,\mathbf{j} = -\left(\frac{\partial \phi}{\partial x}\right)\mathbf{i} - \left(\frac{\partial \phi}{\partial y}\right)\mathbf{j} = -\nabla \phi$$

the negative gradient of ϕ by definition. Since the gradient of a scalar function is always normal to the curve (or the level surface in three dimensions) representing the function, the velocity vectors, and hence streamlines, are always normal to the equipotential lines (or surfaces in three dimensions).

In heat conduction, equipotential lines are lines of constant temperature, and streamlines are lines indicating the direction of heat flow. In electrical conduction, equipotential lines are lines of constant voltage, and the streamlines are lines along which current flows. In fluid flow, equipotential lines are just that—they are *not* lines of constant pressure—and streamlines are lines indicating fluid particle paths for steady flow.

Further differentiation of the preceding partial differential equations gives

$$\frac{\partial^2 \phi}{\partial x^2} = \frac{\partial^2 \psi}{\partial y \partial x} \quad \text{and} \quad \frac{\partial^2 \phi}{\partial y^2} = -\frac{\partial^2 \psi}{\partial x \partial y}$$

and thus for continuously differentiable functions

$$\frac{\partial^2 \phi}{\partial x^2} + \frac{\partial^2 \phi}{\partial y^2} = 0 \quad \text{and} \quad \frac{\partial^2 \psi}{\partial x^2} + \frac{\partial^2 \psi}{\partial y^2} = 0$$

Also

$$\nabla^2 \phi = \nabla \cdot \nabla \phi = \nabla \cdot \left(\frac{\partial \phi}{\partial x} \mathbf{i} + \frac{\partial \phi}{\partial y} \mathbf{j} \right) = \frac{\partial^2 \phi}{\partial x^2} + \frac{\partial^2 \phi}{\partial y^2} = 0$$

Any function $\phi(x,y)$ which satisfies the Laplace equation is called *harmonic* and is a possible velocity potential which describes some irrotational flow. The velocity components of such a flow may be obtained from Eq. 6–1. There are unlimited solutions to the Laplace equation, and the desired one requires insertion of appropriate boundary conditions. Note that it is possible for given velocity components to satisfy the continuity requirements of Eq. 5–2a but not satisfy the irrotational requirements of Eq. 5–12. In this instance, the velocity components would *not* be derivable from a velocity potential ϕ, and the flow might represent that of a real, rotational fluid (with viscosity).

EXAMPLE 6–1. Given $\phi = x^2 - y^2$, find the velocity components and the stream function, and describe the flow.

Solution: The velocity components are $u = -2x$ and $v = 2y$. Since $u = -\partial \psi / \partial y = -2x$, $\psi = 2xy + f(x) + C$. Also, since $v = \partial \psi / \partial x = 2y$, $\psi = 2xy + f(y) + C$. A comparison of these two expressions for ψ indicates that $f(x) = f(y) = 0$, and thus $\psi = 2xy + C$. The value of the constant C does not change the flow pattern; only the numerical value of each of the family of streamlines is changed. The streamlines are rectangular hyperbolas, asymptotic to the x and y axes. The potential lines are rectangular hyperbolas, asymptotic to the lines $x = y$ and $x = -y$. The flow in the second and third quadrants represents two-dimensional flow from left to right, towards the y-z plane.

The flow rate between streamlines is equal to the difference between the values of stream functions representing the streamlines. In Fig. 6–1 the flow rate between streamlines ψ and $\psi + d\psi$ towards the right is the sum of the volumetric flow rate in the $+x$ and the $-y$ directions, from continuity. This is

$$u \, dy - v \, dx = - \, d\psi = | \, d\psi \, |$$

Thus the flow rate between any two streamlines ψ_1 and ψ_2 is

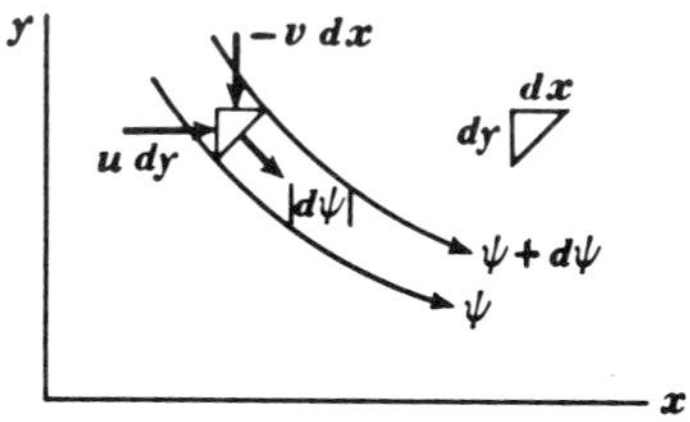

FIG. 6–1. Flow rate between streamlines for incompressible fluid.

$$Q = \int_1^2 | \, d\psi \, | = | \, \psi_2 - \psi_1 \, |$$

6–2. FLOW NETS FOR TWO-DIMENSIONAL FLOW

A set of equipotential lines separated by an amount $\Delta\phi = C$ and a set of streamlines with $\Delta\psi = C$ will form curvilinear squares. The system of curvilinear squares formed by these equipotential lines and streamlines is known as a flow net. With a little practice, flow nets for many fluid flows may be drawn freehand with sufficient accuracy for many purposes.

The method consists of drawing streamlines equally spaced at some section where there is rectilinear flow. The number of intervals or streamlines depends upon the accuracy desired and the effort one is willing to expend—the smaller the increments the greater the accuracy and the greater the effort required to draw the flow net, and conversely. Only in the limit when $\Delta\psi$ and $\Delta\phi$ approach zero will the flow net consist of perfect squares. The larger the intervals, the more the curvilinear squares will depart from perfect squares. Streamlines are drawn by eye and a system of normal equipotential lines are then added. Successive adjustments are made in both streamlines and equipotential lines until the net appears proper. Diagonal lines through the curvilinear squares should also form a mesh of curvilinear squares; this is often used as an added check on the correctness of the flow net.

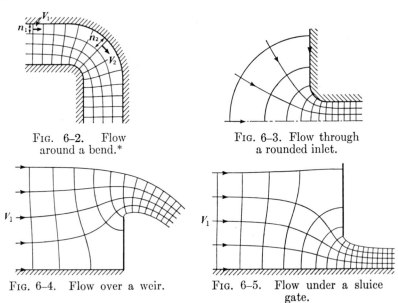

Fig. 6–2.   Flow around a bend.*

Fig. 6–3.   Flow through a rounded inlet.

Fig. 6–4.   Flow over a weir.

Fig. 6–5.   Flow under a sluice gate.

From continuity, $V_1 n_1 = V_2 n_2$ in Fig. 6–2, and thus velocities vary inversely with streamline spacing. From the Bernoulli equation for an

*Flow nets in Figs. 6–2, 6–3, 6–4, and 6–5 are reproduced, with permission, from *Basic Mechanics of Fluids*, by Hunter Rouse, John Wiley & Sons, Inc., 1953.

ideal incompressible fluid when gravity effects are absent, $(\rho V_1{}^2/2) + p_1 = (\rho V_2{}^2/2) + p_2$ and pressure variations may also be determined throughout the flow field once velocity variations are known. If gravity effects are present the complete Bernoulli equation must be used.

For flow around a circular bend, the velocity is greatest ($Vr = C$ for a free vortex from Sec. 5–4) and the pressure least at the inner radius (Fig. 6–2).

The flow into a rounded entrance is shown in Fig. 6–3. Flow from a rounded exit or outlet would be the mirror image of this.

Flow over a weir under the influence of gravity is shown in Fig. 6–4, and flow under a sluice gate is shown in Fig. 6–5.

Flow nets for flow around corners, shown in Fig. 6–6, indicate infinitesimal velocities at the outer corner in view (a) and infinitesimal streamline spacing with infinite velocities at the inner corners in both views (a) and (b).

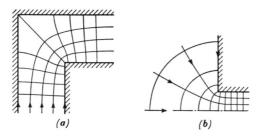

(a)   (b)

FIG. 6–6.   Flow around a corner a) in a duct and b) into a duct.*

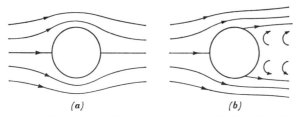

(a)   (b)

FIG. 6–7.   Flow past a circular cylinder; a) ideal fluid without separation and b) real fluid with separation.

Real fluids act like ideal fluids in regions where streamlines converge or diverge only minutely near boundaries. Where divergence of streamlines is appreciable, separation occurs and the flow net will not give a reliable picture of the flow if the boundaries of the separation zone are not known.

*Flow nets in Fig. 6–6 are reproduced, with permission, from *Elementary Mechanics of Fluids*, by Hunter Rouse, John Wiley & Sons, Inc., 1946.

Real fluids tend to overshoot as they pass sharp corners or enter regions where boundaries diverge. An example of this is shown in Fig. 6–7 for flow past a circular cylinder. The flow of an ideal fluid, view (a), is similar to the flow of a real fluid, view (b), over the upstream portion of a cylinder, but the flow of the ideal fluid and of the real fluid differ over the aft portion of a cylinder. In Fig. 6–4 and 6–5 the flow nets have been drawn by assuming that the fluid would separate from the boundaries at the sharp edges.

6–3. EXAMPLES OF IDEAL, TWO-DIMENSIONAL, STEADY FLUID FLOWS

Rectilinear flow. Uniform flow in the $+x$ direction is such that $u = u_s$ and $v = 0$. Then $-\partial\phi/\partial x = u_s$ and $\phi = -u_s x + f(y)$ (neglecting the constant), and $v = -\partial\phi/\partial y = 0$ and ϕ is thus not a function of y. The stream function is obtained from $u = -\partial\psi/\partial y = u_s$, from which $\psi = -u_s y + f(x)$ (again neglecting the constant), and $v = \partial\psi/\partial x = 0$ and ψ is thus not a function of x. The flow net for this flow is shown in Fig. 6–8. Since rectangular and polar coordinates are related by the expressions $x = r \cos \theta$ and $y = r \sin \theta$, the potential and stream functions for uniform flow in the $+x$ direction are

$$\phi = -u_s x = -u_s r \cos \theta$$
$$\psi = -u_s y = -u_s r \sin \theta$$

The velocity potential and stream functions for uniform flow in any direction can always be expressed by first-degree equations in x and y. Thus $\phi = -ux - vy$ and $\psi = -uy + vx$ for the general situation.

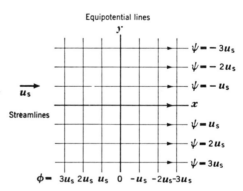

Equipotential lines

FIG. 6–8.   Rectilinear flow in the $+x$ direction.

For example, $\phi = 2x + y$ and $\psi = -x + 2y$ represent flow for which $u = -2$ and $v = -1$ (and $\mathbf{V} = -2\,\mathbf{i} - 1\,\mathbf{j}$) throughout the entire x-y plane.

Source. A line source is a line of unit length between two parallel planes, a unit distance apart, from which fluid flows radially in all directions parallel to the planes [Fig. 6–9 (a)]. The strength of the source is equal to the volumetric flow rate from it. The potential function and the

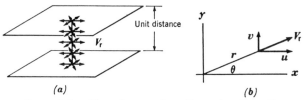

(a)   (b)

FIG. 6–9. Flow from a two-dimensional, or line, source; a) line source, b) flow in the x-y plane.

stream function will be derived. In the x-y plane [Fig. 6–9 (b)] the radial velocity is V_r at a radial distance r from the origin, the location of the source. The volumetric flow rate from this line source of unit length is $q = V_r 2\pi r$. From geometry, the definition of the velocity potential, and the stream function we may write for $r \neq 0$

$$V_r = \frac{q}{2\pi r} = -\frac{\partial \phi}{\partial r} = -\frac{1}{r}\frac{\partial \psi}{\partial \theta}$$

and
$$V_\theta = 0$$

Thus

$$\phi_{source} = -\frac{q}{2\pi}\ln r = -\frac{q}{4\pi}\ln(x^2 + y^2) \tag{6–6}$$

and

$$\psi_{source} = -\frac{q}{2\pi}\theta = -\frac{q}{2\pi}\arctan\frac{y}{x} \tag{6–7}$$

where q equals the strength of the source, and $q/2\pi$ the flow rate per radian.

Sink. A sink is a negative source, and the velocity potential and the stream function for a sink are the negative of those for a source.

$$\phi_{sink} = \frac{q}{4\pi}\ln(x^2 + y^2) = \frac{q}{2\pi}\ln r \tag{6–8}$$

$$\psi_{sink} = \frac{q}{2\pi}\tan^{-1}\frac{y}{x} = \frac{q}{2\pi}\theta \tag{6–9}$$

Vortex. For an irrotational, or free, vortex $Vr = C$ (Sec. 5–4), streamlines are circles about the origin, and equipotential lines are radial lines from the origin. The stream function and velocity potential may be described by interchanging ϕ and ψ in the equations for a source. For a vortex rotating in a positive (counterclockwise) direction,

$$\phi_{vortex} = -C\tan^{-1}\frac{y}{x} = -C\theta \tag{6–10}$$

$$\psi_{\text{vortex}} = \frac{C}{2} \ln (x^2 + y^2) = C \ln r \qquad (6\text{–}11)$$

The strength of a vortex depends on the magnitude of C, since at a given radius, the greater the value of C the greater the rotational velocity. The *strength* is defined as the magnitude of the *circulation*. Circulation, in turn, is defined as the line integral of the product of the velocity component tangent to an element of the closed path around which the integral is taken times the infinitesimal path length. This is

$$\Gamma = \oint |\mathbf{V}| \cos \theta \, | \, dl | = \oint \mathbf{V} \cdot dl \qquad (6\text{–}12)$$

in Fig. 6–10. For the particular case of a path along a circle whose center is at the origin (a vortex streamline), the velocity vector is always constant and tangent to the path of integration, and $dl = r \, d\theta$. Then

$$\Gamma = V \oint dl = V \int_0^{2\pi} r \, d\theta = 2\pi r \, V = 2\pi C$$

For any other closed path which does not include the origin, the circulation for an irrotational vortex is zero.

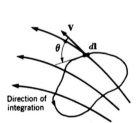

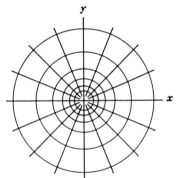

FIG. 6–10. Circulation in a positive direction, with region about which integration is made being to the left of path traversed.

FIG. 6–11. Flow net for a source, sink, and vortex.

Figure 6–11 shows the flow net for a source, a sink, and a vortex. The potential functions and stream functions for rectilinear flow, a source, a sink, and a free vortex, may be added in a number of different ways. The results will be solutions of the Laplace equation and will describe different flow situations. Some typical combinations will be illustrated without derivation.

Half body. The addition of a rectilinear flow and a source flow produces flow around a half body (Fig. 6–12).

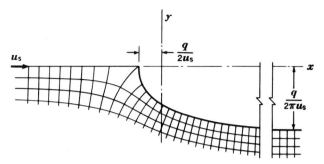

FIG. 6–12. Flow net for one side of a half body.

$$\phi = -u_s x - \frac{q}{4\pi} \ln (x^2 + y^2) = -u_s r \cos \theta - \frac{q}{2\pi} \ln r \quad (6\text{–}13)$$

$$\psi = -u_s y - \frac{q}{2\pi} \tan^{-1} \frac{y}{x} = -u_s r \sin \theta - \frac{q}{2\pi} \theta \quad (6\text{–}14)$$

Doublet. A source and sink of equal strength, when brought together in such a way that the product of their strength and the distance between them remains constant, produce a doublet, or dipole. The constant C (any C, not necessarily the same as for a vortex) is called the strength of the doublet (Fig. 6–13).

To form a doublet from a sink and source brought together along the x axis, the potential function at any point P in Fig. 6–14 is that for the source plus that for the sink.

$$\phi_D = -\frac{q}{2\pi} \ln r + \frac{q}{2\pi} \ln (r + dr) = \frac{q}{2\pi} \ln \left(1 + \frac{dr}{r}\right)$$

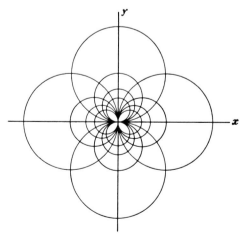

FIG. 6–13. Doublet or dipole.

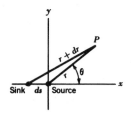

FIG. 6–14. Source-sink combination to form a doublet.

Expansion of $\ln\left(1 + \dfrac{dr}{r}\right)$ in a power series gives

$$\phi_D = \frac{q}{2\pi}\left[\frac{dr}{r} - \frac{1}{2}\left(\frac{dr}{r}\right)^2 + \ldots\right]$$

Neglecting higher powers of dr/r gives

$$\phi_D = \frac{q}{2\pi}\frac{dr}{r} = \frac{(q\,ds)\cos\theta}{2\pi r}$$

Thus

$$\phi_D = C\frac{\cos\theta}{r} = \frac{Cx}{x^2 + y^2} \tag{6–15}$$

Similarly

$$\psi_D = -C\frac{\sin\theta}{r} = \frac{-Cy}{x^2 + y^2} \tag{6–16}$$

Cylinder. Flow past a circular cylinder is obtained by combining a rectilinear flow with a doublet and is shown in Fig. 6–15 for the doublet $C = -u_s R^2$. This is obtained by setting $u = -\partial\phi/\partial x = 0$ at $x = R$ and $y = 0$ in the expression for ϕ for a rectilinear flow and for a doublet from Eq. 6–15.

$$\phi = -u_s x - u_s\frac{R^2 x}{x^2 + y^2} = -u_s r\cos\theta - u_s R^2\frac{\cos\theta}{r} \tag{6–17}$$

$$\psi = -u_s y + u_s\frac{R^2 y}{x^2 + y^2} = -u_s r\sin\theta + u_s R^2\frac{\sin\theta}{r} \tag{6–18}$$

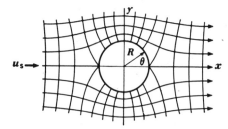

FIG. 6–15. Flow past a circular cylinder.

At any point in the flow, $\mathbf{V} = -\nabla\phi = -(\partial\phi/\partial x)\ \mathbf{i} - (\partial\phi/\partial y)\ \mathbf{j}$, and

$$V = |\ \mathbf{V}\ | = \sqrt{\left(\frac{\partial\phi}{\partial x}\right)^2 + \left(\frac{\partial\phi}{\partial y}\right)^2}$$

Along the surface of the cylinder, $V = 2u_s \sin\theta$.

Cylinder with circulation. Flow around a circular cylinder with circulation is obtained by adding a vortex to the rectilinear flow past the cylinder (a clockwise vortex is used in Fig 6–16). The strength of the vortex is $C = \Gamma/2\pi$.

$$\phi = -u_s\left(x + \frac{R^2 x}{x^2 + y^2}\right) + \frac{\Gamma}{2\pi}\tan^{-1}\frac{y}{x}$$

$$= -u_s\left(r + \frac{R^2}{r}\right)\cos\theta + \frac{\Gamma}{2\pi}\theta \qquad (6\text{–}19)$$

$$\psi = -u_s\left(y - \frac{R^2 y}{x^2 + y^2}\right) - \frac{\Gamma}{4\pi}\ln(x^2 + y^2)$$

$$= -u_s\left(r - \frac{R^2}{r}\right)\sin\theta - \frac{\Gamma}{2\pi}\ln r \qquad (6\text{–}20)$$

With no circulation about the cylinder, the stagnation points (where the velocity is zero) are at $\theta = 0$ and $\theta = \pi$ (Fig. 6–15). As the circulation is increased, the stagnation points move toward each other along the surface of the cylinder until they coincide at $\theta = -\pi/2$. If the circulation is increased more, the stagnation points will be removed from the surface of the cylinder, and fluid will rotate completely around the cylinder. The tangential velocity along the surface of the cylinder is

$$V_\theta = -\left(2u_s \sin\theta + \frac{\Gamma}{2\pi R}\right)$$

(negative because in Fig. 6–16 it is clockwise) from which the location of the stagnation points $V_\theta = 0$ can be related to the circulation by the equation

$$\Gamma = -4\pi u_s R \sin\theta$$

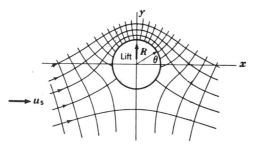

Fig. 6–16. Rectilinear flow and vortex flow (negative, or clockwise) around a circular cylinder produces lift.

A double stagnation point (at $\theta = -\pi/2$) occurs if the velocity due to circulation is twice u_s, from the equation

$$V_{\text{circ}} = \frac{\Gamma}{2\pi R} = -2u_s \sin \theta \Big|_{V_\theta = 0} = 2u_s \Big|_{V_\theta = 0}$$

In all of the preceding situations, if the free-stream velocity u_s is known, the velocity at any other point may be obtained from the velocity potential, the stream function, or direct measurement of the streamline spacing on a flow net. If the pressure p_s is known where the velocity u_s is known, the pressure at other points may be obtained from the Bernoulli equation

$$\rho \frac{u_s{}^2}{2} + p_s = \rho \frac{V^2}{2} + p$$

Drag is defined as the resultant force of a fluid on the surface of a body in a direction parallel to the free-stream velocity of approach u_s. In an ideal fluid, only normal forces due to pressure occur, and for flow past a circular cylinder without circulation, the pressure variation around the surface is given by

$$p - p_s = \rho \frac{u_s{}^2}{2} - \frac{\rho(2u_s \sin \theta)^2}{2} = \frac{\rho u_s{}^2}{2}(1 - 4 \sin^2 \theta)$$

From this,

$$\text{Drag} = - \int_0^{2\pi} (p - p_s) \cos \theta \,(R \, d\theta) = 0$$

and

$$\text{Lift} = - \int_0^{2\pi} (p - p_s) \sin \theta \,(R \, d\theta) = 0$$

For flow past a circular cylinder *with* circulation,

$$p - p_s = \frac{\rho}{2} \left[u_s{}^2 - \left(2u_s \sin \theta + \frac{\Gamma}{2\pi R} \right)^2 \right]$$

and the drag is again zero. The lift for a unit length of cylinder is

$$L = \rho u_s \Gamma \tag{6-21}$$

See Sec. 11–3 for a further discussion of circulation and lift.

Tornado. A tornado may be approximated by a two-dimensional vortex and a sink, except in a region near the origin, and this is an example of good agreement between a real and an ideal fluid. The resultant flow is shown in Fig. 6–17. For the ideal fluid

$$\phi = \frac{q}{2\pi} \ln r - \frac{\Gamma}{2\pi} \theta = \frac{q}{4\pi} \ln (x^2 + y^2) - \frac{\Gamma}{2\pi} \tan^{-1} \frac{y}{x}$$

$$\psi = \frac{q}{2\pi} \theta + \frac{\Gamma}{2\pi} \ln r = \frac{q}{2\pi} \tan^{-1} \frac{y}{x} + \frac{\Gamma}{4\pi} \ln (x^2 + y^2)$$

The tangential velocity from the vortex is $V_\theta = \Gamma/2\pi r$, and the radial velocity from the sink is $V_r = -q/2\pi r$. The resultant velocity is $V = \sqrt{\Gamma^2 + q^2}/2\pi r$, which may also be obtained from

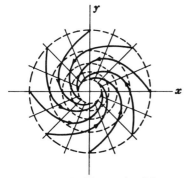

FIG. 6–17. Vortex (positive, or counterclockwise) and sink as a tornado model.

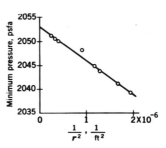

FIG. 6–18. Minimum recorded pressures during passage of tornado. Theoretical model combining vortex and sink indicates linear relation between pressure and $1/r^2$. Measurements verify this.

$$V = \sqrt{\left(\frac{\partial \phi}{\partial x}\right)^2 + \left(\frac{\partial \phi}{\partial y}\right)^2}$$

Thus $Vr = C = \sqrt{\Gamma^2 + q^2}/2\pi$. Combining this with the energy equation for an ideal fluid gives

$$p_2 - p_1 = \frac{\rho C^2}{2}\left(\frac{1}{r_1^2} - \frac{1}{r_2^2}\right)$$

which indicates a linear relation between p and $1/r^2$.

Measurements made during passage of a tornado on June 8, 1953 at eight barograph stations in the NACA Lewis Laboratory near Cleveland, Ohio are tabulated in Table 6–1. Adjustments in position, but not in

TABLE 6–1

MINIMUM PRESSURES FROM MEASUREMENTS DURING
PASSAGE OF A TORNADO*

Station	Corrected minimum pressure, psfa	Distance from path, R feet	$\frac{1}{R^2} \times 10^6$
1	2041.0	764	1.713
2	2044.8	918	1.187
3	2050.6	1591	0.355
4	2043.6	889	1.265
5	2050.3	1545	0.419
6	2039.3	715	1.956
7	2048.4	1050	0.907
8	2051.2	1902	0.276

*Extracted from W. Lewis and P. J. Perkins, "Recorded Pressure Distribution in the Outer Portion of a Tornado Vortex," *Monthly Weather Review*, Vol. 81 (1953), pp. 379–385, with permission of the Weather Bureau, U.S. Department of Commerce.

direction, of the path of the center of the tornado were made, as well as an adjustment to a standard reference pressure for all stations. From the data, $Vr = C = 78 \times 10^3$ ft²/sec, and a graph substantiating the linear relation between p and $1/r^2$ is shown in Fig. 6–18.

6–4. POTENTIAL FLOWS FROM CONFORMAL TRANSFORMATIONS IN THE COMPLEX PLANE

Potential flow patterns may be obtained by combining simple flow patterns, as was done in Section 6–3. This superposition method is valid because of the linearity of the Laplace equation.

A second method of obtaining solutions to the Laplace equation for two-dimensional flow makes use of the functions of a complex variable. By this means a rectangular grid flow net in one complex plane is transformed into the desired flow net in another complex plane. The transformation is called *conformal* because infinitesimal squares in the one plane become similar infinitesimal curvilinear squares in the other plane. In some instances, successive conformal transformations are used to obtain a desired flow pattern.

For example, the rectangular grid in Fig. 6–8 (this is in the so-called w plane) is transformed into the flow of Fig. 6–15 (this is the so-called z plane in which $z = x + iy = r\,e^{i\theta}$) by the complex transformation

$$w = -u_s \left(z + \frac{R^2}{z} \right)$$

$$= -u_s \left(re^{i\theta} + \frac{R^2}{r} e^{-i\theta} \right)$$

which may be separated into two components; ϕ the real component, and ψ the imaginary component, such that $w = \phi + i\psi$. Since by definition

$$e^{i\theta} = \cos\theta + i\sin\theta$$

and

$$e^{-i\theta} = \cos(-\theta) + i\sin(-\theta)$$

$$= \cos\theta - i\sin\theta$$

the transformation becomes

$$w = -u_s\, r\,(\cos\theta + i\sin\theta) - u_s\,\frac{R^2}{r}\,(\cos\theta - i\sin\theta)$$

$$= -u_s\left(r + \frac{R^2}{r}\right)\cos\theta - i\,u_s\left(r - \frac{R^2}{r}\right)\sin\theta$$

so that

$$\phi = -u_s\left(r + \frac{R^2}{r}\right)\cos\theta \qquad\qquad [6\text{–}17]$$

and

$$\psi = -u_s \left(r - \frac{R^2}{r}\right) \sin \theta \qquad\qquad [6\text{-}18]$$

as before in Section 6–3.

This particular conformal transformation may be physically described as resulting from plotting a rectangular grid such as in Fig. 6–8 on a rubber sheet, making a cut along the x axis symmetrically about the y axis and opening the cut to form a circle. The stretched rubber sheet would have the grid lines in the form of the flow net of Fig. 6–15.

If the cut were made along the negative y axis, and the two edges of the cut swung 90 degrees to coincide with the x axis, the stretched rubber sheet would have the grid lines in the form of the flow net for Example 6–1. This is shown in Fig. 6–19. Here, $w = z^2/4$.

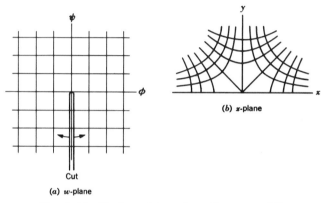

(a) w-plane

(b) x-plane

FIG. 6–19. Conformal transformation $w = z^2/4$.

A third method of analysis involves the use of the Schwarz-Christoffel theorem, often in conjunction with conformal mapping. This theorem provides a means of mapping the interior of a simple closed polygon into the upper half-plane, with the boundary of the polygon becoming the real axis (the x-axis in the complex plane).

Some useful engineering results of this complicated mapping technique were obtained by von Mises for the contraction coefficients for two-dimensional jets of an incompressible fluid in the absence of gravity. The ratio of the resulting cross-sectional area of a jet to the area of the boundary opening is called the coefficient of contraction, C_c. For the flow system shown in Fig. 6–20, von Mises calculated C_c values given in Table 6–2.

Values of contraction coefficients in Table 6–2 agree well with experimental values measured for real fluids. The results listed for two-dimensional flow may be used for axisymmetric jets if the coefficient of contraction is defined by

$$C_c = b_{\text{jet}}/b = (d_{\text{jet}}/d)^2$$

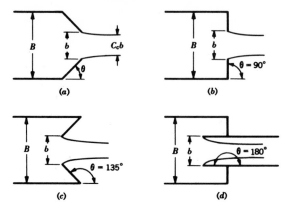

FIG. 6–20. Geometry of two-dimensional jet flow.

TABLE 6–2

COEFFICIENTS OF CONTRACTION FOR TWO-DIMENSIONAL JETS
FOR GEOMETRIES OF FIG. 6–20

b/B	C_c $\theta = 45°$	C_c $\theta = 90°$	C_c $\theta = 135°$	C_c $\theta = 180°$
0.0	0.746	0.611	0.537	0.500
0.1	0.747	0.612	0.546	0.513
0.2	0.747	0.616	0.555	0.528
0.3	0.748	0.622	0.566	0.544
0.4	0.749	0.631	0.580	0.564
0.5	0.752	0.644	0.599	0.586
0.6	0.758	0.662	0.620	0.613
0.7	0.768	0.687	0.652	0.646
0.8	0.789	0.722	0.698	0.691
0.9	0.829	0.781	0.761	0.760
1.0	1.000	1.000	1.000	1.000

and d and D are the diameters corresponding to the widths b and B, respectively. For example, if a small round hole of diameter d is in a large reservoir $(d/D = 0)$, the jet diameter would be $\sqrt{0.611} = 0.782$ times the diameter of the hole, for $\theta = 90$ degrees.

REFERENCES

1. L. M. Milne-Thomson, *Theoretical Hydrodynamics* (New York: The Macmillan Company, 1960).

2. V. L. Streeter, *Fluid Dynamics* (New York: McGraw-Hill Book Company, Inc., 1948).

3. A. H. Shapiro, *The Dynamics and Thermodynamics of Compressible Fluid Flow*, Vol. 1 (New York: The Ronald Press Company, 1953). Part III.

PROBLEMS

6-1. Which of the following scalar functions could represent the velocity potential for an ideal incompressible fluid flow?

a) $f = x - 3y$
b) $f = x^2 + y^2$
c) $f = x^2 - y^2$
d) $f = \sin (x + y)$

e) $f = \sin (x - y)$
f) $f = \ln (x + y)$
g) $f = \ln (x - y)$
h) $f = \arctan (y/x)$

Ans. a), c), and h)

6-2. For the fluid flows of Prob. 6-1, what are a) the stream functions and b) the velocity vectors?

Ans. $\psi_a = 3x + y$
$\mathbf{V}_a = -\mathbf{i} + 3\mathbf{j}$

6-3. For the irrotational flows of Prob. 5-6 determine the velocity potentials.

6-4. Given $u = 3x$, $v = -3y$, and $w = 0$. Find the stream function and the velocity potential function for this flow.

6-5. Describe the flow given by

a) $\psi = -20y$
b) $\psi = 10x$
c) $\psi = 5x - 8.66y$
d) $\psi = x^2$

6-6. Given $u = \sin yt + \ln xy$ and $v = \cos xt - y/x$. a) Is continuity satisfied? b) Is the flow irrotational?

Ans. a) Yes, b) No.

6-7. Given $u = 3y$ and $v = 6x$. a) Does a stream function exist? If so, what is the stream function? b) Are the velocity components derivable from a potential function? If so, what is the potential function?

6-8. Given $\psi = 3x - 5y$. a) Is this a potential flow? b) If so, what is the potential function?

Ans. $\phi = -5x - 3y + C$

6-9. Let $u = -2x$ and $v = 2y + 2$. a) Show that continuity is satisfied. b) Show that the flow is irrotational. c) What is the stream function? d) What is the potential function? e) Plot the flow net and compare with that for Example 6-1.

6-10. For the flow of Example 6-1, a) prove that the flow is irrotational and that continuity is satisfied. b) If the pressure at (3,4) is zero, show that the maximum pressure in the flow field is 50ρ.

6-11. Show that, if the speed of a fluid is constant throughout the x–y plane, the streamlines are parallel straight lines.

6-12. Given a stream function $\psi = y - x$, a) what are the x and y components of velocity at (0,0) and (2,1)? b) What is the volumetric flow rate between streamlines passing through these points? c) What is the difference in pressure between these points for a fluid of density 1.5 slugs/ft³?

6–13. Given $u = 2y$ and $v = 2$. *a*) What is the stream function for this flow? *b*) Sketch the streamline pattern in the upper half plane for the constant in the stream function set equal to zero.

6–14. A fluid is between two parallel plates which are a distance B apart. One plate is at rest and the other moves at a velocity V so that the velocity profile between the plates is given by $u = Vy/B$, where u is the fluid speed at a distance y from the plate at rest. What is the stream function which describes this flow?

6–15. Given the velocity potential

$$\phi = \frac{y^3}{3} - x^2 y$$

a) What is the velocity vector which describes the flow? *b*) Show that the vorticity is everywhere zero. *c*) What is the stream function? *d*) Plot the streamlines and the equipotential lines in the right half-plane ($x \geq 0$) for both ψ and $\phi = 0, \pm 5$, and ± 10 to a scale of 1 in. $= 2$ units.

6–16. Plot the streamlines and the equipotential lines in the upper half-plane ($y \geq 0$) for the flow described in Example 6–1. Let both ψ and $\phi = 0, \pm 2, \pm 4$, and ± 6 to a scale of 1 in. $= 1$ unit.

6–17. The general expression in polar form for the potential function for two-dimensional steady flow around a corner of angle α may be written as

$$\phi = r^{\pi/\alpha} \cos \frac{\pi \theta}{\alpha}$$

a) What is the stream function for this flow? *b*) Show that for $\alpha = \pi$, the flow may be represented by $V = -i$. *c*) For $\alpha = \pi/2$, show that the flow is that of Example 6–1.

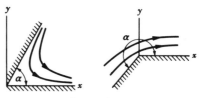

PROB. 6–17.

6–18. What is the magnitude of the velocity at the corner in Prob. 6–17 *a*) for $0 < \alpha < \pi$ and *b*) for $\pi < \alpha < 2\pi$?

Ans.   a) 0; *b*) ∞

6–19. Plot the streamlines and equipotential lines for $\psi = 0, 2, 4$, and 6 and $\phi = 0, \pm 2, \pm 4$, and ± 6, with $\alpha = 3\pi/2$ in Prob. 6–17, to a scale of 1 in. $= 10$ units. Polar graph paper is suggested.

6–20. Show that the vorticity for two-dimensional flow is equal to

$$\frac{\partial^2 \psi}{\partial x^2} + \frac{\partial^2 \psi}{\partial y^2}.$$

6-21. *a*) Draw free-hand, a flow net representing the flow of an ideal incompressible fluid past a 90-deg corner. One equipotential line and two streamlines are shown. *b*) Compare your free-hand sketch with a plot of the streamlines $\psi = 2xy$ and the equipotential lines $\phi = x^2 - y^2$ in Prob. 6-16.

6-22. Suppose Fig. 6-2 represents two-dimensional flow with $V_1 = 5$ ft/sec and $\rho = 1.94$ slugs/ft^3. Estimate the pressure difference between the outer and inner surfaces of the bend.

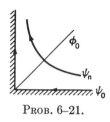

PROB. 6-21.

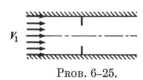

PROB. 6-25.

6-23. From Fig. 6-5, plot the variation in pressure along the bottom of the channel in terms of

$$\frac{\Delta p}{\rho V_1{}^2/2}$$

6-24. The pressure is constant and equal to atmospheric along the upper and lower streamlines for the weir flow beyond the weir plate in Fig. 6-4, and along the upper streamline for the jet issuing from the sluice gate in Fig. 6-5. Explain why the spacing between equipotential lines varies along these streamlines.

6-25. Consider two-dimensional incompressible flow through an orifice in a rectangular duct. *a*) Draw a flow net for ideal fluid flow and make a sketch of the pressure variation along the duct center line. *b*) Draw the streamline pattern for a real fluid flow and make a sketch of the pressure variation along the duct center line. Compare with part *a*).

6-26. Verify that the potential functions for *a*) a source, *b*) a sink, *c*) a doublet, and *d*) an irrotational vortex are harmonic.

6-27. A source of strength 4π is placed at (4,0) and a source of strength 6π is placed at (0,0). *a*) Locate the stagnation point. *b*) What is the velocity vector at (0,8)?

6-28. What are the velocity, the pressure gradient, and the fluid acceleration at the point (2,4) for a two-dimensional source flow of strength 6.28 cfs/ft? Assume $\rho = 1.5$ slugs/ft^3.

6-29. Show that the potential function for a three-dimensional point source of strength Q is $\phi = Q/4\pi r$.

6-30. A line source and a line sink, each of strength 20π cfs/ft, are placed at $y = 0$ and $x = -20$ ft and $x = +20$ ft, respectively, in a uniform flow field with $u_s = 20$ ft/sec. a) What is the stream function for this flow? b) Where are the stagnation points? c) Show that the stream function at the stagnation points is $\psi = 0$. d) What is the velocity field represented by this flow? e) Write the stream function in polar form. f) What is the maximum width of the long thin shape around which the fluid flows? (It flows inside as well.) g) Where is $v = 0$? h) What is the difference between the free-stream pressure and that at $(0,5)$? $\rho = 1.94$ slugs/ft^3.

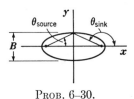

PROB. 6–30.

Ans. a) $\psi = -u_s\, y - \dfrac{q}{2\pi} \arctan \dfrac{y}{x+20} + \dfrac{q}{2\pi} \arctan \dfrac{y}{x-20}$

b) $x = \pm 20.49$ ft, $y = 0$

d) $V = \left[u_s + \dfrac{q}{2\pi}\dfrac{x+20}{(x+20)^2 + y^2} - \dfrac{q}{2\pi}\dfrac{x-20}{(x-20)^2 + y^2} \right] i$

$\quad + \left[\dfrac{10y}{(x+20)^2 + y^2} - \dfrac{10y}{(x-20)^2 + y^2} \right] j$

e) $\psi = -u_s\, r \sin\theta - \dfrac{Q}{2\pi}(\theta_{\text{source}} - \theta_{\text{sink}})$

f) $B = \pi - 2 \arctan(B/40) = 2.992$ ft for small θ_{source}

g) along x and y axes

h) 37.4 psf

6-31. Given the stream function $\psi = 4 \ln(x^2 + y^2)$ representing a two-dimensional vortex, a) what is the magnitude of the velocity at $(1,1)$ and at $(1,3)$? b) What is the difference in pressure intensity between these points for a fluid of density 1.5 slugs/ft^3? c) What is the flow rate in cfs/ft between streamlines passing through these points?

Ans. a) $\sqrt{32}$ and $\sqrt{6.4}$ ft/sec

b) 19.2 psf

c) 6.44 cfs/ft

6-32. For the vortex in Prob. 6–31, a) what are the speeds at $(1,0)$ and $(1,3)$? b) What is the difference in pressure between these points for a fluid of density 1.6 slugs/ft^3? c) What is the flow rate in slugs/sec per ft between streamlines passing through these points?

6-33. A line source in two-dimensional flow of strength q is placed at the origin, and a uniform flow of velocity u_s in the $+x$ direction is added to it to produce flow around a two-dimensional half body (Fig. 6–12). a) Show that the stagnation point is at $x = -q/2\pi u_s$. b) What is the value of the stream function at the stagnation point? c) Show that as $x \to +\infty$, the width of the half body is q/u_s. This is the distance between streamlines for which $\psi = -q/2$.

6-34. Show that the half body of Fig. 6–12 is one-half its maximum width at $x = 0$.

6–35. What is the maximum flow velocity at the surface of the half body of Fig. 6–12? At what value of θ (in polar coordinates) is it located? Give values for $q = 30$ cfs/ft and $u_s = 50$ ft/sec.

6–36. a) Derive an expression for the velocity u along the stagnation streamlines for rectilinear flow past a cylinder of radius R (Fig. 6–15). b) What is the fluid acceleration at $x = -2R$?

6–37. A circular cylinder of radius R is in an infinite ideal fluid which flows past the cylinder with a velocity u_s far from the cylinder (Fig. 6–15). The fluid density is ρ and the free-stream pressure is p_s. a) Show that the resultant force on the cylinder is zero and b) that the force on both the upstream and downstream halves of the cylinder is equal to $2Rp_s - (\rho Ru_s^2/3)$ per unit length of cylinder.

6–38. For what values of θ (Fig. 6–15) is the pressure at the surface of the cylinder the same as the free-stream pressure p_s? (See discussion of the pitot cylinder in Sec. 13–1 and Fig. 13–6.)

6–39. What is the stream function for potential flow past a circular cylinder of radius 0.5 ft normal to a free stream of velocity $u_s = 8$ ft/sec?

6–40. In Prob. 6–39, what is the difference between the maximum and the minimum pressures on the surface of the cylinder for a fluid density of 1.94 slugs/ft³?

6–41. a) What is the strength of the circulation around a cylinder of radius R in a free stream of velocity u_s which will bring the stagnation points together at $\theta = 3\pi/2$? See Fig. 6–16. b) For what values of θ is the pressure on the cylinder equal to the free stream pressure?

6–42. Obtain an expression for the pressure $(p - p_s)/(\rho u_s^2/2)$ in terms of θ, ρ, u_s, R, and T around the surface of a cylinder for steady incompressible flow past the cylinder a) without circulation, b) with stagnation points at $\theta = 5\pi/4$ and $7\pi/4$, and c) with stagnation points coinciding at $\theta = 3\pi/2$. Refer to Fig. 6–16.

6–43. For the three conditions of Prob. 6–42, a) what is the lift force per unit length of cylinder? b) At what values of θ is the pressure on the surface of the cylinder the same as the free-stream pressure p_s?

6–44. Standard air at a free stream velocity of $u_s = 100$ ft/sec flows past a long circular cylinder normal to the flow. A circulation of 200π ft²/sec encircles the cylinder, which has a radius of 1 ft. Find on the surface of the cylinder a) the tangential velocity due to the circulation, b) the maximum air speed, c) the stagnation points, d) the difference between the maximum and the minimum pressure, and e) the lift per foot of length of the cylinder.

6–45. A 6-ft diameter cylinder 10 ft high is rotated about its axis at 120 rpm in a stream of standard air flowing past the cylinder at 30 ft/sec. The rotation produces a circulation 50 per cent as effective as an irrotational vortex having the same peripheral speed at the surface of the cylinder. What is the lift force on the cylinder?

6–46. Suppose the flow pattern of Fig. 6–16 is obtained with flow from *right* to *left*. a) Is the circulation produced by the free vortex in the positive or in the negative sense? b) What would be the potential and the stream functions for this flow?

6–47. The annular space between two long coaxial cylinders is filled with a viscous oil. a) The outer cylinder is rotated at a peripheral speed of V and the inner cylinder is held at rest. Show that the velocity profile in the annular space is that of a rectangular hyperbola (as is true for a free vortex). b) Show that when the inner cylinder is rotated at a peripheral speed of

$$\left[\frac{1}{1 - (R_1/R_2)}\right] V$$

and the outer cylinder is rotated in the same direction at a peripheral speed of

$$\left[\frac{1}{(R_2/R_1) - 1}\right] V$$

the viscous fluid in the annular space between cylinders flows exactly like an ideal fluid in a free vortex. R_1 is the inner and R_2 the outer cylinder radius, respectively.

6–48. The resultant air speed 1200 ft from the center of a tornado is 80 ft/sec. For air of density 0.0022 slug/ft^3, what is the difference in pressure between a point far removed from the tornado and a point 600 ft from its center?

Ans. 28.2 psf

6–49. What is the diameter of a jet of water issuing from a sharp-edged, circular hole, 2 in. in diameter, in the side of a large tank?

6–50. In Fig. 6–20(a), what is the volumetric flow rate per unit width for two-dimensional flow of an incompressible fluid with $b = 0.5$ ft, $B = 1.5$ ft, $\theta = 45$ degrees, and a pressure at B of 8 psig? Neglect viscous effects, and assume $\rho = 1.94$ slugs/ft^3.

Ans. 13.3 ft^3/sec

6–51. Repeat Prob. 6–50 for $\theta = 90$ degrees.

6–52. Repeat Prob. 6–50 for $\theta = 180$ degrees.

6–53. Repeat Prob. 6–50 for a circular duct with a circular hole.

Ans. 5.09 ft^3/sec

6–54. What is the flow rate from a 1.5-ft diameter pipe with a 0.5-ft diameter end cap orifice at its end, when the pressure in the pipe is 8 psig? Water flows without viscous effects.

7

The Boundary Layer in Incompressible Flow

In connection with theories of bird flight, da Vinci (1452–1519) was probably the first to consider air as a resisting medium. Galileo (1564–1642) expressed this quantitatively, though in general incorrectly, in stating that resistance varied directly as the velocity. The calculus of Newton (1642–1727) laid the foundation for the development of the theoretical aspects of fluid mechanics by Euler (1707–1783), Bernoulli (1700–1782), and others. Strangely enough, the results of this classical treatment were in marked contradiction to experience, insofar as the existence of drag forces were concerned.

The earliest experimental work on fluid resistance, following some large-scale experiments by Newton on spheres dropped from a cathedral, was done in the field of ballistics. Here, however, the resistance was largely due to compressible effects rather than viscous effects. Classical hydro- and aerodynamic theory of ideal fluids always produced the same results—zero pressure drop in a pipe and zero drag on any shape in a steady-fluid flow. This last is known as D'Alambert's paradox. It was not until 1904 that Prandtl in Germany was able to reconcile the two schools of thought. He introduced the concept of a thin boundary layer next to a body in which the viscous effects were concentrated. Beyond the boundary layer the viscous effects were considered to be negligible, and the flow could be treated as that of an ideal fluid (Fig. 7–1).

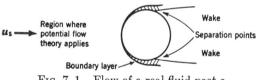

Fig. 7–1. Flow of a real fluid past a circular cylinder.

Potential flow was introduced in the preceding chapter, and results of the ideal fluid theory may be applied to real fluids if the body past which fluid flows is considered to be enlarged by the thickness of the boundary layer, or deformed by separation effects. The present chapter is devoted to a study of the growth of the boundary layer and boundary layer separation.

Boundary layer theory is of extreme importance in modern fluid mechanics and is essential to an understanding of convective heat transfer.

Definitive treatments of boundary layer theory have been given by Schlichting [1,2, and 3] and Prandtl [4]. An introduction to thermal boundary layers is given in Chapter 16.

7–1. DESCRIPTION OF THE BOUNDARY LAYER

The development of a boundary layer can perhaps be best described by a study of flow along a flat plate. Consider a uniform flow of an incompressible fluid at a free-stream velocity u_s approaching the plate (Fig. 7–2).

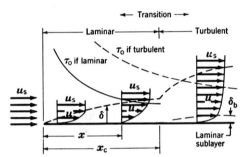

FIG. 7–2. Flow of a viscous fluid along a
flat plate.

When the fluid reaches the leading edge, large shear stresses are set up near the plate surface, and the fluid particles at the plate surface are brought to rest and those for a short distance normal to the plate are retarded because of viscous shear. The region of retarded flow is called the *boundary layer*, and its thickness is designated as δ. For some longitudinal distance x_c, the flow within the boundary layer is laminar. Downstream from this point the boundary layer flow becomes unstable and eventually becomes turbulent. If the velocity u_s for a given fluid is increased, x_c is decreased such that the product $u_s x_c$ remains essentially constant. The value of this constant varies directly with the kinematic viscosity of the fluid, and if different fluids are used, the ratio $u_s x_c/\nu$ is approximately constant. This ratio is one form of the Reynolds number, which is discussed in more detail in Chapter 8.

The boundary layer thickens in the direction of flow, and thus the velocity change from zero at the plate surface to u_s at a distance δ takes place over an increasingly greater distance normal to the plate. The rate of change of velocity determines the velocity gradient at the plate surface and thus the shear stresses as well. This shear stress is

$$\tau_o = \mu \left(\frac{du}{dy}\right)_{y=0} \qquad [2\text{–}7]$$

over the entire plate surface. As the laminar boundary layer thickens, instabilities set in, and these are not damped out, so that a turbulent boundary layer forms. These instabilities were originally predicted by Tollmein and Schlichting in Germany in the early 1930's and verified experimentally by Dryden, Schubauer, and Skramstad in the United States in 1940. The cross components of velocity (normal to the main flow) produce a mixing of the fluid with an accompanying momentum exchange which is absent in laminar flow. For the turbulent boundary layer, the resulting velocity profile is more rounded with a higher velocity gradient at the plate surface, and the boundary layer is thicker and the shear stresses greater in this instance. Actually, a laminar sublayer exists between the plate surface and the turbulent portion of the boundary layer. This is reasonable to expect, since the inertia forces are very small because of the very low velocities near the plate surface, and viscous forces are relatively large, and complete mixing is inhibited by the presence of the plate.

The transition from a laminar to a turbulent boundary layer depends on the roughness of the plate and the turbulence level in the free stream, in addition to the ratio $u_s x_c / \nu$. Either plate roughness; a high turbulence level in the free stream; or, if the free stream is not uniform, a decelerating free stream will cause transition to take place nearer the leading edge of the plate (at a smaller value of x_c). A surface is considered to be hydrodynamically smooth if its roughness elements have no influence on the flow outside the laminar sublayer, but are drowned out by it. Conversely, a surface is considered rough if its roughness elements do have an effect on the flow outside the laminar sublayer. An excellent review of studies on the transition from laminar to turbulent flow was given by Dryden [5].

The drag on the plate due to viscous shear is indicated by the area under the curves of shear stress in Fig. 7-2.. The total drag is obviously dependent upon the location of the transition from laminar to turbulent flow within the boundary layer because of the higher shear in the turbulent region. If transition takes place near the leading edge, the total drag is greater than if transition takes place farther downstream. Methods have been developed to inhibit transition and thus reduce drag. These methods include boundary layer suction through a porous surface and a careful design of the shape of the surface (for other than a flat plate).

The longer the flat plate, the greater is the total drag, but the *average* shear stress decreases with length. If, however, the boundary layer changes from laminar to turbulent, the average shear stress will increase, but will then decrease as the plate length increases. For long plates on which the laminar portion of the boundary layer extends for only a relatively short distance, it is customary to assume a turbulent boundary layer over the entire plate.

Up to this point in our discussion, flow past a flat plate has involved no pressure variations either parallel or normal to the plate. In both the laminar and turbulent portions of the boundary layer, the velocity at a fixed distance y_1 from the plate decreases with x, but when transition occurs, this velocity will increase. Only at the plate surface itself is the velocity zero (Fig. 7–3).

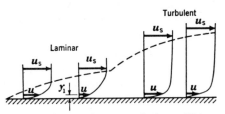

FIG. 7–3. Velocity variation within boundary layer at a fixed distance from a plate.

The pressure gradient is not always zero; it is determined for given boundaries by a solution of the potential flow problem for those boundaries (see Chapter 6). For example, for flow in converging sections the pressure decreases, and for flow in diverging sections the pressure increases in the direction of flow. Flow in a direction of increasing pressure is called flow in a positive, or adverse, pressure gradient and occurs in flow around curved boundaries and towards a stagnation point as well as in diverging ducts. In these instances, the pressure is increased at the expense of a decrease in kinetic energy or velocity, and velocities at a fixed distance from the surface may decrease to zero. When this happens, the boundary layer separates from the surface, and the phenomenon is known as *boundary layer separation*. The separation point is followed by a region called the *wake*, in which intense eddies exist with an accompanying increase in drag or loss of energy.

For flow past a curved surface, the velocity profile has an inflection (change in curvature) beginning where the pressure gradient becomes positive (Fig. 7–4). The particle at y_1 has a decreasing velocity as it flows

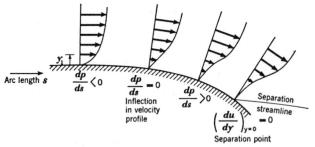

FIG. 7–4. Flow past a curved surface.

along the surface, and it finally comes to rest where the boundary layer separation occurs. If the boundary layer is laminar in the region of the adverse pressure gradient, the velocity at y_1 would be less than if the boundary layer were turbulent at y_1 (Fig. 7–3). Hence the particle in laminar flow would have less kinetic energy and would come to rest farther upstream than if the flow were turbulent in the boundary layer. Separation, then, is retarded if the boundary layer can be made to become turbulent. If drag is due to viscous shear, it is desirable to retard the formation of turbulence in the boundary layer. If drag is largely due to low pressures in the wake, it is desirable to enhance the formation of turbulence in the boundary layer so that the separation point is moved downstream. This retarded separation will create a smaller wake.

Flow in a pipe is similar to flow along a flat plate, except that a negative pressure gradient (pressure drop in the flow direction) exists for incompressible flow in a pipe. If fluid is assumed to enter a pipe in such a way that separation of streamlines from the pipe entrance is avoided, the velocity profile at entrance is quite flat. Thus a boundary layer will grow along the pipe walls. At some point the boundary layers from the walls will meet at the center of the pipe. Beyond this point the velocity profile will not change form, and the flow is called fully developed flow. Again, the velocity gradient and the wall shear are greatest at entrance, and decrease to a steady value at and beyond the fully developed region (see Sec. 10–2). In the entrance region or length, the center-line velocity must increase, since if some fluid is retarded within the boundary layer, continuity requires that the velocity outside the boundary layer be increased. The growth of the boundary layer in pipes is illustrated in Fig. 7–5.

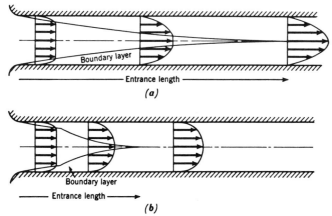

Fig. 7–5. Growth of boundary layer in a pipe (not to scale); a) laminar flow and b) turbulent flow.

When water with a free surface flows over a spillway, the boundary layer builds up in thickness as the water flows down the spillway and rapidly becomes turbulent. When the boundary-layer thickness equals the water depth, air becomes entrained in the water because of the turbulence, and the water becomes frothy in appearance.

7–2. THE PRANDTL BOUNDARY LAYER EQUATIONS

A solution of the Navier-Stokes equations (Eq. 5–39) in simplified form and the continuity equation (Eq. 5–4) for steady, two-dimensional flow in a laminar boundary layer for flow along a flat plate parallel to the flow was made originally by Blasius in 1908 [1]. The boundary layer thickness was assumed to be small as compared with any other characteristic dimension including the radius of curvature (if any) of the boundary. Only those terms in the Navier-Stokes equations of the largest order of magnitude in each equation were retained; those of a lesser order of magnitude were neglected. The simplified Navier-Stokes equations and the continuity equation for two-dimensional flow are known as the *Prandtl boundary layer equations* (see Appendix II for their derivation). With x and u taken parallel to the boundary and y and v normal to it, they may be written as

$$u \frac{\partial u}{\partial x} + v \frac{\partial u}{\partial y} = -\frac{1}{\rho} \frac{\partial p}{\partial x} + \nu \frac{\partial^2 u}{\partial y^2}$$

$$\frac{\partial p}{\partial y} = 0$$

$$\frac{\partial u}{\partial x} + \frac{\partial v}{\partial y} = 0$$

The second condition ($\partial p/\partial y = 0$) implies that the pressure is constant throughout the boundary layer at any given location. The Bernoulli equation applied to the flow outside the boundary layer determines the pressure within the boundary layer at any location. For flow parallel to a flat plate with a constant free stream velocity, the pressure is also constant, so that $\partial p/\partial x = 0$ in the absence of gravity. The Prandtl boundary layer equations then become

$$u \frac{\partial u}{\partial x} + v \frac{\partial u}{\partial y} = \nu \frac{\partial^2 u}{\partial y^2} \quad \text{and} \quad \frac{\partial u}{\partial x} + \frac{\partial v}{\partial y} = 0$$

with boundary conditions at $y = 0$, $u = v = 0$; at $y = \infty$, $u = u_s$.

Solutions of these partial differential equations have been obtained by transforming them into total differential equations [1, 6]. Results of the calculations are given in Table 7–1 and in Fig. 7–8 together with results of approximate methods of analyzing boundary layer flow by the use of the momentum theorem.

7–3. THE MOMENTUM EQUATION FOR THE BOUNDARY LAYER

Items of quantitative interest are the boundary layer thickness and the boundary shear. The shear depends on whether the boundary layer is laminar or turbulent, and thus the transition point becomes of interest as well. Exact solutions of the hydrodynamic equations of motion (the Navier-Stokes equations) for a few limited conditions have been carried out, but are quite complicated. An approximate and surprisingly accurate method introduced by von Karman in 1921 will be described, since it makes use of the momentum theorem already discussed in Chapter 5.

The boundary layer thickness may be expressed in a number of ways.

1. One definition refers to the actual thickness δ of the region of retarded flow, and this definition is useful for analytical calculations.

2. Since the velocity u within the boundary layer approaches the free-stream velocity u_s asymptotically (Fig. 7–2), in experimental measurements of boundary layer velocity profiles the boundary layer thickness δ' is commonly defined as the distance from the boundary to the point where $u = 0.99u_s$.

3. A *displacement thickness* $\delta*$ is defined as the distance the actual boundary would have to be displaced in order that the actual flow rate would be the same as that of an ideal fluid past the displaced boundary. It may be expressed as

$$\delta* = \frac{1}{u_s} \int_0^\delta (u_s - u)\, dy = \int_0^\delta \left(1 - \frac{u}{u_s}\right) dy \qquad (7\text{–}1)$$

4. A *momentum thickness* δ_i is defined as a distance from the actual boundary such that the momentum flux through this distance δ_i is the same as the deficit of momentum flux through the actual boundary layer. This may be expressed as

$$(\rho \delta_i\, u_s)\, u_s = \int_0^\delta \rho(u_s - u)\, u\, dy$$

so that

$$\delta_i = \frac{1}{u_s^2} \int_0^\delta (u_s - u)\, u\, dy$$

or

$$\delta_i = \int_0^\delta \left(1 - \frac{u}{u_s}\right) \frac{u}{u_s}\, dy \qquad (7\text{–}2)$$

If u/u_s is expressed in terms of y, then $\delta*$ and δ_i can be expressed in terms of δ. The value of δ, in turn, may be found from a solution of the boundary layer equations. Definition sketches for the displacement and the momentum thickness of the boundary layer are shown in Fig. 7–6.

The momentum equation for a boundary layer along a flat surface may be derived by applying the momentum theorem to a region of unit width, of infinitesimal length dx, and of height y_2.

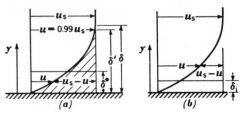

FIG. 7–6. Boundary layer thicknesses defined; *a*) displacement thickness (rectangular area $u_s\delta^*$ equals crosshatched area) and *b*) momentum thickness.

In Fig. 7–7 the mass-flow rate and momentum flux into and out of the region *abcd* are indicated. The mass flow through *bc* is the difference between that through *cd* and *ab*, from continuity. Since streamlines are not exactly parallel to the boundary (Fig. 5–13), some fluid will pass through a line such as *bc* parallel to the boundary. The *x* component of velocity of

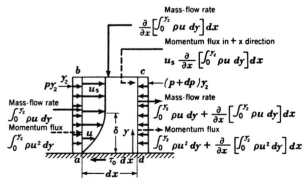

FIG. 7–7. Infinitesimal length of boundary layer.

this mass flow is u_s, and the momentum flux is then as shown. The external forces py_2, $(p + dp)\, y_2$, and $\tau_0\, dx$ are as shown. The pressure is commonly considered to be invariant with y at a given section. Equation 5–14, the momentum equation, becomes

$$\Sigma F_x = \text{net momentum flux out of the region } abcd$$

and thus

$$py_2 - \tau_0\, dx - (p + dp)\, y_2 = \frac{\partial}{\partial x}\left(\int_0^{y_2} \rho u^2\, dy\right) dx - u_s \frac{\partial}{\partial x}\left(\int_0^{y_2} \rho u\, dy\,\right) dx$$

which, when simplified, becomes[1]

$$\tau_0 + y_2 \frac{dp}{dx} = \rho \frac{d}{dx} \int_0^{y_2} (u_s - u)\, u\, dy - \rho \frac{du_s}{dx} \int_0^{y_2} u\, dy \qquad (7\text{–}3)$$

[1]Total derivatives are now used since the quantities vary only with x.

The second term on the left-hand side of this equation may be expressed in terms of the free-stream velocity u_s by applying the Bernoulli equation to the region outside the boundary layer. This equation is valid for ideal incompressible fluid flow and is assumed valid even for real fluids beyond the boundary layer.

$$\rho \frac{u_s^2}{2} + p = \text{constant}$$

or, when differentiated with respect to x,

$$\rho u_s \frac{du_s}{dx} + \frac{dp}{dx} = 0$$

so that
$$y_2 \frac{dp}{dx} = -y_2 \, \rho u_s \frac{du_s}{dx} = -\rho \frac{du_s}{dx} \int_0^{y_2} u_s \, dy$$

Then Eq. 7–3 becomes

$$\tau_0 = \rho \frac{d}{dx} \int_0^\delta (u_s - u) \, u \, dy + \rho \frac{du_s}{dx} \int_0^\delta (u_s - u) \, dy \qquad (7\text{–}4a)$$

The limits of integration have been changed from y_2 to δ, since both integrands vanish beyond δ because of the $(u_s - u)$ term. Equation 7–4a may be written in terms of the displacement thickness δ^* and the momentum thickness δ_i.

$$\tau_0 = \rho \frac{d}{dx} (u_s^2 \, \delta_i) + \rho u_s \frac{du_s}{dx} \delta^* \qquad (7\text{–}4b)$$

For flow past a flat plate with no pressure gradient (u_s is constant) this becomes

$$\tau_0 = \rho \frac{d}{dx} \int_0^\delta (u_s - u) \, u \, dy \qquad (7\text{–}5)$$

and this corresponds with the result of Example 5–7, which can be obtained directly and may be written as

$$F = \int_0^x \tau_0 \, dx = \rho \int_0^\delta (u_s - u) \, u \, dy$$

7–4. THE FLAT PLATE IN A UNIFORM FREE STREAM WITH NO PRESSURE GRADIENTS

Laminar boundary layer. The boundary layer thickness, the local shear or local friction coefficient, and the average shear or average friction coefficient over any length of plate may be obtained for any prescribed shape of velocity profile within the boundary layer. The profiles may be assumed to be similar at successive x-positions, so that

$$\frac{u}{u_s} = f \left(\frac{y}{\delta} \right)$$

This assumption has been verified experimentally. The function f is a judiciously chosen expression which satisfies sufficient boundary conditions.

Three equations for f drived from $u = a + by + cy^2 + dy^3$ are given in the following tabulation, together with the boundary conditions imposed in each instance.

BOUNDARY CONDITIONS		EQUATION	
At $y = 0$	At $y = \delta$		
$u = 0$	$u = u_s$	$u/u_s = y/\delta$	(7-6)
$u = 0$	$u = u_s,\ du/dy = 0$	$u/u_s = 2(y/\delta) - (y/\delta)^2$	(7-7)
$u = 0,\ d^2u/dy^2 = 0$	$u = u_s,\ du/dy = 0$	$u/u_s = (3/2)(y/\delta) - (1/2)(y/\delta)^3$	(7-8)

The condition $d^2u/dy^2 = 0$ at $y = 0$ is obtained from Prandtl's simplification of the Navier-Stokes equations relating inertia, pressure, and viscous forces, and infers that since the velocity in the immediate neighborhood of the wall is very small, only shear forces act on the fluid. This assumption in turn requires that the shear stress is constant for all values of y very near the wall, and thus du/dy is constant and $d^2u/dy^2 = 0$.

The boundary layer thickness δ is obtained by equating the value of boundary shear stress in Eq. 7-5 to its definition, $\tau_0 = \mu\,(du/dy)_{y=0}$.

$$\tau_0 = \rho\,\frac{d}{dx}\int_0^\delta (u_s - u)\,u\,dy = \mu\left(\frac{du}{dy}\right)_{y=0}$$

Using the velocity profile given by Eq. 7-8, this is

$$u_s^2\rho\,\frac{d}{dx}\int_0^\delta \left(1 - \frac{u}{u_s}\right)\frac{u}{u_s}\,dy = \mu\left(\frac{3}{2}\frac{u_s}{\delta}\right)$$

or

$$\frac{39}{280}\rho u_s^2\,\frac{d\delta}{dx} = \frac{3}{2}\mu\,\frac{u_s}{\delta}$$

A separation of variables gives

$$\delta\,d\delta = \frac{140}{13}\frac{\mu}{\rho u_s}\,dx$$

and integration gives

$$\delta = 4.64\sqrt{\frac{\mu x}{\rho u_s}} + C$$

where $C = 0$, since when $x = 0$, $\delta = 0$. In dimensionless form,

$$\frac{\delta}{x} = \frac{4.64}{\sqrt{u_s\,\rho x/\mu}} = \frac{4.64}{\sqrt{u_s\,x/\nu}} \tag{7-9}$$

The displacement thickness, from Eq. 7-1, is

$$\delta^* = \int_0^\delta \left(1 - \frac{u}{u_s}\right)dy$$

and for the profile given by Eq. 7-8,

$$\delta^* = 0.375\,\delta$$

The local skin-friction coefficient c_f is defined as the ratio of the local wall shear stress τ_0 to the dynamic pressure of the free stream.

$$c_f = \frac{\tau_0}{\rho u_s^2/2} \qquad (7\text{--}10a)$$

where

$$\tau_0 = \frac{3}{2}\mu\frac{u_s}{\delta} = \frac{0.323\,\rho u_s^2}{\sqrt{u_s\,x/\nu}}$$

so that

$$c_f = \frac{0.646}{\sqrt{u_s\,x/\nu}} \qquad (7\text{--}10b)$$

The average skin-friction coefficient over any length of plate x is found by its definition, which is the ratio of the total shear force on the plate to the product of the dynamic pressure of the free stream times the area of the plate (which is x for a unit width).

$$C_f = \frac{\text{drag per unit width}}{(\rho u_s^2/2)\,x} = \frac{\int_0^x \tau_0\,dx}{(\rho u_s^2/2)\,x}$$

and when $\tau_0 = 0.323\,\rho u_s^2/\sqrt{u_s\,x/\nu}$ is substituted and the integration performed,

$$C_f = \frac{1.292}{\sqrt{u_s\,x/\nu}} \qquad (7\text{--}11)$$

which is exactly twice the local value at any point x.

A comparison of the values of δ/x, C_f, and δ^*/x, for the three velocity profiles assumed in Eqs. 7–6, 7–7, and 7–8, with a solution by Blasius of a simplified form of the Navier-Stokes equations (known as Prandtl's boundary layer equations), is shown in Table 7–1. As previously mentioned, the ratio $u_s\,x/\nu$ is a form of the Reynolds number based on the length x, and may be designated as Re_x.

A comparison of Eqs. 7–7, 7–8, and the velocity profile obtained from the Blasius solution is shown in Fig. 7–8.

TABLE 7–1
RESULTS OF CALCULATIONS FOR LAMINAR BOUNDARY LAYER

Velocity Profile	$\dfrac{\delta}{x}$	C_f	$\dfrac{\delta^*}{x}$
$\dfrac{u}{u_s} = \dfrac{y}{\delta}$	$\dfrac{3.46}{\mathrm{Re}_x^{1/2}}$	$\dfrac{1.156}{\mathrm{Re}_x^{1/2}}$	$\dfrac{1.73}{\mathrm{Re}_x^{1/2}}$
$\dfrac{u}{u_s} = 2\left(\dfrac{y}{\delta}\right) - \left(\dfrac{y}{\delta}\right)^2$	$\dfrac{5.47}{\mathrm{Re}_x^{1/2}}$	$\dfrac{1.462}{\mathrm{Re}_x^{1/2}}$	$\dfrac{1.83}{\mathrm{Re}_x^{1/2}}$
$\dfrac{u}{u_s} = \dfrac{3}{2}\left(\dfrac{y}{\delta}\right) - \dfrac{1}{2}\left(\dfrac{y}{\delta}\right)^3$	$\dfrac{4.64}{\mathrm{Re}_x^{1/2}}$	$\dfrac{1.292}{\mathrm{Re}_x^{1/2}}$	$\dfrac{1.74}{\mathrm{Re}_x^{1/2}}$
(Blasius)	$\dfrac{4.91}{\mathrm{Re}_x^{1/2}}$	$\dfrac{1.328}{\mathrm{Re}_x^{1/2}}$	$\dfrac{1.73}{\mathrm{Re}_x^{1/2}}$

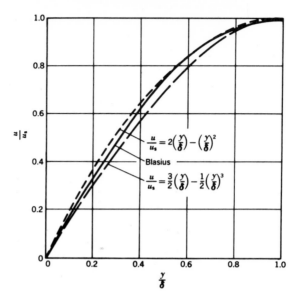

FIG. 7–8. Laminar boundary layer velocity profiles.

There is remarkable agreement between the Blasius solutions and those based on assumed velocity profiles applied to the momentum equation of the boundary layer.

The qualitative results of Sec. 7–1 concerning the growth of the boundary layer and the decrease in shear along the plate are indicated quantitatively in Table 7–1. This table shows the following:

1. The laminar boundary layer thickness, however defined, increases as the square root of the distance x from the leading edge and inversely as the square root of the free-stream velocity u_s.

2. The local and average skin-drag coefficients vary inversely with the square root of both x and u_s.

3. The total drag ($F = C_f \rho u_s{}^2 x/2$ per unit width) varies as the 1.5 power of the free-stream velocity and the square root of the length x.

The boundary layer is laminar for values of $u_s x/\nu$ (the Reynolds number based on x) up to about 300,000 to 500,000, depending on the plate roughness and level of turbulence in the free stream, as mentioned in Sec. 7–1.

EXAMPLE 7–1. Standard air flows past a flat plate at a free-stream velocity of 20 ft/sec. What is the thickness of the boundary layer 1 ft from the leading edge of the plate?

Solution: $\mathrm{Re}_x = u_s x/\nu = (20)\,(1)/1.57 \times 10^{-4} = 12.7 \times 10^4$, and thus the boundary layer may be assumed laminar.

$$\frac{\delta}{x} = \frac{4.91}{\text{Re}_x^{1/2}} = \frac{4.91}{356} = 0.0138$$

The boundary layer thickness is then

$$\delta = (0.0138)(12) = 0.165 \text{ in.}$$

and the displacement thickness is

$$\delta^* = (1.73/356)(12) = 0.058 \text{ in.}$$

Turbulent boundary layer. The thickness of the turbulent boundary layer may be obtained from Eq. 7–5 in a manner similar to that used to obtain the thickness of the laminar boundary layer. The analysis, however, is not so rigorous as that for the laminar case. A different shape of the velocity profile within the boundary layer will have to be used, of course, and the wall shear will be expressed in a form obtained from measurements on turbulent flow in pipes. We will assume that the boundary layer is turbulent from the leading edge of the plate. This is not strictly correct, but for long plates where the laminar boundary layer exists over a relatively small percentage of the total length, the error in making this assumption is very small. Also, a turbulent boundary layer is often artificially generated in many model tests by mounting a wire near the leading edge of the plate or by roughening the leading portion of the plate surface. This reduces the laminar portion of the boundary layer to a negligibly small region. In instances where the laminar portion of the boundary layer is not negligible, the results for the laminar and the turbulent portions will be combined.

Prandtl suggested that the velocity varies as the seventh root of the distance from the wall.

$$\frac{u}{u_s} = \left(\frac{y}{\delta}\right)^{1/7} \tag{7–12}$$

This equation cannot apply at the wall surface, since the velocity gradient at that point is infinite ($du/dy = u_s/7\ \delta^{1/7}\ y^{6/7}$), and this would indicate an infinite shear, which is not physically possible. The laminar sublayer adjacent to the wall is assumed to have a linear velocity profile, and this profile becomes tangent to the seventh-root profile at the outer edge of the laminar sublayer (at $y = \delta_b$) in Fig. 7–9.

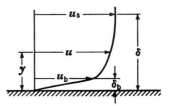

FIG. 7–9. Turbulent boundary layer with laminar sublayer.

The empirical expression of Blasius for the boundary shear is

$$\tau_0 = 0.0225\ \rho u_s^2 \left(\frac{\nu}{u_s\ \delta}\right)^{1/4} \tag{7–13}$$

which was obtained from pipe-flow measurements by assuming that if a pipe were unrolled to form a flat surface, the boundary layer thickness δ would correspond to one-half the pipe diameter.

Equation 7–5 becomes

$$0.0225 \, \rho u_s^2 \left(\frac{\nu}{u_s \, \delta}\right)^{1/4} = \rho u_s^2 \frac{d}{dx} \int_0^\delta \left[1 - \left(\frac{y}{\delta}\right)^{1/7}\right] \left(\frac{y}{\delta}\right)^{1/7} dy$$

Integration and separation of variables gives

$$\delta^{1/4} \, d\delta = 0.232 \left(\frac{\nu}{u_s}\right)^{1/4} dx$$

so that a completely turbulent boundary layer has a thickness given by

$$\frac{\delta}{x} = \frac{0.371}{(u_s \, x/\nu)^{1/5}} \tag{7–14}$$

The displacement thickness is $\delta/8$, or

$$\frac{\delta^*}{x} = \frac{0.046}{(u_s \, x/\nu)^{1/5}} \tag{7–15}$$

and the momentum thickness is $7\delta/72$, or

$$\frac{\delta_i}{x} = \frac{0.036}{(u_s \, x/\nu)^{1/5}} \tag{7–16}$$

As before, the local skin-friction coefficient c_f is

$$c_f = \frac{\tau_0}{\rho u_s^2/2} \tag{7–17a}$$

where, for the turbulent boundary layer,

$$\tau_0 = 0.0225 \, \rho u_s^2 \left(\frac{\nu}{u_s \, \delta}\right)^{1/4} = 0.0288 \, \rho u_s^2 \left(\frac{\nu}{u_s \, x}\right)^{1/5}$$

and thus

$$c_f = \frac{0.0576}{(u_s \, x/\nu)^{1/5}} \tag{7–17b}$$

The average skin-friction coefficient over a finite length of plate x is

$$C_f = \frac{\text{drag per unit width}}{(\rho u_s^2/2) \, x} = \frac{\int_0^x \tau_0 \, dx}{(\rho u_s^2/2) \, x}$$

so that for $5 \times 10^5 < u_s \, x/\nu < 10^7$,

$$C_f = \frac{0.072}{(u_s \, x/\nu)^{1/5}} \tag{7–18}$$

Experimental results for completely turbulent boundary layers indicate that 0.074 is a better value than 0.072. Below the lower limit of the given range of Reynolds number ($\mathrm{Re}_x = u_s \, x/\nu$), the boundary layer is normally laminar, and Blasius' wall shear equation (Eq. 7–13) applies only to the upper limit given.

For $10^7 < u_s \, x/\nu < 10^9$ (Reynolds number between 10^7 and 10^9) an empirical equation obtained by Schlichting [1] agrees quite well with measured data.

Schlichting's equation is

$$C_f = \frac{0.455}{(\log_{10} \text{Re}_x)^{2.58}} \tag{7-19}$$

Other semiempirical equations relating the skin-friction coefficient C_f with Reynolds number $u_s\, x/\nu$ have been given in the literature.

It is seen that for a turbulent boundary layer:

1. The boundary layer thickness increases as the $\frac{4}{5}$ power of the distance from the leading edge, as compared with $x^{1/2}$ for a laminar boundary layer.

2. The local and average skin-friction coefficients vary inversely as the fifth root of both x and u_s, as compared with the square root for a laminar boundary layer.

3. The total drag varies as the $\frac{9}{5}$ power of the free-stream velocity ($u_s{}^{9/5}$) and the $\frac{4}{5}$ power of the plate length ($x^{4/5}$), as compared with $u_s{}^{1.5}$ and $x^{0.5}$ for a laminar boundary layer.

The laminar sublayer. The thickness of the laminar sublayer may be found in terms of the boundary layer thickness δ by considering the linear velocity profile with a resulting constant shear throughout the laminar sublayer. At δ_b the velocity is u_b (Fig. 7-9). The wall shear stress is

$$\tau_0 = \mu \left(\frac{du}{dy}\right)_{y=0} = \mu \left(\frac{u}{y}\right)_{0 \le y \le \delta_b} = \mu\, \frac{u_b}{\delta_b} = 0.0225\, \rho u_s{}^2 \left(\frac{\nu}{u_s\, \delta}\right)^{1/4}$$

from Eq. 7-13, and this also is the value of the shear throughout the laminar sublayer. From this expression

$$\frac{\delta_b}{\delta} = \frac{u_b}{u_s} \frac{1}{0.0225} \left(\frac{\nu}{u_s\, \delta}\right)^{3/4}$$

The seventh-root velocity profile in the turbulent region of the boundary layer must meet the linear velocity profile in the laminar sublayer. At the junction, Eq. 7-12 becomes

$$\frac{\delta_b}{\delta} = \left(\frac{u_b}{u_s}\right)^7$$

Equating these two expressions for δ_b/δ gives

$$\frac{u_b}{u_s} = \frac{1.88}{(u_s\, \delta/\nu)^{1/8}} = \frac{2.13}{(u_s\, x/\nu)^{1/10}}$$

so that

$$\frac{\delta_b}{\delta} = \frac{198}{(u_s x/\nu)^{7/10}} \tag{7-20}$$

Both laminar and turbulent boundary layers. A boundary layer is generally laminar to begin with and changes to a turbulent condition at some downstream point. The total drag, as well as the drag coefficient, may be calculated by adding the drag owing to the laminar boundary layer to the drag owing to the turbulent portion of the boundary layer, assuming that the turbulent portion beyond the transition point acts as though it were turbulent from the leading edge of the plate.

The Prandtl-Schlichting skin-friction equation for a smooth plate is

$$C_f = \frac{0.455}{(\log_{10} \mathrm{Re}_x)^{2.58}} - \frac{A}{\mathrm{Re}_x} \qquad (7\text{--}21)$$

where the value A depends on the critical value of the Reynolds number $(u_s\, x_c/\nu)$ at which the laminar boundary layer becomes turbulent. Values of A for various values of $u_s\, x_c/\nu$ are

$u_s\, x_c/\nu$	10^5	5×10^5	10^6
A	360	1700	3300

Equations 7–18, 7–19, 7–21, and the Blasius equation from Table 7–1 are shown in Fig. 7–10. Measurements by a number of experimenters are in good agreement with the curves shown.

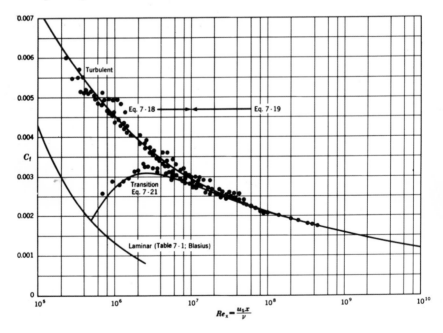

FIG. 7–10. Drag coefficients for a smooth flat plate. Measurements by Wieselsberger, Gerber, Froude, Kempf, and Schoenherr.

For a laminar boundary layer, the roughness of the plate surface does not affect the aforementioned results, although the boundary layer will become turbulent more readily. For a turbulent boundary layer the results apply for smooth plates and for plates whose roughness elements are such that the plate behaves as a smooth plate. Schlichting gives an expression for the maximum height of roughness elements in order that a surface may be still considered hydrodynamically smooth. This is

$$k_{\mathrm{adm}} \leqq 100 \, \frac{\nu}{u_s} \tag{7-22}$$

In all instances of flow along flat plates parallel to the flow, the drag force D is

$$D = C_f \, (\rho u_s{}^2/2) \, A \tag{7-23}$$

where C_f is the skin friction drag coefficient, ρ is the fluid density, u_s is the free stream velocity, and A is the area of the plate subjected to the shearing action of the fluid. The skin friction drag for many surfaces may be approximated by calculating the skin friction drag on an equivalent flat plate.

REFERENCES

1. H. Schlichting, *Boundary Layer Theory* (Translated by J. Kestin), 4th ed. (New York: McGraw-Hill Book Company, Inc., 1960).

2. H. Schlichting, "Boundary-Layer Theory," Section 9 of *Handbook of Fluid Dynamics*, edited by V. L. Streeter (New York: McGraw-Hill Book Company, Inc., 1961).

3. H. Schlichting, "Three-Dimensional Boundary Layer Flow," Proc. Ninth Convention, International Association for Hydraulic Research, Dubrovnic, Yugoslavia, 1961, pp. 1262–1290.

4. L. Prandtl, *Essentials of Fluid Dynamics* (New York: Hafner Publishing Company, 1952).

5. H. L. Dryden, "Transition from Laminar to Turbulent Flow," Section A of *Turbulent Flows and Heat Transfer*, edited by C. C. Lin (Princeton, New Jersey: Princeton University Press, 1959).

6. E. R. G. Eckert and R. M. Drake, *Heat and Mass Transfer* (New York: McGraw-Hill Book Company, Inc., 1959).

PROBLEMS

7-1. Derive Prandtl's equation for a laminar boundary layer by applying the momentum theorem to an element of incompressible fluid of length dx and height dy in the x-y plane in a direction parallel to a flat surface. With a pressure gradient, this is

$$u \, \frac{\partial u}{\partial x} + v \, \frac{\partial u}{\partial y} = -\frac{1}{\rho} \frac{dp}{dx} + \nu \, \frac{\partial^2 u}{\partial y^2}$$

$$\left[\tau_x + \frac{\partial}{\partial y}(\tau_x)dy\right]dx \qquad (\rho v + \frac{\partial(\rho v)}{\partial y}dy)(u + \frac{\partial u}{\partial y}dy\cdot)dx$$

$$p\,dy \rightarrow \boxed{\begin{matrix}dx\\dy\cdot\end{matrix}} \leftarrow(p+dp)dy \quad (\rho u\,dy)u\ \boxed{}\ (\rho u + \frac{\partial(\rho u)}{\partial x}dx)(u + \frac{\partial u}{\partial x}dx)dy$$

$$u \rightarrow$$

$$\overleftarrow{\tau_x\,dx} \qquad\qquad (\rho v\,dx)u$$

Forces on fluid element   Momentum flux into and out of
                                 fluid element

PROB. 7–1.

7–2. Show from the Prandtl boundary layer equations that at a boundary surface, the velocity profile for a laminar boundary layer has an infinite radius of curvature. That is, at $y = 0$, $\partial^2 u/\partial y^2 = 0$.

7–3. Carry out in detail the steps leading from Eq. 7–3 to Eq. 7–4a.

7–4. Determine the ratios of displacement and momentum thickness to the boundary layer thickness (δ^*/δ and δ_i/δ) for the following velocity profiles: a) $u/u_s = y/\delta$; b) $u/u_s = \frac{3}{2}(y/\delta) - \frac{1}{2}(y/\delta)^3$; c) $u/u_s = (y/\delta)^{1/7}$.

Ans. a) $\frac{1}{2}$ *and* $\frac{1}{6}$

7–5. Assume the velocity profile in the laminar boundary layer along a flat plate is given by the expression

$$\frac{u}{u_s} = \sin\left(\frac{\pi y}{2\delta}\right)$$

a) Derive an expression for the boundary layer thickness and for the average drag coefficient C_f. Compare with the results in Table 7–1. b) What is the displacement thickness in terms of the boundary layer thickness?

7–6. Assume $u/u_s = (y/\delta)^{1/8}$ in a turbulent boundary layer. Calculate the boundary layer thickness δ/x and the drag coefficient C_f using Eq. 7–13 for the wall shear stress. Compare results with Eqs. 7–14 and 7–18.

7–7. Repeat Prob. 7–6 assuming $u/u_s = (y/\delta)^{1/9}$.

7–8. How does the ratio of displacement thickness to boundary layer thickness (δ^*/δ) for a laminar boundary layer compare with that for a turbulent boundary layer? Determine a qualitative answer from an inspection of the velocity profiles within the boundary layers, and then check the ratio of Eq. 7–15 to Eq. 7–14 with similar ratios obtained from Table 7–1.

7–9. From the definition of displacement thickness and momentum thickness of a boundary layer (Eqs. 7–1 and 7–2) and from the turbulent velocity profile of Eq. 7–12, derive Eqs. 7–15 and 7–16.

7–10. Carry out in detail the steps leading to Eq. 7–20, which gives the relative thickness of the laminar sublayer.

7–11. Would transition from a laminar boundary layer to a turbulent boundary layer on a flat plate occur nearer to the leading edge for a smooth surface or for a rough surface? Consider all parameters the same except surface roughness. Explain your answer.

7-12. An equation for the velocity profile in a turbulent boundary layer on a flat surface obtained from analysis and experiment is of logarithmic form. It is

$$\frac{u}{\sqrt{\tau_0/\rho}} = 2.5 \ln y + C$$

where $\sqrt{\tau_0/\rho}$ is the so-called shear velocity, y is the normal distance from the boundary, and C is a constant. Suppose wind velocities over flat grassland are measured to be 10.0 and 11.0 ft/sec at 10 and 20 ft, respectively, above the ground. Estimate the wind velocity at a height of 80 ft above the ground a) from the given equation and b) from Eq. 7-12, the ⅐-power law variation.

Ans.   a) 13.0 ft/sec; b) 13.4 ft/sec

7-13. Water at 60 F flows along a smooth flat plate at a free stream velocity of $u_s = 12$ ft/sec. What is the boundary layer thickness a) 4.8 in., b) 4 ft, and c) 40 ft from the leading edge of the plate?

Ans.   b) 0.071 ft

7-14. What are the total thickness δ and the displacement thickness δ^* of the boundary layer along the hull of a Great Lakes ore boat a) 80 ft and b) 160 ft aft of the bow when the boat travels at 10 knots (16.9 ft/sec) in water at 50 F? Assume a flat-plate boundary layer growth.

7-15. The local skin-drag coefficient is defined as the ratio of the local boundary shear stress to the dynamic pressure of the free stream. The velocity profile for laminar flow along a flat plate is $u = ay + by^2 + cy^3$, where y is the normal distance from the plate surface. Write an expression for the local skin-drag coefficient c_f for a fluid of density ρ, kinematic viscosity ν, and a free stream velocity u_s in terms of a, ν, and u_s.

7-16. A smooth flat plate 4 ft long and 2 ft wide is placed in a stream of standard air at 25 ft/sec. Calculate the total drag on the plate (both sides) and the maximum thickness of the boundary layer for both a laminar and a completely turbulent boundary layer. Neglect edge effects.

7-17. Water flows along a smooth flat plate 8 ft long and parallel to the flow. Plot curves on a single graph to show the outer edge of the boundary layer (the boundary layer thickness δ) for a) a free stream velocity $u_s = 0.1$ ft/sec with a laminar boundary layer, b) a free stream velocity $u_s = 10$ ft/sec with a completely turbulent boundary layer, and c) a free stream velocity of 10 ft/sec with a transition from a laminar to a turbulent boundary layer at $\mathrm{Re}_x = 5 \times 10^5$. Use $\nu = 10^{-5}$ ft²/sec. Plot the length x at a scale 1 in. = 1 ft; plot δ full scale.

7-18. In Prob. 7-17, what would be the free stream velocity for air with $\nu = 1.6 \times 10^{-4}$ ft²/sec in order that the curves of δ vs x be identical?

7-19. A smooth flat plate is in a parallel flow stream. What is the ratio of the drag over the upstream half of the plate to that over the entire plate a) for a laminar boundary layer over its entire length and b) for a turbulent boundary layer over its entire length?

Ans.   a) 0.707; b) 0.574

7-20. Water at 70 F, at a free-stream velocity of 4 ft/sec, and with a low turbulence level flows past a smooth, rectangular, flat plate 1 x 10 ft in size. Compare a) the total drag and b) the thickness of the boundary layer at the trailing edge for flow parallel to the 10-ft side with that for flow parallel to the 1-ft side. Neglect edge effects.

7–21. In Prob. 7–19, over what percentage of the plate length will the drag be one-half the total drag for parts a) and b)?

7–22. A 4- x 20-ft smooth flat plate is placed in a parallel flow stream. Assume a completely turbulent boundary layer. Is the total drag greater when the 4-ft side is parallel to the flow or when the 20-ft side is parallel to the flow? Get a qualitative answer from physical reasoning, then check by using Eq. 7–18.

7–23. a) Estimate the skin friction drag on an airship 40 ft in diameter with an effective length of 300 ft at an air speed of 55 mph in standard air. b) What horsepower would be required to propel the craft?

7–24. A 20-ft, smooth wax model of a cargo ship is towed through fresh water at 60 F at a speed of 5 knots (8.45 ft/sec). The wetted hull area is 70 ft². What is the skin-friction drag, assuming a completely turbulent boundary layer equivalent to that on a flat plate?

Ans.   13.6 lb$_f$

7–25. A 15-ft smooth model of an ocean vessel is towed in fresh water at 5.5 knots (9.30 ft/sec). The wetted hull area is 38 ft². What is the skin friction drag in water at 60 F?

7–26. Water at 70 F and at an axial velocity of 50 ft/sec enters the 12.000-in. diameter test section of a water tunnel with a boundary layer thickness equal to that from a starting point 18 in. upstream. The velocity profile is flat over the entire cross section except for the boundary layer. Estimate the increase in axial velocity at the end of a 24-in. test section length due to the growth of the boundary layer. Assume flat plate theory.

7–27. Water enters a round pipe with an essentially flat velocity profile. The boundary layer thickens in the direction of flow (Fig. 7–5), which results in an acceleration of the fluid in the core with an accompanying pressure drop given by the Bernoulli equation. If the walls are made slightly diverging to accommodate the bound-

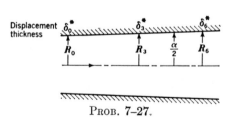

PROB. 7–27.

ary layer growth, the axial pressure may be essentially constant.

Assume water at 70 F enters a 3-ft diameter smooth duct at $u_s = 60$ ft/sec with a turbulent boundary layer equivalent to that 0.75 ft from the leading edge of a flat plate. a) Estimate the duct radius at 3 ft and at 6 ft downstream from the duct entrance for a constant pressure core flow, assuming flat-plate boundary layer growth. b) Why is the Bernoulli equation applicable in the core flow?

Ans.   a) $R_3 = 18.051$ in.; $R_6 = 18.094$ in.

7-28. In order to straighten the flow and reduce the scale of turbulence in a water tunnel, an egg-crate type of flow straightener is formed from thin plates. A number of 4-in. square ducts 2 ft long result. For a flow velocity of 8 ft/sec approaching the straightener and a water temperature of 70 F, calculate a) the displacement thickness of the boundary layer at the downstream end of the straightener (assume no pressure gradient, although a very small one exists); b) the velocity in the core flow at the downstream end of the flow straightener (the velocity increases because of the retardation of flow within the boundary layer); c) the pressure drop through the straightener by applying the Bernoulli equation to the core flow; and d) the pressure drop through the straightener, by determining the drag per duct and writing the momentum theorem between entrance and exit of the duct.

7-29. An incompressible fluid flows past one side of a porous flat surface at a free-stream velocity of u_s and at constant pressure. Fluid is drawn from the boundary layer through the porous surface at a uniform velocity of $v \ll u_s$. The boundary layer velocity profile is given by

$$\frac{u}{u_s} = f\left(\frac{y}{\delta}\right) = f(\eta)$$

Apply the momentum theorem and show that the local skin-friction coefficient may be expressed as

$$c_f = \frac{\tau_0}{\rho u_s^2 /2} = 2\frac{d\delta}{dx}\int_0^1 f(\eta)[1 - f(\eta)]d\eta + \frac{2v}{u_s}$$

Refer to Example 5-7. In this problem the fluid removed at the porous surface has an initial velocity of u_s in the $+x$ direction, but after removal from the flow its velocity in this direction is zero.

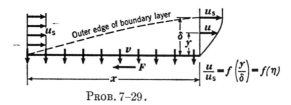

PROB. 7-29.

7-30. How would the results of Prob. 7-29 be affected if fluid is injected into the boundary layer uniformly instead of being removed?

8 | Dimensionless Numbers and Dynamic Similarity

In fluid mechanics, as well as in other physical systems, experimental data are often presented in dimensionless form. These dimensionless numbers may be obtained in various ways. For example, a Reynolds number may be obtained by a formal dimensional analysis of a system in which viscosity plays a predominating role by taking the ratio of the inertia to viscous forces in a flow system or by writing the differential equations of motion (including viscous terms) in dimensionless form. Dynamic similarity between two or more geometrically similar flow systems is said to exist when the appropriate dimensionless numbers are the same for the systems.

8-1. INTRODUCTION

In physical systems, certain quantities, such as mass, length, and time (or force, length, and time), are considered to be fundamental quantities since they cannot be expressed in simpler terms. All other physical quantities may be expressed in terms of these fundamental quantities. Velocity is a length divided by time, dynamic viscosity is a mass divided by length and time, and density is a mass per unit volume (length cubed). The fundamental quantities are said to have dimensions. We measure each fundamental *dimension* in various systems of *units*, such as grams and slugs for mass, angstroms and feet for length, and seconds and years for time.

In any physical system in which two or more quantities are inter-related, it is often convenient to set up dimensionless quantities which in turn are interrelated. The number of dimensionless quantities is always less than the total number of physical quantities, and this fact enables us to correlate experimental data more easily. We may say, for example, that the friction factor for the flow of any incompressible fluid in a smooth pipe depends on the Reynolds number. Such a statement is much simpler than saying that the pressure drop per unit length of pipe for incompressible flow in a smooth pipe depends on the viscosity, density, and average velocity of the fluid and on the pipe diameter. The actual relationship between the dimensionless numbers usually has to be determined from experiment.

We are all familiar with the Mach number, since it appears frequently in the daily press. The Mach number is a dimensionless number, being the ratio of the flow, or flight, velocity to the speed of sound; the inertial to the elastic, or compression, forces in the fluid system; or the kinetic energy of the mean flow to the mean kinetic energy of the gas molecules. Many other dimensionless numbers, though not all, are named in honor of individuals who have done pioneering work in the field associated with the number. Among the dimensionless numbers in the field of fluid mechanics arc, in addition to the Mach number, a) the Reynolds number, Re, in connection with effects of viscosity; b) the Froude number, Fr, in connection with gravity effects; c) the Weber number, We, in connection with surface tension effects; d) the Knudson number, Kn, in conjunction with slip flow in rarefied gases; e) the pressure coefficient, C_p, indicative of pressure variations (the cavitation number or index σ is a special form of a pressure coefficient used in conjunction with cavitation phenomena); and f) the drag and lift coefficients, C_D and C_L, in connection with drag and lift.

In heat transfer, often closely related with fluid mechanics, many other dimensionless numbers are used, noteworthy ones being named after Nusselt, Prandtl, Stanton, Peclet, Schmidt, Eckert, Graetz, and Grashof. This list is by no means complete.

It may be stated that without dimensionless numbers, experimental progress in fluid mechanics (heat transfer as well) would have been almost nil; it would have been swamped by masses of accumulated data.

8–2. DIMENSIONAL ANALYSIS OF FLUID SYSTEMS

The dimensions of a number of quantities used in fluid mechanics are listed in Table 8–1. The MLT and the FLT systems of dimensions are related by the expressions

$$F = Ma = \frac{ML}{T^2} \quad \text{and} \quad M = \frac{FT^2}{L}$$

Either system of dimensions may be used (exclusively) in a dimensional analysis.

We are interested in obtaining the most significant and independent dimensionless groups, or parameters, for the particular physical system being analyzed. Actually, the resulting groups will indicate only how to organize a set of experiments and how to plot the resulting experimental data. We cannot determine how one dimensionless variable will vary with another except by experiment (in a few instances of viscous flow this variation may be calculated analytically).

The so-called π(pi) theorem—commonly called the Buckingham π theorem, but first stated by Vaschy and proved in increasing generality by Buckingham, Riabouchinsky and Martinot-Lagarge, and Birkhoff[1]—will be explained by means of an example.

Suppose we want to analyze the flow of an incompressible fluid in

[1]G. Birkhoff, *Hydrodynamics*, (Princeton, New Jersey: Princeton University Press, 1950).

TABLE 8–1

DIMENSIONS OF VARIOUS QUANTITIES

	FLT	*MLT*
Geometrical characteristics		
Length (diameter, height, breadth, chord, span, etc.)	L	L
Angle	None	None
Area	L^2	L^2
Volume	L^3	L^3
Fluid properties*		
Mass	FT^2/L	M
Density (ρ)	FT^2/L^4	M/L^3
Specific weight (γ)	F/L^3	M/L^2T^2
Kinematic viscosity (ν)	L^2/T	L^2/T
Dynamic viscosity (μ)	FT/L^2	M/LT
Elastic modulus (K)	F/L^2	M/LT^2
Surface tension (σ)	F/L	M/T^2
Flow characteristics		
Velocity (V)	L/T	L/T
Angular velocity (ω)	$1/T$	$1/T$
Acceleration (a)	L/T^2	L/T^2
Pressure (Δp)	F/L^2	M/LT^2
Force (drag, lift, shear)	F	ML/T^2
Shear stress (τ)	F/L^2	M/LT^2
Pressure gradient $(\Delta p/L)$	F/L^3	M/L^2T^2
Flow rate (Q)	L^3/T	L^3/T
Mass flow rate $(\dot{m})$	FT/L	M/T
Work or energy	FL	ML^2/T^2
Work or energy per unit weight	L	L
Torque and moment	FL	ML^2/T^2
Work or energy per unit mass	L^2/T^2	L^2/T^2

*Density, viscosity, elastic modulus, and surface tension depend upon temperature, and therefore temperature will not be considered a property in the sense used here.

a round pipe. We judge that the pressure drop per unit length of pipe (this is the pressure gradient $\Delta p/L$) depends on the pipe diameter D, the pipe roughness k (the effective height of the roughness elements), the average flow velocity V, the fluid density ρ, and the fluid viscosity μ. This may be written as

$$\frac{\Delta p}{L} = f(D, k, V, \rho, \mu)$$

and in terms of dimensions in the FLT system as

$$\frac{F}{L^3} = f\left[(L), (L), \left(\frac{L}{T}\right), \left(\frac{FT^2}{L^4}\right), \left(\frac{FT}{L^2}\right)\right]$$

There are $n = 6$ quantities involved and $m = 3$ fundamental dimensions (F, L, and T). The π theorem states that there will be at least one set of

$n - m$ (equal to 3 here) independent dimensionless groups in a dimensional analysis. The total number of dimensionless groups is

$$n!/(m + 1)! \, (n - m - 1)!$$

which is 15 in this example. The independent groups will be designated as $\pi_1, \pi_2, \cdots$, and π_{n-m}.

Each of the three groups ($n - m = 3$) will consist of m (equal to 3 in this example) quantities in common, and these are called *repeating variables*. Three general rules guide the selection of repeating variables:

a) In a dimensional analysis of any physical system the repeating variables must include among them all of the m fundamental dimensions.

b) For a fluid system, the most significant groups will result if the repeating variables are chosen so that one is a geometrical characteristic, one is a fluid property, and one is flow characteristic (Table 8–1).

c) The dependent variable should not be used as a repeating variable.

After the repeating variables are chosen, each one of the remaining original quantities is included with each one of the π groups. Let D be the geometrical characteristic, ρ the fluid property, and V the flow characteristic ($\Delta p/L$ also results from flow, but a dependent variable should not be used as a repeating variable). Then

π_1 will contain D, ρ, V, and $\Delta p/L$;
π_2 will contain D, ρ, V, and k; and
π_3 will contain D, ρ, V, and μ.

In order that these π's be dimensionless, *any one* quantity in each may appear to the first power, and the others will appear to some unknown power which can be found. Thus let

$$\pi_1 = D^x \, \rho^y \, V^z \, \frac{\Delta p}{L}$$

$$= (L)^x \left(\frac{FT^2}{L^4}\right)^y \left(\frac{L}{T}\right)^z \frac{F}{L^3} = L^0 F^0 T^0$$

in order to be dimensionless. The values of x, y, and z may be obtained by equating exponents of F, L, and T to zero. For this example, these are

$$
\begin{array}{ll}
y + 1 = 0 & \text{for } F \\
x - 4y + z - 3 = 0 & \text{for } L \\
2y - z = 0 & \text{for } T
\end{array}
$$

from which $x = 1$, $y = -1$, and $z = -2$. Thus,

$$\pi_1 = \frac{\Delta p}{L} \frac{D}{\rho V^2}$$

which is commonly known as one-half the friction factor f for a pipe. Similarly, $\pi_2 = k/D$, which is known as the relative roughness of a pipe, and $\pi_3 = \mu/VD\rho$, which is the reciprocal of the Reynolds number for a pipe. Note that the reciprocal, square, square root, and so forth, or a constant times a dimensionless number, is also dimensionless, and the useful form of the result is determined largely by convention or experience. The result of the example may be expressed as

$$\pi_1 = f(\pi_2, \pi_3)$$

or that the friction factor for pipe flow depends on the relative roughness of the pipe and on the Reynolds number of the flow. The actual relationship is determined experimentally (see Figs. 10–6 and 10–7). A different choice of repeating variables (μ and ρ are both fluid properties, and D and k are both geometrical characteristics) would result in a number of different π's, some of the total of 15 possible. The dimensional analysis is equally as valid for any three independent dimensionless groups, although experience in this instance shows that the most significant ones are those just obtained.

As long as the six chosen quantities are the only ones included in a study of fluid flow in pipes, the experimental results will apply to *any* incompressible fluid flowing at *any* velocity in *any* round straight pipe. High velocity gas flow, for example, cannot be correlated with the resulting π's because the compressibility of the fluid, indicated by the elastic modulus K, was omitted. The dimensionless numbers are independent of the system of units used in making the experiments, so the results are applicable to the foot-pound-second system, the centimeter-gram-second system, the kilogram-meter-second system, or any other system. The advantages of using dimensionless parameters are clearly apparent. We have succeeded in expressing six related quantities in terms of three; this enables us to plot the friction factor as a function of the Reynolds number for a family of curves, each representing a given relative roughness, usable in any consistent system of units.

8–3. DYNAMIC SIMILITUDE

Flow systems are considered to be dynamically similar *a*) if they are geometrically similar, and *b*) if the forces acting in one system are in the same ratio to each other as similar forces in the second system. We might also state that flow systems are dynamically similar if the dimensionless parameters obtained in a dimensional analysis of the systems are the same for both. This is essentially the same as conditions *a*) and *b*). Thus, in the example worked out in Sec. 8–2, any two pipe systems for which the Reynolds number and relative roughness are the same will have dynamically similar flows, and the friction factor will be the same for both. This fact indicates that the pressure drop in a large oil pipeline could be determined by making measurements of the pressure drop in a small pipe carrying water.

All types of model tests made of airplanes, missiles, rivers, harbors, breakwaters, pumps, turbines, and so forth are based on the criterion of dynamic similarity. It should be pointed out, however, that many practical problems confront the experimenter, and it is not always possible to have complete dynamic similarity in making model studies in fluid-flow systems.

Among the forces encountered in flowing fluids are those due to inertia, viscosity, gravity, pressure, surface tension, and compressibility. These may be expressed in a semidimensional way in terms of length L, velocity V, density ρ, viscosity μ, gravity g, pressure change Δp, surface tension σ, and compressibility K, rather than simply a force F. Quantities in brackets are retained in order that the type of force may be recognized.

$$\text{Inertia force} = Ma = \frac{\rho L^3\ V^2}{L} = [\rho]L^2\ V^2$$

$$\text{Viscous force} = \tau A = \mu \left(\frac{du}{dy}\right) L^2 = \mu \left(\frac{V}{L}\right) L^2 = [\mu]\ VL$$

$$\text{Gravity force} = Mg = \rho L^3\ [g]$$

$$\text{Pressure force} = (\Delta p)A = [\Delta p]L^2$$

$$\text{Surface tension force} = [\sigma]L$$

$$\text{Compressibility force} = [K]L^2$$

Inertia forces are usually important in any fluid in motion. The ratio of the inertia force to each of the others is then expressed as

$$\frac{\text{Inertia force}}{\text{Viscous force}} = \frac{\rho L^2\ V^2}{\mu VL} = \frac{\rho LV}{\mu}, \text{ the Reynolds number Re}$$

$$\frac{\text{Inertia force}}{\text{Gravity force}} = \frac{\rho L^2\ V^2}{\rho L^3\ g} = \frac{V^2}{Lg} \text{ or } \frac{V}{\sqrt{Lg}}, \text{ the Froude number Fr}$$

$$\frac{\text{Pressure force}}{\text{Inertia force}} = \frac{\Delta p L^2}{\rho L^2\ V^2} = \frac{\Delta p}{\rho V^2} \text{ or } \frac{\Delta p}{\rho V^2/2}, \text{ the pressure coefficient } C_p$$

$$\frac{\text{Inertia force}}{\text{Surface tension force}} = \frac{\rho L^2\ V^2}{\sigma L} = \frac{V^2}{\sigma/\rho L} \text{ or } \frac{V}{\sqrt{\sigma/\rho L}}, \text{ the Weber number We}$$

$$\frac{\text{Inertia force}}{\text{Compressibility force}} = \frac{\rho L^2\ V^2}{KL^2} = \frac{V^2}{K/\rho} \text{ or } \frac{V}{\sqrt{K/\rho}}, \text{ the Mach number M}$$

When inertia and viscous forces govern the flow in a fluid system, dynamic similarity requires that the Reynolds number be the same for each. Large Reynolds numbers indicate large inertia forces compared to viscous forces, and this condition indicates turbulent flow. Small Reynolds numbers indicate relatively small inertia forces compared to viscous forces and are associated with laminar or viscous flow. The length in the Reynolds number is some characteristic length of the system; it may be a pipe diameter, the length from the leading edge of an airfoil, the diameter of a settling particle, and so forth. The velocity is a characteristic velocity; it may be the free-stream velocity or the so-called shear velocity $\sqrt{\tau_0/\rho}$.

When gravity forces govern the flow, the Froude number should be the same in two dynamically similar systems. The length is a characteristic length; it may be the length of a ship if gravity waves are involved or the water depth in open-channel flow. In the latter instance, Froude numbers less than 1 indicate subcritical flow and Froude numbers greater than 1 indicate supercritical flow. Whether the flow is below or above critical depends on the flow velocity as compared to the velocity of an elementary surface wave (see Sec. 12–2).

If surface tension forces are significant, the Weber number should be the same for dynamic similarity. In most large liquid flow systems, surface tension forces rarely affect the flow and thus models of rivers, for example, must be large enough so that surface tension forces do not affect the model flow either. The role of surface tension forces in cavitation is not yet fully understood.

For compressible flow of gases, the Mach number should be the same in two systems in which there is dynamic similarity. Mach numbers less than, the same as, or greater than the speed of a weak pressure wave (an acoustic wave) are associated with subsonic, sonic, or supersonic flow, respectively. The velocity in the Mach number may be the free-stream velocity or the local velocity at some prescribed point other than the free stream. The reference velocity $\sqrt{K/\rho}$ may be the acoustic velocity in the free stream, the acoustic velocity at a stagnation point where the stream velocity is zero, or the acoustic velocity at a point where the stream velocity is sonic (see Chapter 9).

The pressure coefficient will automatically be the same for two flow systems if the other dimensionless numbers are the same for the particular type of modeling being carried out.

EXAMPLE 8–1. Oil ($\nu = 0.00015$ ft²/sec) flows through a 30-in. pipe at an average velocity of 8 ft/sec. At what velocity should water flow in a 3-in. pipe for dynamically similar flow? Water viscosity is 10^{-5} ft²/sec.

Solution: Subscript o and w denote oil and water, respectively.

$$\text{Re}_o = \text{Re}_w$$

$$\frac{V_o D_o}{\nu_o} = \frac{V_w D_w}{\nu_w} \quad \text{or} \quad \frac{(8)(2.5)}{15 \times 10^{-5}} = \frac{V_w(0.25)}{10^{-5}}$$

$$V_w = 5.33 \text{ ft/sec}$$

EXAMPLE 8–2. A river model is built to a scale of $\frac{1}{80}$. What surface velocity in the prototype river is represented by a corresponding surface velocity of 0.6 ft/sec in the river model?

Solution: Subscripts p and m denote prototype and model, respectively.

$$\mathrm{Fr}_p = \mathrm{Fr}_m$$

$$\frac{V_p}{\sqrt{L_p g_p}} = \frac{V_m}{\sqrt{L_m g_m}}$$

and

$$V_p = V_m \left(\frac{L_p}{L_m}\right)^{1/2} = (0.6)(80)^{1/2} = 5.36 \text{ ft/sec}$$

EXAMPLE 8–3. The pressure at the nose of a ¼-scale model torpedo tested in water at 48 ft/sec is 15.5 psi greater than the free-stream pressure upstream of the torpedo nose. The drag of the torpedo is being studied. What would be the pressure on the nose of the prototype torpedo above the free-stream pressure upstream of its nose? Consider the model to be tested in fresh water, and the prototype to run in salt water ($s = 1.025$), both at the same dynamic viscosity.

Solution:

$$\mathrm{Re}_m = \mathrm{Re}_p$$

$$\frac{V_m L_m \rho_m}{\mu_m} = \frac{V_p L_p \rho_p}{\mu_p} \quad \text{and} \quad V_p = V_m \frac{L_m \rho_m}{L_p \rho_p} = (48)\left(\frac{1}{4}\right)\left(\frac{1}{1.025}\right)$$

$$V_p = 11.71 \text{ ft/sec}$$

The pressure coefficient will be the same for the model and prototype.

$$(C_p)_p = (C_p)_m$$

$$\frac{\Delta p_p}{\rho_p V_p^2 / 2} = \frac{\Delta p_m}{\rho_m V_m^2 / 2}$$

$$\Delta p_p = \Delta p_m \frac{\rho_p V_p^2}{\rho_m V_m^2} = (15.5)(1.025)\frac{11.71^2}{48^2} = 0.945 \text{ psi}$$

EXAMPLE 8–4. A missile flying at Mach 3 in standard air (59 F) is studied by means of a ⅒-scale model in a wind tunnel at −40 F. What is the wind tunnel speed, and at what speed does the prototype missile fly?

Solution:

$$M_m = M_p = \frac{V_m}{\sqrt{kRT_m}} = \frac{V_p}{\sqrt{kRT_p}} = 3$$

$$V_m = 3\sqrt{(1.4)(1715)(420)} = 3015 \text{ ft/sec}$$

$$V_p = 3\sqrt{(1.4)(1715)(519)} = 3348 \text{ ft/sec}$$

In addition to the five dimensionless force ratios just given, many other dimensionless numbers exist and are equal in dynamically similar flows. All are obtainable by dimensional analysis of various systems. Among those in fluid systems are the drag and lift coefficients and the cavitation number, or index.

Drag coefficient. Drag may be due to viscous shear (skin-friction drag on an airfoil or ship's hull), to pressure (flow normal to a flat surface), to gravity effects (wave drag of an ocean vessel), or to compressibility effects (high-speed missile). In any case, a dimensional analysis will indicate that the drag coefficient is a function of the Reynolds number, the Froude number, or the Mach number, respectively. For dynamically similar flow, the appropriate one of these three numbers will be the same for model and prototype, and thus the drag coefficient will also be the same for both. This may be expressed as

$$C_{D_m} = C_{D_p} = \frac{D_m}{(\rho_m V_m^2/2)\,A_m} = \frac{D_p}{(\rho_p V_p^2/2)\,A_p}$$

and the drag of a prototype may be estimated by measurement of model drag according to this equation. Appropriate velocity ratios are determined from Table 8–2 by the type of modeling.

TABLE 8–2

MODELING RATIOS

(Subscript m indicates model, subscript p indicates prototype)

RATIO	MODELING PARAMETER				
	Reynolds Number	Froude Number, Undistorted Model*	Froude Number, Distorted Model*	Mach Number, Same Gas	Mach Number, Different Gas
Velocity $\dfrac{V_m}{V_p}$	$\dfrac{L_p}{L_m}\dfrac{\rho_p}{\rho_m}\dfrac{\mu_m}{\mu_p}$	$\left(\dfrac{L_m}{L_p}\right)^{1/2}$	$\left(\dfrac{L_m}{L_p}\right)^{1/2}_V$	$\left(\dfrac{\theta_m}{\theta_p}\right)^{1/2}$	$\left(\dfrac{k_m R_m \theta_m}{k_p R_p \theta_p}\right)^{1/2}$
Angular velocity $\dfrac{\omega_m}{\omega_p}$	$\left(\dfrac{L_p}{L_m}\right)^2\dfrac{\rho_p}{\rho_m}\dfrac{\mu_m}{\mu_p}$	$\left(\dfrac{L_p}{L_m}\right)^{1/2}$	†	$\left(\dfrac{\theta_m}{\theta_p}\right)^{1/2}\dfrac{L_p}{L_m}$	$\left(\dfrac{k_m R_m \theta_m}{k_p R_p \theta_p}\right)^{1/2}\dfrac{L_p}{L_m}$
Volumetric flow rate $\dfrac{Q_m}{Q_p}$	$\dfrac{L_m}{L_p}\dfrac{\rho_p}{\rho_m}\dfrac{\mu_m}{\mu_p}$	$\left(\dfrac{L_m}{L_p}\right)^{5/2}$	$\left(\dfrac{L_m}{L_p}\right)^{3/2}_V\left(\dfrac{L_m}{L_p}\right)_H$	†	†
Time $\dfrac{t_m}{t_p}$	$\left(\dfrac{L_m}{L_p}\right)^2\dfrac{\rho_m}{\rho_p}\dfrac{\mu_p}{\mu_m}$	$\left(\dfrac{L_m}{L_p}\right)^{1/2}$	$\left(\dfrac{L_m}{L_p}\right)_H\left(\dfrac{L_p}{L_m}\right)^{1/2}_V$	$\left(\dfrac{\theta_p}{\theta_m}\right)^{1/2}\dfrac{L_m}{L_p}$	$\left(\dfrac{k_p R_p \theta_p}{k_m R_m \theta_m}\right)^{1/2}\dfrac{L_m}{L_p}$
Force $\dfrac{F_m}{F_p}$	$\left(\dfrac{\mu_m}{\mu_p}\right)^2\dfrac{\rho_p}{\rho_m}$	$\left(\dfrac{L_m}{L_p}\right)^3\dfrac{\rho_m}{\rho_p}$	$\dfrac{\rho_m}{\rho_p}\left(\dfrac{L_m}{L_p}\right)_H\left(\dfrac{L_m}{L_p}\right)^2_V$	$\dfrac{\rho_m}{\rho_p}\dfrac{\theta_m}{\theta_p}\left(\dfrac{L_m}{L_p}\right)^2$	$\dfrac{K_m}{K_p}\left(\dfrac{L_m}{L_p}\right)^2$

*For the same value of gravitational acceleration for model and prototype.
†Of little importance.

EXAMPLE 8–5. The wave drag on a $\frac{1}{16}$-scale model of a merchant ship is determined to be 0.25 lb$_f$ when tested for a prototype speed of 20 ft/sec. What is the wave drag on the prototype? The model is tested in fresh water; the prototype sails in sea water ($s = 1.025$).

Solution:

$$C_{D_m} = C_{D_p} = \frac{D_m}{(\rho_m V_m^2/2)\,A_m} = \frac{D_p}{(\rho_p V_p^2/2)\,A_p}$$

where $V_p/V_m = (L_p/L_m)^{1/2}$ from the Froude law. Then

$$D_p = D_m \frac{\rho_p}{\rho_m}\left(\frac{V_p}{V_m}\right)^2\left(\frac{L_p}{L_m}\right)^2 = 0.25(1.025)(4)^2(16)^2 = 1050 \text{ lb}_f$$

Lift coefficient. The lift coefficient is defined as

$$C_L = \frac{L}{(\rho V^2/2)\, A}$$

where L is the lift and A is the chord area of the lifting surface. The coefficient is obtainable (except for the constant 2) in a dimensional analysis along with a shape parameter and the angle of attack. It is also a function of the Reynolds number, and if these are equal for a given airfoil shape, for example, the lift coefficients will also be the same for two foils.

Cavitation number. The cavitation number is a form of pressure coefficient with a datum, or reference, pressure. This reference pressure may be the vapor pressure, a cavity pressure, or some other reference cavitation pressure. It may be expressed as

$$\sigma = \frac{p - p_{\text{ref}}}{\rho V^2/2}$$

If vapor pressure is the datum,

$$\sigma_v = \frac{p - p_v}{\rho V^2/2}$$

or if a cavity pressure is the datum,

$$\sigma_c = \frac{p - p_c}{\rho V^2/2}$$

It is often assumed that cavitation similarity exists if the cavitation number is the same for two cavitating flow conditions, but this has not been established completely. The cavitation number is used as a modeling parameter for rotating machines (pumps and turbines).

8–4. MODELING RATIOS

It is helpful to determine relationships between velocities, angular velocities, discharges, and times for a model and a prototype. The method used to obtain these will be illustrated and the results tabulated.

Velocity ratios may be obtained directly from the appropriate modeling parameter (Re, Fr, We, or M).

Angular velocity is expressed as a velocity divided by a length, and thus

$$\frac{\omega_m}{\omega_p} = \frac{V_m\, L_p}{L_m\, V_p} = \left(\frac{V_m}{V_p}\right)\left(\frac{L_p}{L_m}\right)$$

A discharge is a velocity times an area, and thus

$$\frac{Q_m}{Q_p} = \frac{V_m\, A_m}{V_p\, A_p} = \left(\frac{V_m}{V_p}\right)\left(\frac{L_m}{L_p}\right)^2$$

Time is the ratio of a length to a velocity, and thus

$$\frac{t_m}{t_p} = \left(\frac{L_m}{V_m}\right)\left(\frac{V_p}{L_p}\right) = \left(\frac{L_m}{L_p}\right)\left(\frac{V_p}{V_m}\right)$$

Distorted models are sometimes used. The size of a river model, for example, is determined by the space available, the reach of the prototype river which is to be modeled, and the discharge required and available. In some instances the model might become quite small, with a scale of $\frac{1}{100}$, for example. Then depths less than 1 ft in the prototype become less than 0.01 ft in the model, and surface tension or viscosity may affect the flow in the model. But if surface tension or viscosity do not affect the flow in the prototype, they should not affect the flow in the model. To avoid this, a distorted model may be used wherein the vertical scale is larger than the horizontal scale, say, $\frac{1}{40}$ or so. Velocity is determined by gravity forces in the vertical direction. Thus for a distorted model the velocity in the model is related to that in the prototype by the equation

$$\frac{V_m}{V_p} = \left(\frac{L_m}{L_p}\right)_V^{1/2}$$

which is the square root of the vertical scale ratio. The discharge is the flow velocity times an area in a vertical plane made up of a vertical length L_V and a horizontal length L_H. Thus

$$\frac{Q_m}{Q_p} = \frac{V_m}{V_p}\frac{A_m}{A_p} = \left(\frac{L_m}{L_p}\right)_V^{1/2}\left(\frac{L_m}{L_p}\right)_H\left(\frac{L_m}{L_p}\right)_V = \left(\frac{L_m}{L_p}\right)_H\left(\frac{L_m}{L_p}\right)_V^{3/2}$$

The time is a horizontal length divided by a velocity, and thus

$$\frac{t_m}{t_p} = \frac{(L_m)_H}{V_m}\frac{V_p}{(L_p)_H} = \left(\frac{L_m}{L_p}\right)_H\left(\frac{L_p}{L_m}\right)_V^{1/2}$$

Some velocity, rotational speed, discharge, and time ratios are given in Table 8–2.

8–5. INCOMPLETE SIMILARITY

In many instances more than one force ratio is involved in a flow system. In general, for these instances complete dynamic similarity is possible only for full-size models, and since this is usually impractical, incomplete similarity results. An example is the study of the drag of a surface ship, for which the drag is due both to viscous shear along the hull and to waves, a gravity phenomenon. In order to keep both the Reynolds number and the Froude number the same for the model and the prototype, the corresponding velocity ratios are equated to obtain

$$\frac{\nu_m}{\nu_p} = \left(\frac{L_m}{L_p}\right)^{3/2}$$

If the model is $\frac{1}{15}$ the size of the prototype, the model fluid viscosity must be $\frac{1}{58}$ the viscosity of water. There is no such liquid. And if the model is tested in water at the same temperature as in the prototype (a practical thing to do), $L_m = L_p$ and a full-size model is then necessary. Actually the model is tested according to the Froude law, and estimates are made of the skin-friction (viscous shear) drag, which amounts to approximately 50 to 80 per cent of the total. (Chapters 7 and 11 illustrate the method of calculating skin-friction drag.) Precise accuracy is not possible. The sequence of calculations is as follows:

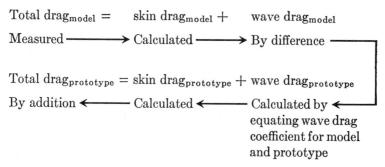

Some limitations of model tests will be described briefly.

Reynolds modeling. Reynolds modeling is used for studies of pipe flow, lift and drag of airfoils, and drag on almost any shape in incompressible flow; and in boundary layer studies in both incompressible and compressible flow. Viscous effects in gases may be modeled at Mach numbers below about 0.3 without interference from compressible effects. Above that, compressible effects enter in, and these must be modeled properly. Surface roughness should be similar in order that the onset of turbulence in the boundary layer occurs similarly in the model and prototype. Also, the level of turbulence in the free streams should be the same. Thus, flying an airplane through still air is not the same as blowing air past the same airplane in a large wind tunnel at the same velocity, although the Reynolds number may be the same for both. Boundary layer transition will not be the same for model and prototype. A larger portion of the wing surfaces (and the fuselage as well) will most likely have a laminar boundary layer when flying in still air than when in the wind tunnel, and thus a smaller portion will have a turbulent boundary layer in still air than in the wind tunnel. Since the drag is greater for a turbulent boundary layer, the total drag on the airplane flying in still air would be less than the total drag on the airplane in the wind tunnel.

Froude modeling. Froude modeling is used for hydraulic turbines, the measurement of the wave resistance of ships, tidal models of harbors, wave phenomena (beach erosion and breakwaters), river models, and water entry phenomena. The difficulty of ship modeling has already been mentioned and is not yet completely solved. In wave-study models, capillarity often enters in, and the viscous damping of waves is also not taken into account exactly. Air entrainment in flow over large dams is not modeled precisely in small models. Exact modeling of bed movement and sediment transport for a movable-bed river is difficult if not impossible to achieve, and this type of modeling is not only a science but an art.

Mach modeling. Mach modeling is done for gas flows at Mach numbers above about 0.3. The viscous effects (Reynolds phenomena) are not entirely absent, even at supersonic flow, because shock interactions with the boundary layer occur, and the thickness of a shock is influenced by the Reynolds number. Condensation shock is by no means governed solely by the Mach number.

8–6. SOME GENERAL EXPRESSIONS FOR DYNAMIC SIMILITUDE

Dimensional analyses applied to a rectilinear flow system and to a rotating system result in a number of dimensionless groups commonly used in practice, some of which have already been discussed.

Rectilinear flow systems. Suppose that a force F (drag or lift, for example) is believed to depend on several linear dimensions of the system, a, b, c, and d; the flow velocity V; the fluid density ρ; the fluid viscosity μ; the acceleration of gravity g; the pressure variations in the system Δp; the fluid surface tension σ; and the fluid compressibility K. Then we may write

$$F = f(a, b, c, d, V, \rho, \mu, g, \Delta p, \sigma, K)$$

There are $12 - 3 = 9$ independent dimensionless groups to be obtained. If a, V, and ρ are chosen as repeating variables, the results of a dimensional analysis are:

$$2\pi_1 = \frac{F}{\rho V^2 a^2/2}, \text{ the drag or lift (or any force) coefficient}$$

$$\pi_2 = \frac{a}{b}$$

$$\pi_3 = \frac{a}{c}$$

$$\pi_4 = \frac{a}{d}$$

$$\pi_5 = \frac{\rho V a}{\mu}, \text{ the Reynolds number Re}$$

$$\pi_6 = \frac{V^2}{ag} \text{ or } \frac{V}{\sqrt{ag}}, \text{ the Froude number Fr}$$

$$2\pi_7 = \frac{\Delta p}{\rho V^2/2}, \text{ the pressure coefficient } C_p$$

$$\pi_8 = \frac{\rho V^2 a}{\sigma} \text{ or } \frac{V}{\sqrt{\sigma/\rho a}}, \text{ the Weber number We}$$

$$\pi_9 = \frac{\rho V^2}{K} \text{ or } \frac{V}{\sqrt{K/\rho}}, \text{ the Mach number M}$$

Thus we may state that

$$\pi_1 = f(\pi_2, \pi_3, \pi_4, \pi_5, \pi_6, \pi_7, \pi_8, \pi_9)$$

or that when constants such as 2 are included,

$$\frac{F}{\rho V^2 a^2/2} = f\left(\frac{a}{b}, \frac{a}{c}, \frac{a}{d}, \frac{\rho Va}{\mu}, \frac{V}{\sqrt{ag}}, \frac{\Delta p}{\rho V^2/2}, \frac{V}{\sqrt{\sigma/\rho a}}, \frac{V}{\sqrt{K/\rho}}\right)$$

or that $\quad C_D$ or $C_L = f\left(\frac{a}{b}, \frac{a}{c}, \frac{a}{d}, \text{ Re, Fr, } C_p, \text{ We, M}\right)$

As previously mentioned, it may not be possible to eliminate all but one or two effects in a flow situation, and in these instances compromises must be made. For example, the drag or lift coefficient for an airfoil (or hydrofoil) section may depend on some geometrical parameters and only the Reynolds number in a low-velocity air stream (compressible and gravity effects are absent). They may depend on both Re and M in a high subsonic gas flow. They may depend on both Re and Fr for a hydrofoil at shallow submergence where surface waves are set up. If the hydrofoil cavitates, the Weber number We and the pressure coefficient in the form of the cavitation number may also be involved.

Rotating systems. Rotating systems include pumps, compressors, turbines, propellers, fluid couplings, torque converters, and so forth. Suppose the volumetric flow rate Q through a rotating machine or system is believed to depend on the efficiency η, the energy per unit mass of fluid $e(H = e/g$ is often called the head on a pump or turbine for incompressible flow), the power supplied P, the rotational speed N, the diameter of the rotor D, the fluid density ρ, the fluid viscosity μ, the fluid compressibility K, the torque T, and the thrust F. Then

$$Q = f(\eta, H, P, N, D, \rho, \mu, K, T, F)$$

We will obtain at least $11 - 3 = 8$ independent dimensionless groups, one of which is already dimensionless (η). Thus there are 7 groups to be found from a dimensional analysis. If D, ρ, and N are chosen as repeating variables, the results are:

$$\pi_1 = \frac{Q}{ND^3}$$

$$\pi_2 = \frac{e}{N^2D^2} \left(\text{generally used in the form } \frac{H}{N^2D^2}\right)$$

$$\pi_3 = \frac{P}{\rho N^3 D^5}$$

$$\pi_4 = \frac{\rho ND^2}{\mu}, \text{ a form of the Reynolds number Re}$$

$$\pi_5 = \frac{K}{\rho N^2 D^2} \text{ or } \frac{ND}{\sqrt{K/\rho}}, \text{ a form of the Mach number M}$$

$$\pi_6 = \frac{T}{\rho N^2 D^5}, \text{ the torque coefficient } C_{\text{torque}}$$

$$\pi_7 = \frac{F}{\rho N^2 D^4}, \text{ the thrust coefficient } C_{\text{thrust}}$$

$\pi_8 = \eta$, the efficiency

Thus we may state that

$$\frac{Q}{ND^3} = f\left(\eta, \frac{H}{N^2 D^2}, \frac{P}{\rho N^3 D^5}, \text{ Re, M, } C_{\text{torque}}, C_{\text{thrust}}\right)$$

The ratio of $\pi_1^{1/2}/\pi_2^{3/4}$ is called the specific speed of a pump.

$$N_{s(P)} = \frac{N\sqrt{Q}}{e^{3/4}} \tag{8-1}$$

This equation is truly dimensionless, but in American pump practice N is commonly expressed in revolutions per minute, Q in gallons per minute, and e in terms of the head H in feet of fluid. Thus Eq. 8–1 is generally stated as

$$N_{s(P)} = \frac{N\sqrt{Q}}{H^{3/4}} \tag{8-2}$$

The specific speed of a pump as used in Eq. 8–2 is not truly dimensionless, but is dimensional owing to the use of H rather than gH and to the units used for N and Q. Since $e = gH$, Eq. 8–1 should be used for rating pumps for use on the moon, for example, where the value of g is different from the value of g on the earth. A pump producing a high head at a relatively low discharge has a low specific speed; this is characteristic of a centrifugal pump. One producing a low head at a relatively large flow rate has a relatively high specific speed; this is characteristic of an axial-flow or propeller-type pump. The intermediate range of moderate heads at moderate discharge is characteristic of mixed-flow pumps. Typical values of specific speed for centrifugal pumps range from about 500 to 5000; for mixed-flow pumps, from 4000 to 10,000; and for axial-flow or propeller pumps, from 10,000 to 15,000 per stage. One stage consists of one rotor or impeller, and the specific speed generally applies to a single stage of a multistage pump.

The ratio $\pi_3^{1/2}/\pi_2^{5/4}$ is called the specific speed of a turbine.

$$N_{s(T)} = \frac{N\sqrt{P}}{\rho^{1/2}\, e^{5/4}} \tag{8-3}$$

Hydraulic turbines pass water, and the value of the water density is generally omitted. The power P is commonly expressed as brake horse-power bhp, and the speed and head are expressed the same as in pump practice. The American turbine practice is to designate the specific speed of a turbine in a dimensional form as

$$N_{s(T)} = \frac{N\sqrt{\text{bhp}}}{H^{5/4}} \tag{8-4}$$

A turbine operating under a high head with a relatively low flow rate has a relatively low specific speed; this is characteristic of a Pelton wheel, or impulse turbine. A turbine operating under a relatively low head at a large flow rate has a relatively high specific speed; this is characteristic of a propeller-type, or Kaplan, turbine. The intermediate range of moderate heads and moderate flow rates is characteristic of a mixed-flow, or Francis, type of turbine. Typical values of specific speed for impulse turbines are about 5; for Francis turbines, from 20 to 100; and for propeller, or Kaplan, turbines, about 100 to 200.

The dimensionless groups listed earlier for rotating systems or machines are applicable to dynamically similar, or homologous, operating conditions for geometrically similar systems. They are widely used in predicting the performance of large units from laboratory tests on small units by pump and turbine manufacturers. They may be used to predict the performance of a given machine at a speed other than the rated speed, assuming equal efficiencies at the two speeds. They may be used to estimate the performance of a pump, for example, with a slightly different impeller diameter from one for which the performance characteristics are known. Some examples will illustrate the principles involved.

EXAMPLE 8-6. A centrifugal pump is rated at 1000 gpm at a head of 135 ft at a speed of 1750 rpm. For the same efficiency of operation, what would the flow rate and head be if the speed of this pump were reduced to 1450 rpm?

Solution: From π_1, $Q_1/N_1 = Q_2/N_2$ since the diameter is the same. Thus $Q_2 = 1000 \ (1450/1750) = 829$ gpm.

From π_2, $H_1/N_1^2 = H_2/N_2^2$ since the diameter is the same. Thus $H_2 = 135$ $[(1450)^2/(1750)^2] = 92.8$ ft.

For an efficiency of 75 per cent, the power required at the rated speed of 1750 rpm is

$$\text{bhp}_1 = \frac{Q\gamma H}{550(\eta)} = \frac{(1000/449)(62.4)(135)}{(550)(0.75)} = 45.5$$

The power required at 1450 rpm may be found by a similar method or from the expression for π_3. Thus,

$$\frac{\text{bhp}_2}{N_2^3} = \frac{\text{bhp}_1}{N_1^3}$$

since the fluid density and the impeller diameter are the same. Therefore,

$$\text{bhp}_2 = 45.5 \frac{(1450)^3}{(1750)^3} = 25.9$$

EXAMPLE 8–7. A model turbine with a 16.5625-in. runner (rotor) is tested under a head of 18.5 ft at a speed of 374 rpm. The measured output is 22.15 hp at an efficiency of 89.3 per cent. The prototype runner diameter is 161 in. What are the head, speed, flow rate, and power output for the prototype turbine for dynamically similar flow? (Actually, the efficiency of the larger unit in this instance, would be about 3 per cent greater than for the model.) What type of turbine is this?

Solution: For geometrical similarity, all linear dimensions are in the same ratio. Thus,

$$H_p = H_m \frac{D_p}{D_m} = 18.5 \frac{161}{16.5625} = 180 \text{ ft}$$

From π_2,

$$N_p = N_m \left(\frac{D_m}{D_p}\right)^{1/2} = 374 \left(\frac{16.5625}{161}\right)^{1/2} = 120 \text{ rpm}$$

The flow rate may be obtained from the expression for π_1, or from the fact that the model test is based on the Froude law, since gravity flow is involved. From π_1, as well as from the Froude law, $Q_p/Q_m = (L_p/L_m)^{5/2}$. The flow in the model is found from Sec. 5–6 to be $Q_m = (\text{bhp}_m)(550)/(62.4)(H_m)(\eta_m)$, where the w term in the energy equation is equivalent to the H term in the dimensionless groups in this section. Substituting, $Q_m = (22.15)(550)/(62.4)(18.5)(0.893) = 11.82 \text{ ft}^3/\text{sec}$. Thus $Q_p = 11.82 (161/16.5625)^{5/2} = 3490 \text{ ft}^3/\text{sec}$. The power output of the prototype turbine at the same efficiency as the model may be found from Sec. 5–6 or from π_3. From π_3,

$$P_p = P_m \left(\frac{N_p}{N_m}\right)^3 \left(\frac{D_p}{D_m}\right)^5 = 22.15 \left(\frac{120}{374}\right)^3 \left(\frac{161}{16.5625}\right)^5 = 63,500 \text{ hp}$$

The specific speed of the model (which is the same as that for the prototype) is

$$N_{s(T)} = \frac{374\sqrt{22.15}}{18.5^{5/4}} = 46$$

indicating a Francis turbine.

REFERENCES

The reader is referred to the following sources for additional information on dimensional analysis and dynamic similarity:

P. W. Bridgman, *Dimensional Analysis* (New Haven, Connecticut: Yale University Press, 1931, Paperback Y-82, 1963).

W. J. Duncan, *Physical Similarity and Dimensional Analysis* (London: Edward Arnold and Co., 1953).

M. Holt, "Dimensional Analysis," Section 15, *Handbook of Fluid Dynamics*, edited by V. L. Streeter (New York: McGraw-Hill Book Company, Inc., 1961).

H. L. Langhaar, *Dimensional Analysis and Theory of Models* (New York: John Wiley and Sons, Inc., 1951).

PROBLEMS

8–1. Show the dimensional equivalence of the following:
a) Energy per unit mass and velocity squared

    b) Time rate of change of energy and force times velocity

    c) Head and energy per unit weight

    d) Viscosity in units of $lb_f \, sec/ft^2$ and slugs/ft sec

    e) The terms p/ρ and h, the enthalpy per unit mass

    f) Energy per unit volume and dynamic pressure

8–2. Determine the dimensions of the constant of proportionality for the following situations:

    a) The speed of sound in a given gas is directly proportional to the square root of the absolute temperature.

    b) The volumetric flow rate over a given rectangular weir is proportional to the $\frac{3}{2}$ power of the head on the weir.

    c) The settling velocity of silt in a reservoir is proportional to the square of the effective silt particle diameter.

    d) In a viscous fluid, the shear stresses are proportional to the velocity gradient.

    e) The drag of a given body is proportional to the square of the velocity of flow past it.

    f) The velocity of flow in an open channel is proportional to the hydraulic radius to the $\frac{2}{3}$ power and to the square root of the slope of the channel bed.

8–3. The velocity of propogation c of surface waves whose height is small compared with the water depth y is assumed to depend on y, the water density ρ, and the acceleration of gravity g. Express these variables as a dimensionless group.

$$Ans. \quad \pi_1 = \frac{c}{\sqrt{gy}}$$

8–4. The velocity of sound c depends on the elastic modulus K of a material and the density ρ of the material. Express these variables as a dimensionless group.

8–5. A shear velocity v_* may be expressed in terms of the boundary shear stress and the fluid density. What is the form of this expression? HINT: Use dimensional analysis to find a group involving τ_0 and ρ which has the dimensions of a velocity, or find a dimensionless group involving v_*, τ_0, and ρ.

8–6. The increase in pressure from the static pressure p_s to the stagnation pressure p_0 for incompressible flow depends on the free stream velocity u_s and the fluid density ρ. Express these variables (Δp, u_s, and ρ) as a dimensionless group.

$$Ans. \quad \pi_1 = \Delta p / \rho \, u_s^2$$

8–7. The increase in temperature from the static temperature T_s to the stagnation temperature T_0 in an adiabatic gas flow depends on the stream velocity V and the heat capacity c_p of the gas. Express these variables (ΔT, V, and c_p) as a dimensionless group.

8–8. The depth y_2 downstream of a hydraulic jump depends on the upstream depth y_1, the unit discharge q (volumetric flow rate per unit width of channel), and the acceleration of gravity g. Express these variables in dimensionless form. Compare with Eq. 12–14.

8–9. The resistance F of a surface ship depends on the ship speed V, the ship length L, the hull surface roughness k, the fluid density ρ, the fluid viscosity μ, and the acceleration of gravity g in connection with wave resistance. Express these variables in dimensionless form.

$$Ans. \quad \frac{F}{\rho V^2 L^2} = f\left(\frac{VL\rho}{\mu}, \frac{k}{L}, \frac{V}{\sqrt{gL}}\right)$$

8–10. The power P required to drive a fan or blower depends on the fluid density ρ, the fluid viscosity μ, the impeller diameter D, the volumetric flow rate Q, and the rotational speed N. Express these variables in dimensionless form. Show that $\rho ND^2/\mu$ is a form of the Reynolds number.

$$Ans. \quad \frac{P}{\rho N^3 D^5} = f\left(\frac{Q}{ND^3}, \frac{\rho ND^2}{\mu}\right)$$

8–11. The size d of spray or drops formed when liquid flows from a nozzle depends on a characteristic velocity in the nozzle V, the nozzle tip diameter D, the fluid density ρ, the fluid viscosity μ, the surface tension between the liquid and air σ, and the acceleration of gravity g. Express these variables in dimensionless form.

8–12. The pressure gradient $\Delta p/L$ for fully developed laminar flow in a circular tube depends on the flow rate Q, the tube diameter D, the fluid viscosity μ and the fluid density ρ. Express these variables in dimensionless form.

8–13. The boundary layer thickness δ on a smooth flat plate in an incompressible flow without pressure gradients depends on the free-stream velocity u_s, the fluid density ρ, the fluid viscosity μ, and the distance from the leading edge of the plate x. Express these variables in dimensionless form. Compare with Eqs. 7–9 and 7–14.

8–14. The fluid velocity u within a boundary layer depends on the free-stream velocity u_s, the fluid density ρ, the fluid viscosity μ, the wall shear stress τ_0, the normal distance from the boundary y, and the distance from the leading edge of the boundary surface x. Express these variables in dimensionless form. Discuss the term y/x in connection with results of Chapter 7, which showed that u/u_s depends on y/δ.

$$Ans. \quad \frac{u}{u_s} = f\left(\frac{u_s \, x\rho}{\mu}, \frac{\tau_0}{\rho u_s{}^2}, \frac{y}{x}\right)$$

8–15. Suppose the transition point x_t between a laminar and a turbulent boundary layer on an airfoil depends on the chord length C, the free-stream velocity u_s, the fluid viscosity ν, the turbulence intensity u' (the root-mean-square values of the turbulent velocity fluctuations about u_s), and the scale of the turbulence L. Show that this may be expressed as

$$\frac{x_t}{C} = f\left(\frac{u_s \, C}{\nu}, \frac{u'}{u_s}, \frac{L}{C}\right)$$

8–16. Laminar flow occurs along a flat surface, passes over a step, and re-attaches itself to a second flat surface parallel to the first at a distance x_R from the step. This reattachment distance x_R depends on the step height s, the free stream velocity u_s, the fluid density ρ, the fluid viscosity μ, and the boundary layer thickness δ at the step. Express these variables in dimensionless form.

$$Ans. \quad \frac{x_R}{s} = f\left(\frac{u_s s \rho}{\mu}, \frac{\delta}{s}\right)$$

8–17. The flow rate Q over a rectangular weir depends on the head on the weir crest H, the weir crest height Z (Fig. 13–15), the breadth of the weir crest b, the fluid density ρ, the fluid viscosity μ, the fluid surface tension σ, and the acceleration of gravity g, which may be considered a flow parameter. Express these variables in dimensionless form, and identify the Froude, Reynolds, and Weber numbers in your results.

8–18. Repeat Prob. 8–10 for a V-notch weir of angle θ (Fig. 13–18), the variable b being replaced by θ.

$$Ans. \quad \frac{Q}{g^{1/2} H^{5/2}} = f\left(\frac{\mu}{\rho g^{1/2} H^{3/2}}, \frac{\sigma}{H^2 g\rho}, \theta, \frac{H}{Z}\right)$$

8–19. The thrust of a ship propeller F depends on the propeller diameter D, the rotational speed N, the fluid density ρ, the fluid viscosity μ, and the speed of the propeller through the fluid V called the advance velocity, and the acceleration of gravity g. Express these variables in dimensionless form.

$$Ans. \quad \frac{F}{\rho D^2 V^2} = f\left(\frac{VD\rho}{\mu}, \frac{V}{ND}, \frac{gD}{V^2}\right)$$

8–20. The lift of a given airfoil shape in a subsonic flow depends on the angle of attack α, the chord length C, the span S, the free stream velocity u_s, the fluid viscosity μ, and the fluid density ρ. Express these variables in dimensionless form.

$$Ans. \quad \frac{L}{\rho u_s^2 CS} = f\left(\alpha, \frac{S}{C}, \frac{u_s \rho C}{\mu}\right)$$

NOTE: The application of the π theorem will give C^2, representing an area, instead of CS, the actual wing area.

8–21. Water at 70 F flows in a 12-in. pipe at an average velocity of 10 ft/sec. For flow at the same Reynolds number, calculate the average flow velocity for a) air at 100 F and 50 psia in a 6-in. pipe and b) gasoline at 50 F in an 8-in. pipe.

$$Ans. \quad a)\ 99\ \text{ft/sec}$$

8–22. Crude oil at 100 F flows in a 16-in. diameter pipe at a rate of 3000 gpm. At what rate should water at 70 F flow in a 4-in. diameter pipe for dynamically similar flow?

8–23. It is desired to estimate the pressure gradient for the flow of crude oil at 60 F at an average velocity of 10 ft/sec in a 18-in. pipeline. Measurements are made of the pressure gradient for water at 70 F flowing in a 3-in. pipe. a) At what velocity should the water flow in order that the water and oil systems be dynamically similar? b) The pressure gradient for the water is measured as 0.037 psi/ft. What is the pressure gradient for the oil?

8–24. Tests in a wind tunnel are to be used to determine the lift and drag of hydrofoils with a 12-in. chord for a boat designed to travel at 60 ft/sec in water at 70 F. In order to avoid compressibility effects in the wind tunnel, assume air at 59 F is to be used at a maximum velocity of 200 ft/sec. What wind tunnel pressure should be used with the 12-in. hydrofoils in the wind tunnel? The hydrofoils are to be run deep so that only viscous effects need to be considered.

8–25. The drag of an airship in standard air at 50 ft/sec is to be studied by means of a $\frac{1}{15}$-scale model. *a)* What is the required pressure in a wind tunnel for an air speed of 200 ft/sec at 59 F? *b)* At what speed should the model be towed in water at 70 F for dynamically similar flow? Towing must be deep to avoid gravity waves, or at high pressure in a water tunnel in order to avoid cavitation.

Ans. *a)* 3.75 atmospheres

8–26. An aircraft is to fly at 25,000 ft (temperature is -30 F and pressure is 785 psfa) at a velocity of 880 ft/sec. A $\frac{1}{20}$-scale model is tested in a high-speed pressurized wind tunnel in which the air is at 50 F. Assume Mach and Reynolds numbers the same in model and prototype. *a)* What is the model test velocity? *b)* What is the pressure in the wind tunnel?

Ans. *a)* $V_m = 960$ ft/sec; *b)* $p_m = 130$ psia

8–27. The drag and bending moment on a structure in a 60-mph wind is to be studied on a $\frac{1}{20}$-scale model in a pressurized wind tunnel where the air is 8 times the density of atmospheric air, but at the same temperature. *a)* What should be the wind speed in the wind tunnel? *b)* What prototype bending moment is indicated by a measured bending moment of 18 lb$_f$ ft on the model?

8–28. A torpedo 20 ft long is to travel at 20 knots (33.8 ft/sec) in water at 70 F. Suppose the drag of this torpedo is to be studied by means of an 8-ft model in a wind tunnel with standard air at the same Reynolds number as that for the prototype. *a)* What would be the air speed in the wind tunnel? *b)* Would this result in a useful model study? Explain.

8–29. Compare the thickness δ of a boundary layer at $x = 6$ ft from the leading edge of a smooth flat plate for flow at a Reynolds number of $Re_x = 2 \times 10^7$ for water at 70 F with that for standard air. $\delta/x = f(Re_x)$.

8–30. A maximum flow rate of 6 ft³/sec is available for a river model. This corresponds to 30,000 ft³/sec for the prototype. What is the maximum size of the model in terms of the prototype size?

Ans. Max $L_m/L_p = 1/30.2$

8–31. A spillway model is built to a scale of $\frac{1}{45}$. When the depth of water over the crest is 2 in., the flow rate is 1.5 ft³/sec. To what head and flow rate in the prototype does this correspond?

8–32. The flow in a river is 50,000 ft³/sec. A distorted model with a horizontal scale of $\frac{1}{70}$ and a vertical scale of $\frac{1}{20}$ is built for laboratory tests. What is the flow rate in the model?

8–33. A tank containing water drains through a 1-in. diameter orifice in 6 min 20 sec. How long would it take for kerosene to drain from a geometrically similar tank through a 4-in. diameter orifice? Neglect viscous effects, and consider only the effect of gravity.

8-34. The tank containing water in Prob. 8-33 is on the moon, where the acceleration of gravity is $\frac{1}{6}$ that on earth. How long will it take for the tank to drain on the moon?

Ans.   15 min 31 sec

8-35. The wave resistance of a $\frac{1}{40}$-scale model of a ship is studied in fresh water. The prototype ship travels at 28 knots (1 knot = 1.69 ft/sec). *a*) What is the model speed? *b*) What wave drag in the prototype corresponds to a wave drag of 2.00 lb$_f$ for the model?

8-36. A 20-ft wax model of a cargo ship is towed through fresh water at 5 knots (8.45 ft/sec) with a total measured drag of 23.5 lb$_f$. The skin-friction drag coefficient is 0.00272, and the wetted surface area is 69.85 ft^2. *a*) What is the skin-friction drag on the model? *b*) What is the wave drag for the model? *c*) What is the wave-drag coefficient for the model? The model is tested according to the Froude number and represents a prototype ship 400 ft long. *d*) What is the speed of the prototype ship? *e*) Estimate the wave drag for the prototype ship. *f*) If the skin-friction drag coefficient for the prototype is 0.0018, what is the skin-friction drag for the prototype? *g*) What is the total drag for the prototype? *h*) What is the horsepower required to tow the model and to propel the prototype at the speed in part *d*)?

Ans.   *e*) 85,000 lb$_f$; *f*) 71,500 lb$_f$; *h*) hp$_m$ = 0.361, hp$_p$ = 10,750

8-37. The relation between head and discharge for water flowing through a 90-deg V-notch weir (Fig. 13–18) is

$$Q = 2.47\ H^{2.48}\ \text{ft}^3/\text{sec}$$

where H is in feet. Suppose crude oil at 70 F flows through the weir at a head of 9 in. *a*) What are the head and discharge for dynamically similar flow of water at 70 F? Inertia, viscous, and gravity forces are involved. *b*) What is the discharge of oil? *c*) What is the effect of viscosity on the flow over a weir? Refer to Prob. 8–11.

Ans.   *a*) H_w = 0.233 ft, Q_w = 0.0666 ft^3/sec; *b*) Q_o = 1.23 ft^3/sec; *c*) Q_w = 1.21 ft^3/sec at a head of 9 in. Flow rate increases slightly with an increase in viscosity.

8-38. A model of a dam for a hydroelectric project is to be built for flow studies. The maximum flow in the river is 120,000 ft^3/sec, and the maximum supply available in the laboratory for model studies is 4 ft^3/sec. What is the largest distorted model that may be built, in relation to the river size, in order that dynamically similar flows may be achieved? The horizontal scale is to be reduced three times that of the vertical scale; that is, $(L_m/L_p)_V = 3(L_m/L_p)_H$.

Ans. $\left(\dfrac{L_m}{L_p}\right)_H = \dfrac{1}{119.4}$

8-39. A $\frac{1}{50}$-scale model of a river contains some bridge piers. The force on one pier in the model is 0.39 lb$_f$. What force would be expected on a full-size pier in the prototype, assuming similarity for inertia and gravity forces?

8-40. A $\frac{1}{1800}$-scale model of a tidal estuary is operated to satisfy the Froude law. What length of time in the model represents 12.4 hr in the prototype? This is approximately a tidal period.

8–41. A tidal model is built to a scale of $\frac{1}{3600}$ horizontally and $\frac{1}{81}$ vertically. For a tidal period of 12.4 hr in nature, what is the tidal period in the model?

Ans. 1.86 min

8–42. An airplane is to fly in standard air at 250 ft/sec. A $\frac{1}{6}$-scale model is made and tested in a wind tunnel with standard air at 1500 ft/sec. Considering inertia, viscous, and compressibility forces, is the flow past the model dynamically similar to that past the prototype? Explain.

8–43. Fundamental studies on boundary layers for compressible flow are made in wind tunnels with air flowing past a model at rest and in firing ranges in which a model is fired through a gas which is at rest. In which type of test would free-flight conditions be better simulated? Discuss your answer.

8–44. One of the advantages of using hydrogen rather than air for cooling electrical generators is the reduction in windage losses. Estimate these losses for hydrogen as a percentage of those for air in a given machine. Assume hydrogen and air at essentially the same pressure and temperature. Power loss is proportional to the product of a drag force and a velocity.

Ans. 7 per cent

8–45. Tests on a $\frac{1}{10}$-scale model of a supersonic body in a wind tunnel at a Mach number of 1.8 indicate a drag coefficient of 0.45. The wind tunnel air in the test section is at -50 F and 2.50 psia. *a)* What is the air speed in the test section of the wind tunnel? *b)* What is the drag of the prototype missile at 50,000 ft ($T = -67$ F and $p = 242$ psfa) compared with that of the model in the wind tunnel at the same Mach number?

Ans. *a)* 1787 ft/sec

8–46. A supersonic firing range consists of a closed chamber containing xenon at 65 F. At what velocity should a small missile be fired through the chamber in order that the steady flow pattern past it be dynamically similar to a free flight at 4000 ft/sec in standard air?

8–47. Write expressions for the ratio of prototype horsepower to model horsepower for dynamically similar flows based on the *a)* Reynolds number, *b)* Froude number, and *c)* Mach number.

8–48. A pump discharges 4000 gpm under a head of 12.1 ft at an efficiency of 82 per cent at 1150 rpm. Estimate the flow rate, head, and brake horsepower for a speed of 1450 rpm, assuming the same efficiency.

Ans. $\text{hp}_{1450} = 29.9$

8–49. A centrifugal pump is rated at 450 gpm at a head of 122 ft when pumping water at 1750 rpm. The pump efficiency is 74 per cent. Estimate the flow rate, head, and brake horsepower at 1450 rpm, assuming the same efficiency.

8–50. The impeller of the centrifugal pump in Prob. 8–49 is 12 in. in diameter. Estimate the pump performance when the impeller diameter is reduced to 11.5 in., assuming the same speed (1750 rpm) and efficiency.

8–51. A 16-in. diameter model of an 8-ft diameter propeller is tested in accordance with the results of Prob. 8–19, with the exception that viscous forces are considered negligible. A torque of 15 lb$_f$ ft at 450 rpm develops a thrust of 55 lb$_f$ at a speed of advance of 8.45 ft/sec. *a*) To what speed of advance and rotational speed for the prototype propeller do these test conditions correspond? *b*) Estimate the thrust and torque for the prototype propeller, assuming the same efficiency and fluid for both model and prototype. *c*) What is the propeller efficiency? This is defined as the ratio of power output to power input.

Ans. *a*) 20.7 ft/sec and 183.7 rpm; *b*) 11,880 lb$_f$ and 19,440 lb$_f$ ft; *c*) 65.7 per cent

8–52. Compute the specific speed for the pumps in *a*) Prob. 8–48, *b*) Prob. 8–49, and *c*) Prob. 8–50.

8–53. A turbine develops 8000 hp under a head of 100 ft at 450 rpm. Estimate the *a*) speed and *b*) power developed under a head of 80 ft. *c*) What type of turbine is this?

Ans. *a*) 402 rpm; *b*) 5700 hp; *c*) $N_{s(T)} = 127$, Kaplan

8–54. A 20-in. diameter turbine wheel is tested at 1008 rpm under a head of 400 ft and delivers 1.46 hp. It is a ½-scale model of a large turbine which is to operate under a net head of 4830 ft. *a*) What is the speed of the prototype turbine? *b*) What is the power output of the prototype turbine at the same efficiency as the model? *c*) What type of turbine is this?

8–55. In making model tests of the following situations, state for each whether the Reynolds number, the Froude number, the Mach number, or a combination of them are significant.

a) Liquid flow in a pipe
b) High-velocity gas flow in a pipe
c) The drag of a parachute
d) Flow over a spillway in a river model
e) The drag of a submarine at a 100-ft depth
f) The total drag on a cargo ship
g) Boundary layer growth on a supersonic missile
h) The movement of sediment in a river
i) Silt settling in a reservoir
j) Beach erosion

9

The Flow of Compressible Gases

Situations in which relatively large variations in fluid density occur with associated large variations in velocity exist in many gas flows and involve thermodynamic effects. The study of this type of flow is often referred to as *gas dynamics*. The behavior of the gas depends to a large extent on the speed of the gas flow in relation to that of a weak pressure wave, measured in terms of the Mach number M. At low subsonic speeds (M < 0.2), the density variations are so small that the flow may be considered incompressible. At higher subsonic speed, the density variations increase and their effects become more and more pronounced. At supersonic speeds (M > 1), the effects are very pronounced, and abrupt changes in velocity and pressure, which increase in magnitude as the Mach number increases, occur across a shock, for example.

The following assumptions will be made in the treatment given in this chapter:

1. Gases will be considered perfect ($p = \rho RT$ and c_p = constant). This simplifies the equations used and gives quite accurate results for moderate pressures, temperatures, or Mach numbers. For pressures below 50 atmospheres or stagnation temperatures below 1000 R, accuracy is good for any Mach number; and for higher pressures and temperatures, errors increase with Mach number, up to a maximum which depends on the pressure and temperature.[1]

2. Flow will generally be considered adiabatic (without heat transfer). In addition it will be considered reversible, and thus isentropic, with the exception of flow across a shock. Diabatic flow (with heat transfer) is discussed in Sec. 9–4.

3. The flow will be considered one-dimensional.

4. Changes in potential energy (elevation) will not be considered, since they are trivial (if not zero) compared to changes in kinetic energy and enthalpy.

5. No external work is done on or by the gas.

With conditions 2, 3, 4, and 5, the steady-flow energy equation (Eq. 5–17a) will have the forms

$$\frac{V_1^2}{2} + h_1 = \frac{V_2^2}{2} + h_2 = h_0 = \text{constant} \tag{9–1a}$$

[1] C. DuP. Donaldson, "Note on the Importance of Imperfect-Gas Effects and Variation of Heat Capacities on the Isentropic Flow of Gases," *NACA R.M* No. L8J14, 1948.

and
$$V\,dV + dh = 0 \qquad (9\text{–}1\text{b})$$

Thus there will be a mutual interchange of kinetic energy with enthalpy, resulting in opposite changes in velocity and temperature.

Straightforward application of the continuity, momentum, and energy equations together with thermodynamic relationships for perfect gases, the isentropic relation $p/\rho^k = $ constant, and the second law of thermodynamics will enable us to make a quantitative study of compressible gas flow. Results will apply with remarkable accuracy to high-speed flight and flow through gas-turbine, steam-turbine, and rocket nozzles. Flow with friction through pipes will be taken up in Sec. 10–9.

9–1. THE VELOCITY OF SOUND

The velocity of a plane, weak, pressure pulse in a gas may be determined by applying the continuity and momentum principles across a wave front traveling in a duct of area A. The momentum theorem applied to the dashed region of Fig. 9–1 (wall shear is negligible) is
$$(p + dp)A - pA = cA\rho\,[-(c - dV) - (-c)]$$

so that
$$dp = \rho c\,dV \qquad (9\text{–}2)$$

From continuity,
$$cA\rho = (c - dV)A(\rho + d\rho)$$

and if the second-order differentials are neglected,
$$\frac{d\rho}{\rho} = \frac{dV}{c} \qquad (9\text{–}3)$$

Combining Eqs. 9–2 and 9–3, and using Eq. 2–12c,
$$c^2 = dp/d\rho = K/\rho$$

For a gas
$$c^2 = \left(\frac{\partial p}{\partial \rho}\right)_{\text{isentropic}} \qquad (9\text{–}4\text{a})$$

Since the changes in pressure and temperature are extremely small, they are considered to be reversible. In addition, the temperature gradients are also small and the process is very rapid, consequently no heat is transferred. Thus the process approaches an isentropic, for which $p/\rho^k = $ constant. The logarithmic form is
$$\ln p - k\ln\rho = \ln\,(\text{constant})$$

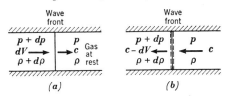

FIG. 9–1. Weak pressure wave in a duct of area A. *a*) Observer at rest. *b*) Observer "riding" on wave front.

from which $$\frac{dp}{d\rho} = \frac{kp}{\rho} = kRT$$

Thus the velocity of sound in a perfect gas is

$$c = \sqrt{\frac{kp}{\rho}} \qquad (9\text{-}4b)$$

$$= \sqrt{kRT} \qquad (9\text{-}4c)$$

$$= \sqrt{\frac{K}{\rho}} \qquad (9\text{-}4d)^2$$

since the isentropic elastic modulus K for a perfect gas is equal to kp.

For air, $c = 49.02 \sqrt{T}$, where c is in feet per second and T is in degrees Rankine.

9–2. THE MACH NUMBER AND ITS RANGES

The Mach number has been defined (Chapter 8) as the ratio of a) the flow velocity to the sound velocity, b) the inertia to the elastic forces in a flow system, or c) the kinetic energy of the mean flow to the mean kinetic energy of the gas molecules. In any case,

$$\mathrm{M} = \frac{V}{c} \qquad (9\text{-}5)$$

The velocity V may be either the local velocity or the relative velocity between the free stream and a body immersed in the stream. For example, a local velocity may be the velocity at the throat or at the exit of a nozzle. The velocity of either an aircraft or a missile in free flight through still air and the free-stream velocity past a test body in a wind tunnel are examples of relative velocity between a stream and a body immersed in the stream.

The reference sonic velocity may be a) the local sonic velocity c determined from the local temperature, b) the sonic velocity c_0 at the stagnation condition, or c) the velocity c^* where the flow is, or would be, sonic. These are interrelated by the steady-flow energy equation [Eq. 9–1a, with $h = c_p T$, $c_p = Rk/(k-1)$ and $c = \sqrt{kRT}$] applied to each of the three states.

$$\frac{V^2}{2} + \frac{1}{k-1} c^2 = \frac{1}{k-1} c_0{}^2 = \frac{k+1}{2(k-1)} c^{*2} \qquad (9\text{-}6)$$

[2]The acoustic velocity in any medium is $c = \sqrt{K/\rho}$. For gas-liquid mixtures the acoustic velocity becomes less than that for either the liquid or gas alone. For a liquid with a small concentration of gas nuclei, the elastic modulus of the mixture is reduced, with no appreciable reduction in density, and thus the acoustic velocity is reduced. For a gas with minute liquid droplets, the density of the mixture is increased, with no appreciable change in elastic modulus, and again the acoustic velocity for the mixture is reduced. The velocity of sound in a 14 per cent water and 86 per cent air mixture is about 100 ft/sec (depending on the pressure, temperature, and impressed frequency) as compared with about 4800 ft/sec for water and about 1100 ft/sec for air. See also Prob. 2-60.

We will use the local sound velocity c as a reference throughout this chapter.

For steady flow, the energy equation for adiabatic flow with the assumptions listed at the beginning of this chapter is

$$\frac{V^2}{2} + h = \text{constant}$$

There are two extreme situations for a given gas condition:

1. If all kinetic energy is converted to enthalpy, the velocity is zero and the temperature is a maximum.
2. If all the enthalpy could be converted to kinetic energy (a hypothetical condition), the temperature would drop to absolute zero, and the velocity would be a maximum.

In the first instance, the velocity is zero and the speed of sound is a maximum; in the second instance, the speed of sound is zero and the velocity is a maximum. This is indicated in three expressions for the constant in the energy equation: 1) for an arbitrary given state where the velocity is V and the temperature T, 2) for the stagnation state, and 3) for the zero-temperature state. With $\Delta h = c_p \Delta T$ and $T = c^2/kR$, the energy equation may be written for these three states as

$$V^2 + \frac{2}{k-1} c^2 = \frac{2}{k-1} c_0^2 = V_{\text{max}}^2 \qquad (9\text{--}7)$$

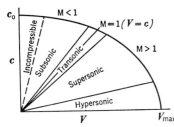

FIG. 9–2. Ellipse showing ranges of compressible gas flow.

A plot of this equation is shown in Fig. 9–2 and is known as the steady-flow adiabatic ellipse. The reader is also referred to the discussion of Fig. 13–9.

9–3. ISENTROPIC FLOW OF A PERFECT GAS

Between any two points or sections in an isentropic flow the following energy, continuity, isentropic, and gas equations apply:

$$\frac{V_1^2}{2} + h_1 = \frac{V_2^2}{2} + h_2 \qquad [9\text{--}1a]$$

$$V_1 A_1 \rho_1 = V_2 A_2 \rho_2 \qquad [5\text{--}6b]$$

$$\frac{p_1}{\rho_1^k} = \frac{p_2}{\rho_2^k} \qquad [3\text{--}13c]$$

$$h_2 - h_1 = c_p(T_2 - T_1) = \frac{Rk}{k-1}(T_2 - T_1) \quad [3\text{--}8 \text{ and } 3\text{--}12]$$

Stagnation temperature. The stagnation temperature exists at a point of zero velocity. Thus if the fluid proceeds to this point adiabatically

$$\frac{V^2}{2} + h = h_0$$

from which $$T_0 = T + \frac{V^2}{2c_p} \qquad (9\text{-}8a)^3$$

and the stagnation temperature rise varies as the square of the gas velocity. Recall that $V^2 = \text{M}^2 c^2 = \text{M}^2 kRT$ and that $c_p = Rk/(k-1)$. Thus

$$\frac{T_0}{T} = 1 + \frac{k-1}{2} \text{M}^2 \qquad (9\text{-}8b)$$

Actually, Eqs. 9–8a and 9–8b are valid for any adiabatic flow of a perfect gas at all Mach numbers, whether reversible or not. Thus they may be applied across a shock wave, which is not reversible, as in Sec. 9–5.

Stagnation pressure. The stagnation pressure p_0 is, by definition, the pressure reached isentropically, and is often called the isentropic stagnation pressure. It is also called the reservoir pressure, since for any flow condition a reservoir pressure p_0 may be imagined from which flow proceeds isentropically to a pressure p and Mach number M. If the flow is entirely isentropic, p_0 is constant throughout the flow; if non-isentropic, p_0 changes from section to section. In an irreversible adiabatic flow p_0 decreases in the direction of flow, and the decrease in p_0 is a measure of the irreversibility of the flow or the increase in entropy of the gas. From Eqs. 3–13b and 9–8b

$$\frac{p_0}{p} = \left(\frac{T_0}{T}\right)^{\frac{k}{k-1}} = \left(1 + \frac{k-1}{2} \text{M}^2\right)^{\frac{k}{k-1}} \qquad (9\text{-}9a)$$

and this is the defining equation for stagnation pressure for *both* subsonic and supersonic flow. Expanding this expression[4] gives, after simplifying,

$$p_0 = p + \frac{\rho V^2}{2}\left[1 + \frac{1}{4}\text{M}^2 + \frac{2-k}{24}\text{M}^4 + \frac{(2-k)(3-2k)}{192}\text{M}^6 + \cdots\right]$$

$$(9\text{-}9b)$$

This may be compared with $p_0 = p + \rho V^2/2$ for incompressible flow.

The term in brackets in Eq. 9–9b indicates the effect of the increase in gas density due to compressibility and is called the *compressibility factor*. Values of this factor for $k = 1.4$ (air, for example) range from 1 as the Mach number approaches zero (no compressibility effects) to 1.276 as the Mach number approaches unity. This means that the dynamic pressure

[3]For air, if $T_0 - T$ is in degrees centigrade and V is in miles per hour,
$$T_0 - T \approx (V_{\text{mph}}/100)^2 \text{ deg C}$$

[4]$(1 + x)^a = 1 + ax + a(a-1)\frac{x^2}{2!} + a(a-1)(a-2)\frac{x^3}{3!} + \cdots$, which is convergent for $x^* < 1$. Mathematically, the resulting expansion given by Eq. 9–9b is valid for $\text{M} < \sqrt{5}$ for a gas with $k = 1.4$. Physically, Eqs. 9–9a and 9–9b are valid only for isentropic flow, and may be applied to subsonic initial flow when flow is *towards* a stagnation point. If flow is *from* a reservoir (a stagnation condition), Eq. 9–9a is valid for any subsequent Mach number and Eq. 9–9b is valid for subsequent Mach numbers less than $\sqrt{5} = 2.236$ (for $k = 1.4$), provided the flow is isentropic.

increases 27.6 per cent over the dynamic pressure if incompressible flow is incorrectly assumed, because of the compressibility of the gas as the Mach number approaches unity.

Duct flow. For incompressible flow, the continuity equation $VA =$ constant indicates that an increase in flow area is associated with a decrease in velocity, and a decrease in flow area is associated with an increase in velocity. For compressible flow this is not always the case, because of the changes in fluid density. The relationship between area and velocity changes is a function of the local Mach number and may be found by combining the continuity, energy, and second-law equations in differential form. These, for isentropic flow, are

$$\frac{dV}{V} + \frac{dA}{A} + \frac{d\rho}{\rho} = 0 \qquad [5\text{--}10]$$

$$V \, dV + dh = 0 \qquad [9\text{--}1b]$$

and
$$dh = \frac{dp}{\rho} \qquad [3\text{--}5]$$

From the second and third of these equations, $\rho = -dp/V \, dV$, and if this is substituted in the first equation,

$$\frac{dA}{A} = -\frac{dV}{V}\left(1 - \frac{V^2}{dp/d\rho}\right) = -\frac{dV}{V}\left(1 - \frac{V^2}{c^2}\right)$$

so that[5]
$$\frac{dA}{dV} = \frac{A}{V}(M^2 - 1) \qquad (9\text{--}10)$$

Whether the area and the velocity decrease or increase is determined by the sign of dA/dV, which in turn depends on the magnitude of the local Mach number. The various possibilities are listed in Table 9–1.

Subsonic gas flow is similar to incompressible flow in so far as the velocity increases if the flow area decreases, and conversely, the velocity decreases if the flow area increases. The velocity may be sonic ($M = 1$) *only* where the area is constant and is not changing, such as in the throat of a nozzle. (Constant-area flow—pipe flow—is discussed in Chapter 10.) For supersonic gas flow, an increase in flow area produces an *increase* in velocity, and a decrease in flow area produces a *decrease* in velocity.

[5]An alternative derivation is as follows: For a nonviscous fluid, the equation of motion may be written as

$$\frac{dp}{\rho} + V \, dV = 0$$

and since $c^2 = dp/d\rho$ we get

$$c^2 \frac{d\rho}{\rho} + V \, dV = 0$$

Combining this equation with the continuity equation (Eq. 5-10) gives

$$\frac{dV}{V}\left(1 - \frac{V^2}{c^2}\right) + \frac{dA}{A} = 0$$

which is equivalent to Eq. 9–10.

TABLE 9–1

AREA AND VELOCITY CHANGES FOR GAS FLOW IN DUCTS (EQ. 9–10)

Mach Number M	$\dfrac{dA}{dV}$	dA	dV	$\dfrac{dV}{dx}$ As a Function of $\dfrac{dA}{dx}$
<1	−	+	−	Velocity decreases
		−	+	Velocity increases
>1	+	+	+	Velocity increases
		−	−	Velocity decreases
=1	0	0		Velocity can be sonic only in the throat of a nozzle or in a pipe (see Sec. 10–10).

Supersonic gas flow is analogous to the flow of traffic in a multilane roadway. If the roadway narrows to fewer lanes, traffic speed is reduced, and if the roadway widens to more lanes, traffic speed is increased.

Additional relationships between changes in velocity, Mach number, temperature, pressure, and area may be obtained by combining the differential forms of the continuity, energy, isentropic, perfect gas, and Mach number equations.

The isentropic relationship $p/\rho^k = $ constant may be written as

$$\frac{dp}{p} - k\frac{d\rho}{\rho} = 0 \qquad (9\text{–}11)$$

The perfect gas equation $p = \rho RT$ may be written as

$$\frac{dp}{p} = \frac{d\rho}{\rho} + \frac{dT}{T} \qquad (9\text{–}12)$$

The Mach number is defined as $\mathbf{M} = V/\sqrt{kRT}$ and may be written as

$$\frac{d\mathbf{M}}{\mathbf{M}} = \frac{dV}{V} - \frac{dT}{2T} \qquad (9\text{–}13)$$

The results of various combinations are

$$\frac{dV}{V} = \left[\frac{1}{1 + \dfrac{k-1}{2}\mathbf{M}^2}\right]\frac{d\mathbf{M}}{\mathbf{M}} \qquad (9\text{–}14)$$

which, since the term in brackets is always positive, indicates that both velocity and Mach number either increase or decrease together.

$$\frac{dT}{T} = \left[\frac{-(k-1)\mathrm{M}^2}{1 + \frac{k-1}{2}\mathrm{M}^2} \right] \frac{d\mathrm{M}}{\mathrm{M}} \tag{9-15}$$

which, since the term in brackets is always negative, indicates that temperature changes are opposite to Mach number changes. That is, temperatures decrease with an increase in Mach number, and temperatures increase with a decrease in Mach number.

$$\frac{dp}{p} = \left[\frac{-k\mathrm{M}^2}{1 + \frac{k-1}{2}\mathrm{M}^2} \right] \frac{d\mathrm{M}}{\mathrm{M}} \tag{9-16}$$

which, since the term in brackets is always negative, indicates that pressure changes are also opposite to Mach number changes.

$$\frac{dA}{A} = \left[\frac{-(1-\mathrm{M}^2)}{1 + \frac{k-1}{2}\mathrm{M}^2} \right] \frac{d\mathrm{M}}{\mathrm{M}} \tag{9-17}$$

which indicates that area changes and Mach number changes depend on the magnitude of the Mach number, since the term in brackets may be either positive or negative. Results are the same as those for Eq. 9–10 listed in Table 9–1 which relate area and velocity changes. For subsonic flow (M < 1), area and Mach number changes are opposite. For sonic flow (M = 1), $dA/A = 0$, and this flow can occur only in a throat where the flow cross section is not changing. For supersonic flow (M > 1), area and Mach number changes are in the same direction (both increase or decrease together).

Flow through nozzles. Gas flowing through a converging or a converging-diverging nozzle is usually supplied from a pressure tank or reservoir in which the velocity is zero or essentially so. Thus the supply reservoir is in a known stagnation condition, and the velocity, temperature, and pressure at any other section in the flow are given by Eqs. 9–1a, 9–8b, and 9–9a, respectively. These may be written as

$$V = \sqrt{2c_p T_0 \left(1 - \frac{T}{T_0}\right)} \tag{9-18a}$$

in terms of the temperature T at any arbitrary section for *any* adiabatic flow. For isentropic flow,

$$V = \sqrt{2c_p T_0 \left[1 - \left(\frac{p}{p_0}\right)^{\frac{k-1}{k}}\right]} \tag{9-18b}$$

in terms of the pressure p at any arbitrary section.

The temperature at any section where the Mach number M is known is

$$T = \frac{T_0}{1 + \frac{k-1}{2}M^2} \tag{9-19}$$

and the pressure at any section where the Mach number M is known is

$$p = \frac{p_0}{\left(1 + \frac{k-1}{2}M^2\right)^{\frac{k}{k-1}}} \tag{9-20}$$

Densities may be calculated from the gas equation $p = \rho RT$ or from

$$\rho = \frac{\rho_0}{\left(1 + \frac{k-1}{2}M^2\right)^{\frac{1}{k-1}}} \tag{9-21}$$

At the section where the velocity is sonic (the throat), the Mach number is unity and the flow is called *critical flow*. If conditions at this section are designated by an asterisk, the critical temperature T^* from Eq. 9–19 is

$$\frac{T^*}{T_0} = \frac{2}{k+1} \tag{9-22}$$

which is valid for *any* adiabatic flow (both isentropic flow and flow with friction). The critical pressure p^* from Eq. 9–20 or from the isentropic relation and Eq. 9–22 is

$$\frac{p^*}{p_0} = \left(\frac{2}{k+1}\right)^{\frac{k}{k-1}} \tag{9-23}$$

which is valid *only* for isentropic flow. Both T^*/T_0 and p^*/p_0 depend only on the specific heat ratio of the gas. For air ($k = 1.4$), $T^*/T_0 = \frac{5}{6}$ and $p^*/p_0 = 0.528$. Thus air flowing from a supply tank (reservoir) will have its temperature reduced to $\frac{5}{6}$ the tank temperature and its pressure reduced to 52.8 per cent of the tank pressure at the location where the velocity becomes sonic ($M = 1$).

If the gas expands (pressure drops), Eq. 9–16 indicates an increase in the Mach number. This is true for both subsonic and supersonic flow. Equations 9–10 and 9–17 indicate that an area reduction in subsonic flow and an area increase in supersonic flow are necessary to accelerate the gas. The relationship between the area A^* where the Mach number is unity (the throat) and the area A at any other section where $M \gtrless 1$ may be obtained by integrating Eq. 9–17 to obtain

$$\frac{A}{A^*} = \frac{1}{M}\left(\frac{1 + \frac{k-1}{2}M^2}{(k+1)/2}\right)^{\frac{k+1}{2(k-1)}} \tag{9-24}$$

which depends only on the Mach number for a given gas.

From continuity,

$$\frac{V}{V^*} = \frac{A^*\rho^*}{A\rho} = M \sqrt{\frac{\dfrac{k+1}{2}}{1 + \dfrac{k-1}{2}M^2}} \tag{9-25}$$

which relates the velocity V at a section where $M \gtrless 1$ to the velocity V^* where the velocity is sonic ($M = 1$).

Note that for isentropic flow, values of T/T_0, p/p_0, ρ/ρ_0, A/A^*, and V/V^* depend only on the Mach number for a given gas, and these functions given in Eqs. 9–8b, 9–9a, 9–21, 9–24, and 9–25, respectively, may be tabulated. An example is shown in Table A–1 (Appendix III) for isentropic flow of a gas for which $k = 1.4$. Gas tables of this type may be used for numerical calculations of flow problems.

The results may easily be applied to the analysis of flow through a given nozzle or to the design of a nozzle for given flow conditions.

For a *converging nozzle* (Fig. 9–3), if the receiver and supply pressures are equal, there will be no flow (Eq. 9–18b). As p_3 is reduced, V_1 will increase to a sonic value. This occurs when p_1 becomes critical (Eq. 9–23). For values of receiver pressure above critical, the nozzle exit pressure and receiver pressure are equal. If the receiver pressure is reduced below the critical pressure, the flow through the nozzle is not affected, since it is sonic at exit and cannot exceed that value. (Suppose V_1 is supersonic. Then the velocity would have to be sonic between the supply tank and nozzle exit. But this is impossible from Eq. 9–10 and Table 9–1, since the area is decreasing and sonic flow cannot occur if the area is changing.) The flow rate is

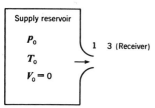

Fig. 9–3. Flow through a converging nozzle.

Mass flow rate $= V_1 A_1 \rho_1$

The exit velocity may be found from Eq. 9–18a or 9–18b. The area A_1 is assumed given. The density ρ_1 may be obtained from Eq. 9–21 or from the gas equation, since if either p_1 or T_1 is given, the other may be found from the isentropic relation. If V_1 is sonic, the mass-flow rate for air flow becomes

$$\dot{m} = c_1 A_1 \frac{p_1}{RT_1} = \sqrt{kRT_1}\,(A_1)\frac{0.528p_0}{R(5T_0/6)} \tag{9-26a}$$

$$= 0.0165 \frac{A_1 p_0}{\sqrt{T_0}} \quad \text{slugs/sec} \tag{9-26b}$$

$$= 0.53 \frac{A_1 p_0}{\sqrt{T_0}} \quad \text{lb}_m\text{/sec} \tag{9-26c}$$

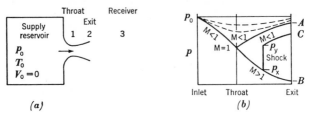

FIG. 9–4. *a*) Flow through a converging-diverging
nozzle. *b*) Axial pressures in nozzle.

If the exit flow is sonic and the receiver pressure less than critical, the
flow becomes supersonic beyond the exit and dissipates itself through a
series of successive shocks outside the nozzle.

The axial pressure distribution between the inlet and throat of a
converging-diverging nozzle shown in Fig. 9–4 applies to a converging
nozzle.

For a *converging-diverging nozzle* (Fig. 9–4), there is no flow if
$p_3 = p_0 (= p_1, = p_2,$ and so forth). As the receiver pressure p_3 is lowered,
flow exists throughout the nozzle, with a minimum pressure and maximum
velocity at the throat. The pressures vary along the axis according to the
dashed lines of Fig. 9–4b. As the receiver pressure is lowered to A,
the flow in the throat will become sonic, and the pressure there will be
critical. Flow will be subsonic both upstream and downstream from the
throat. There is only one other exit pressure (at B) for which isentropic
flow with sonic velocity in the throat may occur. The flow rate is the
same whether the exit pressure is at A or at B, since the throat conditions
are the same in each instance. The flow is supersonic, however, beyond
the throat if the exit pressure is at B. As for a converging nozzle, if the
receiver pressure is below B, a series of successive shocks occur beyond the
end of the nozzle exit and full expansion does not occur within the nozzle.
If the exit pressure is below A but somewhat above B, a shock will be set
up in the nozzle at a point depending on the exit pressure and the
nozzle shape. In this instance the flow may be considered isentropic only
up to the shock and beyond the shock, but not through the shock. It
should be noted that for flow which is non-isentropic owing to viscous or
frictional effects rather than to shocks, the flow in the nozzle throat is
subsonic.

If the throat velocity is sonic, the flow rate is given by Eq. 9–26a.
In general, the mass-flow rate is always given by the product $VA\rho$. Values
of velocity and density may be obtained for any section where the pressure
or temperature is specified.

EXAMPLE 9–1. Air at 100 psia and 100 F flows from a tank through a converging nozzle whose tip area is 0.005 ft². What is the exit pressure, exit temperature, and flow rate if the receiver pressure is *a*) 70 psia and *b*) 14.7 psia? See Fig. 9–3.

Solution: a) Since the receiver pressure is greater than critical (52.8 psia), flow will be subsonic at the nozzle exit, and the pressure $p_1 = 70$ psia.

$$T_1 = T_0 \left(\frac{p_1}{p_0}\right)^{\frac{k-1}{k}} = 560 \left(\frac{70}{100}\right)^{0.286} = 506 \text{ R} = 46 \text{ F}$$

The mass-flow rate $= V_1 A_1 \rho_1$. From Eq. 9–18a,

$$V_1 = \sqrt{2c_p T_0(1 - T_1/T_0)} = \sqrt{(2)(6000)(560)(1 - 0.903)} = 806 \text{ ft/sec}$$

$$\rho_1 = \frac{p_1}{RT_1} = \frac{(70)(144)}{(1715)(506)} = 0.0116 \text{ slug/ft}^3$$

$$\dot{m} = V_1 A_1 \rho_1 = (806)(0.005)(0.0116) = 0.0467 \text{ slug/sec}$$
$$= (32.17)(0.0467) = 1.50 \text{ lb}_m/\text{sec}$$

b) If the receiver pressure is 14.7 psia (below critical), the nozzle exit pressure is critical, so $p_1 = 52.8$ psia. The exit temperature (from Eq. 9–22) is

$$T_1 = T^* = \tfrac{5}{6} T_0 = \tfrac{5}{6} (560) = 466 \text{ R} = 6 \text{ F}$$

The flow rate $= V_1 A_1 \rho_1$, where V_1 is sonic.

$$V_1 = c_1 = 49.02\sqrt{T_1} = 49.02\sqrt{466} = 1060 \text{ ft/sec}$$

$$\rho_1 = \frac{p_1}{RT_1} = \frac{(52.8)(144)}{(1715)(466)} = 0.00951 \text{ slug/ft}^3$$

$$\dot{m} = V_1 A_1 \rho_1 = (1060)(0.005)(0.00951) = 0.0504 \text{ slug/sec}$$
$$= (32.17)(0.0504) = 1.62 \text{ lb}_m/\text{sec}$$

EXAMPLE 9–2. If a converging-diverging nozzle with a throat area of 0.005 ft² and an exit area of 0.01 ft² is attached to the supply tank of Example 9–1, what is the flow rate and exit pressure, temperature, and Mach number for complete expansion in the nozzle? See Fig. 9–4.

Solution: For complete expansion, the exit pressure corresponds to point B in Fig. 9–4b. The flow rate is fixed by sonic flow in the throat, and this is the same as for critical flow in the converging nozzle of Example 9–1. Thus the flow rate is 1.62 lb$_m$/sec.

The ratio of exit area to throat area (the flow is critical in the throat) is

$$\frac{A_2}{A^*} = \frac{0.01}{0.005} = 2$$

and from Table A–1, $M_2 = 2.20$ and the corresponding values of $p_2/p_0 = 0.0935$ and $T_2/T_0 = 0.508$ indicate that $p_2 = 9.35$ psia and $T_2 = 284$ R $= -176$ F.

9–4. DIABATIC FLOW OF A PERFECT GAS WITHOUT FRICTION

Adiabatic flow implies flow without heat transfer to or from the gas or fluid. Diabatic flow is flow in which heat *is* added to or removed from the gas or fluid. In this section we will assume the flow is frictionless, implying a nonviscous (ideal) gas. This condition is approximated in short ducts with large heat transfer. In addition, the gas is assumed to be perfect, and the perfect gas relation $pv = RT$ applies. We will write some differential equations expressing the continuity equation, the Euler equation of motion (applicable only to a nonviscous fluid), the energy equation (including heat transfer), the perfect gas equation, and the definition of the Mach number. These will be combined to give differential equations from which variations in velocity, pressure, density, temperature, and Mach number in the direction of flow may be obtained as a function of Mach number for both heat addition to the gas and heat removal from the gas. Only qualitative results will be illustrated to show the comparison with similar variations in adiabatic flow without friction, as indicated by Eqs. 9–14 through 9–17.

The pertinent equations are

Continuity
$$\frac{dV}{V} + \frac{dA}{A} + \frac{d\rho}{\rho} = 0$$

Euler's equation of motion
$$\frac{dp}{\rho} = -V \, dV$$

Energy
$$dh + V \, dV = dq$$

Perfect gas
$$\frac{dp}{p} = \frac{d\rho}{\rho} + \frac{dT}{T}$$

Mach number
$$\frac{dM}{M} = \frac{dV}{V} - \frac{dT}{2T}$$

These may be combined (after considerable manipulation) to give

$$\frac{dV}{V} = \frac{1}{1 - M^2}\left(\frac{dq}{h} - \frac{dA}{A}\right)$$

$$\frac{dp}{p} = \frac{-kM^2}{1 - M^2}\left(\frac{dq}{h} - \frac{dA}{A}\right)$$

$$\frac{d\rho}{\rho} = \frac{-1}{1 - M^2}\left(\frac{dq}{h} - \frac{dA}{A}\right) - \frac{dA}{A}$$

$$\frac{dT}{T} = \frac{1 - kM^2}{1 - M^2}\left(\frac{dq}{h} - \frac{dA}{A}\right) + \frac{dA}{A}$$

$$\frac{dM}{M} = \frac{1 + kM^2}{2(1 - M^2)}\left(\frac{dq}{h} - \frac{dA}{A}\right) - \frac{dA}{A}$$

where $h = c_p \, T = \dfrac{Rk}{k - 1} \, T = \dfrac{pk}{\rho(k - 1)}$.

Just how the velocity, pressure, temperature, and Mach number will change in the direction of flow depends on whether the flow is subsonic ($M < 1$) or supersonic ($M > 1$) and on whether $(dq/h) - (dA/A)$ is positive, zero, or negative. In the case of density, temperature, and Mach number variations the results will also depend on whether the area increases, decreases, or remains constant (the dA/A terms affect the results).

For a duct of constant cross section ($dA = 0$) without friction but with heat added (dq is positive), the following results are obtained from a determination of the sign of each expression:

1. For the subsonic case, the velocity and Mach number increase and the pressure and density decrease in the direction of flow (the term

$1 - M^2$ is positive). The temperature increases if the Mach number is less than $1/\sqrt{k}$ and *decreases* if the Mach number is greater than $1/\sqrt{k}$ but less than unity. Heat addition has the effect of *cooling* the gas in this range of Mach numbers. (See the discussion of the Rayleigh line in Sec. 15–2.)

2. For the supersonic case, the velocity and Mach number decrease, and the pressure, density, and temperature increase in the direction of flow. In all instances the term $1 - M^2$ is negative, and the sign of dV/V and so forth may be determined easily.

In all instances for diabatic flow, all variables change at an infinite rate at a Mach number $M = 1$, and the results are nonvalid at this point. Thus both subsonic flow and supersonic flow approach the sonic condition as heat is added, but cannot go beyond this condition (subsonic flow cannot become supersonic, and supersonic flow cannot become subsonic).

Results for heat removal should be determined by the student.

For a duct of constant cross section without friction but with heat transfer, the continuity equation, momentum theorem, and energy equations in finite form may be combined with the perfect gas law and the definition of the Mach number to give equations which may be used in making calculations. These are:

Continuity $V_1 \rho_1 = V_2 \rho_2 = $ constant mass flow intensity G

Momentum theorem $p_1 - p_2 = V_1 \rho_1(V_2 - V_1) = V_2 \rho_2(V_2 - V_1)$

from which $p_1 + V_1{}^2\rho_1 = p_2 + V_2{}^2\rho_2$

This equation indicates that the thrust function is constant. In terms of mass-flow intensity G,

$$p_1 + GV_1 = p_2 + GV_2$$

or
$$p_1 + \frac{G^2}{\rho_1} = p_2 + \frac{G^2}{\rho_2} \qquad (9\text{--}27)$$

which indicates that the pressure and velocity as well as pressure and density are linearly related. Equation 9–27 is known as the equation of the Rayleigh line. This is discussed in detail in Chapter 15.

Energy equation $h_1 + \dfrac{V_1{}^2}{2} + q = h_2 + \dfrac{V_2{}^2}{2}$

and since $h + V^2/2$ is the stagnation enthalpy h_0,

$$h_{01} + q = h_{02}$$

from which $q = c_p(T_{02} - T_{01}) \qquad (9\text{--}28)$

and thus the heat transfer directly affects the change in stagnation enthalpy and the stagnation temperature.

Mach number $\dfrac{M_2}{M_1} = \dfrac{V_1\,c_2}{V_2\,c_1} = \dfrac{V_1}{V_2}\sqrt{\dfrac{T_2}{T_1}}$

Perfect gas
$$\frac{p_1}{\rho_1 T_1} = \frac{p_2}{\rho_2 T_2}$$

These equations may be combined to give the ratio of stagnation temperatures and static temperatures in terms of Mach number at two sections between which heat is transferred in a frictionless duct.

$$\frac{T_{02}}{T_{01}} = \frac{T_2}{T_1} \frac{\left(1 + \dfrac{k-1}{2} M_2{}^2\right)}{\left(1 + \dfrac{k-1}{2} M_1{}^2\right)} \tag{9-29}$$

and
$$\frac{T_2}{T_1} = \frac{M_2{}^2}{M_1{}^2} \frac{(1 + kM_1{}^2)^2}{(1 + kM_2{}^2)^2} \tag{9-30}$$

9–5. NORMAL SHOCK WAVES

A normal shock wave is one in which the plane of the shock wave is at right angles to the flow streamlines. Normal shocks may occur in the diverging section of a nozzle, the diffuser throat of a supersonic wind tunnel, in pipes, and forward of a blunt-nosed body. In all instances the flow is supersonic upstream of the shock, and it will be shown that it is always subsonic downstream of the shock.

Equations relating conditions downstream of the shock to conditions upstream may be obtained by writing the continuity, energy, and momentum equations across the shock. As before, a perfect gas will be assumed. The flow through the shock is adiabatic but not reversible, so the isentropic relationship generally will not hold. Actually, the flow *does* approach isentropic flow for very weak shocks (for upstream Mach numbers not greater than about 1.2), but the assumption of irreversible adiabatic flow in all instances makes the results completely general. The shock forms an essential discontinuity, although it has a finite thickness of about two mean-free-path lengths (about 10^{-5} in.) for upstream Mach numbers greater than 2. The thickness increases for weaker shocks, being about 10^{-3} in. at an upstream Mach number of about 1.007. The abrupt change in gas density across the shock may be detected optically, since the index of refraction of the gas depends on the density. Apparatus in common use includes the interferometer, the schleiren, and the spark shadowgraph which detect density changes, density gradients, and the rate of change of density gradients, respectively.

It is common practice to designate conditions upstream of a shock with a subscript x and those downstream by the subscript y, and these are indicated in Fig. 9–5.

The continuity equation is

$$V_x A \rho_x = V_y A \rho_y$$

or
$$V_x \rho_x = V_y \rho_y \tag{9-31a}$$

The energy equation is

$$\frac{V_x^2}{2} + h_x = \frac{V_y^2}{2} + h_y = h_0 \tag{9-32a}$$

which indicates that the stagnation enthalpy is the same on both sides of the shock. For a perfect gas, $h_0 = c_p T_0$, and thus the stagnation temperature for a perfect gas is also the same on both sides of the shock.

The momentum equation applied to the dashed region in Fig. 9–5 is

$$p_x A - p_y A = V_x A \rho_x (V_y - V_x) = V_y A \rho_y (V_y - V_x)$$

or
$$p_x + V_x^2 \rho_x = p_y + V_y^2 \rho_y \tag{9-33a}$$

which indicates that the thrust function is the same on both sides of a normal shock.

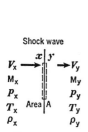

FIG. 9–5. A normal shock.

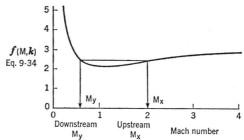

FIG. 9–6. Mach numbers across normal shock ($k = 1.4$).

In terms of the Mach number $M = V/\sqrt{kRT}$, Eqs. 9–31a, 9–32a, and 9–33a become

$$\frac{p_x M_x}{\sqrt{T_x}} = \frac{p_y M_y}{\sqrt{T_y}} \tag{9-31b}$$

$$T_x\left(1 + \frac{k-1}{2} M_x^2\right) = T_y\left(1 + \frac{k-1}{2} M_y^2\right) \tag{9-32b}$$

and
$$p_x(1 + kM_x^2) = p_y(1 + kM_y^2) \tag{9-33b}$$

Eliminating pressure p and temperature T from these we get

$$\frac{1 + kM_x^2}{M_x\left(1 + \dfrac{k-1}{2} M_x^2\right)^{1/2}} = \frac{1 + kM_y^2}{M_y\left(1 + \dfrac{k-1}{2} M_y^2\right)^{1/2}} = f(M, k) \tag{9-34}$$

which indicates that a particular Mach number function is the same on both sides of the shock. This function is plotted in Fig. 9–6.

A thermodynamic analysis indicates that the pressure rises across the shock, and from Eq. 9–33b the Mach number decreases. Thus in Fig.

9–6, points on the right side of the curve minimum (at $M = 1$) represent upstream conditions, and those to the left represent downstream conditions. It is seen that the higher the upstream Mach number, the lower the downstream Mach number, and vice versa. Equation 9–34 may be solved for $M_y{}^2$ to obtain

$$M_y{}^2 = \frac{M_x{}^2 + \dfrac{2}{k-1}}{\dfrac{2k}{k-1} M_x{}^2 - 1} \tag{9–35}$$

which shows that there is one, and only one, downstream Mach number associated with a given upstream Mach number for a given gas. With this expression for $M_y{}^2$, Eqs. 9–32b and 9–33b for the temperature and pressure ratios across the shock become

$$\frac{T_y}{T_x} = \frac{2(k-1)}{(k+1)^2 \, M_x{}^2} \left(1 + \frac{k-1}{2} M_x{}^2\right) \left(\frac{2k}{k-1} M_x{}^2 - 1\right) \tag{9–36}$$

and

$$\frac{p_y}{p_x} = \frac{2k}{k+1} M_x{}^2 - \frac{k-1}{k+1} \tag{9–37}$$

From these,

$$\frac{\rho_y}{\rho_x} = \frac{V_x}{V_y} = \frac{k+1}{2} \frac{M_x{}^2}{1 + \dfrac{k-1}{2} M_x{}^2} \tag{9–38}$$

The ratio of stagnation-to-static pressure for flow towards a stagnation point for $M_x > 1$ may be obtained by a combination of Eqs. 9–37 and 9–9a since the gas must first pass through the shock and then progress to the stagnation pressure from the subsonic condition behind the shock. With the usual subscripts, this ratio may be written as

$$\frac{p_{0y}}{p_x} = \left(\frac{p_y}{p_x}\right) \text{Eq. 9–37} \quad \left(\frac{p_{0y}}{p_y}\right) \text{Eq. 9–9a}$$

$$= \left(\frac{k+1}{2} M_x{}^2\right)^{\frac{k}{k-1}} \left(\frac{2k}{k+1} M_x{}^2 - \frac{k-1}{k+1}\right)^{\frac{1}{1-k}} \tag{9–39}$$

Finally, the reduction in stagnation pressure may be obtained from Eqs. 9–9a, 9–35, and 9–37 by considering a gas to flow from a reservoir at pressure p_{0x} through a suitable nozzle to a supersonic condition, then through a normal shock to a stagnation pressure p_{0y}. Because of the entropy increase across the shock, the reservoir pressure is not recovered, and p_{0y} is less than p_{0x}. From Eq. 9–9a,

$$\frac{p_{0y}}{p_{0x}} = \frac{p_y}{p_x} \left(\frac{1 + \dfrac{k-1}{2} M_y{}^2}{1 + \dfrac{k-1}{2} M_x{}^2}\right)^{\frac{k}{k-1}}$$

If the expression for p_y/p_x in Eq. 9–37 and that for $M_y{}^2$ in Eq. 9–35 are substituted, algebraic simplification gives

$$\frac{p_{0y}}{p_{0x}} = \left(\frac{\dfrac{k+1}{2}M_x{}^2}{1+\dfrac{k-1}{2}M_x{}^2}\right)^{\frac{k}{k-1}} \left(\frac{2k}{k+1}M_x{}^2 - \frac{k-1}{k+1}\right)^{\frac{1}{1-k}} \qquad (9\text{–}40)$$

It should be noted that although a gas may be considered to flow from a stagnation condition to a supersonic condition isentropically such that Eq. 9–9a is valid, a gas may not flow from this same supersonic condition to a stagnation condition through a shock wave in a manner such that Eq. 9–9a applies.

For a normal shock, the values of M_y, p_y/p_x, T_y/T_x, ρ_y/ρ_x, p_{0y}/p_x, and p_{0y}/p_{0x} depend only on the upstream Mach number M_x for a given gas. These values, given in Eqs. 9–35, 9–37, 9–36, 9–38, 9–39, and 9–40, respectively, may be tabulated. An example is given in Table A–2 (Appendix III) for a normal shock in a gas for which $k = 1.4$.

EXAMPLE 9–3. If for the converging-diverging nozzle in Example 9–2 a shock were to exist in the diverging portion of the nozzle where the pressure is 40 psia (p_x in Fig. 9–4b), what is the Mach number just upstream and just downstream of the shock, the pressure just downstream of the shock, and the flow rate in the nozzle?

Solution: From Table A–1, the Mach number where the pressure is $40/100 = 0.4$ of the reservoir pressure for isentropic flow is $M_x = 1.223$. From Table A–2, $M_y = 0.828$ and $p_y/p_x = 1.58$ so that $p_y = 63.2$ psia and the flow rate is the same as in Example 9–1; namely, 0.0505 slug/sec or 1.62 lb$_m$/sec, since the flow is sonic at the same conditions in the throat with or without the shock. Equations 9–9a, 9–35, and 9–37 could be used instead of the tables to find M_x, M_y, and p_y/p_x, respectively.

The density ratio across a normal shock may be expressed in terms of the pressure ratio across the shock by eliminating $M_x{}^2$ in Eqs. 9–37 and 9–38. The result is

$$\frac{\rho_y}{\rho_x} = \frac{\left(\dfrac{k+1}{k-1}\right)\dfrac{p_y}{p_x} + 1}{\dfrac{p_y}{p_x} + \left(\dfrac{k+1}{k-1}\right)} \qquad (9\text{–}41)$$

which is known as the *Rankine-Hugoniot equation.* From Eq. 9–37, as the upstream Mach number M_x approaches infinity, the pressure ratio p_y/p_x also approaches infinity. From Eq. 9–41, the density ratio under these circumstances approaches a finite maximum value, which is 6 for air or any other gas for which $k = 1.4$.

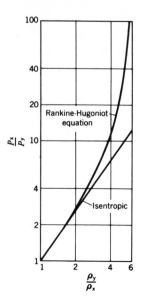

FIG. 9–7. Rankine-Hugoniot and isentropic curves for $k = 1.40$.

A log-log plot of Eq. 9–41 together with the isentropic relation between pressure and density for $k = 1.4$ is shown in Fig. 9–7. The curves show that flow through a normal shock approaches an isentropic flow for weak shocks (flow in which the upstream Mach number M_x approaches unity). This approach to isentropic flow is also indicated by the near-unity values of p_{0y}/p_{0x} in Table A–2 (Appendix III) for M_x values near unity. The strength of a shock may be defined as the ratio of the pressure rise through the shock to the upstream pressure. That is

$$\text{Shock strength} = \frac{p_y - p_x}{p_x} = \frac{p_y}{p_x} - 1 \qquad (9\text{–}42)$$

The entropy increase across a shock may be obtained by integrating Eq. 3–5 ($T\,ds = dh - v\,dp$). This gives

$$s_y - s_x = c_p \ln (T_y/T_x) - R \ln (p_y/p_x)$$

Since $T_{0y} = T_{0x}$, this can be shown to be

$$s_y - s_x = -R \ln (p_{0y}/p_{0x}) \qquad (9\text{–}43)$$

Thus flow through shocks is increasingly irreversible as M_x increases (Table A–2, Appendix III).

Additional treatment of normal shocks is given in Chapter 15, where the Fanno and Rayleigh lines for gas flow are compared with the specific energy and specific thrust diagrams for open channel flow.

9–6. OBLIQUE SHOCKS

An oblique shock is a general form of discontinuity in a supersonic gas flow which is inclined from a direction normal to the oncoming flow. A normal shock is thus a special form of an oblique shock. Oblique shocks occur in most supersonic flows, although there need not necessarily be shocks simply because supersonic flow exists.

An oblique shock may be obtained or visualized by superimposing a tangential component of velocity to the upstream and downstream velocities for a normal shock. This is equivalent to observing the shock while moving along the normal shock front with a velocity V_t (Fig. 9–8). Subscripts 1 and 2 will be used for the upstream and downstream conditions, respectively, rather than x and y in order to distinguish between the normal shock results and the oblique shock results. Subscripts t and n refer to the tangential and normal components, respectively.

Oblique shock equations may be obtained from the continuity, momentum (in both tangential and normal directions), and energy equations; or from a transformation of the normal shock equations. The transforma-

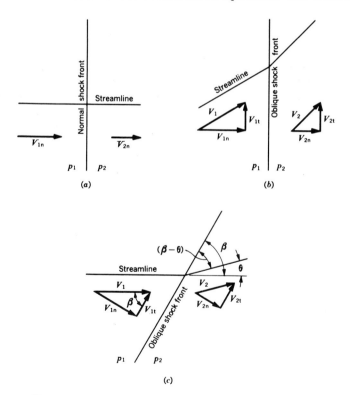

Fig. 9–8. Oblique shock obtained from normal shock.

tion method will be used here. From Fig. 9–8, the upstream Mach number is $M_1 = V_1/c_1$, and $V_{1n} = V_1 \sin \beta$. Thus

$$\frac{V_{1n}}{c_1} = M_1 \sin \beta$$

Also, the downstream Mach number is $M_2 = V_2/c_2$, and $V_{2n} = V_2 \sin (\beta - \theta)$. Thus

$$\frac{V_{2n}}{c_2} = M_2 \sin (\beta - \theta)$$

where β is called the shock angle with respect to the upstream flow direction, and θ is the deflection angle of the streamlines as the fluid passes through the oblique shock. Thus in the normal shock equations (Eqs. 9–35 through 9–38) M_x is replaced by $M_1 \sin \beta$ and M_y is replaced by $M_2 \sin (\beta - \theta)$. This gives for the Mach number downstream of the oblique shock

$$M_2{}^2 = \frac{1}{\sin^2 (\beta - \theta)} \; \frac{M_1{}^2 \sin^2 \beta + \dfrac{2}{k - 1}}{\dfrac{2k}{k - 1} M_1{}^2 \sin^2 \beta - 1} \tag{9-44}$$

The temperature ratio T_2/T_1 is, after rearranging Eq. 9–36,

$$\frac{T_2}{T_1} = 1 + \frac{2(k - 1)}{(k + 1)^2} \; \frac{M_1{}^2 \sin^2 \beta - 1}{M_1{}^2 \sin^2 \beta} \; (kM_1{}^2 \sin^2 \beta + 1) \tag{9-45}$$

The pressure ratio p_2/p_1 is, after rearranging Eq. 9–37,

$$\frac{p_2}{p_1} = 1 + \frac{2k}{k + 1} (M_1{}^2 \sin^2 \beta - 1) \tag{9-46}$$

The density ratio is,

$$\frac{\rho_2}{\rho_1} = \frac{(k + 1) M_1{}^2 \sin^2 \beta}{2 + (k - 1) M_1{}^2 \sin^2 \beta} \tag{9-47}$$

The ratios of thermodynamic properties (temperature, sound speed, pressure, and density) depend only on the normal component of velocity and are not affected by the motion of the observer. The normal component V_{1n} must, of course, be supersonic; that is, $M_1 \sin \beta \geqq 1$. Thus there is a minimum wave angle β for a given upstream Mach number M_1, the maximum wave angle β being that for a normal shock. Hence

$$\sin^{-1} 1/M_1 \leqq \beta \leqq \pi/2 \tag{9-48}$$

A useful relation between M_1, θ, and β may be obtained by noting that in Fig. 9–8, $\tan \beta = V_{1n}/V_{1t}$ and $\tan (\beta - \theta) = V_{2n}/V_{2t}$. From these

$$\frac{\tan (\beta - \theta)}{\tan \beta} = \frac{V_{2n}}{V_{1n}} = \frac{\rho_1}{\rho_2} = \frac{2 + (k - 1) \, M_1{}^2 \sin^2 \beta}{(k + 1) \, M_1{}^2 \sin^2 \beta} \qquad (9\text{-}49)$$

Dividing both numerator and denominator of the last expression by $2M_1{}^2 \sin^2 \beta$ gives, after simplification

$$\frac{1}{M_1{}^2} = \sin^2 \beta - \frac{(k + 1)}{2} \frac{\sin \beta \sin \theta}{\cos (\beta - \theta)} \qquad (9\text{-}50)$$

In this and preceding equations, θ is the deflection or turning angle of the streamlines as they pass through the oblique shock. It could thus be the half-angle of a wedge placed at a zero angle of attack in a supersonic flow, or the angle of a corner inside which a supersonic flow turns. Both these situations are shown in Fig. 9–9.

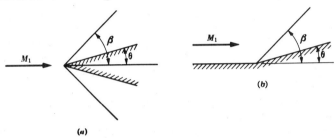

FIG. 9–9. Supersonic flow past a) a wedge, and b) an inside corner.

Equation 9–50 is shown graphically in Fig. 9–10. The curves indicate that for a given M_1 there are two possible wave angles associated with a given half-wedge or deflection angle. The larger wave angle represents a strong shock, and the flow downstream is usually subsonic. The smaller wave angle represents a weak shock, and the flow downstream is usually

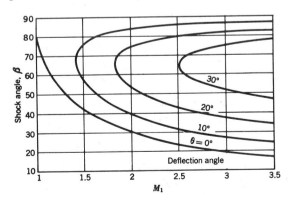

FIG. 9–10. Relation between shock angle, deflection angle, and upstream Mach number for oblique shocks (Eq. 9–50).

supersonic but less than M_1. Also, for a given M_1 there is a maximum half-wedge or deflection angle associated with this M_1. This represents the maximum angle of the half-wedge for which the shock remains attached.

The Rankine-Hugoniot equation (Eq. 9–41) is also valid for oblique shocks, since both pressure and density are thermodynamic properties and do not depend on the motion of an observer. Normal shock tables (Table A–2, Appendix III) may be used for oblique shocks if M_x for a normal shock is taken as $M_1 \sin \beta$ for an oblique shock. Then $M_y = M_2 \sin (\beta - \theta)$ and values of p_y/p_x, ρ_y/ρ_x, T_y/T_x, and p_{0y}/p_{0x} for normal shocks become values of p_2/p_1, ρ_2/ρ_1, T_2/T_1, and p_{02}/p_{01}, respectively.

REFERENCES

The reader is referred to the following sources for additional information on the flow of compressible gases:

A. B. Cambel, "Compressible Flow," Section 8 of *Handbook of Fluid Dynamics*, edited by V. L. Streeter (New York: McGraw-Hill Book Company, Inc., 1961).

N. A. Hall, *Thermodynamics of Fluid Flow* (Englewood Cliffs, N. J.: Prentice-Hall, Inc., 1950).

H. W. Liepmann and A. Roshko, *Elements of Gas Dynamics* (New York: John Wiley and Sons, Inc., 1956).

J. A. Owczarek, *Fundamentals of Gas Dynamics* (Scranton, Pa.: International Textbook Company, 1964).

A. H. Shapiro, *The Dynamics and Thermodynamics of Compressible Fluid Flow*, Vol. 1 (New York: The Ronald Press Company, 1953).

PROBLEMS

9–1. Calculate the velocity of sound at 70 F for each of the gases listed in Table 3–1.   *Ans.* $c_{air} = 1128$ ft/sec,
$c_{hydrogen} = 4277$ ft/sec,
$c_{xenon} = 578$ ft/sec

9–2. Air expands isentropically from a reservoir at 100 psia and 220 F to a pressure of 14.7 psia. *a*) What is the air temperature at this pressure? *b*) What is the speed of sound in the reservoir and in the gas at 14.7 psia?

9–3. Repeat Prob. 9–2 for xenon.

9–4. What is the speed in miles per hour of an object traveling at a free flight Mach number of 2.5 in *a*) air, *b*) hydrogen, and *c*) xenon, all at 70 F?

9–5. An aircraft flies at a Mach number of 0.75. What is its air speed in a standard atmosphere at *a*) 1000 ft where $T = 55.4$ F and *b*) 30,000 ft where $T = -47.9$ F?

Ans. *a*) 835 ft/sec

9–6. What is the speed of sound in the NACA standard atmosphere at *a*) sea level, *b*) 10,000 ft, *c*) 50,000 ft, *d*) 100,000 ft, and *e*) 190,000 ft? Refer to Sec. 4–12

9-7. The sonic velocity in any homogeneous medium is $c = \sqrt{K/\rho}$. Explain why the sonic velocity is reduced a) when a fine mist of water droplets is introduced into air and b) when gas nuclei are introduced into water.

9-8. Small models of missiles are shot through controllable-pressure firing ranges consisting of a gas at rest. a) Which of the gases listed in Table 3-1 would be most suitable in order to keep the missile speed at a minimum? b) What speed is required to achieve a Mach number of 3.0 at 70 F in xenon and in helium? c) What Mach number corresponds to a missile speed of 1500 ft/sec in xenon and in helium at 50 F?

$Ans.$ b) $V_{xenon} = 1734$ ft/sec, $V_{helium} = 9945$ ft/sec

9-9. Three reference temperatures are used to define three Mach numbers for a given flow. These three reference temperatures result in three reference sonic velocities, one for each temperature. These are a) c, the local sonic velocity at the local temperature, b) c^*, the sonic velocity where the flow is changed isentropically to a Mach number of 1, and c) c_0, the sonic velocity at the stagnation point. If at a point in a flow stream of air the velocity is 500 ft/sec and the local temperature is 416 R, what are c, c^*, and c_0?

9-10. Standard air at rest (59 F) is accelerated isentropically. a) What is the Mach number when the velocity becomes 500 ft/sec? b) What is the velocity when the speed becomes sonic? c) What is the theoretical maximum speed attainable?

9-11. Air at rest at 200 F is accelerated isentropically. a) What is the air speed when the Mach number becomes 0.8? b) What is the air speed when the flow becomes sonic? c) What is the Mach number when the air speed becomes 2000 ft/sec?

9-12. Show that the difference between stagnation and static temperature for air is essentially given by

$$T_0 - T \approx \left(\frac{V_{mph}}{100}\right)^2 \quad \text{degrees Centigrade}$$

9-13. Equation 9-9b is valid for isentropic flow of air, hydrogen, nitrogen, and oxygen ($k = 1.4$) for M < 2.236. What are the upper limits of M for the other gases listed in Table 3-1 for which this equation may be used?

9-14. Calculate the compressibility factor at M = ¼, ½, ¾, and 1 for air, methane, and xenon, and plot the results for air. What is the effect of the ratio of specific heat capacities k on the compressibility factor?

9-15. What is the stagnation temperature rise ($T_0 - T$) for a craft traveling at Mach 2 in the NACA standard atmosphere at a) sea level, b) 50,000 ft ($T = -67.6$ F), and c) 190,000 ft ($T = 170$ F)?

$Ans.$ a) 416 F, b) 314 F, c) 504 F

9-16. An aircraft flies in the NACA standard atmosphere at 20,000 ft ($T = -12.3$ F, $\rho = 0.001267$ slug/ft³) at a speed of 500 ft/sec. What is the stagnation pressure rise ($p_0 - p$), a) neglecting compressibility effects and b) including compressibility effects?

9–17. a) Show that the ratio of stagnation density ρ_0 to density ρ, where the Mach number is M, for isentropic flow is

$$\frac{\rho_0}{\rho} = \left(1 + \frac{k-1}{2}M^2\right)^{\frac{1}{k-1}}$$

and by expanding in a power series, show that for very small M

$$\frac{\Delta\rho}{\rho} \approx \frac{1}{2}M^2$$

b) Suppose gas flow is defined as incompressible if the variation in density is no greater than 2 per cent ($\rho_0/\rho \leq 1.02$). What is the maximum Mach number for which the flow may then be considered incompressible? Show that this has no significant dependency on the type of gas. HINT: Calculate the M^4 term in the series expansion for the range of k values in Table 3–1 and compare with the M^2 term.

9–18. Given

$$V\,dV + c^2\frac{d\rho}{\rho} = 0$$

Is this valid for any adiabatic flow or for just isentropic flow? Explain.

9–19. From the energy equation $h_0 = h + V^2/2$, the isentropic relations, the perfect gas equation, and the continuity equation derive a) Eq. 9–18a, b) Eq. 9–18b, c) Eq. 9–22, d) Eq. 9–23, and e) Eq. 9–26b.

9–20. Calculate the critical pressure ratio (Eq. 9–23) for all the gases listed in Table 3–1. Plot a curve relating p^*/p_0 vs k.

9–21. Use Table A–1 to obtain the answers to the following isentropic flows for air: a) At what Mach number is the temperature 8/10 the stagnation temperature? b) At what Mach number is the stagnation pressure 30 per cent greater than the static pressure? c) What Mach numbers could exist at sections in a converging-diverging nozzle at which the areas are 1.4 times the throat area? d) What would be the ratio of the pressure for subsonic flow to that for supersonic flow in part c)? e) What duct area, in terms of throat area, at the exit of a converging-diverging nozzle fed from a reservoir produces an exit velocity twice the throat velocity? f) The density at a section in a nozzle is one-third that at the throat. What is the Mach number at this section? g) What is the temperature at a section in a nozzle where the density is one-third that at the throat (see part f) in terms of the reservoir temperature? h) What ratio of exit area to throat area for a converging-diverging nozzle results in an exit pressure equal to 20 per cent of the pressure in the reservoir which feeds the nozzle?

Ans. a) M = 1.118, c) 0.471 or 1.763, f) M = 2.076

9–22. In an isentropic flow of air, at one point the velocity is 800 ft/sec, $p = 50$ psia, and $T = 140$ F. a) What is the temperature where the Mach number is 2.00? b) Use gas tables to find the pressure where M = 2.00.

9–23. Compute the mass-flow rate for air discharging from a tank at 40 psig and 140 F through a converging nozzle with an exit area of 0.02 ft². The air discharges isentropically into a standard atmosphere.

9–24. An impact tube on an aircraft registers a stagnation pressure of 6 psig where the ambient static pressure is 14.0 psia. The air temperature is 40 F. *a*) What is the free-flight Mach number for the aircraft? *b*) What is its speed? *c*) What is the temperature on the nose of the aircraft?

Ans. c) $T_0 = 94$ F

9–25. An object moves at 500 mph through standard air. What is *a*) the gage pressure and *b*) the temperature at the forward stagnation point?

9–26. A perfect gas ($k = 1.4$, $R = 3000$ ft lb$_f$/slug R) flows from a reservoir at 120 psia and 440 F through a converging nozzle. The flow is isentropic and the reservoir pressure is 14.7 psia. Find *a*) the nozzle exit pressure, *b*) the gas velocity at the nozzle exit, and *c*) the nozzle exit area for a flow of 0.05 slug/sec.

9–27. Air in a tank at 100 psia and 80 F discharges into a standard atmosphere through a converging nozzle. For isentropic flow *a*) what is the exit pressure, *b*) what is the air temperature at the exit of the nozzle, and *c*) what is the exit diameter for a round nozzle discharging 0.05 slug/sec?

9–28. One way to account for viscous, or frictional, effects in gas nozzles is to define an isentropic efficiency as the ratio of kinetic energy at outlet for frictional adiabatic flow to that for isentropic flow between the same pressures. Show that this efficiency, $\eta_n = V_a{}^2/V_i{}^2$, may be written as

$$\eta_n = \frac{2(h_1 - h_a) + V_1{}^2}{2(h_1 - h_i) + V_1{}^2}$$

where subscript 1 refers to initial conditions, *a* to outlet conditions reached adiabatically with friction, and *i* to outlet conditions reached isentropically.

9–29. The isentropic efficiency of a nozzle is 95 per cent (Prob. 9–28). Air in a reservoir at 100 psia and 340 F flows through the nozzle and exhausts at 14.7 psia. The flow is adiabatic. *a*) What would be the exit temperature for isentropic flow? *b*) What would be the exit velocity for isentropic flow? *c*) What is the actual exit velocity? *d*) What is the actual exit temperature?

Ans. a) 2 F, *d*) 19 F

9–30. Air in a reservoir at 120 psia and 100 F discharges through a converging nozzle to the atmosphere. Design the nozzle for a flow rate of 0.1 slug/sec. Specify exit area.

9–31. In Prob. 9–30 design a converging-diverging nozzle for full expansion for the same flow rate. Specify throat and exit areas.

9–32. A converging-diverging nozzle fed from a reservoir has an exit area 3 times the throat area. What is the ratio of exit pressure to reservoir pressure for isentropic flow of *a*) air and *b*) carbon dioxide? $M_{\text{exit}} > 1$.

9–33. Air flows isentropically from a reservoir at 200 psia and 140 F through a converging-diverging nozzle to a receiver at atmospheric pressure. Full expansion takes place within the nozzle. *a*) What is the exit area in terms of the throat area?

b) What would be the exit area in terms of throat area for helium at the same reservoir conditions?

Ans.   a) $A/A^* = 2.303$, b) $A/A^* = 1.923$

9–34. Combustion in the combustion chamber of a rocket produces a pressure of 300 psia and a temperature of 5000 R. The products of combustion may be considered as a perfect gas with $R = 2450$ ft lb$_f$/slug R and a ratio of specific heat capacities $k = 1.26$. The gases pass through a converging-diverging nozzle with a throat area of 0.8 ft^2 and exit at 14.7 psia. a) What is the thrust developed at sea level? b) What is the thrust developed at 20,000 ft ($p = 973$ psfa)? Assume isentropic flow.

Ans.   a) 48,400 lb$_f$

9–35. A gas flows in a duct of constant cross section without friction, but heat removal takes place. How do the velocity, pressure, density, temperature, and Mach number change in the direction of flow for a) subsonic flow and b) supersonic flow? Refer to the differential equations in Sec. 9–4.

9–36. Air flows through a short tube without friction. Heat is supplied to increase the initial Mach number of 0.3 at a temperature of 100 F to a final Mach number of 0.6. How much heat must be supplied per unit mass of air?

Ans.   6000 Btu/slug

9–37. As heat is added to a subsonic frictionless gas flowing in a constant-area duct, the Mach number increases to a maximum of 1.0 before choking occurs. The gas temperature increases to a maximum at a Mach number of $1/\sqrt{k}$, then decreases to T^*, the value associated with a Mach number of 1. a) At what subsonic Mach number is the gas temperature $T = T^*$ for air? b) What is T_{max}/T^* for air?

9–38. Air flows in a constant-area duct without friction at an initial temperature of $T_1 = 100$ F and an initial Mach number of $M_1 = 0.5$. Heat is added to the air at a rate of 773 Btu/slug between sections 1 and 2. a) What is the stagnation temperature at each section? b) What is the ratio of stagnation temperature at each section to that where the Mach number is 1? (Find T_{01}/T_0^* and T_{02}/T_0^*). c) What is the Mach number at section 2?

Ans.   a) $T_{01} = 588$ R, $T_{02} = 688$ R; b) 0.691 and 0.809, respectively; c) $M_2 = 0.591$

9–39. Use Table A–2 to obtain answers to the following situations involving normal shocks in air: a) The stagnation pressure on the nose of a blunt-nosed projectile is 3.5 times the free-stream pressure of the atmosphere. What is the free-flight Mach number? b) What is the Mach number just downstream of the shock in part a)? c) The strength of a shock may be defined as the ratio of the pressure increase across it to the upstream pressure $(p_y - p_x)/p_x$. What Mach number would produce a shock of strength 5? d) The ratio of downstream to upstream stagnation pressure across a normal shock is a direct measure of its irreversibility. The entropy increase is $\Delta s = -R \ln(p_{0y}/p_{0x})$. At what Mach number is the entropy increase 1300 ft lb$_f$/slug R?

Ans.   a) $M_x = 1.523$, c) $M_x = 2.299$

9–40. Use Tables A–1 and A–2 in solving the following situations involving air flow. Consider the flow to be isentropic except across shocks. a) A normal shock occurs in a converging-diverging nozzle fed from a reservoir. The shock occurs where M = 2.2 What is the ratio of the pressure just downstream from the shock to the reservoir pressure p_y/p_{0z}? b) What is the stagnation temperature just downstream from the shock in terms of the reservoir temperature? c) What is the area of the nozzle where the shock forms in part a) in terms of the throat area? d) What is the exit area for conditions of part a) in terms of the throat area for an exit pressure 70 per cent of the reservoir pressure ($p_C = 0.70\ p_0$ in Fig. 9–4b)?

9–41. a) Does the pressure ratio across a normal shock p_y/p_x increase or decrease as the upstream Mach number M_x increases? b) Given the pressure p_x, the temperature T_x, the Mach number M_x, and the ratio of specific heat capacities k for a gas, which of these must be known in order that the Mach number M_y downstream of a normal shock may be calculated? c) At a Mach number of 0.8, is the stagnation pressure for a given flow greater, equal, or less if compressible effects are considered than if they are ignored? d) The Mach number at a given location in a diverging duct is 1.4. Does the Mach number increase, remain the same, or decrease downstream? No shocks are present. e) Repeat part d) for a Mach number of 0.8.

9–42. Derive Eq. 9–43, which gives the entropy increase for flow through a shock.

9–43. Show that the velocities on the two sides of a normal shock may be related by the expression $V_x V_y = (c^*)^2$. HINT: Solve for p_y and p_x in terms of k, ρ, V, and $(c^*)^2$ from Eq. 9–6. Equate $p_y - p_x$ from these and from Eq. 9–33a and simplify, using Eq. 9–31a.

9–44. Air flows adiabatically from a reservoir at 90 psia and 140 F through a converging-diverging nozzle. A shock occurs at a section where the pressure has dropped to 15 psia. What is the pressure just beyond the shock? Assume isentropic flow to the shock.

9–45. Show that the downstream Mach number for a normal shock approaches a limiting minimum value as the upstream Mach number increases without limit. What is this minimum Mach number for a) air, b) carbon dioxide, and c) xenon?

9–46. Explain why the presence of normal shocks in a converging-diverging nozzle fed from a reservoir does not affect the flow rate through the nozzle.

9–47. A converging-diverging nozzle is attached to a pressure tank containing a gas at stagnation conditions. Explain why a shock cannot occur in the converging portion of the nozzle. Assume isentropic flow, except across the shock.

9–48. The stagnation pressure for a missile at a 50,000-ft altitude ($p = 242$ psfa, $T = -67$ F) is 8.42 psig. What is the free-flight Mach number for the missile?

Ans. M = 2.07

9–49. A normal shock occurs in air flowing in a duct at M = 2.5 where the upstream static pressure is 12 psia. a) What is the static pressure downstream of the shock? b) What is the stagnation pressure downstream of the shock? c) What is the decrease in stagnation pressure across the shock? d) What is the increase in static pressure across the shock?

Ans. a) $p_y = 85.5$ psia

9–50. Air from a reservoir at a pressure p_0 flows through a converging-diverging nozzle of throat area $A*$ and an exit area $2.5A*$. A normal shock occurs beyond the throat where $A = 1.45A*$. a) What is the exit Mach number? b) What is the receiver pressure in terms of p_0? c) What receiver pressure would produce isentropic supersonic flow without shocks?

Ans. a) $M_{exit} = 0.303$, b) $p_{exit}/p_{0x} = 0.758$, c) $p_{rec} = 0.0640\, p_0$

9–51. A supersonic aircraft flies horizontally overhead at 10,000 ft at a Mach number of 1.6 in still air. What is the time interval between the instant the aircraft is directly overhead and the instant the shock wave is detected by an observer on the ground? Assume $c = 1100$ ft/sec, and that the aircraft is a point source.

Ans. 7.10 sec

9–52. From Eqs. 9–44, 9–46, and 9–47 show that as M_1 becomes very large

$$M_2{}^2 \rightarrow \frac{k-1}{2k \sin^2 (\beta - \theta)}$$

$$\frac{p_2}{p_1} \rightarrow \frac{2k}{k+1} M_1{}^2 \sin^2 \beta$$

$$\frac{\rho_2}{\rho_1} \rightarrow \frac{k+1}{k-1} \text{ (the same as for a normal shock)}$$

9–53. A two-dimensional wedge is used to measure the Mach number of the flow in a supersonic wind tunnel using air. The total wedge angle is 20 degrees, and the wave angle β is 50 degrees. a) What is the Mach number in the wind tunnel? b) What is the smallest Mach number for which this wedge could be used to determine the Mach number?

Ans. a) $M = 1.62$

9–54. What is the Mach number M_2 downstream of the oblique shock of Prob. 9–53?

9–55. Repeat Prob. 9–53 for $\theta = 20$ degrees and $\beta = 80$ degrees.

9–56. What is the Mach number downstream of the oblique shock of Prob. 9–55?

10

The Flow of Real Fluids in Ducts

10–1. BASIC CONSIDERATIONS

The effects of fluid viscosity on the flow of liquids and gases in ducts are of both theoretical and practical interest. Laminar flow in many instances can be analyzed theoretically, but turbulent flow has thus far defied rigorous analysis. Both theory and experiment have been necessary to reach the present state of understanding of turbulent flow. In either case, viscosity is important, and the Reynolds number with the hydraulic diameter[1] as the characteristic length (Re = VD_h/ν) will be a significant parameter. Uniform flow in circular tubes is laminar up to a Reynolds number of about 2300, then it passes through a transition regime (intermittently laminar and turbulent) before becoming entirely turbulent. For engineering calculations it is generally assumed laminar below a Reynolds number of 2000 and turbulent above 2000.

Duct flow is important because:

1. Studies of turbulent flow in pipes have led to a better understanding of turbulent flow in general. Recall that experimental results from studies of turbulent flow in pipes were used in the analysis of turbulent boundary layers (Eq. 7–13).

2. We need to be able to estimate the head-loss term h_L in the energy equation for incompressible flow in order to determine the power given up by a liquid to a turbine, the power requirements for pumping liquids through pipelines, or the flow rate for a given situation. The term h_L represents the mechanical energy converted to thermal energy and in a thermodynamic sense, it is a loss only in available energy.

3. Flow of real gases is never reversible, and the wall shear stress (commonly referred to as wall friction) affects the flow of gases even in short nozzles, though not appreciably in certain respects. In long pipes, wall friction has a pronounced effect on gas flow.

4. Many systems of engineering interest involve both fluid flow and heat transfer in ducts, and an understanding of the flow process is a necessary prerequisite to an understanding of the heat-transfer process.

5. Flow through cascades (in turbines, compressors, or vaned elbows,

[1] The hydraulic diameter D_h = 4 (Area of the duct cross section) divided by the duct perimeter ($D_h = 4A/P$). Thus for a circular tube the hydraulic diameter equals the tube diameter.

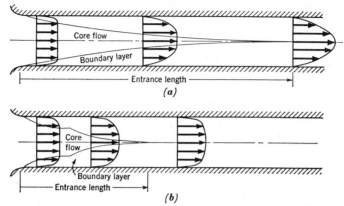

Fig. 10–1. Growth of boundary layer in a pipe (not to scale); a) in laminar flow, b) in turbulent flow.

for example) may be studied as flow *around* a single blade or as duct flow *between* blades.

Incompressible laminar and turbulent flow in both the entrance and the fully developed flow regions in ducts; incompressible flow through contractions, expansions, and pipe fittings; compressible flow in pipes; and flow of mixtures in pipes will be treated in this chapter.

The development of the velocity profile in the entrance region of a pipe was discussed in Sec. 7–1, and the growth of the boundary layer was indicated in Fig. 7–5. The flow was assumed to be one-dimensional at entrance. For both laminar and turbulent flow (shown again in Fig. 10–1), the wall shear stress is very large at entrance and generally decreases in the direction of flow to a fixed value. The magnitude of the pressure gradient dp/dx also generally decreases in the flow direction to a fixed value, but at a rate slightly less than that for the wall shear stress. Finally, the velocity profile also changes, and eventually it becomes adjusted to a fixed profile. The wall shear stress, the pressure gradient, and the velocity profile all approach their fixed values asymptotically, and thus it is difficult to set a precise length for the entrance region. It could be defined as the region or length required for any one of these three quantities to reach a fixed value.

When the wall shear stress, the pressure gradient, and the velocity profile have reached constant conditions, the flow is called fully developed flow.

Fluid flowing with an average velocity V through a cross section in a circular tube has a rate of flow of momentum of $\beta \rho V^2 (\pi D^2/4)$, from Eq. 5–16. The momentum theorem applied to a control volume of length dx in the tube, assumed to be of constant diameter, is (see Fig. 10–2)

$$p \frac{\pi D^2}{4} - (p + dp) \frac{\pi D^2}{4} - \tau_0 \, \pi D \, dx = \frac{\pi D^2}{4} \frac{d}{dx} (\beta \rho V^2) \, dx$$

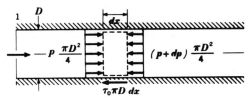

FIG. 10–2. Flow through elemental length of a circular tube.

so that

$$-\frac{dp}{dx} = \frac{4}{D}\tau_0 + \rho V^2 \frac{d\beta}{dx} + \beta\rho V \frac{dV}{dx} \tag{10-1}$$

since $\beta V \, d(\rho V)/dx = 0$ from continuity.

For fully developed, incompressible flow, $d\beta/dx = 0$, $dV/dx = 0$, and the wall shear stress τ_0 which depends on the shape of the velocity profile near the tube wall does not change with x. Thus for this situation

$$-\frac{dp}{dx} = \frac{\Delta p}{L} = \frac{4\tau_0}{D} \tag{10-2}$$

The pressure drops in the direction of flow, and thus dp is negative for a positive dx. The *magnitude* of the pressure drop over a length of tube L is generally designated as $\Delta p = p_1 - p_2$, where section 1 is upstream of section 2. All of the pressure drop for fully developed incompressible flow goes into overcoming wall shear. This wall shear stress may be conveniently determined by measuring the pressure drop over a given length of pipe.

For developing flow in the entrance of a tube, $\beta = 1$ initially and approaches a fully developed value at some distance downstream of the entrance. For incompressible, fully developed flow $\beta = \frac{4}{3}$ for laminar flow in a circular tube and about 1.03 for turbulent flow. Similar values apply for compressible flow. In the entrance region the overall pressure drop overcomes the wall shear and increases the flow momentum. For incompressible flow, Eq. 10–1 becomes

$$-\frac{dp}{dx} = \frac{4\tau_0}{D} + \rho V^2 \frac{d\beta}{dx} \tag{10-3}$$

Flow becomes truly fully developed only after $d\beta/dx = 0$, for only then is there no further change in the shape of the velocity profile. However, the velocity profile near the tube wall becomes fixed before that in the interior of the flow, so that the wall shear becomes fixed while there is still some variation in β and dp/dx. This is why measurements of wall shear stress indicate a shorter entrance length than do measurements of dp/dx or of the velocity near the tube axis.

For compressible flow of a gas beyond the entrance of a circular tube the normalized shape of the velocity profile is essentially constant and thus $d\beta/dx \approx 0$. However, V varies with x because of thermodynamic changes which affect the density ρ. Hence the wall shear stress τ_0 and the pressure gradient dp/dx vary with x, and Eq. 10–1 takes the form

$$-\frac{dp}{dx} = \frac{4\tau_0}{D} + \beta\rho V \frac{dV}{dx} \qquad (10\text{–}4)$$

The pressure drop thus goes into overcoming wall shear and increasing the momentum of the flow. Equation 10–4 will be integrated in Section 10–10.

10–2. FULLY DEVELOPED INCOMPRESSIBLE FLOW IN DUCTS

In engineering practice it is customary to express the pressure gradient (pressure drop per unit length of pipe) in the form of the so-called Darcy-Weisbach equation, which was also developed by a dimensional analysis in Sec. 8–2. This equation is

$$\frac{\Delta p}{L} = \frac{f}{D} \frac{\rho V^2}{2} \qquad (10\text{–}5)$$

where f is the friction factor, $\rho V^2/2$ is the dynamic pressure of the mean flow, and D is the pipe diameter. An alternative form in terms of the head loss due to friction h_f is

$$h_f = \frac{\Delta p}{\gamma} = f\left(\frac{L}{D}\right)\frac{V^2}{2g} \qquad (10\text{–}6)$$

The value of the friction factor has to be known in order that these equations may be used in making calculations. The dimensional analysis of Sec. 8–2 indicated that the friction factor f was a function of the relative roughness (k/D) of the pipe surface and of the Reynolds number of the mean flow $(VD\rho/\mu)$. The friction factor can be determined analytically for laminar flow and semiempirically for turbulent flow. These two methods will be discussed separately, and then the final results will be given in graphical form.

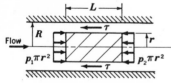

FIG. 10–3. Cylindrical element in round pipe.

For fully developed incompressible flow in a round pipe, the momentum theorem applied to a cylindrical element of length L and radius r (Fig. 10–3) gives

$$p_1\,\pi r^2 - p_2\,\pi r^2 - \tau 2\pi r L = 0$$

or

$$\tau = \frac{p_1 - p_2}{L}\left(\frac{r}{2}\right) \qquad (10\text{–}7)$$

which is valid for both laminar and turbulent flow. Equation 10–7 shows that the shear stress varies linearly with the pipe radius, being zero at the center and a maximum at the pipe walls, where the wall shear stress τ_0 becomes

$$\tau_0 = \frac{p_1 - p_2}{L}\left(\frac{R}{2}\right) = \frac{\Delta p}{L}\left(\frac{D}{4}\right) \qquad [10\text{–}2]$$

A comparison of Eq. 10–7 with Eq. 10–5 shows that the wall shear stress is related to the friction factor by the equation

$$\tau_0 = f \frac{\rho V^2}{8} \tag{10–8}[2]$$

It will be convenient to introduce a shear velocity v_* defined as

$$v_* = \sqrt{\frac{\tau_0}{\rho}} = V \sqrt{\frac{f}{8}} \tag{10–9}$$

For circular tubes the tube diameter D is the characteristic length parameter used in the various equations. For noncircular ducts the hydraulic diameter D_h is used. This is defined as

$$D_h = \frac{4A}{P} \tag{10–10}$$

where A is the cross-sectional flow area and P is the duct perimeter.

10–3. FULLY DEVELOPED LAMINAR INCOMPRESSIBLE FLOW IN DUCTS

Circular tubes. For laminar flow, the shear stress may be expressed not only as in Eq. 10–7 but also in terms of the velocity gradient.

$$\tau = \mu \frac{du}{dy} = -\mu \frac{du}{dr}$$

where u is the varying velocity throughout the cross section and $du/dy = -du/dr$ (since $y = R - r$, $dy = -dr$) is the velocity gradient. Then, from Eq. 10–7,

$$\frac{du}{dr} = -\frac{\tau}{\mu} = -\frac{\Delta p}{L} \frac{r}{2\mu}$$

Integration with the boundary condition $u = 0$ at $r = R$ gives

$$u = \frac{1}{4\mu} \left(\frac{\Delta p}{L}\right) (R^2 - r^2) \tag{10–11a}$$

which indicates a parabolic velocity profile. This equation could also be obtained by integrating the appropriate Navier-Stokes equation in cylindrical coordinates, namely

$$\frac{dp}{dx} = \mu \left(\frac{d^2u}{dr^2} + \frac{1}{r} \frac{du}{dr}\right) = \frac{\mu}{r} \frac{d}{dr} \left(r \frac{du}{dr}\right)$$

with the boundary condition that $u = 0$ at $r = R$.

The maximum velocity $u_{\max}$ is at the center of the tube (at $r = 0$) and is

$$u_{\max} = \frac{\Delta p}{L} \left(\frac{R^2}{4\mu}\right)$$

[2]The friction factor may be defined as the ratio of the local wall shear stress to the dynamic pressure of the mean flow, or $f' = \tau_0/(\rho V^2/2)$. The Darcy-Weisbach friction factor is 4 times this value, or $f = 4f'$.

Thus the velocity profile of Eq. 10–11a could also be written as

$$\frac{u}{u_{\max}} = 1 - \left(\frac{r}{R}\right)^2 \tag{10–11b}$$

The average velocity V is

$$V = \frac{Q}{A} = \frac{\int u\, dA}{A} = \frac{\int_0^R 2\pi r\, u\, dr}{\pi R^2} = \frac{\Delta p}{L}\left(\frac{R^2}{8\mu}\right) = \frac{u_{\max}}{2} \tag{10–12}$$

or one-half the maximum. The pressure gradient, in terms of the flow rate, is

$$\frac{\Delta p}{L} = \frac{128\mu Q}{\pi D^4} \tag{10–13}$$

The friction factor f for laminar flow is obtained by combining Eq. 10–5 and Eq. 10–13 to get

$$f = \frac{64}{VD\rho/\mu} = \frac{64}{\mathrm{Re}_D} \tag{10–14}$$

This expression has been verified experimentally and is valid for engineering calculations of both *smooth and rough* circular pipes for Reynolds numbers up to about 2000. It is possible to achieve laminar flow for Reynolds numbers as high as 40,000 or more in carefully controlled laboratory experiments, but instabilities are usually present in piping systems, which limit laminar flow to Reynolds numbers no greater than about 2000.

Similar relations for fully-developed laminar flow of a power-law non-Newtonian fluid in circular tubes are developed in Appendix I.

TABLE 10–1	TABLE 10–2	TABLE 10–3
FRICTION FACTORS FOR CONCENTRIC ANNULUS [1]	FRICTION FACTORS FOR RECTANGLE [1]	FRICTION FACTORS FOR CIRCULAR SEGMENT [2]

 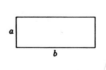 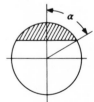

r_1/r_2	$f\,\mathrm{Re}$	a/b	$f\,\mathrm{Re}$	α	$f\,\mathrm{Re}$
0.0001	71.78	0	96.00	0	62.2
0.001	74.68	1/20	89.91	10	62.2
0.01	80.11	1/10	84.68	20	62.3
0.05	86.27	1/8	82.34	30	62.4
0.10	89.37	1/6	78.81	40	62.5
0.20	92.35	1/4	72.93	60	62.8
0.40	94.71	2/5	65.47	90	63.1
0.60	95.59	1/2	62.19	120	63.3
0.80	95.92	3/4	57.89	150	63.7
1.00	96.00	1	56.91	180	64.0

Noncircular ducts. Various methods of analysis have been used to determine the friction factor ($f = [\Delta p/L] [2D_h/\rho V^2]$) and Reynolds number (Re $= VD_h\rho/\mu$) relation for noncircular ducts. Results of these analyses for various cross sections are given in Tables 10–1 through 10–4. Note that flow in a rectangle of zero aspect ratio represents flow between parallel plates, and corresponds to flow in a concentric annulus of radius ratio approaching unity. Also note that a circular sector with $\alpha = 90$ degrees is identical to a circular segment with $\alpha = 90$ degrees.

TABLE 10–4
LAMINAR FLOW FRICTION FACTORS [3]
CIRCULAR SECTOR   ISOCELES TRIANGLE   RIGHT TRIANGLE

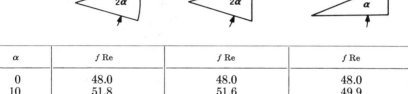

α	f Re	f Re	f Re
0	48.0	48.0	48.0
10	51.8	51.6	49.9
20	54.5	52.9	51.2
30	56.7	53.3	52.0
40	58.4	52.9	52.4
50	59.7	52.0	52.4
60	60.8	51.1	52.0
70	61.7	49.5	51.2
80	62.5	48.3	49.9
90	63.1	48.0	48.0

10–4. FULLY DEVELOPED INCOMPRESSIBLE TURBULENT FLOW IN DUCTS

Circular tubes. In turbulent flow in a pipe, the radial components of velocity cause an interchange of momentum between adjacent layers of fluid, and as a result, the velocity profile is flatter than that for laminar flow. The higher the Reynolds number, the flatter the velocity profile. Since the velocity is zero at the pipe wall, this results in a very large velocity gradient at the pipe wall with a resulting higher wall shear stress than for laminar flow at the same Reynolds number.

The analysis of turbulent flow is not as simple as that for laminar flow. The Navier-Stokes equations may be written for homogeneous turbulence to include velocity and pressure fluctuations. These equations involving statistical correlations of fluctuating quantities are known as the Reynolds equations. The number of unknowns, unfortunately, is greater than the number of equations. G. I. Taylor in 1935 suggested that, in the absence of mean velocity gradients, turbulence was not only homogeneous but also isotropic—independent of the orientation or location of the coordinate axes. The Reynolds equations then became simplified, and theoretical analyses and experimental studies have been enhanced by the assumption of isotropy. A number of statistical theories have received attention, notably those by Taylor, Burgers, von Karman, Howarth, Dryden, Kolmogoroff, and Lin [4], but none has yet received universal acceptance.

A number of phenomological theories have been advanced [5]. These are based on observation of transverse transport of fluid owing to a mixing process in turbulent flow. Saint-Venant in 1843 introduced a mixing coefficient into fluid stress equations. Prandtl in 1925 made use of a mixing length which represents the transverse distance that fluid elements or lumps travel in exchanging momentum. This mixing length may be illustrated by comparing it with the mean distance molecules in a gas move transverse to the mean flow direction between molecular collisions. In 1930, von Karman made use of a similar length parameter. Taylor in 1915 suggested that vorticity was conserved in this lateral transport of fluid elements or lumps, rather than momentum.

Reynolds in about 1880 showed that the turbulent shear stress in two-dimensional flow could be expressed as

$$\tau = -\rho \, \overline{u'v'}$$

where u' and v' are the instantaneous fluctuations of velocity from the mean in a direction parallel to the mean flow and normal to it, respectively. In a velocity gradient, Prandtl suggested that

$$u' \propto l \frac{du}{dy}$$

where l is the mixing length just mentioned, and v' is proportional to u'. Thus the turbulent shear stress could be written as

$$\tau = \rho l^2 \left| \frac{du}{dy} \right| \frac{du}{dy}$$

where the proportionality factor is included in l. Near a boundary the mixing length was considered to vary with y, the normal distance from the boundary, such that $l = \kappa y$. Thus, at the boundary,

$$\tau_0 = \rho \kappa^2 y^2 \left(\frac{du}{dy} \right)^2$$

This equation may be integrated to obtain

$$\frac{u}{\sqrt{\tau_0/\rho}} = \frac{u}{v_*} = \frac{1}{\kappa} \ln y + C$$

where v_* is known as the shear velocity. Experiments show that $\kappa = 0.4$. Thus, since $u = u_{\max}$ at the pipe center line (at $y = R$),

$$\frac{u_{max} - u}{\sqrt{\tau_0/\rho}} = \frac{u_{max} - u}{v_*} = 2.5 \ln \frac{R}{y} \qquad (10\text{--}15)$$

It was assumed by von Karman that the turbulent velocity fluctuations vary with a length l, which he considered to vary with du/dy divided by d^2u/dy^2, and with the mean velocity gradient du/dy. In addition, he assumed the turbulent shear to vary with $\rho l^2 \, (du/dy)^2$ as Prandtl did. Thus von Karman's analysis shows that

$$\sqrt{\frac{\tau}{\rho}} = -\kappa \frac{(du/dy)^2}{d^2u/dy^2}$$

and this gives, upon integration,

$$\frac{u_{max} - u}{\sqrt{\tau_0/\rho}} = \frac{u_{max} - u}{v_*} = -\frac{1}{\kappa}[\ln(1 - \sqrt{1 - y/R}) + \sqrt{1 - y/R}] \quad (10\text{--}16)$$

where $\kappa = 0.36$, which fits experimental data quite well.

Neither Prandtl's nor von Karman's concept is valid at the pipe center line where the transverse momentum transport is zero, or at the pipe wall where the flow is laminar. This laminar region is called the laminar sublayer and was discussed in Sec. 7–4. The results given by Eq. 10–16 apply quite well to very high Reynolds numbers. Turbulent flow at lower Reynolds numbers may be described by a power-law equation of the form of Eq. 7–12.

Three flow regimes are generally considered: 1) The hydraulically smooth regime, in which the roughness elements are submerged within the laminar sublayer (see Sec. 7–4). For this regime, $0 \leq v_*k/\nu \leq 5$. 2) The transition regime, in which the roughness elements protrude partly beyond the laminar sublayer. For this regime, $5 \leq v_*k/\nu \leq 70$. 3) The hydraulically rough regime, in which all roughness elements protrude beyond the laminar sublayer. For this regime, $v_*k/\nu > 70$.[3]

An empirical expression by Blasius for the wall shear stress for turbulent flow in a *smooth* pipe is

$$\tau_0 = 0.0395 \, \rho V^2 \left(\frac{\nu}{VD}\right)^{1/4} = \frac{0.0395 \, \rho V^2}{\mathrm{Re}_D^{1/4}} \qquad (10\text{--}17)$$

where V is the average velocity and D is the pipe diameter. (This was transformed in Eq. 7–13 to apply to a flat plate.) The friction factor is

$$f = \frac{8\tau_0}{\rho V^2} = \frac{0.316}{\mathrm{Re}_D^{1/4}} \qquad (10\text{--}18)$$

and this equation is known as Blasius' law of pipe friction for smooth pipes. It applies for Reynolds numbers no greater than about 100,000 and was obtained by assuming a velocity profile of the form

[3] Note that v_*k/ν is a Reynolds number based on the shear velocity and roughness height k.

$$\frac{u}{u_{\max}} = \left(\frac{y}{R}\right)^{1/n} \qquad\qquad [7\text{--}12]$$

outside or beyond the laminar sublayer (but extending not quite to the pipe center line) with $n \approx 7$, where u is the velocity at a distance y from the pipe wall. Actually, values of n experimentally determined by J. Nikuradse [5] vary from 6 at $\mathrm{Re}_D = 4 \times 10^3$ to 10 at $\mathrm{Re}_D = 3.2 \times 10^6$. This variation in n suggested a logarithmic form for the velocity profile and for the friction formula at higher Reynolds numbers. The result is

$$\frac{1}{\sqrt{f}} = 2 \log (\mathrm{Re}_D \sqrt{f}) - 0.8 \qquad\qquad (10\text{--}19)$$

and this equation is known as Prandtl's law of pipe friction for smooth pipes. Experiments by J. Nikuradse have verified this equation up to a Reynolds number of 3.4×10^6.

For *rough* pipes, the classical experiments are those by J. Nikuradse in which uniform sizes of sand grains were cemented to the inside surfaces of smooth pipes so that a range of relative roughness (k/D, the ratio of sand-grain diameter to pipe diameter) from about 0.001 to 0.033 was obtained. Friction factors and Reynolds numbers were determined for all test runs, and the results are shown in Fig. 10–4.

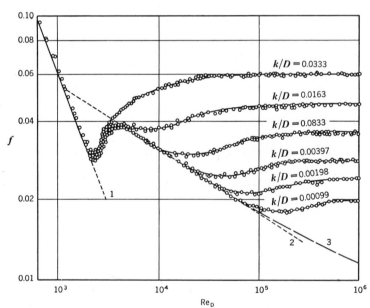

FIG. 10–4. Results of Nikuradse's measurements on pipes artificially roughened with sand grains. Curve *1*: Eq. 10–14, $f = 64/\mathrm{Re}_D$; curve *2*: Eq. 10–18, $f = 0.316/\mathrm{Re}_D^{0.25}$; curve *3*: Eq. 10–19, $1/\sqrt{f} = 2 \log (\mathrm{Re}_D\sqrt{f}) - 0.8$.

The analysis of flow in *rough* pipes (generalized results also apply to smooth pipes) involves the shear velocity v_*, defined as

$$v_* = \sqrt{\frac{\tau_0}{\rho}} = \sqrt{\frac{f}{8}}\, V \qquad (10\text{-}20)$$

In this flow regime, Prandtl's semiempirical analysis gives a universal velocity distribution law as

$$\frac{u_{\max} - u}{v_*} = 5.75 \log \frac{R}{y} = 2.5 \ln \frac{R}{y} \qquad [10\text{-}15]$$

where $u_{\max}$ is the center-line velocity, u is the variable velocity at a distance y from the pipe walls, and R is the pipe radius. From Eq. 10–15 the average velocity V may be calculated as

$$V = u_{\max} - 3.75\, v_* \qquad (10\text{-}21)$$

Combining Eqs. 10–20 and 10–21 gives an expression for the ratio of the center-line velocity to the average velocity as

$$\frac{u_{\max}}{V} = 1 + 1.33 \sqrt{f} \qquad (10\text{-}22)$$

This equation may be used as a means of estimating the average velocity for fully developed turbulent flow in a round pipe from a single measurement of the center-line velocity, although a more accurate determination results from measurements which give the actual velocity profile.

A typical measured velocity profile for fully developed turbulent flow in a circular tube is shown in Fig. 10–5.

In the completely rough regime of flow, a semiempirical analysis also indicates that the velocity profile may be given in terms of the equivalent sand-grain roughness k as

$$\frac{u}{v_*} = 5.75 \log \frac{y}{k} + 8.5 = 2.5 \ln \frac{y}{k} + 8.5 \qquad (10\text{-}23)$$

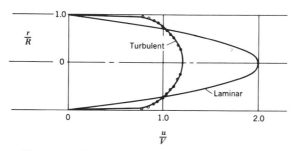

FIG. 10–5. Measured turbulent velocity profile at Re = 80,000 in a smooth circular tube compared with laminar velocity profile at Re < 2000.

When Eq. 10–23 is combined with Eq. 10–21 and the resulting constant adjusted for experimental results of Nikuradse, an expression for the friction factor becomes

$$f = \frac{1}{\left(2 \log \dfrac{D}{2k} + 1.74\right)^2} \tag{10-24}$$

An equation by Colebrook and White encompasses all flow regimes. This equation is

$$\frac{1}{\sqrt{f}} = 1.74 - 2 \log \left(\frac{2k}{D} + \frac{18.7}{\mathrm{Re}_D \sqrt{f}}\right) \tag{10-25}$$

which becomes Eq. 10–24 as Re_D gets very large, and Eq. 10–19 for smooth pipes for which $k \to 0$.

The application of theoretical analyses and test results for turbulent flow in commercial pipes is difficult, because the absolute roughness k of these pipes is not well known. In addition, it is known that roughness spacing and shape, as well as size, affects pipe friction. Experiments on commercial pipes have led to the use of an *equivalent sand-grain roughness* for these pipes, and the results useful for engineering calculations are shown in Fig. 10–6.[4] Calculations are only as accurate as the knowledge of pipe roughness, and estimates of pressure drops or head losses owing to pipe friction may be considered good if they are within 5 or 10 per cent of the actual values. A chart for determining relative roughness is shown in Fig. 10–7.

A study of Figs. 10–4 and 10–6 indicates that 1) for laminar flow, the friction factor depends only on the Reynolds number and is not affected by pipe roughness; 2) for smooth pipes, the friction factor for turbulent flow also depends only on the Reynolds number; 3) for the hydraulically rough regime, the friction factor depends only on the relative roughness of the pipe surface and is not dependent on the Reynolds number; 4) for the transition regime in rough pipes, the friction factor depends on both the relative roughness and the Reynolds number.

Three types of problems may arise in connection with friction losses in pipes. These problems involve the determination of the following:

1. The pressure drop, or head loss, for a given flow of a given fluid in a given pipe. The relative roughness k/D and the Reynolds number are determined and the friction factor obtained from Fig. 10–6. The pressure drop, or head loss, is calculated from Eq. 10–5 or Eq. 10–6.
2. The discharge for a given pipe and fluid with a specified pressure drop, or head loss. Two methods may be used.

[4]An enlarged reproduction of Fig. 10–6 is provided within the inside cover at the back of this book.

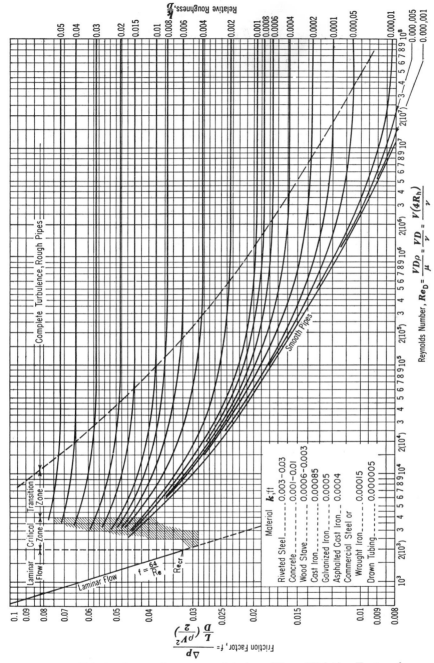

Fig. 10-6. Friction factors for commercial pipe. (From "Friction Factors for Pipe Flow," by L. F. Moody, *Trans. ASME*, Vol. 66, 1944, with permission of the publishers, The American Society of Mechanical Engineers.)

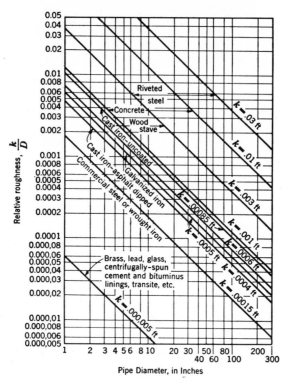

Fig. 10–7. Relative roughness factors for new clean pipes. (From "Friction Factors for Pipe Flow," by L. F. Moody, *Trans. ASME*, Vol. 66, 1944, with permission of the publishers, The American Society of Mechanical Engineers.)

a) A friction factor may be assumed and the velocity calculated from Eqs. 10–5 or 10–6. If the Reynolds number is high, the friction factor will only depend on the relative roughness of the pipe, and this is a good initial assumption. The Reynolds number based on the first estimate of velocity is then calculated and a better friction factor obtained from Fig. 10–6 if the Reynolds number is low enough so that the hydraulically rough regime is not reached. Successive trials will give the desired flow rate.

b) A discharge may be assumed, and the corresponding velocity used to calculate an estimated Reynolds number. The pressure drop, or head loss, may then be determined as in the type problem referred to in *a*) and compared with the specified value. Too large a calculated head loss indicates too large an assumed flow rate, and vice versa. Successive trials may be made until the calculated head loss agrees with the given value, or three trials may be plotted (Q vs. h_f) and the desired flow rate corresponding to the given head loss interpolated graphically.

3. The pipe size required to carry a given flow rate of a given fluid with a specified pressure drop or head loss. A pipe diameter may be assumed and the pressure drop, or head loss, calculated as in the type problem referred to in a) and compared with the given value. If the calculated head loss is too large, the assumed pipe diameter was too small, and vice versa. Successive trials may be made until the calculated head loss agrees with the given value, or three trial solutions may be plotted (D vs. h_f) and the desired pipe diameter obtained by graphical interpolation. The next larger commercial pipe size should be chosen for an engineering design.

EXAMPLE 10–1. What is the pressure drop in 500 ft of 4-in. smooth pipe if oil ($\gamma = 58$ lb$_f$/ft^3, $\mu = 0.001$ slug/ft sec) flows through it at a velocity of a) 2 ft/sec and b) 10 ft/sec?

Solution: a) $\mathrm{Re}_D = VD\rho/\mu = (2)(1/3)(58/32.2)/0.001 = 1200$, indicating laminar flow. Then $f = 64/\mathrm{Re}_D = 0.0533$ and $\Delta p = f(L/D)\rho V^2/2 = 0.0533$ $[500/(1/3)]\,(1.80)(2)^2/2 = 288$ psf $= 2.0$ psi.

b) $\mathrm{Re}_D = 6000$, and $f = 0.0355$ from Fig. 10–6. Then $\Delta p = 0.0355\,[500/(1/3)]$ $(1.8)(10)^2/2 = 4790$ psf $= 33.3$ psi.

EXAMPLE 10–2. What is the flow rate for water at 60 F in a 12-in. cast-iron pipe if the head loss in 1000 ft of pipe is 12 ft? ($k/D = 0.00085$.)

Solution:

Method 1. Assume $f = 0.0188$ for high Re_D. Then $V^2/2g = h_f\,D/fL$ $= (12)(1)/(0.0188)(1000) = 0.639$ ft, and $V = 6.4$ ft/sec. For this velocity, $\mathrm{Re}_D = VD/\nu = (6.4)(1)/1.22 \times 10^{-5} = 5.25 \times 10^5$ and for this Re_D, $f = 0.0194$. Thus $V^2/2g = (12)(1)/(0.0194)(1000) = 0.619$ ft, and $V = 6.30$ ft/sec. The Reynolds number for this velocity is 5.16×10^5, and the friction factor is again 0.0194. Thus the flow rate is $Q = VA = (6.3)(0.7854) = 4.95$ ft^3/sec.

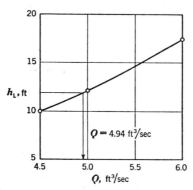

FIG. 10–8.   Example 10–2.

Method 2. If flow rates of 4.5, 5, and 6 ft³/sec are assumed, the corresponding head losses are 9.97, 12.26, and 17.5 ft, respectively. A graphical interpolation gives $Q = 4.94$ ft³/sec (Fig. 10–8).

Noncircular ducts. The results for pressure drop or head loss for fully developed turbulent flow in circular tubes may be generally applied to noncircular ducts if the diameter D is replaced by the hydraulic diameter D_h (Eq. 10–10) in the expressions for relative roughness, Reynolds number, and pressure drop or head loss. They may be used for square ducts, for rectangular ducts where the ratio of the two sides does not exceed about 8, for equilateral triangular ducts, for hexagonal ducts, and for concentric annular ducts with a ratio of inner to outer diameter up to at least 0.75 [6]. For these concentric annular ducts, the friction factor is about 6–8 per cent greater than that for a smooth circular tube at Reynolds numbers from 15,000 to 150,000.

The effect of eccentricity on the friction factor in smooth annular ducts is shown in Fig. 10–9. The eccentricity is defined as $e = s/(r_2 - r_1)$, where s is the distance between the axis of the outer and the inner tube,

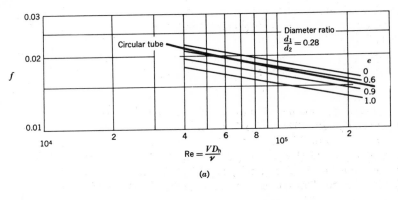

(a)

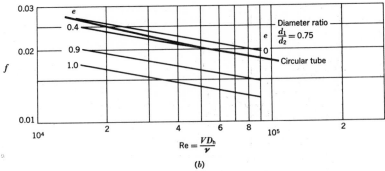

(b)

FIG. 10–9. Friction factor for smooth eccentric annulus compared with friction factor for smooth circular tubes, after V. K. Jonsson [6].

and r_2 and r_1 are the radii of these tubes, respectively. When $e = 0$, the tubes are concentric, and when $e = 1$ the inner tube is in contact with the outer tube.

In ducts with tall, narrow, triangular cross sections, both laminar and turbulent flow may coexist at a section [7], and the analysis of this type of flow is not so straightforward as in ducts more nearly circular.

10–5. STEADY INCOMPRESSIBLE FLOW IN THE ENTRANCE REGION OF DUCTS

In many instances of engineering interest, ducts are short, and a knowledge of entrance flow phenomena is necessary.

Equation 10–3 indicates that for developing flow in the entrance region of a duct, the overall pressure drop overcomes wall shear and increases the flow momentum. In calculating this pressure drop, it is customary to use fully developed friction factors and to add a correction term k_L to account for entrance effects. Thus

$$\frac{p_1 - p}{\rho V^2/2} = \frac{fL}{D_h} + k_L \tag{10–26}$$

where p_1 is the pressure at the duct inlet, and L is the distance from the duct entrance to a location where the pressure is p. The correction term k_L accounts for the development of the velocity profile, incremental viscous dissipation in the entrance region relative to that for fully developed flow, and separation losses, if any. The value of k_L is a function of position along the duct, but becomes a constant in the fully developed flow region. For practical purposes, it is the fully developed value of k_L which is of greatest use and which is referred to in the hydraulic literature as an entrance loss coefficient. It depends on the Reynolds number of the flow, and on the shape of the duct entrance as well as on the shape and surface of the duct itself. Values of k_L have been calculated and measured for laminar flow in ducts, and have been measured for turbulent flow in some ducts.

The length of duct required to attain essentially fully developed conditions is called the hydrodynamic entrance length, L_e. For engineering calculations, it is generally sufficient to associate the entrance length with the distance from the duct entrance which is needed for the pressure gradient to become within a specified percentage of the fully developed pressure gradient.

Values of k_L and of L_e for both laminar and turbulent flow in various ducts will be listed.

Laminar flow. The pressure drop in the entrance length L_e may be obtained from the Bernoulli equation written along the duct axis. This is valid since there is no shear in the core flow in the entrance region (Fig. 10–1a). Thus

$$p_1 - p_e = (\rho u_{max}^2/2) - \rho V^2/2 = \left[\left(\frac{u_{max}}{V}\right)^2 - 1\right](\rho V^2/2)$$

$$(10\text{-}27)$$

For any duct in which the ratio of maximum velocity to average velocity for fully developed flow is known, the pressure drop in the entrance region is given by Eq. 10–27. If values of both f and k_L are known, the entrance length may be obtained by combining Eqs. 10–26 and 10–27. Thus

$$\frac{L_e}{D_h} = \frac{1}{f}\left[\left(\frac{u_{max}}{V}\right)^2 - 1 - k_L\right]$$

$$(10\text{-}28)$$

Friction factors are known as functions of Re (Tables 10–1 through 10–4) and thus values of L_e/D_hRe may be calculated from Eq. 10–28 for ducts in which k_L values are known.

For a *circular tube*, $u_{max}/V = 2$. The value of k_L has been determined both analytically as well as experimentally with an average value of about 1.30 [1]. Thus since f Re = 64, the entrance length for laminar flow in a circular tube is

$$\frac{L_e}{D} = \frac{Re_D}{64}(2^2 - 1 - 1.30) = 0.0265\ Re_D$$

$$(10\text{-}29)$$

The pressure drop for fully developed flow in this length of pipe is

$$\Delta p = \frac{64}{Re_D}\left(\frac{L_e}{D}\right)(\rho V^2/2) = 1.70(\rho V^2/2)$$

and thus the pressure drop in the entrance region is greater than that for fully developed flow in an equal length of pipe by the factor

$$\frac{\Delta p_e}{\Delta p} = 3/1.70 = 1.76$$

$$(10\text{-}30)$$

The average wall shear stress in the entrance region is greater than that for fully developed flow in an equal length of pipe by the factor

$$\frac{(\bar{\tau}_0)_e}{\tau_0} = 1.76 - 2(\beta - 1)/1.70 = 1.76 - 2(1.33 - 1)/1.70$$

$$= 1.37$$

$$(10\text{-}31)$$

These values (1.76 and 1.37) are approximate and apply to the entrance region defined as the region where the pressure gradients and the wall shear stresses, respectively, are developing towards a fixed value. If the entrance region were defined as the region in which the velocity profiles are developing, both values would be lower, although the shear-stress ratio would always be less than the pressure-gradient ratio.

Some values of k_L and L_e/D_h Re for laminar flow in various ducts are given in Tables 10–5 through 10–8.

TABLE 10–5 ENTRANCE EFFECTS, CONCENTRIC ANNULUS (See Table 10–1)		TABLE 10–6 ENTRANCE EFFECTS, RECTANGLE (See Table 10–2)			TABLE 10–7 ENTRANCE EFFECTS, CIRCULAR SEGMENT (See Table 10–3)	

r_1/r_2	k_L	a/b	k_L	$L_e/D_h\mathrm{Re}$	α	k_L
0.0001	1.13	0	0.69	0.0059	0	1.74
0.001	1.07	1/8	0.88	0.0094	10	1.73
0.01	0.97	1/5	1.00	0.0123	20	1.72
0.05	0.86	1/4	1.08	0.0146	30	1.69
0.10	0.81	1/2	1.38	0.0254	40	1.65
0.20	0.75	3/4	1.52	0.0311	60	1.57
0.40	0.71	1	1.55	0.0324	90	1.46
0.60	0.69				120	1.39
0.80	0.69				150	1.34
1.00	0.69				180	1.33

TABLE 10–8
ENTRANCE EFFECTS
(See Table 10–4)

α	CIRCULAR SECTOR k_L	ISOCELES TRIANGLE k_L	RIGHT TRIANGLE k_L
0	2.97	2.97	2.97
10	2.06	2.14	2.40
20	1.71	1.85	2.09
30	1.58	1.79	1.94
40	1.53	1.83	1.88
50	1.50	1.95	1.88
60	1.49	2.14	1.94
70	1.48	2.38	2.09
80	1.47	2.72	2.40
90	1.46	2.97	2.97

Turbulent flow. Both analysis and experiment indicate the same general results for turbulent flow as for laminar flow; namely, that the wall shear stress becomes fixed in a shorter entrance region than the entrance region required for the pressure gradient to become fixed. This region, in turn, is shorter than the region required for the velocity profile to become fixed. The entrance region is shorter, however, for turbulent flow than for laminar flow on any similar basis of comparison.

Values of the entrance loss coefficient k_L in Eq. 10–26 as well as the entrance length L_e are determined experimentally. For a square entrance, flow separation results in a high k_L value of about 0.50–0.55 for circular tubes and concentric annuli [8]. For a rounded entrance, the initial boundary layer flow is generally laminar (Fig. 10–1b) and the entrance region pressure drop does not substantially exceed (it may even be less) the corresponding fully developed pressure drop. Thus k_L values for smooth circular tubes and concentric annuli are about 0.08 or less under these conditions. If an obstruction causes the boundary layer to be turbulent at the tube or annulus entrance, k_L values are larger, depending upon the size of the boundary layer trip.

Entrance lengths for turbulent flow in smooth tubes and concentric annuli are based on the length required for the pressure gradient to become within a specified percentage of the fully developed pressure gradient (5 per cent, for example). On this basis L_e for these ducts (annulus diameter ratio up to 0.75) with square or rounded entrances are about 30 hydraulic diameters or less [6, 8]. The effect of increasing the eccentricity and the diameter ratio for the eccentric annulus is to increase the entrance length; $L_e = 91$ hydraulic diameters for an eccentricity $e = 1.0$ and a diameter ratio of 0.75. The range of Reynolds number for these annulus results is about 15,000 to 150,000.

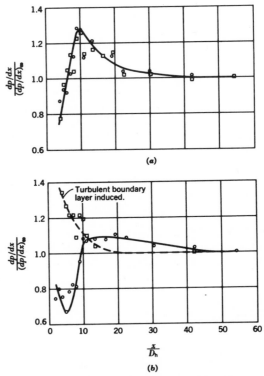

FIG. 10–10. Local pressure gradients in a smooth tube [8]. *a*) Square entrance Re = 60,000–70,000. *b*) Rounded entrance, Re = 49,000.

Fig. 10–10 shows the development of the pressure gradient in the entrance region of a smooth circular tube with a square entrance and with a rounded entrance [8]. The entrance lengths are seen to be about 30 hydraulic diameters or less based on the 5 per cent pressure gradient criterion. For the square entrance the pressure gradient ratio is less than unity at small values of x/D_h because of the effects of pressure recovery downstream of the vena contracta (Fig. 10–11a). It is even negative at x/D_h values nearer zero where the pressure increases in the direction of flow in the expansion following the vena contracta. For the rounded entrance the solid curve in Fig. 10–10b indicates an initial laminar boundary layer which undergoes a transition to turbulence (Fig. 10–1) at the minimum point on the curve. With a boundary layer trip to induce a turbulent boundary layer at the tube entrance, the expected monotonically decreasing ratio of pressure gradients is obtained.

For both laminar and turbulent flow, local as well as average wall shear stresses and local as well as average pressure gradients generally are greater in the entrance region than in the fully developed flow region of a duct. The increase in local or average pressure gradients is greater than the increase in local or average wall shear stresses, since additional pressure drop must be provided to increase the momentum in the entrance region.

10–6. CONTRACTIONS, EXPANSIONS, AND PIPE FITTINGS

Losses in contractions, expansions, and pipe fittings are largely due to separation effects and are known as *form* losses, as contrasted to pipe friction losses due to wall shear. Wall shear also accounts for a large part of the losses in a well-designed contraction, but in any case, the losses are due to the viscosity of the fluid. The losses are generally expressed in terms of the velocity head $V^2/2g$ at the downstream end of the duct element. The effects actually extend for some distance downstream of the loss-producing element, because of the distance required for the velocity profile to reach its fully developed shape. It is customary in engineering calculations, however, to consider the loss as a localized loss and to be concentrated in the immediate neighborhood of the loss-producing section. In all instances except for expansions, the losses are expressed as

$$h_L = k_L \frac{V_2^2}{2g} \qquad (10\text{–}32)$$

where k_L is an experimentally determined loss coefficient. For expansions, the loss may be written as

$$h_L = k_L \frac{(V_1 - V_2)^2}{2g} \qquad (10\text{–}33)$$

section 1 being upstream from section 2.

Losses of this type are often referred to as *minor* losses, but they are minor only for relatively long pipelines. For short pipe systems, they often make up the major part of the total losses.

Contractions. When a real fluid passes around a corner, separation occurs (Fig. 10–11), and the eddies in the separation zone give rise to

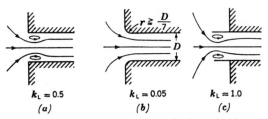

$k_L \approx 0.5$ $k_L \approx 0.05$ $k_L \approx 1.0$

(*a*)   (*b*)   (*c*)

FIG. 10–11. Pipe entrances with pipes flowing full. *a*) Square, *b*) round, and *c*) reentrant.

energy losses. These losses may be minimized by rounding the corners; the optimum is attained when the radius of curvature is ⅐ the pipe diameter. A projecting entrance as shown in Fig. 10–11(*c*) is known as a Borda mouthpiece, for which the contracted flow section is one-half the pipe cross section if the pipe does not flow full (see Prob. 5–115).

Abrupt changes in pipe size produce separation, and the loss coefficient is a function of the diameter ratio D_2/D_1 (Fig. 10–12). Typical values of k_L are given in Table 10–9.

TABLE 10–9
TYPICAL LOSS COEFFICIENTS FOR AN ABRUPT CONTRACTION

D_2/D_1	0.2	0.4	0.6	0.8	0.9
k_L	0.39	0.36	0.29	0.14	0.05

A gradual contraction may be designed with a minimum head loss. Typical examples are contractions for subsonic wind tunnels, water tunnels, and fire nozzles. Separation is to be avoided near the downstream end of

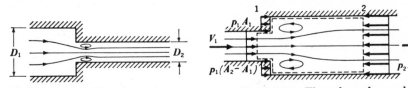

FIG. 10–12. Abrupt decrease in pipe size (contraction).

FIG. 10–13. Flow through a sudden enlargement in a pipe.

wind and water tunnel contractions, especially in a water tunnel, in order that low pressures, which enhance cavitation, may be avoided. In addition, a very flat velocity profile is desired in the test section immediately following the contraction, and this type of profile is typical of a contracting flow stream. Most of the total head at the contraction entrance is pressure head, which is uniform across the section. Most of the total head downstream is velocity head, and since very little of it originates from the nonuniform velocity head upstream, it is very uniform across the downstream section. A typical value of the kinetic energy correction factor α, which is a measure of the flatness of the velocity profile, at the downstream end of a well-designed contraction with $D_2/D_1 = \frac{1}{3}$ is 1.002, indicating a very flat profile. The loss coefficient in this contraction may well be as low as 0.03, based on the downstream velocity head.

Expansions. The head loss in a sudden expansion may be determined by writing the continuity, momentum, and energy equations for the isolated region indicated by dashed lines in Fig. 10-13. These equations are, respectively,

$$V_1 A_1 = V_2 A_2$$
$$p_1 A_1 + p_1(A_2 - A_1) - p_2 A_2 = V_1 A_1 \rho(V_2 - V_1)$$

neglecting wall shear, and

$$\frac{V_1^2}{2g} + \frac{p_1}{\gamma} = \frac{V_2^2}{2g} + \frac{p_2}{\gamma} + h_L$$

The pressure at the point of enlargement is approximately p_1, since the streamline spacing is essentially the same as at section 1. Solving for the head loss gives

$$h_L = \frac{(V_1 - V_2)^2}{2g} \tag{10-34}$$

A submerged pipe discharging into a large reservoir or tank represents a sudden enlargement for which $V_2 \to 0$, and for this the head loss is $h_L = V_1^2/2g$. Thus, one pipe velocity head is lost because of viscous dissipation as the jet leaving the pipe eventually is brought to rest.

The high losses owing to separation in a sudden enlargement may be reduced considerably if the enlargement is made gradual in order that separation be avoided. An enlargement of this type is known as a subsonic diffuser. If the total angle of divergence is made too small, both the wall friction and the fabrication costs will be large. An optimum divergence angle is about 7 or 8 deg, for which the loss coefficient of Eq. 10-33 is about 0.14; it may be as low as 0.06 for a diffuser with a carefully designed parabolic curvature at the inlet with a length equal to one-half or more of the inlet diameter.

Flow in a diffuser is very complex. Diffusers are designed to convert velocity head into pressure head in subsonic wind tunnels, water tunnels, draft tubes for hydraulic turbines, and pump volutes, for example. Their ability to make this conversion is often used as a measure of efficiency and is known as the pressure efficiency, as contrasted to energy efficiency. The pressure efficiency may be written as

$$\eta_p = \frac{p_2 - p_1}{\alpha_1 \dfrac{\rho V_1{}^2}{2} - \alpha_2 \dfrac{\rho V_2{}^2}{2}} \tag{10-35a}$$

and the energy efficiency as

$$\eta_e = \frac{\alpha_1 \dfrac{V_1{}^2}{2g} - h_L}{\alpha_1 \dfrac{V_1{}^2}{2g}} \tag{10-35b}$$

Subscripts 1 and 2 refer to upstream and downstream sections, respectively, where the pressure is p, the velocity V, the kinetic energy correction factor α, the fluid density ρ, and the head loss in the diffuser h_L. In Eq. 10-35b, the efficiency is the ratio of energy at exit to the energy at inlet, the only energy at inlet being kinetic energy since pressure itself does not represent an ability to do work. Also, the pressure recovery for an incompressible fluid is independent of the pressure level at inlet, and thus the pressure intensity at inlet should not be included. Loss coefficients for diffusers are defined in various ways, and care should be exercised in their use.

Studies by Robertson and Ross [9] indicate that the pressure efficiency is lower for a thicker boundary layer at the entrance to a diffuser, and decreases with divergence angle from 5 to 10 deg. The energy efficiency, however, is quite independent of these factors as long as separation is avoided. Typical values range from 83 to 93 per cent for pressure efficiency and from 91.5 to 96.5 per cent for energy efficiency for similar geometries and flows.

Pipe fittings. Losses through pipe fittings may be given in the form of Eq. 10-32 or in terms of an equivalent pipe length. In either instance, calculations are approximate at best, and accurate information would require that direct measurements be made. Typical loss coefficients for various fittings are given in Table 10-10.

The pressure drop, or head loss, owing to energy dissipation in an

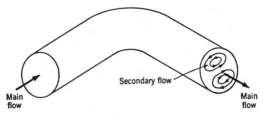

Fig. 10-14. Secondary flow in an elbow.

TABLE 10–10
RESISTANCE COEFFICIENTS FOR
VALVES AND FITTINGS*

Valve or Fitting	k_L
Ball check valve, wide open..........	70
Foot valve, wide open...............	15
Lift check valve, wide open..........	12
Globe valve, wide open..............	10
Angle valve, wide open..............	3.1
Blowoff valve, wide open............	2.9
Swing check valve, wide open........	2.3
Gate valve, wide open...............	0.19
Regular elbow	
screwed.........................	0.9
flanged..........................	0.3
Long-radius elbow	
screwed.........................	0.6
flanged..........................	0.23
Close return bend, screw type........	2.2
Flanged return bend (2 elbows)	
regular radius....................	0.38
long radius......................	0.25

*Reproduced, with permission, from *Tentative Standards of Hydraulic Institute, Pipe Friction*, New York: Hydraulic Institute.
NOTE: The k_L values listed may be expressed in terms of an equivalent pipe length for a given installation and flow by equating $k_L = fL_{eq}/D$ so that $L_{eq} = k_L D/f$.

elbow is largely due to a secondary flow superimposed on the main flow. As a result of centrifugal effects, the fluid in the faster core is directed outwards, and in order to satisfy continuity (the outward flowing fluid must be replaced), the slower fluid near the boundaries is directed inwards. This condition is shown in Fig. 10–14.

10–7. APPLICATIONS

The form of the energy equation as applied to liquids for one-dimensional flow

$$\frac{V_1^2}{2g} + \frac{p_1}{\gamma} + z_1 - w = \frac{V_2^2}{2g} + \frac{p_2}{\gamma} + z_2 + h_L$$

indicates that in the absence of external work, a decrease in total head occurs in the direction of flow. The total head at a section in a pipe system is the sum of the kinetic head and the piezometric head. A line connecting the values of total head at successive points along a piping system is known as the energy grade line (EGL), and a line connecting values of piezometric head at successive points along a piping system is known as the hydraulic grade line (HGL). Although these terms are used in the hydraulic literature, more appropriate terms might be the total head line (THL) and piezometric head line (PHL), respectively. The vertical distance between these lines at any section is the velocity head at that section. The energy or total head line *drops* in the direction of flow by an amount equal to the head loss h_L, which occurs in the direction of flow. For a constant-area pipe, this drop is due to friction, and the slope of the energy grade line is equal to h_L/L. This slope is defined as the sine rather than the tangent of the angle with the horizontal. For entrances, contractions, expansions, pipe fittings, and exits the loss is generally considered to be more or less concentrated at the location of these items, although the effects of the loss-producing elements extend for some distance downstream from each of them. An example of the energy grade line and the hydraulic grade line for a piping system is shown in Fig. 10–15. If a pump is in the system, the energy grade line *rises* an amount equal to the work term w in the energy equation.

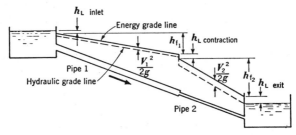

FIG. 10–15. Energy grade line and hydraulic grade line for flow between two open reservoirs.

The height of the hydraulic grade line above the pipe center line represents the pressure head p/γ in the pipe. If the hydraulic grade line is below the pipe center line, the pressure in the pipe is subatmospheric, and the liquid in the pipe is under a partial vacuum. If the hydraulic grade line is below the pipe by a height equal to more than the height h_b of a barometer containing the liquid at the same temperature, vapor pressure will exist in the pipe and flow may cease. This condition, then, limits the height to which a liquid may be siphoned. If the hydraulic grade line is below the pipe center line by an amount h_b or more in a water supply system, for example, either the pressure in the mains must be increased or the particular pipe must be laid at a lower level.

If two or more pipes are in *series*, the same flow passes through each pipe. If the pipes are designated with integer subscripts (1,2,3, and so forth), the total head loss through the entire system is the sum of the losses through each individual pipe and fitting. These statements are expressed as

$$Q_0 = Q_1 = Q_2 = Q_3 = \cdots \tag{10-36a}$$

or

$$Q_0 = V_1 A_1 = V_2 A_2 = V_3 A_3 = \cdots \tag{10-36b}$$

and if h_L is the head loss for fittings and valves,

$$\Sigma h_L = h_{f_1} + h_{f_2} + h_{f_3} + \cdots + h_L \tag{10-37}$$

If two or more pipes are connected in *parallel*, the total flow rate is the sum of that through each individual branch, and the head loss through one branch is the same as for all the others. These statements may be expressed as

$$Q_0 = Q_1 + Q_2 + Q_3 + \cdots \tag{10-38a}$$

or

$$Q_0 = V_1 A_1 + V_2 A_2 + V_3 A_3 + \cdots \tag{10-38b}$$

and

$$h_{L_1} = h_{L_2} = h_{L_3} = \cdots \tag{10-39}$$

The head loss through any one branch may be considered as being due purely to friction, or the valve and fitting losses may be expressed either in terms of an equivalent pipe length or as a loss coefficient times the velocity head in the pipe. Then Eq. 10–39 may be written as

$$\left(f_1 \frac{L_1}{D_1} + \Sigma k_{L_1} \right) \frac{V_1{}^2}{2g} = \left(f_2 \frac{L_2}{D_2} + \Sigma k_{L_2} \right) \frac{V_2{}^2}{2g} = \left(f_3 \frac{L_3}{D_3} + \Sigma k_{L_3} \right) \frac{V_3{}^2}{2g} = \cdots$$

so that

$$\frac{V_2}{V_1} = \sqrt{\frac{(f_1 L_1/D_1) + \Sigma k_{L_1}}{(f_2 L_2/D_2) + \Sigma k_{L_2}}}$$

and so on. The lengths, diameters, and loss coefficients are presumably known, and values of friction factors are estimated as in the type problem referred to in (2) of Sec. 10–4. Then, in order to determine the flow distribution or the head loss through the system, Eqs. 10–38 may be written and V_1 (and thus Q_1), for example, estimated from

$$Q_0 = V_1 A_1 + \frac{V_2}{V_1} V_1 A_2 + \frac{V_3}{V_1} V_1 A_3 + \cdots$$

from which V_2, V_3, and so forth (and thus Q_2, Q_3, and so forth) may also be estimated. A check of the assumed friction factors by calculating the respective Reynolds numbers based on the estimated velocities and the relative roughness of the pipes should be made and the new values of the friction factors used for an improved set of calculations. However, this check is often unnecessary.

EXAMPLE 10–3. New 8-, 12-, and 16-in. cast-iron pipes 2400, 4800, and 7200 ft long, respectively, are connected in parallel. The total flow through the three

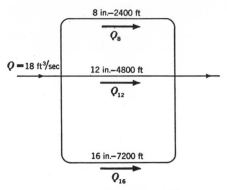

FIG. 10–16. Examples 10–3 and 10–4.
Parallel-pipe system.

pipes is 18 ft³/sec. What is the pressure drop through the system? Since the pipes are long, neglect losses due to fittings and valves. See Fig. 10–16.

Solution: The velocity of flow through each pipe must first be determined, and then the head loss for any one pipe calculated. The relative roughness of the pipes is 0.0013, 0.00085, and 0.00064, respectively. At high Reynolds numbers, the corresponding friction factors are 0.021, 0.0188, and 0.0177, respectively. Thus

$$\frac{V_{12}}{V_8} = \sqrt{\left(\frac{f_8}{f_{12}}\right)\left(\frac{L_8}{L_{12}}\right)\left(\frac{D_{12}}{D_8}\right)} = \sqrt{\left(\frac{0.021}{0.0188}\right)\left(\frac{2400}{4800}\right)\left(\frac{12}{8}\right)} = 0.915$$

$$\frac{V_{16}}{V_8} = \sqrt{\left(\frac{f_8}{f_{16}}\right)\left(\frac{L_8}{L_{16}}\right)\left(\frac{D_{16}}{D_8}\right)} = \sqrt{\left(\frac{0.021}{0.0177}\right)\left(\frac{2400}{7200}\right)\left(\frac{16}{8}\right)} = 0.89$$

The pipe areas are 0.349, 0.7854, and 1.396 ft², respectively. Thus

$$18 = 0.349 V_8 + (0.915)(0.7854) V_8 + (0.89)(1.396) V_8$$

and $V_8 = 7.79$, $V_{12} = 7.13$, and $V_{16} = 6.93$ ft/sec. The corresponding Reynolds numbers are 4.3×10^5, 5.8×10^5, and 7.6×10^5. A recheck of friction factors gives $f_8 = 0.0215$, $f_{12} = 0.0194$, and $f_{16} = 0.0182$. Then $V_{12}/V_8 = 0.912$ and $V_{16}/V_8 = 0.888$. This gives $V_8 = 7.81$, $V_{12} = 7.12$, and $V_{16} = 6.9$ ft/sec, none of which changed significantly. The head loss is

$$h_{f_8} = f_8 \left(\frac{L_8}{D_8}\right)\frac{V_8{}^2}{2g} = (0.0215)\frac{(2400)}{(8/12)}\frac{(7.8)^2}{2g} = 73.5 \text{ ft}$$

$$\Delta p_f = \frac{(73.5)(62.4)}{144} = 31.8 \text{ psi}$$

10–8. EMPIRICAL PIPE-FLOW EQUATIONS

A number of empirical pipe-flow equations for water in pipes have been used, and the equation of Hazen and Williams is perhaps the most widely used. This equation is

$$V = 1.318C \, (R_h)^{0.63} \, S^{0.54} \qquad \text{ft/sec} \qquad (10\text{--}40\text{a})$$

or
$$Q = 1.318C \, (R_h)^{0.63} \, S^{0.54} \, A \qquad \text{ft}^3/\text{sec} \qquad (10\text{--}40\text{b})$$

where R_h = hydraulic radius of the pipe, $A/P (R_h = D/4$ for a round pipe);
S = slope of the energy grade line h_f/L;
A = pipe cross-sectional area;
C = roughness coefficient.

The Darcy-Weisbach equation may be written in a similar form:

$$V = \sqrt{\frac{8g}{f}} \, (R_h)^{0.5} \, S^{0.5} \qquad \text{ft/sec} \qquad (10\text{--}41)$$

The Darcy equation and Hazen-Williams equation give similar results if

$$f = \frac{m}{\text{Re}_D{}^{0.16}} \qquad (10\text{--}42)$$

where C and m are related for various types of pipes according to Table 10–11.

TABLE 10–11
HAZEN-WILLIAMS ROUGHNESS VALUES

Types of Pipe	C	m
Extremely smooth pipes.............	140	0.13
New steel or cast iron...............	130	0.15
Wood, average concrete.............	120	0.17
New riveted steel, clay.............	110	0.20
Old cast iron, brick................	100	0.24
Old steel riveted....................	95	0.27
Badly corroded cast iron............	80	0.37
Very badly corroded iron or steel.....	60	0.63

The Hazen-Williams equation is clumsy to use numerically, and thus an alignment chart (Fig. 10–17) may be used. This chart is made for a value of $C = 100$. Since both V and Q vary linearly with C, the chart may be used for any other value of C if the following rules are applied:

1. If the discharge Q is given, convert it to the flow which would occur if the given pipe had a C of 100, by multiplying the given Q by the ratio of 100 to the actual C value. Then use the chart directly, using the corrected discharge.

2. If the discharge is to be determined, multiply the flow rate obtained from the chart by the actual C value and divide by 100. This gives the actual discharge.

Flow in parallel pipe systems may readily be solved. Since $R_h = D/4$ for a round pipe, we may write Eq. 10–40b as

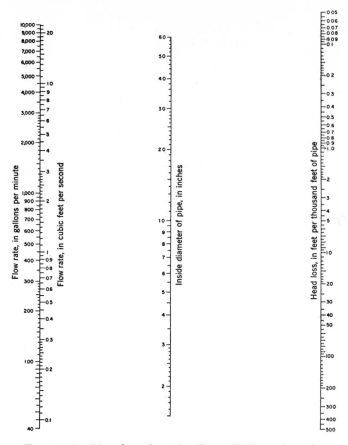

FIG. 10–17. Pipe flow chart for Hazen-Williams formula with $C = 100$.

$$Q = \frac{1.318\pi CD^{2.63}}{4^{1.63}} \left(\frac{h_L}{L}\right)^{0.54}$$

Thus from Eq. 10–38a,

$$Q_0 = h_L^{0.54}(C_1' + C_2' + C_3' + \cdots C_n')$$

where

$$C' = \frac{1.318\pi CD^{2.63}}{4^{1.63}L^{0.54}}$$

which has a fixed value for each pipe. Therefore, any assumed head loss h_L through the parallel system will give flows in each pipe in the correct proportion, though the total may not be correct. The flow in each branch may be corrected by the same factor needed to correct the total flow to the given Q_0, and the head loss may be determined directly from Fig. 10–17.

EXAMPLE 10–4. Determine the head loss across the parallel system of Example 10–3 by using the Hazen-Williams equation or chart.

Solution: Assume that $h_L = 60$ ft in Example 10–3. Then from Fig. 10–17, the flow rates in each pipe are obtained.

For the 8-in. pipe, $h_L/L = 25$ ft/1000 ft, and $Q_8 = (2.04)(1.3) = 2.65$ ft³/sec.
For the 12-in. pipe, $h_L/L = 12.5$ ft/1000 ft, and $Q_{12} = (4.1)(1.3) = 5.3$ ft³/sec.
For the 16-in. pipe, $h_L/L = 8.33$ ft/1000 ft, and $Q_{16} = (6.9)(1.3) = 9.0$ ft³/sec.
The total flow rate for a 60-ft head loss would be 16.95 ft³/sec, and thus a factor of 1.06 applied to each branch will result in a total flow of 18 ft³/sec. Then $Q_8 = (2.65)(1.06) = 2.81$ ft³/sec. Since $C = 130$, a flow rate of $2.81/1.3 = 2.16$ ft³/sec is applied to the chart, and the head loss is found to be $h_L/1000$ ft $= 29$ ft. For a 2400-ft length, $h_L = (29)(2.4) = 70$ ft, which compares favorably with the result of Example 10–3.

10–9. PIPE NETWORKS

Complex pipe networks conveying water may be analyzed quite readily with the aid of the alignment chart of Fig. 10–17. The flow distribution for a given network may be desired, and this is generally an indeterminate problem which must be solved by successive trials, or iterations. In the design of a network, the flow and pressures at various points may be specified, and the pipe sizes determined. This is also an indeterminate type of problem which must be solved by successive trials, or iterations.

A network consists of a finite number of loops containing any number of individual pipes, some of which may be common to two loops. In Fig. 10–18 the simple network has two loops, pipe *2* being common to both loops. Two conditions must be met for a balanced flow in the network:

1. The net flow into any junction must be zero. This means that the flow rate into the junction must equal the flow rate out of the junction.

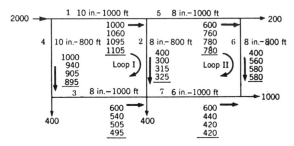

FIG. 10–18. Example 10–5. Flow distribution by Hardy-Cross method. Pipe numbers are labeled. Flow rates are in gallons per minute. See Table 10–12.

2. The net head loss (or pressure drop) around a loop must be zero. If a loop is traversed in either direction, a balanced flow must result in a return to the original condition (head or pressure) at the starting point.

The procedure for determining the flow distribution in a given network involves assigning flows in each pipe so that continuity at each junction is satisfied (condition 1). Then the head loss around each loop is calculated, and if not zero, adjustments to the assumed flows are made either by pure estimate or by a method of iteration known as the Hardy-Cross method. The correction for each loop is given by

$$\Delta Q = -\frac{\text{net head loss for the assumed flows}}{1.85 \ \Sigma h_L/Q_0 \text{ for the assumed flows}}$$

This equation is derived as follows:

In a given loop in a network let Q = actual, or balanced, flow rate and Q_0 = assumed flow rate so that $Q = Q_0 + \Delta Q$. Then, since the Hazen-Williams equation (as well as others) may be expressed as $h_L = nQ^x$, we may write

$$nQ^x = n(Q_0 + \Delta Q)^x$$
$$= n\left[Q_0{}^x + xQ_0{}^{x-1}\,\Delta Q + \frac{x(x-1)}{2}\,Q_0{}^{x-2}\,(\Delta Q)^2 + \cdots\right]$$

If ΔQ is truly small compared to Q_0, terms beyond the second may be neglected. For a balanced loop or network,

$$\Sigma h_L = \Sigma nQ^x = \Sigma nQ_0{}^x + \Delta Q\,\Sigma xnQ_0{}^{x-1} = 0$$

Solving for ΔQ we get

$$\Delta Q = -\frac{\Sigma nQ_0{}^x}{\Sigma xnQ_0{}^{x-1}}$$

$$\Delta Q = -\frac{\Sigma h_L}{1.85 \ \Sigma h_L/Q_0} \tag{10–43}$$

The procedure is as follows:

1. Assume any reasonable flow distribution, in both magnitude and direction, in all pipes so that the total flow into each junction is algebraically zero. This should be indicated on a diagram of the pipe network.

2. Set up a table to analyze each closed loop in the network semi-independently.

3. Compute the head loss h_L in each pipe.

4. For each loop, consider the flow rate Q_0 and the head loss h_L to be positive for clockwise flow in the loop and negative for counter-clockwise flow.

TABLE 10-12
EXAMPLE 10-5

Loop	Pipe	Diam (in.)	L/1000 (ft)	First Trial				Second Trial				Third Trial			
				Q_0 (gpm)	$h_L/1000$ ft (ft)	h_L (ft)	h_L/Q_0	Q_0 (gpm)	$h_L/1000$ ft (ft)	h_L (ft)	h_L/Q_0	Q_0 (gpm)	$h_L/1000$ ft (ft)	h_L (ft)	h_L/Q_0
I	1	10	1.0	+1000	+10.0	+10.0	0.0100	+1060	+11.0	+11.0	0.0104	+1095	+11.6	+11.6	0.0106
	2	8	0.8	+ 400	+ 5.5	+ 4.4	0.0110	+ 300	+ 3.2	+ 2.6	0.0076	+ 315	+ 3.5	+ 2.8	0.0089
	3	8	1.0	− 600	−11.5	−11.5	0.0192	− 540	− 9.5	− 9.5	0.0176	− 505	− 8.4	− 8.4	0.0166
	4	10	0.8	−1000	−10.0	− 8.0	0.0080	− 940	− 8.8	− 7.0	0.0075	− 905	− 8.3	− 6.6	0.0073
						− 5.1	0.0482			− 2.9	0.0431			− 0.6	0.0434

$$\Delta Q = -\frac{-5.1}{(1.85)(0.0482)} = +57 \text{ gpm} \qquad \Delta Q = -\frac{-2.9}{(1.85)(0.0431)} = +36 \text{ gpm} \qquad \Delta Q = -\frac{-0.6}{(1.85)(0.0434)} = +8 \text{ gpm}$$

Loop	Pipe	Diam (in.)	L/1000 (ft)	Q_0 (gpm)	$h_L/1000$ ft (ft)	h_L (ft)	h_L/Q_0	Q_0 (gpm)	$h_L/1000$ ft (ft)	h_L (ft)	h_L/Q_0	Q_0 (gpm)	$h_L/1000$ ft (ft)	h_L (ft)	h_L/Q_0
II	5	8	1.0	+ 600	+11.5	+11.5	0.0192	+ 760	+17.6	+17.6	0.0232	+ 780	+18.5	+18.5	0.0238
	6	8	0.8	+ 400	+ 5.5	+ 4.4	0.0110	+ 560	+10.0	+ 8.0	0.0143	+ 580	+10.8	+ 8.6	0.0148
	7	6	1.0	− 600	−47	−47	0.0783	− 440	−26.5	−26.5	0.0602	− 420	−24	−24	0.0571
	2	8	0.8	− 400	− 5.5	− 4.4	0.0110	− 300	− 3.2	− 2.6	0.0076	− 315	− 3.5	− 2.8	0.0089
						−35.5	0.1195			− 3.5	0.1053			+ 0.3	0.1046

$$\Delta Q = -\frac{-35.5}{(1.85)(0.1195)} = +160 \text{ gpm} \qquad \Delta Q = -\frac{-3.5}{(1.85)(0.1053)} = +18 \text{ gpm} \qquad \Delta Q = -\frac{+0.3}{(1.85)(0.1046)} = -1.5 \text{ gpm}$$

5. Compute the algebraic head loss Σh_L in each loop.

6. Compute the total head loss per unit discharge h_L/Q_0 for each pipe. Determine the sum of the quantities $\Sigma h_L/Q_0 = \Sigma n Q_0^{0.85}$ for each loop. From the definitions of head loss and flow direction, each term in this sum is necessarily positive.

7. Determine the flow correction for each loop from

$$\Delta Q = -\frac{\Sigma h_L}{1.85\,\Sigma h_L/Q_0} \qquad\qquad [10\text{-}43]$$

This correction is to be applied algebraically to each pipe in the loop. For a pipe which is in common with another loop, the flow correction for that pipe is the net effect of the corrections for both loops.

8. Indicate corrected flows on the diagram of the pipe network as in step 1. A check on the corrections of step 7 will be shown by a continuity check at each pipe junction.

9. Repeat steps 1 thru 8 until either the head loss for a loop is balanced within desired limits or the flow corrections are made as small as desirable.

Flow corrections may be made by either of two methods:

1. Corrections for all loops may be made before any corrections are applied. The head loss and the value of h_L/Q_0 for a pipe in common with two loops need be calculated but once and the results used in both loops.

2. Correction for a loop may be applied to each pipe in that loop before calculating correction in the next or successive loops.

EXAMPLE 10-5. Given the pipe network shown in Fig. 10-18, determine the flow rate through each pipe. The pipe sizes and lengths are indicated alongside each pipe. Assume a C value of 100.

Solution: Assumed flow and direction are indicated near each pipe, together with the corrected flows for each trial as indicated in Table 10-12. Corrections were made to the nearest 10 gpm for the first trial and to the nearest 5 gpm thereafter. Final results are shown underlined in Fig. 10-18. This type of problem may be solved readily on automatic computers.

10-10. FLOW OF COMPRESSIBLE GASES IN PIPES WITH FRICTION

Subsonic gas flow in pipes differs from liquid flow in pipes primarily in that the gas density decreases and hence the velocity increases in the direction of flow. The general flow equation for compressible flow in a duct of constant cross section was derived in Sec. 10-1 as Eq. 10-4. The wall shear stress may be expressed in terms of the friction factor from Eq. 10–8, so that the pressure gradient is

$$-\frac{dp}{dx} = \frac{f}{D}\frac{\rho V^2}{2} + \beta \rho V \frac{dV}{dx} \qquad (10\text{--}44)$$

This equation is similar to the Darcy-Weisbach equation (Eq. 10–5) except for the last term on the right, which represents the pressure drop required to increase the flow momentum. The value of β is about 1.03 for fully developed incompressible turbulent flow. Thus a one-dimensional analysis, with $\beta = 1.0$, is justified.

A dimensional analysis would indicate that the friction factor for compressible flow could depend upon the Mach number as well as the relative roughness of the pipe and the Reynolds number. Experiments have shown, however, that the dependence on Mach number for subsonic flow is negligible and that the friction factor may be obtained in the same manner as for incompressible flow.

Equation 10–44 with $\beta = 1$ may be written in dimensionless form as

$$\frac{dp}{\rho V^2/2} + f\frac{dx}{D} + 2\frac{dV}{V} = 0 \qquad (10\text{--}45)$$

This general equation will be integrated directly for isothermal flow and used in the analysis for adiabatic flow in pipes with friction.

Isothermal flow. In order to integrate Eq. 10–45, the variable density and velocity will have to be expressed in terms of the variable pressure, and the variation in the friction factor f will have to be investigated.

If all conditions are known at some upstream section (section *1*), those at any arbitrary section downstream can be expressed in terms of known values at section *1*.

From the perfect gas equation of state,

$$\frac{p}{\rho} = \frac{p_1}{\rho_1} = RT$$

a constant, from which
$$\rho = p\frac{\rho_1}{p_1}$$

From continuity,
$$V\rho = V_1\rho_1$$

then
$$V = \frac{V_1 p_1}{p}$$

The differential form of this last equation (for later use) is

$$\frac{dV}{V} + \frac{dp}{p} = 0 \qquad \text{or} \qquad \frac{dV}{V} = -\frac{dp}{p}$$

The first term in Eq. 10–45 can then be written as

$$\frac{2}{\rho_1 \, V_1{}^2 \, p_1} \, p \, dp$$

The friction factor depends on the relative roughness of the pipe, which is assumed to be constant, and on the Reynolds number $\mathrm{Re} = VD\rho/\mu$, which is also constant, since $V\rho$ is constant, from continuity, and the dynamic viscosity depends only on the temperature, which is constant. Hence the friction factor is constant and can be found in the usual manner for known conditions at any section.

If $L = x_2 - x_1$, Eq. 10–45 can now be integrated to obtain

$$p_1{}^2 - p_2{}^2 = \rho_1 \, V_1{}^2 \, p_1 \left(f \frac{L}{D} - 2 \ln \frac{p_2}{p_1} \right) \qquad (10\text{–}46a)$$

or

$$p_1{}^2 - p_2{}^2 = k \, \mathrm{M_1}{}^2 \, p_1{}^2 \left(f \frac{L}{D} - 2 \ln \frac{p_2}{p_1} \right) \qquad (10\text{–}46b)$$

in terms of the initial Mach number. These equations give the pressure at some distance L downstream of any initial section 1 where conditions are known. The logarithmic term is often small compared to fL/D and may be neglected for a first approximation. Then this first approximation for p_2 should be used to calculate the magnitude of the logarithmic term, and an iterative process used to calculate p_2 precisely.

Equation 10–46b may be solved for fL/D to give

$$f \frac{L}{D} = \frac{1}{k \mathrm{M_1}{}^2} \left[1 - \left(\frac{p_2}{p_1} \right)^2 \right] - 2 \ln \frac{p_1}{p_2} \qquad (10\text{–}47)$$

This equation gives the distance L from section 1 where conditions are known to some downstream section where p_2 is specified. It is a dimensionless equation and indicates that the dimensionless length fL/D is related to the pressure ratio p_2/p_1 by a family of curves, one for each initial Mach number, for a given gas (given k). These relationships are shown in Fig. 10–19.

A dimensional plot of pressure versus length would have the same general appearance as the curves in Fig. 10–19. Equation 10–45, by letting $dV/V = -dp/p$, contains only two differentials, dp and dx. Thus the pressure gradient, which is the slope of the curves of Figs. 10–19 and 10–20, can be shown to be

$$\frac{dp}{dx} = \frac{\dfrac{pf}{2D}}{1 - \dfrac{p}{\rho V^2}} = \frac{\dfrac{f}{D} \dfrac{\rho V^2}{2}}{k \mathrm{M}^2 - 1} \qquad (10\text{–}48)$$

As $\mathrm{M} \to 0$, this is essentially the Darcy equation for liquid pipe flow; thus at low Mach numbers, isothermal flow may be considered as incompressible. The pressure gradients will be within 5 per cent at Mach numbers up to

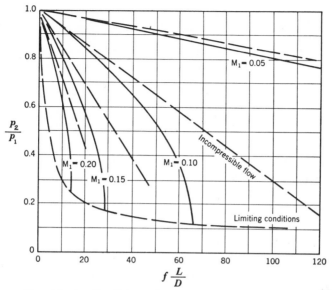

Fɪɢ. 10–19. Conditions along pipe for isothermal flow of a gas at various initial Mach numbers ($k = 1.4$).

0.184 for air. A thermodynamic analysis will indicate that the entropy increases as the fluid goes from 1 to 0 in Fig. 10–20, and decreases from 0 to 3. This latter decrease is impossible since it contradicts the second law of thermodynamics. Thus flow can exist only up to 0, which is called the limiting point. Associated with this limiting point are a limiting Mach number, a limiting or minimum pressure, and a limiting or maximum length of pipe. These will be indicated by asterisks (M*). Flow from 3 to 0 represents supersonic flow.

Limiting or Maximum Mach Number. At the limiting point the pressure gradient is infinite. Thus for dp/dx to be infinite, the denominator of Eq. 10–48 must be zero. Then

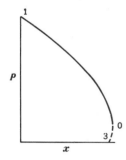

Fɪɢ. 10–20. Pressure along pipe for gas flow. (Curve represents isothermal flow at an initial Mach number of 0.10, but the general shape is characteristic of all types of gas flow in pipes.)

$$M^* = \frac{1}{\sqrt{k}} \qquad (10\text{–}49)$$

and the velocity can increase along the pipe only until the Mach number equals $1/\sqrt{k} = 0.845$ for air, for example.

Limiting or Minimum Pressure. Recall that from continuity

$$V_1 p_1 = Vp = V^*p^*$$

so that
$$\frac{p^*}{p_1} = \frac{V_1}{V^*} = \frac{M_1 c_1}{M^* c^*} = \frac{M_1}{M^*} = M_1 \sqrt{k}$$

since the acoustic velocity remains constant for isothermal conditions. Therefore,

$$\frac{p^*}{p_1} = M_1 \sqrt{k} \qquad (10\text{-}50)$$

and the pressure drops along the pipe to a minimum which depends on the initial Mach number.

Limiting or Maximum Length. The limiting or maximum length of pipe can be found by inserting the expression for the minimum pressure, Eq. 10–50, into the general expression for fL/D, Eq. 10–47, to get

$$\frac{fL^*}{D} = \frac{1}{kM_1^2} - 1 - \ln \frac{1}{kM_1^2} \qquad (10\text{-}51)$$

A number of conclusions may be drawn concerning subsonic isothermal flow:

1. The pressure drops at an increasing rate along the pipe, in contrast with a constant pressure gradient for fully developed liquid flow.

2. The velocity and Mach number increase up to a maximum Mach number of $1/\sqrt{k}$. This increase ceases at a limiting or maximum length, which must be at the end of the pipe. If assumed initial conditions at some upstream section result in a maximum length of pipe which is less than a given pipe length, then the initial conditions will have to be adjusted (lower M_1) so that the **given pipe** length becomes at least equal to or less than the **maximum length** for the adjusted initial conditions.

3. The limiting pressure ratio and the limiting or maximum **length** depend only on the gas (k value) and the initial Mach number. Thus tables may be prepared and used for making pipe calculations. Then

$$\frac{p_2}{p_1} = \frac{M_1}{M_2} \qquad (10\text{-}52)$$

and from Eq. 10–51

$$\frac{fL}{D} = \left(\frac{fL^*}{D}\right)_{M_1} - \left(\frac{fL^*}{D}\right)_{M_2} \qquad (10\text{-}53)$$

These equations relate pressures and lengths between two sections for which the Mach numbers are given.

It is interesting to speculate whether heat is added or removed from the gas as it flows through a pipe. The general energy equation becomes

$$\frac{V_1^2}{2} + q = \frac{V_2^2}{2}$$

and since $V_2 > V_1$ for subsonic flow, q must be positive, and heat is added to the gas. The tendency to cool as a result of expansion is greater than the tendency to heat as a result of wall friction, and therefore heat must be added to maintain a constant temperature. For supersonic flow, $V_2 < V_1$, q is negative, and heat is removed from the gas.

Adiabatic flow. Integration of Eq. 10-45 again requires that the variable density and velocity be expressed in terms of the variable pressure, and the variation of the friction factor must again be investigated.

The momentum equation (Eq. 10-45) when multiplied by $k\mathrm{M}^2/2$ may be written as

$$\frac{dp}{p} + \frac{k\mathrm{M}^2}{2} f \frac{dx}{D} + k\mathrm{M}^2 \frac{dV}{V} = 0$$

The continuity equation in differential form is

$$\frac{dV}{V} + \frac{d\rho}{\rho} = 0$$

The perfect gas equation in differential form is

$$\frac{dp}{p} = \frac{d\rho}{\rho} + \frac{dT}{T}$$

From the definition of the Mach number $\mathrm{M} = V/C = V/\sqrt{kRT}$,

$$\frac{d\mathrm{M}}{\mathrm{M}} = \frac{dV}{V} - \frac{dT}{2T}$$

The energy equation $h + V^2/2 = $ constant may be written in differential form as

$$\frac{dT}{T} + (k-1)\,\mathrm{M}^2\,\frac{dV}{V} = 0$$

We have five simultaneous equations in six differential variables, dp/p, dV/V, $d\rho/\rho$, dT/T, $d\mathrm{M}/\mathrm{M}$, and $f\,dx/D$. The first five (dependent) variables may be expressed in terms of $f\,dx/D$, the independent variable. The results are

$$\frac{dp}{p} = -\frac{1 + (k-1)\mathrm{M}^2}{1 - \mathrm{M}^2} \frac{k\mathrm{M}^2}{2} f \frac{dx}{D}$$

$$\frac{dV}{V} = \frac{1}{1 - \mathrm{M}^2} \frac{k\mathrm{M}^2}{2} f \frac{dx}{D}$$

$$\frac{d\rho}{\rho} = -\frac{1}{1 - \mathrm{M}^2} \frac{k\mathrm{M}^2}{2} f \frac{dx}{D}$$

$$\frac{dT}{T} = -\frac{\mathrm{M}^2(k-1)}{1 - \mathrm{M}^2} \frac{k\mathrm{M}^2}{2} f \frac{dx}{D}$$

and

$$\frac{d\mathrm{M}}{\mathrm{M}} = \frac{1 + \dfrac{k-1}{2}\mathrm{M}^2}{1 - \mathrm{M}^2} \frac{k\mathrm{M}^2}{2} f \frac{dx}{D}$$

A thermodynamic analysis shows that since dx is positive in the direction of flow, f must be positive. Therefore the preceding equations indicate that for subsonic flow ($\mathrm{M} < 1$) the velocity and Mach number increase, while the pressure, density, and temperature decrease in the direction of flow. The opposite is true in each instance for supersonic flow ($\mathrm{M} > 1$).

Limiting or Maximum Mach Number. The equation for dp/p can be solved for the pressure gradient:

$$\frac{dp}{dx} = -\frac{fkp}{2D}\mathrm{M}^2\left[\frac{1 + (k-1)\mathrm{M}^2}{1 - \mathrm{M}^2}\right] = -\frac{f}{D}\frac{\rho V^2}{2}\left[\frac{1 + (k-1)\mathrm{M}^2}{1 - \mathrm{M}^2}\right] \quad (10\text{–}54)$$

As $\mathrm{M} \to 0$, this is essentially the Darcy equation for liquid pipe flow; thus for low Mach numbers, adiabatic gas flow may also be treated as incompressible. The pressure gradients will be within 5 per cent at Mach numbers up to 0.185 for air. Figure 10–20, which is applicable for adiabatic flow as well as isothermal, indicates that the pressure drops to the limiting point 0, and at that point dp/dx is infinite. From Eq. 10–54, the limiting Mach number is 1 for adiabatic flow.

Limiting or Minimum Pressure. To obtain the limiting pressure, we combine the equations for dp/p and $d\mathrm{M}/\mathrm{M}$ to obtain

$$\frac{dp}{p} = -\frac{1 + (k-1)\mathrm{M}^2}{\mathrm{M}\left(1 + \dfrac{k-1}{2}\mathrm{M}^2\right)}d\mathrm{M}$$

which, when integrated between some given section and the point where $\mathrm{M} = 1$ (the limiting point), gives

$$\frac{p^*}{p_1} = \mathrm{M}_1\sqrt{\frac{2\left(1 + \dfrac{k-1}{2}\mathrm{M}_1^2\right)}{k+1}} \quad (10\text{–}55)$$

The integration is evident if $d\mathrm{M} = d\mathrm{M}^2/2\mathrm{M}$.

Limiting or Maximum Length. The expression for $d\mathrm{M}/\mathrm{M}$ can be rearranged to give

$$f\frac{dx}{D} = \frac{1 - \mathrm{M}^2}{k\mathrm{M}^4\left(1 + \dfrac{k-1}{2}\mathrm{M}^2\right)}d\mathrm{M}^2$$

by letting $d\mathrm{M} = d\mathrm{M}^2/2\mathrm{M}$. Integrating between a given section and the point where $\mathrm{M} = 1$,

$$\frac{\bar{f}L^*}{D} = \frac{1 - M_1^2}{kM_1^2} + \frac{k+1}{2k} \ln \frac{(k+1)M_1^2}{2\left(1 + \frac{k-1}{2} M_1^2\right)} \qquad (10\text{-}56)$$

where $\bar{f}$ is the average friction factor. At high Reynolds numbers, especially for rough pipes, the friction factor depends only on the pipe roughness, and thus the friction factor could conceivably be constant for adiabatic flow. If not,

$$\bar{f} = \frac{1}{L^*} \int_0^{L^*} f \, dx$$

The value of f at section 1 may be assumed to equal $\bar{f}$, and after solving for conditions at some downstream point, the value of f throughout the entire pipe can be examined and an appropriate average value used to recalculate downstream conditions.

Limiting Temperature and Velocity. The preceding expressions for dT/T, dV/V, and dM/M can be solved simultaneously by eliminating $f \, dx/D$ to obtain, after integration,

$$\frac{T^*}{T_1} = \frac{2\left(1 + \frac{k-1}{2} M_1^2\right)}{k+1} \qquad (10\text{-}57)$$

and

$$\frac{V^*}{V_1} = \frac{1}{M_1} \sqrt{\frac{2\left(1 + \frac{k-1}{2} M_1^2\right)}{k+1}} \qquad (10\text{-}58)$$

These equations may be used in the following manner: for the flow conditions known at some arbitrary section 1, the limiting conditions can be calculated. These limiting conditions are the same for corresponding flow conditions at any other section. Therefore

$$\frac{p_2}{p_1} = \frac{p^*/p_1}{p^*/p_2}$$

$$\left(\frac{\bar{f}L}{D}\right)_{1-2} = \left(\frac{\bar{f}L^*}{D}\right)_1 - \left(\frac{\bar{f}L^*}{D}\right)_2$$

$$\frac{T_2}{T_1} = \frac{T^*/T_1}{T^*/T_2}$$

$$\frac{V_2}{V_1} = \frac{V^*/V_1}{V^*/V_2}$$

Flow near the limiting condition would be very nearly adiabatic, because the high heat-transfer rates required to maintain isothermal flow would be very difficult to achieve.

If adiabatic flow is assumed for a given initial subsonic condition, the pressure at any downstream point where the Mach number is M_2 is always slightly less than it would be if the flow were assumed to be isothermal. The ratio is

$$\frac{p_2 \text{ ad}}{p_2 \text{ iso}} = \left[\frac{1 + (k - 1)M_1^2/2}{1 + (k - 1)M_2^2/2}\right]^{1/2} \tag{10-59}$$

which is less than 1 for subsonic flow and depends on the ratio of specific heat capacities k for the gas and on the initial and downstream Mach numbers. For air with $M_2 = 0.854$ (the limiting Mach number for isothermal flow), $p_2 \text{ ad}/p_2 \text{ iso} \geqq 0.934$. Similarly, if adiabatic flow is assumed for a given initial subsonic condition, the temperature is always slightly less at any prescribed point where the Mach number is M_2 than if isothermal flow is assumed. The ratio is

$$\frac{T_2 \text{ ad}}{T_2 \text{ iso}} = \frac{1 + (k - 1)M_1^2/2}{1 + (k - 1)M_2^2/2} \tag{10-60}$$

which is less than 1 for subsonic flow. For air with $M_2 = 0.854$, $T_2 \text{ ad}/T_2 \text{ iso} \geqq 0.875$, and for $M_2 = 0.5$ this ratio $\geqq 0.952$.

Therefore, except at high Mach numbers, subsonic isothermal and subsonic adiabatic flow do not differ appreciably.

EXAMPLE 10-6. It is desired to pump methane ($k = 1.31$, $R = 3095$ ft lb$_f$/slug R) through a 12-in. commercial steel pipe. The discharge from a compressor is at a pressure of 120 psia, a temperature of 100 F (the viscosity is 2.5×10^{-7} slug/ft sec), and a velocity of 60 ft/sec. For both isothermal and adiabatic flow with friction, find a) the minimum pressure possible; b) the maximum length of pipe possible; c) the maximum velocity possible; d) the pressure, temperature, velocity, and Mach number at a distance equal to one-half the maximum length from the compressor; and e) the location of a second compressor if the compressor inlet pressure is 30 psia.

Solution:

$$\left.\begin{array}{l} p_1 = 120 \text{ psia} \\ T_1 = 100 \text{ F} \end{array}\right\} \rho_1 = \frac{p_1}{RT_1} = 0.00996 \text{ slug/ft}^3$$

$$c_1 = \sqrt{kRT_1} = \sqrt{(1.31)(3095)(560)} = 1508 \text{ ft/sec}$$

$$M_1 = \frac{V_1}{c_1} = \frac{60}{1508} = 0.0398$$

$$Re_1 = \frac{V_1 D\rho_1}{\mu_1} = \frac{(60)(1)(0.00996)}{2.5 \times 10^{-7}} = 2.4 \times 10^6$$

$$\frac{k}{D} = 0.00015 \text{ so that } f_1 = 0.0134$$

Isothermal Flow	Adiabatic Flow

Isothermal Flow

a) $\dfrac{p^*}{p_1} = M_1 \sqrt{k} = 0.0398 \sqrt{1.31}$

$= 0.0456$

$p^* = (0.0456)(120) = 5.48$ psia

b) $\dfrac{fL^*}{D} = \dfrac{1}{kM_1{}^2} - 1 - \ln \dfrac{1}{kM_1{}^2}$

$= \dfrac{1}{(1.31)(0.0398)^2} - 1 - \ln \dfrac{1}{(1.31)(0.0398)^2}$

$= 481 - 1 - 6.2$

$= 474$

$L^* = \dfrac{474 D}{f} = \dfrac{474(1)}{0.0134}$

$L^* = 35,400$ ft

c) $V^* = c^* M^* = \dfrac{1508}{\sqrt{1.31}} = 1318$ ft/sec

d) At $L_2 = 17,700$ ft,

$\dfrac{fL_2}{D} = 237$

$1 - \left(\dfrac{p_2}{p_1}\right)^2 = kM_1{}^2 \left(f\dfrac{L_2}{D} + 2 \ln \dfrac{p_1}{p_2}\right)$

Adiabatic Flow

a) $\dfrac{p^*}{p_1} = M_1 \sqrt{\dfrac{2\left(1 + \dfrac{k-1}{2} M_1{}^2\right)}{k+1}}$

$= 0.0398 \sqrt{\dfrac{2\left[1 + \dfrac{0.31}{2}(0.0398)^2\right]}{2.31}}$

$= 0.0370$

$p^* = 0.0370 (120) = 4.44$ psia

b) $\dfrac{\overline{fL^*}}{D} = \dfrac{1 - M_1{}^2}{kM_1{}^2} + \dfrac{k+1}{2k} \ln \dfrac{(k+1) M_1{}^2}{2\left(1 + \dfrac{k-1}{2} M_1{}^2\right)}$

$= \dfrac{1 - 0.00159}{1/481} + \dfrac{2.31}{2.62} \ln \dfrac{(2.31)(0.00159)}{2(1.000246)}$

$= 480 - 3.53$

$= 476.5$

$L^* = \dfrac{476.5 D}{\overline{f}} = \dfrac{(476.5)(1)}{0.0134} = 35,600$ ft

When T^* is found, Re* will be calculated and f^* determined. A new $\overline{f}$ may then give a slightly different L^*.

c) $V^* = c^* = \sqrt{kRT^*}$ where

$T^* = T_1 \dfrac{2\left(1 + \dfrac{k-1}{2} M_1{}^2\right)}{k+1}$

$= 560 \dfrac{2(1.000246)}{2.31} = 485$ R

$V^* = \sqrt{(1.31)(3095)(485)} = 1402$ ft/sec

Thus

$Re^* = \dfrac{V^* \rho^* D}{\mu^*} = \dfrac{V_1 \rho_1 D}{\mu^*}$

$Re^* = \dfrac{(60)(0.00996)(1)}{2.3 \times 10^{-7}} = 2.6 \times 10^6$

$f^* = 0.0133$ and $\overline{f} = 0.01335$

$L^* = \dfrac{476.5 D}{f} = 35,700$ ft, a truer value.

d) At $L = 17,850$ ft,

$\dfrac{p_2}{p_1} = \dfrac{p^*/p_1}{p^*/p_2} = \dfrac{0.0370}{\text{function of } M_2}$

Eq. 10-56 with $fL_2/D = 238.2$ is solved for $M_2 = 0.056$.

Isothermal Flow	Adiabatic Flow

Isothermal Flow

For a first approximation,

$$1 - \left(\frac{p_2}{p_1}\right)^2 = \frac{1}{481}(237) = 0.492$$

$$\frac{p_2}{p_1} = 0.713$$

and $+2\ln(p_1/p_2) = +0.68$, and a recalculation gives

$$\frac{p_2}{p_1} = 0.712$$
$$p_2 = (0.712)(120) = 85.5 \text{ psia}$$
$$T_2 = 100 \text{ F} = 560 \text{ R}$$
$$V_2 = \frac{V_1 \rho_1}{\rho_2} = V_1 \frac{p_1}{p_2} = 60\left(\frac{120}{85.5}\right)$$
$$= 84.3 \text{ ft/sec}$$

e) If $p_3 = 30$ psia,

$$\left(\frac{fL}{D}\right)_{1-3} = \frac{1}{k M_1{}^2}\left[1 - \left(\frac{p_3}{p_1}\right)^2\right] - 2\ln\frac{p_1}{p_3}$$

$$= 481\left[1 - \frac{1}{16}\right] - 2\ln 4$$

$$= 448$$

$$L_3 = \frac{448\,D}{f} = 33{,}400 \text{ ft}$$

Adiabatic Flow

$$\frac{p^*}{p_2} = M_2 \sqrt{\frac{2\left(1 + \dfrac{k-1}{2}M_2{}^2\right)}{k+1}}$$

$$p_2 = \frac{4.44}{0.056\sqrt{2[1 + 0.155(0.00314)]/2.31}}$$
$$= 85.0 \text{ psia}$$

$$T_2 = \frac{T^*}{2\left(1 + \dfrac{k-1}{2}M_2{}^2\right)\Big/(k+1)}$$

$$= \frac{485}{0.866} \approx 560 \text{ R}$$

and the temperature has not dropped noticeably. Since $c_1 \approx c_2$,

$$V_2 = V_1\frac{M_2}{M_1}$$

$$= 60\left(\frac{0.056}{0.0398}\right) = 84.4 \text{ ft/sec}$$

e) If $p_3 = 30$ psia, $(fL/D)_3$ is a function of M_3, which can be found by trial from Eq. 10–55 to be $M_3 = 0.1585$.

$$\left(\frac{fL^*}{D}\right)_3 = \frac{1 - M_3{}^2}{k M_3{}^2} - \frac{k+1}{2k}\ln\frac{2\left(1 + \dfrac{k-1}{2}M_3{}^2\right)}{(k+1)\,M_3{}^2}$$

$$= 27.1$$

$$L_3{}^* = \frac{(27.1)(1)}{0.0133} = 2040 \text{ ft}$$

$$L_3 = (L^*)_1 - (L^*)_3 = 35{,}700 - 2040$$
$$= 33{,}660 \text{ ft}$$

The results of Example 10–6 indicate that for given initial conditions: a) the minimum pressure for adiabatic flow is slightly less than that for isothermal flow; b) the maximum length for both types of flow is essentially the same, that for adiabatic flow being less than 1 per cent greater than for isothermal flow; c) the pressure and temperature at a point halfway to the limiting point are essentially the same for either type of flow; d) the rate of pressure drop is very large near the limiting point, and practical considerations rule out the advisability of having pipes longer than 80 to 90 per cent of the maximum length; and e) for practical purposes, since there is always some uncertainty in the values of the friction factor, and purely isothermal or purely adiabatic flow in pipes is rarely if ever achieved, either isothermal or adiabatic flow may be assumed in making engineering calculations.

10–11. FLOW OF MIXTURES IN PIPES

Two-phase flow in pipes (gas-liquid, solids in liquids, and solids in gases) is quite complicated, and in most instances is not well understood. There are some situations, however, in which either empirical results or experiments based on dimensional analysis which result in semiempirical equations have been found useful. The hydraulic conveying of paper pulp and solids will be discussed briefly.

Paper stock. Wood fibers for making paper are suspended in water as a means of handling and are conveyed in pipelines at consistencies (ratio of weight of air-dry pulp to the weight of water in a given total volume of mixture) up to about 6 per cent. The effect of the presence of the wood fibers is to increase the wall shear of the more or less homogeneous mixture as compared to that for water flowing alone. The pressure drop, or head loss, due to friction is not noticeably affected for consistencies below about 1.3 per cent.

Experiments have been made on a practical basis with consistencies as one of the major parameters. An analysis and check [10] of experiments conducted in Germany [11] resulted in correlations that can be expressed in terms of the Darcy-Weisbach equation. The friction factor is a function of the type of pulp and a pseudo-Reynolds number. The effective friction factor to be used in the equation

$$h_f = f \frac{L}{D} \left(\frac{V^2}{2g} \right)$$

is given by

$$f = \frac{250 \, K'}{\text{Re}'^{1.63}} \tag{10–61}$$

In this expression K' depends on the type of paper pulp, and is
  1.0 for unbleached sulphite, Southern kraft, and cooked groundwood;
  0.9 for soda, sulphate, bleached sulphate, and reclaimed paper;
  1.2 for Canadian kraft and groundwood.
The value of the pseudo-Reynolds number for $1.3 < C < 6$ is

$$\text{Re}' = \frac{D^{0.205} V \gamma}{C^{1.157}} \tag{10–62}$$

where D = pipe diameter in feet;
  V = average flow velocity in feet per second;
  γ = specific weight of water (62.4 lbf/ft³);
  C = stock consistency in per cent.

EXAMPLE 10–7. Compare the pressure drop for a flow of 600 gpm of soda pulp at a consistency of 3 per cent in a 6-in. diameter steel pipe 100 ft long with the pressure drop for water in the same pipe at the same flow rate.

Solution: For soda pulp, $K' = 0.9$.

$$V = Q/A = \frac{600}{(449)(0.1963)} = 6.81 \text{ ft/sec}$$

$$\text{Re}' = \frac{(0.5^{0.205})(6.81)(62.4)}{3^{1.157}} = 103$$

$$f = \frac{(250)(0.9)}{103^{1.63}} = 0.118$$

Thus for the mixture,

$$\Delta p = \gamma_m f \frac{L}{D} \left(\frac{V^2}{2g}\right) = (62.4)(0.118)(200)(0.719) = 1060 \text{ psf} = 7.36 \text{ psi}$$

For water alone,

$$\text{Re} = VD/\nu = (6.81)(0.5)/1.22 \times 10^{-5} = 2.8 \times 10^5$$

and for steel pipe, $f = 0.017$.

For water alone,

$$\Delta p = \gamma f \frac{L}{D} \left(\frac{V^2}{2g}\right) = (62.4)(0.017)(200)(0.72) = 153 \text{ psf} = 1.06 \text{ psi}$$

Thus the pressure drop for the pulp mixture is nearly 7 times that for water alone.

Solids. In the hydraulic conveying of solids in pipes (sand, gravel, and coal, for example) two flow regimes are generally considered.

1. *Homogeneous* transport applies to fine particles which are maintained in suspension, and the mixture flows like a homogeneous fluid. In laminar flow, however, the particles may settle out. For turbulent flow, the usual methods for calculating head loss apply if the density and apparent viscosity of the mixture are used. The concentration of fine particles should be low so that the mixture does not become non-Newtonian.

2. In *heterogeneous* flow, particles may tend to slide at the surface of a more or less stationary bed formed by the settled particles along the bottom of a horizontal pipe, or they may move as a sliding bed. For this regime it is possible to estimate head losses, but the actual physical situation is not well understood.

An empirical equation from Worster and Durand [12] for this type of flow gives the relative increase in pressure gradient for a mixture compared to that for water alone. This equation is

$$\frac{(\Delta p/L)_m - (\Delta p/L)_w}{(\Delta p/L)_w} = 121 C \left[\frac{gD(s_s - 1)}{V^2} \frac{V_s}{\sqrt{gd(s_s - 1)}}\right]^{1.5} \qquad (10\text{--}63)$$

where subscripts m, w, and s refer to mixture, water, and solids, respectively;

C = particle concentration by volume;

D = pipe diameter;

s_s = specific gravity of the solids;

V = mean flow velocity of the water;

V_s = settling velocity of the particles in still water;

d = particle diameter (or equivalent) for which 85 per cent of the particles are smaller (15 per cent are larger than d).

This equation has been verified in tests with sand, gravel, and manganese dioxide up to $\frac{3}{16}$ in. in mean diameter in pipes from 1 to 3 in. in diameter, with $\frac{1}{12}$-in. sand and $\frac{1}{2}$-in. coal in 3-in. pipes, and with $\frac{1}{12}$-in. sand and 1-in. coal in 6-in. pipes [12, 13]. Specific gravities of coal, sand, gravel, and manganese dioxide are 1.4, 2.6, 2.6, and 4.1, respectively.

Equation 10–63 indicates that the increase in pressure drop for a slurry of solids in water varies inversely as the cube of the flow velocity. The equation also involves the ratio of two forms of the Froude number. One form is based on the flow velocity and the pipe diameter, the other on the settling velocity of the particles and the particle diameter. The expression has not been verified for slurries with a wide variation of particle sizes, and thus should be used with caution in those instances.

EXAMPLE 10–8. Estimate the pressure drop for water at 10 ft/sec in a 1-ft pipe, 1000 ft long, carrying $\frac{1}{2}$-in. diameter gravel at a concentration of 10 per cent by volume. The settling velocity of this gravel is about 1.15 ft/sec.

Solution: From Eq. 10–63,

$$\frac{\Delta p_m}{\Delta p_w} - 1 = (121)(0.1) \left[\frac{(32.2)(1)(1.6)}{10^2} \frac{1.15}{\sqrt{(32.2)(\frac{1}{24})(1.6)}} \right]^{1.5}$$
$$= 3.11$$

Thus $\Delta p_m/\Delta p_w = 4.11$. For water alone, $Re_D = VD/\nu = (10)(1)/1.22 \times 10^{-5} = 8.2 \times 10^5$, and the pipe may be considered smooth since gravel flows in it. Then $f = 0.012$ and $\Delta p_w = (fL/D)(\rho V^2/2) = (0.012)(1000)(1.94)(100/2) = 1160$ psf $= 8.0$ psi. The pressure drop for the mixture is $\Delta p_m = (4.11)(8) = 33$ psi.

In order to use Eq. 10–63, the settling velocity of the particles must be determined by direct measurement. Natural particles are rarely spheres, and the drag on nonspherical particles, such as sand and gravel, is greater than that on spherical particles of the same material and mass.

Over a wide range of Reynolds numbers the drag coefficient for spheres (Fig. 11–4) and nonspherical particles is essentially constant, and the settling velocity for a given shape of material varies as the square root of its size. Then $V_s/\sqrt{d}$ in Eq. 10–63 is a constant, regardless of particle size, and the equation may be applied to any size distribution of particles, so long as they are not so small that the drag coefficient increases. An average value of $V_s/\sqrt{d}$ measured for a number of particles would be used in estimating the pressure drop for a heterogeneous mixture of solids in water.

REFERENCES

1. T. S. Lundgren, E. M. Sparrow and J. B. Starr, "Pressure Drop Due to the Entrance Region in Ducts of Arbitrary Cross Section," *Trans. Am. Soc. Mech. Engrs., Journal of Basic Eng.,* Vol. 86, Series D, No. 3 (1964), pp. 620–626.

2. E. M. Sparrow and A. Haji-Sheikh, "Flow and Heat Transfer in Ducts of Arbitrary Shape with Arbitrary Thermal Boundary Conditions," to be published in *Journal of Heat Transfer, Trans. Am. Soc. Mech. Engrs.*

3. E. M. Sparrow and A. Haji-Sheikh, "Laminar Heat Transfer and Pressure Drop in Isosceles Triangular, Right Triangular, and Circular Sector Ducts," *Journal of Heat Transfer, Am. Soc. Mech. Engrs.,* Vol. 87, Series C, No. 3 (1965), pp. 426–427.

4. S. K. Friedlander and L. Topper, Editors, *Turbulence: Classical Papers on Statistical Theory* (New York: Interscience Publishers, Inc., 1961).

5. H. Schlichting, *Boundary Layer Theory*, translated by J. Kestin (New York: McGraw-Hill Book Company, Inc., 1960).

6. V. K. Jonsson, "Experimental Studies of Turbulent Flow Phenomena in Eccentric Annuli," Ph. D. Thesis, University of Minnesota (1965).

7. E. R. G. Eckert and R. M. Drake, *Heat and Mass Transfer* (New York: McGraw-Hill Book Company, Inc., 1959), pp. 159–160.

8. R. M. Olson and E. M. Sparrow, "Measurements of Turbulent Flow Development in Tubes and Annuli with Square or Rounded Entrances," *A.I.Ch.E. Journal*, Vol. 9 (1963), pp. 766–770.

9. J. M. Robertson and D. Ross, "Effect of Entrance Conditions on Diffuser Flow," *Trans. Am. Soc. Civil Engrs.,* Vol. 118 (1953), pp. 1068–1097.

10. Durst, Chase, and Jenness, "An Analysis of Data on Stock Flow in Pipes," *J. Tech. Assn. of Pulp and Paper Industries*, Vol. 35, No. 12.

11. W. Brecht and H. Heller, "A Study of the Pipe Friction Losses of Paper Stock Suspensions," *Ibid.,* Vol. 33, No. 9.

12. R. A. Smith, "Experiments on the Flow of Sand-Water Slurries in Horizontal Pipes," *J. Inst. of Chem. Engrs.,* Vol. 33 (1955), pp. 85–92.

13. *Ibid.,* and D. M. Newitt, J. F. Richardson, M. Abbott, and R. B. Turtle, "Hydraulic Conveying of Solids in Horizontal Pipes," and Discussion by R. C. Worster, *Ibid.,* pp. 93–113.

PROBLEMS

10–1. If crude oil at 60 F is pumped through a 6-in. diameter pipeline at a rate of 224 gpm, is the flow laminar or turbulent?

10–2. Water at a viscosity of 1.86×10^{-5} slug/ft sec flows through a $\frac{1}{4}$-in. ID tube at a rate of 1 gpm. Calculate the Reynolds number, and determine whether the flow is laminar, turbulent, or possibly transition flow.

10–3. Explain qualitatively why the total force resulting from the pressure drop in the entrance region of a horizontal pipe is greater than the total shear force along the pipe wall. Assume incompressible flow.

10–4. Show that the hydraulic diameter for a) an annulus is equal to the difference in diameters of its two tubes, and b) a rectangular duct is twice the duct area divided by the sum of its sides ($D_h = 2ab/(a + b)$ in Table 10–2).

10–5. The pressure drops 100 psi in a 6-in. pipe over a length of 5000 ft. What is the wall shear stress for the flow of a) water, and b) crude oil? What is the shear velocity for c) water, and d) crude oil?

Ans. a) and b) 0.36 lb$_f$/ft^2, c) 0.431 ft/sec

10–6. Standard air flows at an average velocity of 110 ft/sec in a smooth brass tube 1.400 in. ID. a) What is the Reynolds number of the flow? b) What is the friction factor? c) What is the pressure gradient? d) What is the wall shear stress? e) What is the shear velocity?

Ans. e) 5.29 ft/sec

10–7. Repeat Prob. 10–6 for water flowing at 80 F in a smooth 2-in. tube at an average velocity of 10 ft/sec.

10–8. Crude oil at 87 F flows in a 1-in. pipe. a) What is the maximum flow rate, in gallons per minute, for which the flow may be considered laminar? b) What is the pressure drop in 100 ft of pipe? c) What is the deflection of a water manometer connected across 100 ft of this pipe?

Ans. c) 5.75 ft

10–9. Oil with a kinematic viscosity of $\nu = 0.0004$ ft^2/sec flows through an inclined tube 1 in. in diameter at an average velocity of 4 ft/sec. What is the inclination of the tube if the pressure inside the tube is constant along its length? HINT: Find arctan h_L/L.

Ans. 13.25 deg

10–10. Unavis J-43 hydraulic fluid at 75 F flows at a rate of 10 gpm through a pipe 1 in. in diameter. At what slope will the pipe convey the oil at constant pressure?

10–11. An oil flows from a large open cup through a vertical tube 18 in. long with an inside diameter of $\frac{1}{32}$ in. at a rate of 0.1 in.^{3}/min. The oil surface in the cup is 24 in. above the end of the tube. What is the kinematic viscosity of the oil? Assume fully developed laminar flow throughout the entire tube, and neglect the exit velocity head. Verify the validity of these assumptions.

Ans. $\nu = 5.02 \times 10^{-5}$ ft^2/sec

10–12. a) Compare the cost of pumping fuel oil through 500 ft of 4-in. commercial steel pipe at 100 gpm at 50 F with that at 100 F. b) Would it be economical to heat the oil from 50 F to 100 F in order to reduce pumping costs? For fuel oil, $c_p = 0.56$ Btu/lb$_m$ F.

10–13. At what radial distance from the pipe axis will the velocity be equal to the mean velocity for fully developed laminar flow?

10–14. Laminar flow exists in a round pipe. If the flow rate is reduced, what effect does this have on the a) wall shear stress and b) friction factor?

10–15. Laminar flow occurs in the annulus between two coaxial cylinders of radius R_1 and R_2 $(R_2 > R_1)$, respectively. The pressure drop over a length L is Δp. Show that the average velocity of flow is

$$V = \frac{\Delta p}{8\mu L} \left[(R_1{}^2 + R_2{}^2) - \frac{(R_2{}^2 - R_1{}^2)}{\ln R_2/R_1} \right]$$

where μ is the dynamic viscosity of the fluid. HINT: Let τ be the shear stress at a radius r. Apply the momentum theorem to a cylindrical shell in the annular region to get

$$\frac{dp}{dL} + \frac{1}{r}\frac{d(\tau r)}{dr} = 0$$

Since τ is a function of r only and p of L only, integrate first with respect to r, then with respect to r again substituting $\tau = -\mu(du/dr)$ and multiplying through by dr/r with boundary conditions $u = 0$ at $r = R_1$ and at R_2. This gives an expression for the varying velocity $u = u(r)$.

10–16. In Prob. 10–15, show that for $R_2/R_1 = 2$, $f = 95.2/\text{Re}$ for fully developed laminar flow in an annulus. In general

$$f\,\text{Re} = \frac{64\,[(R_2/R_1) - 1]^2}{(R_2/R_1)^2 + 1 - \dfrac{(R_2/R_1)^2 - 1}{\ln\,(R_2/R_1)}}$$

10–17. Oil $(\rho = 1.75$ slugs/ft^3 and $\nu = 0.003$ ft^2/sec) flows in a 2×2-in. square duct at an average velocity of 12.0 ft/sec. What is the pressure drop per 100 ft of duct length?

10–18. What is the pressure drop per 100 ft of 1×4-in. rectangular duct for the flow of Prob. 10–17?

10–19. Given a circular duct and a noncircular duct, both having the same perimeter P. A given fluid of viscosity ν flows at a rate Q through both ducts. a) Show that the Reynolds number is the same for both flow situations, and is $\text{Re} = Q/P\nu$. b) Show that the pressure gradient for the flow in the noncircular duct is related to that for the flow in the circular duct by the expression

$$\frac{(\Delta p/L)_n}{(\Delta p/L)_c} = \frac{f_n}{f_c} \left(\frac{A_c}{A_n}\right)^3$$

where subscripts c and n refer to the circular and noncircular ducts, respectively. In general the friction factors are not the same for laminar flow (Eq. 10–14 and Tables 10–1 through 10–4), but are the same for turbulent flow in smooth ducts (see page 234).

10–20. Univis J-43 hydraulic fluid at 150 F flows through a 1-in. ID smooth tube. The pressure drop over a 50-ft length is 0.50 psi. What is the flow rate in ft^3/sec?

Ans. 0.0104 ft^3/sec

10–21. Explain why the friction factor decreases as the velocity of a given fluid increases in a circular tube for fully-developed laminar flow.

10–22. Laminar flow exists in a long 1-in. ID circular tube. What is the effect on the pressure gradient of inserting a 0.01-in. diameter wire at the tube axis?

10–23. An oil ($\nu = 0.0004$ ft^2/sec and $\rho = 1.80$ slugs/ft^3) flows at an average velocity of 10 ft/sec in an equilateral triangle duct 1 in. on each side. What is the pressure drop in 50 ft of this duct?

10–24. Use Fig. 10–6 to obtain answers to the following questions. *a)* For what flow regime does the pressure drop in a pipe vary as the square of the flow rate? *b)* What is the friction factor at $Re_D = 10^5$ for a smooth pipe? For $k/D = 0.0001$? For $k/D = 0.001$? *c)* Over what range of Reynolds numbers is the friction factor constant for a 6-in. cast-iron pipe? *d)* Suppose the absolute roughness of a given pipe were to increase over a period of years to 3 times its initial value. Would this have greater effect on the pressure drop for a given turbulent flow at high Reynolds numbers or at low Reynolds numbers? *e)* For what flow regime does f depend only on Re_D? *f)* For what flow regime does f depend only on k/D? *g)* For what flow regime does f depend on both Re_D and k/D? *h)* The friction factor is 0.06 for a smooth pipe. What is the friction factor for a pipe of relative roughness $k/D = 0.001$ at the same Reynolds number? *i)* Repeat part *h)* for $f = 0.015$.

10–25. When the flow rate through a given smooth pipe is 4 ft^3/sec, the friction factor is 0.06. What friction factor can be expected if the flow rate is increased to 24 ft^3/sec?

10–26. What is the pressure drop per mile of pipe when water at 50 F flows in a 12-in. ID cast-iron pipe at a flow rate of 7.84 ft^3/sec?

Ans. 68.6 psi.

10–27. What is the pressure drop per 1000 ft of pipeline for the flow in Prob. 10–1?

10–28. What is the head loss and the pressure drop per mile of 24-in. commercial steel pipe through which gasoline at 60 F flows at an average velocity of 15 ft/sec?

10–29. Water flows in a new, horizontal 12-in. cast-iron pipe. In checking for the magnitude of a leak in the pipeline, two pressure gages 2000 ft apart upstream of the leak indicate a pressure difference of 20.0 psi. Two gages 2000 ft apart downstream of the leak indicate a pressure difference of 19.0 psi. Estimate the magnitude of the leak.

Ans. 0.173 ft^3/sec

10–30. Crude oil ($s = 0.87$ and $\nu = 5 \times 10^{-5}$ ft^2/sec) is to be pumped through a 12-in. diameter class H cast-iron pipe. This pipe will safely withstand approximately 350 psig internal pressure. How far apart should pumping stations be placed for a flow rate of 50,000 barrels per day (1 barrel = 42 gal)?

10–31. A 4-in. ID smooth pipe carries olive oil at an average velocity of 4.5 ft/sec. What is the pressure gradient when the oil temperature is *a)* 65 F, and *b)* 100 F? *c)* Explain why the pressure gradient is reduced so little for the warmer, less viscous oil.

10–32. Water flows in a 6-in. pipe at a rate of 3.14 ft³/sec. The total head drops 12.5 ft between two sections 100 ft apart along the pipe. *a*) What is the friction factor? *b*) What is the relative roughness of the pipe? *c*) Identify the pipe material, assuming it is in new condition.

10–33. Water at 70 F flows in a 6-in. galvanized pipe. What flow rate will produce a pressure drop of 13.0 psi in 1000 ft of horizontal pipe?

Ans. $Q = 1.34$ ft³/sec

10–34. Water flows in a 2-in. ID smooth pipe at 75 F. A piezometer tube 50 ft upstream from the free discharge at the end of the pipe shows water to rise 12.0 ft above the pipe centerline at the discharge end. What is the flow rate?

10–35. Water flows in a 1.38-in. ID pipe at 60 F. For a flow rate of 0.05 ft³/sec there is a head loss of 4.63 ft in a 40-ft length of pipe. What is the relative roughness of the pipe? From this, identify the pipe material.

10–36. The total head drops 18 ft in a length of 1500 ft of 12-in. cast-iron pipe. What is the flow rate for water at 70 F?

10–37. What flow rate of water at 50 F will result in a pressure drop of 2.5 psi in 1000 ft of cast-iron pipe 2 ft in diameter?

10–38. Fully developed flow at a flow rate Q exists in a pipe of diameter D_1 and length L. The pressure drop is Δp_1. What would be the pressure drop in terms of Δp_1 for the same Q and L if the pipe diameter were doubled for *a*) laminar flow, and *b*) turbulent flow?

10–39. It is desired to convey a hydraulic fluid ($\nu = 10^{-4}$ ft²/sec and $s = 0.848$) at a rate of 40 gpm through a smooth pipe with a pressure drop of 2 psi per 100 ft of pipe. What size pipe should be used?

10–40. Diesel oil ($s = 0.85$ and $\nu = 5 \times 10^{-5}$ ft²/sec) is to be pumped from a tanker to a storage tank through 600 ft of cast-iron pipe at a rate of 500 gpm. The oil level in the storage tank is 75 ft higher than that in the tanker. The pump in the tanker can develop a discharge pressure of 60 psig. Considering only pipe friction losses, what size pipe will be necessary?

10–41. Fully-developed flow in a smooth pipe is at an average velocity of 2 ft/sec. What is the maximum (centerline) velocity when *a*) Re $=1600$, and *b*) Re $=10^5$?

Ans. *a*) 4 ft/sec

b) 2.35 ft/sec

10–42. Fully-developed flow in a 12-in. cast-iron pipe exists at an average velocity of 6 ft/sec. What is the centerline velocity for *a*) fuel oil at 50 F, and *b*) crude oil at 70 F?

10–43. The wall shear stress and hence the pressure gradient may be estimated for fully developed turbulent flow from velocity measurements. Water flows at $V = 0.86 \ u_{\max} = 7.00$ ft/sec in a 6-in. pipe. *a*) What is the wall shear stress? *b*) What is the pressure drop in 100 ft of pipe? *c*) If the pipe is smooth, estimate the water temperature.

10-44. From Eqs. 10-15a and 10-21 show that

$$\frac{V - u}{v_*} = 2.5 \ln \frac{R}{y} - 3.75$$

10-45. Measurements in fully developed turbulent flow of a liquid in a pipe indicate that the velocity midway between the pipe wall and the pipe axis is 0.9 times the center-line velocity. *a)* What is the average velocity of flow in terms of the center-line velocity? *b)* What is the relative roughness of the pipe?

Ans. *a)* $V = 0.783\, u_m$, *b)* $k/D = 0.0147$

10-46. Direct measurements indicate that for fully developed turbulent flow in a circular tube of relative roughness 0.0018 and a smooth tube at Re = 82,000 the average velocity corresponds to that at $y/R = 0.25$. At what value of y/R is the velocity equal to the average velocity for *a)* the power-law velocity profile $u/u_m = (y/R)^{1/7}$, and *b)* the universal velocity profile given by Eq. 10-15?

10-47. A 2- by 4-ft rectangular air duct is made of smooth aluminum sheet. It conveys 19,200 ft³/min of standard air. What is the pressure drop in 500 ft of this duct?

10-48. Compare the pressure gradient in a rectangular duct with that for a circular duct, the flow rate and duct perimeter being the same in each instance. Consider aspect ratios of 1:1, 2:1, 3:1, and 4:1 for the rectangular duct.

Ans. 7.87 for the 4:1 aspect ratio

10-49. Standard air flows through a 2- by 4-ft rectangular duct made of smooth aluminum sheet at a rate of 9600 ft³/min. What diameter of round duct of the same material would convey this flow with the same pressure gradient?

10-50. Air at 100 F and 14.7 psia flows at 10 ft/sec through a 3.5- by 14-in. smooth duct in the space between studs in the wall of a house. What diameter round duct of the same material would convey the same flow with the same pressure gradient? Round leaders commonly are used between a furnace and the wall ducts.

10-51. Standard air flows at an average velocity of 100 ft/sec in the annular space between smooth circular tubes 4 in. and 1 in. in diameter, respectively. What is the pressure drop per 100 ft of length *a)* for a concentric annulus, and *b)* for an eccentricity of 1.0?

10-52. Water at 150 F flows through the annular space between smooth circular tubes 4 in. and 3 in. in diameter, respectively, at an average velocity of 5 ft/sec. What is the pressure drop per 100 ft of length for *a)* a concentric annulus, and *b)* an eccentricity of 0.9?

Ans. *a)* 3.9 psi

10-53. A fluid of constant density ρ enters a pipe of radius R with a uniform velocity V. At a downstream section the velocity varies with the radius r according to the equation

$$u = 2V\left(1 - \frac{r^2}{R^2}\right)$$

Let the pressures at sections 1 (inlet) and 2 (downstream section) be p_1 and p_2, respectively. Show that the frictional force of the pipe walls on the fluid between sections 1 and 2 is

$$F = \pi R^2 \left(p_1 - p_2 - \frac{1}{3} \rho V^2 \right)$$

10–54. Fuel oil at 85 F drains from a tank through 5 ft of 1-in. diameter pipe. The level of oil in the tank is 6 ft above the exit end of the tube. *a)* What is the flow rate through the tube if fully developed flow is assumed to exist throughout the entire pipe? Assume exit velocity head is negligible, then confirm it. The entrance is well rounded. *b)* What is the entrance length for conditions assumed in part *a)*? *c)* Will the flow rate calculated in part *a)* be changed significantly if the additional pressure drop in the entrance region is taken into account?

Ans. a) 4.10 gpm, *b)* 0.74 D, *c)* No

10–55. Suppose a 2-in. pipe is used instead of a 1-in. pipe in Prob. 10–54. *a)* What is the flow rate if fully developed flow is assumed to exist throughout the entire pipe and the exit velocity is neglected? *b)* What is the flow rate if fully developed flow is assumed to exist but the exit velocity head is considered? *c)* What is the flow rate if the additional pressure drop in the entrance region and the exit velocity head are both included? *d)* Which flow condition (*a, b,* or *c*) most closely resembles the true physical situation? Note that the entrance length is about 5 diameters or ⅙ the pipe length.

10–56. Fuel oil passes through a heat exchanger consisting of 150 tubes in parallel. Each tube is 10 ft long and 1 in. ID. The oil enters at 75 F and leaves at 110 F ($\nu = 7.2 \times 10^{-3}$ and 2.0×10^{-3} ft²/sec, respectively) at a mean velocity of 6 ft/sec. Assume heat transfer takes place such that the viscosity varies linearly along each tube. Estimate the power required to pump the oil through the tube bundle, considering only the pressure drop or head loss in the tubes themselves, *a)* assuming fully developed flow throughout the tubes and *b)* assuming the oil enters each tube one-dimensionally and that the velocity profile develops within the tubes.

10–57. Some ducts are to be provided with pressure taps to measure the friction factor for fully-developed laminar flow. Each duct is attached to a supply reservoir with a short rounded entrance. Estimate the minimum distance from the tank to the location of the first pressure tap to ensure fully-developed flow based on pressure gradient for flow at Re = 2000 for *a)* a circular tube, *b)* a square duct, and *c)* a ⅕ rectangle.

10–58. What is the ratio of maximum to average velocity for fully-developed laminar flow in *a)* a ¼ rectangle, and *b)* a square?

Ans. a) 1.77

10–59. What is the ratio of the maximum to average velocity for fully-developed laminar flow between parallel plates ($a/b = 0$ for a rectangular duct)?

10–60. What is the average wall shear stress in the entrance region for laminar flow in a circular tube of diameter D, an average flow velocity V, and a fluid density ρ? Compare the result with the wall shear stress for fully-developed flow, $\tau_0 = (16/\text{Re}) (\rho V^2/2)$, and Eq. 10–31.

10–61. Water flows at 6 ft³/sec through a contraction from a 12-in. pipe to a 6-in. pipe. Compare *a*) the head loss and *b*) the pressure drop through a sudden contraction with that for a well-designed gradual contraction.

10–62. Derive Eq. 10–34 from the continuity, momentum, and energy equations for flow through a sudden enlargement. Assume one-dimensional flow.

10–63. Water flows through an 8-in. pipe which enlarges abruptly to 16 in. in diameter. A differential manometer containing mercury is connected across the enlargement and shows a deflection of 5 in. What is the flow rate?

10–64. A pipe whose area is 0.5 ft² enlarges abruptly to a pipe of 1 ft² area. A few diameters downstream the second pipe is enlarged abruptly to a third pipe of 2 ft² in area. The pressure rise from the first to the third pipe (a few diameters downstream from the last enlargement) is 3.5 psi. What is the flow rate if the pipes are horizontal and convey water? Assume one-dimensional flow, and neglect pipe friction.

Ans. 14.4 ft³/sec

10–65. Water flows at a rate of 6 ft³/sec in a horizontal 6-in. pipe which is enlarged to a 12-in. pipe. Estimate the head loss and pressure rise between the two pipes for *a*) a sudden enlargement, *b*) a 7-deg diffuser with an abrupt change from the 6-in. pipe to the diffuser cone, and *c*) a 7-deg diffuser with a parabolic transition between the 6-in. pipe and the diffuser cone.

10–66. The measured pressure rise through a 6- to 12-in. diameter diffuser in a water tunnel is $0.82 \, \rho V_1{}^2/2$, where V_1 is the average velocity at the upstream end. Kinetic energy correction factors at the upstream and downstream ends are $\alpha_1 = 1.004$ and $\alpha_2 = 1.56$, respectively. *a*) What is the pressure efficiency? *b*) What is the energy efficiency?

10–67. A 6-in. pipe is joined to a 12-in. pipe by a reducing flange. For water flowing at a rate of 4 ft³/sec, what is the head loss *a*) when the water flows from the smaller to the larger pipe, and *b*) when the water flows from the larger to the smaller pipe?

Ans. a) 3.64 ft

10–68. Water drains from a large tank through a 2-in. galvanized pipe 4 ft long under a head of 12 ft. The actual pipe diameter is 2.067 in. ID, and the friction factor may be taken as $f = 0.03$. The pipe flows full at exit. What is the flow velocity in the pipe for *a*) a rounded entrance, and *b*) a reentrant type of entrance (Fig. 10–11)?

10–69. A liquid flows in a pipe with $k/D = 0.002$ at a Reynolds number of 10^5. This pipe is replaced by a similar pipe of two-thirds the diameter of the original pipe. What is the flow velocity in the smaller pipe in terms of that in the original larger pipe if the pressure drop is the same in each instance? Both pipes are of the same length.

Ans. $V_{small} = 0.77 \, V_{large}$

10–70. A pipe is replaced by one twice its diameter. How will the flow rate for the larger pipe compare with that for the smaller pipe, assuming the head loss across each pipe to be the same? Consider both laminar and turbulent flow in both smooth and rough pipes.

10–71. A total flow of 30 ft³/sec of water at 70 F passes through two asphalt-dipped cast-iron pipes connected in parallel. One is 12 in. in diameter and 1000 ft long, the other is 16 in. in diameter and 2000 ft long. What is the flow rate through the 12-in. pipe? Consider only wall friction losses.

10–72. Consider two identical open tanks, one with a vertical discharge pipe of length L_1 and the other with a vertical discharge pipe of length $L_2 = L_1 + \Delta L$. Both pipes flow full. Let the water depth in each tank be h feet, the pipe diameters be D, the entrance loss coefficient be k_L, and the friction factor f be the same in each pipe. Show that the flow velocity V_1 in the short pipe is related to the flow velocity V_2 in the longer pipe by a) $V_1 > V_2$ if $hf/D > 1 + k_L$, b) $V_1 = V_2$ if $hf/D = 1 + k_L$, and c) $V_1 < V_2$ if $hf/D < 1 + k_L$.

NOTE: One might ask whether an open tank will drain more quickly through a short drainpipe or through a long drainpipe. Results for a vertical pipe indicate that whether the flow rate from one tank is greater than from the other is independent of the pipe length.

10–73. A 24-in. riveted steel pipe ($k = 0.003$ ft) 30,000 ft long connects two open reservoirs whose levels differ by 150 ft. a) What is the flow rate from the higher to the lower reservoir? b) What horsepower would be required to pump 10,000 gpm from the upper to the lower reservoir? c) What horsepower would be required to pump 10,000 gpm from the lower to the higher reservoir?

10–74. In Prob. 10–73 c), what per cent saving in power would result if an 18-in. riveted steel pipe 20,000 ft long is connected in parallel to two-thirds the existing 24-in. pipe for a total flow of 10,000 gpm?

10–75. Sketch the total head lines and the piezometric head lines for the flow situations in Prob. 10–73 a), b), and c), and in Prob. 10–74.

10–76. Determine the flow distribution and the pressure drop through the pipe system in Example 10–3 for a total flow rate of 30 ft³/sec. For turbulent flow in the hydraulically rough regime, how does the total flow through a group of given pipes connected in parallel affect the relative distribution of flow through the individual pipes?

10–77. A 24-in. riveted steel pipe ($k = 0.003$ ft) 15,000 ft long in series with an 18-in. riveted steel pipe 10,000 ft long connects two reservoirs whose levels differ by 100 ft. What is the flow rate from the higher to the lower reservoir?

The Hazen-Williams equation for pipe flow in the form of the alignment chart of Fig. 10–17 should be used for Prob. 10–78 through Prob. 10–89.

10–78. Refer to Table 10–11 and Fig. 10–17 to obtain answers to the following water flow systems. a) What is the pressure drop in 500 ft of 6-in. old cast-iron pipe for a flow rate of 350 gpm? *b)* Repeat part *a)* for new cast-iron pipe. *c)* What size new riveted steel pipe will convey 4 ft³/sec with a head loss of 10.4 ft per 1000 ft of pipe? *d)* What flow rate will produce a pressure drop of 10 psi in 500 ft of old cast-iron pipe 6 in. in diameter? *e)* Repeat part *d)* for new steel pipe. *f)* What is the flow rate between two open reservoirs 100 ft different in elevation which are connected by 3000 ft of 10-in. new riveted steel pipe? Consider only pipe friction losses.

Ans.   *a)* 3.70 psi, *f)* 2140 gpm

10–79. Solve Prob. 10–71.

10–80. Solve Prob. 10–73.

10–81. Solve Prob. 10–74.

10–82. A storage reservoir for a town water supply is located 20 miles from the service reservoir at the edge of the town and its surface is 300 ft above that of the service reservoir. The initial design was for a flow of 4,000,000 gal/day. An increase to 6,000,000 gal/day was later required. The increased flow was to be accommodated by a second pipe of the same diameter as the first in parallel with it over a part of the 20-mile distance, with a wye connection at the junction. What should be the length of the added pipe? Assume smooth riveted steel pipe. Use *a)* the Darcy-Weisbach equation with *k* = 0.003 ft and *b)* the Hazen-Williams equation with *C* = 110.

10–83. A pipeline splits into two parallel branches. One branch consists of an 8-in. pipe 1000 ft long in series with a 12-in. pipe 1000 ft long. The second branch consists of a 10-in. pipe 1000 ft long. Assume *C* = 100. What is the pressure drop through the parallel system for a total flow of 1500 gpm?

10–84. A 6-in. pipe 200 ft long is connected to an open upper reservoir and is in series with a 12-in. pipe 300 ft long which discharges into a lower reservoir. The reservoir surfaces differ by 50 ft in elevation. Assume old cast-iron pipe and consider the head loss at a square entrance to the 6-in. pipe, the sudden enlargement, and the exit from the 12-in. pipe to the lower reservoir. What is the flow rate?

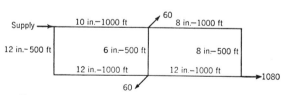

PROB. 10–85. Note: Flow rates are in gallons
per minute.

10–85. Determine the flow through each pipe in the network. Assume *C* = 100 for all pipes. Will the flow distribution be different if *C* is other than 100 but the same for all pipes?

10–86. Determine the flow through each pipe and the pressure drop from A to B. Assume $C = 100$.

Ans. 5.0 psi

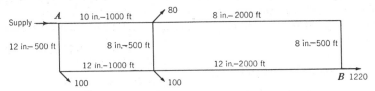

PROB. 10–86. Note: Flow rates are in gallons per minute.

10–87. Determine the flow through each pipe in the network. Assume $C = 100$.

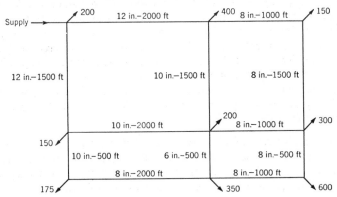

PROB. 10–87. Note: Flow rates are in gallons per minute.

10–88. Draw pressure contours at 1-psi intervals on a scale drawing of the pipe network. Assume $C = 100$.

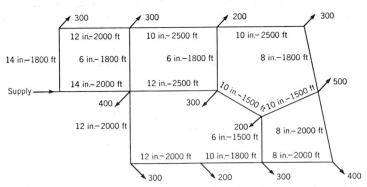

PROB. 10–88. Note: Flow rates are in gallons per minute.

10–89. Determine the flow through each pipe in the network. Assume $C = 100$ for all pipes.

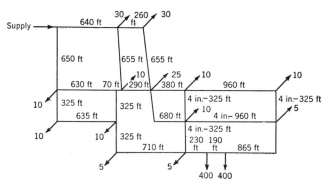

PROB. 10–89. Note: Flow rates are in gallons per minute.
All pipes are 6-in. diameter except as noted.

10–90. Two reservoirs differ in elevation by 60 ft. They are connected with 1000 ft of 6-in. commercial steel pipe with the following fittings: a square entrance, two flanged elbows, and two gate valves. Estimate the flow rate when the valves are wide open. Assume water at 60 F.

10–91. Draw the total head line and the piezometric head line for the flow in Prob. *a)* 10–64, *b)* 10–90.

10–92. Subsonic flow of a gas occurs at constant temperature in a pipe with friction. *a)* Does the magnitude of the pressure gradient dp/dx increase, remain constant, or decrease in the direction of flow? *b)* Does the Reynolds number increase, remain the same, or decrease in the direction of flow? *c)* Does the Mach number increase, remain the same, or decrease in the direction of flow? *d)* Is heat added to the gas or removed from it in order that the temperature be maintained constant?

10–93. Plot curves of p_1/p_2 vs. fL/D similar to those in Fig. 10–19 for $M_1 = 0.1$ for $k = 1.3$ and $k = 1.67$ in order to show the effect of the ratio of specific heat capacities on isothermal flow in a pipe with friction.

10–94. A straight pipe in which gas flows is inclined at an angle θ with the horizontal. *a)* Show that Eq. 10–45 becomes

$$\frac{dp}{\rho V^2/2} + \frac{f\,dx}{D} + \frac{g\sin\theta\,dx}{V^2/2} + 2\frac{dV}{V} = 0$$

b) Show that the pressure gradient for isothermal flow becomes

$$\frac{dp}{dx} = \frac{\dfrac{pf}{2D} + \dfrac{pg\sin\theta}{V^2}}{1 - \dfrac{p}{\rho V^2}}$$

c) Show that the limiting pressure for isothermal flow in an inclined pipe is the same as for a horizontal pipe (Eq. 10–50).

10–95. For given initial conditions, compare the dimensionless limiting length fL^*/D for carbon dioxide with that for xenon at $M_1 = 0.01$ and at $M_1 = 0.1$.

Generalize your results in a qualitative statement concerning the effect of the ratio of specific heat capacities k on the limiting length.

10–96. Calculate the ratio of $\bar{f}L^*/D$ for adiabatic flow to the value of fL^*/D for isothermal flow of air at initial Mach numbers of *a*) 0.05, *b*) 0.1, *c*) 0.2, *d*) 0.3, *e*) 0.4, and *f*) 0.5. Make a qualitative statement regarding the limiting length for adiabatic flow versus that for isothermal flow of a given gas in a given pipe with given initial conditions.

Ans. *a*) 1.0035, *f*) 1.31

10–97. The friction factor f is constant for isothermal flow of a gas in a pipe with friction. For subsonic adiabatic flow, is $\bar{f} \leqq f_1$, or is $\bar{f} \geqq f_1$; that is, how does the average friction factor compare with the initial value?

10–98. The Mach number for air flow in a pipe increases from 0.3 to 0.7 because of pipe friction. The initial pressure $p_1 = 20$ psia. What is the pressure at the section where $M_2 = 0.7$ *a*) if the flow is isothermal and *b*) if the flow is adiabatic?

Ans. *a*) 8.57 psia
b) 8.25 psia

10–99. What is $\bar{f}L^*/D$ for adiabatic flow in a pipe with friction *a*) for the initial Mach number M_1 approaching zero, *b*) for M_1 approaching 1, and *c*) for very large values of M_1 (supersonic flow)? $k = 1.4$.

Ans. *c*) 0.822

10–100. Air enters a 1-ft diameter commercial steel pipe from a compressor at 240 F and 200 psia, at an average velocity of 40 ft/sec. *a*) What is the limiting length for isothermal flow? *b*) What is the limiting length for adiabatic flow?

Ans. *a*) 55,100 ft

10–101. The limiting Mach number for adiabatic flow in a pipe with friction is 1.0. In Prob. 10–100, what is the Mach number *a*) 100 ft and *b*) 1000 ft from the limiting length for adiabatic flow?

10–102. The limiting Mach number for isothermal flow of air in a pipe with friction is 0.845. In Prob. 10–100, what is the Mach number *a*) 100 ft and *b*) 1000 ft from the limiting length for isothermal flow?

Ans. *b*) M = 0.203

10–103. The Mach number for air flow in a pipe increases from 0.1 to 0.6 because of pipe friction. The pressure at the section where $M_1 = 0.1$ is $p_1 = 80$ psia. What is the pressure at the section where $M_2 = 0.6$ *a*) if the air temperature remains constant and *b*) if no heat is transferred to or from the air within the pipe (adiabatic but not isentropic flow)?

10–104. Methane flows through an 8-in. insulated pipe at a rate of 25 lb$_m$/sec. At inlet the pressure is 100 psia and the temperature is 120 F. Calculate *a*) the initial Mach number, *b*) the Mach number at a section where the temperature is 100 F, and *c*) the pressure at the section where $T = 100$ F.

Ans. *c*) 34.5 psia

10–105. Repeat Prob. 10–104 for air flow.

10–106. Air enters a 6-in. commercial steel pipe at 150 psia, 140 F, and 60 ft/sec. Over what length of pipe will the Mach number increase to a value of 0.1 for a) isothermal flow and b) adiabatic flow? c) What is the pressure at $M_2 = 0.1$ for part a)? d) What are the minimum pressures for parts a) and b)? e) What is the maximum length of pipe for parts a) and b)?

10–107. Air at 100 psia and 100 F enters a 6-in. diameter commercial steel pipe at a velocity of 29 ft/sec. The flow is isothermal. a) What is the initial Mach number M_1? b) What is the limiting length of pipe? c) What is the minimum pressure attainable? d) What is the pressure at $0.8L^*$?

Ans. d) 45.2 psia

10–108. Methane ($k = 1.31$ and $R = 3095$ ft lb$_f$/slug R) enters a 6-in. diameter commercial steel pipe at 150 psia, 100 F ($\mu = 2.5 \times 10^{-7}$ slug/ft sec), and 50 ft/sec. What is the pressure 6000 ft downstream for a) isothermal flow, b) adiabatic flow, and c) incompressible flow?

Ans. a) and b) 128 psia

10–109. Repeat Prob. 10–108 a) for air flow.

10–110. The limiting pressure for assumed entrance conditions for gas flow in a pipe is 5 psia. Suppose the limiting length of pipe discharges into the atmosphere (14.7 psia). Discuss whether the assumed flow could exist, and if not, what changes must occur.

10–111. The limiting length for assumed entrance conditions for gas flow in a pipe is 10,000 ft. Suppose the actual pipe length is 14,000 ft. Discuss whether the assumed flow could exist, and if not, what changes must occur.

10–112. Methane ($k = 1.31$ and $R = 3095$ ft lb$_f$/slug R) is to be delivered at a rate of 6.65 lb$_m$/sec at a pressure of 2 atmospheres through 5 miles of 6-in. pipe. Assume isothermal flow at 60 F with $f = 0.015$. Calculate the inlet pressure required at the upstream end of the pipe.

10–113. Repeat Prob. 10–112 for air flow.

11 | Dynamic Drag and Lift

In this chapter, the fluid forces acting on a body in a flow stream owing to the relative motion between the fluid and the body are considered. Buoyant and gravity forces on the body are not included since they are static and not dynamic effects, and they act regardless of the relative motion between the fluid and the body.

11-1. FLUID FORCES ON A BODY IN A FLOW STREAM

When an extensive, incompressible viscous fluid flows past a body submerged in it or when a body moves through this fluid at rest, two types of forces act over the surface of the body. These surface forces are due to pressure and to viscous shear. Over any infinitesimal area of the body surface, the pressure force is normal to that area, and the viscous shear force is parallel or tangent to the area. The components of these forces when taken *in the direction of motion* of the body (or of the approaching fluid with respect to the body) and then summed up over the entire body surface result in what is called *profile drag*. Waves may be set up at a liquid surface as a result of the motion of a body (a ship, boat, or hydrofoil, for example) and drag owing to these waves is called *wave drag*. In compressible gas flow, compression shocks contribute to what is also called wave drag.

If the components of the pressure and viscous shear forces over an infinitesimal area are taken *normal* to the direction of motion of the body (or of the fluid with respect to the body) and summed up over the entire body surface, the resulting force is called *lift*. Associated with this lift force on an airfoil or blade element of finite span is a drag force called *induced drag*.

In a steady flow of an ideal (nonviscous) fluid of infinite extent, only forces from pressure exist, and the drag force in all instances except free-cavity flows is zero. Lift, however, may be produced in an ideal fluid by superimposing an irrotational vortex, or circulation, around the body. In fact, vortices, or circulation, are required in order to produce lift in a *viscous* fluid as well as in an ideal (nonviscous) fluid.

11-2. DRAG

In the absence of wave or induced drag, the total drag is the profile drag, which in turn is due to pressure and viscous shear. The profile drag may be due entirely to viscous shear, entirely to pressure, or to a combination of both. In the latter instance, viscous shear forces may play an important role, however, in the development of the boundary layer and in influencing the point of separation of the boundary layer from the surface of the body. This in turn affects the size of the wake and the pressure within it, both of which partially determine the pressure drag. Positive pressures over the leading portion of the body also contribute to pressure drag.

The drag is expressed as the product of a drag coefficient, the dynamic pressure of the free stream, and some characteristic area. The drag coefficient was found in Chapters 7 and 8 to be a function of a number of parameters including the body shape, Reynolds number, Mach number, Froude number, surface roughness, and free-stream turbulence. In any instance, the drag is expressed as

$$\text{Drag} = C \frac{\rho u_s^2}{2} A \qquad (11\text{--}1)$$

where C = drag coefficient (the drag coefficient was defined in Sec. 8–3 as the ratio of the drag force to the force represented by the product of the dynamic pressure of the free stream and some area);

C_f = skin-friction drag coefficient;

C_D = drag coefficient for other forms of drag;

$\rho u_s^2/2$ = dynamic pressure of the free stream;

A = area being sheared for pure skin-friction drag, the chord area for lifting vanes, or the projected frontal area for other shapes.

Skin-friction drag. Pure, viscous shear drag was discussed in Chapter 7 for parallel flow past a smooth flat plate. The drag coefficient C_f was shown to depend on whether the boundary layer was laminar or turbulent. If the boundary layer is laminar, C_f depends on the Reynolds number of the flow based on the free-stream velocity u_s and the length of the plate x. If the boundary layer is turbulent, C_f depends on the Reynolds number of the flow, the roughness of the plate, and on the location of the transition from a laminar to a turbulent boundary layer, which in turn depends on the plate roughness and on the turbulence level of the free stream.

Resulting curves of drag coefficient as a function of Reynolds number for smooth flat surfaces are given in Fig. 7–10, and again in Fig. 11–1, which also includes an approximate curve for rough surfaces typical of a ship's hull [1].

Additional information on ship resistance may be found in books on naval architecture [2].

The skin-friction drag of surface ships, submarines, airships, and so forth, in addition to flat surfaces, may be approximated using the data of Fig. 11–1.

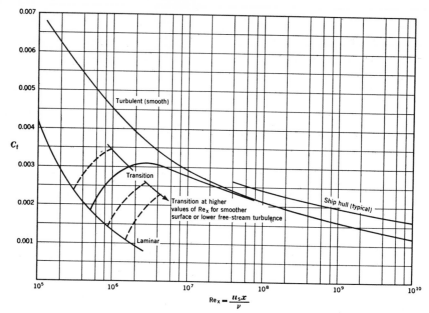

FIG. 11–1. Drag coefficients for plane surfaces parallel to flow.

EXAMPLE 11–1. A 15-ft smooth model of an ocean vessel is towed in fresh water at 5.5 knots (9.3 ft/sec) with a total measured drag of 17 lb$_f$. The wetted surface of the hull is 38 ft². Estimate the skin-friction drag.

Solution: The skin-friction drag may be estimated by considering the wetted surface of the hull as a flat plate 15 ft long with a total area of 38 ft².

$$\mathrm{Re}_x = u_s\, x/\nu = (9.3)(15)/1.21 \times 10^{-5} = 1.15 \times 10^7$$

From Fig. 11–1, $C_f = 0.0029$. Then the skin-friction drag is

$$\mathrm{Drag}_{\mathrm{friction}} = C_f(\rho u_s^2/2)\, A = (0.0029)(1.94)(9.3^2/2)(38) = 9.25\ \mathrm{lb}_f$$

Pressure drag. Pure pressure drag exists for flow past a flat plate normal to a stream. Any shear forces act normal to the approaching stream and thus do not contribute to the drag force directly. They may, however, affect the growth of the boundary layer along the surface and have a minute effect on the pressure distribution.

The drag coefficient for pure pressure drag depends on the shape of the surface and the Reynolds number of the flow based on some characteristic dimension D. The flow pattern and pressure distribution for two-dimensional flow around a plate of infinite length L is shown in Fig. 11–2. The drag coefficient for a finite plate depends on the ratio of D/length, as well as Re_D, because of end effects. For values of D/L from 0.4 to 1.0 at $\mathrm{Re}_D > 1000$, $C_D \approx 1.16$, which is slightly greater than that for a circular

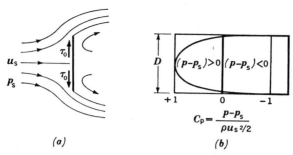

FIG. 11–2. Two-dimensional flow past a flat plate normal to the free stream. *a*) Flow pattern. Note that shear force is normal to the free-stream velocity u_s. *b*) Pressure distribution (according to measurements by Fage and Johansen).

disc ($C_D = 1.12$) for the same range of Re_D. Figure 11–3 indicates the effect of D/L on C_D for a rectangular plate normal to the flow.

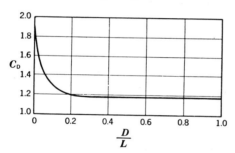

FIG. 11–3. Effect of shape on drag coefficient for rectangular plate normal to the flow stream (according to measurements by Wieselsberger and Flachsbart).

EXAMPLE 11–2. Calculate the drag force on a 10-ft billboard 100 ft wide at ground level in a 60-mph wind normal to the billboard. Assume standard air.

Solution: The drag will be one-half that for a 20- x 100-ft rectangle, since the flow is essentially the same as that past the top half of a 20- x 100-ft rectangle.

$$Re_D = u_s D/\nu = (88)(20)/1.57 \times 10^{-4} > 10^3$$

From Fig. 11–3, $C_D = 1.2$ for $D/L = 0.2$. Thus the drag is

$$\text{Drag} = (1.2)(0.00238)(88^2/2)(10 \times 100) = 11{,}000 \text{ lb}_f$$

For $D/L = 0.1$, $C_D = 1.3$, and this would apply if the air flows around all edges of the billboard.

Combined skin friction and pressure drag (profile drag). The flow

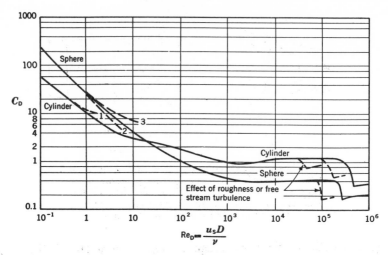

FIG. 11–4. Drag coefficients for spheres and infinite circular cylinders. Curve *1*: Lamb's solution for cylinder. Curve *2*: Stokes' solution for sphere (Eq. 11–3). Curve *3*: Oseen's solution for sphere (Eq. 11–4).

past a circular cylinder or a sphere may be analyzed analytically with certain approximations for laminar flow. Results of experiments for turbulent flow may be explained on the basis of boundary layer growth and separation. It is informative to look into these flows in some detail. Typical curves relating drag coefficients with Reynolds number are shown in Fig. 11–4. Each curve represents the results of numerous measurements.

The curve for very slow motion (called creeping motion) for the cylinder is from a solution of the Navier-Stokes equations by Lamb [3]. He obtained a drag coefficient given by

$$C_D = \frac{8\pi}{2\mathrm{Re}_D - \mathrm{Re}_D \ln \mathrm{Re}_D}$$

which is valid for Re_D less than about 0.5 [4].

A similar solution for a sphere was made by Stokes in 1850 and gave the drag as

$$\mathrm{Drag} = 3\mu u_s \pi D \tag{11–2}$$

and is valid for $\mathrm{Re}_D < 0.1$. Combining Eqs. 11–1 and 11–2, we find that for this range of Reynolds number

$$C_D = \frac{24}{\mathrm{Re}_D} \tag{11–3}$$

Stokes' solution also showed that one-third of the drag was pressure drag and two-thirds was due to viscous shear.

Oseen in 1910 made an improvement in the Stokes solution by including, in part, the inertia terms Stokes omitted. Oseen's solution gave

$$C_D = \frac{24}{\text{Re}_D}\left(1 + \frac{3}{16}\,\text{Re}_D\right) \tag{11-4}$$

which is valid for $\text{Re}_D < 1$.[1]

It is interesting to note that experimental results lie midway between the Stokes and Oseen curves in Fig. 11–4. Thus, since the plot is logarithmic, the experimental data follow the equation

$$C_D = \frac{24}{\text{Re}_D}\left(1 + \frac{3}{16}\,\text{Re}_D\right)^{\frac{1}{2}} \tag{11-5}$$

quite accurately for Reynolds numbers up to 100.

If a sphere falls through a fluid of infinite extent (fluid dimensions much greater than the sphere diameter), the buoyant and drag forces at terminal or steady velocity are equal to the gravity force on the sphere. Thus for $\text{Re}_D < 0.1$ Stokes' law will apply and

$$\gamma_f\,\frac{\pi D^3}{6} + 3\mu u_s\,\pi D = \gamma_s\,\frac{\pi D^3}{6}$$

Thus, if the fall velocity u_s, the fluid and sphere specific weights γ_f and γ_s, respectively, and the sphere diameter D are known, the fluid viscosity is

$$\mu = \frac{D^2(\gamma_s - \gamma_f)}{18\,u_s} \tag{11-6}$$

and this equation provides an extremely simple method for measuring dynamic viscosity. If the fluid is of finite extent, the influence of the boundaries of the container is such as to indicate an apparent drag coefficient higher than that in an infinite fluid. If, for example, the sphere falls in the center of a vertical cylinder of diameter D_c, the relative velocity of the fluid adjacent to the sphere increases, the drag increases, and the sphere will fall slower than in an infinite fluid. The measured velocity u_m should be corrected to its equivalent velocity in an infinite fluid u_s by the equation

$$u_s = \left(1 + 2.4\,\frac{D}{D_c}\right)u_m \tag{11-7}$$

For a number of particles uniformly distributed in a fluid, mutual interference will cause them to fall more slowly than if each particle fell alone. The settling velocity of natural particles such as sand and gravel is less than that for equivalent spheres, since the drag coefficient increases with increasing departure from a spherical shape.

EXAMPLE 11–3. A $\frac{1}{16}$-in. steel sphere ($\rho_s = 15.15$ slugs/ft³) falls at a steady velocity of 0.01056 ft/sec in an oil of density $\rho_f = 1.684$ slugs/ft³ contained in a vertical cylinder 3.75 in. in diameter. What is the oil viscosity?

[1]The Stokes, Oseen, and experimental curves coincide at low Re_D, and it is difficult to place an upper limit to the range of validity of Eqs. 11–3 and 11–4. At $\text{Re}_D = 1$, the Oseen equation gives a C_D 18 per cent higher than the Stokes equation; experimental data lie between them.

Solution: From Eq. 11–7,

$$u_s = \left(1 + 2.4\frac{0.0625}{3.75}\right)(0.01056) = 0.0110 \text{ ft/sec}$$

From Eq. 11–6,

$$\mu = \frac{(0.0625/12)^2(15.15 - 1.684)(32.17)}{(18)(0.0110)} = 0.0594 \text{ slug/ft sec}$$

Equation 11–6 is valid, since

$$\text{Re}_D = \frac{u_s D\rho_f}{\mu} = \frac{(0.0110)(0.0625/12)(1.684)}{0.0594} = 0.00162 < 0.1$$

and is well within the range of validity for the Stokes equation.

As the Reynolds number increases (this may be produced by an increase in u_s for a given sphere in a given fluid), the laminar boundary layer separates from the aft portion of the sphere and a laminar wake is established. Further increase in Re_D results in a turbulent wake, with a rather constant drag coefficient, such that the drag varies approximately as u_s^2. In this region, vortices are formed and shed in alternate directions behind the sphere or cylinder. This formation and shedding of vortices causes a time-varying asymmetry in the pressure distribution around the aft surface which, in turn, results in alternating transverse forces that may set the body in vibration. Shapes other than spheres and cylinders also exhibit these characteristics. The singing of telephone wires and power lines and the fluttering of Venetian blinds are well-known examples. Near $\text{Re}_D = 300,000$ the laminar boundary layer suddenly becomes turbulent, and the boundary layer separation point moves aft, resulting in a smaller wake and hence smaller drag. This movement of the separation point accounts for the sudden drop in the drag coefficient near a Reynolds number of 300,000 for the sphere and about 500,000 for the cylinder.

The boundary layer may become turbulent at a Reynolds number lower than these values if the sphere or cylinder is rough, or if the turbulence level, or intensity, in the flow stream is increased.

The drag curve for rough spheres or for a high turbulence intensity in the free stream is indicated in Fig. 11–4. This reduction in drag coefficient is taken advantage of in the roughening of golf balls.

The shift in separation point for flow past a sphere or circular cylinder is indicated in Fig. 11–5. Fluid particles near the boundary at A are moving faster in a turbulent boundary layer than in a laminar boundary layer. Thus they have more kinetic energy with which to overcome the adverse pressure gradient (increasing pressure) behind the sphere or cylinder. Hence, the particles in the turbulent boundary layer are able to move further aft before coming to rest and being separated from the boundary. As a result, there is a smaller wake and less drag.

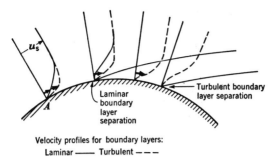

Velocity profiles for boundary layers:
Laminar ——— Turbulent — — —

Fig. 11–5. Separation of laminar and turbulent
boundary layer from a cylinder.

This same general situation exists for any body shape for which the drag is significantly affected by a wake.

In the 1920's, the turbulence level, or intensity, in subsonic wind tunnels was measured by determining the critical value of Re_D at which the drag decreased suddenly (or for which the drag coefficient became 0.3, for example) for a smooth sphere mounted on a force-measuring system in the wind tunnel. The higher the intensity of turbulence, the lower was this critical Reynolds number. This was surely an ingenious device. Recent developments in hot-wire anemometry have made possible more detailed studies of turbulence fluctuations and intensities.

Wave drag. When a boat or ship travels on the surface of water, bow and stern waves are generated. Energy is required to generate these waves, and this energy originates from the propulsion system of the boat or ship. The propulsion system, then, supplies the energy or force to overcome the skin-friction drag (plus that of the miscellaneous appurtenances such as rudder and propeller shaft support struts) and to set up these surface waves. That portion of the total drag attributed to wave generation is called the *wave drag.* Wave drag also exists for seaplane hulls, and for submarines and hydrofoils submerged but at a depth shallow enough for surface waves to form.

Wave drag is not measured directly, but it is taken as the residual drag remaining after all drag which can be calculated or estimated is subtracted from the total measured drag. There are, of course, sources of uncertainty in these estimates.

EXAMPLE 11–4. A 15-ft smooth model of an ocean vessel is towed in fresh water at 5.5 knots (9.3 ft/sec) with a total measured drag of 17 lb$_f$. The wetted surface of the hull is 38 ft^2. Estimate the wave drag, considering skin friction to be the only other drag force.

Solution: The wave drag is

$$\text{Drag}_{\text{wave}} = \text{Drag}_{\text{total}} - \text{Drag}_{\text{friction}} = 17 - 9.25 = 7.75 \text{ lb}_f$$

since $\text{Drag}_{\text{friction}}$ was 9.25 lb$_f$ in Example 11–1.

In supersonic gas flows, the drag of airfoils is influenced by Mach waves (shock patterns), and this type of drag is also called wave drag.

Drag may be measured directly on a model or determined from velocity and pressure measurements in the wake with the application of the momentum equation.

One of the most complete compilations of drag coefficient data is that by Hoerner [5]. An interesting discussion of drag is contained in a short paperback *Shape and Drag* by Shapiro [6].

11–3. LIFT

The phenomenon of lift produced in an ideal (nonviscous) fluid by the addition of a free vortex (circulation) around a cylinder in a rectilinear flow stream described in Sec. 6–3 is known as the Magnus effect. It was mentioned by Newton in 1672 and was investigated experimentally by Magnus in 1853. In a real (viscous) fluid, this effect may be produced by a ping-pong ball, for example, by making it spin as it travels through the air. Because the relative velocity between the air and the ball is zero at the surface of the ball, the spin of the ball produces a circulation approximating a free vortex outside the boundary layer. A top spin produces a downward force, and a bottom spin an upward force. Spin about a vertical axis produces a sideward force, known as a "hook" or "slice" in golf, for example. In the case of both the ideal fluid and the real fluid, a circulation is necessary for the production of a lift force. Figure 11–6 illustrates the effect of bottom spin on a ping-pong ball.

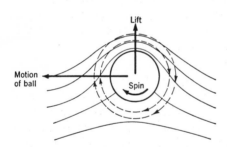

FIG. 11–6. Effect of bottom spin on a ball moving in a viscous fluid.

Lift is expressed as the product of a lift coefficient, the dynamic pressure of the free stream, and the chord area of the lifting vane. The lift coefficient was found in Chapter 8 to depend on a number of parameters, including the shape and angle of attack of the vane, Reynolds number, Mach number, Froude number for shallow hydrofoils, and aspect ratio.

The lift force is generally defined by the equation

$$\text{Lift} = C_L \left(\frac{\rho u_s^2}{2} \right) A \tag{11–8}$$

where C_L = lift coefficient;

$\rho \dfrac{u_s^2}{2}$ = dynamic pressure of the free stream;

A = chord area of the lifting vane.

Lifting vanes are shapes which produce lift, and include such things as kites, airfoils, hydrofoils, and propeller blades. Because all lifting vanes are fundamentally the same, it is sufficiently informative to study the behavior of an airfoil.

It was shown in Sec. 6–3 that the lift on a circular cylinder in a nonviscous fluid of density ρ, with a free-stream velocity u_s, and with a circulation of strength Γ was

$$\text{Lift} = \rho u_s \, \Gamma \qquad\qquad [6\text{--}21]$$

per unit length of cylinder.

The Kutta (1902)-Joukowski (1905) theorem extends this result to include any shape under the same flow conditions. The problem here is to determine the circulation for a given situation or shape of lifting vane. Qualitatively, this may be stated with reference to Fig. 11–7, which shows the flow lines past an airfoil at a given angle of attack α, with and without circulation. The circulation required to swing the trailing stagnation streamline A tangent to the trailing edge of the airfoil is the desired quantity. The addition of circulation results in a higher velocity and lower pressure over the upper surface and a lower velocity and higher pressure over the lower surface of the airfoil. The result is a lift force upwards.

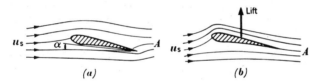

(a)   *(b)*

Fig. 11–7. Ideal fluid flow past an airfoil. *a)* Without circulation. No lift or drag. *b)* With circulation. Lift but no drag. Circulation added to flow pattern in *(a)* to produce flow pattern in *(b)*.

Joukowski discovered a mathematical method for transforming circles into airfoil shapes and was thus able to transform the streamline pattern around a circular cylinder into the streamline pattern around the airfoils. This method enabled him to calculate the theoretical lift for these "transformed" airfoils. Von Karman and von Mises improved Joukowski's mathematical models so that shapes more closely resembling actual wing sections were obtained. Joukowski's theory indicated that the lift coefficient for an airfoil in an ideal fluid when the airfoil thickness and camber approach zero (becoming a flat plate) is

$$C_L = 2\pi \sin \alpha_0 = 2\pi\alpha_0 \qquad\qquad (11\text{--}9)$$

for small angles of attack. The angle α_0 is the difference between the actual angle of attack and the angle of attack for which the lift is zero. For a flat

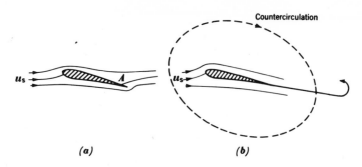

FIG. 11–8. Starting vortex a) at beginning of motion
and b) after establishment of vortex.

plate and symmetrical airfoils without camber (curvature), α_0 is the same
as α, since the lift is zero for zero angle of attack. Equation 11–9 states
that the slope of a line relating C_L (ordinate) to α_0 (abscissa) is 2π, and this
is very closely approximated in practice for thin airfoils at small values
of α (stall conditions must be avoided).

Thus ideal fluid theory predicts actual lift performance amazingly
well but gives zero drag in all instances in an infinite fluid.

The theory of lift in a real (viscous) fluid is largely credited to
Lanchester (in about 1907) and its improvement to Prandtl later on. An
airfoil in a real fluid must create its own circulation, or vortex field, just as
the spinning ping-pong ball, in order to experience lift. The starting
vortex is indicated in Fig. 11–8. As the motion begins, it is very slow and
approaches that of irrotational flow in an ideal fluid. The fluid particles
passing around the trailing edge must move very rapidly and must approach
a stagnation condition at A. But because of the viscosity of the fluid, they
have less velocity than if the fluid were ideal, and the fluid separates from
the trailing edge of the airfoil in the form of a vortex [Fig. 11–8(b)]. As
this vortex passes from the airfoil, an opposing reaction starts a countercirculation opposite in direction to that of the trailing vortex. It is this
induced countercirculation which produces the lift.

For a finite lifting vane (the preceding discussion applies to a vane of
infinite span), additional explanations are necessary, since a vortex cannot
terminate within the fluid. The lift of a finite wing is zero at its tips, and
thus the circulation would appear to be zero there also, so that the vortex
system cannot extend out to infinity. A closed vortex loop is necessary, and
this loop consists of tip vortices which trail behind the airfoil tips back to
the starting vortex. This condition is shown schematically in Fig. 11–9.
The starting vortex degenerates to zero with time because of viscous
dissipation, and the vortex pattern is thus more horseshoe-shaped than
rectangular or toroidal.

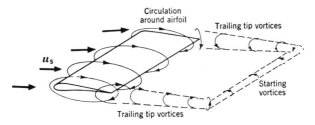

Fig. 11–9. Closed-loop vortex pattern for finite wing.

The tip vortices have low-pressure cores, and for ship propellers, they may be photographed or seen as threadlike cavities in the shape of helixes peeling off the blade tips. Under certain conditions they may be observed as vapor trails behind aircraft flying at high altitudes. Air within the vortex core expands and cools, and vapors may condense out to become visible.

Induced drag. For an airfoil of finite span, the tip vortices produce a downwash, which is a motion normal to that of the approaching stream. The resulting flow vector is inclined from that representing the motion of the airfoil in the fluid (see Fig. 11–10). Thus the true drag and lift are also inclined from the direction of motion. The component of the force L' in the direction of the vector u_s is called the *induced* drag. The greater the aspect ratio (span/chord) the less the induced drag. For testing purposes, the induced drag may be essentially eliminated by the use of end plates on a finite foil. Work must be expended to produce the trailing tip vortices and this is at the expense of drag on the foil, much in the same manner as wave drag for a surface ship.

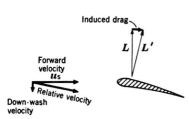

Fig. 11–10. Downwash (for an airfoil of finite span) which produces induced drag.

Common methods of plotting experimental lift-drag data include graphs of C_L and C_D vs. α and polar diagrams. Typical data so plotted are shown in Fig. 11–11. One of the most desirable characteristics of an airfoil is a high lift-drag ratio, and the corresponding angle of attack for the maximum value of this ratio is easily obtained by determining the point of tangency for a line passing through the origin. This is point A in Fig. 11–11(b). Also, the drag at zero lift is the profile drag, and thus the additional drag at finite lift is the induced drag. At $\alpha = 8$ deg, for example, the induced drag is as indicated in Fig. 11–11(b). In Fig. 11–11(c), the slope of the polar diagram and the stall angle are seen to increase slightly with the Reynolds number. Figure 11–11(d) shows the effect of changes in aspect ratio of the airfoil.

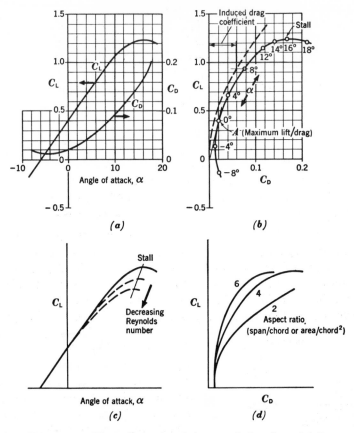

FIG. 11–11. Three-dimensional characteristics of an airfoil of finite length. *a*) Typical lift and drag coefficients for an airfoil. *b*) Typical polar diagram. *c*) Effect of Reynolds number on lift coefficient and stall angle. *d*) Effect of aspect ratio.

Propeller blades. A propeller is a lifting vane for which both lift and drag on a blade element contribute towards thrust and torque. A blade element of a typical ship propeller is shown in Fig. 11–12. If the forward motion of the propeller in still water is u_s, the water approaches the blade element parallel to the shaft at this velocity. If the peripheral speed of the propeller is $u_t = \omega r$, the water approaches the blade at a tangential velocity u_t, the resulting relative motion being represented by the vector u_R. The angle of attack is α, and the blade angle at the particular radius shown is β. The resulting lift and drag forces on the blade element are as shown in Fig. 11–12. The thrust, parallel to the shaft for a blade element of length Δr is

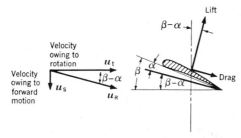

FIG. 11–12. Section of propeller blade
at radius r.

$$\text{Thrust} = \text{Lift cos } (\beta - \alpha) - \text{Drag sin } (\beta - \alpha) \qquad (11\text{--}10)$$

and the torque is

$$\text{Torque} = [\text{Lift sin } (\beta - \alpha) + \text{Drag cos } (\beta - \alpha)]\, r \qquad (11\text{--}11)$$

These equations indicate that both thrust and torque are influenced by both lift and drag. The total thrust and torque, of course, is due to that of all blade elements for all blades comprising the entire propeller.

There is an optimum angle of attack for the particular foil section which makes up the propeller blade. At a given value of u_s, u_t will vary linearly with the radial distance to a blade element, and thus $\beta - \alpha$ will vary. If α is to be constant, the blade angle β must vary, and this accounts for the twist in propeller blades.

If the driving motor or engine runs best at a given fixed speed, then u_t is fixed for each blade element, and variations in forward speed will vary u_s and hence the angle $\beta - \alpha$. In order to keep α constant, the blade angle β should be controlled as a function of forward speed u_s. Thus controllable-pitch propellers for airplanes, propeller pumps, and propeller turbines are often used.

Measurement of lift. Lift of airfoils may be calculated or they may be measured directly in a wind tunnel or under noncavitating conditions in a water tunnel or towing basin. For two-dimensional flow, measurements in a tunnel may be made indirectly by an integration of pressures measured over the walls of the tunnel test section or, in general, by an integration of the pressures over the airfoil section.

The algebraic difference between the predominantly negative pressures on the top surface of the foil and the predominantly positive pressures on the bottom surface will result in a net force normal to the chord of the airfoil. As a first approximation, the component of this force normal to the approaching free stream is the net lift on the airfoil.

If p_x is the surface pressure at a distance x from the leading edge of an

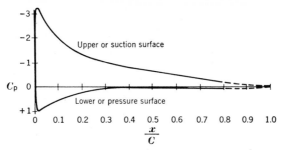

FIG. 11–13. Dimensionless plot of measured distribution over an NACA 0015 airfoil at 8-deg angle of attack. $\mathrm{Re}_x \approx 6 \times 10^4$.

airfoil of chord length C, p_s is the free-stream pressure, ρ is the free-stream density, and u_s is the free-stream velocity of approach, then the surface pressures may be expressed as a dimensionless pressure coefficient

$$C_p = \frac{p_x - p_s}{\rho u_s^2/2} = 1 - \left(\frac{u_x}{u_s}\right)^2 \qquad (11\text{–}12)$$

A typical dimensionless plot of measurements made on an NACA 0015 airfoil (symmetrical foil with maximum thickness 15 per cent of the chord length) in a small wind tunnel is shown in Fig. 11–13. The average height of the area between curves, expressed dimensionlessly in the same manner as C_p, is called the normal force coefficient C_N. In terms of the angle of attack α, the lift coefficient is

$$C_L = C_N \cos \alpha - C_C \sin \alpha \qquad (11\text{–}13)$$

where C_C is the chordwise force coefficient normal to C_N. Since $C_C \sin \alpha$ is usually very small compared to $C_N \cos \alpha$,

$$C_L \approx C_N \cos \alpha \qquad (11\text{–}14)$$

The average height of the area between the pressure curves for the top and bottom surfaces of the airfoil represents C_N and is found as follows:

$$C_N = \frac{\text{area between curves}}{\text{length equivalent to } x/C = 1.0 \times \text{length equivalent to } C_p = 1.0}$$

where the area and lengths are expressed in terms of the same linear unit.

A determination of C_L at an angle of attack of 8 deg from pressure measurements gave $C_L = 0.85$, as compared to 0.87 from Eq. 11–9 ($C_L = 2\pi \sin \alpha$). The theoretical value is 0.88. Thus calculations from ideal fluid theory agree well with measured values of lift.

According to the Bernoulli equation, the maximum rise in pressure from the free-stream value p_s is the dynamic pressure. Thus at a stagnation point on an airfoil, the maximum value of $p_x - p_s$ is $\rho u_s^2/2$, and the maximum value of the pressure coefficient C_p in Eq. 11–12 is unity. This is shown in Fig. 11–13.

The low pressures indicated in Fig. 11–13 for the upper, or suction, surface provide most of the lift for this particular foil. Associated with these low pressures are high velocities, so that at high subsonic free-stream velocities, local velocities along the foil surface may become supersonic and shocks may affect the flow. For hydrofoils, the low pressures may cause cavitation, which is undesirable for the profile represented by Fig. 11–13.

The theory of lift and an extensive presentation of the characteristics of subsonic airfoils is given by Abbott and von Doenhoff [7]. Authentic, nontechnical books on drag and lift applied to aerodynamics have been written by Sutton [8] and von Karman [9].

11–4. SIMILARITY CONSIDERATIONS

The principles of dynamic similarity discussed in Chapter 8 imply that all pertinent dimensionless groups obtained in a dimensional analysis should be the same for a model and its prototype or for any two or more dynamically similar flow situations. Thus,

$$C_L \text{ or } C_D = f(\text{Re, M, Fr, We, } k/L, \sigma, \text{ shape, free-stream turbulence level})$$
$$(11\text{–}15)$$

where Re, M, Fr, and We are the Reynolds, Mach, Froude, and Weber numbers and apply when viscous, compressibility, gravity, or surface tension forces, respectively, affect the flow, k/L is the relative roughness based on some characteristic length L, and σ is the cavitation number (see Sec. 8–3). Then, as a first approximation, the lift or drag coefficients for two situations may be said to be the same if the other parameters are the same. For example, the drag of a smooth sphere in an incompressible fluid of large extent in the absence of cavitation is such that

$$C_D = f(\text{Re})$$

and the drag coefficient for any sphere in any fluid at a given Reynolds number is fixed, and is the same for any other sphere in any other fluid at that same Reynolds number. This statement is true if the turbulence level, or intensity, in the free stream in both instances is the same. Differences show up at a Reynolds number of about 300,000, as described in Sec. 11–2. Thus the flow about a sphere falling in a fluid at rest may *not* be the same as for the sphere at rest in a fluid flowing past at the same relative velocity. Boundary layer transition and separation affect both drag and lift for many body shapes, and drag and lift may not be the same in two flow situations unless *all* parameters in Eq. 11–15 are the same. Honeycombs are often added upstream of test sections in water and wind tunnels to reduce the turbulence intensity and scale.

The proper cavitating pressure for liquids to be used in determining the cavitation number (Sec. 8–3) is not well established except for steady cavities. Hence, model tests conducted at the same cavitation number as for the prototype do not necessarily result in similarity of flow. For steady cavities, similarity is better than for incipient cavitation.

It should be emphasized that any effect which does not affect the flow in one system should have no effect in a dynamically similar system. For example, airfoils tested in water at a given Reynolds number must not cavitate if correlation with performance in air is to be made; model torpedoes in a wind tunnel at a given Reynolds number must not be tested at velocities high enough so that Mach number effects are present.

EXAMPLE 11–5. The drag of a 3-ft model of a 21-ft torpedo is measured in a wind tunnel at 59 F and 4 atmospheres pressure. The prototype speed is 20 knots (34.8 ft/sec). Estimate the model speed.

Solution: Assume $\mathrm{Re}_m = \mathrm{Re}_p$ so that

$$\frac{V_m L_m \rho_m}{\mu_m} = \frac{V_p L_p}{\nu_p}$$

and

$$V_m = V_p \left(\frac{L_p}{L_m}\right) \left(\frac{\mu_m/\rho_m}{\nu_p}\right)$$

$$= 34.8 \left(\frac{21}{3}\right) \left(\frac{0.0373 \times 10^{-5}/0.00952}{1.21 \times 10^{-5}}\right)$$

$$= 789 \text{ ft/sec}$$

This corresponds to a Mach number of $M = 789/1116 = 0.71$, and thus compressibility effects would exist for the model, and the flow would *not* be dynamically similar.

Suppose a ship is to be tested by means of a model. Both viscous and gravity forces (skin-friction and wave drag) are to be included. If both the Reynolds number and the Froude number are the same for model and prototype, equating velocity ratios (Table 8–2) indicates that

$$\frac{\nu_m}{\nu_p} = \left(\frac{L_m}{L_p}\right)^{\frac{3}{2}}$$

Unless the model is essentially the same size as the prototype, no liquid satisfying this ratio for model tests is available. If water is used, the model would be nearly the same size as the prototype. In practice, the model test is based on the Froude number, and skin-friction drag is calculated for both the model and prototype, as described in Sec. 8–5.

EXAMPLE 11–6. Estimate the prototype wave drag and skin-friction drag in sea water ($\rho = 1.99$ slugs/ft^3) for the tests of Examples 11–1 and 11–4 for a prototype ship length of 300 ft.

Solution: The wave-drag coefficient is the same for both $(C_{w_m} = C_{w_p})$, and from Table 8–2 for the Froude law, $V_p = V_m (L_p/L_m)^{1/2} = (9.3)(4.46) = 41.6$ ft/sec. Equating wave-drag coefficients yields

$$\left[\frac{\text{Drag}_w}{\rho(V^2/2)A}\right]_m = \left[\frac{\text{Drag}_w}{\rho(V^2/2)A}\right]_p$$

so that
$$\text{Drag}_{w_p} = \text{Drag}_{w_m} \left(\frac{\rho_p}{\rho_m}\right)\left(\frac{V_p^2}{V_m^2}\right)\left(\frac{A_p}{A_m}\right)$$

$$= 7.75 \left(\frac{1.99}{1.94}\right)(20)(20^2)$$

$$= 63,500 \text{ lb}_f$$

The skin-friction drag for the prototype ship at 41.6 ft/sec (24.5 knots) is

$$\text{Drag}_s = C_f \left(\frac{\rho V^2}{2}\right)A$$

where $\text{Re}_x = VL/\nu = (41.6)(300)/1.21 \times 10^{-5} = 1.03 \times 10^9$, and from Fig. 11–1, $C_f = 0.00195$. Thus the drag is

$$\text{Drag}_s = (0.00195)(1.99)(41.6^2/2)\,[(38)(20^2)]$$
$$= 51,100 \text{ lb}_f$$

The total prototype drag is 114,600 lb$_f$ as compared to 17 lb$_f$ for the model.

Lift forces for models and prototypes are determined by equating lift coefficients for dynamically similar flow, at the same Reynolds number for low velocities in a gas or for noncavitating liquid flows, or at the same Mach number for high subsonic gas velocities as well as supersonic gas velocities. Thus, if lift measurements are made on a model airfoil,

$$C_{L_m} = C_{L_p} = \frac{\text{Lift}_m}{\rho_m(V^2/2)_m A_m} = \frac{\text{Lift}_p}{\rho_p(V^2/2)_p A_p}$$

REFERENCES

1. Harold E. Saunders, Captain, U. S. Navy (retired), *Hydrodynamics in Ship Design*, Vol. 2. (New York: The Society of Naval Architects and Marine Engineers, 1957), p. 100, used with permission of the publishers.

2. K. M. S. Davidson, "Resistance and Powering," Chapter 11 of *Principles of Naval Architecture*, edited by H. E. Rossell and L. B. Chapman (New York: The Society of Naval Architects and Marine Engineers, 1941).

3. H. Lamb, *Hydrodynamics* (London: Cambridge University Press, 1932), pp. 614–616.

4. J. M. Robertson, *Hydrodynamics in Theory and Application* (Englewood Cliffs: Prentice-Hall, Inc., 1965), p. 628.

5. S. F. Hoerner, *Fluid-Dynamic Drag* (Midland Park, N. J.: S. F. Hoerner, 1958).

6. A. H. Shapiro, *Shape and Flow* (New York: Doubleday and Company, Inc., Anchor Books, 1961).

7. I. H. Abbott and A. E. von Doenhoff, *Theory of Wing Sections* (New York: McGraw-Hill Book Company, Inc., 1949).

8. O. G. Sutton, *The Science of Flight* (Baltimore: Penguin Books, Inc., 1955).

9. T. von Karman, *Aerodynamics* (Ithaca: Cornell University Press, 1954).

PROBLEMS

11-1. A 2 x 8-ft smooth flat plate is towed deep in fresh water at 60 F and at 10 ft/sec. The wave drag is negligible for deep towing. Calculate the drag force *a)* when the plate is normal to the direction of motion, *b)* when the plane of the plate and the 2-ft side are parallel to the direction of motion, and *c)* when the plane of the plate and the 8-ft side are parallel to the direction of motion. Assume boundary-layer transition occurs at $Re_x = 5 \times 10^5$ for parts *b)* and *c)*. Neglect edge effects.

                                            Ans.   *a)* 1860 lb$_f$, *b)* 9.3 lb$_f$

11-2. Repeat Prob. 11-1 *b)* and *c)* for a completely turbulent boundary layer, neglecting edge effects as before.

11-3. A target consisting of a hollow cylinder 10 ft in diameter and 40 ft long is towed by an airplane at 180 mph in standard air. What horsepower is required to overcome skin-friction drag, assuming flat-plate theory applies to the boundary layer growth on both the inside and the outside surface of the hollow cylinder?

                                                Ans.   220 hp

11-4. A submarine 300 ft long has a surface area of 19,500 ft² and travels at 10 knots (16.9 ft/sec) submerged in sea water at 50 F. What is the skin-friction drag, assuming it to be equivalent to that of a flat plate of the same length and area? Assume the roughness to be that of a typical ship hull.

11-5. An airship 200 ft long has a surface area of 15,000 ft² and travels at 60 mph in standard air. What is the power required to overcome skin-friction drag, assuming the drag to be equivalent to the drag on a smooth flat plate of the same length and area?

                                                Ans.   46.5 hp

11-6. A ship 160 ft long has a wetted hull area of 3200 ft². A smooth ⅟₁₆-scale model is made and towed at 4 ft/sec in fresh water at 60 F. *a)* What is the skin-friction drag on the model? *b)* The model test is based on the Froude number. What is the skin-friction drag on the prototype ship in sea water at 60 F at a speed corresponding to the speed of the model?

11-7. What is the total wind force on a 20 × 80-ft billboard when standard air at 60 mph blows normal to it?

                                                Ans.   17,400 lb$_f$

11-8. Compare the drag force on a 10 x 50-ft billboard at ground level with the drag force on the same billboard mounted high in the air if a high wind is blowing normal to the plane of the billboard.

11-9. Repeat Prob. 11-8 for a 10 x 100-ft billboard.

11-10. The drag coefficient for a finite plate or cylinder normal to a fluid stream is less than the drag coefficient for an infinite plate or cylinder. Explain the reason for this, based on the pressure distributions in Figs. 11-2(b) and 13-6(a), respectively.

11-11. Show that the drag force on a circular billboard is essentially the same as on a square billboard of equal area in a given high wind normal to the plane of the billboards.

11-12. a) What is the terminal velocity of a 200-lb$_f$ man-and-parachute combination in standard air for a parachute 14 ft in diameter having a drag coefficient of $C_D = 1.1$? b) From what height would a man have to jump to attain this same velocity in free flight (neglect air resistance)?

Ans. a) 31.5 ft/sec

11-13. The drag coefficient of a parachute is $C_D = 1.33$. How large a parachute would be required to limit the terminal velocity of a 240-lb$_f$ man-and-parachute combination to a value no greater than the free-fall velocity from a 9-ft height?

11-14. Show that the terminal velocity of a sphere in laminar motion (Stokes' law is considered applicable) falling in a fluid of large extent is

$$u_s = \frac{gd^2(\rho_s - \rho_f)}{18\mu}$$

where g is the gravitational acceleration, d is the sphere diameter, ρ_s and ρ_f are the densities of the sphere and fluid, respectively, and μ is the fluid viscosity. Describe how you could use this equation to determine the viscosity of a fluid.

11-15. A $\frac{1}{16}$-in. diameter aluminum sphere ($\rho = 5.45$ slugs/ft³) falls steadily at a velocity of 0.01 ft/sec in an oil with a density of 1.75 slugs/ft³. Determine the dynamic viscosity of the oil. Assume the oil is of large extent and that the flow is laminar, then verify the laminar-flow assumption.

11-16. During a heavy rain, silt-laden water flows into a large reservoir with a maximum depth of 20 ft. Assume the finest particles have a diameter of 0.00036 in. and a specific gravity of 2.65. Estimate the time required for all the silt to settle to the bottom of the reservoir (water viscosity is 2×10^{-5} slug/ft sec).

Ans. 21.5 hr

11-17. A sphere of aluminum ($s = 2.81$) and a sphere of magnesium ($s = 1.82$) fall freely in water. What should be the ratio of their diameters in order that steady-fluid motion around each should be dynamically similar?

11-18. A $\frac{1}{16}$-in. steel sphere ($\rho = 15.15$ slugs/ft³) falls steadily through a vertical distance of 3 ft in 83.5 sec in an oil with a density of 1.88 slugs/ft³. The oil is contained in a vertical cylinder 3.75 in. in diameter. What is the dynamic viscosity of the oil? Verify any assumptions made.

Ans. $\mu = 0.0172$ slug/ft sec

11-19. A $\frac{1}{64}$-in. smooth aluminum sphere ($\rho = 5.45$ slugs/ft³) falls steadily through a vertical tube 3.75 in. in diameter at a velocity of 0.020 ft/sec. The tube contains an oil with a density of 1.64 slugs/ft³. What is the dynamic viscosity of the oil? Verify any assumptions made.

11–20. When determining the dynamic viscosity of a fluid by measuring the terminal velocity u_s of a sphere falling through the fluid, the Reynolds number may be above that for which Stokes' law is valid. When $0.1 < \text{Re} < 100$, show that if Eq. 11–5 is used for the drag coefficient, the viscosity may be found from the equation

$$\mu^2 + \left(\frac{3}{16} u_s D\rho\right)\mu - \mu_1^2 = 0$$

where μ_1 is the viscosity if Stokes' law were valid (Eq. 11–6).

11–21. A ⅛-in. smooth steel sphere ($\rho = 15.15$ slugs/ft³) falls steadily at a velocity of 1.20 ft/sec in a large container of oil with a density of 1.65 slugs/ft³. Find the viscosity of the oil under the following conditions: *a)* Assume laminar flow so that Stokes' law applies. *b)* Assume the Reynolds number is too large for Stokes' law to be valid. Refer to Prob. 11–20.

11–22. Show that for a sphere falling steadily in a fluid

$$C_D u_s^2 = \frac{4Dg}{3}\left(\frac{\rho_s}{\rho_f} - 1\right)$$

The terminal velocity of falling spheres may be obtained from this equation for $\text{Re} > 0.1$ by trial (assume u_s, calculate Re, obtain C_D, compute $C_D u_s^2$ and compare with required value).

11–23. Assume hailstones are smooth spheres with $s = 0.75$. What is the terminal velocity of hailstones in standard air for diameters of *a)* 0.1 in., *b)* 0.5 in., and *c)* 1.0 in.? Make a statement regarding the terminal velocity of hailstones as a function of diameter for the range of Reynolds numbers involved.

11–24. A smooth 1-in. diameter sphere of specific gravity 7.91 falls through castor oil ($s = 0.97$, $\mu = 0.01$ slug/ft sec). What is the terminal velocity of the sphere?

11–25. What is the settling velocity of a 0.007-in. diameter sand sphere ($s = 2.65$) in stagnant water at 70 F? Note: If Stokes' law is assumed, it will be seen that $\text{Re} > 0.1$ and Eq. 11–5 should be used for C_D.

11–26. What is the terminal velocity of a billiard ball (2.375 in. in diameter, 7-oz. weight) in water at 50 F?

11–27. Determine the size of a spherical water droplet which can be suspended in standard air with an upward air current of 1.0 ft/sec.

11–28. A rubber balloon weighing 0.008 lb_f is filled with helium and becomes a sphere of 1.24-ft diameter. It is held by a string in a horizontal wind blowing at 10 ft/sec. The air and helium are both at 75 F, the air pressure is 14.7 psia, and the helium pressure is 15.0 psia. *a)* What is the drag force on the balloon? *b)* What angle does the string make with the vertical at the balloon? *c)* What is the aerodynamic lift coefficient?

Ans. *a)* 0.059 lb_f, *b)* 46.6 deg, and *c)* $C_L = 0$

11–29. Design a sphere for measuring the speed of offshore tidal currents 2 ft from the bottom of the sea by making use of the drag of a sphere. For example, assume the sphere to be mounted on a vertical rod and the bending moment measured with strain gages. Use the largest smooth or rough sphere practicable for water at 50 F flowing at velocities from 1 to 5 ft/sec.

11–30. The drag of a golf ball in flight is less than the drag for a smooth sphere of the same size because the golf ball is rough. Is there any advantage in roughening the surface of a spherical water supply tank supported 120 ft above the ground in order to reduce the bending moment on the support column in a high wind? Explain.

11–31. Explain why the drag of a rough sphere or cylinder is less than the drag of a smooth sphere or cylinder at Reynolds numbers near 200,000.

11–32. Explain why the drag of a cylinder in a fluid stream normal to its axis and at high Reynolds numbers may be reduced by the addition of a tapered afterbody, forming a short strut.

11–33. A streamlined body falls at a steady velocity in the atmosphere and has a laminar boundary layer over most of its length. Because of an external disturbance, the boundary layer suddenly becomes predominantly turbulent. Will the velocity of fall increase, remain the same, or decrease? Explain.

11–34. Explain how the drag on a 1-ft diameter, 50-ft tall exhaust stack could be the same in a 20-mph crosswind as in a 28-mph crosswind.

11–35. What is the maximum bending moment on a 14-in. diameter cylindrical piling in 40 ft of sea water in an average tidal current of 5 knots (1 knot = 1.69 ft/sec)?

11–36. What horsepower is required to overcome the drag on a ⅜-in. diameter radio aerial 4 ft long on an automobile traveling at 60 mph in standard air?

11–37. Draw a sketch illustrating the effect of top spin on a ping-pong ball moving through air.

11–38. The angle of attack at zero lift for a lifting vane is −3 deg. The vane is placed in a standard air stream at 90 mph at an angle of attack of +4 deg. The chord length is 1.5 ft. What is the theoretical lift coefficient and the lift per foot of span?

$$Ans. \quad C_L = 0.766$$

11–39. A lifting vane with a 3-ft chord has a circulation of 300 ft²/sec in standard air at a free-stream velocity of 100 ft/sec. What is a) the theoretical lift per foot of span, b) the theoretical lift coefficient, and c) the angle of attack measured from the angle of zero lift?

11–40. An airfoil with an area of 0.8 ft² is tested in a pressurized wind tunnel ($p = 5$ atmospheres and $T = 80$ F) at a free-stream velocity of 220 ft/sec. The measured lift is 210 lb$_f$ and the measured drag is 9.5 lb$_f$. a) What is the lift coefficient C_L? b) What is the drag coefficient C_D?

11–41. An airplane has a wing loading of 15 lb_f/ft^2. The wing characteristics are shown in Fig. 11–11(a) and 11–11(b). What is the necessary air speed for level flight in standard air for an angle of attack of 4 deg?

$Ans.$ 137 ft/sec

11–42. A small aircraft with a wing loading of 12 lb_f/ft^2 flies at 100 mph in standard air. The airfoil characteristics are shown in Fig. 11–11(a) and 11–11(b). At what angle of attack should the wing be designed to fly?

11–43. A small aircraft weighs 1800 lb_f and has wings of 100 ft^2 total area with characteristics shown in Fig. 11–11(a) and 11–11(b). What is the air speed for level flight in standard air if the wings are designed for a maximum lift-drag ratio?

11–44. Show that the drag on a given aircraft for level flight is independent of the altitude at which level flight occurs.

11–45. Compare the horsepower required to maintain level flight for a given aircraft at 10,000 ft ($\rho = 0.001756$ slug/ft³) with the horsepower required to maintain level flight at 5000 ft ($\rho = 0.002049$ slug/ft³). Make a qualitative statement regarding the horsepower requirements for maintaining level flight of a given airplane as a function of altitude.

$Ans.$ $hp_{10,000}/hp_{5000} = 1.08$

11–46. Show that the power required to propel a given airfoil supporting a given load is proportional to $C_D/C_L^{3/2}$ and is therefore independent of speed.

11–47. For the airfoil whose characteristics are shown in Fig. 11–11(a) and 11–11(b), plot $C_L^{3/2}/C_D$ and C_L/C_D as ordinates and the angle of attack α as abscissa. a) At what angle of attack is the power required for propulsion a minimum? Refer to Prob. 11–46. b) Show that the power required at the angle of attack for maximum lift-drag ratio is greater than the power required at the angle of attack which gives minimum power.

11–48. The NACA 23012 airfoil has the following characteristics (from NACA Report 669):

α	-4	0	$+4$	$+8$	$+12$
C_L	-0.281	$+0.122$	$+0.523$	$+0.919$	$+1.32$
C_D	0.0075	0.0061	0.0074	0.0101	0.0164

α	$+16$	$+17$	$+18$	$+20$
C_L	$+1.67$	$+1.74$	$+1.30$	$+1.21$
C_D	0.0317	0.0403	0.153	0.201

a) Plot C_L, 10 C_D, and L/D as ordinates and α as abscissa. b) What is the stall angle? c) What is the maximum value of L/D, and at what angle of attack does it occur? d) Plot the polar diagram for this airfoil.

11–49. The NACA 2412 airfoil has the following measured characteristics at $Re = 3 \times 10^6$ (from NACA Technical Note 404):

α	c_L	c_D	α	c_L	c_D
−3.4	−0.178	0.0096	11.8	1.328	0.0201
−1.7	−0.026	0.0092	13.4	1.457	0.0261
−0.4	+0.133	0.0090	15.0	1.566	0.0352
+1.1	0.288	0.0090	15.8	1.589	0.0422
2.6	0.439	0.0095	19.8	1.307	0.2269
5.6	0.744	0.0110	26.8	1.003	0.4189
8.7	1.049	0.0143			

a) Plot c_L, 10 c_D, and L/D as ordinates and α as the abscissa. *b*) What is the stall angle? *c*) What is the maximum value of L/D, and at what angle of attack does it occur? *d*) Plot the polar diagram for this airfoil.

Ans. *b*) 15.8 deg, *c*) 73.4 at 8.7 deg.

11–50. Measured pressure coefficients on an NACA 4412 airfoil at an 8-deg angle of attack are as follows (from NACA Report 563):

$100\frac{x}{C}$	C_p		$100\frac{x}{C}$	C_p	
	Lower Surface	Upper Surface		Lower Surface	Upper Surface
100	0.134		20.0	0.321	−1.239
98.0	0.167	+0.120	14.9	0.345	−1.308
94.9	0.180	+0.079	10.0	0.402	−1.391
89.9	0.203	−0.009	4.9	0.568	−1.547
74.9	0.231	−0.285	2.9	0.748	−1.647
64.9	0.244	−0.456	1.7	0.916	−1.743
50.0	0.252	−0.690	0.9	1.013	−1.793
40.0	0.265	−0.880	0.4	0.905	−1.740
29.9	0.293	−1.071	0.0	0.157	−1.000

a) What is the measured lift coefficient according to Eq. 11–14? *b*) What is the measured lift coefficient according to Eq. 11–13? From the given data, $C_C = -0.100$.

11–51. What is the maximum speed of an NACA 0015 hydrofoil at an angle of attack of 8 deg (Fig. 11–13) in fresh water at 60 F and at a 4.6-ft submergence in order that cavitation be avoided? Assume cavitation begins when the minimum pressure on the surface of the hydrofoil equals the vapor pressure of the water. Barometric pressure is 14.6 psia.

11–52. A 20-ft smooth wax model of a cargo ship is towed in fresh water at 66 F. The total drag force at a velocity of 4.56 ft/sec is measured to be 5.95 lb_f. The wetted surface of the model hull is 77.5 ft². *a*) What is the skin-friction drag of this model? *b*) What is the residual wave drag for this model? The model tests

are conducted according to the Froude law, and the power output of the propellers
driving a similar cargo ship 400 ft long in sea water at 59 F is to be determined.
c) What is the skin-friction drag for the prototype ship? d) What is the wave drag
for the prototype ship? e) What is the required power output of the prototype
propellers?

$Ans.$ a) 4.77 lb$_f$, e) 1320 hp

11–53. Define a) skin-friction drag, b) pressure drag, c) profile drag, d) induced
drag, and e) wave drag.

12

Open-Channel Flow

Flow in an open channel involves the flow of a liquid (water, in most instances of engineering interest) in which the cross-sectional flow area may change in the direction of flow and for which the surface is always at atmospheric pressure. The forces causing flow are due to gravity, and the forces retarding flow are due to viscous shear along the channel bed. Thus both the Froude number and the Reynolds number are involved. Flow in rivers, flumes, culverts not full, canals, and irrigation systems are examples of flow in open channels. We will consider steady flow in prismatic channels, in channels made up of successive prismatic channels, and in Sec. 12–7, flow in channel transitions. A prismatic channel has a constant cross section and constant bed slope though the flow cross section may vary in the direction of flow because of changes in depth. Similarities exist between flow in open channels and gas flow in pipes and nozzles, and these similarities are discussed in Chapter 15.

12–1. BASIC CONSIDERATIONS

For steady uniform flow (no fluid acceleration), the gravity and viscous forces are in equilibrium for any elemental length of channel (Fig. 12–1).

The momentum theorem applied in a direction parallel to the bed may be expressed as

$$(\gamma A \ dx) \sin \theta - \tau_0 P \ dx = 0$$

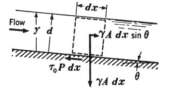

Fig. 12–1. Equilibrium of forces in an open channel.

since forces owing to pressure cancel out. From this, the average bed shear stress is

$$\tau_0 = \gamma R_h S \tag{12–1}$$

where R_h = the hydraulic radius, the ratio of flow cross-sectional area A to the wetted perimeter P;

S = slope of the channel bed;

τ_0 = mean bed shear stress, commonly referred to as the average unit tractive force in open-channel hydraulics.

The vertical distance from the channel bed to the water surface is designated as y, and the depth normal to the bed as d. For channels which drop less than 14 ft per 100 ft, y and d differ by less than 1 per cent, and y will be used to designate depth. Also, the slope S_b of the channel bed mathematically should be the ratio of change in elevation per horizontal distance. However, for small slopes (less than 0.14), the sine and tangent differ by no more than 1 per cent. In open-channel flow analyses, slopes of the bed, water surface, and energy grade lines are generally expressed as $\sin \theta$, θ being the angle between these and the horizontal. Thus, they represent drop per unit length of channel bed.

Even though open-channel flow differs from pipe flow in some respects (cross sections are variable, the surface is at constant atmospheric pressure, and gravity forces are involved), there are striking similarities with regards to viscous effects. Recall from Eq. 10–8 that $\tau_0 = f\rho V^2/8$, and thus, from Eq. 12–1,

$$f = \frac{8\gamma R_h S}{\rho V^2} = \frac{8g R_h S}{V^2}$$

where $S = h_f/L$ and represents the slope of the energy grade line for both pipes and open channels. Measurements on both triangular and rectangular smooth open channels show that the friction factor f is related to the Reynolds number $V4R_h/\nu$ by the *same* curves as for smooth pipes in Fig. 10–6. Typical results are shown in Fig. 12–2.

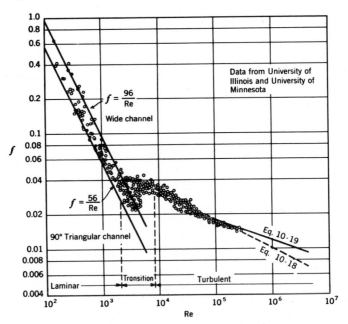

Fig. 12–2. The friction-factor vs. Reynolds-number relationship from experiments in smooth channels. (By permission from V. T. Chow, *Open-Channel Hydraulics*, New York: McGraw-Hill Book Company, Inc., 1959.)

In rough channels, the friction factor is increased for laminar flow and is influenced by the shape of the channel in the turbulent regime. This is probably owing to secondary flow, which involves cross currents superimposed on the mean flow direction.

The gravity effects may be indicated in terms of the Froude number, which is the ratio of the inertia to gravity forces in the system.

$$Fr = \frac{V}{\sqrt{gy_h}} \qquad (12\text{--}2)$$

in which V is the mean flow velocity and y_h is the hydraulic depth. In general, the hydraulic depth is the area of the flow cross section divided by the surface width ($y_h = A/b_s$) and is equal to the actual depth for a rectangular channel. The Froude number is also the ratio of the mean flow velocity V to the velocity $\sqrt{gy_h}$ of an elementary surface wave, known as a small gravity wave. Thus, 1) if the Froude number is less than unity, the flow is *subcritical*, or *tranquil*; 2) if the Froude number is equal to unity, the flow is *critical*; and 3) if the Froude number is greater than unity, the flow is *supercritical*, *rapid*, or *shooting*.

Flow regimes of interest include uniform flow, gradually varied flow, and rapidly varied flow (Fig. 12–3). In addition, the flow may be either steady or unsteady. Only steady flow will be considered here.

Uniform flow exists only in long channels and requires that the depth, cross-sectional area, and hence mean velocity be constant from section to section. In gradually varied flow, these changes take place gradually from section to section, so that the streamlines are essentially parallel and pressures within the flow are hydrostatic. A fundamental assumption in gradually varied flow is that over comparatively short reaches (lengths) of channel, energy losses are considered the same as for uniform flow at the average depth. In rapidly varied flow, changes in depth, flow area, and hence average velocity take place in such short reaches of channel that streamlines have pronounced curvature, and pressures within the flow are not hydrostatic. In abrupt changes in channel boundaries and in hydraulic jumps, energy losses are

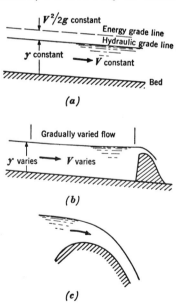

Fig. 12–3. Types of open-channel flow. *a*) Uniform flow, *b*) gradually varied flow, and *c*) rapidly varied flow.

high because of separation and intense turbulence; but for curvilinear flow without separation, such as in faired transitions in channel boundaries or in flow over a weir or free overfalls, energy losses are small and often may be neglected.

The velocity in an open channel varies from zero along the wetted perimeter to a maximum at or near the surface, depending upon the shape of the cross section. Some typical velocity variations are indicated in Fig. 12–4. The velocity head in terms of average velocity V should properly

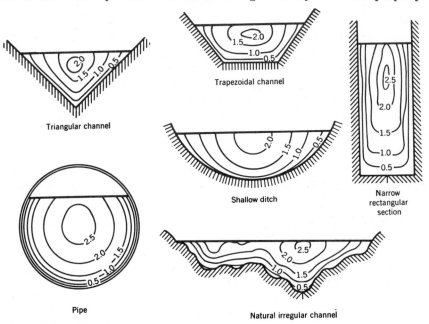

Triangular channel

Trapezoidal channel

Shallow ditch

Narrow rectangular section

Pipe

Natural irregular channel

Fig. 12–4. Typical velocity variations in open channels. (By permission from V. T. Chow, *Open-Channel Hydraulics*, New York: McGraw-Hill Book Company, Inc., 1959.)

be written as $\alpha V^2/2g$ (Sec. 5–5), where α varies from 1.0 to about 1.2 under normal conditions. We will assume one-dimensional flow with $\alpha = 1.0$ in this chapter.

If streamlines are parallel or essentially so (as for uniform flow and gradually varied flow), the pressures within the flow are hydrostatic and determined solely by the depth. For curvilinear streamlines (in rapidly varied flow), the pressures within the flow are less than hydrostatic for convex flow and greater than hydrostatic for concave flow because of centrifugal effects. For channels of large slopes, the pressures within the flow are also less than hydrostatic, the pressure head at any vertical distance y from the surface being

$$h = y \cos^2 \theta$$

where θ is the angle the water surface makes with the horizontal. We will consider in detail only those situations where the pressures within the flow are hydrostatic.

12-2. VELOCITY OF AN ELEMENTARY WAVE

The velocity of a solitary elementary wave on the surface of a liquid may be determined by applying the continuity and Bernoulli equations to a wave with reference axes at rest with respect to the wave (Fig. 12-5).

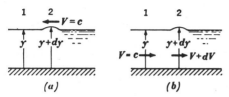

FIG. 12-5. Elementary surface wave. *a)* Observer at rest and *b)* observer moving with wave.

The continuity equation is

$$Vy = (V + dV)(y + dy)$$

or

$$\frac{dV}{V} + \frac{dy}{y} = 0$$

The Bernoulli equation written between sections *1* and *2* is

$$\frac{V^2}{2g} + y = \frac{(V + dV)^2}{2g} + (y + dy)$$

or

$$V\,dV + g\,dy = 0$$

which is equivalent to Eq. 5-18.

Combining the differential forms of the continuity and Bernoulli equations gives (for $V = c$) the wave velocity, or celerity, for waves whose height is small compared with the water depth,[1] for $dy/y \ll 1$

$$c = \sqrt{gy} \qquad\qquad (12\text{-}3a)$$

A more general derivation for nonrectangular channels gives

$$c = \sqrt{gy_h} \qquad\qquad (12\text{-}3b)$$

where y_h is the hydraulic depth.

12-3. UNIFORM FLOW

In uniform flow [Fig. 12-3(a)], the depth and average velocity remain

[1]In Sec. 9-1, the sonic velocity in a gas was derived by using the continuity and momentum equations and was shown to be that of a pressure wave which was very small compared with the ambient pressure.

constant, and thus the channel bed, water surface, and energy grade line are parallel ($S_b = S_w = S_e = S$). This type of flow rarely occurs in a natural stream and exists only in relatively long man-made channels. It may be supercritical or subcritical, but uniform critical flow is very unstable and undulations in the water surface permit only an *average* uniform critical flow to occur. Even though uniform flow is not common, its treatment is necessary because many nonuniform flows approach a uniform flow condition, and uniform flow criteria are used in analyzing nonuniform flow.

It would be desirable to have a uniform-flow equation which would include all the fluid, geometrical, and flow parameters, but none has been developed as yet. The equation most commonly used is the Manning formula relating the average flow velocity V, the channel slope S, the channel roughness n, and the hydraulic radius R_h of the channel cross section. This equation is

$$V = \frac{1.49}{n} R_h{}^{2/3} S^{1/2} \tag{12-4a}$$

and since $Q = VA$, $$Q = \frac{1.49}{n} R_h{}^{2/3} S^{1/2} A \tag{12-4b}$$

The Manning equation is related to the Darcy-Weisbach equation for pipe flow (Eq. 10-6). The Darcy-Weisbach equation may be written as

$$V = \sqrt{\frac{8g}{f}} R_h{}^{1/2} S^{1/2}$$

so that $$\frac{1}{\sqrt{f}} = \frac{1.49}{\sqrt{8g}} \frac{R_h{}^{1/6}}{n} \tag{12-5}$$

Since Manning's n is a measure of roughness, it would seem illogical that it have dimensions of $T/L^{1/3}$, which results from Eq. 12-5 if the value of 1.49 is dimensionless. However, if 1.49 has dimensions of $\sqrt{g}$, then the dimension of n is $L^{1/6}$, and $n/R_h{}^{1/6}$ then represents a relative roughness similar to $k/D = k/4R_h$ for a pipe. In both instances (pipe flow as well as open-channel flow), flow at high Reynolds numbers for relatively rough surfaces is essentially independent of the Reynolds number. Thus *the Froude number is the significant parameter for open-channel flows of most engineering interest.* Manning's experimental work (1889) was in metric units, and in order to use the same value of n in metric and English units, the factor 1.49 (the cube root of the number of feet in a meter) is introduced.

Other uniform-flow equations (notably by Ganguillet and Kutter in 1869, Bazin in 1897, and Powell in 1950) have been proposed and used, but they have not received such wide acceptance as Manning's equation.

The determination of an accurate value of Manning's n is difficult, since the value depends on surface roughness, vegetation in the channel bed, channel irregularity, channel alignment, silting and scouring, obstructions, the size and shape of channel, the stage (water surface level) and discharge, seasonal changes, and suspended materials and bed load carried in the stream.

Typical values of n are listed in Table 12–1. We will assume that the same average roughness value n applies to the entire wetted perimeter of a channel. This is not always the case (as for man-made channels with different bottom and sides, flooded streams where the flooded surface is usually rougher than the main stream, and ice-covered channels) but the treatment of these other cases is beyond the scope of this text.

Manning's equation indicates that for a given channel slope, roughness, and cross section a shape which has a minimum perimeter will convey the maximum flow. Or a given flow will require a minimum cross section to convey it when the perimeter is also a minimum. Minimizing the perimeter gives the most efficient cross section, the semicircle being the best. Fabricated channels or flumes may be made semicircular, rectangular, or trapezoidal in cross section. In any case, *the most efficient section is one for*

TABLE 12–1*

TYPICAL VALUES OF MANNING'S n

Closed Conduits Flowing Partly Full	
Smooth brass	0.010
Corrugated metal storm drains	0.024
Concrete culvert	0.013
Unfinished concrete	0.014
Clay drain tile	0.013
Rubble masonry	0.025
Lined or Built-up Channels	
Unpainted steel	0.012
Planed wood	0.012
Unplaned wood	0.013
Trowel-finished concrete	0.013
Unfinished concrete	0.017
Rough concrete	0.020
Glazed brick	0.013
Brick in cement mortar	0.015
Excavated Channels	
Clean earth (straight channel)	0.022
Earth with weeds (winding channel)	0.030
Natural Streams	
Clean and straight	0.030
Weedy reaches, deep pools	0.100

*With permission from Ven Te Chow, *Open-Channel Hydraulics* (New York: McGraw-Hill Book Company, Inc., 1959).

which the hydraulic radius is one-half the depth. This condition is automatically met for a semicircle. For a rectangular channel, the width should equal twice the depth $(b = 2y)$. For a trapezoidal channel, a half-hexagon is most efficient.

The *normal* depth y_n for an open channel is the depth corresponding to uniform flow and may be obtained from Manning's equation (Eq. 12–4a). The corresponding mean velocity is the *normal velocity* V_n. For most channels, both the normal depth and velocity increase with an increase in total discharge Q. This statement is true for any channel for which the roughness n is considered constant and for which the flow cross section increases at a rate greater than the corresponding increase in wetted perimeter, with an increase in depth. Since

$$V = \frac{1.49}{n} \left(\frac{A}{P}\right)^{2/3} S^{1/2}$$

differentiation with respect to y_n gives

$$\frac{dV}{dy_n} = \frac{1.49}{n} S^{1/2} \left(\frac{2}{3}\right) \left(\frac{A}{P}\right)^{-1/3} \left[\frac{P\dfrac{dA}{dy_n} - A\dfrac{dP}{dy_n}}{P^2}\right] \qquad (12\text{--}6)$$

If the term in brackets is negative, the mean velocity decreases with an increase in depth; if it is zero, the velocity remains constant with an increase in depth; if it is positive—and this is usually the case—the velocity increases with an increase in depth. For a rectangular channel, the term in brackets in Eq. 12–6 is b^2/P^2; for a triangular channel, it is $(1/2) \sin \theta$; and for a trapezoidal channel, it is $(b^2 + 2\, by_n \tan \theta + 2\, y_n^2 \tan \theta/\cos \theta)/P^2$ (Fig. 12–6). In each of these instances, dV/dy_n is positive and both velocity and discharge increase with depth.

Criteria for the design of an open channel for uniform flow depend on whether the channel is nonerodible, erodible, or grass-lined. Important criteria in the design of nonerodible channels are lining costs (which depend

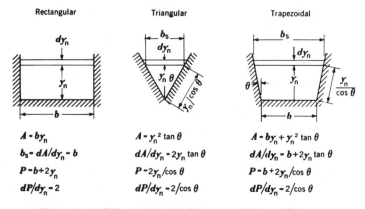

FIG. 12–6. Effect of depth changes on flow sections.

on the channel shape as well as the lining material), minimum flow velocities in order to avoid deposition of sediment which might be carried in the stream, and free-board requirements. In erodible channels, the maximum flow velocities are limited by the probability of bed scouring. Grass linings are used in erodible channels to prevent bed erosion, and such a channel may be designed on the basis of stability of the bed or for maximum capacity.

EXAMPLE 12–1. A rectangular trowel-finished concrete channel 18 ft wide and laid on a slope of 0.002 carries water at a uniform depth of 4 ft. a) What is the average shear stress τ_0 along the channel perimeter? b) What is the average flow velocity? c) What is the flow regime? d) To what value of friction factor f does $n = 0.013$ correspond?

Solution: a) From Eq. 12–1,

$$\tau_0 = \gamma R_h S = 62.4 \ (72/26) \ 0.002 = 0.346 \text{ psf}$$

b) From Table 12–1, $n = 0.013$ and

$$V = \frac{1.49}{0.013} \left(\frac{72}{26}\right)^{2/3} 0.002^{1/2} = 10.1 \text{ ft/sec}$$

c)
$$\text{Fr} = \frac{V}{\sqrt{gy}} = \frac{10.1}{\sqrt{(32.2)(4)}} = 0.89$$

which is less than 1, and the flow is subcritical.

d) From Eq. 12–5,

$$f = \frac{8gR_h S}{V^2} = \frac{8gn^2}{1.49^2 R^{1/3}} = \frac{(8)(32.2)(0.013^2)}{(1.49^2)(1.404)} = 0.014$$

12–4. SPECIFIC ENERGY AND SPECIFIC THRUST

Specific energy. The total energy per unit weight of fluid at any section in a flow stream for an arbitrary streamline in a channel of small slope is the total head—the sum of the velocity head, pressure head, and potential head. If the potential head is taken with respect to the channel bed, the total head or energy is called the *specific energy*. It is expressed in the form of Eq. 5–30b (see Fig. 12–7) as

$$E = \frac{V^2}{2g} + \frac{p}{\gamma} + z$$

and since $\frac{p}{\gamma} + z = y$ for any streamline in the section,

$$E = \frac{V^2}{2g} + y \tag{12-7a}$$

For a rectangular channel, the total discharge Q divided by the channel width b is called the unit discharge q. From the continuity equation,

$$V = \frac{Q}{A} = \frac{Q}{yb} = \frac{q}{y}$$

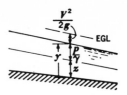

FIG. 12-7.   Specific-energy
nomenclature.

so that the specific energy for a rectangular channel is

$$E = \frac{q^2}{2gy^2} + y \qquad (12\text{--}7b)$$

For a given unit discharge (q constant), the specific energy is a function of the depth of flow [$E = E(y)$]. A plot of this relationship is called a specific-energy diagram, which consists of a family of similar curves each representing a given unit discharge. Examples are shown in Fig. 12–8.

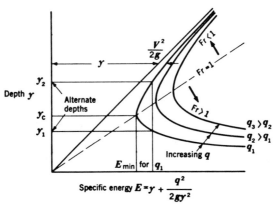

FIG. 12–8. Specific-energy diagram.

From Eq. 12–7b, as y approaches zero, E approaches an infinite value, and as y becomes very large, E approaches y. Each curve in Fig. 12–8 indicates that there are two depths, y_1 and y_2, for example, for which the specific energy is the same. These depths are called *alternate depths*. Also, each curve has a point of minimum specific energy at which the alternate depths coincide. At this minimum point $dE/dy = 0$, since the slope of the curve is infinite. From Eq. 12–7b, at $E_{\min}$,

$$\left(\frac{dE}{dy}\right)_{E_{\min}} = -\frac{2q^2}{2gy^3} + 1 = 0$$

so that

$$y_{E_{\min}}^3 = \frac{q^2}{g}$$

The velocity head at this point is

$$\frac{V^2}{2g} = \frac{q^2}{2gy^2} = \frac{gy^3}{2gy^2} = \frac{y}{2}$$

or

$$V = \sqrt{gy}$$

This equation corresponds to a Froude number of unity, and thus *flow at minimum specific energy is critical flow*. This statement is often considered to be a definition of critical flow. The minimum specific energy E_{min} *for a given unit discharge* is

$$E_{min} = y_c + \frac{V_c^2}{2g} = y_c + \frac{y_c}{2} = \frac{3}{2} y_c \qquad (12\text{--}8)$$

The critical depth for a given unit discharge is

$$y_c = \left(\frac{q^2}{g}\right)^{1/3} \qquad (12\text{--}9a)$$

and the critical velocity for a given unit discharge is

$$V_c = \sqrt{gy_c} \qquad (12\text{--}10)^2$$

Horizontal distances from the ordinate to the specific energy curve in Fig. 12–8 represent the depth (from the ordinate to the 45-deg line) plus the velocity head (from the 45-deg line to the curve). Thus for a given unit discharge at depths greater than critical, the velocities are less than critical so that the Froude number is less than 1 and the flow is called subcritical. For depths less than critical, the velocities are greater than critical so that the Froude number is greater than 1 and the flow is called supercritical.

A *mild* slope is one on which uniform flow occurs at depths greater than critical; a *critical* slope is one on which uniform flow occurs at critical depth; and a *steep* slope is one on which uniform flow occurs at a depth less than critical. Thus, whether a channel slope is mild, critical, or steep

[2] For a nonrectangular channel

$$E = \frac{Q^2}{2gA^2} + y \qquad \text{and} \qquad \frac{dE}{dy} = -\frac{2Q^2}{2gA^3}\frac{dA}{dy} + 1$$

where $\frac{dA}{dy} = b_s$, the surface width (Fig. 12–6). Thus,

$$\frac{Q^2 b_s}{gA^3} = 1 \qquad (12\text{--}9b)$$

for *minimum specific energy*, which represents critical flow. From this,

$$\frac{V^2 A^2 b_s}{gA^3} = 1 \qquad \text{or} \qquad V = \sqrt{\frac{gA}{b_s}} = \sqrt{gy_h}$$

which agrees with Eq. 12–2 for a Froude number of 1.

does not depend solely on the inclination of the channel bed but on the type of uniform flow it produces. This criteria is similar to the criterion for a hydraulically smooth or rough surface—it depends on the flow as well as the actual surface roughness.

The specific-energy diagram is very useful in analyzing gradually varied flow and is helpful in showing depth variations in rapidly varied flow.

Thrust function. The thrust function was defined in Sec. 5–4 as[3]

$$F = pA + \rho V^2 A$$

For a unit width of rectangular channel (Fig. 12–9),

$$pA = \left(\frac{\gamma y}{2}\right)(y)$$

and

$$\rho V^2 A = \left(\frac{\gamma}{g}\right)\left(\frac{q^2}{y^2}\right)(y)$$

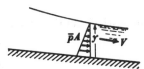

The thrust function per specific weight of fluid f is called the *specific thrust function*, or specific thrust, and is

Fig. 12–9.   Thrust-function nomenclature.

$$f = \frac{y^2}{2} + \frac{q^2}{gy} \qquad (12\text{–}11)$$

For a given unit discharge q, the specific thrust function depends only on the depth $[f = f(y)]$. A plot of this relationship is called a specific-thrust diagram and consists of a family of similar curves, each applying to a given unit discharge. Examples are shown in Fig. 12–10. As is true for

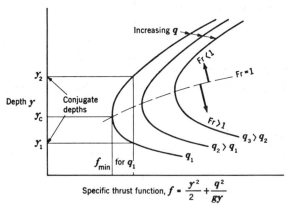

Fig. 12–10. Specific-thrust diagram.

specific energy, here also two depths (y_1 and y_2, for example) exist for which the specific thrust is the same for a given unit discharge. These

[3]By convention, we will use gage pressures here.

depths are called *conjugate*, or *sequent*, depths. Each curve has a minimum value of specific thrust at which the conjugate, or sequent, depths coincide. At this minimum point, $df/dy = 0$. From Eq. 12–11,

$$\frac{df}{dy} = y - \frac{q^2}{gy^2} = 0$$

so that

$$y_{f_{\min}}^3 = \left(\frac{q^2}{g}\right)$$

which is the same condition as for minimum specific energy. Thus minimum specific thrust also corresponds to critical flow.

Expressions for the specific thrust function for nonrectangular channels are more complicated than those for specific energy because the pA term involves the depth to the centroid of the cross section.

Examples of the use of the specific-energy and thrust-function curves are shown in Fig. 12–11. For uniform flow [Fig. 12–11(a)], the depth of flow and velocity are both constant; from Eqs. 12–7a and 12–11, the specific

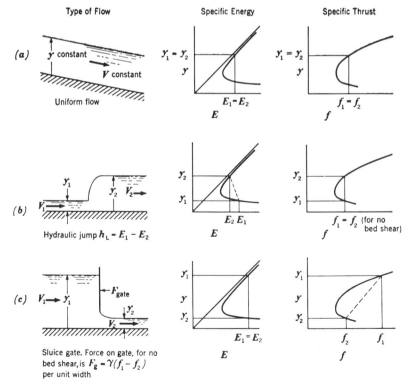

FIG. 12–11. Examples of application of specific-energy and specific-thrust diagrams.

energy and specific thrust are both constant. For a hydraulic jump [Fig. 12-11(b)], the specific thrust is constant for flow on a horizontal bed without bed shear (see Sec. 12–6). The conjugate, or sequent, depths may then be obtained from the specific-thrust curve. When these depths are located on the specific-energy curve, the change in specific energy, which represents the head or energy loss through the jump, may be obtained. For flow under a sluice gate on a horizontal channel [Fig. 12–11(c)], the energy equation indicates a constant specific energy, and the alternate depths may be obtained from the specific-energy curve. These depths, located on the specific-thrust curve, indicate the change in specific thrust, which represents the force of the sluice gate on the fluid.

EXAMPLE 12–2. An unfinished concrete trapezoidal channel has a 12-ft bottom width and sides inclined 45 deg from the horizontal. It is laid on a slope of 0.001. The flow rate is 500 ft^3/sec. a) What is the normal depth? b) What is the flow regime? c) What is the critical depth for this flow? d) What would be the critical slope for this channel?

Solution: a) From Manning's equation,

$$Q = \frac{1.49}{0.017} \left(\frac{12y_n + y_n{}^2}{12 + 2\sqrt{2}y_n}\right)^{2/3} (0.001)^{1/2} (12y_n + y_n{}^2)$$

The value of y_n may be found by a trial solution by inserting various assumed values of y until the calculated flow rate is 500 ft^3/sec, or by plotting the flow rate obtained from three assumed values of y and interpolating the resulting curve.

Assumed y, ft	4.00	4.50	5.00	4.75	4.90
Calculated Q, ft^3/sec	347	429	517	473	499

A plot of y vs. Q for $y = 4$, 4.5, and 5 ft also indicates that $y_n = 4.90$ ft.

b)

$$Fr = \frac{V}{\sqrt{gy_h}}$$

where $V = Q/A = 500/82.8 = 6.04$ ft/sec and $y_h = A/b_s = 82.8/(12 + 2y_n) = 3.80$ ft. Thus

$$Fr = \frac{6.04}{\sqrt{(32.2)(3.80)}} = 0.55$$

which is less than 1 so the flow is subcritical.

c) The condition which has to be met is that $Q^2/g = A^3/b_s$ (Eq. 12-9b). Thus

$$\frac{500^2}{32.2} = \frac{(12y_c + y_c{}^2)^3}{12 + 2y_c}$$

and a trial solution gives $y_c = 3.42$ ft.

d) Uniform flow would occur at critical depth and critical velocity. Thus $V_c = Q/A_c = 500/52.74 = 9.49$ ft/sec or

$$(y_h)_c = \left(\frac{A}{b_s}\right)_c = \frac{52.74}{18.86} = 2.80 \text{ ft}$$

so $\qquad V_c = (\sqrt{gy_h})_c = \sqrt{(32.2)(2.80)} = 9.49$ ft/sec

From Manning's equation,

$$V = \frac{1.49}{n} (R_h)^{2/3} S^{1/2}$$

where $R_h = (A/P)_c = 52.74/21.69 = 2.43$ ft. Then

$$S_c = \frac{V^2 n^2}{1.49^2 R_h^{4/3}} = \frac{(9.49^2)(0.017^2)}{(1.49^2)(2.43^{4/3})} = 0.00359$$

12-5. GRADUALLY VARIED FLOW

In gradually varied flow, the depth varies, and changes in depth take place over relatively long reaches of a channel. Whether the depth increases or decreases in the direction of flow is of interest, and this may be determined qualitatively if the sign of dy/dx is known (y is the depth and x is the distance in the flow direction, positive in the direction of flow). If dy/dx is positive, the depth will increase, and if dy/dx is negative, the depth will decrease in the direction of flow. If dy/dx is zero, the depth is constant and the flow is uniform. In addition to finding the change in depth qualitatively, the actual water surface profile may be calculated by any of a number of methods, one of which will be described here.

Depth variation. An expression for the rate of change of depth with downstream distance for a wide rectangular channel (two-dimensional flow) is

$$\frac{dy}{dx} = S_b \frac{1 - \left(\frac{y_n}{y}\right)^{10/3}}{1 - \left(\frac{y_c}{y}\right)^3} \qquad (12\text{-}12a)$$

The bed slope S_b is defined as positive when the bed drops in the direction of flow, and the sign of dy/dx is thus determined by the magnitude of the actual depth as compared with the normal depth y_n and the critical depth y_c. The derivation of Eq. 12-12a involves the combination of the Manning equation with a differential expression for the total head or energy. The total head or energy at a section is referred to an arbitrary datum where $z = 0$ (Fig. 12-12).

This total head or energy H for any channel is

$$H = \frac{V^2}{2g} + y + z_b$$

and for a rectangular channel

$$H = \frac{q^2}{2gy^2} + y + z_b$$

Differentiation with respect to x gives

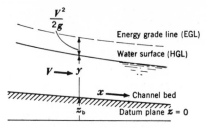

FIG. 12–12. Total head at a
section in an open channel.
S_e = slope of energy grade
line
S_w = slope of water surface
S_b = slope of channel bed

$$\frac{dH}{dx} = -\frac{2q^2}{2gy^3}\frac{dy}{dx} + \frac{dy}{dx} + \frac{dz_b}{dx}$$

In this expression dH/dx is the slope of the energy grade line $-S_e$ and dz_b/dx is the slope of the channel bed $-S_b$. The slope S_e is

$$S_e = \frac{q^2 n^2}{1.49^2\, y^{10/3}}$$

since $R_h = y$ for a rectangular channel which is very wide compared to the depth.
Thus

$$\frac{dy}{dx} = \frac{S_b\left(1 - \dfrac{q^2 n^2}{1.49^2\, y^{10/3}}\dfrac{1}{S_b}\right)}{1 - \dfrac{q^2}{gy^3}} \tag{12–12b}$$

In the numerator

$$\frac{q^2 n^2}{1.49^2\, y^{10/3}\, S_b} = \frac{q^2 n^2}{1.49^2\, y^{10/3}}\;\frac{1}{\left(y_n{}^2\,\dfrac{1.49^2}{n^2}\,y_n{}^{4/3}\right)} = \left(\frac{y_n}{y}\right)^{10/3}$$

and in the denominator

$$\frac{q^2}{gy^3} = \left(\frac{y_c}{y}\right)^3$$

so that

$$\frac{dy}{dx} = S_b\,\frac{1 - \left(\dfrac{y_n}{y}\right)^{10/3}}{1 - \left(\dfrac{y_c}{y}\right)^3}$$

for a wide rectangular channel.

The sign of dy/dx may be found for various depths on mild, steep, critical, horizontal, and adverse slopes. The procedure and results are shown in Table 12–2. An examination of the magnitude of dy/dx in Eq. 12–12 when the depth y is very large, nearly normal, nearly critical, or very small will indicate the general shapes of the resulting varied-flow water-surface profiles shown in Fig. 12–13. The twelve profile types are the only ones possible for gradually varied flow. Their use is indicated in the following examples.

TABLE 12–2

DEPTH VARIATIONS FOR GRADUALLY VARIED FLOW

Slope	$\dfrac{y_n}{y}$	Sign of Numerator	$\dfrac{y_c}{y}$	Sign of Denominator	Sign of $\dfrac{dy}{dx}$	Depth	Type of Surface Profile
Mild	<1	$+$	<1	$+$	$+$	Increases	M-1
$y_n > y_c$	>1	$-$	<1	$+$	$-$	Decreases	M-2
	>1	$-$	>1	$-$	$+$	Increases	M-3
Steep	<1	$+$	<1	$+$	$+$	Increases	S-1
$y_n < y_c$	<1	$+$	>1	$-$	$-$	Decreases	S-2
	>1	$-$	>1	$-$	$+$	Increases	S-3
Critical	<1	$+$	<1	$+$	$+$	Increases	C-1
$y_n = y_c$	>1	$-$	>1	$-$	$+$	Increases	C-3
Horizontal		$-$*	<1	$+$	$-$	Decreases	H-2
$y_n = \infty$		$-$*	>1	$-$	$+$	Increases	H-3
Adverse	<1	$-$†	<1	$+$	$-$	Decreases	A-2
$y_n < 0$	<1	$-$†	>1	$-$	$+$	Increases	A-3

*From Eq. 12–12b.
†$S_b < 0$.

EXAMPLE 12–3. What is the water-surface profile for flow passing from a long mild slope to a long steep slope?

Solution: In Fig. 12–14, uniform flow, an M-1 or M-2 curve terminating at a depth greater than critical at the change in bed slope is impossible on the mild slope because it would have to be followed by an S-1 curve which would never reach normal depth on the steep slope. An M-2 curve reaching critical depth upstream from the change in bed slope is also impossible because the flow cannot remain critical to the change in bed slope (critical uniform flow cannot occur on a mild slope). Neither can it become less nor more than critical, because if it did, the surface would immediately return towards critical along an M-2 or M-3 curve. Therefore, the only possible profile is an M-2 curve passing through critical depth at the location of the change in bed slope, followed by an S-2 curve asymptotic to the normal depth line on the steep slope.

EXAMPLE 12–4. A number of surface profiles are shown in Fig. 12–15. Their correctness and the impossibility of other profiles should be verified.

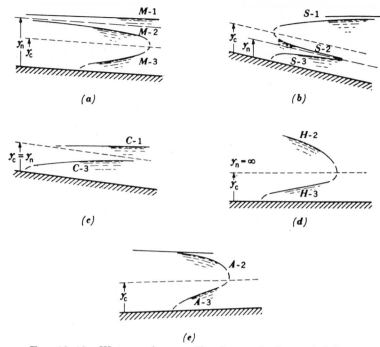

FIG. 12–13. Water-surface profiles for gradually varied flow;
for a) mild slope, b) steep slope, c) critical slope, d) horizontal
slope, and e) adverse slope.

Profiles in Fig. 12–15 indicate that 1) flow on a long steep slope is
uniform *upstream* from either a change in bed slope or a change in bed
roughness and 2) flow on a long mild slope is uniform *downstream* from
either a change in bed slope or a change in bed roughness.

Surface profiles for short channels depend largely on the headwater
and tailwater conditions and generalized results usually cannot be given.

Computation of water surface profiles for gradually varied flow.
Definite points on the surface profiles shown in Fig. 12–13 may be deter-

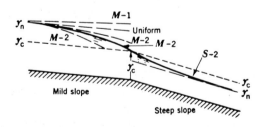

FIG. 12–14. Flow from a long mild slope
to a long steep slope.

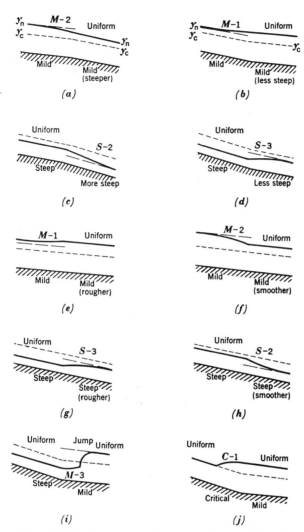

Fig. 12–15. Examples of water surface profiles
for gradually varied flow on changes in bed slope.

mined by a variety of methods. In the so-called direct-step method, the distance between two sections where depths are assigned may be estimated by assuming that the slope of the energy grade line for this distance is 1) the same as for uniform flow at a velocity equal to the average of those at the two sections ($\overline{S}_e = \overline{V}^2\, n^2/1.49^2\, \overline{R}^{4/3}$) or 2) equal to the average of the slope of the energy grade lines corresponding to uniform flow at the two sections [$\overline{S}_e = (S_{e1} + S_{e2})/2$, where S_{e1} and S_{e2} are found from Manning's equation].

In Fig. 12–16, the energy equation written for the flow between sections *1* and *2* is

$$\frac{V_1{}^2}{2g} + y_1 + z_{b1} = \frac{V_2{}^2}{2g} + y_2 + z_{b2} + h_L$$

Grouping terms gives $\left(\dfrac{V_2{}^2}{2g} + y_2\right) - \left(\dfrac{V_1{}^2}{2g} + y_1\right) = (z_{b1} - z_{b2}) - h_L$

or $$E_2 - E_1 = S_b\,\Delta x - \overline{S}_e\,\Delta x$$

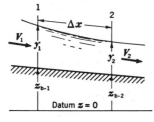

Fig. 12–16. Nomenclature for computing gradually varied flow profiles.

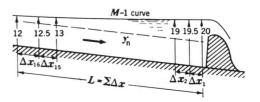

Fig. 12–17. Backwater curve.

so that $$\Delta x = \frac{E_2 - E_1}{S_b - \overline{S}_e} \tag{12–13}$$

Calculations are made either upstream or downstream from a section where the depth is known. For *M-1*, *M-2*, *H-2*, and *A-2* curves, calculations generally proceed upstream; for *M-3*, *S-1*, *S-2*, *S-3*, *C-1*, *C-3*, *H-3*, and *A-3* curves, calculations generally proceed downstream. For an assumed flow and channel slope, shape, and roughness, the accuracy obtained depends largely on the size of depth increments chosen. The smaller the depth increments, the more accurate are the results because of the assumptions made regarding energy loss. The depth increments should be smaller as the profile approaches uniform depth. If the length of a varied-flow profile between sections where the depths are y_0 and y_k is to be calculated, accuracy would be better if depth increments of $(y_0 - y_k)/20$ were used instead of $(y_0 - y_k)/4$, for example. The calculation effort would be five times greater if 20 rather than 4 intervals were used. This need not be so, however, since the values of Δx increase or decrease monotonically in a well-behaved manner. Thus the value of Δx between y_0 and y_1, y_4 and y_5, y_9 and y_{10}, y_{14} and y_{15}, y_{19} and y_{20} may be calculated and a curve of the various values of Δx versus interval number plotted. The values of Δx for depth intervals between those calculated may be interpolated from the graph. Maximum accuracy with minimum effort may thus be achieved. The method is illustrated in Example 12–5.

EXAMPLE 12–5. Water flows in a 50-ft wide rectangular channel at a rate of 4000 ft³/sec. The bed slope is 0.001 and the roughness coefficient is $n = 0.025$. A dam increases the depth to 20 ft immediately upstream. What is the distance upstream to a point where the depth is 12 ft?

Solution: From the Manning equation, the normal depth is 10.95 ft, and from Eq. 12–9a, the critical depth is 5.84 ft. Thus $y > y_n > y_c$ so that the water-surface profile is an *M-1* curve. Calculation proceeds as indicated in Table 12–3 and Fig. 12–17.

Using sixteen intervals of 0.5 ft each, the total length is calculated as 13,101

TABLE 12–3

CALCULATION OF VARIED-FLOW PROFILE FOR EXAMPLE 12–5

y	A	V	$\dfrac{V^2}{2g}$	E	P	R	$R^{4/3}$	$S_e = \dfrac{V^2}{\dfrac{1.49^2}{n^2}R^{4/3}}$	$\bar{S}_e$	ΔE	$S_b - \bar{S}_e$	Δx

Using Sixteen Intervals

y	A	V	$\dfrac{V^2}{2g}$	E	P	R	$R^{4/3}$	S_e	$\bar{S}_e$	ΔE	$S_b - \bar{S}_e$	Δx
20	1000	4.00	0.2485	20.248	90.0	11.111	24.7	0.0001820				599
19.5	975	4.105	0.262	19.762	89.0	10.94	24.4	0.0001940	0.0001880	0.486	0.0008120	610*
19												622*
18.5												634*
18												646*
17.5	875	4.57	0.3245	17.825	85	10.29	22.45	0.0002615				660
17	850	4.71	0.345	17.345	84	10.11	21.90	0.0002850	0.0002732	0.480	0.0007268	678*
16.5												702*
16												730*
15.5												764*
15	750	5.34	0.4425	15.443	80	9.375	19.75	0.000405				815
14.5	725	5.52	0.474	14.974	79	9.175	19.3	0.000444	0.000425	0.469	0.000575	870*
14												945*
13.5												1050*
13												1220*
12.5	625	6.40	0.637	13.137	75	8.34	16.9	0.000681				1556
12	600	6.667	0.690	12.690	74	8.11	16.33	0.000765	0.000723	0.447	0.000277	13,101 ft

Using Three Intervals

y	A	V	$\dfrac{V^2}{2g}$	E	P	R	$R^{4/3}$	S_e	$\bar{S}_e$	ΔE	$S_b - \bar{S}_e$	Δx
20				20.248				0.0001820				3115
17.5				17.825				0.0002615	0.0002217	2.423	0.0007783	3570
15				15.443				0.000405	0.000333	2.382	0.000667	6640
12				12.690				0.000765	0.000585	2.753	0.000415	13,325 ft

Using One Interval

y	A	V	$\dfrac{V^2}{2g}$	E	P	R	$R^{4/3}$	S_e	$\bar{S}_e$	ΔE	$S_b - \bar{S}_e$	Δx
20				20.248				0.0001820				
12				12.690				0.000765	0.0004735	7.558	0.0005265	14,330 ft

*These values are obtainable from a plot of Δx vs. y in Fig. 12–18.

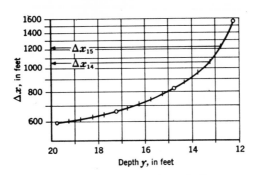

FIG. 12–18. Interpolation of distances between assigned depths for backwater curve.

ft. With three intervals of 2.5 or 3 ft, the total length is 13,325 ft. With only one depth interval of 8 ft, the length is calculated to be 14,330 ft. The use of larger depth increments generally results in an *overestimation* of the length of the varied-flow profile for subcritical flow, and the use of larger depth increments generally results in an *underestimation* of the length of a varied-flow profile for supercritical flow.

12–6. HYDRAULIC JUMP

A hydraulic jump may occur in channels of any slope and may be found at the foot of spillways and below sluice gates. In all instances, the flow is supercritical upstream of the jump and subcritical downstream of the jump. Equations relating conditions downstream of the jump to conditions upstream may be obtained by writing the continuity, momentum, and energy equations across the jump. If we assume a horizontal channel so that there are no gravity forces, and neglect bed shear for the short reach of channel over which the jump exists, we find that the depth ratio across the jump and the downstream Froude number depend only on the upstream Froude number. Also, the loss of available energy per unit weight of fluid passing through the jump depends only on the depths upstream and downstream.

For the region in which the momentum change takes place (Fig. 12–19) in a unit width of rectangular channel, the continuity equation is

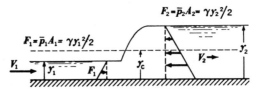

FIG. 12–19. Hydraulic jump.

$$V_1\, y_1 = V_2\, y_2$$

and the momentum equation is

$$\gamma \frac{y_1^2}{2} - \gamma \frac{y_2^2}{2} = \frac{V_1\, y_1 \gamma}{g}\, (V_2 - V_1)$$

so that we get, after combining,

$$\frac{y_1^2}{2} + \frac{q^2}{gy_1} = \frac{y_2^2}{2} + \frac{q^2}{gy_2}$$

which indicates that the thrust function is constant across the jump, in the absence of gravity and bed shear.

The energy equation is[4]

$$E_1 = E_2 + h_L$$

or

$$\frac{q^2}{2gy_1^2} + y_1 = \frac{q^2}{2gy_2^2} + y_2 + h_L$$

The momentum equation may be arranged to yield

$$y_2^2 + y_1\, y_2 - \frac{2q^2}{gy_1} = 0$$

(since one root of the momentum equation is the trivial case for which $y_1 = y_2$), a quadratic whose solution gives

$$\frac{y_2}{y_1} = \frac{1}{2}\left(\sqrt{1 + \frac{8q^2}{gy_1^3}} - 1\right) = \frac{1}{2}\left(\sqrt{1 + 8\,\mathrm{Fr}_1^2} - 1\right) \qquad (12\text{--}14)$$

Since the momentum equation is symmetrical in y_1 and y_2, it may also be written as

$$y_1^2 + y_2\, y_1 - \frac{2q^2}{gy_2} = 0$$

which is another quadratic, whose solution gives

$$\frac{y_1}{y_2} = \frac{1}{2}\left(\sqrt{1 + \frac{8q^2}{gy_2^3}} - 1\right) = \frac{1}{2}\left(\sqrt{1 + 8\,\mathrm{Fr}_2^2} - 1\right) \qquad (12\text{--}15)$$

Equations 12–14 and 12–15 indicate that for a given unit discharge, the smaller the upstream depth, the greater is the downstream depth, and vice versa. As the upstream depth approaches critical ($\mathrm{Fr}_1 \rightarrow 1$), the depth ratio approaches unity. The strength of the jump is expressed in terms of the depth ratio y_2/y_1 or in terms of the upstream Froude number Fr_1.

---

[4]The term h_L represents the mechanical energy converted to thermal energy and, in a thermodynamic sense, it is a loss only in available energy.

The energy loss through the jump is

$$h_L = E_1 - E_2 \tag{12-16}$$

$$= \frac{q^2}{2gy_1^2} - \frac{q^2}{2gy_2^2} + (y_1 - y_2) = \frac{q^2}{2g}\left(\frac{1}{y_1^2} - \frac{1}{y_2^2}\right) + (y_1 - y_2)$$

and since
$$\frac{q^2}{g} = \frac{y_1 \, y_2 \, (y_1 + y_2)}{2}$$

from the quadratic equation obtained from the momentum equation, the head loss or energy loss through the jump is

$$h_L = E_1 - E_2 = \frac{(y_2 - y_1)^3}{4\, y_1\, y_2} \tag{12-17}$$

The hydraulic jump is illustrated on the specific-energy and thrust-function diagrams in Fig. 12–11(b).

Equations 12–14, 12–15, and 12–17 are strictly valid only for one-dimensional flow for which the momentum and energy correction factors (α and β in Sec. 5–5 and 5–4) are assumed to be unity. Actually, the velocity profile upstream of the jump is more nearly one-dimensional than that downstream. Secondly, the bed shear was assumed zero, and this is less true the longer the jump. The ratio of jump length to downstream depth is about 6 for upstream Froude numbers greater than about 4. Measurements of velocity profiles indicate values of y_2/y_1 from a more exact analysis, which includes the true momentum and the bed shear, to be uniformly less than the approximate value given by Eq. 12–15 [1]. The exact and approximate values agree at $Fr_1 = 1$, and the exact value is about 5 per cent less than the approximate value at $Fr_1 = 8$.

In addition to these effects, gravity effects increase as the bed slope increases.

A hydraulic jump can be controlled by a sill, a broad-crested weir, an abrupt rise in the channel floor, or an abrupt drop in the channel floor. In each instance, analysis is made by means of the continuity, momentum, and energy equations. Stilling basins of special design are often used to stabilize the location of a jump and as a means of dissipating energy [2].

Oblique jumps may form in channels where side contractions or expansions occur.

A hydraulic bore is an example of a moving hydraulic jump and may occur in a river emptying into the sea (a tidal estuary) in which case the phenomenon is called a tidal bore. The wall of water travels upstream, and if q represents the unit discharge passing through the bore, Eqs. 12–14 and 12–15, as well as those used in their development, apply. The velocities relative to the moving jump are V_1 and V_2.

Example 12–6. Estimate the location of a hydraulic jump downstream of a spillway in the channel of Example 12–5 (for the same flow rate) and calculate the energy and power dissipation in the jump. Assume the dam to be 14 ft high, that critical flow occurs at its crest, and that no energy losses occur on the spillway (Fig. 12–20).

Solution: $E_1 + 14 = E_2$, or

$$\left(\frac{3}{2}\right) 5.84 + 14 = \frac{q^2}{2gy_2{}^2} + y_2$$

so that $y_2{}^3 - 22.76\, y_2{}^2 + 99.7 = 0$. Roots of this cubic equation are $+22.56$, $+2.20$, and -2.00 ft, and thus $y_2 = 2.20$ ft. (The roots $+22.56$ and -2.00 ft are

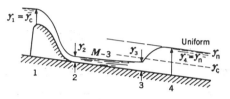

Fig. 12–20. Location of hydraulic jump below spillway.

physically impossible.) The depth y_4 is the normal depth of 10.95 ft, and this is the depth downstream of a jump for which the upstream depth is y_3. From Eq. 12–15,

$$y_3 = \frac{y_4}{2}\left(\sqrt{1 + \frac{8q^2}{gy_4{}^3}} - 1\right) = 2.66 \text{ ft}$$

The length of the *M-3* profile from a depth of 2.20 ft to 2.66 ft is the distance to the jump. The calculations are shown in Table 12–4.

TABLE 12–4
CALCULATION FOR *M-3* CURVE OF EXAMPLE 12–6

y	A	V	$\dfrac{V^2}{2g}$	E	P	R	$R^{4/3}$	S_e	ΔE	$\bar{S}_e$	$\lvert S_b - \bar{S}_e\rvert$	Δx, ft
2.20	110	36.35	20.55	22.75	54.4	2.022	2.555	0.1452				
									2.40	0.1314	0.1304	18.4
2.35	117.5	34.05	18.00	20.35	54.7	2.15	2.77	0.1176				
									1.94	0.1070	0.1060	18.3
2.50	125	32.0	15.91	18.41	55.0	2.27	2.98	0.0965				
									1.72	0.0877	0.0867	19.8
2.66	133	30.05	14.03	16.69	55.32	2.405	3.22	0.0789				

Total length $= 56.5$ ft

In one step,

$$\Delta x = \frac{E_2 - E_3}{\lvert S_b - \bar{S}_e \rvert} = \frac{22.75 - 16.69}{\lvert 0.001 - 0.11205 \rvert} = \frac{6.06}{0.111} = 54.6 \text{ ft}$$

The energy loss in the jump is $E_3 - E_4 = 4.91$ ft lb$_f$/lb (more easily obtained from Eq. 12–17) $= 24{,}500$ ft lb/sec per foot width. The power loss is 44.4 hp per foot width.

12–7. CHANNEL TRANSITIONS

The continuity, momentum, and energy equations together with the specific-thrust and specific-energy diagrams may be used to determine the changes in water surface which occur when the channel bottom is raised, when the channel width is increased or decreased, or when a combination of both exists. We will assume that the transitions are gradual so that energy losses may be neglected. Flow in channel transitions is rapidly varied flow.

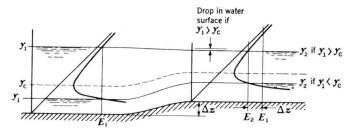

Fɪɢ. 12–21. Effect of rise in channel bed on water-surface elevation.

If the channel bottom is raised a height Δz and the width remains constant (Fig. 12–21), then q is constant and the energy equation is

$$E_1 = E_2 + \Delta z$$

A specific-energy curve (q is constant) may be slid along the channel bottom. If the flow upstream of the rise is subcritical, the depth will decrease in order that the specific energy E may decrease, and if the flow upstream of the rise is supercritical, the depth must increase in order that the specific energy may decrease. As the magnitude of Δz is increased, $E_1 - E_2 = \Delta z$ also increases, and E_2 eventually corresponds to $E_{\min}$, indicating critical flow over the rise. The Δz which produces critical flow is the maximum rise in the bottom that is possible without causing a backwater (M-1 curve) if the upstream flow is subcritical. Additional increase in Δz beyond $E_1 - E_{\min}$ requires an increase in depth, since more specific energy is needed than is available for a depth of the assumed value of y_1. The flow then remains critical over the rise as Δz is increased. If the flow is supercritical upstream and $\Delta z > (E_1 - E_{\min})$, a jump will form upstream of the rise, and the flow will then be subcritical and hence the surface will drop slightly as the flow passes over the rise in the channel floor (Fig. 12–22).

In any case the specific-thrust diagram may also be slid along the channel bed and the net force (per unit width of channel) of the channel transition on the flow stream is the difference in thrust function upstream and downstream of the rise times the specific weight of the water $[F = \gamma(\Delta f)]$.

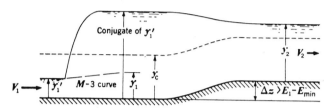

Fig. 12–22. Supercritical flow upstream of rise in channel bed. If $\Delta z > E_1 - E_{min}$, the jump will occur some distance upstream of the rise in the channel bed. On a horizontal bed, the jump will occur where the depth y_i' is less than y_1 (on a M-3 curve) in order that the specific energy E_1' be greater than E_1.

If the channel sides are contracted, the unit discharge increases but the specific energy remains constant (assuming no losses). As the unit dis-

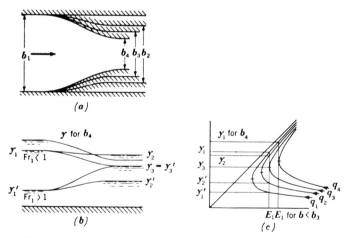

Fig. 12–23. Flow through a constricted channel. a) Plan view, b) elevation, and c) specific energy.

charge q increases, the depth changes as indicated on successive curves for increasing q on a specific-energy diagram. For a given initial flow, there is a unit discharge q_{max} (q_3 in Fig. 12–23) such that E_{min} for this q_{max} corresponds to the initial specific energy E_1. This condition results in critical flow in the constricted section. Making the channel width even narrower will cause a backwater (*M-1* curve) if the upstream flow is subcritical, and the depth will correspond to that value of specific energy on the q_1 curve which is E_{min} for the unit discharge in the constricted section (q_4, for example).

If the upstream flow is supercritical, the depth in the constriction increases as the unit discharge q increases and also becomes critical (for q_3, for example). Further reduction in width causes a jump to form upstream, with a drop in the water surface as for subcritical flow entering the constriction.

EXAMPLE 12–7. Water flows at a rate of 200 ft³/sec in a rectangular channel, (Fig. 12–24) 10 ft wide at a depth of 4 ft. A streamlined pier 2 ft wide and 12 ft long is placed in the middle of the stream. Estimate the depth adjacent to the pier, assuming the drag on the pier to be 1/10 the hydrostatic force on its projected area (the drag coefficient is about 0.05 based on the chord area of the pier).

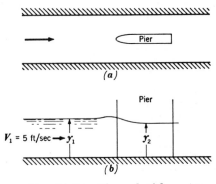

FIG. 12–24. Channel with center pier. *a*) Plan view and *b*) elevation.

Solution:

$$y_{c_1} = \left(\frac{q_1^2}{g} \right)^{1/3} = 2.315 \text{ ft}$$

so that the upstream flow is subcritical. The energy equation is

$$E_1 = E_2 + h_L \quad \text{or} \quad \frac{V_1^2}{2g} + y_1 = \frac{V_2^2}{2g} + y_2 + h_L$$

The continuity equation is

$$V_1 b_1 y_1 = V_2 b_2 y_2$$

The momentum equation is

$$\frac{\gamma y_1^2}{2} b_1 - \frac{\gamma y_2^2}{2} b_2 - \frac{1}{10} \frac{\gamma y_1^2}{2} (2) = Q \frac{\gamma}{g} (V_2 - V_1)$$

The unknowns are V_2, y_2, and h_L. The continuity and momentum equations yield $y_2 = 3.67$ ft and $V_2 = 6.81$ ft/sec. Then $h_L = E_1 - E_2 = 0$. This indicates that the energy loss resulting from the pier exists largely in the wake of the pier, although a different approximation to the drag on the pier would alter the value of h_L slightly.

12–8. SPECIALIZED EXAMPLES OF OPEN-CHANNEL FLOW

Open-channel flow in culverts may be analyzed by using methods already discussed. Flow over steep spillways often involves an aeration process which results in two-phase flow of air and water. Brief mention of these is made to indicate typical fields of engineering interest and research.

Flow in culverts. A culvert should be designed to convey a given discharge with the least head. The flow through a culvert is open-channel flow if the culvert does not flow full and is pipe flow if the culvert does flow full. Factors which determine which type of flow occurs include the size, shape, roughness, length, and slope of the culvert; the inlet and outlet water surface elevations; and the inlet and outlet culvert geometries.

For a long culvert on a steep slope, the control of flow is considered to be at the inlet for part-full flow because the flow will be critical there, and the culvert length, roughness, and outlet conditions will not affect the flow. If the culvert flows full, the control of flow is considered to be owing to culvert friction, although the inlet and outlet losses are also involved but to a lesser degree.

For a long culvert on a mild or horizontal slope with a free outlet, the control of flow is at the outlet for part-full flow because critical flow will occur at the outlet, and the flow will depend on the culvert friction as well as the inlet geometry. If the culvert flows full, control is the same as for a culvert on a long steep slope flowing full.

For a short culvert with a free outlet, part-full flow exists for low inlet heads with both a square and a round inlet (these represent the two extremes of inlet geometry) and for any head on a culvert with a square inlet. A short culvert with a free outlet and a rounded inlet will flow full if the head is about 1.5 diameters above the culvert invert (the bottom of the culvert inlet).

Whether the culvert is on a mild or a steep slope may be determined from the conditions for critical flow (Eq. 12–9b).

$$\frac{Q^2}{g} = \frac{A^3}{b_s} \qquad [12\text{–}9\text{b}]$$

which, when combined with the Manning equation (Eq. 12–4b) for critical flow $\left(Q = \dfrac{1.49}{n} R_h{}^{2/3} S_c{}^{1/2} A, \text{ where } S_c \text{ is the critical slope} \right)$ gives the critical slope in dimensionless form. For a circular culvert (subscript o refers to the entire culvert),

$$\frac{S_c}{\left(\dfrac{n^2}{D^{1/3}}\right)} = \frac{72.9 \left(\dfrac{A}{A_o}\right)}{\left(\dfrac{b_s}{D}\right)\left(\dfrac{R_h}{R_{ho}}\right)^{4/3}} \qquad (12\text{--}18)$$

For a square culvert of sides d and water depth y,

$$\frac{S_c}{\left(\dfrac{n^2}{d^{1/3}}\right)} = \frac{14.6 \left(\dfrac{y}{d}\right)}{\left(\dfrac{\dfrac{y}{d}}{1 + 2\left(\dfrac{y}{d}\right)}\right)^{4/3}} \qquad (12\text{--}19)$$

Equations 12–18 and 12–19 are plotted in Fig. 12–25, and the uniform flow regime or culvert slope for a given flow may be determined from this figure by calculating the value of $S/(n^2/D^{1/3})$ or $S/(n^2/d^{1/3})$ for a given culvert. This given culvert may be on a mild or steep slope, depending on the depth of flow.

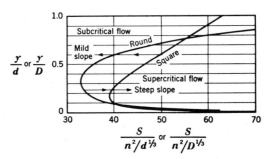

FIG. 12–25. Flow regimes and culvert slope for various depths of flow in square and round culverts.

Once the slope of the culvert is determined, the control point may be established for open-channel flow. For pipe flow, the steady-flow energy equation applied between the headwater and culvert exit may be used to determine the flow for a given head or the head required to produce a specified flow rate. The inlet design is of especial importance for long steep culverts and for short culverts when the headwater is more than about one-half the culvert diameter ($D/2$ for a round culvert and $d/2$ for a square culvert) above the culvert crown at inlet [3].

EXAMPLE 12–8. A 3-ft diameter concrete culvert ($n = 0.011$) is laid on a slope of 0.01. What will be the flow regime for part-full flow?

Solution:

$$\frac{S}{n^2/D^{1/3}} = \frac{0.01}{(0.011)^2/3^{1/3}} = 119$$

From Fig. 12–25, the culvert is steep for nearly all depths, and the flow will be supercritical with flow control at the culvert inlet.

EXAMPLE 12–9. A 4-ft square culvert of unfinished concrete is 100 ft long and has a bottom slope of 0.008. What will be the flow regime for part-full flow?

Solution:

$$\frac{S}{n^2/d^{1/3}} = \frac{0.008}{(0.017)^2/4^{1/3}} = 44$$

From Fig. 12–25, the culvert is on a mild slope and the flow will be subcritical for $0.05 > y/d > 0.43$. Flow control will be at the outlet, and if the outlet is free, critical flow will occur there. For y/d between 0.05 and 0.43 the culvert is on a steep slope, the flow will be supercritical, and flow control will be at the inlet where flow will be critical.

Air-entrained flow on steep slopes. When water flows down a steep slope, the boundary layer thickens in the direction of flow. When the boundary layer thickness is equal to the depth of flow, a self-aeration process results in a two-phase flow with a frothy appearance. The aeration process is related to the turbulence conditions within the flow. The mixture consists of bubbles entrained in the water in a lower region near the channel bed, with increasing air concentration in the vertical direction, through a transition region, and to an upper region in which water particles move through air.

There are indications of a bulking effect for aerated flow. The flow velocity, however, is greater for air-entrained flow than for non-aerated flow of water at the same water flow rate. Experiments indicate that the same form of discharge equation may be used for aerated flow as for nonaerated flow with the same value of roughness coefficient if appropriate depths are used in each instance.

REFERENCES

1. Hunter Rouse, T. T. Siaa, and S. Nagaratnam, "Turbulence Characteristics of the Hydraulic Jump," Hydraulics Division ASCE, *Proceedings Paper 1528*, Vol. 84, No. HY1 (Feb. 1928), pp. 1–30, and discussion by D. R. F. Harleman, Hydraulics Division ASCE, *Proceedings Paper 1856*, Vol. 84, No. HY6 (Nov. 1958), pp. 52–55.

2. E. A. Elevatorski, *Hydraulic Energy Dissipators* (New York: McGraw-Hill Book Company, Inc., 1959).

3. Lorenz G. Straub, Alvin G. Anderson, and Charles E. Bowers, "Importance of Inlet Design on Culvert Capacity," *Technical Paper No. 13, Series B,* University of Minnesota, St. Anthony Falls Hydraulic Laboratory, August, 1953; or "Culvert Hydraulics," *Research Report 15-B,* Highway Research Board, National Academy of Sciences—National Research Council, Washington, D. C., 1953, pp. 53–71.

The reader is referred to the following sources for additional information on open channel flow:

B. A. Bakhmeteff, *Hydraulics of Open Channels* (New York: McGraw-Hill Book Company, Inc., 1932).

V. T. Chow, *Open-Channel Hydraulics* (New York: McGraw-Hill Book Company, Inc., 1959).

F. M. Henderson, *Open Channel Flow* (New York: The Macmillan Company, 1966).

PROBLEMS

12–1. Show that the expression for the average bed shear stress in an open channel (Eq. 12–1) is also a valid expression for the wall shear stress for incompressible flow in a pipe.

12–2. Water flows at a rate of 800 ft³/sec in a rectangular channel 16 ft wide. What are the Froude number and the type of flow if the depth is *a*) 2 ft, *b*) 4 ft, and *c*) 6 ft? *d*) At what depth will the flow be critical?

12–3. Water flows in a trapezoidal channel. The base is 10 ft wide, the sides slope 45 deg, and the flow depth is 5 ft. What are the Froude number and the type of flow for a flow rate of *a*) 500 ft³/sec and *b*) 1000 ft³/sec?

12–4. Water flows at a rate of 300 ft³/sec in a trapezoidal channel with a base 12 ft wide and sides sloping 60 deg from the horizontal. What are the Froude number and the type of flow for a flow depth of *a*) 4 ft and *b*) 2 ft? *c*) At what depth will the flow be critical?

$$Ans. \quad a) \; Fr = 0.50, \text{ subcritical; } c) \; y_c = 2.57 \text{ ft}$$

12–5. The value of Manning's n is rather insensitive to large variations in the absolute roughness k. *a*) Show from Eqs. 10–24 and 12–5 that

$$\log_{10} \frac{2R_h}{k} = \frac{1.49}{4\sqrt{2g}} \left(\frac{R_h^{1/6}}{n} \right) - 0.87$$

b) Plot a relation between $2R_h/k$ and $R_h^{1/6}/n$ on log-log paper for a range of $R_h^{1/6}/n$ from 40 to 120, a three-fold range in n for a given R_h. *c*) What is the range in absolute roughness k for the range in n plotted in part *b*)?

$$Ans. \quad c) \; 5170{:}1$$

12–6. What range in absolute surface roughness k is indicated by a range in Manning's n from 0.012 to 0.024 for a hydraulic radius of 4 ft? Refer to Prob. 12–5.

12–7. Calculate the area A, the perimeter P, the hydraulic radius R_h, the surface breadth b_s, and the hydraulic depth y_h for the following channel sections. *a*) Rectangular, 6 ft deep and 9 ft wide. *b*) Rectangular, 9 ft deep and 6 ft wide.

c) Trapezoidal, one-half a hexagon, 6 ft deep. *d*) Trapezoidal, 6 ft deep, 16-ft base width, sides sloping 60 deg from the horizontal. *e*) Triangular, 6 ft deep, $\theta = 45$ deg [Fig. 12–6(*b*)]. *f*) Parabolic, $y = 0.1x^2$, depth = 6 ft.

Ans. *c*) $A = 62.4$ ft², $P = 20.8$ ft, $R_h = 3$ ft, $b_s = 13.86$ ft, and $y_h = 4.50$ ft

12–8. For uniform flow in an open channel with $n = 0.014$, laid on a slope of 0.006, and having a cross-sectional area of $A = 80$ ft², what is the flow rate *a*) for a rectangular channel with a width $b = 20$ ft and depth $y = 4$ ft, *b*) for a half hexagon, and *c*) for a semicircle?

12–9. Water flows uniformly 3 ft deep in a rectangular open channel 20 ft wide. The channel is of unfinished concrete and has a bed slope of 0.010. Is the flow subcritical, critical, or supercritical?

12–10. What is the unit discharge for uniform flow in a very wide rectangular channel with $n = 0.013$ laid on a slope of 0.001 for a flow depth of 4 ft?

Ans. $q = 36.6$ cfs/ft

12–11. A rectangular channel 10 ft wide discharges 200 cfs when the depth is 4 ft. What is the flow rate when the depth is 6 ft?

12–12. Uniform flow in a rectangular channel 10 ft wide with a bed slope of 0.0004 and $n = 0.0149$ occurs at a 3-ft depth. What is the Froude number of the flow?

12–13. A rectangular open channel 20 ft wide has $n = 0.0149$, a uniform flow depth of 4 ft, and a bottom slope of 0.0036. Will an elementary surface wave travel upstream?

12–14. What size (to the nearest foot) circular concrete culvert ($n = 0.013$) will convey 500 cfs on a slope of 0.001 when flowing half full?

12–15. The depth downstream from a sluicegate in an unfinished concrete rectangular channel 8 ft wide is 1.5 ft. The flow rate is 35 cfs. *a*) For what channel slope will the depth remain at 1.5 ft? *b*) How will the depth change if the channel slope is 1/600? *c*) How will the depth change if the slope is 1/1200?

Ans. *a*) $S = 0.00099$

12–16. Uniform flow occurs in an open channel with a 90-degree V shape at a rate of 10 cfs. The roughness value is $n = 0.012$. At what slope of the channel will the flow be critical?

Ans. $S_c = 0.0037$

12–17. For a given flow rate Q, channel slope S, and roughness n, show that the total vertex angle for a triangular channel for minimum perimeter (and hence channel material) is 90 deg.

12–18. Uniform flow occurs at a depth of 2.2 ft in a rectangular channel 12 ft wide on a slope of 0.002. The channel is made of unfinished concrete. Is the flow subcritical or supercritical?

Ans. Fr = 0.64, subcritical

12–19. What is the minimum slope on which a rough concrete rectangular open channel will convey 600 ft³/sec at an average velocity of 5 ft/sec? Hint: The minimum slope is associated with a maximum hydraulic radius.

12–20. What is the minimum slope on which a trapezoidal channel of unfinished concrete will convey 300 ft³/sec at an average velocity of 6 ft/sec?

12–21. Determine the size of rough concrete channels with a bed slope of 5 ft per mile and having the most efficient cross sections which will convey 100 ft³/sec. Consider *a*) rectangular, *b*) semicircular, and *c*) trapezoidal cross sections.

12–22. It is desired to convey 30 ft³/sec of water in a rectangular channel on a slope of 0.01. What are the dimensions of the channel when a minimum of unplaned timber is used in its construction?

Ans. $y = 1.316$ ft, $b = 2.632$ ft

12–23. A flow of 1 cfs is conveyed in a 90-deg triangular channel (sides slope 45 deg) made of structural aluminum ($n = 0.010$) and at a slope of 0.010. *a*) What is the normal depth? *b*) What is the Froude number?

12–24. At what depth will uniform flow occur in a rectangular channel 20 ft wide, laid on a slope of 0.001, and lined with unfinished concrete for a flow of 1000 ft³/sec? Is the slope of the channel mild or steep?

Ans. $y_n = 7.02$ ft

12–25. Find *a*) the normal depth and *b*) the Froude number for a flow of 250 ft³/sec in a rough concrete, trapezoidal channel. The bottom width is 8 ft and the sides slope 60 deg from the horizontal. The bed slope is 20 ft per mile.

12–26. What is the normal depth for a unit discharge of 40 cfs/ft in a wide, rough concrete channel having a bed slope of 0.002?

12–27. What is the normal depth for a flow of 600 ft³/sec in a rough concrete, trapezoidal channel with a bottom width of 12 ft and a bed slope of 0.008? Consider sides sloping *a*) 90 deg from the horizontal (rectangular), *b*) 60 deg from the horizontal, and *c*) 45 deg from the horizontal.

12–28. A rectangular channel 20 ft wide conveys 200 cfs at a depth of 5 ft. *a*) What is the critical depth for this flow? *b*) What is the Froude number? *c*) What is the specific energy of the flow? *d*) If $n = 0.012$, what slope will produce uniform flow?

12–29. Water flows 4 ft deep at an average velocity of 8 ft/sec in a rectangular channel. *a*) What is the Froude number? *b*) What is the specific energy? *c*) What is the alternate depth? *d*) What is the specific thrust? *e*) What is the conjugate depth?

Ans. *b*) $E = 4.994$ ft, *d*) $f = 15.95$ ft²

12–30. A rectangular channel 25 ft wide with $n = 0.020$ conveys 600 cfs. At what slope will the flow be critical?

Ans. $S_c = 0.00546$

12-31. Repeat Prob. 12–30 for a trapezoidal channel with a bottom width of 25 ft and sides sloping 45 deg.

12-32. Derive an expression relating critical depth and critical velocity for a triangular channel.

$$Ans. \quad V_c = \sqrt{g \, y_c/2}$$

12-33. Water flows at a rate of 120 cfs in a rectangular channel 8 ft wide. a) What is the maximum depth for supercritical flow? b) What is the specific energy for a depth of 4 ft? c) What is the alternate depth for part b)?

12-34. The Froude number is 0.6 at a flow depth of 4 ft in a rectangular channel. a) What is the critical depth for this flow rate? b) For what flow rate would the 4-ft depth be critical?

$$Ans. \quad a) \quad y_c = 2.85 \text{ ft}$$
$$b) \quad q = 45.4 \text{ cfs/ft}$$

12-35. Show that for a nonrectangular channel, the specific thrust function is
$$f = A\bar{y} + Q^2/Ag$$
where A is the channel cross section and $\bar{y}$ is the depth to the centroid of this section.

12-36. Plot curves of specific energy versus depth for flow in a rectangular channel at unit discharges of a) $q = 20$ cfs/ft, b) $q = 30$ cfs/ft, and c) $q = 40$ cfs/ft. Use a scale of 1 in. = 1 ft and plot for depths up to 7 ft. From the graphs determine the critical depth for each unit discharge and compare with calculated values.

12-37. Plot curves of specific thrust versus depth for flow in a rectangular channel at unit discharges of a) $q = 20$ cfs/ft, b) $q = 30$ cfs/ft, and c) $q = 40$ cfs/ft. Use a scale of 1 in. = 1 ft for depths and 1 in. = 5 ft² for specific thrust and plot for depths up to 7 ft. From the graphs determine the critical depth for each unit discharge and compare with calculated values.

12-38. The unit discharge in a rectangular channel is 40 cfs/ft and the depth is 6 ft. From the graphs plotted in Probs. 12–36 and 12–37, or from numerical computations, determine a) the alternate depth and b) the conjugate, or sequent, depth.

12-39. The unit discharge in a rectangular channel is 20 cfs/ft and the depth is 7 ft. From the graphs plotted in Probs. 12–36 and 12–37, or from numerical calculation, determine a) the alternate depth and b) the conjugate, or sequent, depth.

12-40. The depth upstream from a sluice gate [Fig. 12–11(c)] in a rectangular channel is 7 ft. From the curves plotted in Probs. 12–36 and 12–37 determine the depth downstream from the sluice gate and the force on the sluice gate per foot of channel width for flow at each unit discharge plotted.

12-41. Water flows over the crest of a spillway (from a mild to a steep slope) at a critical depth of 2.5 ft. Calculate the flow over a spillway 60 ft wide.

12-42. Water flows 8-ft deep in a rectangular channel 12 ft wide at a rate of 480 ft³/sec. a) What is the critical depth for this flow? b) Is the flow subcritical, critical, or supercritical? c) At what other depth could the water flow with the same specific energy?

12-43. Equation 12-7a is plotted in Fig. 12-8 as E versus y for various values of constant unit discharge q. If the specific energy E is constant, the unit discharge q is a function of depth y. *a*) Show that for flow at constant specific energy, $q = y\sqrt{2g(E - y)}$. *b*) Show that the flow is critical for maximum q, and that for flow at constant specific energy, $y_c = 2E/3$. *c*) Show that

$$\frac{q}{q_{max}} = \frac{3}{2}\frac{y}{E}\sqrt{3\left(1 - \frac{y}{E}\right)}$$

d) Plot a dimensionless curve of y/E versus q/q_{max} for flow at constant specific energy.

12-44. What is the critical slope for a flow of 820 ft³/sec in a rectangular channel 20 ft wide for a roughness coefficient of $n = 0.015$?

Ans. $S_c = 0.00322$

12-45. A V-shaped, 90-deg, triangular channel has a slope $S = 0.0001$, a roughness $n = 0.0149$, a flow rate $Q = 0.5$ ft³/sec, and each side slopes 45 deg from the horizontal. *a*) What is the normal depth? *b*) At what depth would the specific energy be a minimum? *c*) Is the flow in part *a*) subcritical or supercritical?

12-46. A rectangular channel 18 ft wide conveys 540 ft³/sec at a depth of 5 ft. *a*) What is the critical depth? *b*) Is the given flow subcritical or supercritical? *c*) What is the Froude number of the flow? *d*) What is the specific energy? *e*) If Manning's $n = 0.012$, what slope would be required to maintain uniform flow? *f*) Is this slope a mild or a steep slope?

Ans.   *a*) $y_c = 3.04$ ft; *b*) subcritical, since $y > y_c$; *c*) Fr = 0.473;
d) $E = 5.56$ ft; *e*) $S = 0.000493$; *f*) mild, since uniform flow
is subcritical.

12-47. A dam in the channel of Prob. 12-24 increases the depth to 12 ft. What is the depth 4000 ft upstream from the dam?

Ans. $y = 9.17$ ft

12-48. Repeat Example 12-5 for a bed slope of 0.002.

12-49. A trapezoidal channel of rough concrete has a bottom width of 12 ft, a bed slope of 0.0025, and sides which slope 45 deg from the horizontal. The channel conveys 500 ft³/sec. A dam increases the depth to 6 ft. *a*) What is the normal depth? *b*) What is the depth 400 ft upstream from the dam? *c*) What is the depth 800 ft upstream from the dam?

Ans. *a*) $y_n = 4.17$ ft, *b*) $y = 5.20$ ft, *c*) $y = 4.59$ ft

12-50. Verify the correctness of the water surface profiles and the impossibility of other profiles for each flow situation shown in Fig. 12-15.

12-51. A hydraulic jump forms in a long, unfinished concrete channel 10 ft wide and laid on a slope of 0.001. The flow rate is 200 ft³/sec. What is the depth just upstream of the jump? Assume uniform flow downstream of the jump.

Ans. $y_1 = 1.12$ ft

12-52. At a section in a wide channel the depth is 3 ft and the velocity is

12 ft/sec. If a hydraulic jump occurs, would it be upstream or downstream of this section? Explain.

12–53. For a hydraulic jump in a rectangular channel, show that the Froude number upstream Fr_1 and the Froude number downstream Fr_2 are related by the equation

$$Fr_2{}^2 = \frac{8\ Fr_1{}^2}{(\sqrt{1 + 8Fr_1{}^2} - 1)^3}$$

12–54. By equating both unit discharge and specific thrust upstream and downstream of a hydraulic jump, show that

$$\frac{1 + 2Fr_1{}^2}{Fr_1{}^{4/3}} = \frac{1 + 2Fr_2{}^2}{Fr_2{}^{4/3}} = f(Fr)$$

Plot Fr versus $f(Fr)$ and compare with Fig. 9–6, a similar plot for normal shocks in a gas.

12–55. Water flows 4 ft deep at an average velocity of 15 ft/sec in a rectangular channel 25 ft wide. What downstream depth is necessary to form a hydraulic jump?

12–56. Water enters a long, wide rectangular channel at the foot of a spillway at a velocity of 24 ft/sec and a depth of 0.50 ft. The channel has a bed slope of $1/1600$ and $n = 0.0165$. *a)* What is the normal depth for the channel? This is the depth downstream of the hydraulic jump which will form. *b)* How far from the foot of the spillway will the jump form?

12–57. Water in a wide rectangular channel flows at an average velocity V_1 and at a depth of y_1. A surge traveling upstream at a velocity V_s produces an increase in depth to y_2 and a velocity V_2 relative to a reference at rest. *a)* Write continuity and momentum equations for a steady-state flow system and show that

$$\frac{(V_1 + V_s)^2}{gy_1} = \frac{y_2}{2y_1}\left(1 + \frac{y_2}{y_1}\right)$$

b) Show that if $y_2/y_1 > 1$, $(V_1 + V_s) > \sqrt{gy_1}$, indicating a Froude number relative to the surge front greater than unity. *c)* Show that as $y_2/y_1 \rightarrow 1$, $(V_1 + V_s) \rightarrow \sqrt{gy_1}$. Thus a small surge travels at a velocity $\sqrt{gy_1}$ relative to the water over which it moves.

12–58. Water in a wide river flows at an average velocity of 12 ft/sec at a mean depth of 12 ft. A tidal bore produces a change in depth of 3 ft. At what velocity does the bore travel upstream?

$$Ans.\quad V_{bore} = 11.33\ ft/sec$$

12–59. A tidal bore travels upstream in a wide river at 6 mph. The river depth upstream of the bore is 8 ft, and downstream of the bore the river depth is 10 ft. What is the average velocity of the flow in the river upstream of the bore?

12–60. Water flows from a sluice gate at a depth less than critical. It proceeds downstream on a horizontal channel which extends a great distance, then drops off suddenly. Assume critical flow at the drop-off (actually the flow is critical a very short distance upstream from the drop-off). Identify the water surface profiles, and describe how to determine the location of the hydraulic jump.

12–61. In Prob. 12–60 the depth at the contracted section below the sluice gate [y_2 in Fig. 12–11(c)] is 1.00 ft, the horizontal channel is 10 ft wide and 1000 ft long, $n = 0.014$, and $q = 32$ cfs/ft. Locate the hydraulic jump.

      Ans. $L = 152$ ft downstream from the contracted section below the sluice gate.

12–62. Through a smooth transition between two rectangular channels the width increases from 10 ft to 12 ft, but the water surface does not change in elevation. If the upstream depth is 5 ft, how much is the bed of the channel raised in the transition? Neglect losses.

      Ans. $\Delta z = 10$ in.

12–63. Water flows at a depth of 5 ft in a rectangular channel 10 ft wide. A smooth hump 1 ft high in the channel bed produces a drop of 6 in. in the water surface. What is the flow rate? Neglect losses.

12–64. Water flows at an average velocity of 8 ft/sec at a depth of 6 ft in a rectangular channel. What is the change in depth and the change in stage (water surface level) for a) a smooth rise of $\frac{1}{2}$ ft in the channel bed and b) a smooth drop of $\frac{1}{2}$ ft in the channel bed?

12–65. Repeat Prob. 12–64 for flow at 16 ft/sec at a depth of 2 ft.

12–66. An essentially horizontal channel narrows down from 10 ft to 5 ft in width. The depth in the upstream 10-ft section is 2 ft. a) What is the depth in the 5-ft section for a flow of 480 ft³/sec? Assume no losses. b) Sketch specific-energy diagrams for this channel and locate appropriate depths [see Fig. 12–23(c)].

12–67. The flow rate in a constant-width rectangular channel is 29.5 cfs/ft. A sill raises the bottom of the channel 1 ft. What is the depth of flow over the sill for an initial depth upstream of a) 6 ft and b) 1.5 ft? Assume no losses. c) Locate appropriate depths on a specific-energy diagram.

      Ans. a) $y = 4.79$ ft, b) $y = 1.67$ ft

12–68. The bottom of a constant-width rectangular channel is raised gradually. The depth and velocity upstream of the raised bed are 10 ft and 10 ft/sec, respectively. a) For no losses, what is the maximum height the bottom may be raised without affecting the flow depth upstream? b) For the condition of part a) what is the horizontal component of force acting on the curved portion of the raised bed per unit width of channel? Neglect bed shear.

12–69. A rectangular channel 4 ft wide conveys 40 cfs uniformly at a depth of 2.8 ft. What is the widest streamlined obstruction which may be placed in the center of the channel which will not cause a backwater? Increasing the width of the pier will increase the flow velocity adjacent to it until critical flow occurs.

12–70. Give a verbal definition (use no equations) of the following terms as applied to open channel flow. a) Uniform flow. b) Normal depth. c) Hydraulic radius. d) Hydraulic grade line. e) Specific energy. f) Mild slope. g) Critical slope. h) Steep slope. i) Critical depth. j) Hydraulic jump.

13

Flow Measurements

It is both desirable and necessary in many instances to know the magnitude of various flow parameters such as speed or velocity, pressure, temperature, and volumetric, or mass-flow rate, in a fluid system. These instances might include 1) manufacturing process control; 2) rating tests of equipment such as pumps, turbines, fans, blowers, propellers, airfoils, and so forth; 3) hydrological studies of rainfall and drainage in watershed areas and the apportioning and control of water in irrigation systems; 4) establishment of costs when fluids are sold to a customer, such as water, gas, steam for processing or heating, and liquid fuels; and 5) experimental work in research and development programs.

Fluid-flow measurement techniques are becoming more and more complex because of the greater demand for more detailed information and because of the need for remote measurements using telemetering techniques, which involve electronic methods. Measurement systems consist of three component parts: a sensing device, a transmitting medium or system, and an indicating or recording device. This chapter generally will deal with only those components which involve fluids or fluid systems. A treatment of electrical or electronic components is not within the scope of the text.

Included in this chapter are discussions of velocity measurements and flow-rate measurements. Flow measurements might be considered a science of coefficients, because we generally apply the Bernoulli equation for liquid flow and the steady-flow energy equation for isentropic gas flow (in each instance a frictionless fluid is assumed) and then compare the actual behavior of a real (viscous) fluid with the ideal fluid by means of velocity or discharge coefficients. In many instances real fluids behave very much like ideal fluids, so that these coefficients are then nearly unity.

13–1. VELOCITY MEASUREMENTS

The velocity at a point or a number of points throughout a section in a fluid stream is often needed in order to establish the velocity profile. This velocity profile may be of interest in the fundamental studies of boundary layers or wakes, or it may be necessary in order to obtain the average velocity throughout the section from an integration of the velocity profile in order to determine the flow rate. A point velocity is almost impossible to measure, since any sensing device occupies a finite region. However, if the area of flow occupied by the sensing element is very small compared with the total area of the flow stream, we may consider the measured velocity to be essentially a point velocity. For example, a current meter sweeping out an 8-in. circle in a river would measure essentially a point velocity, while in a 12-in. pipe it would not. A 12-in. anemometer measuring wind speeds would indicate essentially a point velocity in the atmosphere, while in a 24-in. duct it would not. A ¼-in. tube facing upstream in a 6-in. pipe would indicate essentially a point velocity in the central flow area of the pipe, but measurements near the pipe wall, where the velocity gradient is large, would require a tube such as a small hypodermic needle to measure point velocities.

It is essential that the presence of the sensing device in the flow stream will not affect the flow being measured, and this requirement also limits the size of instrument which may be used satisfactorily.

Velocities are commonly measured indirectly by measuring the difference between the stagnation and free-stream pressures, by the speed of rotating vaned wheels, by the cooling effect on a thin cylinder in crossflow, and by the angle of oblique shocks in a supersonic gas. In some instances velocities are measured directly by determining the distance traveled by a group of fluid particles in a measured time interval.

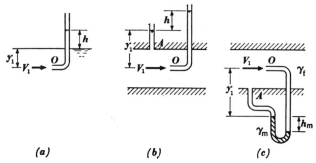

(a) (b) (c)

FIG. 13–1. Pitot tube. In a) an open liquid stream, b) a pipe, and c) a pipe, connected to a manometer.

Pitot tube. If a bent open tube is placed to face upstream in an open liquid stream, the liquid will rise in the tube a height h (capillary effects are assumed absent) as in Fig. 13–1(a). The Bernoulli equation written from a point upstream from the submerged end of the tube and the end of the tube itself is

$$\frac{\rho V_1{}^2}{2} + p_1 = p_0 \tag{13–1}$$

since a stagnation condition exists within the tube. Since $p_1 = \gamma y_1$ and $p_0 = \gamma(y_1 + h)$, Eq. 13–1 may be solved for the stream velocity.

$$V_1 = \sqrt{\frac{2\gamma h}{\rho}} = \sqrt{2gh} \tag{13–2}$$

If the stream velocity at a point in a pipe is to be measured [Fig. 13–1(b)], the same equation is obtained. If the static pressure is high, y_1 is large and reading of the piezometric heights y_1 and $y_1 + h$ may be difficult (y_1 would be about 231 ft for water at a pressure of 100 psig in a pipe).[1]

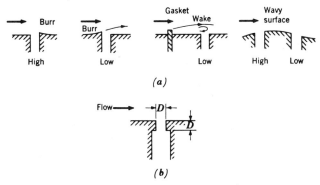

FIG. 13–2. Piezometer tap geometries. a) Poor taps. Measured pressures are referred to actual pressures. b) Good tap.

The tubes in Fig. 13–1(b) may be connected to a simple manometer as in Fig. 13–1(c) to result in a more convenient system. The difference between stagnation and static (free-stream) pressure is

$$p_0 - p_1 = h_m(\gamma_m - \gamma_f)$$

where h_m is the manometer deflection, and γ_m and γ_f are the specific weights of the manometer and flowing fluids, respectively. The stream velocity becomes

$$V_1 = \sqrt{2gh_m \frac{\gamma_m - \gamma_f}{\gamma_f}} = \sqrt{\frac{2(p_0 - p_s)}{\rho}} \qquad (13\text{--}3)$$

The total head or impact tube and its opening should be as small as possible in order that essentially a point velocity be measured. If Re = $ur/\nu < 50$ (r is the radius of the tube opening) laminar flow effects around the tube will cause the indicated stagnation pressure to be in error [1].

The system shown in Fig. 13–1(c) may be incorporated into a single instrument known as a *combined pitot tube*. This tube consists of two concentric cylinders bent into a L-shape and with various head forms, such that the inner cylinder is at the stagnation pressure and the annular region

---

[1]The shape of piezometer taps, such as at A in Fig. 13–1(b), is critical. They should be made in a smooth region, far removed from internal projections such as flange gaskets, flanges themselves, wavy surfaces, and so forth. No burrs resulting from drilling should project into the flow stream. Good and poor piezometer taps are shown in Fig. 13–2.

between cylinders is at the free-stream pressure. Sketches of two common head forms for a combined pitot tube are shown in Fig. 13–3. Different head forms have been used to improve accuracy for various angles of yaw (angle between free-stream velocity vector and pitot tube). The indicated static pressure is subject to some uncertainty because the static holes may be exposed to a pressure slightly different from that of the free stream. If the flow is turbulent, the high-frequency velocity and pressure variations have the effect of indicating a velocity higher than the time-average velocity, and it is common to use a coefficient C_v, so that

$$V_1 = C_v \sqrt{2gh_m \frac{\gamma_m - \gamma_f}{\gamma_f}} \qquad (13\text{--}4)$$

Unless an instrument is carefully calibrated, C_v is usually assumed to be unity. One calibration method consists of towing a pitot tube at a measurable speed through still water or air, in which case the turbulence

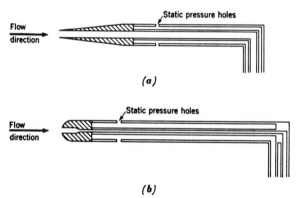

FIG. 13–3. Combined pitot tubes. *a)* Brabbee's design and *b)* Prandtl's design. Prandtl's design is accurate over a greater range of yaw than Brabbee's design.

level of the fluid would be zero, though the instrument may not produce exactly the same manometer deflection in a moving turbulent stream under otherwise identical flow conditions.

It should be pointed out that velocity fluctuations are manifested as pressure fluctuations, and these are generally damped out (depending on their frequency) if a liquid manometer system is used with the pitot or impact tube. A pressure transducer mounted in the instrument and connected to an electronic circuit is necessary if fluctuating pressures are to be measured with any degree of accuracy.

In a gas flow, compressibility must be considered, and the appropriate equation for *subsonic* flow is Eq. 9–9a. This equation may be written as

$$V_1 = \sqrt{\frac{2kRT_1}{k-1}\left[\left(\frac{p_0}{p_1}\right)^{\frac{k-1}{k}} - 1\right]} \qquad (13\text{-}5)$$

or in terms of the Mach number being measured.

$$M_1 = \sqrt{\frac{2}{k-1}\left[\left(\frac{p_0}{p_1}\right)^{\frac{k-1}{k}} - 1\right]} \qquad (13\text{-}6)$$

For these high-velocity gas flows, the free-stream static pressure p_1 must be known, since it is the value $p_0 - p_1$ which is measured with the manometer. From these values the ratio p_0/p_1 may be obtained.

For a *supersonic* gas stream, the pitot tube equation is given by Eq. 9–39 as

$$\frac{p_0}{p_1} = \left(\frac{k+1}{2}M_1^2\right)^{\frac{k}{k-1}}\left(\frac{2k}{k+1}M_1^2 - \frac{k-1}{k+1}\right)^{\frac{1}{1-k}} \qquad (13\text{-}7)$$

and the Mach number corresponding to the measured value of p_0/p_1 may be found from gas tables (Table A–2, for example). The conventional static tube will not indicate the free-stream pressure, since it is in a subsonic region behind the shock which forms forward of the tube. The static pressure of the free stream must be obtained by other means.

EXAMPLE 13–1. What water velocity is indicated for a deflection of 3.5 in. on a mercury manometer connected to a combined pitot tube?

Solution: From Eq. 13–3,

$$V_1 = \sqrt{(2)(32.17)(3.5/12)(13.56 - 1)} = 15.36 \text{ ft/sec}$$

EXAMPLE 13–2. A pitot tube in air at a temperature of 5.5 F at 15,000 ft ($p_1 = 8.3$ psia) indicates a difference between stagnation and static pressure of 4.7 psi. What is the velocity and Mach number being measured?

Solution:

$$\frac{p_0}{p_1} = \frac{8.3 + 4.7}{8.3} = 1.566 < 1/0.528$$

so the flow is subsonic. From Eq. 13–6 or Table 9–2,

$$M_1 = 0.828 \quad \text{and} \quad V_1 = M_1 c_1 = 0.828\sqrt{(1.4)(1715)(465.5)}$$

so that $V_1 = 877$ ft/sec.

A pitot tube may be used in a mixture of gas bubbles and liquid (such as air and water) for gas concentration C no greater than about 0.6 by volume if the concentration is known. The pitot tube, connecting tubing, and manometers must be free of bubbles. The velocity being measured is the mean velocity of the mixture and is

$$V_{\text{mixture}} = \sqrt{\frac{2(p_0 - p_1)}{(1 - C)\rho_{\text{liquid}}}} = \sqrt{\frac{2gh_m}{(1 - C)}\left(\frac{\gamma_m}{\gamma_{\text{liquid}}} - 1\right)} \qquad (13\text{-}8)$$

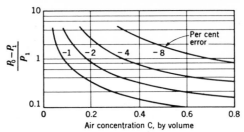

<FIG. 13–4>. Effect of neglecting air compressibility on measurement of velocity of an air-water mixture with a combined pitot tube.

where h_m is the manometer deflection and γ_m and γ_{liquid} are the specific weights of the manometer fluid and the flowing liquid, respectively.

Errors due to compressible effects are negligible for high concentrations at low velocities or low concentrations at higher velocities. Equation 13–8 is within the indicated accuracy for conditions as shown in Fig. 13–4. If the gas fraction in a gas-liquid mixture is assumed to flow isentropically to a stagnation point, the steady-flow energy equation applied to the mixture may be shown to result in

$$\frac{V_1^2}{2} = \frac{p_0 - p_1}{\rho_w(1 - C)} + \frac{C}{1 - C}\left(\frac{p_1}{\rho_w}\right)\left[\frac{k}{k - 1}\left(\frac{p_0}{p_1}\right)^{\frac{k-1}{k}} - \frac{1}{k - 1} - \left(\frac{p_0}{p_1}\right)\right] \quad (13\text{–}9)$$

The last term expresses the effect of gas compressibility, and the error in neglecting it (as in Eq. 13–8) is the ratio of the second to the first term on the right-hand side of Eq. 13–9. The expression,

Error =

$$\sqrt{1 + \frac{C}{(p_0 - p_1)/p_1}\left[\frac{k}{k-1}\left(\frac{p_0 - p_1}{p_1} + 1\right)^{\frac{k-1}{k}} - \frac{1}{k-1} - \left(\frac{p_0 - p_1}{p_1} + 1\right)\right]} - 1$$

$$(13\text{–}10)$$

is plotted in Fig. 13–4.

Pitot cylinder. A small cylinder mounted in a pipe so that it is free to move along the diameter of the pipe and which has a small hole at a forward stagnation point (leading edge of the cylinder) may be used in conjunction with a wall piezometer tap to measure the difference between stagnation and static pressure. A cylinder of this type is known as a pitot cylinder (Fig. 13–5). If velocity measurements are made at a number of points, the velocity profile may be determined and the flow rate calculated.

Equation 13–4, with $C_v = 1.00$, may be used for the pitot cylinder as well as the pitot tube. The flow area obstructed by the cylinder should be

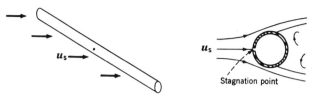

FIG. 13-5. Pitot cylinder.

kept small, preferably less than about 2 or 3 per cent, in order that choking effects may be minimized. The piezometer tap should not be in the plane of the pitot cylinder for the same reason. The static pressure in this plane will be measured too low if the piezometer tap is in the choked section.

The pressure field around a cylinder, shown in Fig. 13-6(a), is such that if the pressure tap or slots in it are placed 35 deg to 40 deg above and below the stagnation point and are connected to opposite sides of a differential manometer (or other pressure differential indicator), the cylinder then becomes a sensitive device for determining flow direction. When the manometer deflection is zero, the point 0 faces directly upstream. A slight change in direction of the velocity vector u_s unbalances the manometer, since the pressure at one tap rises and that at the other drops. This device is used in aircraft to indicate rate of climb and in ducts to detect spiral flows.

In order to obtain an average velocity from measurements made at

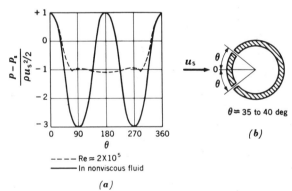

FIG. 13-6. a) Pressure field around a cylinder. b) Cylinder used as a direction indicator.

various points throughout a flow cross section, it is often convenient to take the measurements at the centroids of equal subareas. The measurements may then be averaged arithmetically to obtain the average flow velocity. The accuracy of the result depends, of course, on taking sufficient point velocities. In axisymmetric flow in round pipes, point velocities should be taken midway between equal increments of $\Delta(r^2)$. If ten readings are taken, they should be made at distances from the pipe axis equal to 0.05, 0.15, 0.25,   , and 0.95 R^2, and velocities measured at these points may be averaged directly. If n readings are taken to represent the individual velocities u_i of n subareas, the average velocity V is

$$V = \frac{1}{n} \sum_{i=1}^{i=n} u_i \qquad (13\text{--}11)$$

If the velocity profile itself is obtained from measurements, the average velocity may be obtained by a graphical integration of the area under the velocity vs. r^2 curve or by the use of Simpson's rule or the trapezoidal rule.

A reasonably good, though not accurate, estimate of the average velocity for fully developed flow in a pipe may be made by a measurement of the center-line velocity at a section (preceded by a long section of straight pipe). An estimate of the ratio of maximum to average velocity may be made from Eq. 10–22, but it is at best an estimate, especially if the pipe roughness is not known or if fully developed flow cannot be assured.

Length-time measurements. The distance traversed by a group of fluid particles in a given time interval is a measure of the fluid velocity,

Fig. 13–7. Surface flow pattern for water approaching spillway of model of a dam. (Courtesy of Dr. Lorenz G. Straub.)

averaged over the measured distance. If a salt solution is injected into a stream, its transit time between two sets of electrodes may be measured because of the change in fluid resistivity as the salt slug passes the electrode pairs. This method has been used in large turbine penstocks over rather large distances and in aerated flows where minute cloudlets of salt solution are injected at a rate of 20 injections per second and the transit time between electrodes 3 in. apart in the flow path are recorded by electronic means [2].

Turbulent flow patterns in liquids may be observed by adding non-soluble droplets of a fluid whose density is the same as that of the flowing liquid and taking photographs with a known time exposure. If paper punchings (confetti) are spread over the surface of a liquid stream, the surface flow pattern may be obtained from a photograph of known time exposure. Both the magnitude and direction of motion of the surface may be obtained. A typical photograph of this type for flow approaching the spillway of a dam model is shown in Fig. 13–7.

Current meters and anemometers. Cones on current meters used in water and hemispheres on anemometers used in air are attached to radial arms mounted on a central shaft as shown in Fig. 13–8.

A flow stream in the plane of rotation from any direction will create drag on all cones or cups. The drag on cone A (and cup A) is greater than that on cone B (and cup B), so that the net torque rotates the assemblies as shown. The speed of rotation is generally indicated by means of an electrical contact made once each revolution, and the number of contacts per unit time interval is a direct measure of the average speed of the fluid in the region traversed by the meters. A precalibration by towing the instruments through still water (or air) enables the speed to be determined. The direction of flow is not obtained.

A second type of current meter or anemometer consists of windmill-type vanes mounted in a support so that the fluid flow is parallel to the axis of rotation. Measuring techniques and calibration are similar to those for the cone or cup type of instrument.

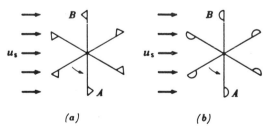

(a)   *(b)*

FIG. 13–8. *a)* Current meter used in water and *b)* anemometer used in air.

Hot-wire anemometers. A hot-wire anemometer makes use of the convection cooling on a heated cylinder held normal to a gas stream. This cooling is a function of the gas and wire temperatures and the free-stream velocity. Wires of 0.0005 to 0.005 in. in diameter and 0.25 to 0.5 in. long are held by a forked probe and exposed to the fluid stream. Two methods of measurement are used:

1) The wire resistance is kept constant by adjusting the current flow through it, and the velocity is determined by measuring the current and using a calibration of the instrument.

2) The current flow through the wire is kept constant, and the change in wire resistance from convection cooling is measured in terms of the voltage drop across it. Fluctuations in velocity may be detected and recorded on an oscillograph by suitable circuits.

Hot-wire anemometers have been used for measuring velocity profiles where the velocity gradients are large. This measurement is possible because of the small size of the sensing device. They are also used in measuring turbulence intensities in gas flows.

Oblique shocks in a gas. If an infinitesimal disturbance travels in a gas at a speed V, greater than the speed of a sound wave c, a Mach cone will be generated by the wave fronts issuing from the point disturbance P (Fig. 13–9). The spherical sound waves emanating from P as it moves

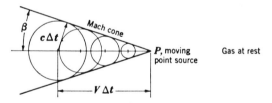

Fig. 13–9. Mach cone.

towards the right are indicated. In a time Δt the wave front travels a distance $c\Delta t$, while the source P travels a distance $V\Delta t$. Thus the sine of the half-angle of the Mach cone is

$$\sin \beta = \frac{c\Delta t}{V\Delta t} = \frac{1}{\mathrm{M}} \qquad (13\text{–}12)$$

Since a real disturbance is finite, Eq. 13–12 is not exact, and the Mach number determined from it will be less than the actual value.

If the point source is at rest with a supersonic gas flowing past it, a Mach cone similar to that in Fig. 13–9 will be generated (it will be opposite in direction to that shown if the gas flows to the right).

It is common practice to place either a wedge (two-dimensional flow) or a cone (three-dimensional flow) at zero incidence in a supersonic gas stream, and the Mach number of the free stream may then be obtained by measuring the wedge half-angle θ and the oblique shock-angle β (Fig.

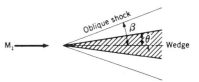

FIG. 13–10. Mach number measurement with wedge.

13–10). The wedge or cone half-angle θ must be small enough so that the bow wave remains attached to the wedge or cone tip. For this condition, the continuity and momentum equations together with the system geometry may be written to show that the free-stream Mach number M_1 for a bow wave on a wedge (two-dimensional flow) may be determined from the equation

$$\frac{1}{M_1{}^2} = \sin^2\beta - \left(\frac{k+1}{2}\right) \frac{\sin\beta \sin\theta}{\cos(\beta-\theta)} \qquad [9\text{–}49]$$

Relationships for a cone are more complicated than for a wedge. However, Eq. 13–12 is a better approximation for an attached shock on a cone than on a wedge. It is difficult to determine the free-stream Mach number from a detached bow wave.

Shock waves are photographed by means of interferometers (these detect density changes across the shock), schlieren systems (these detect density gradients), and shadowgraph systems (these detect the gradient of the density gradient).

EXAMPLE 13–3. A Mach angle β of 20 deg on a wedge of half-angle 8 deg are measured on a schlieren photograph of a two-dimensional wedge in the test section of a supersonic wind tunnel. What is the Mach number of the air flow?

Solution: From Eq. 13–12,

$$\frac{1}{M_1{}^2} = (0.342)^2 - \frac{(1.4+1)}{2} \frac{(0.342)(0.139)}{(0.987)} = 0.0585$$

Thus, $M_1 = 4.13$.

Eq. 13–12 gives $M_1 = 1/0.342 = 2.92$, which is not correct, since a wedge rather than a point or line disturbance is used.

13–2. LIQUID FLOW RATES IN PIPES

Liquid flow rates in pipes may be measured by means of a number of devices. Many, such as disk meters of the type used in homes for metering water and the rotameter (which consists of a float in a vertical diverging tube), are direct reading and will not be treated here.

A constriction or an elbow in a pipeline will produce measurable piezometric pressure differences along the pipe walls, and these pressure differences may be used as a means of determining the flow rate. Two methods of approach may be used.

1) The Bernoulli equation (one-dimensional flow with no losses in the form of energy dissipation) and the continuity equation may be written between a section in the pipe and the constricted section, and an expression for the flow rate obtained by combining them. An estimate of the ratio of the actual flow rate to the calculated flow rate may be made from previous (published) experiments and applied. From this an estimate of the flow rate in the given system may be obtained.

2) The flow meter may be calibrated, either by the manufacturer or by the user before or after installation. The same fluid and the same range of flows as in the actual installation should be used for the calibration.

Actual calibration (the second method) is necessary for precise measurements, although good estimates (often within 1 or 2 per cent) may be possible by using the first method. A given meter may not be exactly geometrically or dynamically similar to one which has been previously calibrated, and thus the flow coefficients may not be the same.

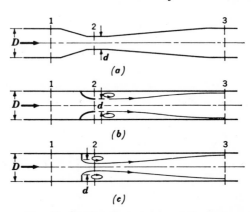

Fig. 13–11. Pipe flow meters. *a*) Venturi, *b*) nozzle, and *c*) orifice.

Analysis of venturi, nozzle, and orifice meters. The Bernoulli and continuity equations applied between sections *1* and *2* of Fig. 13–11 are

$$\frac{V_1^2}{2g} + \frac{p_1}{\gamma} + z_1 = \frac{V_2^2}{2g} + \frac{p_2}{\gamma} + z_2$$

and $$V_1 A_1 = V_2 A_2$$

Solving for V_2 gives

$$V_2 = \frac{1}{\sqrt{1 - (A_2/A_1)^2}} \sqrt{2g\left[\left(\frac{p_1}{\gamma} + z_1\right) - \left(\frac{p_2}{\gamma} + z_2\right)\right]}$$

where the term in brackets inside the radical represents the change in piezometric head Δh between sections *1* and *2*. This change in piezometric head may be measured by means of a differential manometer, for which the deflection is a direct measure of Δh regardless of the inclination of the meter axis (it may be horizontal, vertical, or inclined). The ideal flow rate may be expressed as

$$Q_{ideal} = \frac{A_2\sqrt{2g\,\Delta h}}{\sqrt{1 - (A_2/A_1)^2}} \qquad (13\text{--}13)$$

This equation cannot be exactly correct, because the steady-flow energy equation for liquids should be written as

$$\alpha_1 \frac{V_1^2}{2g} + \frac{p_1}{\gamma} + z_1 = \alpha_2 \frac{V_2^2}{2g} + \frac{p_2}{\gamma} + z_2 + h_L$$

The terms neglected in the Bernoulli equation (α_1, α_2, and h_L) are affected by viscous effects and the boundary roughness.

A flow coefficient K applied to Eq. 13–13 gives a simple form for the actual flow rate Q.

$$Q = K\left(\frac{\pi d^2}{4}\right)\sqrt{2g\,\Delta h} \qquad (13\text{--}14)$$

where d is the diameter of the meter throat. This is the diameter at section *2* for the venturi and the nozzle in Fig. 13–11, and at the orifice plate upstream of section *2* for the orifice meter. The value of K is a function of the following:

1) The type of meter.
2) The ratio of meter throat diameter to pipe diameter, d/D. For the venturi and nozzle it includes the so-called approach velocity factor $\sqrt{1 - (A_2/A_1)^2}$. For the orifice it includes this approach velocity factor and, in addition, the contraction of the jet from the orifice plate to the *vena contracta* at section *2* (Fig. 13–11).
3) The viscous effects and the pipe roughness contained in the kinetic energy correction factors α_1 and α_2 and the head loss term h_L, all of which were neglected in the Bernoulli equation. These effects may be expressed in terms of the Reynolds number at the meter throat (in some instances the Reynolds number for the pipe is used).

Thus we may write

$$K = K\left(\text{meter shape}, \frac{d}{D}, \text{Re}_d\right)$$

Typical values of the flow coefficients are shown in Fig. 13–12. From Eq. 13–14,

$$K = \frac{Q}{\frac{\pi d^2}{4}\sqrt{2g\,\Delta h}}$$

and the Reynolds number may be written as

$$\mathrm{Re}_d = \frac{Vd}{\nu} = \frac{Qd}{\frac{\pi d^2}{4}\nu} = K\frac{d\sqrt{2g\,\Delta h}}{\nu} \tag{13-15}$$

A family of lines representing constant values of $d\sqrt{2g\,\Delta h}/\nu$ is superimposed on the K vs. Re_d graph of Fig. 13–12. Thus, for a given piezometric head change Δh across a meter of throat diameter d for a fluid of viscosity ν the value of $d\sqrt{2g\,\Delta h}/\nu$ may be calculated, and the intersection of this line with the appropriate meter curve gives the value of K for the meter. The flow rate may then be estimated from Eq. 13–14.

In these meters the throat pressures should not be allowed to become so low that cavitation occurs. In addition, low pressures may cause leakage of air into the manometer lines and cause errors, whereas very slight leakage of liquid out of the lines for high-pressure installations would cause no measurable errors.

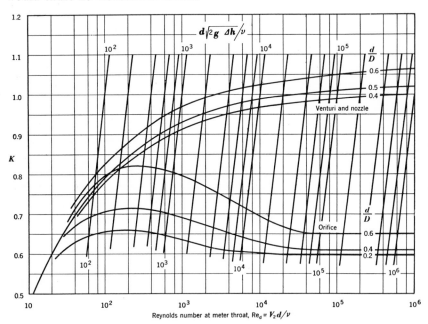

FIG. 13–12. Approximate flow coefficients for pipe meters.

EXAMPLE 13–4. A mercury manometer connected across a 3-in. nozzle meter in a 6-in. pipe indicates a deflection of 6.0 in. Estimate the flow rate for water at 60 F.

Solution:

$$\Delta h = \frac{6}{12} \left(\frac{\gamma_m - \gamma_w}{\gamma_w} \right) = \frac{6}{12} (13.56 - 1) = 6.28 \text{ ft}$$

Then

$$d \sqrt{2g \, \Delta h}/\nu = \frac{(0.25) \sqrt{(64.4)(6.28)}}{1.22 \times 10^{-5}} = 4.1 \times 10^5$$

and from Fig. 13–12, $K = 1.02$. From Eq. 13–14, the flow rate is

$$Q = (1.02)(0.0491) \sqrt{(64.4)(6.28)} = 1.01 \text{ ft}^3/\text{sec}$$

For an orifice, $K = 0.62$, and the flow rate would be $Q = 0.61 \text{ ft}^3/\text{sec}$.

The total piezometric pressure drop or total head loss across the entire meter (from section *1* to *3* in Fig. 13–11) is greatest for the orifice and least for the venturi for the same flow rate and meter size. The loss from section *2* to *3* for the orifice is essentially that of a sudden enlargement from the *vena contracta* to the pipe. For the nozzle, it is also essentially that of a sudden enlargement, but from the lower throat velocity (compared with that for the orifice) to the pipe. For the venturi, it is essentially that of a gradual enlargement (a conical diffuser of about 6 to 7 deg is generally used).

It should be reemphasized that these meters should be calibrated carefully for precise flow-rate measurements.

Elbow meter. Flow through an elbow in a pipeline results in a higher pressure at the outer wall surface than at the inner wall surface. This pressure difference is a function of the flow rate. The piezometric or pressure-head difference measured by means of suitable piezometer taps may be indicated on a differential manometer and used as an indication of flow rate. The elbow meter is inexpensive, since it is already a part of the piping system, and when carefully calibrated it is an accurate meter. A typical calibration consists of a logarithmic plot of manometer deflection vs. volumetric flow rate. A typical installation is shown in Fig. 13–13.

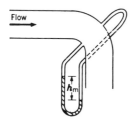

Fig. 13–13. Elbow meter.

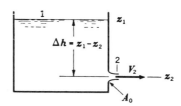

Fig. 13–14. Flow from a free orifice.

13–3. LIQUID FLOW RATES IN OPEN TANKS OR OPEN CHANNELS

Flow from open tanks or in open channels is due to gravity, and changes in velocity along a free surface are produced as a result of changes in potential head.

As for pipe meters, estimates of flow rates may be made by using flow coefficients applied to the results of employing the Bernoulli and continuity equations, but precise measurements must be based on careful calibration of the meter.

Open tanks. Flow of a liquid from a circular orifice at the side of an open tank is estimated by writing the Bernoulli equation from a point on the free surface to the contracted jet, where the streamlines are parallel (from point *1* to point *2* in Fig. 13–14). The velocity at *1* is essentially zero, and the pressures at *1* and *2* are both atmospheric. Thus the Bernoulli equation is

$$z_1 = \frac{V_2{}^2}{2g} + z_2$$

so that

$$V_2 = \sqrt{2g\,\Delta h}$$

and

$$Q_{\text{ideal}} = A_2\sqrt{2g\,\Delta h} \tag{13–16}$$

The steady-flow energy equation contains a term h_L which is not included in the Bernoulli equation. The actual velocity is

$$V_{2\text{ actual}} = \sqrt{2g(\Delta h - h_L)}$$

A simple expression for the actual flow rate is

$$Q = KA_0\sqrt{2g\,\Delta h} \tag{13–17}$$

where A_0 = the area of the orifice hole;

K = a flow coefficient, which depends on the magnitude of h_L, which in turn is affected by the roughness of the inside surface of the tank near the orifice hole and by the flow rate which depends on Δh, and the contraction of the jet from the orifice to section *2*.

For an ideal fluid,

$$\frac{A_2}{A_0} = \frac{\pi}{\pi + 2} = 0.611 \tag{13–18}$$

and for a real fluid the contraction depends on the sharpness of the orifice hole as well as the tank surface roughness just inside the orifice hole. A typical value of K for a sharp-edged orifice is about 0.60.

Weirs. A weir is a partial obstruction in an open channel over which the liquid accelerates with a free liquid surface. Flow over a sharp-crested weir was illustrated in Fig. 6–4 by means of a flow net. The Bernoulli

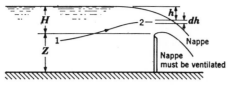

FIG. 13-15. Sharp-crested suppressed weir.

equation written for a suppressed weir (it extends across the full width of a channel) along a streamline (see Fig. 13-15) is

$$\frac{V_1^2}{2g} + (H + Z) = \frac{V_2^2}{2g} + (H + Z - h)$$

and we get

$$V_2 = \sqrt{2g(h + V_1^2/2g)}$$

Assumptions made in this derivation include 1) no losses and 2) parallel streamlines without contraction over the weir crest. The flow rate through an element of width b and height dh is

$$dQ = V_2 b \, dh$$

$$= b\sqrt{2g} \sqrt{(h + V_1^2/2g)} \, dh$$

Integration from $h = 0$ to $h = H$ gives

$$Q_{\text{ideal}} = \frac{2}{3} b \sqrt{2g} \left[\left(H + \frac{V_1^2}{2g}\right)^{3/2} - \left(\frac{V_1^2}{2g}\right)^{3/2} \right] \qquad (13\text{--}19)$$

As before, a simple expression may be written as

$$Q = K \frac{2}{3} b \sqrt{2g} \, H^{3/2} \qquad (13\text{--}20)$$

where K depends on 1) the so-called approach velocity head $V_1^2/2g$, which in turn depends on the ratio of weir head H to weir crest height Z as well as H itself and 2) the contraction of the streamlines just beyond the weir crest.

Numerous values for K (or a similar coefficient) have been published in hydraulic literature, and a rational analysis by von Mises [3] indicates K to have the form

$$K = 0.611 + 0.075 \frac{H}{Z} \qquad (13\text{--}21)$$

EXAMPLE 13-5. Estimate the flow rate over a sharp-crested weir with a ventilated nappe. The weir is a suppressed weir 12 ft wide, the weir crest is 6 ft high, and the head H is 1.2 ft.

Solution: From Eq. 13-21,

$$K = 0.611 + 0.075 \frac{1.2}{6} = 0.626.$$

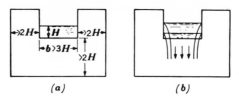

FIG. 13–16. Contracted weir. *a*) Proportions and *b*) jet contraction.

Thus, from Eq. 13–20,

$$Q = (0.626)(2/3)(12) \sqrt{64.4} \ (1.2)^{3/2} = 52.8 \ \text{ft}^3/\text{sec}$$

A weir may be narrower than the channel in which it is installed and is then called a weir with side contractions, or a contracted weir. An empirical equation of Gourley and Crimp for a contracted weir of the type shown in Fig. 13–16 is

$$Q = 3.10 \ b^{1.02} \ H^{1.47} \tag{13–22}$$

A Cipolletti weir has sides sloping in order to avoid the varying contraction of the jet with head, as shown in Fig. 13–16(*b*). This weir is shown in Fig. 13–17. An empirical equation for a Cipolletti weir is

$$Q = 3.37 \ bH^{1.5} \tag{13–23}$$

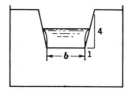

FIG. 13–17.
Cipolletti weir.

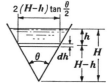

FIG. 13–18. V-notch weir.

A V-notch weir is useful for increased accuracy at low flow rates and for higher flow rates as well. From Fig. 13–18, the flow through an element of area dh high and $2(H - h) \tan \dfrac{\theta}{2}$ wide is

$$dQ = 2 \sqrt{2gh} \ (H - h) \tan \frac{\theta}{2} \ dh$$

Integration from $h = 0$ to $h = H$ gives

$$Q_{\text{ideal}} = \frac{8}{15} \sqrt{2g} \tan \frac{\theta}{2} \ H^{5/2}$$

if the velocity of approach is neglected. Applying a flow coefficient K, which depends on the geometry of the system and the roughness of the upstream face of the weir plate, gives

$$Q = K \left(\frac{8}{15}\right) \sqrt{2g} \tan \frac{\theta}{2} H^{5/2} \qquad (13\text{--}24)$$

Typical values of K vary from about 0.58 to 0.62 and decrease with H for values of H less than about 0.2 ft. A typical flow equation for a 90-deg V-notch weir is

$$Q = 2.5 \, H^{2.5} \qquad (13\text{--}25)$$

Critical flow sections. Whenever gradually varying flow in an open channel is critical (at a Froude number of 1.0), the flow rate may be determined from Eq. 12–9a to be

$$q = V_c \, y_c = \sqrt{g y_c{}^3} \qquad (13\text{--}26a)$$

and the total flow rate for a channel of width b is

$$Q = b \sqrt{g y_c{}^3} \qquad (13\text{--}26b)$$

Sluice gate. Flow through a sluice gate (Fig. 13–19) is similar to flow through the upper half of a two-dimensional slot or orifice, and the streamline pattern or flow net was shown in Fig. 6–5. The theoretical contraction of the flow is, from Eq. 13–18,

$$\frac{y_2}{y_s} = 0.611$$

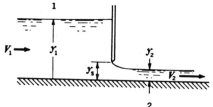

FIG. 13–19. Sluice gate.

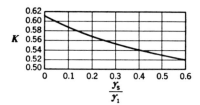

FIG. 13–20. Approximate flow coefficients for a sluice gate. (By permission from Hunter Rouse, *Elementary Mechanics of Fluids*, New York: John Wiley & Sons, Inc., 1946.)

The Bernoulli equation and continuity equation written for one-dimensional flow between sections *1* and *2* of Fig. 13–19 are

$$\frac{V_1{}^2}{2g} + y_1 = \frac{V_2{}^2}{2g} + y_2$$

and

$$V_1 \, y_1 = V_2 \, y_2$$

so that

$$V_2 = \frac{1}{\sqrt{1 - (y_2/y_1)^2}} \sqrt{2g(y_1 - y_2)}$$

and for a width b,

$$Q_{ideal} = \frac{by_2}{\sqrt{1 - (y_2/y_1)^2}} \sqrt{2g(y_1 - y_2)} \qquad (13\text{--}27)$$

A simple form of discharge equation is obtained by introducing the flow coefficient K, so that

$$Q = Kby_s \sqrt{2gy_1} \qquad (13\text{--}28)$$

where K depends on the system geometry (y_1, y_2, and y_s) and is approximately as shown in Fig. 13–20 as a function of y_s/y_1.

EXAMPLE 13–6. Estimate the flow rate under a sluice gate 10 ft wide. The upstream depth is 18 ft, and the gate opening is 2 ft.

Solution: $y_s/y_1 = 1/9$, and from Fig. 13–20, $K = 0.585$. Thus,

$$Q = (0.585)(10)(2) \sqrt{(64.4)(18)} = 398 \text{ ft}^3/\text{sec}$$

13–4. SUBSONIC GAS FLOW RATES IN PIPES

Gas flow rates in pipes may be measured on a mass-flow basis. As for liquid flow rates, gas flow meters should be calibrated for accurate measurements, but estimates may be made from published data on flow meters.

In Fig. 13–11, the steady-flow energy equation, the continuity equation, and the isentropic equation may be applied between sections *1* and *2* for the venturi meter and the nozzle meter. These equations are

$$\frac{V_1^2}{2} + h_1 = \frac{V_2^2}{2} + h_2$$

$$V_1 A_1 \rho_1 = V_2 A_2 \rho_2$$

and $\qquad \dfrac{T_2}{T_1} = \left(\dfrac{p_2}{p_1}\right)^{\frac{k-1}{k}} \qquad$ or $\qquad \dfrac{p}{\rho^k} = \text{constant}$

Combining these equations gives the mass-flow rate in terms of quantities at section *2* and at section *1*.

$$\dot{m}_{ideal} = \frac{A_2 \sqrt{2k\, p_1 \rho_1 \left[\left(\dfrac{p_2}{p_1}\right)^{2/k} - \left(\dfrac{p_2}{p_1}\right)^{\frac{k+1}{k}}\right]}}{\sqrt{1 - \left(\dfrac{A_2}{A_1}\right)^2 \left(\dfrac{p_2}{p_1}\right)^{2/k}}}$$

This equation may be written in a simpler form, comparable to that used for liquid flow, by introduction of the flow coefficient K (the same as for liquid flow) and an expansion factor Y. Then,

$$\dot{m} = KYA_2 \sqrt{2\rho_1 (p_1 - p_2)} \qquad \text{(slug/sec)} \qquad (13\text{--}29a)$$

$$= 32.2 \, KYA_2 \sqrt{2\rho_1(p_1 - p_2)} \qquad (\text{lb}_\text{m}/\text{sec}) \qquad (13\text{–}29b)$$

where, for the venturi and nozzle meters,

$$Y = \sqrt{ \frac{ \left(\frac{k}{k-1}\right) \left(\frac{p_2}{p_1}\right)^{2/k} \left[1 - \left(\frac{p_2}{p_1}\right)^{\frac{k-1}{k}}\right] \left[1 - \left(\frac{d}{D}\right)^4\right] }{ \left[1 - \left(\frac{p_2}{p_1}\right)\right] \left[1 - \left(\frac{d}{D}\right)^4 \left(\frac{p_2}{p_1}\right)^{2/k}\right] } } \qquad (13\text{–}30)$$

and K is obtained from Fig. 13–12. Equation 13–30 indicates that Y is a function of three dimensionless ratios, that is,

$$Y = Y\left(k, \frac{p_2}{p_1}, \frac{d}{D}\right)$$

Thus for a given gas (given k), Y should be a unique function of p_2/p_1 for any specified value of d/D. A graph of the expansion factor Y is shown in Fig. 13–21. The effect of the compressible flow (actually the gas expands in passing to the meter throat) is to *reduce* the flow rate of a gas for given initial conditions and pressure drop, as compared with the flow rate if incompressible flow were assumed. The minimum pressure in the venturi

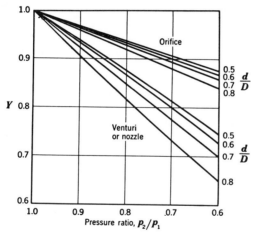

FIG. 13–21. Approximate expansion factors for $k = 1.4$.

or nozzle throat is the critical pressure of the gas, which, in terms of the stagnation pressure p_0, is

$$\frac{p_c}{p_0} = \left(\frac{2}{k+1}\right)^{\frac{k}{k-1}} \qquad [9\text{–}23]$$

Test results give the expansion factor as

$$Y = 1 - \frac{1}{k}\left[0.41 + 0.35\left(\frac{d}{D}\right)^4\right]\left(1 - \frac{p_2}{p_1}\right) \qquad (13\text{--}31)$$

for an orifice meter [4]. Values are plotted in Fig. 13–21.

REFERENCES

1. C. W. Hurd, K. P. Chesky, and A. H. Shapiro, "Influence of Viscous Effects on Impact Tubes," *Am. Soc. Mech. Engrs., Journal of Appl. Mech.*, Vol. 20 (1953), p. 257.

2. Lorenz G. Straub, John M. Killen, and Owen P. Lamb, "Velocity Measurements of Air-Water Mixtures," *Trans. Am. Soc. of Civil Engrs.*, Vol. 119 (1954), pp. 207–220.

3. Hunter Rouse, *Elementary Mechanics of Fluids* (New York: John Wiley and Sons, Inc., 1946), p. 93.

4. *Fluid Meters, Their Theory and Application*, 5th ed. (New York: The American Society of Mechanical Engineers, 1959.)

PROBLEMS

13–1. A combined pitot tube is placed in a jet of water and is connected to a mercury manometer which shows a deflection of 18.00 in. What is the velocity of the water in the jet?

13–2. A combined pitot tube is placed in a stream of standard air and is connected to a differential manometer containing methyl alcohol ($s = 0.80$). The manometer deflection is 3.75 in. What is the measured air speed?

13–3. A combined pitot tube connected to a micromanometer produces a deflection of 0.570 in. of water when placed in an air stream at atmospheric pressure and 100 F. What is the velocity of the air stream?

Ans. $V = 51.9$ ft/sec

13–4. An oil ($s = 0.9$, $\mu = 0.001$ slug/ft sec) flows in a 6-in. pipe. The center-line velocity is measured with a combined pitot tube with water as the gage fluid in a differential manometer attached to the pitot tube. The manometer deflection is 27.0 in. *a)* What is the center-line velocity? *b)* Estimate the volumetric flow rate.

13–5. A pitot-static tube on an airplane is connected to a differential manometer which reads 6.00 in. water when the plane flies in standard air. What is the speed of the airplane?

13–6. A combined pitot tube mounted on an airplane is calibrated to read air speed in miles per hour when used in standard air. What is the true air speed for an indicated air speed of 180 mph at *a)* 5000 ft, where $\rho = 0.002049$ slug/ft³, and *b)* 10,000 ft, where $\rho = 0.001756$ slug/ft³?

Ans. a) $V = 194$ mph

13–7. A total pressure tube is placed in a pipe carrying mercury. The difference in pressure between this tube and a wall pressure tap is indicated by a deflection of 3.00 in. on a mercury-water manometer. What is the velocity of the mercury?

13–8. What is the dynamic pressure head in inches of water for standard air flowing at 5 ft/sec?

13–9. What is the smallest impact tube which may be used to measure the velocity in Prob. 13–8?

Ans. 0.0375 in. ID

13–10. The difference between stagnation and static pressure measured with an impact tube and a static pressure tap is 8.55 cm alcohol ($s = 0.800$) for air at 78 F and 2095 psfa. What is the air velocity?

13–11. Repeat Prob. 13–10 for a deflection of 37.45 cm alcohol. Check for compressible effects.

13–12. The stagnation pressure measured with a stagnation tube in a wind tunnel is 3 psi above the static pressure measured at a static-pressure tap at the wall. The test section is at a pressure of 3 atmospheres. What is the Mach number of the flow?

13–13. A combined pitot tube is mounted on an airplane moving through air at 13 psia and 25 F. The stagnation pressure measured by the tube is *a*) 0.5 psig, *b*) 5.0 psig, *c*) 10.0 psig, and *d*) 15.0 psig. What are the respective flight velocities and Mach numbers?

Ans. *b*) $V = 754$ ft/sec, M $= 0.698$

13–14. A combined pitot tube is used to measure the average velocity (with respect to time) of a 50-per-cent mixture of air and water in a steep open channel. The deflection of a differential mercury manometer connected to the tube is 8.00 in. What is the measured velocity of the mixture?

13–15. Repeat Prob. 13–14 for an air concentration of .60 per cent and a manometer deflection of 14.00 in.

Ans. $V = 50.6$ ft/sec

13–16. The stagnation hole in a pitot cylinder and a wall pressure tap are connected to a differential manometer containing acetylene tetrabromide. Various point velocities along the pipe radius are to be determined for the flow of water in a round pipe. Manometer readings h_m are taken for various radial locations of the stagnation hole in the pitot cylinder as follows:

r/R	0	0.2	0.4	0.6	0.8	0.9	0.95
h_m, in.	21.5	20.62	16.62	9.55	4.08	2.19	1.46

What is the average velocity?

13–17. A point disturbance in air produces a Mach cone with a half-angle of 50 deg. What is the Mach number of the flow?

13–18. Show that Eq. 9–49 is valid for a point source, for which $\theta = 0$ deg, and becomes equivalent to Eq. 13–12.

13–19. A 20-deg, two-dimensional wedge produces an oblique shock at an angle of 135 deg from the free-stream velocity vector in an air stream. What is the free-stream Mach number?

Ans. M $= 1.77$

13–20. A 15-deg wedge in a supersonic air flow produces a wave angle $\beta = 50$ deg. *a)* What is the Mach number of the flow? *b)* What other wave angle could exist for this Mach number? Refer to Fig. 9–10.

13–21. A 4-in. diameter meter is installed in a 10-in. diameter pipe in which water at 70 F flows at a rate of 2 ft³/sec. What deflection on a mercury manometer connected across the meter would occur for *a)* a venturi meter and *b)* an orifice meter?

• 13–22. The maximum flow of water at 70 F expected in a 6-in. venturi meter in a 12-in. pipe sloping 45 deg from the horizontal is 8 ft³/sec. What deflection of a mercury manometer would occur if the upstream piezometer tap is *a)* 2 ft and *b)* 3 ft from the throat piezometer tap, measured parallel to the meter center line?

Ans. $h_m = 24.2$ in. for both *a)* and *b)*

13–23. Water at 70 F flows through a 6-in. diameter meter in a 10-in. diameter pipe. A differential manometer connected across the meter shows a deflection of 9.00 in. What is the flow rate for *a)* a venturi or a nozzle meter and *b)* an orifice meter? The manometer fluid is mercury.

13–24. In Prob. 13–23, crude oil at 70 F flows through the meters and the manometer deflection is 3.20 in. What is the flow rate for *a)* a venturi or a nozzle meter and *b)* an orifice meter?

Ans. *b)* $Q = 2.02$ ft³/sec

13–25. A 3-in. nozzle meter is installed in a 6-in. water pipeline. What diameter orifice would produce the same deflection on a manometer connected across the meters for the same flow rate of 1.50 ft³/sec through each meter?

13–26. A mercury manometer connected across a 3-in. orifice in a 6-in. pipe shows a deflection of 12.00 in. for a certain flow of water. What would be the deflection on the same manometer for the same flow rate through a 3-in. nozzle meter in the pipe?

13–27. Water flows in a 6-in. pipe with a 3-in. nozzle meter. The drop in piezometric head from the pipe to the meter throat is 14.4 ft of water. *a)* What is the flow rate? *b)* What is the head loss from the meter inlet to the throat? *c)* What is the head loss from the meter throat to a point downstream of the nozzle? Assume it to be equivalent to a sudden enlargement loss.

13–28. A venturi meter, a nozzle meter, and an orifice meter of the same throat diameter are in series in a pipe, but far apart so there is no mutual interference. Across which meter will the total head loss be the greatest for a given flow? Explain your answer.

13–29. A 3-in. nozzle meter is installed in a 6-in. water pipeline. A differential mercury manometer shows a deflection of 9.00 in. Calculate the flow rate through the pipe and estimate the *total* head loss resulting from the meter installation.

Ans. $h_L = 5.76$ ft

13-30. Crude oil at 57 F flows through a 6-in. pipe. The flow rate is measured by means of a differential mercury manometer attached to *vena contracta* taps across a 3.6-in. orifice. The manometer deflection is 2.25 in. What is the flow rate?

13-31. A maximum flow of 3 ft³/sec of water at 70 F in a 12-in. pipe is to be measured with a nozzle or an orifice meter. The maximum deflection of a differential manometer containing acetylene tetrabromide ($s = 2.964$) is limited to 24 in. What is the smallest diameter *a*) nozzle and *b*) orifice which may be installed?

13-32. A calibration of an elbow meter (Fig. 13-13) is as follows:

Manometer deflection h_m, in.	3.00	6.00	12.00	24.00	48.00
Flow rate, ft³/sec	0.130	0.190	0.277	0.405	0.570

What is the calibration equation, assuming it to be of the form $Q = Kh_m{}^n$ ft³/sec, where h_m is in feet?

13-33. Water flows from a circular orifice in a large tank under a head of 40 ft. The orifice diameter is 4.00 in. For a flow of 480 ft³ in 3 min, what is the discharge coefficient?

Ans. $C_d = 0.602$

13-34. Estimate the unit discharge (q in units of cfs/ft) for flow over a sharp-crested weir with a well-ventilated nappe for a head of 0.8 ft and a crest height of *a*) 1 ft, *b*) 2 ft, and *c*) 4 ft. Explain the resulting effect of crest height on flow rate on the basis of the variation in the approach velocity V_1 (Eq. 13-19).

Ans. *a*) $q = 4.93$ cfs/ft

13-35. What is the crest height for a suppressed, sharp-crested weir in a channel 6 ft wide for a total water depth upstream of 5 ft when the flow rate is 125 ft³/sec?

13-36. A sharp-crested weir with a crest height $Z = 3$ ft in a channel 9 ft wide has a coefficient K which is given by Eq. 13-21. Although K does not vary exponentially with H/Z, an approximate equation for the weir flow is $Q = C_1 H^n$. What is a relation between Q, in cubic feet per second, and H, in feet, for values of H from 1 to 2 ft?

Ans. $Q = 30.6\, H^{1.56}$

13-37. Repeat Prob. 13-36 for a crest height $Z = 4$ ft.

13-38. The effect of side contractions on the flow rate over a weir may be illustrated by comparing the flow rate over *a*) a suppressed weir, *b*) a contracted weir, and *c*) a Cipolletti weir, each with the same base width b and a large crest height Z to minimize the effects of approach velocity. Calculate the flow rate over these three weirs for $b = 3$ ft, $H = 1.0$ ft, and $Z = 6$ ft.

13-39. What is the flow rate through a 90-deg, V-notch weir for a head of *a*) 3 in. and *b*) 14 in.?

Ans. *a*) $Q = 0.078$ ft³/sec

13–40. A depth recorder for a 90-deg, V-notch weir is to be used to record flow rates varying between 1 and 20 ft^3/sec. What is the required range of the depth recorder?

13–41. The water depth upstream of a given sharp-crested weir varies, of course, with the discharge. Variations in upstream water level may be reduced by the use of a weir crest longer than the channel width. This weir crest may be in the shape of a V, a W, or square U's connected to inverted square U's, for example. Calculate the variation in water level upstream of a sharp-crested suppressed weir in a wide river for flow rates from 0 to 40 cfs/ft of channel width for a weir crest length a) equal to the channel width, b) twice the channel width, and c) four times the channel width. Assume $K = 0.63$ at maximum discharge.

13–42. The flow rate in a laboratory model 6 ft wide reaches 4.00 cfs. a) What is the head on a rectangular weir if the velocity of approach is neglected? b) How long a weir (see Prob. 13–41) would be necessary to limit the head to 0.05 ft?

13–43. The flow rate in a river model is 0.15 cfs/ft of channel width. How long a sharp-crested, suppressed weir crest should be installed in order to limit the head on the weir to a) ½ in. and b) ¼ in.? Refer to Prob. 13–41.

Ans. b) 15.2 times the channel width

13–44. Calculate the flow rate under a sluice gate 6 ft wide with an upstream depth of 12 ft and a gate opening of 1 ft.

13–45. A flow rate of 20 cfs/ft issues from a sluice gate with a 2-ft opening. What is the depth upstream of the sluice gate?

13–46. A flow rate of 40 cfs/ft is to flow under a sluice gate when the maximum allowable head upstream is 22 ft. At what opening should the gate be set?

Ans. $y_s = 1.80$ ft

13–47. Repeat Prob. 13–46 for a unit discharge of 60 cfs/ft.

13–48. Air at 40 psig and 100 F flows in an 8-in. pipe. The pressure drop to the throat of a 4-in. venturi meter is 8 psi. What is the flow rate?

Ans. $\dot{m} = 0.352$ slug/sec

13–49. Air enters an 8 × 4-in. diameter venturi meter at 50 psig and 80 F. The throat pressure is 40 psig. What is the flow rate in slug per second?

13–50. Repeat Prob. 13–49 for an orifice meter.

13–51. Methane at 75 psig and 120 F flows through a 10-in. pipe. The differential pressure between the inlet and the 6-in. throat of a nozzle meter is 18 psi. What is the flow rate? $\mu = 2.49 \times 10^{-7}$ slug/ft sec.

13–52. Repeat Prob. 13–51 for an orifice meter.

13–53. The flow of methane at 80 F ($\mu = 2.34 \times 10^{-7}$ slug/ft sec) and 18 psia in a 12-in. pipe at an average velocity of 50 ft/sec is to be measured with an orifice meter in the pipeline. The maximum pressure differential across the meter is to be 3.60 psi. What is the smallest diameter orifice which may be used?

14

Turbomachines

A rotating machine or turbomachine is one which adds energy to or extracts energy from a fluid by virtue of a rotating system of blades within the machine. The rotating element is called a rotor in a compressor, an impeller in a pump, a rotor in a gas or steam turbine, and a runner in a hydraulic turbine. Centrifugal, axial-flow, and mixed-flow pumps and compressors; fans and blowers; and water, steam, or gas turbines are examples of rotating machines. The general theory of rotating machines will be introduced in this chapter, and then attention will be focused on the operating characteristics of hydraulic machines.

14–1. GENERAL THEORY

Energy is transferred from the rotor or impeller in a compressor or pump and from the fluid to the rotor or runner in a turbine. The fluid leaves the rotor with a resultant velocity V_2 at a radius R_2 and enters with a resultant velocity V_1 at a radius R_1. These velocities have components in three mutually perpendicular directions: 1) axial, or parallel to the axis of rotation of the rotor; 2) radial or meridional, which is normal to the axis of rotation and passes through it; and 3) tangential, which is normal to both the axial and the meridional directions. (The tangential component is often called the whirl component.) These are designated by subscripts a, m, and t, respectively. Only the tangential components contribute to the rotation of the rotor, and the change in angular momentum, or moment of momentum, per unit mass of the fluid passing through the rotor is $V_{2t} R_2 - V_{1t} R_1$. From Newton's second law, this is equal to the torque on the rotor for steady flow. The energy transfer E per unit weight of fluid equals the product of torque times the angular velocity divided by the acceleration of gravity g. Thus

$$E = \frac{(V_{2t} R_2 - V_{1t} R_1)\, \omega}{g} \tag{14-1}$$

Since $\omega r = U$, the peripheral velocity of the rotor, Eq. 14–1 may be written as

$$E = \frac{V_{2t} U_2 - V_{1t} U_1}{g} \tag{14-2}$$

Equations 14–1 and 14–2 are known as the Euler equations for a pump or compressor and represent the energy transferred to the fluid by the impeller or rotor. For a turbine the equations may be written with the subscripts

369

interchanged to represent the energy transferred to the rotor or runner by the fluid.

With reference to Fig. 14–1, the relationships between velocities may be written

$$V_{2m}{}^2 = V_2{}^2 - V_{2t}{}^2 = V_{2r}{}^2 - (U_2 - V_{2t})^2$$

from which
$$U_2 V_{2t} = \frac{V_2{}^2 + U_2{}^2 - V_{2r}{}^2}{2}$$

where V_{1r} and V_{1r} represent the velocity of the fluid relative to the impeller blades at exit and entrance, respectively. Similarly, at the impeller inlet,

$$U_1 V_{1t} = \frac{V_1{}^2 + U_1{}^2 - V_{1r}{}^2}{2}$$

With these relations, Eq. 14–2 becomes

$$E = \frac{V_2{}^2 - V_1{}^2}{2g} + \frac{U_2{}^2 - U_1{}^2}{2g} + \frac{V_{1r}{}^2 - V_{2r}{}^2}{2g} \qquad (14\text{–}3)$$

which indicates that E is the sum of the difference in the squares of the absolute fluid velocity, the peripheral rotor velocity, and the relative fluid velocity, respectively. The first term represents the change in kinetic energy of the fluid, the second term represents the pressure change from centrifugal effects, and the third term represents the pressure change owing to relative kinetic energy. The second and third terms are considered as static-pressure effects.

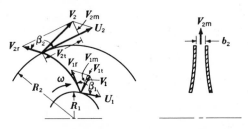

FIG. 14–1.   Flow through a centrifugal pump impeller.

In a radial-flow or mixed-flow impeller, all three terms in Eq. 14–3 are effective. In an axial-flow machine, the fluid enters and leaves at the same radius so that $U_2 = U_1$, and only the first and third terms are effective. In a tangential-flow machine, only the first term is effective.

It is common to designate gas turbines or compressors on the basis of the relative importance of the second and third terms in Eq. 14–3 compared with all three terms, though it may be applied to hydraulic machines as well. The ratio of the second and third terms to all three terms is called the *reaction*.

$$\text{Reaction} = \frac{\dfrac{U_2{}^2 - U_1{}^2}{2g} + \dfrac{V_{1r}{}^2 - V_{2r}{}^2}{2g}}{E} \qquad (14\text{--}4)$$

Rotating machines may be classified according to a) whether the fluid does work on the rotor or runner (a turbine), or the rotor or impeller transfers energy to the fluid (a compressor or pump), b) the predominant flow direction through the rotor (axial, radial, tangential, or mixed), or c) the reaction.

Radial-flow compressor or centrifugal pump. From Eq. 14–2, the maximum energy transfer occurs when the angular momentum or whirl at inlet is zero, so that $V_{1t} = 0$. Thus from Fig. 14–1, when the inlet whirl is zero, Eq. 14–2 may be written as

$$E = \frac{V_{2t}\, U_2}{g} = \frac{[U_2 - V_{2m}\cot(180 - \beta_2)]U_2}{g} = \frac{U_2{}^2}{g} + \frac{U_2 V_{2m}}{g}\cot\beta_2 \quad (14\text{--}5a)$$

From continuity, the volumetric flow rate through the machine is

$$Q = 2\pi R_2\, b_2 V_{2m}$$

and if V_{2m} from this expression is substituted into Eq. 14–5a,

$$E = \frac{U_2{}^2}{g} + \frac{U_2 \cot\beta_2}{2\pi R_2\, b_2\, g}\, Q \qquad (14\text{--}5b)$$

indicating that for a given impeller at a prescribed peripheral speed E is a function only of the discharge Q.

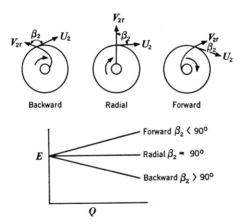

FIG. 14–2. Euler performance curves
for centrifugal pump.

For a backward-curved impeller blade $\beta_2 > 90°$, $\cot\beta_2$ is negative, and E decreases with an increase in Q. For a radial blade $\beta_2 = 90°$, $\cot\beta_2 = 0$, and E is constant. For a forward-curved blade $\beta_2 < 90°$, $\cot\beta_2$

is positive, and E increases as Q increases. The so-called Euler performance curves for a centrifugal pump or compressor are shown in Fig. 14–2.

Axial-flow compressors or pumps. In an axial-flow machine, the axial component of velocity is generally constant ($U_1 = U_2$) and Eqs. 14–2 and 14–3 become

$$E = \frac{U}{g}(V_{2t} - V_{1t}) = \frac{V_2{}^2 - V_1{}^2}{2g} + \frac{V_{1r}{}^2 - V_{2r}{}^2}{2g} \qquad (14\text{--}6)$$

respectively. If neither V_{1t} nor V_{2t} is zero, the fluid has a whirl component at both inlet and outlet. Equation 14–6 indicates that the absolute velocity of the fluid increases and the relative velocity decreases as the fluid passes through the impeller blades. Figure 14–3 shows axial flow through an impeller and indicates the effect of the blade angle at inlet and outlet on the quantity $V_{2t} - V_{1t}$, which is a direct measure of the energy transfer.

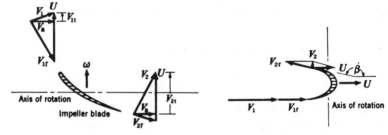

FIG. 14.3. Velocity diagrams   FIG. 14–4. Velocity dia-
for axial-flow pump.   gram for tangential-flow
                                            turbine.

Axial-flow turbine. Equation 14–6 applies with subscripts reversed.

Tangential-flow turbine. An impulse turbine involves only a tangential velocity at inlet with a small axial component at the exit of the runner. The fluid enters and leaves at the same radius, so that $U_1 = U_2$, and with essentially the same relative velocity, so that $V_{1r} \approx V_{2r}$. Thus there is no pressure change, and an impulse turbine has zero reaction. The energy transferred is solely due to a jet striking the impeller blades, and the change in momentum takes place at constant radius. The energy transfer per unit weight of fluid is, from Eq. 14–2,

$$E = \frac{U}{g}(V_{1t} - V_{2t}) = \frac{U}{g}[(U + V_{1r}) - (U + V_{2r}\cos\beta)]$$

and since $V_{1r} \approx V_{2r}$,

$$E = \frac{U}{g}V_{1r}(1 - \cos\beta) \qquad (14\text{--}7)$$

Equation 14–7 may be obtained from the momentum theorem directly (Fig. 14–4). The force on the blade is $F = Q\rho(V_{1r} - V_{2r}\cos\beta)$, where

$V_{1r} \approx V_{2r}$ as before. The power is $P = FU = Q\rho V_{1r} U(1 - \cos\beta)$. The energy per unit weight of fluid is $E = P/Q\gamma = (U/g)V_{1r}(1 - \cos\beta)$, which is identical to Eq. 14-7.

14-2. ENERGY EQUATION AND SYSTEM CHARACTERISTICS FOR PUMPS

The total energy added to a fluid by a pump impeller is greater than the net energy or head added to the fluid by the pump itself. Energy or head losses occur owing to secondary flow within the pump impeller and passages, flow separation, disk friction in a centrifugal pump, and leakage. These losses reduce the pump head to a value less than the impeller head.

The energy or head added to a fluid by a pump is obtained from the energy equation (Eq. 5-30b) applied between the inlet section *1* and the outlet section *2*.

$$-w = \frac{V_2{}^2 - V_1{}^2}{2g} + \frac{p_2 - p_1}{\gamma} + (z_2 - z_1) \qquad \text{[5-30b]}$$

or
$$H = H_v + H_p + H_z \qquad (14\text{-}8)$$

where the increase in total head H results largely from an increase in the pressure head H_p, rather than the velocity head H_v or potential or elevation head H_z. The ratio of the power represented by the total net head H to the power input to the pump is the over-all efficiency of the pump.

$$\eta = \frac{\text{output}}{\text{input}} = \frac{Q\gamma H}{(550)(\text{horsepower input})} \qquad (14\text{-}9)$$

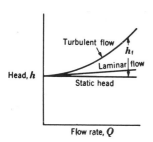

FIG. 14-5. Piping system demand or characteristic curves.

The pump supplies energy to increase the potential head or pressure head of the fluid in the system, to overcome head losses, or both. The system demand increases linearly with discharge for laminar flow, and almost parabolically with discharge for turbulent flow (Fig. 14-5). Any pump or combination of pumps operates at the intersection of the system characteristic or demand curve and the characteristic performance curve for the pump or combination of pumps. Typical performance curves are given in Sec. 14-3. The discharge and head corresponding to the point of maximum efficiency are called the *normal*, or *rated*, discharge and head, respectively.

14-3. PUMP PERFORMANCE CHARACTERISTICS

The actual performance characteristics of pumps are not obtained from the theory presented in Sec. 14-1 but are obtained by direct measurements made on the particular pump or on a model of the pump. It is customary to express the head, efficiency, and brake horsepower (horse-power input) as functions of capacity or flow rate, either in tabular or graphical form.

Centrifugal pumps. A centrifugal pump is so named because the head added by the impeller to the fluid is due largely to centrifugal effects. It is generally a high head, low capacity type of pump. A centrifugal pump having medium head and medium capacity characteristics is shown in Fig. 14–6. Fluid enters the eye of the impeller in an essentially axial direc-

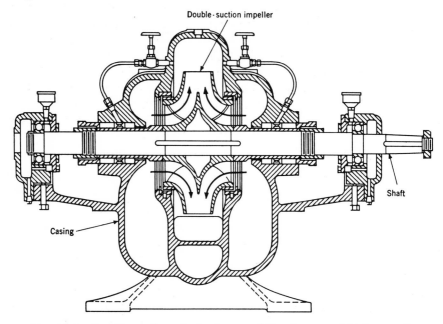

Fig. 14–6. Double-suction, single-stage centrifugal pump of high capacity and relatively low head. (Courtesy Worthington Corporation.)

tion, with a tangential component (whirl or prerotation) caused by viscous effects. The fluid flows outwards through diverging passages between the impeller blades and disks and leaves the impeller periphery at a high pressure and a rather high velocity as it enters the casing, or volute. The flow within the impeller is a combination of a source flow and a forced-vortex flow. The purpose of the volute is to convert the kinetic head, represented by the high discharge velocity, into pressure head before the fluid leaves the pump discharge pipe. If the casing contains fixed guide vanes, the pump is called a diffuser or turbine pump.

A centrifugal pump may have a single suction or a double suction, depending on whether the fluid enters the impeller from one or both axial directions, respectively. In a double-suction pump, end thrust on the pump

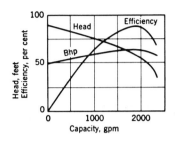

Fig. 14–7. Performance curves for a centrifugal pump.

shaft is essentially eliminated and impeller inlet velocities are reduced for a given impeller size. More than one impeller may be mounted on one shaft, and in this multistage-type pump the fluid discharging from one impeller and its volute enters the eye of the following impeller, and so forth. The total head added by a multistage pump is the sum of the heads added by each stage.

Typical performance curves for a centrifugal pump are shown in Fig. 14–7. Efficiencies are as high as 85 per cent for large pumps.

Centrifugal pumps may be classified according to the shape of their head-discharge curves (Fig. 14–8) or their power-discharge curves (Fig. 14–9). The terminology in Fig. 14–8 refers to the change in head for a decreasing discharge. Curves a, c, and d are called stable characteristics

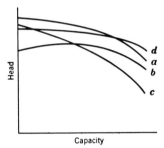

Fig. 14–8. Centrifugal-pump classification based on shape of head-capacity curve. a) Rising curve. b) Drooping curve. c) Steep curve. d) Flat curve.

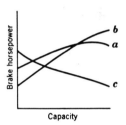

Fig. 14–9. Centrifugal-pump classification based on shape of power-capacity curve. a) Nonoverloading with reduction in head. b) Overloading with reduction in head and increase in capacity. c) Overloading with increase in head and decrease in capacity. Refer to Fig. 14–8.

because only one head is associated with a given discharge. Conversely, curve b is called an unstable characteristic. The stability of operation, however, depends on the system characteristic or demand curves (Fig. 14–5) as well as the pump characteristic curve. Pump b of Fig. 14–8 would probably be unstable if used in parallel with a similar pump or when the system characteristic curve is quite flat (head essentially independent of flow rate, as when the head losses are small). It might be stable in a system with low static head compared with higher head losses.

The power-capacity curves labeled a, b, and c in Fig. 14–9 correspond to the head-capacity curves labeled a, b, and c in Fig. 14–8. Curve a is called a nonoverloading characteristic, since the power decreases when the head is either increased or decreased. Curve b is called an overloading curve with a reduction in head, and curve c is called an overloading curve with an increase in head.

Axial-flow pump. An axial-flow pump is a propeller-type pump (Fig. 14–10). It may have three sets of blades: 1) inlet guide vanes to remove any tangential velocity component, 2) impeller blades, and 3) outlet vanes

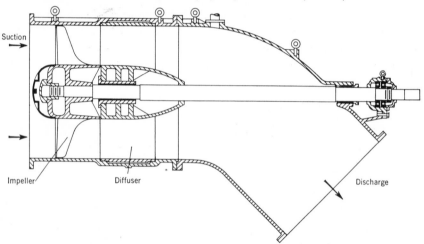

FIG. 14–10. Horizontal axial-flow pump. (Courtesy Worthington Corporation.)

to remove the tangential or whirl component of velocity at the pump discharge. Larger pumps are often made with controllable-pitch impeller blades so that good efficiency can be achieved over a wide range of flow rates. An axial-flow pump is a high-capacity, low-head type pump. Typical performance curves are shown in Fig. 14–11. Efficiencies are typically as high as 75 per cent. The head-capacity curve often has an unstable characteristic, and the power-capacity curve is of type c in Fig. 14–9.

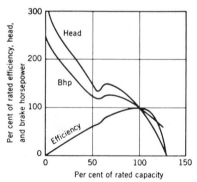

FIG. 14–11. Typical performance curves for an axial-flow pump. (Courtesy Worthington Corporation.)

Mixed-flow pump. A mixed-flow pump, shown in Fig. 14–12, has characteristic curves between those of a centrifugal pump and an axial-flow pump.

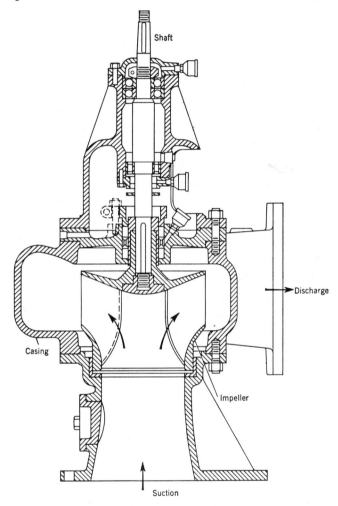

Shaft

Discharge

Casing

Impeller

Suction

Fig. 14–12. Pump with mixed-flow impeller. (Courtesy Worthington Corporation.)

14–4. PUMP AND SYSTEM COMBINATIONS

When two similar pumps are connected in series, the resulting characteristic curves are similar to those obtained by multistaging a number of impellers on a single shaft. For a given capacity, the total head is the sum of the heads added by each individual pump or stage. When two or more similar pumps are in parallel, the total capacity is increased to two or more times the capacity of each individual pump for the same head. The resulting head-capacity operating point will depend on the system characteristic curves as well as the combined pump characteristic curves (Fig. 14–13). One pump will operate at point A, and two pumps will operate at point B. In neither instance will the head or capacity double for the series or parallel combination of two pumps, respectively.

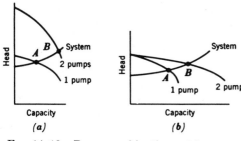

FIG. 14–13. Pump combinations with system characteristics. a) Series. b) Parallel.

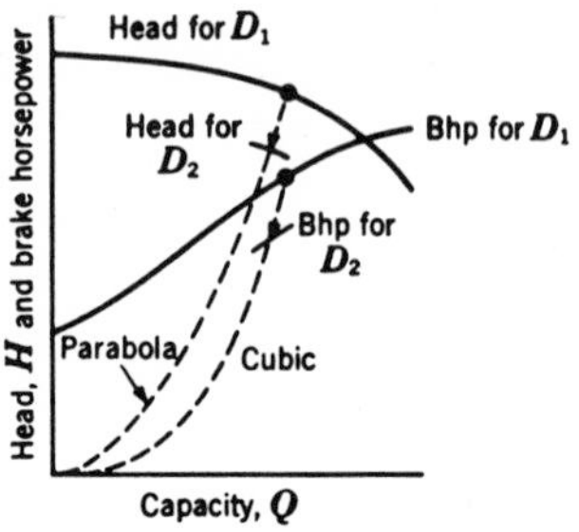

FIG. 14–14. Effect of change in impeller diameter for centrifugal pump.

14–5. DIMENSIONLESS PARAMETERS AND DYNAMIC SIMILARITY FOR PUMPS

The dimensional analysis of rotating machines in Sec. 8–6 (which should be reviewed) showed that for dynamically similar or homologous conditions, certain dimensionless parameters remain constant. These are

$$\frac{Q_1}{N_1 D_1{}^3} = \frac{Q_2}{N_2 D_2{}^3} \tag{14–10}$$

$$\frac{H_1}{N_1{}^2 D_1{}^2} = \frac{H_2}{N_2{}^2 D_2{}^2} \tag{14–11}$$

$$\frac{P_1}{\rho_1 N_1{}^3 D_1{}^5} = \frac{P_2}{\rho_2 N_2{}^3 D_2{}^5} \tag{14–12}$$

and $$N_{s(P)} = \frac{N_1 \sqrt{Q_1}}{H_1{}^{3/4}} = \frac{N_2 \sqrt{Q_2}}{H_2{}^{3/4}} \tag{14–13}$$

These parameters may be used to relate the characteristics of different size but similar pumps operating under dynamically similar conditions (model and prototype units, for example).

For a *given* pump, if the speed N is changed and the efficiency is assumed to remain constant, then Q varies as N, or

$$\frac{Q_1}{Q_2} = \frac{N_1}{N_2} \tag{14–14}$$

H varies as N^2, or $$\frac{H_1}{H_2} = \left(\frac{N_1}{N_2}\right)^2 \tag{14–15}$$

P varies as N^3, or
$$\frac{P_1}{P_2} = \left(\frac{N_1}{N_2}\right)^3 \qquad (14\text{--}16)$$

These equations permit an estimate of the pump performance characteristics for speeds other than those for which characteristics are known from direct measurement (see Example 8–6).

The efficiency of large pumps is generally greater than the efficiency of a geometrically similar small pump. The relation between these efficiencies is given approximately by

$$(1 - \eta_1)\,(N_1 D_1{}^2)^{1/5} = (1 - \eta_2)\,(N_2 D_2{}^2)^{1/5} = \text{constant} \quad (14\text{--}17)$$

For a pump in which the impeller diameter is reduced in order to obtain slightly different characteristics at a given speed (this is common practice among pump manufacturers), the following relationships apply:

$$\frac{Q_1}{Q_2} = \frac{D_1}{D_2} \qquad (14\text{--}18)$$

$$\frac{H_1}{H_2} = \left(\frac{D_1}{D_2}\right)^2 \qquad (14\text{--}19)$$

$$\frac{P_1}{P_2} = \left(\frac{D_1}{D_2}\right)^3 \qquad (14\text{--}20)$$

From these relations, the characteristic curves for a given impeller in a pump may be converted to characteristic curves for a smaller impeller, so long as the change in diameter is no greater than about 20 per cent. Points on a given head-discharge curve for diameter D_1 are transferred to corresponding points on the head-discharge curve for D_2 along parabolas, and points on a given power-discharge curve for diameter D_1 are transferred to corresponding points on the power-discharge curve for diameter D_2 along cubics (Fig. 14–14).

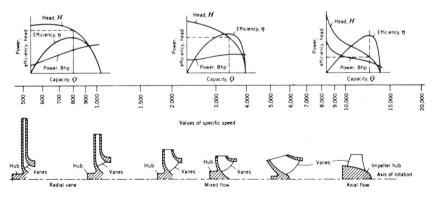

Fig. 14–15. Pump characteristics and specific speed for impellers of various designs. (Courtesy Worthington Corporation.)

Specific speeds in the United States are generally expressed as a nondimensionless number with the speed N in revolutions per minute, discharge Q in gallons per minute, and head H in feet at normal, or rated, capacity and head for a single stage. Typical values of specific speeds for various types of pump impellers, together with corresponding pump characteristic curves, are shown in Fig. 14–15.

14–6. PUMP CAVITATION

It is generally assumed, as a first approximation, that when the absolute pressure at some point within a liquid reaches the vapor pressure corresponding to the liquid temperature, cavities will form. These cavities will contain vapor, undissolved gas, or both. The phenomena of cavity formation or formation and collapse is known as cavitation. Cavities may exist in a more or less steady state (steady with respect to a moving blade element) or as intermittent bubbles. Cavitation, if severe enough, will affect pump performance, cause noisy operation, enhance vibration, and erode metal from the impeller.

There will be some point in the liquid within the pump where the pressure is a minimum, generally in a zone of flow separation, and as the ambient pressure is reduced vapor pressure will be reached and cavitation initiated at this point. Corresponding to this condition will be a fixed absolute pressure at the pump inlet or suction side for a given discharge through the pump. The value of the total head at the center line of the pump inlet (velocity head plus pressure head) minus the vapor-pressure head of the liquid is called the *net positive suction head* (NPSH) for the pump.

$$\text{NPSH} = \frac{V_1^2}{2g} + \frac{p_1}{\gamma} - \frac{p_v}{\gamma} \qquad (14\text{–}21)$$

As the net positive suction head is decreased for a given pump and flow rate, a value will be reached for which cavitation is considered detrimental; that is, the efficiency drops or the pump loses its prime. This point is called the *minimum* net positive suction head (NPSH_{min}) and is a function of the flow rate through a given pump as well as the type of pump. If a pump is operated above the minimum net positive suction head, it will not cavitate detrimentally.

The cavitation number σ for a pump is defined as the net positive suction head divided by the total head against which the pump operates, or

$$\sigma = \frac{\text{NPSH}}{H} \qquad (14\text{-}22)$$

The critical cavitation number σ_c corresponds to the minimum net positive suction head. Thus

$$\sigma_c = \frac{\text{NPSH}_{min}}{H} \qquad (14\text{–}23)$$

The cavitating characteristics of a pump as designated by its minimum net positive suction head or critical cavitation number determine the required static suction lift for a pump installation. Some terms associated with a pump installation are defined in Fig. 14–16.

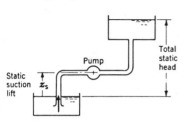

The energy equation for flow between the free surface of the lower sump in Fig. 14–16 and the pump inlet (section *1*) in terms of absolute pressures is

$$0 + \frac{p_a}{\gamma} + 0 = \frac{V_1^2}{2g} + \frac{p_1}{\gamma} + z_s + h_L$$

Fig. 14–16. Pump installation.

where p_a is the atmospheric pressure and h_L is the head loss in the intake. From this equation and the definition of net positive suction head in Eq. 14–21,

$$\mathrm{NPSH} = \frac{V_1^2}{2g} + \frac{p_1}{\gamma} - \frac{p_v}{\gamma} = \frac{p_a}{\gamma} - z_s - h_L - \frac{p_v}{\gamma}$$

and the minimum value of the static suction lift z_s is

$$z_s = \frac{p_a}{\gamma} - \frac{p_v}{\gamma} - \mathrm{NPSH}_{\min} - h_L \qquad (14\text{-}24\mathrm{a})$$

$$= \frac{p_a}{\gamma} - \frac{p_v}{\gamma} - \sigma_c H - h_L \qquad (14\text{-}24\mathrm{b})$$

If z_s is negative, the pump must be located below the level of the lower sump.

14–7. HYDRAULIC TURBINES

Hydraulic turbines are used to extract energy from water as it passes through the rotating turbine runner. The momentum of the water results from the velocity gained at the expense of potential energy or head as the water flows from a higher to a lower elevation. Available heads range from several thousand feet to ten feet or less. Hydraulic turbines are generally connected directly to an electric power generator, although in some instances they may be attached to wheels for grinding wood pulp, for example. As opposed to variable-speed operation of pumps, turbines generally run at a carefully controlled constant speed, depending on the type and design of turbine and generator and the local alternating-current power frequency.

The available water supply often varies throughout the year, while the power demand remains more uniform. Regulation of the flow resulting from runoff of seasonal rainfall may occur as a result of natural conditions, such as chains of large lakes, or by means of dams to create storage reservoirs.

The *gross*, or *total*, *head* on a hydroelectric plant is the difference between headwater and tailwater elevations (this varies from time to time) when the turbines are not in operation. The over-all hydraulic plant efficiency is the ratio of the power output of the turbines to the total available water power input based on the flow rate and gross head. The *net*, or *effective*, *head* is generally considered to be the difference in head between the entrance to the turbine and the tailwater. Thus the turbine itself is not charged with head losses in the penstock or intake passages between the headwater and the turbine. The net head for an impulse turbine is generally assumed to be the total head (velocity plus pressure) at the entrance to the turbine nozzle.

Hydraulic turbines may be classified according to *a*) whether they are impulse (zero reaction) or reaction turbines, *b*) the predominate flow direction of the water as it passes through the turbine runner, and *c*) the specific speed (see Sec. 8–6) $N_{s(T)} = N\sqrt{\text{Bhp}}/H^{5/4}$, defined at rated or normal capacity.

14–8. HYDRAULIC TURBINE CHARACTERISTICS

Three general types of hydraulic turbines, based on the flow direction through the runner, are in current use. These are the Pelton turbine (impulse), the Francis turbine (reaction), and the propeller turbine (reaction). Figure 14–17 shows these three types and the flow direction through the runners.

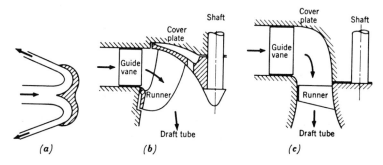

Fig. 14–17. Flow through turbine blades. *a*) Impulse turbine, *b*) Francis turbine, and *c*) Kaplan or fixed-blade propeller turbine. (Courtesy Allis-Chalmers Manufacturing Co.)

Impulse turbine. The Pelton wheel is a type of impulse turbine in current use. It is a tangential-flow turbine with a low specific speed (Fig. 14–18). A modern Pelton wheel is shown in Fig. 14–19. Water at a high head is converted into a high-velocity jet in a carefully designed nozzle. The tangential jet strikes a series of vanes or buckets on a rotating wheel, and the momentum change resulting from the jet deflection creates

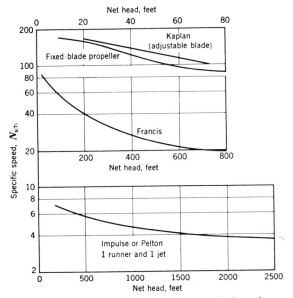

FIG. 14-18. Recommended upper limits of specific speed. (Courtesy Allis-Chalmers Manufacturing Co.)

a force over the bucket surface and hence a torque to rotate the wheel (see Fig. 14-4 and the figure for Prob. 5-105). The jet is unconfined and at atmospheric pressure as it passes through the turbine. The theoretical head or energy per unit weight of water is given by Eq. 14-7, and the theoretical power output of the wheel is

$$P_{th} = Q\rho V_{1r}\, U(1 - \cos\beta) \tag{14-25a}$$

$$= Q\rho(V_1 - U)U(1 - \cos\beta) \tag{14-25b}$$

where Q is the flow rate, V_1 is the jet velocity, U is the peripheral blade velocity, and β is the blade angle at exit. The theoretical efficiency is the ratio of the theoretical power output to the power input in the form of kinetic energy of the jet.

$$\eta_{th} = \frac{Q\rho(V_1 - U)U(1 - \cos\beta)}{Q\gamma V_1^2/2g}$$

$$\eta_{th} = 2\left(1 - \frac{U}{V_1}\right)\frac{U}{V_1}(1 - \cos\beta) \tag{14-26}$$

which is independent of the flow rate and depends only on the speed ratio U/V_1 for a given turbine wheel. It can be shown that the theoretical efficiency is a maximum when $V_1 = 2U$ (see Prob. 5-105). The actual efficiency of the turbine depends on windage losses, mechanical losses in the

FIG. 14–19. Pelton wheel. (Courtesy Allis-Chalmers Manufacturing Co.)

bearings, and hydraulic losses in the nozzle and on the blades. The power output is based on the flow rate Q and the net head H_1 at the nozzle entrance.

$$P = \frac{Q\gamma H_1}{550}\eta \qquad (14\text{--}27)$$

A Pelton wheel generally operates under a high head (gross heads over 5000 ft exist in European installations, and up to 3700 ft in American installations) and requires a correspondingly long penstock or supply pipe. Certain relationships exist between the jet and pipe diameter and the pipe length for maximum power. Since the power input to the turbine depends on both the flow rate Q and the jet velocity V_1, it is apparent that too small a jet will provide a small flow rate even though the jet velocity is large, and too large a jet will provide a low jet velocity even though the flow rate is large. In either instance the power input is reduced.

If the losses in the long penstock or supply pipe are considered to be pipe friction h_f only, the net head H at the nozzle entrance is the difference between the total, or gross, head H_t and h_f.

$$H = H_t - f\frac{L}{D_p}\frac{V_p^2}{2g}$$

where V_p is the velocity and D_p is the diameter of the pipe. The power P_1 in the jet is

$$P_1 = \frac{Q\gamma H}{550} = \frac{\gamma A_1 V_1}{550} \left(H_t - f \frac{L}{D_p} \frac{V_1{}^2}{2g} \frac{D_1{}^2}{D_p{}^2} \right) \tag{14-28}$$

which is a maximum when $dP_1/dA_1 = 0$ or when $H_t = 3h_f$. The power is a maximum when the net head H at the nozzle is two-thirds the gross head H_t. For no losses in the nozzle, $H = V_1{}^2/2g$. Thus, for optimum operation it can be shown that the jet diameter D_1 is related to the penstock diameter D_p by the relation

$$D_1 = \left(\frac{D_p{}^5}{2fL} \right)^{1/4} \tag{14-29}$$

Hence, for a given penstock or pipe diameter there exists a fixed jet diameter D_1 for maximum power

FIG. 14-20. Francis turbine runner. (Courtesy Allis-Chalmers Manufacturing Co.)

Reaction turbines. A Francis-type reaction turbine is a radial- or mixed-flow turbine with fixed runner blades and is most efficient at intermediate specific speeds (Figs. 14–17 and 14–18). The radial-flow type has the lowest specific speed and is essentially the reverse of a centrifugal pump. The mixed-flow type has higher specific speeds and is the reverse of a mixed-flow pump. In both instances, however, the efficiency of the Francis turbine (90 per cent or more) is higher than the efficiency of the corresponding pump. This is largely owing to the greater losses in the diverging flow through the pump impeller and volute than in the converging flow through the scroll and runner in the turbine. A Francis turbine runner is shown in Fig. 14–20.

The propeller-type reaction turbine is an axial-flow turbine with either fixed or adjustable blades and a high specific speed (Figs. 14–17 and 14–18). It is essentially the reverse of an axial-flow pump. A Kaplan turbine runner has adjustable blades and is shown in Fig. 14–21.

FIG. 14–21. Kaplan turbine runner. (Courtesy Allis-Chalmers Manufacturing Co.)

In reaction turbines the water flows from the headwater supply through a penstock (in some instances there is effectively none), through a guide case or scroll, inward past adjustable guide vanes or wicket gates in the guide case, through the turbine runner, and out through a diverging draft tube to the tailrace. In both types of reaction turbine the water is given a whirl component before entering the runner, and as the water passes through the runner, energy is absorbed by it in accordance with Eq. 14–3.

The diverging draft tube is used to reduce the velocity of the water as it enters the tailrace. This in turn reduces the head loss in the system. However, the absolute pressure of the water as it leaves the turbine runner is less with a draft tube than with a constant-area discharge tube. The draft tube requires a lower setting of the turbine in order to avoid cavitation. The cavitation number is often called the Thoma number, or the plant sigma, and is defined as

$$\sigma = \frac{H_a - H_v - z_s}{H} \tag{14-30}$$

where H_a is the atmospheric pressure head, H_v is the vapor pressure head, z_s is the static draft head (comparable to the static suction lift for a pump) and is the height from the tailwater to the bottom of a Francis-turbine

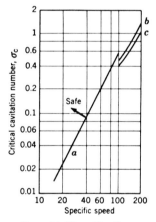

Fig. 14–22. Cavitation limits for reaction turbines. *a*) Francis, *b*) fixed-blade propeller, and *c*) Kaplan.

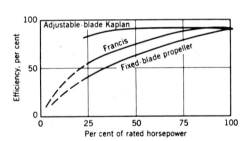

Fig. 14–23. Performance curves for reaction turbines.

runner and to the center of a propeller-turbine runner, and H is the net available head. (The value of $H_a - H_v$ is the height of a water barometer.) Typical lower limits of cavitation number for reaction turbines are shown in Fig. 14–22. Figure 14–23 shows typical efficiencies of reaction turbines.

14–9.   DIMENSIONLESS PARAMETERS AND   DYNAMIC SIMILARITY FOR TURBINES

Dynamic similarity is considered to exist when the dimensionless ratios involving discharge Q, speed N, head H, and size D in Eqs. 14–10, 14–11, and 14–12; the specific speed $N_{s(T)} = N\sqrt{\text{Bhp}}/H^{5/4}$; and the cavitation number of Eq. 14–30 are the same in homologous units. Almost all large turbines are custom-built, and model tests are conducted in order that the performance of the prototype may be predicted with reliability. The similarity parameters apply only if the efficiency is the same for similar units. It is well known that larger units are more efficient than small units. An expression by Moody relating efficiencies of models and prototypes is

$$\frac{1 - \eta_m}{1 - \eta_p} = \left(\frac{D_p}{D_m}\right)^{1/5} \tag{14–31}$$

Example 8–7 illustrates the use of similarity criteria for turbine tests.

REFERENCES

The reader is referred to the following sources for additional information on turbomachinery:

H. Addison, *Centrifugal and Rotodynamic Pumps* (London: Chapman and Hall, Ltd., 1948).

T. Baumeister, "Turbomachinery," Section 19 of *Handbook of Fluid Dynamics*, edited by V. L. Streeter (New York: McGraw-Hill Book Company, Inc., 1961).

J. W. Daily, "Hydraulic Machinery," Chapter 13 of *Engineering Hydraulics*, edited by H. Rouse (New York: John Wiley and Sons, Inc., 1950).

D. H. Norrie, *An Introduction to Incompressible Flow Machines* (New York: American Elsevier Publishing Company, Inc., 1963).

D. G. Shepherd, *Principles of Turbomachinery* (New York: The Macmillan Company, 1956).

PROBLEMS

14–1. A centrifugal pump impeller has a 16-in. diameter, a 1-in. width at exit ($b_2 = 1$ in.), a blade angle $\beta_2 = 150$ deg, and rotates at 1450 rpm. The flow rate is 1600 gpm. *a*) Calculate the meridional or radial, the relative, and the absolute fluid velocities at the impeller exit. *b*) For no inlet whirl, what head is added to water by the impeller? *c*) What horsepower is required to rotate the impeller?

Ans.   a) $V_{2m} = 10.2$ ft/sec, $V_{2r} = 20.4$ ft/sec, $V_2 = 84.1$ ft/sec; *b*) $E = 262$ ft; *c*) 106 hp

14–2. Repeat Prob. 14–1 for a speed of 1150 rpm.

14-3. Repeat Prob. 14-1 for an impeller diameter of 14 in.

14-4. Repeat Prob. 14-1 for a blade angle $\beta_2 = 135$ deg.

14-5. A centrifugal pump impeller has a 9-in. diameter with a $\frac{3}{8}$-in. width at exit. $\beta_2 = 145$ deg. The speed is 1700 rpm and the flow rate through the pump is 225 gpm. Calculate the radial, relative, and absolute fluid velocities at the impeller exit.

14-6. Water flows through the impeller of a centrifugal pump (Fig. 14-1). The flow rate is $Q = 800$ gpm, $R_1 = 2$ in., $R_2 = 8$ in., $b_2 = 0.75$ in., $\beta_2 = 120$ deg, and $N = 1150$ rpm. Assume no inlet whirl. a) What horsepower is required to rotate the impeller? b) Determine the blade angle β_1 at inlet which will make the relative velocity vector V_{1r} tangent to the blade. This condition provides what is known as a shockless entry.

14-7. Show that the reaction of an axial-flow machine is the average of the *tangential components* of the relative fluid velocities V_{1r} and V_{2r} divided by the peripheral blade velocity U. Show that this may also be expressed as

$$\text{Reaction}_{\text{axial flow}} = 1 - \frac{V_{1t} + V_{2t}}{2U}$$

Refer to Fig. 14-3.

14-8. A centrifugal pump with a 4-in. diameter suction pipe and a 3-in. diameter discharge pipe has a measured capacity of 300 gpm, a suction-side vacuum of 8 in. mercury, and a discharge pressure of 35 psig. The suction and discharge pipes are at the same elevation. The measured power input is 9.1 hp. What is the pump efficiency?

14-9. A centrifugal pump has a 6-in. suction pipe and a 5-in. discharge pipe. It is tested at 490 gpm with a measured input of 13.4 hp. The suction pressure is measured with a mercury manometer (Fig. 4-3) with a deflection $h_m = 8.00$ in. and the upper mercury meniscus is 12.0 in. below the suction pipe centerline ($y = 12.0$ in.). The discharge pressure is 31 psig. What is the pump efficiency?

14-10. A centrifugal pump delivers 600 gpm against a head of 100 ft at 1750 rpm. What are the corresponding values of a) discharge and b) head at a speed of 1650 rpm?

14-11. Under what conditions would two similar pumps in parallel in a system deliver essentially twice the discharge of a single pump connected in the same system?

14-12. A 14.125-in. diameter impeller in a centrifugal pump has the following characteristics at 1750 rpm:

Q, gpm	200	300	400	500
H, feet	205	201	191	167

a) Plot the characteristic curve for a speed of 1450 rpm for this pump. b) What impeller diameter would produce a head of 160 ft at 365 gpm at a speed of 1750 rpm? *c*) What brake horsepower would be required in part *b*) for an efficiency of 70 per cent?

$$Ans. \quad b) \ 12.92 \ in., \quad c) \ 21.1 \ hp$$

14–13. A 13.5-in. diameter impeller in a centrifugal pump has the following characteristics at 1750 rpm:

Q, gpm	200	300	350	400
H, feet	177	165	156	147

a) Plot characteristic curves for a speed of 1150 for this pump. *b*) What diameter impeller would produce a head of 140 ft at 300 gpm at a speed of 1750 rpm? *c*) What brake horsepower would be required in part *b*) for an efficiency of 72 per cent?

14–14. A 12-in. diameter impeller in a centrifugal pump delivers 450 gpm at a head of 100 ft at 1750 rpm and requires 14 hp to drive it. *a*) What would be the corresponding capacity and head if the impeller diameter is reduced to 11 in.? *b*) What horsepower would be required in part *a*)? Assume no change in efficiency.

14–15. A pump with a 25-in. impeller is to deliver 13,000 gpm at a head of 102 ft at 860 rpm. A model pump with a 6-in. impeller is run at 1750 rpm. *a*) What are the corresponding capacity and head for the model, assuming homologous conditions? *b*) For an assumed efficiency of 80 per cent for both model and prototype, what horsepower will be required to drive each? *c*) Calculate the specific speed and determine what type of pump this is.

$$Ans. \quad b) \ hp_m = 2.81, \ hp_p = 419; \quad c) \ N_{s(P)} = 3050, \ mixed\text{-}flow \ pump$$

14–16. A 6-in. model of a centrifugal pump has an efficiency of 66 per cent. Estimate the efficiency of similar pumps *a*) 9 in. and *b*) 12 in. in diameter at the same speed.

$$Ans. \quad a) \ 71 \ per \ cent$$

14–17. A pump for which $\sigma_c = 0.08$ pumps against a total head of 200 ft. The water temperature is 100 F, the barometric pressure is 14.5 psia, and the head loss in the suction pipe is 3 ft. What is the maximum value of the static suction lift?

$$Ans. \quad z_s = 12.5 \ ft$$

14–18. Repeat Prob. 14–17 for a water temperature of 180 F ($\gamma = 60.6 \ lb_f/ft^3$ and $p_v = 7.51$ psia).

14–19. Select the type of pump appropriate for the following operating conditions: *a*) 1450 rpm, 200 gpm, 50-ft head; *b*) 720 rpm, 10,000 gpm, 8-ft head; and *c*) 1150 rpm, 1000 gpm, 30-ft head.

14–20. Plot a curve of the theoretical efficiency for an impulse turbine as a function of speed ratio U/V_1 for a blade angle $\beta_2 = 165$ deg.

14–21. In Eq. 14–28, let $A_1 V_1 = Q$ and $dP_1/dA_1 = 0$. Show that $H_t = 3h_f$ for maximum power.

14–22. Verify Eq. 14–29.

14–23. A water jet 2.5 in. in diameter at a velocity of 200 ft/sec drives an impulse wheel whose diameter is 60 in. at a speed of 360 rpm. The jet is deflected through an angle of 165 deg. What horsepower is delivered to the turbine runner?

14-24. A penstock for an impulse turbine is 4000 ft long, 2 ft in diameter, has a total head of 1200 ft, and $f = 0.024$. What is the optimum diameter of the jet? Neglect losses in the nozzle.

14-25. Plot the jet velocity, jet horsepower, and flow rate as ordinates versus jet diameter from 0 to 2 ft as abscissa for the conditions of Prob. 14-24. Verify that maximum power occurs when $H_t = 3h_f$.

14-26. A reaction turbine develops 35,000 hp at 514 rpm under a head of 850 ft. For a barometer reading of 28.00 in. mercury and a maximum water temperature of 60 F ($p_v = 0.26$ psia), what is the maximum height of the bottom of the turbine runner above the tailwater?

Ans. $z_s = 8.1$ ft

14-27. A fixed-blade propeller turbine develops 45,000 hp at 85.7 rpm under a head of 48 ft. For the water and atmospheric conditions of Prob. 14-26, what is the maximum height of the turbine runner with respect to the tailwater?

14-28. A Kaplan turbine with a 22-ft diameter propeller develops 36,000 hp at 75 rpm under a head of 36 ft. *a*) At what speed should a 2-ft diameter model be run under a head of 18 ft for homologous conditions? *b*) What flow rate should exist for the model, assuming an efficiency of 93 per cent for both prototype and model? *c*) What horsepower will be developed by the model? *d*) What is the specific speed?

14-29. Verify Eqs. 14-10, 14-11, and 14-12 on the basis of similarity of vector diagrams (Fig. 14-1) for dynamically similar or homologous machines.

14-30. A 6-in. model of a Francis turbine has an efficiency of 90 per cent. Plot a curve showing expected efficiencies for homologous units 10, 20, and 30 times the size of the model.

14-31. Tests on a 16-in. diameter turbine runner under a head of 24 ft at 400 rpm for a flow rate of 17.8 cfs show a power output of 40.0 hp. *a*) What is the specific speed? *b*) What type of turbine runner is this? *c*) If a 36-in. runner is used under a head of 120 ft, what is the speed, discharge, and horsepower for a homologous condition? Include effect of a slightly greater efficiency for the larger turbine.

14-32. Select the type of hydraulic turbine appropriate for the following conditions: *a*) 100 rpm, 35,000 hp, 92-ft head; *b*) 360 rpm, 20,000 hp, 2245-ft head; and *c*) 125 rpm, 40,000 hp, 70-ft head.

Ans. a) $N_s = 66$, Francis turbine

NOTE: Reference is made to Probs. 5-97, 5-98, and 5-100 through 5-105 in Chapter 5 and to Probs. 8-48, 8-49, 8-50, 8-52, 8-53, and 8-54 in Chapter 8.

15

Varied Flow in Open Channels and Gas Flow in Pipes and Nozzles

One-dimensional flow of water in an open channel is similar in many respects to the one-dimensional flow of a gas in pipes and in nozzles. The trivial situation is uniform flow in an open channel and the flow of a gas in a pipe at such low velocities that the gas flow is essentially incompressible, and thus uniform as well. In uniform open-channel flow, the slope of the water surface is constant in the direction of flow, and for uniform gas flow in a pipe, the pressure gradient dp/dx is constant. These water-surface and pressure gradients may be expressed quantitatively by means of the Manning equation (Eq. 12–4a) for open-channel flow and by the Darcy-Weisbach equation (Eq. 10–5) for pipe flow.

Similarities of greater interest exist between nonuniform flow of water in open channels (see Chapter 12) and 1) isentropic gas flow in nozzles where friction is neglected (Sec. 9–3), 2) adiabatic gas flow in pipes with friction (Sec. 10–10), 3) diabatic flow of gases in pipes without friction (Sec. 9–4), and 4) shocks in gas flow (Sec. 9–5). Gradually varying and rapidly varying open-channel flow in prismatic channels, in otherwise prismatic channels but with changing bottom slopes in the direction of flow, and in channels with bottom and side constrictions have analogous counterparts in high-velocity gas flows in pipes and in nozzles. In all instances, the same basic equations of continuity, energy, and momentum are applicable. The flow patterns or behavior depend in all instances on the ratio of the local flow velocity to that of a weak disturbance. This weak disturbance consists of an elementary surface wave in open-channel flow and of an acoustic or sound wave in gas flow. Thus the controlling parameters are the local Froude number and the local Mach number, respectively. We will consider only rectangular channels in order to use the actual depth rather than the hydraulic depth (cross section area of flow divided by the surface width) for nonrectangular channels.

15–1. FROUDE AND MACH NUMBERS

In Chapter 8 the Froude number was defined as the ratio of inertia to gravity forces in a flow system, and on this basis, the resulting expression for the Froude number is

$$\text{Fr} = \frac{V}{\sqrt{gL}} \qquad (15\text{-}1)$$

where V is the average flow velocity at a section and L is a characteristic length. In Sec. 12–2, the velocity of an elementary wave on the free surface of water (a wave whose height Δy is much smaller than the water depth y) was shown to be

$$c_{\text{wave}} = \sqrt{gy} \qquad (15\text{-}2)$$

The Froude number, then, in a rectangular channel is the ratio of the average flow velocity at a section to that of an elementary (small) surface wave at that section. Thus, if a small pebble is dropped into flowing water, the upstream portion of the circular surface wave will travel upstream if the Froude number is less than unity, it will remain essentially at rest if the Froude number is equal to unity, and it will travel only downstream if the Froude number is greater than unity. In any case, the downstream portion of the circular surface wave will travel downstream superimposed on the stream flow. Flows at Froude numbers less than unity, equal to unity, and greater than unity are called subcritical, critical, and super-critical flows, respectively.

In Chapter 8, the Mach number was defined as the ratio of inertia to compressible forces in a flow system, and on this basis, the resulting expression is

$$\text{M} = \frac{V}{\sqrt{K/\rho}} \qquad (15\text{-}3)$$

where V is the local flow velocity, K is the bulk compression modulus, and ρ is the fluid density. In Sec. 9–1, the velocity of a very weak pressure disturbance (an acoustic wave in which the change in pressure Δp is much smaller than the ambient pressure p) was shown to be

$$c = \sqrt{K/\rho} = \sqrt{kp/\rho} \qquad (15\text{-}4)$$

$$= \sqrt{kRT} \qquad \text{for a perfect gas}$$

The Mach number in a gas is, then, the ratio of the fluid velocity to that of a very weak pressure wave. Thus a sound wave will travel upstream if the local Mach number is less than unity, it will not travel upstream if the local Mach number is unity, and it will travel only downstream if the local Mach number is greater than unity. In each instance, the sound wave will travel downstream with the gas and will be superimposed on the gas flow. Flows at Mach numbers less than unity, equal to unity, and greater than unity are called subsonic, sonic, and supersonic flows, respectively.

15–2. SPECIFIC ENERGY AND THE FANNO LINE; SPECIFIC THRUST AND THE RAYLEIGH LINE

The continuity, energy, and momentum equations applied to both open-channel flow and to gas flow, together with gas relations which give entropy as a function of pressure and density and enthalpy as a function of entropy and density, may be used to produce some useful graphical comparisons between these flows.

Specific energy. The specific energy E in an open channel was defined in Sec. 12–3 as the total energy of an open channel with respect to the channel bed. This relation is indicated in Fig. 15–1 as

$$E = \frac{V^2}{2g} + \frac{p}{\gamma} + z = \frac{V^2}{2g} + y \qquad (15\text{–}5a)$$

For a unit width of channel, the unit discharge is $q = Vy$ and may be considered as the constant flow-rate intensity (in volumetric flow rate per unit width). If this term is substituted in Eq. 15–5a, the specific energy may be expressed in terms of the depth y for a constant unit discharge.

$$E = \frac{q^2}{2gy^2} + y \qquad (15\text{–}5b)$$

For a constant unit discharge, $E = E(y)$ from the energy and continuity equations, and a plot of this relation is shown in Fig. 15–1(b). At any depth, the horizontal distance to the 45-deg line ($y = E$) represents the depth, and the horizontal distance from the line $y = E$ to the specific-energy curve represents the velocity head. At the minimum specific energy (point A), $dE/dy = 0$, and from Eqs. 15–5 this is equivalent to

$$\frac{V^2}{2g} = \frac{y}{2} \qquad \text{or} \qquad \frac{V}{\sqrt{gy}} = 1$$

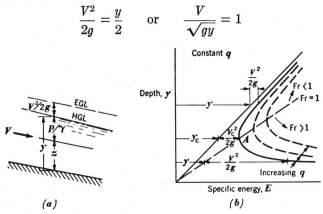

FIG. 15–1.   Specific energy in an open channel.   a) Nomenclature and b) diagram.

Thus the minimum specific energy represents critical flow at a Froude number of unity. Also, flow at depths greater than the critical depth (along the upper part of a specific-energy curve) is subcritical with $Fr < 1$, and flow at depths less than critical (along the lower part of a curve) is supercritical with $Fr > 1$.

The Fanno line. For adiabatic flow of a gas in a pipe with friction, the continuity and energy equations, together with gas relations, may be combined and plotted graphically to give the Fanno line, which is similar to the specific-energy curve for open-channel flow.

The continuity equation is $V\rho = G$, a constant mass-flow intensity (in slugs/ft^2 sec, for example). The energy equation, in the absence of heat transfer, work, and potential energy changes, is

$$h + \frac{V^2}{2} = h_0 \tag{15-6a}$$

where h is the enthalpy and h_0 the stagnation or total enthalpy which is constant for this adiabatic flow. Substituting the value of V from the continuity equation into Eq. 15-6a gives

$$h = h_0 - \frac{G^2}{2}\left(\frac{1}{\rho}\right)^2 \tag{15-6b}$$

which is the equation of the Fanno line shown in Fig. 15-2(a). This Fanno line is a constant (h_0) minus a parabolic quantity $(G^2/2)(1/\rho)^2$. Also shown in Fig. 15-2(a) is a family of constant entropy curves for which $s = s(p, \rho)$. If the curve is replotted with enthalpy h vs. entropy s, the result is as shown in Fig. 15-2(b).

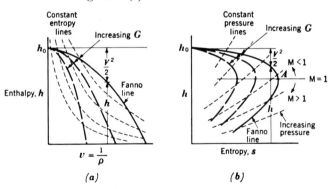

FIG. 15-2. Fanno line. *a*) h vs. $1/\rho$. *b*) h vs. s.

At point A, $ds/dh = 0$, and from the second law of thermodynamics as expressed by Eq. 3-5 ($T\,ds = dh - dp/\rho$), at point A, $dh = dp/\rho$. Substituting this value of dh, at point A, in the differential form of the energy equation ($dh + V\,dV = 0$), we get

$$\frac{dp}{\rho} + V \, dV = 0$$

This equation corresponds to the equation of motion in a frictionless fluid in the absence of gravitational effects, which is true for point A. From continuity, $\rho \, dV + V \, d\rho = 0$, so that

$$\frac{dp}{\rho} + V \, dV = \frac{dp}{\rho} - \frac{V^2 \, d\rho}{\rho} = 0$$

and thus at point A,

$$V^2 = \frac{dp}{d\rho} \qquad \text{at constant entropy} \qquad (15\text{-}7)$$

This equation shows that the velocity at point A is sonic, and the Mach number at point A is unity. This condition corresponds to a Froude number of unity at point A in Fig. 15-1(b). Since from Eq. 9-14 the velocity and Mach number either both increase or both decrease, and since the velocity along the upper part of the Fanno line on the h-s (enthalpy-entropy) diagram in Fig. 15-2(b) is less than sonic, the upper part of the Fanno line in Fig. 15-2(b) represents subsonic flow with $M < 1$, and the lower part of the Fanno line represents supersonic flow with $M > 1$. From the second law of thermodynamics, the entropy of the gas must increase for adiabatic flow with friction. Therefore, subsonic flow is in a direction of increasing Mach number, and supersonic flow is in a direction of decreasing Mach number, both flows approaching $M = 1$ as a limit (see Sec. 10-10). From the family of pressure lines in Fig. 15-2(b), subsonic flow is accompanied by a decreasing pressure, while supersonic flow is accompanied by an increasing pressure.

Similarly, from Fig. 15-1(b), subcritical flow in an open channel and supercritical flow in an open channel approaching point A, where $\text{Fr} = 1$, are accompanied by decreasing and increasing depths, respectively.

Specific thrust function in open-channel flow. The continuity and momentum (thrust function) equations applied to an open channel yield a graphical representation of the specific-thrust function. From Sec. 12-3, these equations are

$$Vy = q$$

indicating a constant unit discharge, or volumetric flow-rate intensity, and

$$F = \frac{\gamma y^2}{2} + \rho V^2 y$$

The specific-thrust function is the thrust function divided by the specific weight of the fluid and is

$$f = \frac{y^2}{2} + \frac{q^2}{gy} \qquad (15\text{-}8)$$

For a constant unit discharge, $f = f(y)$ from the continuity and thrust function, and a plot of this specific-thrust function is shown in Fig. 15–3(b).

At the minimum specific thrust (point B), $df/dy = 0$, and from Eq. 15–8, this is equivalent to

$$y_B{}^3 = \frac{q^2}{g} \quad \text{or} \quad y_B = \frac{V^2}{g}$$

Thus $V/\sqrt{gy_B} = 1$, which is the same condition as for minimum specific energy, and corresponds to critical flow at which Fr $= 1$. As for specific energy, the upper part of the specific-thrust function curve (above B) represents subcritical flow for which Fr < 1, and the lower part of the specific-thrust function curve (below B) represents supercritical flow for which Fr > 1.

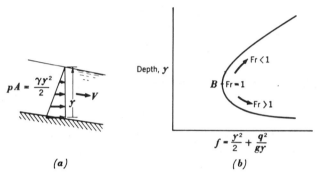

FIG. 15–3.   Specific thrust in an open channel. a)
Pressure term in thrust function. b) Specific thrust
function.

Rayleigh line.   For diabatic flow in a constant area duct without friction, the continuity and momentum equation (thrust function), together with gas relations, give an equation whose graph is called the Rayleigh line.   Diabatic flow without friction implies flow with heat transfer which is reversible.

From continuity, $V\rho = G$, a constant mass-flow rate intensity.   From the momentum theorem, the thrust function is constant in the absence of external drag or friction.   Thus

$$p + \rho V^2 = \text{constant}$$

Combining the continuity and thrust-function equations gives

$$p + \frac{G^2}{\rho} = \text{constant} \tag{15-9}$$

Both entropy and enthalpy are functions of pressure and density, and

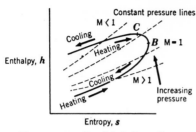

therefore Eq. 15–9 may be plotted as shown in Fig. 15–4.

Point B in Fig. 15–4 corresponds to a sonic velocity and a Mach number of unity, just as point B on the specific-thrust curve of Fig. 15–3(b) corresponds to critical flow with a Froude number of unity. The sonic condition at point B may be shown by differentiating Eq. 15–9 to obtain

$$dp = \frac{G^2}{\rho^2}\, d\rho = 0$$

so that

$$\frac{dp}{d\rho} = \frac{G^2}{\rho^2} = V_B{}^2$$

Then $V_B = \sqrt{dp/d\rho}$, and since $ds = 0$ (entropy constant) at point B, the velocity at point B is sonic and the Mach number is unity. The upper part of the Rayleigh curve corresponds to subsonic flow, and the lower part to supersonic flow. The flow is without friction and thus is reversible, so that heat addition (heating) is associated with an entropy increase, and heat removal (cooling) is associated with an entropy decrease. (For reversible flow, $ds = dQ/T$.) Thus, flow with heat addition is towards a sonic condition, and heat removal is away from a sonic condition, for both subsonic and supersonic flow. This conclusion is compatible with the conclusions reached in Sec. 9–4 for diabatic flow. Note from Fig. 15–4 that for heating at points between the highest point on the Rayleigh line (point C) and point B, the enthalpy of the gas decreases. This means that heating in this region will cool the gas. Conversely, heat removal in this region between points B and C will warm the gas. From Sec. 9–4, point C corresponds to a Mach number of $1/\sqrt{k}$. These conclusions are coincident with those reached in Sec. 9–4 in the analysis of the differential equations for diabatic flow in a pipe without friction which were developed there.

15–3. HYDRAULIC JUMP AND NORMAL SHOCK

A hydraulic jump normal to a stream is similar to a normal shock in a gas flow, and hydraulic jumps oblique to a stream flow direction are similar to oblique shocks in a gas flow.

Hydraulic jump. In Sec. 12–6, the hydraulic jump was shown to occur with constant specific thrust and with a decrease in specific energy, and is the only way in which supercritical flow may become subcritical without passing through a channel transition (Sec. 12–7). The conditions on a specific-energy and a specific-thrust diagram were shown in Fig. 12–11(*b*), and are shown again in Fig. 15–5.

The energy equation written across a jump on a horizontal bed is

$$E_1 = E_2 + h_L$$

so that the head loss (energy dissipation per unit weight of fluid) is

$$h_L = E_1 - E_2$$

which is indicated in Fig. 15–5. The Froude number changes from a value greater than unity to a value less than unity. The depths on each side of the jump were shown in Sec. 12–6 to be a function of the upstream Froude number Fr_1.

$$\frac{y_2}{y_1} = \frac{1}{2}\left(\sqrt{1 + 8Fr_1^2} - 1\right) \tag{15–10}$$

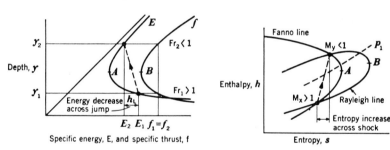

FIG. 15–5. Hydraulic jump.   FIG. 15–6. Normal shock.

Normal shock. In Sec. 9–5, the normal shock was shown to occur at a constant thrust function (constant momentum flux or transport). It can also be shown that the entropy change across the shock is positive in the direction of flow for upstream Mach numbers M_x greater than unity. This increase in entropy is required by the second law of thermodynamics. (Actually, for weak shocks—Mach numbers no greater than about 1.2—the increase in entropy is extremely small, so that the flow is nearly isentropic.) Since the mass-flow rate, energy, and thrust function or momentum flux are all constant across a normal shock (see Sec. 9–5), conditions on each side of the shock must lie on *both* the Fanno line and the Rayleigh line. Thus for a given mass-flow intensity G, the intersections of the Fanno and Rayleigh lines locate upstream and downstream conditions for a normal shock (Fig. 15–6).

Either adiabatic flow in a pipe with friction or diabatic flow (with heat transfer) in a pipe without friction may be initially subsonic,and may then proceed towards the sonic condition along a Fanno line or a Rayleigh line towards point A or B, respectively. These are limiting points, and they provide choking effects which may change the initial assumed conditions in

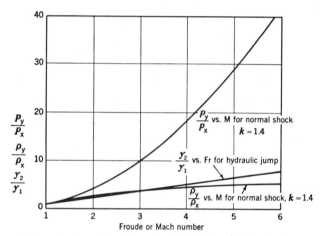

$\dfrac{p_y}{p_x}$

$\dfrac{\rho_y}{\rho_x}$

$\dfrac{y_2}{y_1}$

Froude or Mach number

Fig. 15–7.   Depth ratio for hydraulic jump for various Froude numbers, and pressure and density ratio across normal shock for various Mach numbers $(k = 1.4)$.

the pipe if the gas tries to reach these limiting conditions upstream from the end of the pipe. Different Fanno and Rayleigh lines would then apply, since the mass-flow intensity G would change. If the gas starts out supersonic (on the lower part of the lines), the gas may proceed to A or B as a limit if the back pressure beyond the end of the pipe does not prevent this. If the back pressure is at p_1, for example, a shock will form within the pipe, and the gas may proceed towards A or B at subsonic flow ($M < 1$).

The pressures across a normal shock were shown in Sec. 9–5 to be a function of the upstream Mach number M_x (Eq. 9–37).

$$\frac{p_y}{p_x} = \frac{2k}{k+1}\,M_x{}^2 - \frac{k-1}{k+1} \qquad (15\text{–}11)$$

Figure 15–7 shows the depth ratios for a hydraulic jump as a function of the upstream Froude number, together with the pressure and density ratios for a normal shock as a function of the upstream Mach number. It may be noted that the depth ratio across a hydraulic jump increases almost linearly with the Froude number, while the pressure ratio across a normal shock increases as the square of the Mach number.

15–4. SOME EXAMPLES OF SIMILAR FLOWS

There are various instances in which open-channel flows are similar to gas flows. Some examples are illustrated in Figs. 15–8, 15–9, and 15–10.

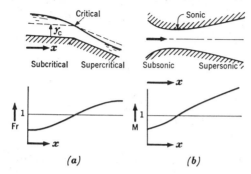

FIG. 15–8. Flow from subcritical to supercritical in an open channel and from subsonic to supersonic in a nozzle. *a)* Flow from a mild to a steep slope in an open channel. *b)* Gas flow in a converging-diverging nozzle with low back pressure.

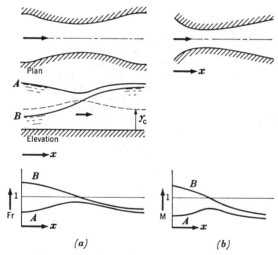

FIG. 15–9. Flow through channel constriction to a high tailwater and gas flow through a converging-diverging nozzle with a high back pressure. *a)* Constriction in channel of constant bed slope, with high tailwater. Curve *A* represents initially subcritical flow; curve *B*, supercritical flow. *b)* Converging-diverging nozzle, with high back pressure. Curve *A* represents initially subsonic flow; curve *B*, supersonic flow.

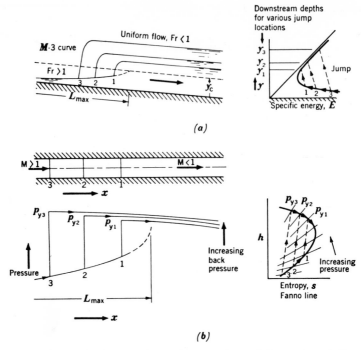

(a)

(b)

FIG. 15-10. Hydraulic jump in open channel for various tail-water elevations, and shock in pipe for various back pressures. *a*) Supercritical open channel flow on a mild slope with various tailwater elevations. Location of jump is dependent upon tail-water elevation. L_{max} refers to length of *M-3* curve for super-critical flow. *b*) Supersonic gas flow entering pipe with friction, adiabatic flow, with various back pressures. Location of shock in pipe is dependent upon back pressure. L_{max} refers to maximum length for supersonic flow.

REFERENCE

E. Preiswerk, "Application of the Methods of Gas Dynamics to Water Flows with Free Surface, Part I, Flows with no Energy Dissipation," *NACA TM* 934, 1940. "Part II, Flows with Momentum Discontinuities (Hydraulic Jumps)," *NACA, TM* 935, 1940.

16 | Convective Heat Transfer

16-1. THE THERMAL BOUNDARY LAYER

When a fluid at one temperature flows past a surface at another temperature, heat transfer takes place from one to the other. The fluid temperature T varies from the free-stream temperature T_s to the wall temperature T_w, the variation taking place in a region known as the

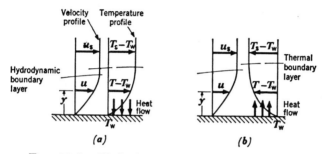

FIG. 16-1. Hydrodynamic and thermal boundary layers. *a*) Wall temperature below free-stream temperature. *b*) Wall temperature above free-stream temperature.

thermal boundary layer (Fig. 16-1). Heat flows by conduction at the wall surface, either from the wall to the fluid or from the fluid to the wall, according to the well-known relation

$$q = -k \frac{\partial T}{\partial y} \tag{16-1}$$

where q = the heat transferred per unit time and unit area;
$\quad k$ = the thermal conductivity of the fluid in energy per unit area, unit time, and unit temperature difference for a unit thickness of fluid[1];
$\quad \dfrac{\partial T}{\partial y}$ = the temperature gradient at the wall surface.

Heat flows in a direction of decreasing temperature (negative temperature gradient) and thus the negative sign is required in Eq. 16-1. If the wall temperature is higher than the free-stream temperature of the fluid, the heat transferred from the wall is carried away within the thermal boundary layer of the fluid. If the wall temperature is lower than the free-stream

[1]In this chapter, k is *not* the ratio of specific-heat capacities.

temperature of the fluid, the heat transferred to the wall is carried to it within the thermal boundary layer. Heat transfer of this type is called *heat transfer by convection*. If the fluid motion is produced by external means (by a pump or blower, for example), the heat transfer is due to *forced convection*. If the fluid is set in motion because of buoyancy effects owing to changes in fluid density which result from the heat transfer, the heat transfer is due to *free convection*. In either case, it is customary to define a heat-transfer coefficient h by the equation

$$q = h(T_w - T_s) \tag{16-2}$$

where h has the dimensions of energy per unit time, unit area, and unit temperature difference. The heat-transfer coefficient h depends on the fluid property values, such as specific heat capacity, thermal conductivity, viscosity, and density; the fluid flow characteristics, such as pressure gradient and whether the flow is laminar or turbulent; and the geometry of the system.

Of primary interest is the determination or prediction of the magnitude of the heat-transfer coefficient h or its dimensionless equivalent, the *Nusselt number* hL/k, for various conditions (where L is a characteristic length similar to that used for the Reynolds number). In addition, the thickness of the thermal boundary layer δ_t is also of interest. The skin-friction coefficient and the thickness of the hydrodynamic boundary layer are analogous to the heat-transfer coefficient and the thickness of the thermal boundary layer. A thermal boundary layer is always accompanied by a hydrodynamic boundary layer, while a hydrodynamic boundary layer need not be accompanied by a thermal boundary layer. The ratio of the thickness of the thermal to the hydrodynamic boundary layer, δ_t/δ, depends inversely on a dimensionless fluid property known as the *Prandtl number* ($\mathrm{Pr} = c_p\mu/k$). The Prandtl number is much less than unity for liquid metals, nearly unity for gases, and up to 10,000 or more for some viscous oils. Therefore, the thermal boundary layer is much thicker than the hydrodynamic boundary layer for liquid metals, about equal to it for gases, and much thinner than the hydrodynamic boundary layer for viscous oils.

A dimensional analysis would show that the forced-convection heat-transfer coefficient for flow past a flat plate depends on the Reynolds number of the flow and on the Prandtl number of the fluid.

$$\mathrm{Nu} = f(\mathrm{Re}, \mathrm{Pr}) \tag{16-3}$$

Also, the thickness of the thermal boundary layer for this flow may be shown to depend on the thickness of the hydrodynamic boundary layer and on the Prandtl number for a plate heated over its entire length.

$$\frac{\delta_t}{\delta} = f(\mathrm{Pr}) \tag{16-4}$$

For fully developed flow in a tube, the Nusselt number is a constant, and the thermal and the hydrodynamic boundary layer are both equal to the tube radius.

Exact solutions of the boundary-layer momentum and energy equations may be made, but a simpler approximate method, similar to that employed in Chapter 7 for the hydrodynamic boundary layer, can be used to obtain useful results.

In order to illustrate the interrelationships between the thermal and hydrodynamic boundary layers, an approximate boundary-layer analysis for laminar flow over a flat plate and in a tube, and the Reynolds analogy for turbulent flow over a flat plate and in a tube will be given.

16–2. FLOW OVER A FLAT PLATE WITH NO PRESSURE GRADIENTS

The boundary-layer heat-flow equation is obtained by making a heat balance on a region of unit width, of infinitesimal length dx, and height y_2 (y_2 is greater than either δ or δ_t). Assumptions include steady two-dimensional flow, constant fluid properties, and velocities in the boundary layer small so that temperature changes owing to dissipation from viscous shear may be considered negligible. It should be noted that for a constant property fluid, the heat transfer does not change or affect the fluid-flow pattern.

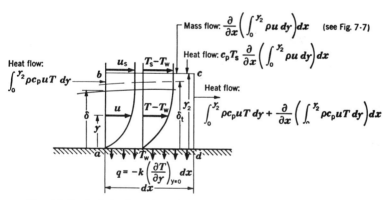

Fig. 16–2. Infinitesimal length of boundary layer with heat balance.

The net heat flow (flow in minus flow out) must be zero. Thus, from Fig. 16–2.

$$\rho c_p T_s \frac{\partial}{\partial x}\left[\int_0^{y_2} u\,dy\right]dx - \rho c_p \frac{\partial}{\partial x}\left[\int_0^{y_2} uT\,dy\right]dx - k\left(\frac{\partial T}{\partial y}\right)_{y=0}dx = 0$$

so that the heat flow equation for the boundary layer is

$$\frac{\partial}{\partial x}\int_0^{y_2}(T_s - T)u\,dy = \frac{k}{\rho c_p}\left(\frac{\partial T}{\partial y}\right)_{y=0} \tag{16–5}$$

Laminar Flow. The thermal boundary-layer thickness δ_t and the local (h) or average ($\bar{h}$) heat-transfer coefficient may be obtained for any prescribed shape of temperature and velocity profiles within the boundary layer. The velocity profile (see Sec. 7–4) may be assumed to be

$$\frac{u}{u_s} = \frac{3}{2}\left(\frac{y}{\delta}\right) - \frac{1}{2}\left(\frac{y}{\delta}\right)^3 \qquad [7\text{–}8]$$

Temperature profiles may be assumed to be of the form

$$T - T_w = a + by + cy^2 + dy^3$$

with appropriate boundary conditions similar to those used for the various velocity profiles in Sec. 7–4. The results are tabulated in Table 16–1.

TABLE 16–1

TEMPERATURE PROFILES IN LAMINAR BOUNDARY LAYER

BOUNDARY CONDITION		EQUATION	
At $y = 0$	At $y = \delta_t$		
$T = T_w$	$T = T_s;\ \dfrac{dT}{dy} = 0$	$\dfrac{T - T_w}{T_s - T_w} = 2\left(\dfrac{y}{\delta_t}\right) - \left(\dfrac{y}{\delta_t}\right)^2$	(16–6)
$T = T_w;\ \dfrac{\partial^2 T}{\partial y^2} = 0$	$T = T_s;\ \dfrac{dT}{dy} = 0$	$\dfrac{T - T_w}{T_s - T_w} = \dfrac{3}{2}\left(\dfrac{y}{\delta_t}\right) - \dfrac{1}{2}\left(\dfrac{y}{\delta_t}\right)^3$	(16–7)

The condition $\partial^2 T/\partial y^2 = 0$ at $y = 0$ is obtained from a simplification of the boundary-layer energy equation for steady flow.

$$u\frac{\partial T}{\partial x} + v\frac{\partial T}{\partial y} = \frac{k}{\rho c_p}\frac{\partial^2 T}{\partial y^2} \qquad (16\text{–}8)$$

The tangential velocity u and the normal velocity v are both zero at the wall and thus at $y = 0$, $\partial^2 T/\partial y^2 = 0$.

The integral of Eq. 16–5 need be carried out only from $y = 0$ to $y = \delta_t$, since beyond that point the fluid temperature is the free-stream temperature ($T = T_s$) and the integrand is zero whether $u = u_s$ or not. The value of the integral of Eq. 16–5 becomes

$$I_{\text{Eq. 16–6}} = u_s\left(T_s - T_w\right)\delta\left[\frac{1}{8}\left(\frac{\delta_t}{\delta}\right)^2 - \frac{1}{120}\left(\frac{\delta_t}{\delta}\right)^4\right] \qquad (16\text{–}9)$$

using Eq. 16–6, and

$$I_{\text{Eq. 16–7}} = u_s\left(T_s - T_w\right)\delta\left[\frac{3}{20}\left(\frac{\delta_t}{\delta}\right)^2 - \frac{3}{280}\left(\frac{\delta_t}{\delta}\right)^4\right] \qquad (16\text{–}10)$$

using Eq. 16–7. If $\delta_t < \delta$, the $(\delta_t/\delta)^4$ terms in Eqs. 16–9 and 16–10 may be neglected, since they will be small compared to the $(\delta_t/\delta)^2$ terms. Equation 16–9 or 16–10 may be differentiated and the results, together with the values of $\delta(d\delta/dx)$ and δ^2 obtained from Eq. 7–9 inserted into Eq. 16–5 to obtain

$$\left(\frac{\delta_t}{\delta}\right)^3 + \frac{4}{3}x\frac{d\left(\frac{\delta_t}{\delta}\right)^3}{dx} = \frac{52}{35}\frac{k}{c_p\mu} = \frac{52}{35}\frac{1}{\mathrm{Pr}}$$

if the temperature profile of Eq. 16–6 is used. A solution of this differential equation in δ_t/δ is

$$\left(\frac{\delta_t}{\delta}\right)^3 = \frac{52}{35\,\mathrm{Pr}} + Cx^{-3/4}$$

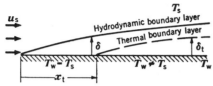

FIG. 16–3. Plate heated beyond
$x = x_t$.

If the plate is at the same temperature as the fluid up to a point x_t from the leading edge (Fig. 16–3), the constant of integration is

$$C = -\frac{52}{35\,\mathrm{Pr}\,x_t^{3/4}}$$

Therefore the ratio of thermal to hydrodynamic boundary-layer thickness is

$$\frac{\delta_t}{\delta} = \frac{1}{0.88\,\mathrm{Pr}^{1/3}}\left[1 - \left(\frac{x_t}{x}\right)^{3/4}\right]^{1/3} \qquad \text{for } \delta_t < \delta \qquad (16\text{--}11)$$

Note that $x_t = 0$ if the plate is heated or cooled over its entire length.

To get the heat-transfer coefficient, Eqs. 16–1 and 16–2 are equated to give

$$h = \frac{k}{T_s - T_w}\left(\frac{\partial T}{\partial y}\right)_{y=0} = \frac{2k}{\delta_t} = \frac{2k}{\delta\left(\frac{\delta_t}{\delta}\right)}$$

Inserting Eq. 7–9 for δ and Eq. 16–11 for δ_t/δ gives the local heat-transfer coefficient.

$$h = \frac{0.376\,k\,\mathrm{Pr}^{1/3}}{x\left[1 - \left(\frac{x_t}{x}\right)^{3/4}\right]^{1/3}}\,\mathrm{Re}_x^{1/2} \qquad (16\text{--}12a)$$

The dimensionless heat-transfer coefficient, the Nusselt number, is

$$\mathrm{Nu}_x = \frac{hx}{k} = \frac{0.376\,\mathrm{Pr}^{1/3}\,\mathrm{Re}_x^{1/2}}{\left[1 - \left(\frac{x_t}{x}\right)^{3/4}\right]^{1/3}} \qquad (16\text{--}12b)$$

If the temperature profile given by Eq. 16–7 is used, the coefficient for

δ_t/δ in Eq. 16–11 becomes $1/1.03$ instead of $1/0.88$, and the coefficient for Nu_x in Eq. 16–12b becomes 0.332 instead of 0.376. Exact solutions of the energy equation (Eq. 16–8) agree quite well with the value 0.332 for a range of Prandtl numbers from 0.6 to 15 [1].

For a plate heated or cooled over its entire length, the average value of the heat-transfer coefficient is twice the local value at the downstream end. Using the value of h from Eq. 16–12a,

$$\bar{h} = \frac{1}{x} \int_0^x h \, dx = 2h \qquad (16\text{–}12c)$$

Turbulent Flow. An analogy between momentum transfer and heat transfer by turbulent motion of masses of fluid particles was derived by Reynolds in 1874. If a mass G of fluid moves through a unit area per unit time from one layer at a temperature T_1 and velocity u_1 to another layer at a temperature T_2 and velocity u_2, the heat transported is

$$q_{\text{turb}} = Gc_p \, (T_1 - T_2)$$

and the apparent shear stress, obtained from equating the force per unit area to the change of momentum flux, is

$$\tau_{\text{turb}} = G \, (u_1 - u_2)$$

Eliminating G gives

$$q_{\text{turb}} = \tau_{\text{turb}} \, c_p \, \frac{T_1 - T_2}{u_1 - u_2}$$

which may be written in differential form as

$$q_{\text{turb}} = \tau_{\text{turb}} \, c_p \, \frac{dT}{du} \qquad (16\text{–}13)$$

This is known as *Reynolds' analogy*.

Within the laminar sublayer the shear stress is, by definition,

$$\tau_{\text{lam}} = \mu \, \frac{du}{dy}$$

and the heat flow from the boundary (at the wall) is, from Eq. 16–1,

$$q_w = -k \left(\frac{dT}{dy} \right)_{y=0}$$

Combining these equations (using the shear stress at the wall, τ_w) gives

$$q_w = -\tau_{\text{lam}} \, \frac{k}{\mu} \left(\frac{dT}{du} \right) \qquad (16\text{–}14)$$

If $k/\mu = c_p$ (true for a fluid for which the Prandtl number is unity), Eqs. 16–13 and 16–14 indicate that the heat flow in the turbulent and laminar regions may be given by the same equation. Then from Eq. 16–14,

$$\frac{q_w}{\tau_w \, c_p} \, du = -dT \qquad (16\text{–}15a)$$

and this equation may be integrated from the wall ($u = 0$ and $T = T'_w$) to the free stream ($u = u_s$ and $T = T_s$) to give

$$\frac{q_w}{T_w \, c_p} \, u_s = (T_s - T_w) \tag{16-15b}$$

From Eq. 16-2, the magnitude of $h = q/(T_w - T_s)$ and from Eq. 7-10a, $c_f = \tau_w/(\rho u_s^2/2)$, so that

$$h = \frac{q}{T_w - T_s} = \frac{\tau_w \, c_p}{u_s} = \frac{c_f}{2} \, \rho u_s c_p \tag{16-16}$$

This equation may be written in terms of the dimensionless heat-transfer coefficient, the Nusselt number, as

$$\mathrm{Nu}_x = \frac{hx}{k} = \mathrm{Re}_x \, \mathrm{Pr} \, \frac{c_f}{2} \tag{16-17a}$$

which gives the local value of the Nusselt number in terms of the local Reynolds number, the Prandtl number, and the local skin-friction coefficient. The value of the local skin-friction coefficient c_f is given by Eq. 7-17b. The Nusselt number may thus be written as

$$\mathrm{Nu}_x = \frac{hx}{k} = 0.0288 \, \mathrm{Pr} \left(\frac{u_s x}{\nu}\right)^{4/5} \tag{16-17b}$$

for a Prandtl number approximately equal to unity. Comparison with Eq. 16-12b for the laminar case with $x_t = 0$ indicates (since $h = k \, \mathrm{Nu}_x/x$) 1) a higher heat-transfer coefficient for turbulent flow than for laminar flow at the same Reynolds number and 2) the heat-transfer coefficient decreases with $x^{-1/2}$ for laminar flow, and less rapidly with $x^{-1/5}$ for turbulent flow.

For fluids with a Prandtl number other than unity, the equations are slightly different. For a range of Pr from 0.6 to about 50, Eq. 16-17a and Eq. 16-17b are quite valid if Nu_x is replaced by $\mathrm{Nu}_x \mathrm{Pr}^{2/3}$ [2]. Equation 16-17b then becomes

$$\mathrm{Nu}_x = 0.0288 \, \mathrm{Pr}^{1/3} \, \mathrm{Re}_x^{4/5} \tag{16-17c}$$

For a plate heated or cooled over its entire length, the average value of the heat-transfer coefficient is 1.25 times the local value at the downstream end. Using the value of h from Eq. 16-17c,

$$\bar{h} = \frac{1}{x} \int_0^x h \, dx = 1.25h \tag{16-17d}$$

EXAMPLE 16-1. Air at a free-stream velocity of 40 ft/sec, a temperature of 80 F, and atmospheric pressure flows past a smooth flat plate which is held at a constant temperature of 260 F. Estimate the heat transfer rate per foot width over the first 2 ft of length for a) a laminar boundary layer with velocity and temperature profiles given by Eqs. 7-8 and 16-7, respectively, and b) a turbulent boundary layer over the entire 2 ft.

Solution: The property values at the mean temperature of $(80+260)/2=170$ F are: $\rho = 0.00196$ slug/ft^3, $\mu = 4.3 \times 10^{-7}$ slug/ft sec (Fig. 2–2), $c_p = 6060$ ft lb$_f$/slug F, and $k = 0.01735$ Btu/hr ft F. Then $\mathrm{Re}_x = u_s x \rho/\mu = 3.64 \times 10^5$ and $\mathrm{Pr} = c_p \mu/k = 0.697$.

a) $\mathrm{Nu}_x = 0.332 \, \mathrm{Pr}^{1/3} \, \mathrm{Re}_x^{1/2} = 178$, and from Eq. 16–12c, $\overline{\mathrm{Nu}}_x = 2\mathrm{Nu}_x = 356$. Then $\bar{h} = \overline{\mathrm{Nu}}_x k/x = 3.09$ Btu/hr ft^2 F, and $Q = \bar{h}A(T_w - T_s) = (3.09)(2)(260-80) = 1110$ Btu/hr.

b) From Eq. 16–17c, $\mathrm{Nu}_x = 0.0288 \, \mathrm{Pr}^{1/3} \, \mathrm{Re}_x^{4/5}$, since $\mathrm{Pr} \neq 1$. $\mathrm{Nu}_x = 720$. From Eq. 16–17d, $\overline{\mathrm{Nu}}_x = 1.25 \, \mathrm{Nu}_x$ for a completely turbulent boundary layer. Thus $\overline{\mathrm{Nu}}_x = 900$, $\bar{h} = \overline{\mathrm{Nu}}_x k/x = 7.8$ Btu/hr ft^2 F, and $Q = \bar{h}A(T_w - T_s) = (7.8)(2)(260 - 80) = 2500$ Btu/hr.

Note that although the local value of the heat-transfer coefficient at $x = 2$ ft for completely turbulent flow is about 4 times that for laminar flow, the average value for a completely turbulent boundary layer is only about 2.5 times that for a laminar boundary layer.

16–3. FLOW IN A PIPE

As in the case of flow past a flat plate, velocity and temperature profiles may be used to analyze laminar flow in pipes and the Reynolds' analogy used to analyze turbulent flow.

Laminar Flow. For fully developed laminar flow, the velocity profile is given by Eq. 10–11a as a parabola.

$$\frac{u}{u_s} = 2\left(\frac{y}{R}\right) - \left(\frac{y}{R}\right)^2 \tag{16–18}$$

The heat flow by conduction through a peripheral area $2\pi r \, dx$ (Fig. 16–4) is

$$Q = -k \, 2\pi r \, dx \, \frac{dT}{dy} \tag{16–19}$$

If a suitable expression for the temperature profile is obtainable, the heat-transfer coefficient h, defined by

$$q = h(T_b - T_w) \tag{16–20}$$

may be derived by combining Eqs. 16–19 and 16–20. The temperature T_b is

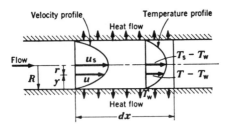

FIG. 16–4. Laminar flow in a pipe with heat transfer.

called the *bulk temperature*, defined by

$$T_b = \frac{\int Tu \, dA}{\int u \, dA} \tag{16-21}$$

and represents the temperature obtained by mixing the fluid passing a section in a given time interval.

As in the case of a flat plate, a temperature profile of the form

$$T - T_w = a + by + cy^2 + dy^3$$

may be assumed, with boundary conditions $T - T_w = 0$ at $y = 0$, $T - T_w = T_s - T_w$ and $dT/dy = 0$ at $y = R$. In addition, if $r = R - y$ is substituted in Eq. 16–19 and the equation solved for dT/dy and differentiated, it is found that

$$\frac{d^2T}{dy^2} = \frac{1}{R}\left(\frac{dT}{dy}\right)_{y=0}$$

This equation indicates that the curvature of the temperature profile is *not* zero at the wall, as was true for the flat plate. These conditions yield a temperature profile whose dimensionless form is invariant in the direction of flow.

$$\frac{T - T_w}{T_s - T_w} = \frac{6}{5}\left(\frac{y}{R}\right) + \frac{3}{5}\left(\frac{y}{R}\right)^2 - \frac{4}{5}\left(\frac{y}{R}\right)^3 \tag{16-22}$$

When this equation is differentiated and introduced into Eq. 16–19, the heat flow per unit area of pipe wall is shown to be

$$q = -k\left(\frac{dT}{dy}\right)_{y=0} = \frac{6}{5}k\frac{(T_s - T_w)}{R} \tag{16-23}$$

From Eqs. 16–18, 16–21, and 16–22 the bulk temperature is expressible as

$$T_b - T_w = 0.583(T_s - T_w)$$

Thus the local heat-transfer coefficient is

$$h = \frac{q}{T_b - T_w} = \frac{6}{5}\frac{k(T_s - T_w)}{R(T_b - T_w)} = \frac{12}{5}\left(\frac{k}{0.583D}\right) = 4.12\frac{k}{D} \tag{16-24}$$

The dimensionless heat-transfer coefficient (the Nusselt number) based on the diameter as the characteristic length is constant and does not vary in the direction of flow for a fully developed velocity and temperature profile for laminar flow in a pipe.

$$\mathrm{Nu}_D = \frac{hD}{k} = 4.12 \tag{16-25a}$$

Exact calculations by Graetz and Nusselt give

$$\mathrm{Nu}_D = 3.65 \tag{16-25b}$$

Turbulent flow. The Reynolds' analogy for fully developed turbulent flow of fluids having a Prandtl number near unity gives the Nusselt number in terms of the pipe Reynolds number, the Prandtl number, and the friction factor. This relationship is

$$\mathrm{Nu}_D = \mathrm{Re}_D \, \mathrm{Pr} \frac{f}{8} \qquad (16\text{--}26)$$

This relation is obtained by integrating Eq. 16–15a from the pipe wall ($u = 0$ and $T = T_w$) to the bulk conditions ($u = V$ and $T = T_b$) to get

$$\frac{q_w}{\tau_w \, c_p} V = T_b - T_w \qquad (16\text{--}27)$$

From the definition of the heat-transfer coefficient for a pipe given in Eq. 16–20,

$$q_w = h(T_b - T_w) \qquad [16\text{--}20]$$

we obtain from Eqs. 16–20 and 16–27,

$$V h = \tau_w \, c_p$$

The wall shear stress in a pipe is defined in Eq. 10–8 as

$$\tau_w = \frac{f \rho V^2}{8}$$

so that

$$\frac{h}{\rho V c_p} = \frac{f}{8}$$

This equation may be expanded to the form

$$\left(\frac{hD}{k}\right)\left(\frac{\mu}{D\rho V}\right)\left(\frac{k}{\mu c_p}\right) = \frac{f}{8}$$

which is equivalent to Eq. 16–26.

Agreement with experimental data for gases is rather good if Nu_D in Eq. 16–26 is replaced by $\mathrm{Nu}_D \mathrm{Pr}^{2/3}$. Equation 16–26 then becomes

$$\mathrm{Nu}_D = \mathrm{Re}_D \, \mathrm{Pr}^{1/3} \frac{f}{8} \qquad (16\text{--}28)$$

EXAMPLE 16–2. Air at 1000 F and atmospheric pressure flows through a 2-in. diameter wrought-iron pipe at an average velocity of 20 ft/sec. Estimate the heat-transfer coefficient. At 1000 F, $\mu = 7.64 \times 10^{-7}$ slug/ft sec, $k = 0.0337$ Btu/hr ft F, Pr = 0.69, and $\rho = 0.000845$ slug/ft^3.

Solution: $\mathrm{Re}_D = VD\rho/\mu = 3690$, and thus the flow is probably turbulent, although it might possibly be laminar. If laminar, $\mathrm{Nu}_D = 3.65$ from Eq. 16–25b. If turbulent, $\mathrm{Nu}_D = \mathrm{Re}_D \mathrm{Pr}^{1/3} f/8$. The relative roughness of the pipe is $0.00015/(\tfrac{1}{6})$ = 0.0009, and the friction factor is $f = 0.042$. Thus $\mathrm{Nu}_D = (3690)(0.69)^{1/3}$ $(0.042/8) = 17.1$. Since $h = \mathrm{Nu}_D k/D$, for laminar flow $h = 0.74$ and for turbulent flow $h = 3.46$ Btu/hr ft^2-F. These results apply to the fully developed flow region only. Higher heat-transfer rates exist in the entrance region.

16–4. RÉSUMÉ

Only a brief introduction for a few simplified cases of forced convective heat transfer has been given in order to show how the fundamental principles, applied to approximate analyses of hydrodynamic boundary layers, may be extended to include approximate analyses of thermal boundary layers. These approximate analyses present a more physical picture than would be possible in the more exact solutions of the simplified equations for laminar flow (Eq. 16–8 and also Sec. 7–2). Heat transfer in turbulent flow generally involves a rational analysis combined with empirical data.

REFERENCES

1. E. R. G. Eckert and R. M. Drake, *Heat and Mass Transfer* (New York: McGraw-Hill Book Company, Inc., 1959), p. 188.

2. A. P. Colburn, "A Method of Correlating Forced Convection Heat Transfer Data and a Comparison with Fluid Friction," *Trans. Am. Inst. Chm. Engrs.*, Vol. 29 (1933), pp. 174–210.

3. F. Kreith, *Principles of Heat Transfer*, 2d ed. (Scranton, Pa.: International Textbook Company, 1965).

PROBLEMS

16–1. Show that the Prandtl number ($Pr = c_p\mu/k$) is dimensionless.

16–2. Compute the Prandtl number for air at 80 F for $c_p = 6000$ ft lb$_f$/slug F and $k = 0.01516$ Btu/hr ft F.

Ans. 0.71

16–3. Compute the Prandtl number for air at 260 F for $c_p = 6060$ ft lb$_f$/slug F and $k = 0.01944$ Btu/hr ft F.

16–4. Compute the Prandtl number for water at 68 F for $c_p = 0.999$ Btu/lb$_m$ F and $k = 0.345$ Btu/hr ft F.

Ans. 7.03

16–5. Compute the Prandtl number for water at 200 F for $c_p = 1.00$ Btu/lb$_m$ F and $k = 0.392$ Btu/hr ft F.

16–6. Derive the temperature profiles given by Eqs. 16–6 and 16–7 from $T - T_w = a + by + cy^2 + dy^3$ and the boundary conditions given in Table 16–1.

16–7. Show that the integral of Eq. 16–5 is given by Eqs. 16–9 and 16–10 for the temperature profiles of Eqs. 16–6 and 16–7, respectively, and the velocity profile of Eq. 7–8.

16–8. Derive the differential equation in δ_t/δ following Eq. 16–10.

$$\left(\frac{\delta_t}{\delta}\right)^3 + \frac{4}{3}x\frac{d\left(\frac{\delta_t}{\delta}\right)^3}{dx} = \frac{52}{35}\frac{k}{c_p\mu} = \frac{53}{35}\frac{1}{Pr}$$

by differentiating Eq. 16–9, using values of $\delta(d\delta/dx)$ and δ^2 from Eq. 7–9, the value of $(\partial T/\partial y)_{y=0}$ from Eq. 16–6, and inserting into Eq. 16–5.

16–9. Show that Eq. 16–11 is a solution of the differential equation in δ_t/δ derived in Prob. 16–8.

16–10. For a linear velocity distribution $\left(\dfrac{u}{u_s} = \dfrac{y}{\delta}\right)$ within a laminar boundary layer for a fluid flowing past a flat plate, the boundary layer thickness is, from Table 7–1,

$$\frac{\delta}{x} = \frac{3.46}{\mathrm{Re}_x^{1/2}}$$

Assume a linear temperature profile as well $\left(\dfrac{T - T_w}{T_s - T_w} = \dfrac{y}{\delta_t}\right)$ with a constant wall temperature T_w.

a) Show that

$$\frac{\delta_t}{\delta} = \frac{1}{\mathrm{Pr}^{1/3}}$$

b) Show that

$$\mathrm{Nu}_x = \frac{1}{3.46}\,\mathrm{Re}_x^{1/2}\,\mathrm{Pr}^{1/3}$$

16–11. Show that the average heat-transfer coefficient $\bar{h}$ for laminar flow along a flat plate heated or cooled over its entire length is twice the local value of the heat-transfer coefficient h at any arbitrary distance x from the leading edge; that is, verify Eq. 16–12c.

16–12. Show that from Eq. 16–16, $\mathrm{Nu}_x = \dfrac{hx}{k} = \mathrm{Re}_x\mathrm{Pr}\,\dfrac{c_f}{2}$ (Eq. 16–17a).

16–13. Assume that a boundary layer is turbulent from the leading edge of a flat plate, and that heat transfer takes place according to Eq. 16–17b. Show that the average value of the heat-transfer coefficient over a distance x from the leading edge is 1.25 times the local value of the heat-transfer coefficient at x; that is, show that

$$\overline{\mathrm{Nu}}_x = 1.25\,\mathrm{Nu}_x \qquad \text{or} \qquad \bar{h} = 1.25\,h$$

16–14. Derive the temperature profile for fully developed laminar flow in a pipe given by Eq. 16–22 from $T - T_w = a + by + cy^2 + dy^3$ and the given boundary conditions.

16–15. Verify the expression for the bulk temperature $T_b - T_w = 0.583$ $(T_s - T_w)$ using the laminar velocity and temperature profiles given by Eqs. 16–18 and 16–22, respectively.

16–16. For a parabolic velocity profile for laminar flow in a pipe given by Eq. 16–18, and a linear temperature profile given by

$$\frac{T - T_w}{T_s - T_w} = \frac{y}{R}$$

show that the bulk temperature T_b is given by the expression

$$T_b - T_w = \frac{7}{15}(T_s - T_w)$$

This means that the heat content of the fluid is the same as though the temperature were uniform across the section at a value equal to

$$\frac{7}{15}(T_s - T_w) + T_w$$

16–17. Air at 60 F and atmospheric pressure flows past a flat plate at 90 ft/sec. The plate is at a constant temperature of 140 F and is 2 ft long and 1 ft wide. Estimate the heat flow rate to the air. Note: At the mean air temperature of 100 F, $k = 0.0174$ Btu/hr ft F and Pr $= 0.72$. Also, $\overline{\mathrm{Nu}}_x = 1.25\,\mathrm{Nu}_x$.

Ans. 2840 Btu/hr

16–18. Repeat Prob. 16–17 using water at the same temperature. For water at 100 F, $k = 0.364$ Btu/hr ft F and Pr $= 4.52$.

16–19. Water flows through a smooth 4-in. diameter pipe at an average velocity of 4 ft/sec and an average temperature of 60 F. The pipe temperature is 140 F. What is the heat-transfer coefficient for fully developed flow? Note: At the mean water temperature of 100 F, $k = 0.364$ Btu/hr ft F and Pr $= 4.52$.

16–20. Air at atmospheric pressure flows through a 6- by 12-in. rectangular duct at an average velocity of 40 ft/sec and an average temperature of 120 F. The smooth duct surface is at a temperature of 280 F. What is the heat-transfer coefficient? Note: At the mean air temperature of 200 F, $k = 0.0174$ Btu/hr ft F and Pr $= 0.72$.

Supplementary Reading

The following would be fruitfully read by any student taking a first course in fluid mechanics:

PRANDTL, LUDWIG, *Essentials of Fluid Dynamics*. New York: Hafner Publishing Company, 1952.

ROUSE, HUNTER, and HOWE, J. W., *Basic Mechanics of Fluids*. New York: John Wiley and Sons, Inc., 1953.

ROUSE, HUNTER, and INCE, SIMON, *History of Hydraulics*. Iowa City: Iowa Institute of Hydraulic Research, State University of Iowa, 1957.

SCHLICHTING, HERMANN, *Boundary Layer Theory*. New York: McGraw-Hill Book Co., Inc., 1961. Introduction and Chapters 1 and 2.

SUTTON, O. G., *The Science of Flight*. Baltimore: Penguin Books Inc., 1955.

VON KARMAN, THEODORE, *Aerodynamics*. Ithaca: Cornell University Press, Cornell University, 1954.

Nomenclature

a	linear acceleration	F	force
A	area	F	thrust function
A	constant	g	acceleration of gravity
b	breadth	g_c	factor of proportionality
b_s	surface breadth	G	mass flow intensity
B	breadth	h	convection heat transfer coefficient
B	constant	h	enthalpy per unit mass
c	wave velocity	h	head
c_f	local skin friction coefficient	h	height
c_p	specific heat capacity at constant pressure	H	head
c_v	specific heat capacity at constant volume	i	$\sqrt{-1}$
		i	unit vector in x direction
C	chord length	I	moment of inertia
C	concentration	j	unit vector in y direction
C	constant	J	mechanical equivalent of heat
C	Hazen-Williams pipe roughness coefficient	k	ratio of specific heat capacities ($k = c_p/c_v$)
C_c	contraction coefficient	k	roughness height
C_D	drag coefficient	k	thermal conductivity
C_f	average skin friction coefficient	k	unit vector in z direction
C_L	lift coefficient	k_L	loss coefficient
C_p	pressure coefficient	K	compressibility (or elastic modulus)
C_v	coefficient of velocity	K	consistency index for non-Newtonian fluids
d	depth normal to flow in an open channel	K	flow coefficient
d	diameter	l	length
D	diameter	l	mixing length
D	drag force	L	length
D_h	hydraulic diameter	L	lift force
e	base of natural logarithms	L_e	entrance length
e	eccentricity	m	mass
e	energy per unit mass	$\dot{m}$	mass flow rate
E	energy transfer per unit weight in a rotating machine	M	mass (dimensional representation)
E	specific energy in an open channel	n	direction normal to streamline
f	force	n	flow behavior index for non-Newtonian fluids
f	friction factor		
f	function	n	Manning roughness coefficient
f	specific thrust function	n	polytropic exponent

N rotational speed

N_s specific speed

p pressure (p_a, atmospheric; p_v, vapor; p_g, gage; p_c, critical; p_0, stagnation; p_s, free stream)

P perimeter

P power

q heat transfer per unit mass

q heat transfer per unit time and area

q unit discharge in an open channel

Q heat transferred

Q volumetric flow rate

r radius

R gas constant

R radius

R_h hydraulic radius

s arc length

s entropy per unit mass

s specific gravity relative to water

s streamline direction

s surface

S slope (S_c, critical; S_b, bed; S_e, energy grade line)

t thickness

t time

T temperature (T_0, stagnation; T_b, bulk; T_s, free stream; T_w, wall)

T time (dimensional representation only)

T torque

u internal energy per unit mass

u variable velocity at a section (u_s, free stream; u_b, edge of laminar sublayer)

u x-component of velocity

U peripheral velocity of a rotor or runner

v specific volume

v y-component of velocity

v_* shear velocity

V average velocity at a section

V velocity in general (V_c, critical; V_n, normal velocity for uniform flow in an open channel)

V volume

w $\phi + i\psi$ (in ϕ-ψ plane)

w work per unit mass (or per unit weight)

w z-component of velocity

W total weight

x flow direction

X body force

y coordinate normal to flow, or depth (y_c, critical; y_h, hydraulic; y_n, normal)

Y body force

Y expansion factor

z elevation above datum plane

z $x + iy$ (in x-y plane)

Z body force

Z compressibility factor for gases

Z weir crest height

GREEK LETTERS

α angle

α angle of attack

α angular acceleration

α energy correction factor

β blade angle

β momentum correction factor

β wave angle

γ specific weight

Γ circulation

δ boundary layer thickness (δ^*, displacement; δ_i, momentum; δ_b, sublayer; δ_t, thermal)

Δ increment of a quantity

∂ partial derivative

ϵ eddy viscosity

η efficiency

θ angle

θ temperature (dimensional representation only)

θ deflection angle

κ proportionality factor in turbulent flow

μ dynamic viscosity

ν kinematic viscosity

π	dimensionless group		ϕ	velocity potential
π	3.1416		ψ	stream function
ρ	mass density		ω	angular velocity
Σ	summation		∇	vector operator del
σ	cavitation number or index			
σ	surface tension			
τ	shear stress (τ_0, at boundary; τ_w, at wall for convective heat transfer)			

SUBSCRIPTS

0	at boundary ($y = 0$)		N	normal
0	stagnation condition		o	oil
a	atmospheric		p	pressure
a	axial		p	prototype
b	bulk		P	pump
b	sublayer		r	radial
c	cavity		R	radial
c	critical		s	in direction parallel to streamline
CG	center of gravity		s	free stream
D	diameter		s	shear
D	drag		s	solid
e	entrance		s	specific (speed)
f	flowing		t	tangential
f	friction		t	thermal
F	force		T	tangential
g	gas		T	turbine
g	gravity		V	vertical
H	horizontal		w	wall
L	lift		w	water
L	loss		x	in x direction
m	manometer		x	upstream of normal shock
m	meridional		y	downstream of normal shock
m	mixture		y	in y direction
m	model		z	in z direction
n	normal		θ	normal to radial direction

DIMENSIONLESS NUMBERS OR GROUPS

Fr	Froude number		Re	Reynolds number
M	Mach number		Re'	pseudo-Reynolds number
Nu	Nusselt number		We	Weber number
Pr	Prandtl number		σ	cavitation number or index

I | Laminar Flow of a Power-Law Fluid

From Fig. 10–3 the shear stress for steady, fully developed flow in a circular tube given by Eq. 10–7 may be equated to the shear stress for a power-law fluid given by Eq. 2–10. From this may be obtained a general expression for the shape of the velocity profile, the average velocity and volumetric flow rate in terms of the pressure gradient, and the friction factor. The results may then be compared with those for laminar flow of a Newtonian fluid in a circular tube given in Section 10–3. When $n = 1$, the general results for a power-law fluid are those for a Newtonian fluid.

Equating Eq. 2–10 to 10–7 gives

$$\tau = -K \left(\frac{du}{dr}\right)^n = \frac{\Delta p}{L} \frac{r}{2}$$

so that

$$du = -\left(\frac{\Delta p}{2LK}\right)^{1/n} \int r^{1/n} \, dr$$

Integration with boundary conditions $u = 0$ at $r = R$ gives

$$u = \left(\frac{\Delta p}{2LK}\right)^{1/n} \left(\frac{n}{n+1}\right) R^{1+1/n} \left[1 - \left(\frac{r}{R}\right)^{1+1/n}\right] \qquad \text{(AI–1)}$$

The average velocity V is

$$V = \frac{2\pi \int u r \, dr}{\pi R^2} = R^{1+1/n} \left(\frac{\Delta p}{2LK}\right)^{1/n} \left(\frac{n}{3n+1}\right) \qquad \text{(AI–2)}$$

The maximum velocity, u_m, occurs at $r = 0$, and is

$$u_m = R^{1+1/n} \left(\frac{n}{n+1}\right) \left(\frac{\Delta p}{2LK}\right)^{1/n} \qquad \text{(AI–3)}$$

Thus we have the following ratios of point to average velocity

$$\frac{u}{V} = \frac{3n+1}{n+1} \left[1 - \left(\frac{r}{R}\right)^{\frac{n+1}{n}}\right] \qquad \text{(AI–4)}$$

of average to maximum velocity

$$\frac{V}{u_m} = \frac{n+1}{3n+1} \qquad \text{(AI–5)}$$

and of point to maximum velocity

$$\frac{u}{u_m} = 1 - \left(\frac{r}{R}\right)^{\frac{n+1}{n}} \tag{AI–6}$$

For $n = 0$, $u/u_m = 1$, $V/u_m = 1$, and a one-dimensional velocity profile is indicated.

For $n = \frac{1}{2}$, $u/u_m = [1 - (r/R)^3]$, $V/u_m = \frac{3}{5}$, and the velocity profile is a cubic equation.

For $n = 1$, $u/u_m = [1 - (r/R)^2]$, $V/u_m = \frac{1}{2}$, and the velocity profile is a parabola, as was obtained in Section 10–3.

For $n \rightarrow \infty$, $u/u_m = 1 - (r/R) = y/R$, $V/u_m = \frac{1}{3}$, and the velocity profile consists of straight lines. These velocity profiles are shown in Fig. AI-1.

The volumetric flow rate, Q, is

$$Q = VA = \frac{\pi n}{3n + 1} \left(\frac{R^{3n+1}}{2K} \frac{\Delta p}{L}\right)^{\frac{1}{n}} \tag{AI–7}$$

The friction factor, f, is

$$f = \frac{8\tau_0}{\rho V^2} = \frac{8}{\rho V^2} K \left(\frac{du}{dy}\right)^n$$

where

$$\frac{du}{dy} = -\frac{du}{dr} = \frac{3n + 1}{n} \left(\frac{2V}{D}\right) = \frac{3n + 1}{4n} \left(\frac{8V}{D}\right)$$

Thus

$$f = \frac{8}{\rho V^2} K \left(\frac{3n + 1}{4n}\right)^n \left(\frac{8V}{D}\right)^n$$

$$= \frac{64}{D^n V^{2-n} \rho/\mu'} \tag{AI–8a}$$

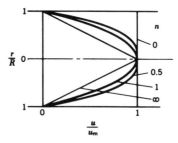

FIG. AI-1. Velocity profiles for power-law fluids for fully-developed flow in circular tubes.

$$= \frac{64}{Re'} \qquad \qquad \text{(AI–8b)}$$

where $\mu' = 8^{n-1} K \left(\frac{3n + 1}{4n} \right)^n$.

For a Newtonian fluid, $n = 1$, $\mu' = K = \mu$, and the value of f is the same as that given in Eq. 10–14.

II | The Prandtl Boundary Layer Equations

The Navier-Stokes equations were simplified by Prandtl in 1904. He stated that viscous effects were concentrated in a thin layer of fluid along solid boundaries. By estimating the order of magnitude of the terms in the Navier-Stokes equations, he simplified them by keeping only terms of magnitude 1 and dropping those of smaller magnitude, δ or less. His method will be shown for two-dimensional steady boundary layer flow.

The boundary layer thickness is assumed to be small as compared with any characteristic dimension of the boundary—the size of a body immersed in the fluid, for example. Distances in the x-direction and velocities u in that direction (including the free stream velocity u_s) are assumed to be of order 1, whereas distances in the y-direction and velocities v in that direction are assumed to be of order δ. The continuity equation with the order of magnitude of each term written beneath it is

$$\frac{\partial u}{\partial x} + \frac{\partial v}{\partial y} = 0$$
$$\frac{1}{1} \qquad \frac{\delta}{\delta}$$

Both terms are seen to be of order 1.

Outside the boundary layer the Bernoulli equation applies, and the differential form of this equation, with the order of magnitude of each term written beneath it, is

$$\frac{\partial p}{\partial x} + \rho\, u_s\, \frac{\partial u_s}{\partial x} = 0$$
$$1\ 1\ \ \frac{1}{1}$$

Thus $\partial p/\partial x$ is of order 1 when the density is assumed to be of order 1.

The Navier-Stokes equation for the x-direction (Eq. 5–39a) is, neglecting gravity,

$$u\frac{\partial u}{\partial x} + v\frac{\partial u}{\partial y} = -\frac{1}{\rho}\frac{\partial p}{\partial x} + \nu\left(\frac{\partial^2 u}{\partial x^2} + \frac{\partial^2 u}{\partial y^2}\right)$$
$$1\frac{1}{1} \quad \delta\frac{1}{\delta} \qquad 1\ 1 \qquad 1 \quad \frac{1}{\delta^2}$$

The first term in parentheses is negligible as compared with the second term. The term containing viscosity must be of the same order of magnitude as the other terms in the equation, and thus the viscosity ν is of the order δ^2. This means that a low-viscosity fluid is required in order to obtain boundary-layer flow.

The Navier-Stokes equation for the y-direction (Eq. 5–39b) is, again neglecting gravity,

$$u \frac{\partial v}{\partial x} + v \frac{\partial v}{\partial y} = - \frac{1}{\rho} \frac{\partial p}{\partial y} + \left(\frac{\partial^2 v}{\partial x^2} + \frac{\partial^2 v}{\partial y^2} \right)$$

$$1 \frac{\delta}{1} \qquad \delta \frac{\delta}{\delta} \qquad 1 \qquad \delta^2 \left(\frac{\delta}{1} \qquad \frac{\delta}{\delta^2} \right)$$

The term $\partial p/\partial y$ must be of the order of magnitude of δ, and thus may be neglected as compared with the terms in the x-component Navier-Stokes equation. This indicates that the pressure gradients across the boundary layer may be neglected.

The simplified Navier-Stokes equations thus become

$$u \frac{\partial u}{\partial x} + v \frac{\partial u}{\partial y} = - \frac{1}{\rho} \frac{\partial p}{\partial x} + \nu \frac{\partial^2 u}{\partial y^2}$$

$$\frac{\partial p}{\partial y} = 0$$

$$\frac{\partial u}{\partial x} + \frac{\partial v}{\partial y} = 0$$

These are the Prandtl boundary layer equations for steady, two-dimensional incompressible flow.

III | Tables for Compressible Gas Flow

TABLE A–1*
ISENTROPIC FLOW, $k = 1.4$

M	$\dfrac{p}{p_0}$	$\dfrac{T}{T_0}$	$\dfrac{\rho}{\rho_0}$	$\dfrac{A}{A^*}$	$\dfrac{V}{V^*}$
0	1.0000,0	1.00000	1.0000,0	∞	0
.01	.9999,3	.99998	.9999,5	5,7.874	.01096
.02	.9997,2	.99992	.9998,0	2,8.942	.02191
.03	.9993,7	.99982	.9995,5	1,9.300	.03286
.04	.9988,8	.99968	.9992,0	14.,482	.04381
.05	.9982,5	.99950	.9987,5	11.5,915	.05476
.06	.9974,8	.99928	.9982,0	9.6,659	.06570
.07	.9965,8	.99902	.9975,5	8.2,915	.07664
.08	.9955,3	.99872	.9968,0	7.2,616	.08758
.09	.9943,5	.99838	.9959,6	6.4,613	.09851
.10	.9930,3	.99800	.9950,2	5.8,218	.10943
.11	.9915,7	.99758	.9939,8	5.2,992	.12035
.12	.9899,8	.99714	.9928,4	4.8,643	.13126
.13	.9882,6	.99664	.9916,0	4.4,968	.14216
.14	.9864,0	.99610	.9902,7	4.18,24	.15306
.15	.9844,1	.99552	.9888,4	3.91,03	.16395
.16	.9822,8	.99490	.9873,1	3.67,27	.17483
.17	.9800,3	.99425	.9856,9	3.46,35	.18569
.18	.9776,5	.99356	.9839,8	3.27,79	.19654
.19	.9751,4	.99283	.9821,7	3.11,22	.20738
.20	.9725,0	.99206	.9802,7	2.96,35	.21822
.21	.9697,3	.99125	.9782,8	2.82,93	.22904
.22	.9668,5	.99041	.9762,1	2.70,76	.23984
.23	.9638,3	.98953	.9740,3	2.59,68	.25063
.24	.9607,0	.98861	.9717,7	2.49,56	.26141
.25	.9574,5	.98765	.9694,2	2.40,27	.27216
.26	.9540,8	.98666	.9669,9	2.31,73	.28291
.27	.9506,0	.98563	.9644,6	2.23,85	.29364
.28	.9470,0	.98456	.9618,5	2.16,56	.30435
.29	.9432,9	.98346	.9591,6	2.09,79	.31504
.30	.9394,7	.98232	.9563,8	2.035,1	.32572
.31	.9355,4	.98114	.9535,2	1.976,5	.33638
.32	.9315,0	.97993	.9505,8	1.921,8	.34701
.33	.9273,6	.97868	.9475,6	1.870,7	.35762
.34	.9231,2	.97740	.9444,6	1.822,9	.36821
.35	.9187,7	.97608	.9412,8	1.778,0	.37879
.36	.9143,3	.97473	.9380,3	1.735,8	.38935
.37	.9097,9	.97335	.9347,0	1.696,1	.39988
.38	.9051,6	.97193	.9312,9	1.658,7	.41039
.39	.9004,4	.97048	.9278,2	1.623,4	.42087
.40	.8956,2	.96899	.9242,8	1.590,1	.43133
.41	.8907,1	.96747	.9206,6	1.558,7	.44177
.42	.8857,2	.96592	.9169,7	1.528,9	.45218
.43	.8806,5	.96434	.9132,2	1.500,7	.46256
.44	.8755,0	.96272	.9094,0	1.474,0	.47292

*The values in this table were originally calculated and reported in M.I.T. Meteor Report No. 14, Bureau of Ordnance, U.S. Navy Department, December, 1947, by A. H. Shapiro, W. R. Hawthorne, and G. M. Edelman.

NOTE: Linear interpolation may be made a) for values without a comma and b) to the left of comma for values containing a comma.

TABLE A–1 (*continued*)

M	$\dfrac{p}{p_0}$	$\dfrac{T}{T_0}$	$\dfrac{\rho}{\rho_0}$	$\dfrac{A}{A^*}$	$\dfrac{V}{V^*}$
.45	.8702,7	.96108	.9055,2	1.448,7	.48326
.46	.8649,6	.95940	.9015,7	1.424,6	.49357
.47	.8595,8	.95769	.8975,6	1.401,8	.50385
.48	.8541,3	.95595	.8934,9	1.380,1	.51410
.49	.8486,1	.95418	.8893,6	1.359,4	.52432
.50	.8430,2	.95238	.8851,7	1.339,8	.53452
.51	.8373,7	.95055	.8809,2	1.321,2	.54469
.52	.8316,6	.94869	.8766,2	1.303,4	.55482
.53	.8258,9	.94681	.8722,7	1.286,4	.56493
.54	.8200,5	.94489	.8678,8	1.270,3	.57501
.55	.8141,6	.94295	.86342	1.255,0	.58506
.56	.8082,2	.94098	.85892	1.240,3	.59508
.57	.8022,4	.93898	.85437	1.226,3	.60506
.58	.7962,1	.93696	.84977	1.213,0	.61500
.59	.7901,2	.93491	.84513	1.200,3	.62491
.60	.78400	.93284	.84045	1.188,2	.63480
.61	.77784	.93074	.83573	1.176,6	.64466
.62	.77164	.92861	.83096	1.165,6	.65448
.63	.76540	.92646	.82616	1.155,1	.66427
.64	.75913	.92428	.82132	1.145,1	.67402
.65	.75283	.92208	.81644	1.1356	.68374
.66	.74650	.91986	.81153	1.1265	.69342
.67	.74014	.91762	.80659	1.1178	.70307
.68	.73376	.91535	.80162	1.1096	.71268
.69	.72735	.91306	.79662	1.1018	.72225
.70	.72092	.91075	.79158	1.0943,7	.73179
.71	.71448	.90842	.78652	1.0872,9	.74129
.72	.70802	.90606	.78143	1.0805,7	.75076
.73	.70155	.90368	.77632	1.0741,9	.76019
.74	.69507	.90129	.77119	1.0681,4	.76958
.75	.68857	.89888	.76603	1.0624,2	.77893
.76	.68207	.89644	.76086	1.0570,0	.78825
.77	.67556	.89399	.75567	1.0518,8	.79753
.78	.66905	.89152	.75046	1.0470,5	.80677
.79	.66254	.88903	.74524	1.0425,0	.81597
.80	.65602	.88652	.74000	1.0382,3	.82514
.81	.64951	.88400	.73474	1.0342,2	.83426
.82	.64300	.88146	.72947	1.0304,6	.84334
.83	.63650	.87890	.72419	1.0269,6	.85239
.84	.63000	.87633	.71890	1.0237,0	.86140
.85	.62351	.87374	.71361	1.0206,7	.87037
.86	.61703	.87114	.70831	1.0178,7	.87929
.87	.61057	.86852	.70300	1.0153,0	.88817
.88	.60412	.86589	.69769	1.0129,4	.89702
.89	.59768	.86324	.69237	1.0108,0	.90583

TABLE A–1 (*continued*)

M	$\dfrac{p}{p_0}$	$\dfrac{T}{T_0}$	$\dfrac{\rho}{\rho_0}$	$\dfrac{A}{A^*}$	$\dfrac{V}{V^*}$
.90	.59126	.86058	.68704	1.0088,6	.91460
.91	.58486	.85791	.68171	1.0071,3	.92333
.92	.57848	.85523	.67639	1.0056,0	.93201
.93	.57212	.85253	.67107	1.0042,6	.94065
.94	.56578	.84982	.66575	1.0031,1	.94925
.95	.55946	.84710	.66044	1.0021,4	.95781
.96	.55317	.84437	.65513	1.0013,6	.96633
.97	.54691	.84162	.64982	1.0007,6	.97481
.98	.54067	.83887	.64452	1.0003,3	.98325
.99	.53446	.83611	.63923	1.0000,8	.99165
1.00	.52828	.83333	.63394	1.0000,0	1.00000
1.01	.52213	.83055	.62866	1.0000,8	1.00831
1.02	.51602	.82776	.62339	1.0003,3	1.01658
1.03	.50994	.82496	.61813	1.0007,4	1.02481
1.04	.50389	.82215	.61288	1.0013,0	1.03300
1.05	.49787	.81933	.60765	1.0020,2	1.04114
1.06	.49189	.81651	.60243	1.0029,0	1.04924
1.07	.48595	.81368	.59722	1.0039,4	1.05730
1.08	.48005	.81084	.59203	1.0051,2	1.06532
1.09	.47418	.80800	.58685	1.0064,5	1.07330
1.10	.46835	.80515	.58169	1.0079,3	1.08124
1.11	.46256	.80230	.57655	1.0095,5	1.08914
1.12	.45682	.79944	.57143	1.0113,1	1.09699
1.13	.45112	.79657	.56632	1.0132,2	1.10480
1.14	.44545	.79370	.56123	1.0152,7	1.11256
1.15	.43983	.79083	.55616	1.0174,6	1.1203
1.16	.43425	.78795	.55112	1.0197,8	1.1280
1.17	.42872	.78507	.54609	1.0222,4	1.1356
1.18	.42323	.78218	.54108	1.0248,4	1.1432
1.19	.41778	.77929	.53610	1.0275,7	1.1508
1.20	.4123,8	.77640	.53114	1.0304,4	1.1583
1.21	.4070,2	.77350	.52620	1.0334,4	1.1658
1.22	.4017,1	.77061	.52129	1.0365,7	1.1732
1.23	.3964,5	.76771	.51640	1.0398,3	1.1806
1.24	.3912,3	.76481	.51154	1.0432,3	1.1879
1.25	.3860,6	.76190	.50670	1.0467,6	1.1952
1.26	.3809,4	.75900	.50189	1.0504,1	1.2025
1.27	.3758,6	.75610	.49710	1.0541,9	1.2097
1.28	.3708,3	.75319	.49234	1.0581,0	1.2169
1.29	.3658,5	.75029	.48761	1.0621,4	1.2240
1.30	.3609,2	.74738	.48291	1.0663,1	1.2311
1.31	.3560,3	.74448	.47823	1.0706,0	1.2382
1.32	.3511,9	.74158	.47358	1.0750,2	1.2452
1.33	.3464,0	.73867	.46895	1.0795,7	1.2522
1.34	.3416,6	.73577	.46436	1.0842,4	1.2591

TABLE A–1 (*continued*)

M	$\dfrac{p}{p_0}$	$\dfrac{T}{T_0}$	$\dfrac{\rho}{\rho_0}$	$\dfrac{A}{A^*}$	$\dfrac{V}{V^*}$
1.35	.3369,7	.73287	.45980	1.0890,4	1.2660
1.36	.3323,3	.72997	.45527	1.0939,7	1.2729
1.37	.3277,4	.72707	.45076	1.0990,2	1.2797
1.38	.3231,9	.72418	.44628	1.1042,0	1.2865
1.39	.3186,9	.72128	.44183	1.1095,0	1.2932
1.40	.3142,4	.71839	.43742	1.1149	1.2999
1.41	.3098,4	.71550	.43304	1.1205	1.3065
1.42	.3054,9	.71261	.42869	1.1262	1.3131
1.43	.3011,9	.70973	.42436	1.1320	1.3197
1.44	.2969,3	.70685	.42007	1.1379	1.3262
1.45	.2927,2	.70397	.41581	1.1440	1.3327
1.46	.2885,6	.70110	.41158	1.1502	1.3392
1.47	.2844,5	.69823	.40738	1.1565	1.3456
1.48	.2803,9	.69537	.40322	1.1629	1.3520
1.49	.2763,7	.69251	.39909	1.1695	1.3583
1.50	.2724,0	.68965	.39498	1.1762	1.3646
1.51	.2684,8	.68680	.39091	1.1830	1.3708
1.52	.2646,1	.68396	.38687	1.1899	1.3770
1.53	.2607,8	.68112	.38287	1.1970	1.3832
1.54	.2570,0	.67828	.37890	1.2042	1.3894
1.55	.2532,6	.67545	.37496	1.2115	1.3955
1.56	.2495,7	.67262	.37105	1.2190	1.4016
1.57	.2459,3	.66980	.36717	1.2266	1.4076
1.58	.2423,3	.66699	.36332	1.2343	1.4135
1.59	.2387,8	.66418	.35951	1.2422	1.4195
1.60	.23527	.66138	.35573	1.2502	1.4254
1.61	.23181	.65858	.35198	1.2583	1.4313
1.62	.22839	.65579	.34826	1.2666	1.4371
1.63	.22501	.65301	.34458	1.2750	1.4429
1.64	.22168	.65023	.34093	1.2835	1.4487
1.65	.21839	.64746	.33731	1.2922	1.4544
1.66	.21515	.64470	.33372	1.3010	1.4601
1.67	.21195	.64194	.33016	1.3099	1.4657
1.68	.20879	.63919	.32664	1.3190	1.4713
1.69	.20567	.63645	.32315	1.3282	1.4769
1.70	.20259	.63372	.31969	1.3376	1.4825
1.71	.19955	.63099	.31626	1.3471	1.4880
1.72	.19656	.62827	.31286	1.3567	1.4935
1.73	.19361	.62556	.30950	1.3665	1.4989
1.74	.19070	.62286	.30617	1.3764	1.5043
1.75	.18782	.62016	.30287	1.3865	1.5097
1.76	.18499	.61747	.29959	1.3967	1.5150
1.77	.18220	.61479	.29635	1.4071	1.5203
1.78	.17944	.61211	.29314	1.4176	1.5256
1.79	.17672	.60945	.28997	1.4282	1.5308

TABLE A-1 (*continued*)

M	$\dfrac{p}{p_0}$	$\dfrac{T}{T_0}$	$\dfrac{\rho}{\rho_0}$	$\dfrac{A}{A^*}$	$\dfrac{V}{V^*}$
1.80	.17404	.60680	.28682	1.4390	1.5360
1.81	.17140	.60415	.28370	1.4499	1.5412
1.82	.16879	.60151	.28061	1.4610	1.5463
1.83	.16622	.59888	.27756	1.4723	1.5514
1.84	.16369	.59626	.27453	1.4837	1.5564
1.85	.16120	.59365	.27153	1.4952	1.5614
1.86	.15874	.59105	.26857	1.5069	1.5664
1.87	.15631	.58845	.26563	1.5188	1.5714
1.88	.15392	.58586	.26272	1.5308	1.5763
1.89	.15156	.58329	.25984	1.5429	1.5812
1.90	.14924	.58072	.25699	1.5552	1.5861
1.91	.14695	.57816	.25417	1.5677	1.5909
1.92	.14469	.57561	.25138	1.5804	1.5957
1.93	.14247	.57307	.24862	1.5932	1.6005
1.94	.14028	.57054	.24588	1.6062	1.6052
1.95	.13813	.56802	.24317	1.6193	1.6099
1.96	.13600	.56551	.24049	1.6326	1.6146
1.97	.13390	.56301	.23784	1.6461	1.6193
1.98	.13184	.56051	.23522	1.6597	1.6239
1.99	.12981	.55803	.23262	1.6735	1.6285
2.00	.12780	.55556	.23005	1.6875	1.6330
2.01	.12583	.55310	.22751	1.7017	1.6375
2.02	.12389	.55064	.22499	1.7160	1.6420
2.03	.12198	.54819	.22250	1.7305	1.6465
2.04	.12009	.54576	.22004	1.7452	1.6509
2.05	.11823	.54333	.21760	1.7600	1.6553
2.06	.11640	.54091	.21519	1.7750	1.6597
2.07	.11460	.53850	.21281	1.7902	1.6640
2.08	.11282	.53611	.21045	1.8056	1.6683
2.09	.11107	.53373	.20811	1.8212	1.6726
2.10	.10935	.53135	.20580	1.8369	1.6769
2.11	.10766	.52898	.20352	1.8529	1.6811
2.12	.10599	.52663	.20126	1.8690	1.6853
2.13	.10434	.52428	.19902	1.8853	1.6895
2.14	.10272	.52194	.19681	1.9018	1.6936
2.15	.10113	.51962	.19463	1.9185	1.6977
2.16	.09956	.51730	.19247	1.9354	1.7018
2.17	.09802	.51499	.19033	1.9525	1.7059
2.18	.09650	.51269	.18821	1.9698	1.7099
2.19	.09500	.51041	.18612	1.9873	1.7139
2.20	.09352	.50813	.18405	2.0050	1.7179
2.21	.09207	.50586	.18200	2.0229	1.7219
2.22	.09064	.50361	.17998	2.0409	1.7258
2.23	.08923	.50136	.17798	2.0592	1.7297
2.24	.08784	.49912	.17600	2.0777	1.7336

TABLE A–1 (*continued*)

M	$\dfrac{p}{p_0}$	$\dfrac{T}{T_0}$	$\dfrac{\rho}{\rho_0}$	$\dfrac{A}{A^*}$	$\dfrac{V}{V^*}$
2.25	.08648	.49689	.17404	2.0964	1.7374
2.26	.08514	.49468	.17211	2.1154	1.7412
2.27	.08382	.49247	.17020	2.1345	1.7450
2.28	.08252	.49027	.16830	2.1538	1.7488
2.29	.08123	.48809	.16643	2.1734	1.7526
2.30	.07997	.48591	.16458	2.1931	1.7563
2.31	.07873	.48374	.16275	2.2131	1.7600
2.32	.07751	.48158	.16095	2.2333	1.7637
2.33	.07631	.47944	.15916	2.2537	1.7673
2.34	.07513	.47730	.15739	2.2744	1.7709
2.35	.07396	.47517	.15564	2.2953	1.7745
2.36	.07281	.47305	.15391	2.3164	1.7781
2.37	.07168	.47095	.15220	2.3377	1.7817
2.38	.07057	.46885	.15052	2.3593	1.7852
2.39	.06948	.46676	.14885	2.3811	1.7887
2.40	.06840	.46468	.14720	2.4031	1.7922
2.41	.06734	.46262	.14557	2.4254	1.7957
2.42	.06630	.46056	.14395	2.4479	1.7991
2.43	.06527	.45851	.14235	2.4706	1.8025
2.44	.06426	.45647	.14078	2.4936	1.8059
2.45	.06327	.45444	.13922	2.5168	1.8093
2.46	.06229	.45242	.13768	2.5403	1.8126
2.47	.06133	.45041	.13616	2.5640	1.8159
2.48	.06038	.44841	.13465	2.5880	1.8192
2.49	.05945	.44642	.13316	2.6122	1.8225
2.50	.05853	.44444	.13169	2.6367	1.8258
2.51	.05763	.44247	.13023	2.6615	1.8290
2.52	.05674	.44051	.12879	2.6865	1.8322
2.53	.05586	.43856	.12737	2.7117	1.8354
2.54	.05500	.43662	.12597	2.7372	1.8386
2.55	.05415	.43469	.12458	2.7630	1.8417
2.56	.05332	.43277	.12321	2.7891	1.8448
2.57	.05250	.43085	.12185	2.8154	1.8479
2.58	.05169	.42894	.12051	2.8420	1.8510
2.59	.05090	.42705	.11418	2.8689	1.8541
2.60	.05012	.42517	.11787	2.8960	1.8572
2.61	.04935	.42330	.11658	2.9234	1.8602
2.62	.04859	.42143	.11530	2.9511	1.8632
2.63	.04784	.41·957	.11403	2.9791	1.8662
2.64	.04711	.41772	.11278	3.0074	1.8692
2.65	.04639	.41589	.11154	3.0359	1.8721
2.66	.04568	.41406	.11032	3.0647	1.8750
2.67	.04498	.41224	.10911	3.0938	1.8779
2.68	.04429	.41043	.10792	3.1233	1.8808
2.69	.04361	.40863	.10674	3.1530	1.8837

TABLE A-1 (*continued*)

M	$\dfrac{p}{p_0}$	$\dfrac{T}{T_0}$	$\dfrac{\rho}{\rho_0}$	$\dfrac{A}{A^*}$	$\dfrac{V}{V^*}$
2.70	.04295	.40684	.10557	3.1830	1.8865
2.71	.04230	.40505	.10442	3.2133	1.8894
2.72	.04166	.40327	.10328	3.2440	1.8922
2.73	.04102	.40151	.10215	3.2749	1.8950
2.74	.04039	.39976	.10104	3.3061	1.8978
2.75	.03977	.39801	.09994	3.3376	1.9005
2.76	.03917	.39627	.09885	3.3695	1.9032
2.77	.03858	.39454	.09777	3.4017	1.9060
2.78	.03800	.39282	.09671	3.4342	1.9087
2.79	.03742	.39111	.09566	3.4670	1.9114
2.80	.03685	.38941	.09462	3.5001	1.9140
2.81	.03629	.38771	.09360	3.5336	1.9167
2.82	.03574	.38603	.09259	3.5674	1.9193
2.83	.03520	.38435	.09158	3.6015	1.9220
2.84	.03467	.38268	.09059	3.6359	1.9246
2.85	.03415	.38102	.08962	3.6707	1.9271
2.86	.03363	.37937	.08865	3.7058	1.9297
2.87	.03312	.37773	.08769	3.7413	1.9322
2.88	.03262	.37610	.08674	3.7771	1.9348
2.89	.03213	.37448	.08581	3.8133	1.9373
2.90	.03165	.37286	.08489	3.8498	1.9398
2.91	.03118	.37125	.08398	3.8866	1.9423
2.92	.03071	.36965	.08308	3.9238	1.9448
2.93	.03025	.36806	.08218	3.9614	1.9472
2.94	.02980	.36648	.08130	3.9993	1.9497
2.95	.02935	.36490	.08043	4.0376	1.9521
2.96	.02891	.36333	.07957	4.0763	1.9545
2.97	.02848	.36177	.07872	4.1153	1.9569
2.98	.02805	.36022	.07788	4.1547	1.9593
2.99	.02764	.35868	.07705	4.1944	1.9616
3.00	.027,22	.357,14	.076,23	4.23,46	1.964,0
3.10	.023,45	.342,23	.068,52	4.65,73	1.986,6
3.20	.020,23	.328,08	.061,65	5.12,10	2.007,9
3.30	.0174,8	.314,66	.055,54	5.6,287	2.027,9
3.40	.0151,2	.301,93	.050,09	6.1,837	2.046,6
3.50	.0131,1	.289,86	.045,23	6.7,896	2.064,2
3.60	.0113,8	.278,40	.040,89	7.4,501	2.080,8
3.70	.0099,0	.267,52	.0370,2	8.1,691	2.096,4
3.80	.0086,3	.257,20	.0335,5	8.9,506	2.111,1
3.90	.0075,3	.247,40	.0304,4	9.7,990	2.125,0
4.00	.0065,8	.238,10	.0276,6	10.7,19	2.138,1
4.10	.0057,7	.229,25	.0251,6	11.7,15	2.150,5
4.20	.0050,6	.2208,5	.0229,2	12.7,92	2.162,2
4.30	.0044,5	.2128,6	.0209,0	13.9,55	2.173,2
4.40	.0039,2	.2052,5	.0190,9	15.2,10	2.183,7

TABLE A–1 (*continued*)

M	$\dfrac{p}{p_0}$	$\dfrac{T}{T_0}$	$\dfrac{\rho}{\rho_0}$	$\dfrac{A}{A^*}$	$\dfrac{V}{V^*}$
4.50	.0034,6	.1980,2	.0174,5	16.5,62	2.193,6
4.60	.0030,5	.1911,3	.0159,7	18.0,18	2.203,0
4.70	.0027,0	.1845,7	.0146,3	19.5,83	2.211,9
4.80	.0024,0	.1783,2	.0134,3	21.2,64	2.220,4
4.90	.0021,3	.1723,5	.0123,3	23.0,67	2.228,4
5.00	.00189	.16667	.01134	25.000	2.2361
6.00	.0₃633	.12195	.00519	53.180	2.2953
7.00	.0₃242	.09259	.00261	104.143	2.3333
8.00	.0₃102	.07246	.00141	190.109	2.3591
9.00	.0₄474	.05814	.0₃815	327.189	2.3772
10.00	.0₄236	.04762	.0₃495	535.938	2.3904
∞	0	0	0	∞	2.4495

NOTE: .0₃495 signifies .000495.

TABLE A-2*
NORMAL SHOCK, $k = 1.4$

M_x	M_y	$\dfrac{p_y}{p_x}$	$\dfrac{\rho_y}{\rho_x}$	$\dfrac{T_y}{T_x}$	$\dfrac{p_{0y}}{p_{0x}}$	$\dfrac{p_{0y}}{p_x}$
1.00	1.0000,0	1.0000,0	1.0000,0	1.0000,0	1.00000	1.8929
1.01	.9901,3	1.0234,5	1.0166,9	1.0066,5	.99999	1.9152
1.02	.9805,2	1.0471,3	1.0334,4	1.01325	.99998	1.9379
1.03	.9711,5	1.0710,5	1.0502,4	1.01981	.99997	1.9610
1.04	.9620,2	1.0952,0	1.0670,9	1.02634	.99994	1.9845
1.05	.9531,2	1.1196	1.0839,8	1.03284	.99987	2.0083
1.06	.9444,4	1.1442	1.10092	1.03931	.99976	2.0325
1.07	.9359,8	1.1690	1.11790	1.04575	.99962	2.0570
1.08	.9277,2	1.1941	1.13492	1.05217	.9994,4	2.0819
1.09	.9196,5	1.2194	1.15199	1.05856	.9992,1	2.1072
1.10	.9117,7	1.2450	1.1691	1.06494	.9989,2	2.1328
1.11	.9040,8	1.2708	1.1862	1.07130	.9985,8	2.1588
1.12	.8965,6	1.2968	1.2034	1.07764	.9982,0	2.1851
1.13	.8892,2	1.3230	1.2206	1.08396	.9977,6	2.2118
1.14	.8820,4	1.3495	1.2378	1.09027	.9972,6	2.2388
1.15	.8750,2	1.3762	1.2550	1.09657	.9966,9	2.2661
1.16	.8681,6	1.4032	1.2723	1.10287	.9960,5	2.2937
1.17	.8614,5	1.4304	1.2896	1.10916	.9953,4	2.3217
1.18	.8548,8	1.4578	1.3069	1.11544	.9945,5	2.3499
1.19	.8484,6	1.4854	1.3243	1.12172	.9937,1	2.3786
1.20	.8421,7	1.5133	1.3416	1.1280	.9928,0	2.4075
1.21	.8360,1	1.5414	1.3590	1.1343	.9918,0	2.4367
1.22	.8299,8	1.5698	1.3764	1.1405	.9907,3	2.4662
1.23	.8240,8	1.5984	1.3938	1.1468	.9895,7	2.4961
1.24	.8183,0	1.6272	1.4112	1.1531	.9883,5	2.5263
1.25	.8126,4	1.6562	1.4286	1.1594	.9870,6	2.5568
1.26	.8070,9	1.6855	1.4460	1.1657	.9856,8	2.5876
1.27	.8016,5	1.7150	1.4634	1.1720	.9842,2	2.6187
1.28	.7963,1	1.7448	1.4808	1.1782	.9826,8	2.6500
1.29	.7910,8	1.7748	1.4983	1.1846	.9810,6	2.6816
1.30	.7859,6	1.8050	1.5157	1.1909	.9793,5	2.7135
1.31	.7809,3	1.8354	1.5331	1.1972	.9775,8	2.7457
1.32	.7760,0	1.8661	1.5505	1.2035	.9757,4	2.7783
1.33	.7711,6	1.8970	1.5680	1.2099	.9738,2	2.8112
1.34	.7664,1	1.9282	1.5854	1.2162	.9718,1	2.8444
1.35	.7617,5	1.9596	1.6028	1.2226	.9697,2	2.8778
1.36	.7571,8	1.9912	1.6202	1.2290	.9675,6	2.9115
1.37	.7526,9	2.0230	1.6376	1.2354	.9653,4	2.9455
1.38	.7482,8	2.0551	1.6550	1.2418	.9630,4	2.9798
1.39	.7439,6	2.0874	1.6723	1.2482	.9606,5	3.0144
1.40	.7397,1	2.1200	1.6896	1.2547	.9581,9	3.0493
1.41	.7355,4	2.1528	1.7070	1.2612	9556,6	3.0844
1.42	.7314,4	2.1858	1.7243	1.2676	.9530,6	3.1198
1.43	.7274,1	2.2190	1.7416	1.2742	.9503,9	3.1555
1.44	.7234,5	2.2525	1.7589	1.2807	.9476,5	3.1915

*The values in this table were originally calculated and reported in M.I.T. Meteor Report No. 14, Bureau of Ordnance, U. S. Navy Department, December, 1947, by A. H. Shapiro, W. R. Hawthorne, and G. M. Edelman.

NOTE: Linear interpolation may be made a) for values without a comma and b) to the left of comma for values containing a comma.

TABLE A–2 (*continued*)

M_x	M_y	$\dfrac{p_y}{p_x}$	$\dfrac{\rho_y}{\rho_x}$	$\dfrac{T_y}{T_x}$	$\dfrac{p_{0_y}}{p_{0_x}}$	$\dfrac{p_{0_y}}{p_x}$
1.45	.7195,6	2.2862	1.7761	1.2872	.9448,3	3.2278
1.46	.7157,4	2.3202	1.7934	1.2938	.9419,6	3.2643
1.47	.7119,8	2.3544	1.8106	1.3004	.9390,1	3.3011
1.48	.7082,9	2.3888	1.8278	1.3070	.9360,0	3.3382
1.49	.7046,6	2.4234	1.8449	1.3136	.9329,2	3.3756
1.50	.7010,9	2.4583	1.8621	1.3202	.9297,8	3.4133
1.51	.6975,8	2.4934	1.8792	1.3269	.9265,8	3.4512
1.52	.6941,3	2.5288	1.8962	1.3336	.9233,1	3.4894
1.53	.6907,3	2.5644	1.9133	1.3403	.9199,9	3.5279
1.54	.6873,9	2.6003	1.9303	1.3470	.9166,2	3.5667
1.55	.6841,0	2.6363	1.9473	1.3538	.9131,9	3.6058
1.56	.6808,6	2.6725	1.9643	1.3606	.9097,0	3.6451
1.57	.6776,8	2.7090	1.9812	1.3674	.9061,5	3.6847
1.58	.6745,5	2.7458	1.9981	1.3742	.9025,5	3.7245
1.59	.6714,7	2.7828	2.0149	1.3811	.8988,9	3.7645
1.60	.66844	2.8201	2.0317	1.3880	.8952,0	3.8049
1.61	.66545	2.8575	2.0485	1.3949	.8914,4	3.8456
1.62	.66251	2.8951	2.0652	1.4018	.8876,4	3.8866
1.63	.65962	2.9330	2.0820	1.4088	.8838,0	3.9278
1.64	.65677	2.9712	2.0986	1.4158	.8799,2	3.9693
1.65	.65396	3.0096	2.1152	1.4228	.87598	4.0111
1.66	.65119	3.0482	2.1318	1.4298	.87201	4.0531
1.67	.64847	3.0870	2.1484	1.4369	.86800	4.0954
1.68	.64579	3.1261	2.1649	1.4440	.86396	4.1379
1.69	.64315	3.1654	2.1813	1.4512	.85987	4.1807
1.70	.64055	3.2050	2.1977	1.4583	.85573	4.2238
1.71	.63798	3.2448	2.2141	1.4655	.85155	4.2672
1.72	.63545	3.2848	2.2304	1.4727	.84735	4.3108
1.73	.63296	3.3250	2.2467	1.4800	.84312	4.3547
1.74	.63051	3.3655	2.2629	1.4873	.83886	4.3989
1.75	.62809	3.4062	2.2791	1.4946	.83456	4.4433
1.76	.62570	3.4472	2.2952	1.5019	.83024	4.4880
1.77	.62335	3.4884	2.3113	1.5093	.82589	4.5330
1.78	.62104	3.5298	2.3273	1.5167	.82152	4.5783
1.79	.61875	3.5714	2.3433	1.5241	.81711	4.6238
1.80	.61650	3.6133	2.3592	1.5316	.81268	4.6695
1.81	.61428	3.6554	2.3751	1.5391	.80823	4.7155
1.82	.61209	3.6978	2.3909	1.5466	.80376	4.7618
1.83	.60993	3.7404	2.4067	1.5542	.79926	4.8083
1.84	.60780	3.7832	2.4224	1.5617	.79474	4.8551
1.85	.60570	3.8262	2.4381	1.5694	.79021	4.9022
1.86	.60363	3.8695	2.4537	1.5770	.78567	4.9498
1.87	.60159	3.9130	2.4693	1.5847	.78112	4.9974
1.88	.59957	3.9568	2.4848	1.5924	.77656	5.0453
1.89	.59758	4.0008	2.5003	1.6001	.77197	5.0934

TABLE A-2 (*continued*)

M_x	M_y	$\dfrac{p_y}{p_x}$	$\dfrac{\rho_y}{\rho_x}$	$\dfrac{T_y}{T_x}$	$\dfrac{p_{0y}}{p_{0x}}$	$\dfrac{p_{0y}}{p_x}$
1.90	.59562	4.0450	2.5157	1.6079	.76735	5.1417
1.91	.59368	4.0894	2.5310	1.6157	.76273	5.1904
1.92	.59177	4.1341	2.5463	1.6236	.75812	5.2394
1.93	.58988	4.1790	2.5615	1.6314	.75347	5.2886
1.94	.58802	4.2242	2.5767	1.6394	.74883	5.3381
1.95	.58618	4.2696	2.5919	1.6473	.74418	5.3878
1.96	.58437	4.3152	2.6070	1.6553	.73954	5.4378
1.97	.58258	4.3610	2.6220	1.6633	.73487	5.4880
1.98	.58081	4.4071	2.6369	1.6713	.73021	5.5385
1.99	.57907	4.4534	2.6518	1.6794	.72554	5.5894
2.00	.57735	4.5000	2.6666	1.6875	.72088	5.6405
2.01	.57565	4.5468	2.6814	1.6956	.71619	5.6918
2.02	.57397	4.5938	2.6962	1.7038	.71152	5.7434
2.03	.57231	4.6411	2.7109	1.7120	.70686	5.7952
2.04	.57068	4.6886	2.7255	1.7203	.70218	5.8473
2.05	.56907	4.7363	2.7400	1.7286	.69752	5.8997
2.06	.56747	4.7842	2.7545	1.7369	.69284	5.9523
2.07	.56589	4.8324	2.7690	1.7452	.68817	6.0052
2.08	.56433	4.8808	2.7834	1.7536	.68351	6.0584
2.09	.56280	4.9295	2.7977	1.7620	.67886	6.1118
2.10	.56128	4.9784	2.8119	1.7704	.67422	6.1655
2.11	.55978	5.0275	2.8261	1.7789	.66957	6.2194
2.12	.55830	5.0768	2.8402	1.7874	.66492	6.2736
2.13	.55683	5.1264	2.8543	1.7960	.66029	6.3280
2.14	.55538	5.1762	2.8683	1.8046	.65567	6.3827
2.15	.55395	5.2262	2.8823	1.8132	.65105	6.4377
2.16	.55254	5.2765	2.8962	1.8219	.64644	6.4929
2.17	.55114	5.3270	2.9100	1.8306	.64185	6.5484
2.18	.54976	5.3778	2.9238	1.8393	.63728	6.6042
2.19	.54841	5.4288	2.9376	1.8481	.63270	6.6602
2.20	.54706	5.4800	2.9512	1.8569	.62812	6.7163
2.21	.54572	5.5314	2.9648	1.8657	.62358	6.7730
2.22	.54440	5.5831	2.9783	1.8746	.61905	6.8299
2.23	.54310	5.6350	2.9918	1.8835	.61453	6.8869
2.24	.54182	5.6872	3.0052	1.8924	.61002	6.9442
2.25	.54055	5.7396	3.0186	1.9014	.60554	7.0018
2.26	.53929	5.7922	3.0319	1.9104	.60106	7.0597
2.27	.53805	5.8451	3.0452	1.9194	.59659	7.1178
2.28	.53683	5.8982	3.0584	1.9285	.59214	7.1762
2.29	.53561	5.9515	3.0715	1.9376	.58772	7.2348
2.30	.53441	6.0050	3.0846	1.9468	.58331	7.2937
2.31	.53322	6.0588	3.0976	1.9560	.57891	7.3529
2.32	.53205	6.1128	3.1105	1.9652	.57452	7.4123
2.33	.53089	6.1670	3.1234	1.9745	.57015	7.4720
2.34	.52974	6.2215	3.1362	1.9838	.56580	7.5319

TABLE A-2—(*Continued*)

M_x	M_y	$\dfrac{p_y}{p_x}$	$\dfrac{\rho_y}{\rho_x}$	$\dfrac{T_y}{T_x}$	$\dfrac{p_{0y}}{p_{0x}}$	$\dfrac{p_{0y}}{p_x}$
2.35	.52861	6.2762	3.1490	1.9931	.56148	7.5920
2.36	.52749	6.3312	3.1617	2.0025	.55717	7.6524
2.37	.52638	6.3864	3.1743	2.0119	.55288	7.7131
2.38	.52528	6.4418	3.1869	2.0213	.54862	7.7741
2.39	.52419	6.4974	3.1994	2.0308	.54438	7.8354
2.40	.52312	6.5533	3.2119	2.0403	.54015	7.8969
2.41	.52206	6.6094	3.2243	2.0499	.53594	7.9587
2.42	.52100	6.6658	3.2366	2.0595	.53175	8.0207
2.43	.51996	6.7224	3.2489	2.0691	.52758	8.0830
2.44	.51894	6.7792	3.2611	2.0788	.52344	8.1455
2.45	.51792	6.8362	3.2733	2.0885	.51932	8.2083
2.46	.51691	6.8935	3.2854	2.0982	.51521	8.2714
2.47	.51592	6.9510	3.2975	2.1080	.51112	8.3347
2.48	.51493	7.0088	3.3095	2.1178	.50706	8.3983
2.49	.51395	7.0668	3.3214	2.1276	.50303	8.4622
2.50	.51299	7.1250	3.3333	2.1375	.49902	8.5262
2.51	.51204	7.1834	3.3451	2.1474	.49502	8.5904
2.52	.51109	7.2421	3.3569	2.1574	.49104	8.6549
2.53	.51015	7.3010	3.3686	2.1674	.48709	8.7198
2.54	.50923	7.3602	3.3802	2.1774	.48317	8.7850
2.55	.50831	7.4196	3.3918	2.1875	.47927	8.8505
2.56	.50740	7.4792	3.4034	2.1976	.47540	8.9162
2.57	.50651	7.5391	3.4149	2.2077	.47155	8.9821
2.58	.50562	7.5992	3.4263	2.2179	.46772	9.0482
2.59	.50474	7.6595	3.4376	2.2281	.46391	9.1146
2.60	.50387	7.7200	3.4489	2.2383	.46012	9.1813
2.61	.50301	7.7808	3.4602	2.2486	.45636	9.2481
2.62	.50216	7.8418	3.4714	2.2589	.45262	9.3154
2.63	.50132	7.9030	3.4825	2.2693	.44891	9.3829
2.64	.50048	7.9645	3.4936	2.2797	.44522	9.4507
2.65	.49965	8.0262	3.5047	2.2901	.44155	9.5187
2.66	.49883	8.0882	3.5157	2.3006	.43791	9.5869
2.67	.49802	8.1504	3.5266	2.3111	.43429	9.6553
2.68	.49722	8.2128	3.5374	2.3217	.43070	9.7241
2.69	.49642	8.2754	3.5482	2.3323	.42713	9.7932
2.70	.49563	8.3383	3.5590	2.3429	.42359	9.8625
2.71	.49485	8.4014	3.5697	2.3536	.42007	9.9320
2.72	.49408	8.4648	3.5803	2.3643	.41657	10.0017
2.73	.49332	8.5284	3.5909	2.3750	.41310	10.0718
2.74	.49256	8.5922	3.6014	2.3858	.40965	10.1421
2.75	.49181	8.6562	3.6119	2.3966	.40622	10.212
2.76	.49107	8.7205	3.6224	2.4074	.40282	10.283
2.77	.49033	8.7850	3.6328	2.4183	.39945	10.354
2.78	.48960	8.8497	3.6431	2.4292	.39610	10.426
2.79	.48888	8.9147	3.6533	2.4402	.39276	10.498

TABLE A–2—(*Continued*)

M_x	M_y	$\dfrac{p_y}{p_x}$	$\dfrac{\rho_y}{\rho_x}$	$\dfrac{T_y}{T_x}$	$\dfrac{p_{0y}}{p_{0x}}$	$\dfrac{p_{0y}}{p_x}$
2.80	.48817	8.9800	3.6635	2.4512	.38946	10.569
2.81	.48746	9.0454	3.6737	2.4622	.38618	10.641
2.82	.48676	9.1111	3.6838	2.4733	.38293	10.714
2.83	.48607	9.1770	3.6939	2.4844	.37970	10.787
2.84	.48538	9.2432	3.7039	2.4955	.37649	10.860
2.85	.48470	9.3096	3.7139	2.5067	.37330	10.933
2.86	.48402	9.3762	3.7238	2.5179	.37013	11.006
2.87	.48334	9.4431	3.7336	2.5292	.36700	11.080
2.88	.48268	9.5102	3.7434	2.5405	.36389	11.154
2.89	.48203	9.5775	3.7532	2.5518	.36080	11.228
2.90	.48138	9.6450	3.7629	2.5632	.35773	11.302
2.91	.48074	9.7127	3.7725	2.5746	.35469	11.377
2.92	.48010	9.7808	3.7821	2.5860	.35167	11.452
2.93	.47946	9.8491	3.7917	2.5975	.34867	11.527
2.94	.47883	9.9176	3.8012	2.6090	.34570	11.603
2.95	.47821	9.9863	3.8106	2.6206	.34275	11.679
2.96	.47760	10.055	3.8200	2.6322	.33982	11.755
2.97	.47699	10.124	3.8294	2.6438	.33692	11.831
2.98	.47638	10.194	3.8387	2.6555	.33404	11.907
2.99	.47578	10.263	3.8479	2.6672	.33118	11.984
3.00	.47519	10.333	3.8571	2.6790	.32834	12.061
3.50	.45115	14.125	4.2608	3.3150	.21295	16.242
4.00	.43496	18.500	4.5714	4.0469	.13876	21.068
4.50	.42355	23.458	4.8119	4.8751	.09170	26.539
5.00	.41523	29.000	5.0000	5.8000	.06172	32.654
6.00	.40416	41.833	5.2683	7.9406	.02965	46.815
7.00	.39736	57.000	5.4444	10.469	.01535	63.552
8.00	.39289	74.500	5.5652	13.387	.00849	82.865
9.00	.38980	94.333	5.6512	16.693	.00496	104.753
10.00	.38757	116.500	5.7143	20.388	.00304	129.217
∞	.37796	∞	6.0000	∞	0	∞

Index